Alaska

Jim DuFresne, Aaron Spitzer

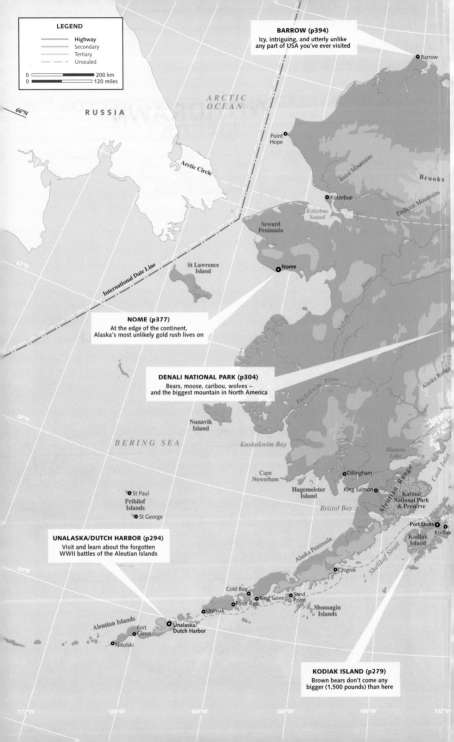

LEGEND

- Highway
- Secondary
- Tertiary
- Unsealed

0 — 200 km
0 — 120 miles

ARCTIC OCEAN

RUSSIA

66°N

BARROW (p394)
Icy, intriguing, and utterly unlike any part of USA you've ever visited

Barrow

Point Hope

Arctic Circle

Bald Mountains

Brooks

Endicott Mountains

Kotzebue

Kotzebue Sound

Seward Peninsula

International Date Line

St Lawrence Island

62°N

Nome

Yukon River

NOME (p377)
At the edge of the continent, Alaska's most unlikely gold rush lives on

DENALI NATIONAL PARK (p304)
Bears, moose, caribou, wolves – and the biggest mountain in North America

Alaska Range

River

Kuskokwim

Nunavik Island

58°N

BERING SEA

Kuskokwim Bay

Iliamna Lake

Cape Newerham

Dillingham

King Salmon

Hagemeister Island

Katmai National Park & Preserve

Cook Inlet

St Paul
Pribilof Islands
St George

Bristol Bay

Aleutian Range

Port Lions
Kodiak
Kodiak Island

UNALASKA/DUTCH HARBOR (p294)
Visit and learn about the forgotten WWII battles of the Aleutian Islands

54°N

Alaska Peninsula

Shelikof Strait

Chignik

Cold Bay
False Pass
King Cove
Unimak
Sand Point
Shumagin Islands

Aleutian Islands

Fort Glenn
Unalaska/ Dutch Harbor

Nikolski

KODIAK ISLAND (p279)
Brown bears don't come any bigger (1,500 pounds) than here

172°W   168°W   164°W   160°W   156°W   152°W

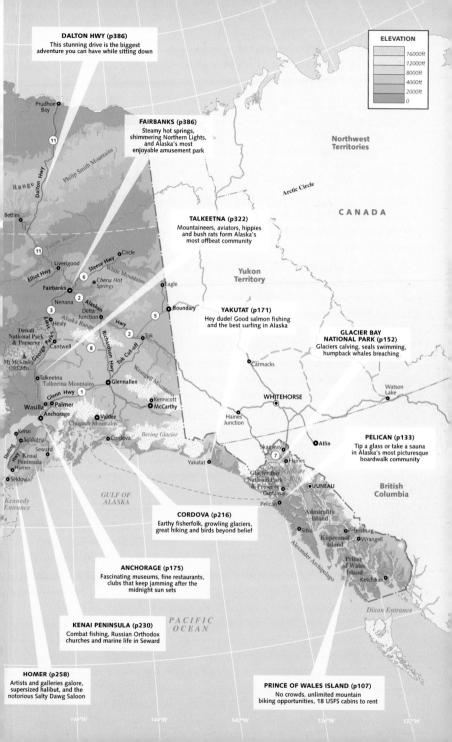

DALTON HWY (p386)
This stunning drive is the biggest adventure you can have while sitting down

FAIRBANKS (p386)
Steamy hot springs, shimmering Northern Lights, and Alaska's most enjoyable amusement park

TALKEETNA (p322)
Mountaineers, aviators, hippies and bush rats form Alaska's most offbeat community

YAKUTAT (p171)
Hey dude! Good salmon fishing and the best surfing in Alaska

GLACIER BAY NATIONAL PARK (p152)
Glaciers calving, seals swimming, humpback whales breaching

PELICAN (p133)
Tip a glass or take a sauna in Alaska's most picturesque boardwalk community

CORDOVA (p216)
Earthy fisherfolk, growling glaciers, great hiking and birds beyond belief

ANCHORAGE (p175)
Fascinating museums, fine restaurants, clubs that keep jamming after the midnight sun sets

KENAI PENINSULA (p230)
Combat fishing, Russian Orthodox churches and marine life in Seward

HOMER (p258)
Artists and galleries galore, supersized halibut, and the notorious Salty Dawg Saloon

PRINCE OF WALES ISLAND (p107)
No crowds, unlimited mountain biking opportunities, 18 USFS cabins to rent

ELEVATION

16000ft
12000ft
8000ft
4000ft
2000ft
0

Northwest Territories

Arctic Circle

CANADA

Yukon Territory

Prudhoe Bay

Bettles

Livengood
Circle
Steese Hwy
White Mountains
Chena Hot Springs
Fairbanks
Nenana
Healy
Delta Junction
Alaskan Hwy
Eagle
Boundary
Carmacks
Watson Lake
Denali National Park & Preserve
Cantwell
Mt McKinley (20,320ft)
Talkeetna
Talkeetna Mountains
Glennallen
Wrangell Mountains
Kennicott
McCarthy
WHITEHORSE
Wasilla
Palmer
Anchorage
Chugach Mountains
Valdez
Cordova
Bering Glacier
Haines Junction
Kenai
Soldotna
Seward
Kenai Peninsula
Homer
Seldovia
Kennedy Entrance
GULF OF ALASKA
Yakatat
Skagway
Haines
Atlin
Glacier Bay National Park & Preserve
Gustavus
Pelican
JUNEAU
British Columbia
Admiralty Island
Sitka
Kupreanof Island
Petersburg
Wrangell
Alexander Archipelago
Prince of Wales Island
Ketchikan
PACIFIC OCEAN
Dixon Entrance

Philip Smith Mountains
Dalton Hwy
Range
Yukon River
Elliot Hwy
Alaska Range
George Pks Hwy
Glenn Hwy
Steese Hwy
Richardson Hwy
Tok Cut-off
Tok
Alaskan Hwy

148°W   144°W   140°W   136°W   132°W

Destination Alaska

Alaska can overwhelm you when you least expect it. The Alaska Airlines' Anchorage–Juneau milk run is a three-hour flight that leapfrogs between towns, spending no more than a half hour in the air at a time. If you're blessed with a high pressure system, Flight 66 is more than just transportation; it's one of Alaska's best flightseeing tours.

On such clear days you will be mesmerized by what lies below: mountains and majestic Mt St Elias; miles of remote beach along a thunderous Gulf of Alaska; countless glaciers winding through a maze of jagged peaks; and lakes with so many icebergs they look like frozen margaritas. More than from anywhere else, Alaska appears so vast, so rugged and so pure. From this vantage point, it rarely displays even a hint of humanity – no highways, no cities, no cruise ships.

Travelers who make the long journey north are usually drawn to Alaska by its fabled reputation and gold-rush history, but once they arrive are stunned by what they see. Cities may be few and serious theater almost nonexistent, but Alaska has a way of overwhelming you when North America's tallest mountain is suddenly on fire by the alpenglow of a clear evening, when a glacier discharges an iceberg the size of a small house, when an 800lb bear catches a 10lb salmon in midair.

These are experiences that can permanently change your way of thinking. So can chartering a flight to access a wilderness cabin, leaving behind all traces of civilization for a few days. So can a simple walk in the woods.

It's not in restaurants or art galleries or other indoor attractions where you'll experience Alaska. It's outdoors where the state's grandeur and size will leave you shaking your head at a land that is so big and still so wild.

MARK NEWMAN

Highlights

Absorb breathtaking mountain scenery on the
White Pass & Yukon Route Railroad (p168)

In a conquering mood? Climb the 'Great
One', Mt McKinley (p62)

Cruise alongside glaciers at Glacier Bay
National Park and Preserve (p152)

OTHER HIGHLIGHTS

- Paddle on an unguided journey along the
  Upper Noatak river, surrounded by dramatic
  mountain peaks (p392)
- Surround yourself in wilderness by staying
  overnight in a United States Forestry Service
  cabin (p65)

Enjoy a flightseeing tour over
Denali National Park (p314)

ERNEST MANEWAL

Hike the extinct volcano, Mt Edgecumbe (p127), or fish in the nearby tidepools

OTHER HIGHLIGHTS

■ Try your hand at 'combat fishing' alongside other diehard fishing folk, lined elbow to elbow, at one of the most abundant places for salmon, Kenai River (p248)

■ Release the daredevil within: don the crampons and grab an ice-axe to embark on a half-day glacier trekking guided tour (p240).

MARK NEWMAN

Go wildlife watching in Denali National Park, home to one of Alaska's 13 caribou herds (p310)

Facing page: Enjoy the ultimate light show, the aurora borealis (northern lights; p359)

MARK NEWMAN

Be awestruck by the expanse of Muir Glacier (p153) in Glacier Bay National Park & Preserve

RALPH LEE HOPKI

Emblematic bird of the States, the bald eagle, Kachemak Bay, near Homer Spit (p260)

MARK NEWMAN

DAVID TIPL

Horned puffin, located on islands across Kachemak Bay (p271)

OTHER HIGHLIGHTS

- Visit the remote Pribilof Islands to see the well-established seal colony (p299)
- Enjoy a whale-watching cruise (p128) from both above and below the water surface with glass-bottomed boats in Sitka, a mecca for marine life enthusiasts

MARK NEWM

Grizzly bear (p50) in pursuit of salmon

Head-to-head moose (p51)

MARK NEWM

Regional Map Contents

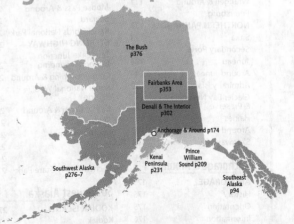

The Bush
p376

Fairbanks Area
p353

Denali & The Interior
p302

Anchorage & Around p174

Kenai
Peninsula
p231

Prince
William
Sound p209

Southwest Alaska
p276–7

Southeast
Alaska
p94

Contents

The Authors

JIM DUFRESNE
Coordinating Author, Southeast Alaska, Anchorage & Around, Southwest Alaska

Jim has lived, worked and wandered across Alaska. He's even cashed a Permanent Fund Dividend check. As the sports and outdoors editor of the *Juneau Empire*, he was the first Alaskan sportswriter to win a national award from Associated Press. As a guide for Alaska Discovery he has witnessed Hubbard Glacier shed icebergs the size of pick-up trucks from its 8-mile-wide face. Jim now lives in Michigan but is constantly returning to the Far North to write books on Alaska including Lonely Planet's *Hiking in Alaska*.

My Favorite Trip

As soon as I stepped off the ferry at Tenakee Springs, I popped into the public bathhouse at the end of the wharf. Two locals were soaking in the hot springs and invited me to join them. They didn't have to ask twice. I had my clothes off and was in that soothing water before introductions took place. By the time the MV *LeConte* departed an hour later I had soaked, wandered the main street and chatted to a few residents. That's why I love this run from Sitka to Juneau. The scenery of forested mountains and breaching whales is excellent but, best of all, you get to spend a little time in places like Tenakee Springs, Angoon and Hoonah. Tiny towns, real Alaska.

AARON SPITZER
Prince William Sound, Kenai Peninsula, Denali & the Interior, Fairbanks & Around, the Bush

Aaron loves bad latitudes. He was Indiana-born and raised and, when 13 years old, induced his mother to embark on an Arctic adventure: a road trip through Canada's Northwest Territories. A decade later he went to Alaska, organizing Denali National Park tours, and being a kayak guide, Juneau bookseller and Bush Alaska's *Tundra Drums* managing editor. For pleasure, he scared himself silly in the woods and waters, fleeing at times from bears, sea lions, moose, mosquitoes and an Alaska Railroad locomotive barreling towards him. Aaron lives in Yellowknife, Northwest Territories, Canada.

LONELY PLANET AUTHORS

Why is our travel information the best in the world? It's simple: our authors are independent, dedicated travelers. They don't research using just the Internet or phone, and they don't take freebies in exchange for positive coverage. They travel widely, to all the popular spots and off the beaten track. They personally visit thousands of hotels, restaurants, cafés, bars, galleries, palaces, museums and more – and they take pride in getting all the details right, and telling it how it is. For more, see the authors section on www.lonelyplanet.com.

Getting Started

Alaska is big, but keep your luggage small and your itinerary simple. Some travelers, so overwhelmed by the size of the state, put off a trip until they have an entire summer and subsequently never get there. Why wait? Just pick a region and you'll be immersed in mountains, wildlife as well as Alaska's wilderness culture. You will be so invigorated by Alaska's grandeur and beauty, and the variety of outdoor adventure, you'll be planning another trip before you're home.

WHEN TO GO

See Climate Charts (p399) for more information.

Alaska is working hard to promote winter tourism but it just hasn't caught on. The traditional season for heading north is still June through August when the weather is at its best, the days are long and everybody – tourists and locals alike – are outside playing. July and August are also the period of high prices, 'No Vacancy' signs and a Disneyland-like atmosphere at the entrance of Denali National Park. Consider beginning or ending your trip during the shoulder season of May and September. Alpine trails are still snow-covered in May and the Southeast can be a rainy place in late September but the demand for lodging is down, most outdoor activities are still possible and prices are easier to stomach. In recent years, probably due to global warming, May has been a particularly dry and sunny month.

Alaska is a large and diverse place and has a climate to match. In the Interior and Fairbanks average temperatures in the summer range from 55°F to 75°F, with a brief period in July to August when they top 80°F or even 90°F. Yet six months later the temperature can drop to -60°F. The Southeast and Prince William Sound have high rainfall and temperatures that only vary 40°F during the year. Anchorage, which is shielded by the Kenai Mountains, has an annual rainfall of 15in and average temperatures of 60°F to 70°F from June to August. The Bush, north of the Arctic Circle, is cool most of the summer, with temperatures around 45°F, and annual rainfall is less than 4in.

Throughout most of Alaska, summers are a beautiful mixture of long days and short nights, making the great outdoors even more appealing. On summer solstice (June 21) Anchorage enjoys more than 19 hours of

---

DON'T LEAVE HOME WITHOUT...

- Protection – fleece, rain gear and a hat – against Alaska's climate (p399).

- Hiking equipment – a pack, boots, water bottle, etc. Avoid having to purchase this equipment at 'absorbent' Alaskan prices.

- Passport and visas – Since 9/11, US entrance requirements have been changed and even Canadians need a passport to enter (p408).

- Casual clothes – the number of upscale restaurants with a dress code is limited to a handful in Anchorage. Leave the black tie at home.

- Cell phone – it will work in most towns and cities. Plus they've been a lifesaver for people lost in the wilderness (p407).

- Swiss Army knife – despite being in the mountains or the city. Just make sure you pack it in your check-in luggage.

sunlight, Fairbanks almost 22 hours. The midnight sun allows activities at hours undreamed of in most other places – 10-mile hikes after dinner or softball games at midnight. It also causes most people, even those with the best window shades, to wake up at 4am or 5am.

Arriving in Alaska in April is possible in the Southeast and the Kenai Peninsula, but much of the state will be enduring spring breakup – when warm weather 'breaks up' ice – a time of slush and mud. Stay during October and you're guaranteed rain most of the time in the Southeast and Southcentral regions and snow in the Interior and Fairbanks.

COSTS & MONEY

Alaska is traditionally known for having the highest cost of living in the country, though places like San Francisco and New York City have caught up with Alaska, if not surpassed it. Two reasons for the high prices in Alaska: the long distances needed to transport everything and the high cost of labor. Also keep in mind that tourism in Alaska is basically a three-month season. If the prices seem inflated, they have to be to cover the nine months when many restaurants and motels are barely scraping by.

The best way to avoid the high prices is to avoid the labor cost. Use public transport; stay in campgrounds or hostels, and enjoy your favorite brew around a campfire at night. The restaurants, bars, hotels and taxi companies, with their inflated peak-season prices, will quickly drain your funds. A rule of thumb for Alaskan prices is that they gradually increase the further north you travel. Overall, the Southeast is cheaper than most places in the Interior and Haines is a bargain in Alaska tourism. Anchorage can be extremely affordable if you live there, outrageous if you are a tourist because of the high cost of accommodations and restaurants in the summer. When traveling in the Bush be prepared for anything, even mediocre rooms that cost $200 a night.

A budget traveler who camps and stays in hostels, cooks two meals a day and participates in low-cost activities such as hiking can travel in Alaska for $50 to $60 a day. A family of four, staying in budget motels, eating twice a day in restaurants and renting a car, should expect daily expenses of $250 or higher. These rates do not include extra activities such as a 90-minute flightseeing tour ($190 per person).

TRAVEL LITERATURE

Alaska's wild nature has inspired a lot of authors throughout the years, both homegrown and the famous.

Coming into the Country (1977), written by John McPhee, is the best portrait of Alaska ever written. McPhee shifts from the wilderness to urban Alaska to a winter spent in remote Eagle in observing Alaskans during the 1970s.

Arctic Dreams (2001), a National Book Award winner, is a compelling look at the Far North and author Barry Lopez' personal journey to a land of stunted trees and endless days.

Going to Extremes (1989) presents Joe McGinniss' humorous and moving journey north. It uncovers the surreal qualities and contradictions of the Last Frontier and a colorful cast of characters who live there.

Into the Wild (1997), Jon Krakauer's bestseller, recounts why a young man from a well-to-do family abandons civilization and walks alone into the Denali wilderness. The book is as much about what he was seeking as it is about why he died.

HOW MUCH?

Halibut fishing charter $200

One-hour flightseeing tour $150

Salmon bake dinner $20-28

Whale watching cruise $120

kayak rental $50-60 per day

TOP TENS

Glaciers

So many glaciers in Alaska, so many ways to experience them…

- Childs Glacier (Cordova, p221) One of the closest tidewater glaciers you can view. Watch out when it calves.
- Mendenhall Glacier (Juneau, p139) Alaska's famous drive-in glacier
- LeConte Glacier (Petersburg, p121) Alaska's famous drive-in glacier
- Ruth Glacier (Talkeetna, p314)) Fly the length of this glacier, even land on it, on your way to view Mt McKinley
- Juneau Ice Field (Juneau, (p143) Take a helicopter trip to the mother of all glaciers and then ride a dog sled across it

- Spencer Glacier (Girdwood, p195) Alaska Railroad tour that includes rafting in front of the glacier
- Matanuska Glacier (Glenn Hwy, p343) Strap on the crampons, grab an ice-axe and go glacier trekking
- Grewingk Glacier (Homer, p272) Camp within view of a glacier
- Columbia Glacier (Valdez, p214) Sure it's retreating but tour boats can still get you within view of all that ice
- Glacier Bay (Gustavus, p153) Spend a day cruising the holy grail of glacier lovers

Festivals & Events

Alaskan summers are short so they're packed with events (for a more complete list go to p402).

- Little Norway Festival (Petersburg, p122) Mid-May
- Kodiak Crab Festival (Kodiak, p283) Late May
- Summer Solstice Festival (Moose Pass, p235) June 21
- Nalukataq Festival (Barrow, p395) Late June
- Independence Day (aka Fourth of July; McCarthy, Gustavus or any of the small towns)

- Girdwood Forest Faire (Girdwood, p197) Early July
- Golden Days (Fairbanks, p362) Late July
- Talkeetna Bluegrass Festival (Talkeetna, p326) Early August
- Southeast Alaska State Fair (Haines, p160) Mid-August
- Alaska State Fair (Palmer, p205) Late August

Wildlife Viewing Spots

For many, the highlight of a trip to Alaska is the wildlife. Here are the best places to see something wild.

- Denali Park Road (Denali National Park, p310) Mountain sheep, moose, caribou, brown bears
- Brooks Falls (Katmai National Park, p290) Brown bears
- St Paul Island (Pribilof Islands, p299) Seabirds and fur seals
- Kenai Fjords National Park (Seward, p242) Whales, sea lions and seals
- Chilkat River (Haines, p161) Bald eagles

- Anan Creek (Wrangell, p111) Black and brown bears
- Arctic Ocean (Barrow, p395) Polar bears
- Frederick Sound (Petersburg, p121) Humpback whales
- Fort Abercrombie State Historical Park (Kodiak, p281) Tidal pool marine life
- Ship Creek (Anchorage or practically any stream in July, p178) Salmon

Caribou Rising (2004), written by Rick Bass, looks at the porcupine caribou herd, the Gwich'in culture (a particular Alaska Native group) and why the oil industry doesn't belong in the Arctic National Wildlife Refuge.

Working on the Edge (1993) sets itself apart from the lots of books on commercial fishing because it details the classic mind-boggling tales of the rich rewards and high risks of king crabbing in the Bering Sea during the boom years of the 1980s.

In *As Far as You Can Go Without a Passport* (1992), author Tom Bodett, before he was a spokesman for Motel 6, was a carpenter living in Homer, using his good-natured and self-deprecating humor to pen essays about Alaska.

INTERNET RESOURCES

Highly computer literate and extremely remote – Alaska was made for the Internet.

Alaska Public Lands Information Centers (www.nps.gov/aplic/center) Before you hit the trail, head here for information on national parks, state parks and other public land.

Alaska Travel Industry Association (www.travelalaska.com) The official tourism marketing arm for the state has its vacation planner online with listings of B&Bs, motels, tours and more.

Alaska Wilderness Recreation and Tourism Association (www.awrta.org) Tour companies and outfitters committed to responsible tourism and minimizing visitor impact.

Alaskan Center (www.alaskan.com) Tourist information as well as bus, ferry, air and train schedules.

Linkup Alaska (www.linkupalaska.com) A web directory with links to more than 100 Alaskan sites, including most of the visitor centers in the state.

Lonely Planet (www.lonelyplanet.com) In the Thorn Tree, you can post questions before you go and then dispense advice when you get back. The Travel Links section connects you to the most useful travel resources elsewhere on the Web.

Itineraries
CLASSIC ROUTES

THE GREAT ALCAN
One to Two Months

This is the classic Alcan (Alaska Hwy) adventure, one of America's most scenic road trips. Mile 1 of the legendary road is in Dawson Creek and it's a 1390-mile, five-day drive to **Delta Junction** (p334). Collect your certificate for having survived the Alcan and then push onto **Fairbanks** (p354) for three days of R&R. Recover with a long soak in **Chena Hot Springs** (p370) and catch gold fever by visiting **Gold Dredge No 8** (p362) near Fairbanks.

Follow the George Parks Hwy south, for a few days of wildlife watching at **Denali National Park** (p304) and a day at Talkeetna for a flightseeing tour of **Mt McKinley** (p324). Treat yourself to a fine meal and a soft bed in **Anchorage** (p185) and check out the **Alaska Native Heritage Center** (p179).

Go to Whittier and enjoy a glacier cruise of **Prince William Sound** (p227) before boarding the **Alaska Marine Highway ferry** (p413) for a two-day trip across the Gulf of Alaska to **Juneau** (p134). See **Mendenhall Glacier** (p150) and climb **Mt Roberts** (p139). Jump back on the ferry to reach beautiful **Sitka** (p123) for a couple of days and then Petersburg to take in a **whale-watching cruise** (p121). Stop at Ketchikan for a boat tour of stunning **Misty Fiords National Monument** (p79) and then head to Bellingham, WA, to end an odyssey that involved driving 2000 miles and sailing seven days on the state ferry.

This is the road trip that every adventurer dreams about: driving to Alaska. It's almost 2000 miles on the road beginning with the Alcan in Canada, seven days on the Alaska Marine Highway ferry and a whole lot of spectacular scenery.

CRUISING SOUTHEAST ALASKA   Two Weeks

This is an easy-to-plan trip to a very scenic region of Alaska but you must reserve your space on the **Alaska Marine Highway ferry** (p413) months in advance. Alight the ferry in Bellingham, Washington, and enjoy the coastal scenery for two days before disembarking for two days at **Ketchikan** (p96). If it's not raining spend a day climbing **Deer Mountain** (p100) and enjoy lunch on the peak, to panoramic views of the Inside Passage. Make sure you take in the **Great Alaskan Lumberjack Show** (p104).

Catch the ferry to **Wrangell** (p111) and take a wild jet-boat tour up the **Stikine River** (p115), North America's fastest navigable river. Continue to Sitka on the ferry for an afternoon at **Sitka National Historic Park** (p126) and another on a **whale watching cruise** (p128).

Head over to Juneau and rent a car one day to view **Mendenhall Glacier** (p150) and to enjoy the scenery from 100 miles of coastal roads. Climb Mt Roberts and then take the **Mt Roberts tramway** (p137) back to the city. That evening enjoy one of the city's **salmon bakes** (p145).

Climb aboard the high-speed catamaran, **MV Fairweather**, (p148), for two days in Skagway, the historic start of the Klondike Gold Rush. Board the **White Pass & Yukon Route Railroad** (p168) for a day trip to Lake Bennett and in the evening catch the rollicking **Days of '98 Show with Soapy Smith** (p170). Backtrack to Juneau and on your final day join a cruise to **Tracy Arm** (p143) to view glaciers, icebergs and seals. Fly home from Juneau because you've run out of days to take the state ferry back.

Don't like to drive? Hop on a ferry in Bellingham and spend two weeks cruising one of the most interesting slices of Alaska, the practically roadless Southeast. Pack the hiking boots because there are great trails within easy walking distance of downtown Juneau, Ketchikan and Sitka.

AN ALEUTIAN ADVENTURE   Two Weeks

For an Alaska most visitors never see, head to this slice of the Bush, an area that RVers can't reach and cruise ships don't go to. Fly into Anchorage and begin the journey by traveling by bus or plane to **Homer** (p258). Schedule an extra day in Homer and spend it exploring **art galleries** (p263) or hiking in **Kachemak Bay State Park** (p272) across the bay.

Take the **Alaska Marine Highway ferry** (p148) to **Kodiak** (p279) and spend an extra day kayaking and **whale watching** (p283). Or splurge on a flight-seeing trip in order to view the giant **Kodiak brown bears** (p286) that roam the Kodiak National Wildlife Refuge.

Before you leave Kodiak stock up on snacks and a good book and board the MV *Tustumena* for its once-a-month run out to **Aleutian Islands** (p285). For the next three days enjoy the immense bird and marine life, including whales, sea lions and dolphins, that the ship passes and the quick stops to a handful of small Alaska Native villages along the **Lower Peninsula** (p294).

Leave the boat when it arrives at the end of the run to spend two days in **Unalaska** (p294). Start the day out at the Aleutian WWII Visitor Center to learn about the 'Forgotten War' and then hike up Mount Ballyhoo to see the gun mounts and other military remains at the **WWII National Historic Area** (p296). Visit the **Museum of the Aleutians** (p296) or rent a mountain bike to explore the outskirts of Unalaska Island. At night, head for the bar and mingle with commercial fishermen at **Latitude** (p298).

End your trip with a one-way flight back to **Anchorage** (p175).

One of the most amazing American ferry trips. Sail from Homer to Kodiak to see the famed Kodiak brown bears. Continue on the MV *Tustumena*, stopping at remote villages along the Lower Peninsula before disembarking at Unalaska for a chapter of WWII history few people have read.

RVING SOUTHCENTRAL   **10 Days**

Alaska is the dream of every RVer and you can be a road hog even if you don't own one. Fly into **Anchorage** (p175) and rent a recreation vehicle (RV) for 10 days that you have reserved well in advance. Stop at one of the city's large supermarkets, pack your RV with groceries and the local brew and then beat it out of town.

Head 45 miles north and spend the afternoon exploring **Hatcher Pass** (p206) and establish your camp in **Palmer** (p202). Follow the Glenn Hwy east, stopping to go glacier trekking on **Mantanuska Glacier** (p343). Spend the night at the first state campground that appeals to you before reaching **Glennallen** (p342).

Travel south on the Richardson Hwy and follow the McCarthy Rd east to the Kennicott River, 127 miles from Glennallen. Spend the next day exploring the quaint village of McCarthy and the amazing mining ruins at **Kennecott** (p347). Return to Richardson Hwy and head south. Check out **Worthington Glacier** (p351) and then spend the night camping in the alpine at **Blueberry Lake State Recreation Area** (p351).

Continue south into Valdez and stay an extra day to splurge on a **Columbia Glacier cruise** (p214). Load your RV on the **Alaska Marine Highway ferry** (reserve this in advance; p216) and sail across Prince William Sound to **Whittier** (p224). On the same day drive 90 miles south to Seward passing through scenic Turnagain Pass. You have two days in **Seward** (p236); book a halibut charter, or kayak in Resurrection Bay but on the afternoon of the second day hightail it back to **Anchorage** (127 miles; p175) to turn in the RV before the dealer closes.

Fly into Anchorage, rent a recreational vehicle then hightail it out of town. This itinerary covers a 650-mile drive in the 10 days to see the great copper mines of Kennecott, explore glaciers near Valdez and try your luck hooking a halibut in Seward.

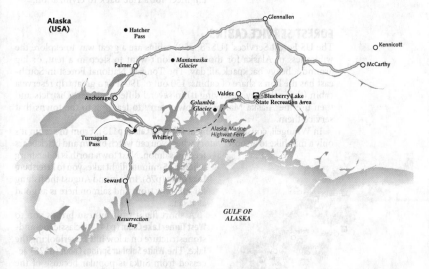

TAILORED TRIPS

ALASKA RAILROADING

Alaska doesn't have a lot of railroads but what it does have passes through some of the most amazing scenery in the country. For history buffs, the **White Pass & Yukon Route Railroad** (p168) is a must on any itinerary. The narrow-gauge line was built in 1900, during the height of the Klondike Gold Rush, putting the Chilkoot Trail out of business. From Skagway the train climbs steeply to 2885ft through the mountains until it reaches White Pass and then chugs along to serene Lake Bennett.

The most popular ticket is the Alaska Railroad's run from Anchorage to **Fairbanks** (p416), stopping at **Denali National Park** (p304) along the way.

But the most scenic rail route is the 114-mile run from Anchorage to Seward. The train ride begins by skirting Turnagain Arm and then climbs an alpine pass and comes within view of three glaciers before reaching Seward on Resurrection Bay.

For a uniquely Alaskan experience, board the Alaska Railroad's *Hurricane Turn* in **Talkeetna** (p195). The small train offers one of the country's last flag stop service as it follows the Susitna River wilderness to Hurricane. Along the way you'll see backpackers, homesteaders, even hunters with a moose at the side of the tracks, flagging down the engineer for a ride back to civilization.

FOREST SERVICE CABINS

The US Forest Services' (USFS, p59) cabins are a great way to explore the wilderness of Alaska for those who don't want to sleep in a tent, or lug around a heavy backpack all day. The Tongass National Forest in Southeast has the lion's share of cabins; 150 out of 190. For a great trip reserve a cabin (that's the key, reserving it) in several different Forest Districts and then use the Alaska Marine Highway ferry to leap fog to the towns that service them.

In Wrangell, consider staying at **Anan Bay Cabin** (p113). From the cabin it's only a mile hike to an observatory where you can watch brown and black bears

feed on salmon. Next town north is Petersburg where a 15-minute flight takes you to **Petersburg Lake Cabin** (p76). In July and August the fishing for rainbow trout and salmon here is as good as it gets.

A short flight from Juneau brings you to **West Turner Lake Cabin** (p141), a classic log-and-stone structure on a low bluff overlooking the lake. The **White Sulphur Springs Cabin** (p128) accessed from Sitka is popular because of the adjacent hot springs bathhouse. Bring a good bottle of wine and in the evening you'll be sipping and soaking. This is wilderness?

GOLD FEVER

Alaska is nothing else if it isn't wild-eyed miners bent over an icy stream desperately swirling a large pan in search for instant wealth. You can still join them.

The best place to catch gold fever is on Nome's **Golden Sands Beach** (p379). It's open to recreational mining and every summer dozens of miners set up camp and use sluice boxes and pans to pull gold flakes from the sand. You can stroll the beach, talk to them and see their vials of dust. Nearby is one of the many dredges in the area.

There are also areas designated for recreational mining adjacent to the north end of the **Resurrection Trail** (p138) in the Kenai Peninsula and **Fairbanks** (p361). To inspect gold nuggets first hand, the **University of Alaska Museum** (p360) or the **Circle District Historical Society Museum** (p372). To feel the pain that prospectors endured to find gold, hike the **Chilkoot Trail** (p66) from Skagway, the first step for thousands in 1898 during the Klondike Gold Rush.

For a lesson on panning techniques, there is **Indian Valley Mine** (p196) near Anchorage, Gold Rush Gold Camp at Fox or Juneau's **Last Chance Mining Museum** (p137). And finally, if you want to purchase a gold pan, well, stop at almost any hardware store in Alaska.

HOT SPRINGS

Even if it's not winter, hot springs can be a welcome relief after a long day on the road. That's the reason Alaska Natives and gold miners had identified most of Alaska's hot springs before the first wave of tourists even showed up.

Fairbanks is the access point to three that are reached by road, one even by a paved road – **Chena Hot Springs** (p370). These springs are by far the most developed in the area and include a lodge, restaurant and a bar that serves cold, cold beer from when you're done soaking in the 110°F hot tub.

For a more rustic adventure and remote setting follow the Elliot Hwy 152 miles to **Manley Hot Springs** (p373) where bathing takes place in a huge, thermal-heated greenhouse that's a veritable Babylonian garden of grapes, Asian pears and hibiscus flowers. Deep in this jungle are three spring-fed concrete tubs, each burbling at different temperatures. A deliriously un-Alaskan setting as there ever was one.

The public bathhouse at **Tenakee Springs** (p132) is another unusual hot springs. This small Southeast village, which is little more than a row of houses on pilings as well as a ferry dock, is situated on a spring that bubbles out of the ground at 108°F.

Locals have long since built a free bathhouse around them, posted with separate hours for men and women.

Snapshot

Alaska may be remote and disconnected from the rest of the USA but its problems and its controversies are America's worries and America's issues. People don't have to live in Alaska to have an opinion on whether the Arctic National Wildlife Refuge (ANWR) should be drilled for oil (p30). When Girl Scout Troop 34 of Fairbanks set traps in the wild to make beaver hats, part of the state's 'Take a Kid Trapping' program, it resulted in a national controversy that climaxed 5000 miles away with heated exchanges in 2004 between People for the Ethical Treatment of Animals (PETA) and the Girl Scouts' national headquarters in Connecticut.

Organizers of the Iditarod, the famous 1100-mile dogsled race, discovered the same when animal rights groups from Florida howled about the length of the race and forced some sponsors to drop out. Perhaps the most controversial plan in Alaska was Governor Frank Murkowski's decision to resume the state's wolf-control program in an effort to increase the number of moose available for human consumption in rural areas. In 2004, biologists killed almost 150 wolves, either by land-and-shoot or aerial shooting, and were directed to take another 300 around Tok. Connecticut-based Friends of Animals has already promised to organize a travel boycott to Alaska until the shootings stop.

Alaskans, however, are not as concerned about wolves or beavers, which are abundant in the state, as they are about surviving and earning a living. Alaska still has one of the highest unemployment rates (more than 7%) in the country. Even with oil topping $60 a barrel in 2005, providing Alaska with a much needed infusion of tax revenue, the state budget is still awash with red ink, and services, from snow removal to school funding, are being sliced. That's why the vast majority of Alaskans are in favor of opening ANWR to the oil industry and building a natural gas pipeline across the state, from the deposits in the North Slope south. The pipeline represents jobs, an economic boom and new revenue in place where there is no state tax on income, sales, inheritance or property. However, the US Senate blocked the energy bill in favor of drilling in late 2005.

But what worries many Alaskans the most is the age of their politicians. Alaska is a pork-barrel state and its elder statesman, US Senator Ted Stevens, is 82 and will not run again in the late-2006 senate election. Congressman Don Young, who also knows how to bring the bacon home due to his lengthy stay in the US Congress, is 72. Alaskans wonder what will happen when they have to send fresh faces to Washington, DC, and how bleak the future will be without the pork, when all they have are beans.

Whether or not ANWR is opened up, or a pipeline is built, Alaskans will prevail. They always do because the gold-rush spirit that first populated the state is as strong as ever. Alaskans may come for the gold or other opportunities to get rich quick but more times than not they stay for the mountains, the wildlife and some of the most impressive scenery in the world that has a way of softening even the surliest sourdough.

History

Alaska's history is a strange series of spurts and sputters, booms and busts. Although today Alaska is viewed as a wilderness paradise and an endless source of raw materials, in the past it has often been regarded as a frozen wasteland, a home suitable only for polar bears. Whenever some natural resource has been uncovered, however, a short period of prosperity and exploitation has followed: first with sea otter skins, then gold, salmon and oil, and, most recently, untouched wilderness. After each resource had been exhausted (some would say raped) the land slipped back into oblivion.

EARLY ALASKANS

The first Alaskans migrated from Asia to North America between 30,000 and 40,000 years ago, during an ice age that lowered the sea level and created a 900-mile land bridge linking Siberia and Alaska. The nomadic groups who crossed the bridge were not bent on exploration but on following the animal herds that provided them with food and clothing.

The first major invasion, which came across the land bridge from Asia, was by the Tlingits and the Haidas, who settled throughout the Southeast and British Columbia, and the Athabascans, a nomadic tribe that lived in the Interior. The other two major groups were the Inupiat who settled the north coast of Alaska and Canada (where they are known as Inuit) and the Yupik who settled southwest Alaska. The smallest group of Alaska natives to arrive was the Aleuts of the Aleutian Islands. The Inupiat, Yupik and Aleuts are believed to have migrated 3000 years ago and were well established by the time the Europeans arrived.

A track from a three-toed, meat-eating dinosaur, dating back 70 million years, was discovered in Denali National Park in 2005.

The Tlingit and Haida cultures were advanced; the tribes had permanent settlements, including large clan dwellings that housed related families. These tribes were noted for their excellent wood carving, especially carved poles, called totems, which can still be seen today in the Totem Heritage Center (p98) in Ketchikan, Sitka National Historical Park (p126) and many other places in the Southeast. The Tlingits were spread across the Southeast in large numbers and occasionally went as far south as Seattle in their huge dugout canoes. Both groups had few problems gathering food, as fish and game were plentiful in the Southeast.

Life was not so easy for the Aleuts, Inupiat and Yupik. With much colder winters and cooler summers, these people had to develop a highly effective sea-hunting culture to sustain life in the harsh regions of Alaska. This was especially true for the Inupiat, who could not have survived the winters without their skilled ice-hunting techniques. In spring, armed with only jade-tipped harpoons, the Inupiat, in skin-covered kayaks called *bidarkas* and *umiaks,* stalked and killed 60-ton bowhead whales. Though motorized boats replaced the kayaks and modern harpoons the jade-tipped spears, the whaling tradition still lives on in places like Barrow.

The indigenous people, despite their harsh environment, were numerous until non-Natives, particularly fur traders and whalers, brought guns, alcohol and disease that destroyed the Alaska Natives' delicate relationship with nature and wiped out entire villages. At one time an estimated

TIMELINE	1741	1784
	Explorer Vitus Bering, sent by Peter the Great, becomes first European to discover Alaska	Russians establish first European settlement at Three Saints Bay on Kodiak Island

FIVE WHO SHAPED ALASKA

Michael J Heney (1864–1910) Heney built two Alaskan railroads that were considered impossible by the leading engineers of his day. With little more than picks, shovels and blasting powder, Heney built the White Pass & Yukon Railroad (WP&YR) in only two years during the height of the Klondike Gold Rush, reaching Whitehorse in 1900. Six years later he arrived at a Prince William Sound cannery, named it Cordova and then proceeded to build the Copper River & Northwestern Railroad (CR&NW) to the Kennecott copper mines. Although only 195 miles long, the CR&NW was an engineering marvel on the scale of the Alcan (the Alaska Hwy) and the Trans-Alaska Pipeline.

James Wickersham (1857–1939) Wickersham didn't arrive in Alaska until he was 42 but went on to become one of the most influential Alaskans in the early 20th century. In 1900, Wickersham was sent to Eagle City as a newly appointed judge, the only one in a judicial district that stretched 300,000 sq miles from the Arctic to the tip of the Aleutians. For the next 30 years he provided justice in an often lawless place and then served as Congressional delegate. He introduced the first Alaskan statehood bill in 1916, put together the first serious attempt to climb Mt McKinley and played a key role in establishing what is now Denali National Park.

William Egan (1914–84) Egan was born in Valdez where he worked as a miner, grocer and cannery worker before being elected to six terms in the Territorial Legislature. While in Juneau he lobbied hard for statehood and served as president of the state constitutional convention. After Alaska became the 49th state of the union, Egan was elected its first governor in 1959 and re-elected in 1962 and 1970. He is the only Alaskan governor born and educated in Alaska.

Jay Hammond (1922–2005) Hammond was a pilot, trapper, hunting guide, commercial fisherman and, from 1975 to 1982, governor of Alaska. He was elected on a platform of permanently saving a portion of the oil money that was about to gush down the Trans-Alaska Pipeline and while in office worked tirelessly for the creation of the Permanent Fund. Today the wildly popular program pays every man, woman and child in Alaska an annual share of the state's oil wealth just for living there.

Jimmy Carter (1924–) Carter was on the eve of leaving the presidency in 1980 when he signed the Alaska National Interest Lands Conservation Act (ANILCA), knowing incoming President Ronald Reagan had promised to veto the bill. Often called the most significant land conservation measure in the history of the USA, the statute protected 106 million acres of federal lands in Alaska, doubling the size of the country's national park and refuge system and tripling the amount of land designated as wilderness. ANILCA expanded the national park system in Alaska by over 43 million acres and created 10 new national parks.

20,000 Aleuts lived throughout the islands of the Aleutian chain. In only 50 years the Russians reduced the Aleut population to less than 2000. The whalers who arrived at Inupiat villages in the mid-19th century were similarly destructive, introducing alcohol that devastated the lifestyles of entire villages. When the 50th anniversary of the Alaska Highway was celebrated in October 1992, many Alaska Natives and Canadians called the event a 'commemoration,' not a 'celebration,' due to the destruction that the link to Canada and the rest of the USA brought (disease, alcohol and a cash economy), further changing their nomadic lifestyle.

The last shot of the Civil War was shot in the Bering Sea by the CSS *Shenandoah* on June 22, 1865, 74 days after Appomattox.

AGE OF EXPLORATION

Thanks to the cold and stormy North Pacific, Alaska was one of the last places in the world to be mapped by Europeans. Because of this, explorers from several countries attempted to lay claim to the land and its resources by establishing a fort or two.

Spanish admiral Bartholeme de Fonte is credited by many with making the first trip into Alaskan waters in 1640, but the first written record of the state was made by Vitus Bering, a Danish navigator sailing for the Russian tsar. In 1728 Bering's explorations demonstrated that America

1804	1867
Alexander Baranof builds the capital of the Russian-American Company at Sitka	USA purchases Alaska from Russia for $7.2 million

and Asia were two separate continents. Thirteen years later, commanding the *St Peter,* he went ashore near Cordova, becoming the first European to set foot in Alaska. Bering and many of his crew died from scurvy during that journey, but his lieutenant survived to return with fur pelts and tales of fabulous seal and otter colonies – Alaska's first boom was under way. Russian fur merchants wasted little time in overrunning the Aleutian Islands and quickly established a settlement at Unalaska and then Kodiak Island. Chaos followed, as bands of Russian hunters robbed and murdered each other for furs while the peaceful Aleuts, living near the hunting grounds, were almost annihilated through massacres and forced labor. By the 1790s Russia had organized the Russian-American Company to regulate the fur trade and ease the violent competition.

The British arrived when Captain James Cook began searching the area for the Northwest Passage. Cook sailed north from Vancouver Island to Southcentral Alaska in 1778, anchoring at what is now Cook Inlet for a spell before continuing on to the Aleutian Islands, Bering Sea and the Arctic Ocean. The French sent Jean-Francoise Galaup, comte de La Perouse, who in 1786 made it as far as Lituya Bay, now part of Glacier Bay National Park. The wicked tides within the long, narrow bay caught the exploration party off guard, capsizing three longboats, killing 21 sailors and discouraging the French from colonizing the area.

www.archives.gov /education/lessons /alaska/cancelled-check .html – view the actual cancelled check and receipt for the purchase of Alaska from Russia in 1867.

Having depleted the fur colonies in the Aleutians, Aleksandr Baranov, who headed the Russian-American Company, moved his territorial capital from Kodiak to Sitka in the Southeast where he built a stunning city, 'an American Paris in Alaska.' At one point, Baranov oversaw (some would say ruled) an immensely profitable fur empire that stretched from Bristol Bay to Northern California. When the British began pushing north into Southeast Alaska, he built a second fort near the mouth of the Stikine River in 1834. That fort, which was named St Dionysius at the time, evolved into the small lumbering and fishing town of Wrangell.

SEWARD'S FOLLY

By the 1860s Russian control of Alaska had become problematic. The Russians found themselves badly overextended: their involvement in Napoleon's European wars, a declining fur industry and the long lines of shipping between Sitka and the heartland of Russia were draining their national treasury. The country made several overtures to the USA to purchase Alaska but it wasn't until 1867 that Secretary of State William H Seward, with extremely keen foresight, signed a treaty to purchase the state for $7.2 million – less than 2¢ an acre.

library.state.ak.us/hist /goldrush/table .html – Alaska State Library's catalogue of gold rush photos from 1893-1916.

By then the US public was in an uproar over the purchase of 'Seward's Ice Box' or 'Walrussia,' and, on the Senate floor, the battle to ratify the treaty lasted six months before the sale was approved. On October 18, 1867, the formal transfer of Alaska to the Americans took place in Sitka. Alaska remained a lawless, unorganized territory for the next 20 years, with the US Army in charge at one point and the US Navy at another.

This great land, remote and inaccessible to all but a few hardy settlers, stayed a dark, frozen mystery to most people. Eventually its riches were uncovered. First whaling began, then the phenomenal salmon runs, with the first canneries built in 1878 at Klawock on Prince of Wales Island.

1878	1880
First salmon cannery in Alaska established at Klawock	Led by a Tlingit chief, Richard Harris and Joe Juneau discover gold, and Juneau is founded

THE ALASKAN GOLD RUSH

What brought Alaska into the world limelight was gold. The promise of quick riches and frontier adventures was the most effective lure Alaska has ever had and, to some degree, still has today. Gold was discovered in the Gastineau Channel in the 1880s, and the towns of Juneau and Douglas sprang up overnight. Circle City, in the Interior, emerged in 1893, when gold was discovered in Birch Creek. Three years later, one of the world's most colorful gold rushes took place in the Klondike region of Canada's Yukon Territory.

Often called 'the last grand adventure,' the Klondike Gold Rush occurred when the country and much of the world was suffering a severe recession. When the banner headline of the *Seattle Post-Intelligencer* bellowed 'GOLD! GOLD! GOLD! GOLD!' on July 17, 1897, thousands of people quit their jobs and sold their homes to finance a trip through Southeast Alaska to the newly created boomtown of Skagway. From this tent city almost 30,000 prospectors tackled the steep Chilkoot Trail (p66) to Lake Bennett, where they built crude rafts to float the rest of the way to the goldfields; an equal number of people returned home along the route, broke and disillusioned.

The number of miners who made fortunes was small, but the tales and legends that emerged were endless. The Klondike stampede, though it only lasted from 1896 to the early 1900s, was Alaska's most colorful era and forever earned the state the reputation of being the country's last frontier.

Within three years of the Klondike stampede Alaska's population doubled to 63,592, including more than 30,000 non-Native people. Nome, another gold boomtown, was the largest city in the territory, with 12,000 residents while gold prompted the capital to be moved from Sitka to Juneau.

WORLD WAR II

In June 1942, only six months after their attack on Pearl Harbor, the Japanese opened their Aleutian Islands campaign by bombing Dutch Harbor for two days and then taking Attu and Kiska Islands. Other than Guam, it was the only foreign invasion of US soil during WWII and is often dubbed 'the Forgotten War' because most Americans are unaware of what took place in Alaska. The battle to retake Attu Island was a bloody one. After 19 days and landing more than 15,000 troops, US forces recaptured the plot of barren land, but only after suffering 2300 casualties and 549 deaths. Of the more than 2300 Japanese on Attu, fewer than 30 surrendered with many taking their own lives.

What had quickly become apparent to both sides was the role the capricious Aleutian weather played in the campaign. Soldiers shot their own troops in the fog; unable to penetrate fog and clouds, ships were thrown against rocks and sunk in heavy seas; pilots met the sides of mountains in low overcast skies. Bad weather literally saved Kodiak, keeping Japanese pilots at bay the night they planned to bomb it.

THE ALCAN & STATEHOOD

Following the Japanese attack on the Aleutian Islands in 1942, Congress panicked and rushed to protect the rest of Alaska. Large army and air force bases were set up at Anchorage, Fairbanks, Sitka and Whittier, and

Warren G. Harding, the first US president to visit Alaska, died only two weeks after leaving Alaska in 1923 with many blaming the 20-hour days for his sleepless-exhausted state.

Good Times Girls of the Alaska/Yukon Gold Rush (2003), by Lael Morgan, is the intriguing story of the women who followed the stampeders north. One prostitute ended up marrying the mayor of Fairbanks and hosting President Warren Harding.

1898	1915
Klondike Gold Rush turns Skagway into Alaska's largest city; Nome gold rush begins	Anchorage is founded when Ship Creek is chosen as a survey camp to build the Alaska Railroad

BOOM & BUST GOLD TOWNS

Circle (pop 99) In 1896 Circle was the largest mining town on the Yukon River, with a population of 700, eight dance halls, an opera house and a library. But like Hope, the Klondike Gold Rush quickly turned Circle into little more than a ghost town.

Hope (pop 165) Established as a mining camp for prospectors working Resurrection Creek in the Kenai Peninsula, Hope was a frenzy of activity, stores and saloons in 1896. Alas it was short-lived as the miners quickly deserted Hope for the Klondike Gold Rush in the Yukon.

Nome (pop 3473) The Golden Sands beach turned tiny Nome into a tent city of 20,000 almost overnight. In 1900 the US Census reported it was the largest town in Alaska with 12,488 permanent residents.

Ruby (pop 190) Originally founded as a supply point on the Yukon River for gold prospectors, a gold strike on Ruby Creek in 1907 and another on nearby Long Creek in 1911 briefly had Ruby's population topping 1000.

Skagway (pop 870) Thanks to the Klondike Gold Rush, the population exploded to 20,000 in 1898, making Skagway Alaska's largest city until Nome swiped the title.

thousands of military personnel were stationed in Alaska. But it was the famous Alcan (also known as the Alaska Hwy) that was the single most important project of the military expansion. The road was built by the military, but Alaska's residents benefited, as the Alcan aided their ability to access and make use of Alaska's natural resources.

In 1916 Alaska's territorial legislature submitted its first statehood bill but the stock market crash of 1929 and then WWII delayed action and kept Congress occupied with more demanding issues. But the growth brought on by the Alcan and to a lesser degree the new military bases pushed Alaska firmly into the 20th century and renewed its drive for statehood. On January 3, 1959, President Dwight Eisenhower proclaimed Alaska the USA's 49th state.

Alaska entered the 1960s full of promise when disaster struck: the most powerful earthquake ever recorded in North America (registering 9.2 on the Richter scale) hit Southcentral Alaska on Good Friday morning in 1964. More than 100 lives were lost, and damage was estimated at $500 million. In Anchorage office buildings sank 10ft into the ground, and houses slid more than 1200ft off a bluff into Knik Arm. A tidal wave virtually obliterated the community of Valdez. In Kodiak and Seward, 32ft of the coastline slipped into the Gulf of Alaska, and Cordova lost its entire harbor as the sea rose 16ft.

www.nps.gov/aleu – The National Park Service site devoted to the 'Forgotten War' of the Aleutian Islands during WWII.

THE ALASKAN BLACK-GOLD RUSH

The devastating 1964 earthquake left the newborn state in a shambles, but a more pleasant gift from nature soon rushed Alaska to recovery and beyond. In 1968 Atlantic Richfield discovered massive oil deposits underneath Prudhoe Bay in the Arctic Ocean. The value of the oil doubled after the Arab oil embargo of 1973, but it couldn't be tapped until there was a pipeline to transport it to the warm-water port of Valdez. And the pipeline couldn't be built until the US Congress, which still administered most of the land, settled the intense controversy between industry, environmentalists and Alaska Natives over historical claims to the land.

The Alaska Native Claims Settlement Act of 1971 was an unprecedented piece of legislation that opened the way for a consortium of

1935	1942
Depression-era families arrive in the Matanuska Valley to begin farming and Palmer is established	Japanese bomb Dutch Harbor during WWII and Americans build the Alcan (Alaska Hwy)

BUILDING THE ALCAN

A land link between Alaska and the rest of the USA was envisioned as early as 1930 but it took WWII to turn the nation's attention north to embark on one of the greatest engineering feats of the 20th century: constructing a 1520-mile road through remote wilderness.

Deemed a military necessity and authorized by President Franklin Roosevelt only two months after the attack on Pearl Harbor, the Alcan was designed to be an overland route far enough inland to be out of range of airplanes transported on Japanese aircraft carriers. The exact route followed old winter roads, trap lines and pack trails, and by March 9, 1942, construction had begun. Within three months, more than 10,000 troops, most of them from the US Army Corps of Engineers, were in the Canadian wilderness. The soldiers felled trees, put down gravel, struggled with permafrost and built pontoon bridges, all at a breakneck pace. They endured –30°F in April, snowfalls in June and swarms of mosquitoes and gnats for most of the summer. They worked 16-hour days, spent nights in pup tents and went weeks without hearing from commanders in base camps, much less from their families.

Despite the harsh conditions, the speed with which the Alcan was built is astounding. With most crews working out of two main camps, Whitehorse and Fort St John, a regiment from the west met a regiment from the east on September 23 at Contact Creek, today Mile 588 of the highway. When a final link was completed near Kluane Lake in late October, the Alcan was open, having been built in only eight months and 12 days.

The official dedication of the Alcan took place on November 20, 1942, at Soldier's Summit near Kluane Lake, at which time an Army truck departed from the ceremony and arrived at Fairbanks the next day. It became the first vehicle to travel the entire highway but has since been followed by thousands more, many of them with travelers looking for adventure and grandeur on North America's great wilderness road trip.

oil companies to undertake the construction of the 789-mile pipeline. The Trans-Alaska Pipeline took three years to build, cost more than $8 billion – in 1977 dollars – and, at the time, was the most expensive private construction project ever undertaken in the world. At the peak of construction, the pipeline employed 28,000 people, doing '7-12s' (seven 12-hour shifts a week).

The oil began to flow on June 20, 1977, and for a decade oil gave Alaska an economic base that was the envy of every other state, accounting for as much as 80% of state government revenue. In the explosive growth period of the mid-1980s, Alaskans enjoyed the highest per-capita income in the country. The state's budget was in the billions. Legislators in Juneau transformed Anchorage into a stunning city, with sports arenas, libraries and performing-arts centers, and provided virtually every bush town with a million-dollar school. From 1980 to 1986, this state of only a half-million residents generated revenue of $26 billion.

DISASTER AT VALDEZ

For most Alaskans, the abundant oil made it hard to see beyond the gleam of the oil dollar. Reality hit them hard in 1989, when the *Exxon Valdez*, a 987ft Exxon oil supertanker, rammed Bligh Reef a few hours out of the port of Valdez. The ship spilled almost 11 million gallons of North Slope crude into the bountiful waters of Prince William Sound. Alaskans and the rest of the country watched in horror as the oil spill quickly

1959	1964
Alaska officially becomes 49th state of the USA on January 3	North America's worst earthquake takes place on Good Friday, devastating Southcentral Alaska

became far too large for booms to contain, spreading 600 miles from the grounding site. State residents were shocked as oil began to appear from the glacier-carved cliffs of Kenai Fjords to the bird rookeries of Katmai National Park. The spill eventually contaminated 1567 miles of shoreline and killed an estimated 645,000 birds and 5000 sea otters.

Today the oil, like other resources exploited in the past, is simply running out. That pot of gold called Prudhoe Bay began its decline in 1988 and now produces less than half of its 1987 peak of two million barrels a day. The end of the Cold War and the subsequent downsizing of the US military in the early 1990s was more economic bad news for Alaska. Alaskan state revenues, once the envy of every other state governor in the country, went tumbling along with the declining oil royalties. In 1982 the Alaska state government enjoyed oil revenue of more than $3.5 billion. Since the 1990s the oil-dependent state government has managed a balanced budget only twice.

ALASKA IN THE 21ST CENTURY

Many Alaskans see the Arctic National Wildlife Refuge (ANWR) and the construction of a natural gas line from the North Slope to the Lower 48 as the solution to the economic problems brought about by the state's dwindling oil reserves.

Large mining projects and more roads are also being pushed for economic development as Alaska faces its greatest debate – the exploitation of its remaining wilderness. The fury over wilderness usage reached a climax when, on the eve of his departure from office in 1980, President Jimmy Carter signed the Alaska National Interest Lands Conservation Act (ANILCA) into law, setting aside 106 million acres for national parks and preserves with a single stroke of the pen.

At the core of the dispute are issues of both 'locking up the land' and federal interference in the livelihood of Alaskans. Squabbles over subsistence and the right of rural residents to enjoy longer seasons and bigger harvests in an effort to live off the land, resulted in Alaska becoming the first state in which the federal government took control of fish and game management on its land. That occurred in 1999 and Alaskans are still incensed over interference from Washington, DC, a foreign capital to most of them.

And that's ironic because Alaska is right up there with West Virginia as a pork-barrel state, thanks to the lengthy service of its politicians in the nation's capital. Senator Ted Stevens has been in office since 1968 and Congressman Don Young, Alaska's only representative, since 1973. 'Uncle Ted,' as Alaskans fondly refer to their senator, has been the top-ranked lawmaker for bringing home 'pork' every year since Citizens Against Government Waste began keeping track in 2000. As chairman of the powerful Senate Appropriations Committee, the watchdog group estimates the senator brought $645 million to the state in 2005 – $984 for each resident. That includes $1.5 million for a bus stop in Anchorage and $231 million for a bridge connecting Ketchikan to its airport.

Therefore the looming crisis for Alaska in the 21st century may not be Prudhoe Bay drying up but aging politicians. Young is 72 years old, while Stevens is 82 and has already announced he will not run again in

Out of the Channel: The Exxon Valdez Oil Spill In Prince William Sound (1999), by John Keeble, is an indepth account of the diaster and Exxon's response and cover-up which the author contends did more damage than the original spill.

1968	1980
Oil and natural gas discovered at Prudhoe Bay on the North Slope	President Jimmy Carter signs the Alaska National Interests Lands Conservation Act (ANILCA), sparing millions of acres of wilderness

DRILLING FOR OIL IN THE LAST GREAT WILDERNESS

Alaska is a battleground for environmental issues but none tugs more at the nation's conscience than the push to drill for oil in the Arctic National Wildlife Refuge (ANWR). Yellowstone National Park sees more visitors in a weekend than this refuge does in a year, yet the battle over oil has turned ANWR into a sacred icon: America's last great wilderness.

And either you're for drilling in the refuge or you're not. There's no middle ground in this debate.

The refuge was created under President Dwight D Eisenhower in the 1950s and expanded to 19.6 million acres by President Jimmy Carter in 1980. It's often labeled by environmentalists as America's Serengeti, a pristine wilderness inhabited by 45 species of mammals, including grizzly bears, polar bears and wolves. Millions of migratory birds use the refuge to nest and every spring the country's second-largest caribou herd, 150,000 strong, gives birth to 40,000 calves there.

But there is also oil in the refuge, concentrated in its fragile coastal plains that span 1.5 million acres along the Beaufort Sea. Geologists believe the ANWR has the largest untapped reserve in the country, rivaling the massive Prudhoe Bay fields to the west when they were first explored. The US Geological Survey has estimated the amount of recoverable oil at between 5.6 billion and 16 billion barrels.

The oil industry, salivating over such a large field, contends only 8% of the refuge would be affected by its infrastructure; roads, pipelines, trucks, drilling platforms, an entire town to house workers, an occasional spill. And once fully developed, the ANWR would produce 1.5-million barrels a day for 20 years, or as much as the USA imports from Saudi Arabia, according to the American Petroleum Institute.

Environmentalists contend that the refuge would never quench more than 2% of the US' thirst for oil and that increased gasoline mileage requirements on vehicles alone, especially gas-guzzling SUVs, would result in bigger energy savings and sooner than the ANWR ever would. Drilling the refuge would not put the country on a course of 'energy independence.'

The battle raged from the earliest days of President Ronald Reagan in the 1980s until 2005. A combination of historically high gas prices at the pump that year and a persistent President George W Bush, an oil man from Texas, finally convinced the US Senate, which had long opposed developing ANWR, to include it in an energy bill.

One columnist compared such an industrial invasion to addicts hocking 'the family heirlooms to keep their drug habit going.' The US' habit happens to be oil and many people fear that opening the ANWR will encourage the oil industry to campaign for drilling rights in areas presently closed; off the California coast, in the Great Lakes or even the Rocky Mountains.

Ironically the ANWR would have no effect on today's high gas prices as it will take at least 10 years for the first arctic oil to reach refineries. By then the coastal plains – a marshy table-land that supports the state's greatest concentration wildlife and is the biological heart of the refuge – could be forever marred with the thumbprint of a dig-and-drill president and a nation addicted to its oil.

In late 2005 the energy bill was blocked by the US Senate, so the ANWR is still protected.

November 2006. In 2002 Frank Murkowski traded a 22-year career in the US Senate for the Alaska governorship. Murkowski's daughter, Lisa, has replaced him in the Senate and many observers expect Senator Stevens' son, Ben, a state representative from Anchorage, to do the same for his father. Politics in Alaska is almost like a monarchy. But while they may have the same name it will be years before they'll have that magic touch in bringing federal dollars back to the Far North.

1989	2000
Exxon Valdez grounds on Bligh Reef and spills 11 million gallons of oil into Prince William Sound	Largest Permanent Fund check ever, $1963, is sent to every man, woman and child in Alaska

The Culture

Alaska is large, young and rough around the edges – not exactly qualities that spark a renaissance of cultural enlightenment. But its scenery is so grand, its mountains so tall and its nature so wild that it has always had a way of pulling the passionate, adventurous and creative-minded north.

REGIONAL IDENTITY

There are Alaskan Natives and there are Texans who have moved up to work in the oil industry. There's bush Alaska and there's Anchorage. There are tree huggers, there are probusiness conservatives and there are miners who won't hesitate to reduce a stream to rubble in search of gold. Alaska is as diverse as it is large.

Most of Alaska is rural bush, small villages and roadless areas where transportation is either by a boat or on a snowmobile in the winter. Yet more than 60% of residents live in the four largest cities. You can still find Alaskans in a log cabin in the middle of nowhere supporting themselves with a trapline. But for the most part that's myth. The majority of residents live in neighborhoods, work a nine-to-five job and look forward to playing softball on the weekends.

And most likely they're newcomers. An estimated 30% of the state's population was born in Alaska, including only one of its seven elected governors. Such a transient population creates a melting pot of ideas, philosophies and priorities. If nothing else, Alaskans are opinionated; the glut of letters to the editor in the *Anchorage Daily News* is proof of that.

Rural or urban, Alaskans tend to be individualistic in their lifestyles, following few outside trends, rather adhering to what their harsh environment dictates. Mother Nature and those −30°F winter days, not California, are responsible for the Alaskan dress code. Only in Juneau can you step into a fancy restaurant and see attire that includes brown rubber boots.

The word 'Alaska' comes from the Aleut term 'Alyeska,' which means 'The Great Land.'

ALASKA'S PERMANENT FUND

Few things amaze visitors more than learning that Alaska gives residents money for living there. The annual checks date back to when Alaskans approved a constitutionally protected Alaska Permanent Fund: money set aside from all mineral-lease royalties but particularly Prudhoe Bay. At the urging of then-governor Jay Hammond, the state legislature created a Permanent Fund Dividend (PFD) payment program and in 1982 began handing out the interest from the fund. In 2005 the PFD was $845 for every man, woman and child who lived in Alaska. The largest check arrived in 2000 – $1963. For people who have lived in Alaska since 1982 the PFD has padded their bank accounts by $24,000.

The Permanent Fund now contains $31 billion and earns more revenue for the state than Prudhoe Bay. The arrival of the checks every October is known as 'Dividend Days,' a time when kids skip school, long lines form at the banks and villages empty out because suddenly there is $600 million to spend on airline tickets.

The checks are so beloved that when asked in 1999 to sacrifice just a small portion of the PFD to ease the state's growing budget deficit, 83% of Alaskans voted 'no.' This is a problem in a place with no state tax on income, sales or property and many Alaskans concede that the solution to their budget deficit will have to be another oil boom, ie in the Arctic National Wildlife Refuge, or statewide taxes. There isn't a politician between the Arctic and the Aleutians who has the stomach to tamper with the PFD.

www.state.ak.us/local
/kids – The State of
Alaska's website for kids,
featuring great videos of
Alaskan wildlife.

That individualistic attitude and a good dose of liberalism was respon-sible for Alaska's great social experiment; from 1975 until 1991 marijuana was legal in Alaska if it was used in the privacy of the home. But over the years Alaskans have moved to the right, voting for Republican presidents, fighting tax increases despite record state budget deficits and becoming one of the first states to pass a constitutional amendment banning same-sex marriages.

LIFESTYLE

In recent years, May in the Southeast, normally a rainy period, has been unusually sunny and warm, causing many residents to suffer from what one called 'solar anxiety.' It's so nice outside you'd better drop every-thing, leave work early and go play. Alaskans are clearly opportunists.

Visitors will find most of the locals they meet in towns and cities have lifestyles similar to their own. They work, they love their weekends, they live in a variety of homes big and small, they participate in double coupon days at supermarkets. Even in remote villages there are satellite TV dishes, the latest hip-hop CD and Internet access to the rest of the world.

The difference is that they live in Alaska and they make the most of it. In rural Alaska many fish for salmon because they live a partially subsistent lifestyle and the fish are there, swimming past their village. In Fort Yukon, north of Fairbanks, almost 90% of the 600 residents are Alaska Natives, unemployment often exceeds 18% and the median household income is only $29,000 in a place where everything costs more. They survive by catching salmon in the Yukon River and hunting caribou on the tundra.

Anchorage, on the other hand, is like a midsize city in northern Min-nesota, only it's surrounded by mountains. Its population is 10% Alaska Native, 6% African American, 6% Asian and 78% of European descent. This is as diverse as you get in Alaska. Unemployment is less than 7%, average household income tops $60,000. Yet many residents still fish for salmon because it's there: cheap protein swimming through the heart of the city in Ship Creek.

The furthest north
supermarket in USA is in
Barrow, a $4 million store
constructed on stilts to
prevent central heating
from thawing
the permafrost.

This opportunistic attitude has been a driving force across Alaska's history and is responsible for its lifestyle today. In the summer Alaskans play because the weather is nice and the days are long. In the winter they linger at the office because the temperature is often below 0°F.

They love the outdoors and cherish their great parks. But the majority of Alaskans have few problems with drilling the pristine wilderness of the Arctic National Wildlife Refuge or clear-cutting Tongass National Forest. They want to live in Alaska so they need to make a living in Alaska, survive in a land where there is little industry or farming. They see trees and oil as an opportunity to do that. To most Alaskans that's not a contradiction. That's life in the Far North.

POPULATION

Alaska, the largest state in the USA, has the third-smallest population. It is also the most sparsely populated state. Population density is 1.1 persons per sq mile; in the rest of the country it's 80 persons per sq mile. Lots of land, few people, but that's changing. Between 1990 and 2000 the state's population increased 14%, a rate higher even than California. As late as the mid-1980s Alaska had the fewest residents of any state in the country. Now it has surpassed Wyoming and Vermont, and is closing in on North Dakota.

Alaskans are overwhelmingly urban (74%) but they are four years younger than the national average: the median age is 32 years old. And

ALASKA NATIVES

Long before Bering's journeys to Alaska (p24), Alaska Natives had made their way there and established a culture and lifestyle in one of the world's harshest environments. Despite modernization and the rapid advances of communications in what had been a remote region of the world, they have managed to retain much of their culture and traditional ceremonies.

More than 102,000 indigenous people, half of whom are Inupiat, live in Alaska but the percentage of the population that is Alaska Native is steadily decreasing. Prior to 1940 they were the majority of the population in Alaska. During WWII they became a minority and today they represent less than 16%. They are no longer tribal nomads but live in permanent villages ranging in size from 20 people to several hundred. Ironically, the largest center of indigenous people in Alaska isn't Barrow but Anchorage, home to 21,000 Alaska Natives.

The biggest challenge facing Alaska Natives today is preserving their culture, particularly their languages, from the onslaught of Western commercialism. Of the 20 Alaska Natives languages, 16 are in danger of becoming extinct. That's because only 36% of Alaska Natives still use their native language. Among those living in Anchorage and Fairbanks it's only 17%. To combat this, cultural centers, such as the Alaska Native Heritage Center (p179) in Anchorage, have embarked on programs to interview elders and to permanently preserve languages, while the University of Alaska has created the Alaska Native Language Center, offering courses such as Athabascan linguistics.

Most travelers to Alaska encounter indigenous culture at Alaska Native museums such as Ketchikan's Totem Heritage Center (p98), in gift shops (p406) where they purchase indigenous art or from package tours to large towns like Barrow. To experience the rich culture and the subsistent way of life of small villages you either have to have a contact there or travel with somebody who does, such as an outfitter. Although Alaska Natives, especially the Inupiat, are very hospitable, there can be tension and suspicion of strangers in isolated bush communities.

along with Nevada, Alaska is still the only state that can boast more men, almost 52%, than women. That leads to the most popular saying among Alaskan women: 'the odds are good but the goods are odd.'

SPORTS

The biggest spectator sport in Alaska is the Iditarod (p34 and p34). Not preparing to be in Alaska in March? There are other spectator sports in Alaska including the great American pastime: baseball. The Alaska Baseball League is made up of five semipro teams of highly regarded college players trying to get a jump on others competing for spots in the major leagues. Teams include Fairbanks' **Alaska Goldpanners** (www.goldpanners.com) and **Anchorage Bucs** (www.anchoragebucs.com), and among the major leaguers who have played in Alaska are sluggers Barry Bonds and Mark McGwire.

Even the smallest towns have a sports bar with a wide-screen TV and patrons cheering on Alaska's adopted home teams: Seattle Mariners, Seattle Seahawks and other pro clubs based in the US Northwest. The state's most unusual sporting event is the **World Eskimo-Indian Olympics** (www.weio.org) in July, when several hundred native athletes converge on Fairbanks to compete in such things as greased pole walking, seal skinning and Indian stick pulling.

MULTICULTURALISM

Slowly Alaska is becoming diversified. The state's most rapid growth occurred after WWII, creating a society that in the 1950s was largely a mix of Alaska Natives and military-minded Whites. Since then the percentages of both indigenous people (see above) and especially the military, due to base closures, have drastically decreased.

THE IDITAROD

In 1948 Joe Redington Sr arrived in Alaska with just $18 in his pocket and used $13 of it to cover a filing fee for a 101-acre homestead in Knik. By accident – some say fate – Redington's homestead was located only a few hundred feet from the historic Iditarod Trail, an old dogsled mail route from Seward to Nome. Redington was fascinated by the Iditarod Trail and the famous 'serum run' that saved the town of Nome from diphtheria in 1925, when mushers used the trail to relay the medical supplies across Alaska.

Worried that snowmobiles might replace sled dogs, Redington proposed an Anchorage–Nome race along the historic trail and then worked tirelessly to stage the first 1100-mile Iditarod in 1973. Alaska's 'Last Great Race,' the world's longest sled dog event, was born.

Despite some rocky times, the Iditarod has endured. It's held in early March, when the temperatures are usually in the low teens and the snow coverage is good. Most visitors to Alaska catch the race at the start – 4th Ave and E St in Anchorage – but that is strictly ceremonial. The mushers run their teams for only a few miles and then truck them up to Wasilla or Willow for a restart of the event.

From there they follow one of two routes of the historic trail, crossing two mountain ranges, following a frozen Yukon River for 150 miles and passing through dozens of small native villages before arriving to cheering crowds in Nome. Although some animal-rights groups protest nationally and contend that such distances are cruel, these sled dogs are the canine equivalents of magnificent, well-trained athletes. In 2005, 79 teams entered the race with 63 reaching Nome and the winner covering 1161 miles in nine days and 18 hours.

Redington made his Iditarod debut in 1974 at age 57 and completed the route in 23 days for 11th place. He went on to run the Iditarod 19 times. His best time was 12 days, two hours and 57 minutes. His final race was in 1997 when, at age 80, the 'Father of the Iditarod' completed the grueling race across the Alaskan wilderness in 13 days.

Alaska is still predominantly white, almost 71%, with African Americans representing less than 4% of the population and Hispanics 4.2%. Asians represent the most significant immigration growth, particularly in communities connected to the commercial fishing industry; in Kodiak they represent 17% of the population, in Unalaska 27%.

Alaska's cultural tensions aren't between sourdough (old-timer) and cheechako (newcomer) but rather between rural and urban, and in particular Alaska Natives and the rest of the state. Sensitive issues such as subsistence rights can bring on spirited debates but rarely more than that.

MEDIA

Alaska's largest daily is the **Anchorage Daily News** (www.adn.com), a top-rated publication that won the Pulitzer prize in the 1970s for stories on the Trans-Alaska Pipeline, which serves as a statewide newspaper. The rest of Alaska's 30 daily, weekly and trade newspapers are scattered around the state and most are eight pages of local news, softball scores and ads.

Radio stations are widespread in Alaska. There are more than 20 stations in the Anchorage area alone, broadcasting everything from jazz to religion. In smaller towns, public radio is a particularly important outlet for news and entertainment. Although always facing the state budget knife, **Alaska Public Radio Network** (www.akradio.org) is surviving with 17 stations in communities as far-flung as Barrow, Kotzebue, Sand Point and Fort Yukon.

RELIGION

For the most part, every religion that mainstream America practices in the Lower 48 can be found in Alaska. One of the most interesting religions, however, is Russian Orthodox, which is the most enduring aspect of a unique period in Alaska's history. After Russian merchants and traders had decimated indigenous populations in the mid- to late 18th century, missionaries arrived as Russia's rulers' answer to the brutal subjugation. They managed to convert the indigenous people of Southwest, Southcentral and Southeast Alaska to a new religious belief.

These beliefs are as strong today as they have ever been. There are active Russian Orthodox congregations in 80 Alaskan communities, with the familiar onion domes of their churches seen in Juneau, Sitka, Kodiak and Unalaska, among other places.

ARTS

The winters are long and the scenery is spectacular. This more than anything else has been the basis for the arts in Alaska. Though to visitors the cultural scene may seem small or even nonexistent in places, it has a long tradition in the Far North, beginning with Alaska Natives and continuing today thanks to tourism and the Alaskan lifestyle, which lends itself to creative souls in places such as Homer, Girdwood and Haines.

www.alaskanativeartists
.com – An online co-op
of Alaskan Natives that
promotes and sells their
traditional and
contemporary artwork.

Native Arts & Crafts

Alaska's indigenous people are renowned for their traditional arts and crafts, primarily because of their ingenious use of local natural materials. Roots, ivory tusks, bone, birch bark, grasses and soapstone have been used creatively to produce ceremonial regalia and artwork items.

Thanks to a flourishing arts market, prompted by increased tourism to the state, Alaska Native arts have become an important slice of the economy in many Bush communities. The Inupiat and Yupik, having the fewest resources to work with, traditionally made their objects out of sea-mammal parts; their ivory carvings and scrimshaw work are world renowned.

The Aleuts of the Aleutian Islands are known for their bentwood hats; the Athabascans of the Interior produce elaborate beadwork; and the Tlingit, Haida and Tsimshian of Southeast Alaska are responsible for the great totems and clan houses.

THE RISE AND FALL OF TOTEMS

Ironically, Europeans stimulated and then nearly halted the art of totem-carving by Alaska Natives in the Southeast. Totem poles are carved from huge cedar trees and are used to preserve family history or make a statement about a clan. They invariably were raised during a potlatch, a ceremony in which a major event was held, designed to draw clans from throughout the region.

The first record of a totem is a sketch produced in a 1791 journal of sailor John Bartlett, aboard the vessel *Gustavus III* while at North Island of Queen Charlotte, BC. By the end of that century totem carving was flourishing after clans had acquired steel knives, axes and other cutting tools through fur trading. But between 1880 and 1950 the art form was almost wiped out when a law forbidding potlatches took effect. When the law was repealed in 1951, a revival of totem carving took place and still continues today.

Average totem heights range from 20ft to 65ft and red cedar is preferred by carvers due to its massive size, straight grain and ease of cutting. Generally, the oldest totems are 50 to 60 years old. Beyond that most poles rot and tumble due to the heavy precipitation and acidic soil of Southeast Alaska.

There probably isn't a community in Southeast Alaska without a totem or two, but Ketchikan has by far the most impressive collections of them at Totem Heritage Center (p98), Saxman Totem Park (p105) and Totem Bight State Park (p105). The tallest totem in the world, however, stands in tiny Kake (p132) and is 132ft high.

But perhaps no single item represents indigenous art better than Alaskan basketry. Each group produces stunning baskets in very distinctive styles, made solely from the materials at hand. Athabascans weave baskets from willow roots and birch bark; the Tlingits use cedar bark; the Inupiat use grasses and baleen, a glossy, hard material that hangs from the jaws of whales.

Cup'ig Eskimo Dictionary (2004), by the Alaska Native Language Center of the University of Alaska, Fairbanks: a collection of 4000 words that can be referenced in English or Cup'ig, a rare Yupik dialect.

The Aleuts are perhaps the most renowned basket weavers. Using rye grass, which grows abundantly in the Aleutian Islands, they are able to work the pliable but very tough material into tiny, intricately woven baskets. The three styles of Aleut baskets (Attu, Atka and Unalaska) carry a steep price in shops but can be viewed at several southwest cultural centers including the Alutiiq Museum (p280) in Kodiak and Museum of the Aleutians (p296) in Dutch Harbor.

Be conscious of the most widespread problem: native art rip-offs. Much of what is being passed off as authentic art has in reality been mass-produced in China, Taiwan or Bali. If you're considering purchasing native art, try to find a legitimate shop and look for the Authentic Native Handicraft from Alaska symbol (see p406). If the price of a soapstone carving seems too good to be true, then it probably is.

Literature

Two of the best-known writers identified with Alaska were not native to the land nor did they spend much time there; but Jack London and Robert Service witnessed Alaska's greatest adventure and turned the experience into literary careers.

London, an American, departed for the Klondike Gold Rush in 1897 hoping to get rich panning gold (opposite). Service, a Canadian bank teller, was transferred to Dawson City in 1902 and then wrote his first book of verse, *The Spell of the Yukon*. The work was an immediate success and contained his best known ballads, 'The Shooting of Dan McGrew' and 'The Cremation of Sam McGee.' Both portray the hardship and violence of life during the gold rush and are recited not just in the Yukon but probably more often on stages and certainly more often in bars across Alaska.

Today's contemporary standouts of Alaskan literature are not memorized nearly as much as Service but are no less elegant in capturing the spirit of the Far North. Among them is Velma Wallis, an Athabascan born in Fort Yukon. Wallis' best novel is *Two Old Women*, a moving tale of two elderly women abandoned by their migrating tribe during a harsh winter. Other works that touch the soul of Alaska include *At the End of This Summer*, by John Haines, a collection of poems he wrote in the 1950s from his homestead near Fairbanks, *The Man Who Swam with Beavers*, by Nancy Lord, a collection of short stories inspired by Alaska Native legends, and Nick Jans' *Tracks of the Unseen: Meditations on Alaska Wildlife, Landscape and Photography*.

Catch and Release: The Insiders Guide to Alaska Men (1997), by Jane Haigh, Kelly Hegarty-Lammers and Patricia Walsh. Three lifelong Alaskans dispel the myth of the 'Alaska Man' in a fun and witty style.

Small cabins and long winter nights filled with sinister thoughts have also given rise to Alaska's share of mystery writers. For a whodunit with a wilderness touch try Dana Stanebow's ex-DA investigator Kate Shugak in *A Cold Day for Murder*, Sue Henry's musher-turned-crime-solver Jessie Arnold in *Murder on the Iditarod Trail* or John Stradley's PI Cecil Younger in *Cold Water Burning*.

Theater & Dance

For many visitors, theater in Alaska is a group of actors who first serve the local salmon bake and then perform a tongue-in-cheek, melodramatic play. But the 49th state also has a committed – though small – theatrical

JACK LONDON'S ALASKA

Raised by his mother in Oakland, California, Jack London quit school at 14 to seek adventures that included trying his hand as an oyster pirate, visiting Japan as a sailor and riding the rails throughout the USA as a hobo. He eventually resumed his education at the University of California at Berkeley but quit school again in 1897 to seek his fortune in the Klondike Gold Rush. He endured the Chilkoot Trail, reached the Yukon gold fields and staked a claim that November. But the following spring London developed a severe case of scurvy and eventually used a small boat to float 1500 miles down the Yukon River to St Michael where he sailed to California. He stayed in the Far North only a year and like most miners returned home penniless but with a head full of stories and tales.

His first book, *The Son of the Wolf,* appeared in 1900 and his two classics followed shortly after that: *Call of the Wild* (1903) and *White Fang* (1906). The central characters of London's best-known novels are dogs. Buck is stolen to be a sled dog in Alaska in *Call of the Wild* while *White Fang*, half-dog, half-wolf, curbs his natural hostility and learns to love after a new world is opened up to him. Using the colorful Klondike as a backdrop, London's classics focus on the struggles between man and nature and learning to survive in the harsh Alaskan wilderness.

London's books quickly gained a wide audience in the USA and around the world. He went on to produce 50 books of fiction and nonfiction in only 17 years to become the country's highest-paid writer of the day. He is also one of the most extensively translated of American authors. Despite his success, London led a tumultuous life that included financial problems and disparaging reviews. He died aged only 40 in 1916.

community that writes, produces and performs plays. The best-known stage in Alaska is Juneau's **Perseverance Theatre** (www.perseverancetheatre.org). Founded in 1979, the company presents classic and original plays, and has become the state's leader in fostering work by Alaskan writers. That includes *How I Learned to Drive*, which premiered at the Perseverance Theatre in 1996 and won playwright Paula Vogel a Pulitzer prize in 1998.

Serious theater can be found in several other Alaskan communities as well. Anchorage has a number of performing groups, including the **Alaska Dance Theatre** (www.alaskadancetheatre.org) and the **Eccentric Theatre Company** (www.cyranos.org), while further north there is the **Fairbanks Shakespeare Theatre** (www.fairbanks-shakespeare.org). For more on Alaskan theaters contact the **Alaska State Council of the Arts** (☎ 907-269-6610; www.educ.state.ak.us/aksca).

Music

The Anchorage Bowl has the residents to pull in well-known artists, from Third Day to Emmylou Harris, with most of them playing at Atwood Concern Hall, Sullivan Sports Arena or even Chilkoot Charlie's (p191). You can also catch nationally known acts, particularly country bands, at the Alaska State Fair Borealis Theatre in Palmer and Fairbanks' Carlson Center. Beyond that a band has to be on the downside of its career before it arrives in towns such as Juneau, Ketchikan or Kodiak.

Homegrown artists, and we're not talking Jewel here, make up an important segment of the Alaskan music scene and are the reason for the state's numerous music festivals. Among the best are the Alaska Folk Festival (p143) that has been held in Juneau for more than 30 years, the Sitka Summer Music Festival (p129), the Talkeetna Bluegrass Festival (p326) and the Bald Eagle Music Festival (p161).

www.mosquitonet .com/%7Egcn – A comprehensive site that covers Alaskan folk musicians and festivals.

Architecture

Since Alaska's best known architectural style is a log cabin with outdoor plumbing, the world doesn't look towards Alaska for progressive designs

TOP TEN ALASKA PHOTO OPPORTUNITIES

Even if you have only a point-and-shoot camera, they'll think you're a pro at home if you bring back one of these shots:

- The reflection of Mt McKinley in Wonder Lake at Denali National Park (p310)
- Giant icebergs calving off Childs Glacier at the end of the Copper River Hwy (p221)
- Brown bears snagging salmon on top of Brooks Fall at Katmai National Park (p290)
- Madam Dolly beckoning you into her brothel museum on Ketchikan's Creek St (p98)
- An angler catching a salmon in Ship Creek with the Anchorage skyline in the background (p178)
- Backpackers scrambling up the Golden Stairway of the Chilkoot Trail (p66)
- A humpback whale breaching during a whale-watching tour in Southeast Alaska (p120)
- The red buildings and towering shafts of the Kennecott Copper Mine ruins (p347)
- The rich colors of the midnight sun over the Arctic Ocean in Barrow (p394)
- Salmon choking any small stream along coastal Alaska (p54)

of buildings and cities. That could change. In late 2005 work began on the $110 million expansion of the Anchorage Museum of History and Art (p178) and by 2009 it will be an innovative showcase of Alaska's culture. What used to be a single, squarish building will be enlarged by a series of additions of various heights and lengths, and staggered to create what the lead architect described as 'slipping volumes.' Surrounding it will be 2 acres of birch forest and tidal pools.

Glass walls housing exhibits, large windows framing views of Anchorage and an observation area where visitors can gaze on the Alaska Range, even Mt McKinley on a clear day, will make the museum both 'transparent and translucent.' From the inside you can experience the grandeur of Alaska that surrounds Anchorage. From the outside you will get a sense of the treasures waiting to be explored before you even enter what is surely to become Alaska's architectural gem.

Painting & Sculpture

Despite the growing wave of cruise ships and the chains of gift stores that follow them, Alaska's community of artists is alive and well and its work can be seen and purchased in many towns including Ketchikan, Homer, Haines and Girdwood. Among the most prominent of Alaska's contemporary painters are Juneau's Rie Munoz, with her distinctly colorful, whimsical style portraying Alaskan life; Anchorage's Byron Birdsall, best known for his surreal landscapes; and Ketchikan's Ray Troll, whose fishy paintings and prints have been compared to Gary Larson's *Far Side* cartoons.

Cinema & TV

Alaska is no stranger to Tinsel Town. Over the years, the 49th state has been used as a cinematic backdrop for movies, TV shows, documentaries and even an episode of *Baywatch*. The most recent feature film shot on location there was *The Big White*, with Robin Williams, Holly Hunter and Woody Harrelson arriving in Skagway in 2004 to work on the dark comedy about a travel agent who lives in Alaska. Williams was also the killer in *Insomnia* (2002), in which Al Pacino plays a police officer sent to a small Alaskan town to investigate a murder. On the lighter side was

Mystery, Alaska (1999), in which Russell Crowe leads the locals of a hockey-crazed small Alaskan town in a game against an NHL squad.

But what really gave the state a boost wasn't a film but a TV show. *Northern Exposure* was an Emmy-winning series about a New York doctor who had to repay the state of Alaska for financing medical school by working in the fictional town of Cicely. The show was a huge hit in the mid-1990s and today people still arrive in Alaska asking the whereabouts of Cicely. Most Alaskans send them to Talkeetna.

Food & Drink

First the bad news: food in Alaska is expensive. The prices in super-markets will raise eyebrows and restaurant menus can be downright shocking at times. The good news, however, is that what they catch and grow in Alaska – king crab, giant prawns (shrimps), 50lb cabbages – is big and delightfully tasty. But the best news is that Alaskans love to eat. Their restaurant scene may not have the sophistication of New York City but their portions are big, their ales hearty and their seafood always fresh and wild.

www.dnr.state.ak.us/ag /index.htm – the Alaska Division of Agriculture website has information on farmers markets, state fairs, and when and where to buy Alaskan produce.

STAPLES & SPECIALTIES

Alaska is the land of seafood, and by that we mean fish that are actually caught in the sea. It's illegal to even think about salmon farming in this state much less raise fish in overcrowded pens. In some supermarkets, the display cases of seafood – king crab legs ($15 per pound), sockeye salmon steaks ($8 to $10 per pound), spot prawns ($12 per pound) – rivals those filled with steaks and chops.

Seafood also sneaks its way into the lunch menu. Alaskans, like most Americans, love their burgers and fries at noon, but many are happy with just a bowl of the seafood chowder: thick, creamy and loaded with everything from clams and shrimps to crab, salmon and halibut. If it's served in a sourdough bread bowl, you're set for the rest of the day.

Sourdough is one of Alaska's best-known specialties. Turn-of-the-century prospectors were dependent on the yeasty starter to make their breads and hot cates rise. Because the sourdough supply is replenished with additional flour and water after each use it would remain active and fresh, well, indefinitely. Today there's hardly a restaurant in Alaska that doesn't serve sourdough pancakes along with the usual eggs, omelettes and sausage for breakfast. Some chefs, with a wink of their eye, claim their sourdough dates back to the Klondike Gold Rush. The ultimate treat in the morning is sourdough pancakes riddled with fresh blueberries and smoth-ered in maple syrup. This is legendary but affordable Alaskan cuisine that makes breakfast the best-value meal in this land of high prices.

Alaska Sourdough (1976), by Ruth Allman, is the longtime classic devoted to Alaska's best-known contribution to frontier cuisine.

Seafood & Shellfish

Menus at restaurants are dominated by seafood. The traditional main is the 'Captain's Platter,' a plate heaped with a deep fried offering of halibut, shrimp and clams. But in recent years Alaskans have become health-conscious and much more creative. Now it's not shocking to see halibut teriyaki served on steamed rice at a café, or almond-crusted cod with raspberry sauce at its upscale counterpart down the street.

Halibut and three species of salmon – king, coho (silver) and sockeye (red) – are the most commonly served fish. But other types can also be enjoyed, including rockfish, sablefish (black cod), pollock and sole. Shellfish – clams, mussels and scallops with giant ones coming from the Bering Sea – are also very common, as are snow, tanner and Dungeness crabs and a variety of shrimps and prawns.

The ultimate feast for many, however, is a pound of steamed king crab legs, which effectively replaces lobster in the Far North, dipped in drawn butter. Such a treat will set you back $30 to $50 depending on the restaurant, but fresh king crab is so good that it's why some visitors end up as Alaskans.

Game

Alaskans adore their wild game. But unless you hunt or know somebody who does there isn't really much opportunity for the average visitor to indulge in tasting such local favorites as mountain goat, caribou and deer. Moose is such prized game that state troopers maintain lists of residents who are ready at a minute's notice to chainsaw one killed in a car crash. It's much too valuable and much too enormous to leave as road kill.

Most 'game' seen in restaurants is either Alaska-bred buffalo or reindeer. Buffalo burgers, a healthy alternative to beef burgers, are available throughout the state. Even more popular is reindeer sausage, a spicy mix of ground reindeer and pork. It accompanies eggs on the breakfast menu or can be found grilling on almost every hotdog cart in Alaska. With a heap of sauerkraut and a squeeze of spicy brown mustard, it's the quickest lunch in the state.

Alaska accounts for almost half of the world's harvest of wild salmon; in 2004 that amounted to 194 million fish.

Ethnic Food

An influx of Asians migrating to Alaska has resulted in most towns having at least one ethnic restaurant. Chinese restaurants are widespread throughout the state, even in communities such as Nome and Unalaska. Many offer what Alaskans love most: all-you-can-eat lunch and dinner buffets, featuring a dozen mains, fried rice, spring rolls, egg drop soup and unlimited trips. With lunch priced around $8 to $10 and dinner $12 to $14, these are among Alaska's best-value eating options. Many supermarkets maintain Oriental food counters where a main and fried rice is $5 to $7.

Sushi bars are also on the rise and, with the state's abundance of fresh seafood, can be especially good, even in out-of-the-way places such as Kodiak. Thai, Vietnamese and Korean restaurants can already be found in Anchorage and it won't be long before they carve a niche in other Alaskan cities.

What Real Alaskans Eat (2003), by Stephen Lay, is a tongue-in-cheek history of why Alaskans eat what they do. Mixed into the text are recipes for everything from roasted beaver tail to bear-fat biscuits.

DRINKS

Whatever you sip, it is brewed and fermented in Alaska. Alaskans even make wine; not out of grapes of course, because they don't have the climate to grow them, but a handful of wineries in Anchorage, Kodiak (p281) and Haines (p159) are making it out of rhubarb, strawberries, blueberries and fireweed flower.

TRAVEL YOUR TASTEBUDS

You know you're in Alaska if you're eating...

Birch syrup Tapped from paper birch trees, it's lighter and not as sweet as maple syrup but has its own distinct flavor. Look for it in Haines, home of **Birchboy Products** (www.birchboy.com).

Squaw candy This is salmon jerky, fillets that have been dried or smoked and are very chewy. Although it's a staple for rural Alaskans in winter, you can purchase it in gift shops.

Spam Alaskans love that chopped-ham-in-a-can because it (seemingly) keeps forever. Dine on Spam du jour or Spam nachos at Anchorage's Mr Whitekeys' Fly by Night Club (p193).

Fiddleheads After a long winter, locals love to pick these young ferns, appearing tightly curled and just above the ground. They're like woodsy brussel sprouts.

We dare you to try...

Muktuk This is an Inupiat delicacy that is made up of the outer skin of a whale and the attached blubber. It has the consistency of stale Jell-O and, needless to say, is an acquired taste. Head to Barrow if you want a sample.

Coffee & Espresso

The coffee craze that began in Seattle has reached Alaska. Espresso shops are everywhere: even in small towns such as McCarthy you can find somebody with an espresso machine. Anchorage has dozens of espresso shops, including drive-thrus where off-to-work employees line up every morning for a quick caffeine hit.

www.anchoragepress
.com – the online edition
of the *Anchorage Press*
has reviews of restau-
rants, microbrew beers
and clubs in Alaska's
largest city.

Alcohol

The legal drinking age in Alaska is 21 years. Except for 70 Alaska Native towns that are dry (alcohol is prohibited) or are damp (the sale of alcohol is prohibited), finding an open bar or liquor store is never very difficult; in fact, only the churches outnumber the bars. The abundance of drinking establishments and the long, dark winters explain why Alaska has the highest alcoholism rate in the USA.

Bars in the larger cities vary in their decor, and many offer music and dancing. The bars in smaller towns are good places to have a brew and mingle with commercial fishermen, loggers or other locals. Bar hours vary, but there are always a few places that open their doors at 9am and don't close until 5am.

The usual US beer (Miller, Budweiser etc) is served but Alaska's micro-breweries are growing and it's unusual if a bar doesn't have at least one microbrew on tap. Alaska's largest brewery is Juneau's Alaskan Brewing Co (p149) and its Alaska Amber is now seen all over the state and even as far away as California and Arizona. In bars a pint of microbrew is $4 to $5, in stores a six-pack is $8 to $10. Beer lovers who want to try most of the state's microbrews should head to Haines in May for the Great Alaska Craft Beer & Home Brew Festival (p160).

CELEBRATIONS

Even when the festival isn't about food, food is always a big part of Alaskan celebrations. Petersburg's Little Norway Festival (p122) celebrates Norwegian Independence Day in May but is best known for the seafood and shrimp feeds staged at night. Alaska's oldest food celebration is the Kodiak Crab Festival (p283). The week-long event was first held in 1958 and today still features lots of cooked king crab. The most unusual gastronomic event is the Great Alaska Beer Train. On a special run in early October, the **Alaska Railroad** (☎ 907-265-2494; www.akrr.com) departs Anchorage for Portage, loaded with Alaskan appetizers, microbrews and a lot of happy people.

About 15 million acres of
soil in Alaska is suitable
for farming but only a
million acres of it is
currently being farmed.

WHERE TO EAT & DRINK

The mainstay of Alaskan restaurants, particularly in small towns, is the main street café. It opens early in the morning, sometimes at 4am if it's catering to charter-fishing captains, serving eggs, bacon, pancakes and oatmeal, and continue with hamburgers, french fries and grilled sandwiches for lunch. There is almost always halibut and salmon on the dinner menu. Sit at the counter or squeeze into the booth and indulge in large portions and strong coffee.

Most small towns also have a hamburger hut, a small shack or trailer with picnic tables outside serving burgers, hot dogs, wraps or fried fish, as well as a pizza parlor with a blackboard menu of pizzas, calzones, hot subs, and beer and wine. All will be open well into the evening.

Cities will have bistros and upscale restaurants, many located along the waterfront with a cozy bar on one side and tables on the other. During the summer they generally serve dinner from 4pm until as late as 10pm. There

---

ALASKAN SALMON BAKES

One popular eating event during summer in much of the state, but especially in the Southeast, is the salmon bake. This is an outdoor affair, set up next to a gurgling stream, with locally caught salmon that is grilled, smothered with somebody's homemade barbecue sauce and served all-you-can-eat style. A dinner costs $20 to $25, is strictly something tourists do, but is often the dining highlight of many trips to Alaska. One of the most adventurous salmon bakes is at Taku Glacier Lodge (p145), which begins with a 15-minute floatplane flight from Juneau and includes flying over a glacier.

---

will also be Asian restaurants (many with split hours – 11am to 2pm and 4pm to 9pm) that will do as much take-out as sit-down business.

Quick Eats

You'll find street vendors selling hot dogs, reindeer sausages and sometimes deep-fried halibut in larger cities, especially those with cruise ship traffic. Most large supermarkets will have ready-to-eat items, delis and even Asian food bars for meals that are quick and affordable. And of course there are always fast-food chains; McDonalds, Burger King and Wendy's are present and increasing.

VEGETARIANS & VEGANS

Alaska is not the land of milk and honey – or vegetables and tofu – for vegetarians and vegans. Part of it is cultural; subsistence – living off the land by hunting and fishing – is still widely practiced in Alaska. And part of it is the fact that there is so little agriculture in the state.

While places catering to vegans are rare, you will find at least one health food store in most midsize towns and cities as well as a number of restaurants advertising 'vegetarian options.' If fish is part of your diet, there's no need to worry. Most menus list as many salmon and halibut mains as beef and pork, if not more. Alternatively, search out Chinese and other Asian restaurants for the best selection of meatless dishes. Also keep in mind that Carrs, Safeway and other large supermarkets often have well-stocked salad bars, self-serve affairs at $5 per pound.

Alaska Cabbage: More Than Just Sauerkraut (1995), by University of Alaska Fairbanks Cooperative Extension Service, is a good pamphlet to have if somehow you end up with a 90lb cabbage from the Mat-Su Valley.

EATING WITH KIDS

Like elsewhere in the USA, most Alaskan restaurants welcome families and tend to cater for children, with high chairs, kids menus (smaller sizes and reduced prices) and waiters quick with a cloth when somebody spills their drink. Upscale places, where bringing an infant would be frowned upon, are limited to a handful in Anchorage, Juneau and Fairbanks. Among the best places to take children for dinner is a salmon bake (above) or a dockside restaurant such as Juneau's Doc Water's Pub (p146) where they can be entertained by the constant traffic of fishing boats and floatplanes while waiting for their food.

HABITS & CUSTOMS

Alaskans don't differ greatly in their habits and customs from other Americans when it comes to mealtime. They eat three meals a day, most of them at home, snack in between, use a fork, knife and spoon and eat kohlrabi only when someone tells them to.

Restaurants are naturally busy on Fridays and Saturdays but reservations are not that important. The exceptions are fine restaurants in Anchorage and cruise ship ports such as Juneau, Ketchikan and Skagway,

www.alaskaseafood .org – the Alaska Seafood Marketing Institute's website is loaded with recipes, seafood facts, nutritional information and even has a kids section.

where three or four boats can suddenly triple the town's population and fill every place that posts a menu.

Tipping is expected in Alaska, and insulting if you leave a $1 tip on a $25 meal. The tourism season is far too short for waiters to earn a living on their wages alone. Tip 15% on breakfast, lunch and café dinners; $20 at an upscale restaurant. Don't forget to tip your bartender even if your time at the bar didn't involve food. When a pint of beer is $4 to $5, a $1-a-drink tip is not too outrageous.

Finally, Alaska is gradually going smoke free. Many cities have already banned smoking in all restaurants and bars. Double check before you light up after a fine meal.

Environment

Large and wild, undeveloped and pure, Alaska has one main attraction – its environment: land without roads, wildlife without cages. Visitors don't travel this far north for the state's restaurants or cultural scene. They want to see the tallest mountain in North America, witness a glacier calving icebergs the size of small cars, hook a 40lb fish. Many arrive solely to sneak away from all traces of civilization, hoping to encounter as much of Alaska's bountiful wildlife as they can.

THE LAND

In geological time, the Alaskan landmass is relatively young and still active. The result of plate tectonics, where the Pacific Plate (the ocean floor) drifts under the North American Plate, Alaska is very mountainous.

The state represents the northern boundary of the chain of Pacific Ocean volcanoes known as the 'Ring of Fire' and is the most seismically active region of North America. It's estimated that 11% of the world's earthquakes occur in Alaska, which averages more than 50 a day, with Valdez experiencing a major one – 5.0 or higher on the Richter scale – almost annually. Most of the state's volcanoes lie in a 1500-mile arc from the Alaska Peninsula, 120 miles southwest of Anchorage, to the tip of the Aleutian Islands. This area contains more than 65 volcanoes, 46 of them active in the last 200 years.

Colliding plates also created three impressive mountain systems that arch across the state. The Coast Range, a continuation of Washington State's Olympic Range, which includes the St Elias Range, the Chugach and Kenai Mountains, sweeps along the southern edge of Alaska before dipping into the sea southwest of Kodiak Island. The Alaska and Aleutian Ranges parallel the same arc, and the Brooks Range skirts the Arctic Circle.

In between the Alaska Range and the Brooks Range is Interior Alaska, an immense plateau rippled by foothills, low mountains and great rivers, among them the Yukon River, the third longest in the USA at 2300 miles. North of the Brooks Range is the North Slope, a tundra that gently descends to the Arctic Ocean.

Southeast Alaska

Southeast Alaska is a 500-mile coastal strip that extends from north of Prince Rupert Island to the Gulf of Alaska. In between are the hundreds of islands of the Alexander Archipelago and a narrow strip of coast separated from Canada's mainland by the glacier-filled Coast Range.

Winding through the middle of the region is the Inside Passage waterway, the lifeline for its isolated communities. High annual rainfall and mild temperatures have turned the Southeast into a rain forest broken up by mountains, glaciers and fjords.

Prince William Sound & Kenai Peninsula

Like the Southeast, much of this region (also known as Southcentral Alaska) is a mixture of rugged mountains, glaciers, steep fjords and lush forests. This mix of terrain, and the fact that much of it can be reached by road, makes Southcentral Alaska the state's most popular recreational area. The weather along the coastline can often be rainy and stormy, but summers are usually mild and in August you'll experience generally sunny weather.

www.lnt.org – the Leave No Trace Center for Outdoor Ethics is an organization dedicated to promoting responsible outdoor recreation and respect for America's wilderness areas.

The Great Kobuk Sand Dunes comprise a 25-sq-mile swath of sand 40 miles above the Arctic Circle. Remnants of ancient glaciers, some dunes rise 100 ft high.

Southwest Alaska

Stretching 1500 miles, from Kodiak Island to the international date line, Southwest Alaska is an island-studded region that includes the Aleutian Islands, the Alaska Peninsula and Bristol Bay. The region forms the northern rim of the Pacific Ocean's Ring of Fire and contains 46 active volcanoes. It is also rich in wildlife, including the largest bears in the world and the richest salmon runs in Alaska.

Denali & the Interior

Roadside Geology of Alaska (1988), by Cathy Connor & Daniel O'Haire, explores the geology you see from the road, covering everything from earthquakes to why there's gold on the beaches of Nome – not dull reading by any means.

Three major highways – the George Parks, Glenn and Richardson Hwys – cut across Alaska's Interior and pass numerous recreational areas, including Denali National Park & Preserve. Boxed in by the Alaska Range to the north and the Wrangell and Chugach Mountains to the south with the Talkeetna Mountains cutting through the middle, the Interior has a rugged appearance matching that of Southeast and Southcentral Alaska but with less rain and cloudy weather.

The Bush

This is the largest slice of Alaska, including the Brooks Range, Arctic Alaska and Western Alaska on the Bering Sea. The remote, hard-to-reach Bush is separated from the rest of the state by mountains, rivers and vast roadless distances, offering a glimpse of a lifestyle unaffected by the state's tourist industry. The climate in the summer can range from a dry and chilly 40°F in the nightless Arctic tundra to the wet and fog of the considerably warmer Bering Sea coast, a flat landscape of lakes and slow-moving rivers.

ALASKA'S GLACIERS

They may be rapidly retreating due to global warming but Alaska's glaciers are still one of its most popular attractions. These rivers of ice form when the snowfall in the mountains exceeds the rate of melting. As the snow builds up, it becomes a solid cap of ice that, because of gravity, flows like a frozen river often on a layer of meltwater that is as thin as a sheet of paper. Because glacial ice absorbs all the colors of the spectrum except blue, which it reflects, glacial ice often appears blue. The more overcast the day, the bluer glacial ice appears. If it's raining on the day you are to view a glacier, rejoice; the blues will never be more intense.

Alaska is one of the few places in the world where active glaciation occurs on such a grand scale. There are an estimated 100,000 glaciers in Alaska, covering 29,000 sq miles, or 5% of the state, and containing three-quarters of all its fresh water.

The largest glacier is the Bering Glacier, which stretches more than 100 miles, from the St Elias Range to the Gulf of Alaska. If you include the Bagley Ice Field, where the Bering Glacier begins, this glacial complex covers 2250 sq miles, making it larger than Delaware. Just to the east is the Malaspina Glacier complex, which is 60 miles long and 1200ft thick.

Tidewater glaciers extend into the sea or a lake, causing them to shed icebergs in an explosion of water. The southernmost tidewater glacier in North America is the LeConte Glacier, near Petersburg in the Southeast. La Perouse Glacier, in Glacier Bay National Park, is the only one that discharges icebergs directly into the Pacific Ocean. The largest collection of tidewater glaciers is in Prince William Sound, where 20 of them are active.

The longest tidewater glacier is Hubbard, which begins in Canada and stretches 76 miles to Russell Fjord, near Yakutat. It might also be one of the most active. In 1986 Hubbard rapidly advanced across the fjord, reaching the shoreline on the other side. For most of that year, Russell Fjord was technically a lake, until the ice dam dramatically broke.

Active tidewater glaciers can be easily viewed from tour boats. The best places to go for such a day cruise are Glacier Bay National Park (p152), Kenai Fjords National Park (p244) or Prince William Sound (p227), out of Whittier. For ways to experience a glacier, see p14.

CLIMATE

The oceans surrounding 75% of the state, the mountainous terrain and the low angle of the sun give Alaska an extremely variable climate and daily weather that is infamous for its unpredictability.

In the Interior and up around Fairbanks precipitation is light, but temperatures can fluctuate by more than 100°F during the year. Fort Yukon holds the record for the state's highest temperature, at 100°F in June 1915, yet it once recorded a temperature of –78°F in winter. Fairbanks regularly has the odd summer's day that hits 90°F and always has nights during winter that drop below –60°F.

The Southeast and much of Southcentral have a temperate maritime climate; much like Seattle only wetter. Juneau averages 57in of rain or snow annually, and Ketchikan gets 154in a year, most of which is rain, as the temperatures are extremely mild even in winter.

Shielded by the Kenai Mountains from Southcentral Alaska's worst weather, the Anchorage Bowl receives only 14in of rain annually and enjoys a relatively mild climate: January averages 13°F, July about 58°F. Technically a subarctic desert, Anchorage does have more than its share of overcast days, especially in early and late summer.

For visitors the most spectacular part of Alaska's climate is its long days. At Point Barrow, Alaska's northernmost point, the sun doesn't set for 2½ months, from May to August. In other Alaskan regions, the longest day is on June 21 (the summer solstice), when the sun sets for only two hours in Fairbanks and for five hours in the Southeast. Even after sunset in late June, it is replaced not by night but by a dusk that still allows good visibility.

> The heaviest recorded annual snowfall in Alaska was 974.5in at Thompson Pass, north of Valdez, in the winter of 1952–53.

WILDLIFE

Even from the road, most people see more wildlife during their trip in Alaska than they do in a lifetime elsewhere. But to increase such sightings you should know what you're looking for and where to look for the species you want to see (p50). The best wildlife areas are highlighted in Getting Started (p14).

> Guide to the Birds of Alaska (1995), by Robert Armstrong, is the birder's bible in the Far North covering all 443 species of Alaska's birds.

NATIONAL, STATE & REGIONAL PARKS

One of the main attractions of Alaska is public land where you can play and roam over an area of 384,000 sq miles, more than twice the size of California. The agency with the most public land is the Bureau of Land Management (BLM; 133,594 sq miles) followed by the US Fish and Wildlife Service (USFWS; 120,312 sq miles) and the National Park Service (84,375 sq miles).

Alaska's 15 national parks in particular are the state's crown jewels, as far as most travelers are concerned. The park system attracts more than two million visitors a year with the most popular units being **Klondike Gold Rush National Historical Park** (☎ 907-983-9224; www.nps.gov/klgo), which draws 844,000 visitors to Skagway, and **Denali National Park** (☎ 907-683-2294; www.nps.gov/dena), home of Mt McKinley. Other popular units are **Glacier Bay National Park** (☎ 907-697-2230; www.nps.gov/glba), a highlight of every cruise ship itinerary in the southeast, and **Kenai Fjords National Park** (☎ 907-224-3175; www.nps.gov/kefj) in Seward.

Alaska State Parks oversees 121 units that are not nearly as renowned as most national parks and thus far less crowded at trailheads and in campgrounds. The largest is the 1.6-million-acre **Wood-Tikchik State Park** (☎ 907-269-8698; www.alaskastateparks.org), a roadless wilderness north of Dillingham. The most popular unit is **Chugach State Park** (☎ 907-345-5014; www.alaskastateparks .org), the 495,000-acre unit that is Anchorage's after-work playground.

> www.aurorawebcam .com – like aurora webcasts from Fairbanks and a gallery of great photos and viseos of the northern lights.

MAJOR PARKS OF ALASKA

Park	Features	Activities	Page
Misty Fiords National Monument	steep fjords, 3000ft sea cliffs, lush rain forest	boat cruises, kayaking, cabin rentals, flightseeing	p79
Tracy Arm-Fords Terror Wilderness Area	glaciers, steep fjords, a parade of icebergs, marine wildlife	boat cruises, kayaking, wildlife watching	p143
Admiralty Island National Monument	wilderness island, chain of lakes, brown bears, marine wildlife	bear viewing, kayaking, canoeing, cabin rentals	p150
Glacier Bay National Park Preserve	tidewater glaciers, whales, Fairweather Mountains	kayaking, camping, whale watching, lodge, boat cruises	p152
Chugach State Park	Chugach Mountains, alpine trails, Eklutna Lake	backpacking, mountain biking, paddling, hiking, campgrounds	p182
Independence Mine State Historical Park	Talkeetna Mountains, alpine scenery, gold mine ruins, visitor center	mine tours, hiking	p206
Kenai Fjords National Park	tidewater glaciers, whales, marine wildlife, steep fjords, cabin rental	boat cruises, kayaking, hiking	p242
Kachemak Bay State Park	glaciers, protected coves, alpine areas, cabin rentals	kayaking, backpacking, boat cruises	p272
Kenai National Wildlife Refuge	chain of lakes, Russian River, moose, campgrounds	fishing, canoeing, wildlife watching, hiking	p247
Katmai National Park & Preserve	Valley of 10,000 Smokes, volcanoes, brown bears, lodge	fishing, bear watching, backpacking, kayaking	p289
Denali State Park	alpine scenery, trails, views of Mt McKinley, campgrounds	backpacking, hiking, camping	p327
Denali National Park	Mt McKinley, brown bears, caribou, Wonder Lake, campgrounds	wildlife viewing, backpacking, hiking, park bus tours	p304
Wrangell-St Elias National Park	mountainous terrain, Kennecott mine ruins, glaciers	backpacking, flightseeing, rafting, mine tours	p345
Chena River State Recreation Area	Chena River, alpine areas, granite tors, campgrounds, cabin rentals	backpacking, canoeing, hiking	p369
Gates of the Arctic National Park	Brooks Range, Noatak River, treeless tundra, caribou	rafting, canoeing, backpacking, fishing	p391
Kodiak National Wildlife Refuge	giant bears, rich salmon runs, wilderness lodges, cabin rentals	bear watching, flightseeing, cabin rentals	p286

Both the BLM and the USFWS oversee many refuges and preserves that are remote, hard to reach and not set up with visitor facilities such as campgrounds and trails. The major exception is the **Kenai National Wildlife Refuge** (☎ 907-262-7021; kenai.fws.gov), whose 14 campgrounds and great fishing are an easy drive from Anchorage and a popular weekend destination for locals and tourists alike.

For more pretrip information see p60 or contact the **Alaska Public Lands Information Center** (☎ 907-271-2737; www.nps.gov/aplic/center), a clearing house for information on all of Alaska's public lands.

ENVIRONMENTAL ISSUES

Due to Alaska's size and its huge tracts of wilderness, its environmental issues are, more often than not, national debates. And the entire country is closely watching its most serious environmental problem: the effects of global warming on Alaska.

Alaska's temperatures are rising, causing its glaciers to retreat at alarming rates. Portage Glacier can no longer be viewed from its visitor center; famed Columbia Glacier is expected to reach land by 2010. The warmer temperatures have caused the tree line to move north into the North Slope tundra and a four-million-acre infestation of the spruce bark beetle in the Kenai Peninsula. Global warming has led to the Mat-Su Valley being invaded by grasshoppers and caused the permafrost to begin disappearing, leaving behind a quagmire that results in villages sliding into the ocean. The Arctic sea ice is also melting; bad news for polar bears who struggle to find food on land and the reason many scientists believe they will be extinct in 50 years.

Alaska's other environmental issues are also hotly contested and include drilling for oil in the Arctic National Wildlife Refuge (see p30) and Governor Frank Murkowski's push to stimulate the economy by building roads across a mostly roadless state. Tugging more at the heartstrings of outside environmentalists is the state's decision to resume its wolf-control program to increase the number of moose available to rural residents living a subsistence lifestyle. Despite 'howl-in' protests by Friends of Animals and threats of a tourism boycott, state biologists have killed almost 500 wolves in 2004–06, either by land-and-shoot or aerial shooting.

For more information on environmental issues, contact these conservation organizations:

Alaska Sierra Club (☎ 907-276-4048; www.alaska.sierraclub.org)
Southeast Alaska Conservation Council (☎ 907-586-6942; www.seacc.org)
Wilderness Society (☎ 907-272-9453; www.wilderness.org)

www.alaskanha.org – The Alaska Natural History Association website sells a wide selection of books on Alaska's environment.

arcticcircle.uconn.edu – a great introduction to the way of life, history and issues concerning Arctic Alaska, including the Arctic National Wildlife Refuge.

Alaskan Wildlife

With a relatively small human population concentrated in a handful of cities, Alaska is one of the few places in the USA where entire ecosystems are still intact and ancient migratory routes uninterrupted. Some species that are threatened or endangered elsewhere – brown bears and bald eagles, to name but two – are thriving in the 49th state. More caribou live in Alaska (900,000) than people (655,435), and birds are in no short supply either. More than 400 species have been seen in the state, with 20 million shorebirds and waterfowl migrating through the Copper River Delta near Cordova every spring. Pods of humpback whales spend summers in the icy straits of Southeast Alaska. Come August, streams and rivers are choking with millions of spawning salmon.

Welcome to Barrow! Polar bears occasionally wander into Barrow, but one bear actually closed down the city's airport in 2004 when it casually strolled across the tarmac.

While the numbers are impressive, it's important to remember that Alaska's wildlife is spread over an area the size of a small continent. Some species, particularly large land mammals, need a vast territory to survive the harsh climactic conditions and the short growing season of their food supply. Many species migrate as the seasons change, while others are concentrated in specific locations across the state.

LAND MAMMALS
Bears

Visitors to Alaska have a love–hate relationship with the bears. Nothing makes you more afraid in the backcountry than the thought of encountering a bear, but you would hate leaving the state without having seen one in the wild. After a handful of bear encounters, most people develop a healthy respect for these magnificent animals. There are three species of bear in Alaska – brown, black and polar bears – and most likely you'll see brown bears, since these have the greatest range.

Backcountry Bear Basics (1997), by Dave Smith, is a worthwhile reference book to read if you are nervous about sharing the wilderness with bears.

At one time, brown bears and grizzly bears were listed as separate species, but now both are classified as Ursus arctos. The difference isn't as much genetics as size. Browns live along the coast where abundant salmon runs help them grow to a large size (often exceeding 800lb). The famed Kodiak brown bear has been known to stand 10ft tall and tip the scales at 1500lb. Grizzlies are browns found inland, away from the rich salmon runs. Normally a male weighs from 500lb to 700lb, and females half as much.

The color of a brown bear can range from almost black to blond, with the darker individuals resembling black bears. One way biologists tell them apart is by measuring the upper rear molar. The length of the crown of this tooth in a brown is always more than 1¼in. A less dangerous approach is to look for the prominent shoulder hump, easily seen behind the neck when a brown bear is on all fours.

There are more than 40,000 brown bears in Alaska. They live everywhere in the state except for some islands in the Aleutians, the Bering Sea and Frederick Sound in the Southeast. In June and July you can see brown bears fishing along rivers. In late summer and early fall, bears will often move to the tundra and to open meadows to feed on berries.

Though black bears are the USA's most widely distributed bruin, their range is far more limited in Alaska. They live in most forested areas of the state, but not north of the Brooks Range, on the Seward Peninsula or on many large islands like Kodiak and Admiralty.

The average male weighs 180lb to 250lb and can range in color from black to a rare creamy white color. A brown or cinnamon black bear often appears in Southcentral Alaska, leaving many backpackers confused about what the species is. Beyond measuring that upper rear molar, look for the straight facial profile to confirm it's a black bear.

Black bears, as well as brown, are creatures of opportunity when it comes to eating. Bears are omnivorous, and their common foods include berries, grass, sedge, salmon and any carrion they happen to find on their travels.

Polar bears (*Ursus maritimus*) have always captured our interest because of their large size and white color, but they're not easy to encounter. Plan on stopping at the zoo in Anchorage or an expensive sidetrip to Barrow if you want to see one. Polar bears occur only in the northern hemisphere and almost always in association with Arctic Sea ice.

A male normally weighs between 600lb and 1200lb but occasionally it tops 1400lb. The polar bear's adaptations to a life on the sea ice include its white, water-repellent coat, dense underfur, specialized teeth for a carnivorous diet (primarily seals) and hair that almost completely covers the bottom of its feet.

Moose

These are improbable-looking mammals: long-legged to the extreme but short-bodied, with a huge rack of antlers and a drooping nose. Standing still, they look uncoordinated until you watch them run or, better still, swim – then their speed and grace are astounding. They're the world's largest members of the deer family, and the Alaskan species is the largest of all moose. A newborn weighs in at 35lb and can grow to more than 300lb within five months; cows weigh from 800lb to 1200lb and bulls from 1000lb to more than 1500lb.

Moose may live to over 20 years old in the wild, and often travel 20 miles to 40 miles to forage for their main diet of birch, willow, alder and aspen saplings. In the spring and summer, you often encounter them feeding in lakes, ponds and muskegs, with those huge noses below the water as they grab for aquatic plants and weeds.

The moose population ranges from an estimated 120,000 to 160,000, and historically moose have always been the most important game animal in Alaska. Athabascans survived by utilizing the moose as a source of food, clothing and implements, and professional hunters in the 19th century made a living by supplying moose meat to mining camps.

Moose are widespread throughout the state and range from the Stikine River in the Southeast to the Colville River on the North Slope. They're most abundant in second-growth birch forests, on timberline plateaus and along the major rivers of Southcentral Alaska and the Interior. Moose are frequently sighted along the Alcan, and Denali National Park (p310) is an excellent place to watch them. But the best place to see the biggest moose is the Kenai Peninsula, especially if you take time to paddle the Swanson River or Swan Lake canoe routes in the Kenai National Wildlife Refuge (p247).

Caribou

Although an estimated 900,000 caribou live in Alaska's 32 herds, these animals are quite difficult to view as they travel from the Interior north to the Arctic Sea. Often called the 'nomads of the north,' caribou range in weight from 150lb to more than 400lb. They migrate hundreds of miles annually between their calving grounds, rutting areas and winter home. In the summer, they feed on grasses, grasslike sedges, berries and small shrubs of the tundra. In the winter they eat a lot of lichen called 'reindeer moss.'

The principal predators of caribou are wolves, and some wolf packs on the North Slope have been known to follow caribou herds for years,

Animal Tracks of Alaska (1993), by Chris Stall, is a must for anybody who plans to do a fair amount of hiking or beachcombing in Alaska. You'll see wildlife tracks everywhere.

Bears don't hibernate but go into a stage of 'dormancy'. This is a deep sleep while denning during winter; some stay dormant for seven months.

Alaska's Sitka black-tailed deer is a favorite of hunters, but it's not the abundant source of meat like a 1,000lb moose. Most deer in Alaska weigh 100lb.

picking off the young, the old and the victims of disabling falls caused by running in tightly massed herds. The caribou are crucial to the Inupiat and other Alaska Natives, who hunt more than 30,000 a year to support their subsistence lifestyle.

The best place for the average visitor to see caribou is Denali National Park (p310). Occasionally you can see them from the park road, but, if the day is warm and still, you'll often encounter them above the tree line, where they head to seek relief from insects. In late spring look for them around the remaining patches of snow.

Perhaps one of the greatest wildlife events left in the world today is the migration of the Western Arctic herd of caribou, the largest such herd in North America, with almost 500,000 animals. The herd uses the North Slope for its calving area, and in late August many of the animals begin to cross the Noatak River on their journey southward. During that time, the few visitors lucky enough to be on the river are often rewarded with the awesome experience of watching 20,000 or more caribou crossing the tundra toward the Brooks Range.

The Alaska Department of Fish and Game produces *Anchorage Wildlife Viewing Hot Spots*. Sure, Anchorage is a big city, but there's still plenty of wildlife around town

Mountain Goats

The mountain goat is the single North American species in the widespread group of goat antelopes. All are characterized by short horns and a fondness for the most rugged alpine terrain.

Although mountain goats are often confused with Dall sheep, they are easily identified by their longer hair, black horns and deep chest. They're quite docile, making them easy to watch in the wild, and their gait, even when they're approached too closely, is a deliberate pace. In the summer they normally frequent high alpine meadows, grazing on grasses and herbs.

In Alaska mountain goats range through the bulk of the Southeast, fanning out north and west into the coastal mountains of Cook Inlet as well as the Chugach and Wrangell Mountains. Good locations to see them include Glacier Bay (p152) and Wrangell-St Elias National Park (p345). Public scopes in Juneau's Marine Park (p138) allow visitors to look for goats on Mt Juneau.

www.nps.gov/aplic /forkids.htm – this great site helps children learn about Alaskan wildlife before they head to the Far North.

Dall Sheep

These are more numerous and widespread than mountain goats – they number close to 80,000 – and live principally in the Alaska, Wrangell, Chugach, and Kenai mountain ranges. Often Dall sheep are seen in Denali National Park (p304) when the park shuttle bus crosses Polychrome Pass on its way to Wonder Lake.

Rams are easy to see thanks to their massive curling horns, which grow throughout their lives. The horns – like claws, hooves and fingernails – grow from the skin, and as rams mature, continue their ever-increasing curl, reaching a three-quarters curl in five years and a full curl in seven years.

It's spectacular to watch rams in a horn-clashing battle, but contrary to popular belief, they're not fighting for a female, just for social dominance. Dall sheep prefer rocky, open, alpine tundra regions. In the spring and fall, however, they tend to move to lower slopes where the grazing is better. The best time to spot rams and see them clash is right before the rut (their mating period), which begins in November.

Wolves

While the wolf is struggling to survive throughout most of the USA, its natural distribution and numbers still seem to be unaffected by human undertakings in Alaska. Throughout history no animal has been more misunderstood than the wolf. A pack of wolves is no match for a healthy 1200lb moose; wolves can usually only catch and kill the weak, injured or young, thus strengthening the herd they are stalking.

Eight thousand wolves live in packs, in almost every region in Alaska. Most adult males average 85lb to 115lb, and their pelts can be either grey, black, offwhite, brown and yellow, with some tinges approaching red. Wolves travel, hunt, feed and operate in the social unit of a pack. In the Southeast their principal food is deer; in the Interior it's moose; in Arctic Alaska it's caribou.

Even if you're planning to spend a great deal of time away from the road wandering in the wilderness, your chances of seeing wolves are rare. You might, however, find evidence of them in their doglike tracks, their howls at night and the remains of their wild kills.

Beavers & River Otters

Around lakes and rivers you stand a good chance of seeing river otters and especially beavers, or at the very least the lodges and dams beavers build. Both live throughout the state except in the North Slope. Often larger than their relatives further south, otters range from 15lb to 35lb, and beavers weigh between 40lb and 70lb, although 100lb beavers have been recorded in Alaska.

FISH & MARINE MAMMALS
Whales

The three most common whales seen in coastal waters are the 50ft-long humpback, with its humplike dorsal fin and long flippers; the smaller bowhead whale; and the gray whale. At one time Glacier Bay was synonymous with whale watching. But today tour boats head out of almost every Southeast Alaska port loaded with whale-watching passengers. You can also join such wildlife trips in Kenai Fjords National Park (p244) near Seward and in Kodiak (p282), where some outfitters combine kayaking and whale watching.

Seals

The most commonly seen marine mammals are seals, which often bask in the sun on an ice floe. Six species of seal exist in Alaska, but most visitors will encounter just the harbor seal, the only seal whose range includes the Southeast, Prince William Sound and the rest of the Gulf of Alaska. The average weight of a male is 200lb – achieved through a diet of herring, flounder, salmon, squid and small crabs.

Two other species, ringed seals and bearded seals, occur for the most part in the northern Bering, Chukchi and Beaufort Seas where sea ice forms during winter. Although travel on land or ice is laborious and slow for seals, they're renowned divers. During a dive a seal's heartbeat may slow from a normal 55 to 120 beats per minute to just 15. This allows them to stay underwater for more than five minutes, often reaching depths of 300ft or more. Biologists have recorded harbor seal dives of 20 minutes or longer.

Dolphins & Porpoises

Many visitors also see dolphins and harbor porpoises, even from the decks of the ferries. Occasionally, ferry travelers spot a rare treat: a pod of orcas (killer whales), whose high black-and-white dorsal fins make them easy to identify from a distance. Orcas, which can be more than

cybersalmon.fws .gov – cyber Salmon is the US Fish & Wildlife Service site dedicated to all things fishy.

Humpback whales eat up to two tons of krill and small fish per day during their summer stay in Alaska.

www.alaskasealife.org /New/research/round island.php – view two-ton walruses jostling or just laying around on Round Island through a live video feed.

20ft long, are actually the largest members of the dolphin family, which also includes the beluga or white whale. Belugas range in length from 11ft to 16ft and often weigh more than 3000lb. The 50,000 belugas that live in Alaskan waters travel in herds of more than 100. Their range includes the Arctic waters north of Bristol Bay and also Cook Inlet, where most visitors will see them, especially in Kenai, which has a beluga observation area (p250).

Salmon

Salmon runs are where thousands of fish swim upstream to spawn, and rank among Alaska's most amazing and common sights. From late July to mid-September, many coastal streams are choked with salmon. You won't see just one fish here and there, but thousands – so many that they have to wait their turn to swim through narrow gaps of shallow water. Five kinds of salmon populate Alaskan waters: sockeye (also referred to as red salmon), king or chinook, pink or humpie, coho or silver, and chum.

Alaska has the longest salmon run in the world, with some chum salmon swimming more than 2000 miles up the Yukon River before they actually spawn.

BIRDS
Bald Eagles

The most impressive bird in Alaska's wilderness is the bald eagle – with a white tail and head, and a wingspan that often reaches 8ft – which has become the symbol of the nation. While elsewhere the bird is on the endangered species list, in Alaska it thrives. The eagle can be sighted almost daily in most of the Southeast and is common in Prince William Sound. The bird is also responsible for a spectacle that exceeds even the salmon runs, when in November more than 4000 eagles migrate to the Chilkat River (p163) near Haines to feed on a late salmon run . Bare trees, without a leaf remaining, can support 80 or more white-headed eagles, with up to four or five to a branch.

Ptarmigan

The state bird of Alaska is the ptarmigan, a cousin of the prairie grouse. Three species of the ptarmigan can be found throughout the state in high treeless country. The birds are easy to spot during the summer, as their wings remain white while their head and chest turn brown. In the winter they sport pure white plumage.

Seabirds & Waterfowl

Alaskan seabirds include the playful horned puffin, six species of auklet and three species of albatross, which boast a wingspan of up to 7ft. The optimum way to see a variety of seabirds, including the rare blackfooted

---

BIRDING IN ALASKA

More than anything, Alaska is a haven for winged wildlife – 437 species of bird have been identified in the state – and thus birders.

The Pribilof Islands in the Bering Sea (p299) attract birders from around the world. If you can't afford that trip, visit Potter Marsh south of Anchorage, a sanctuary that attracts more than 100 species annually. If you're truly serious about birding, then try to come to Alaska during the spring migration in May and attend either the Copper River Delta Shorebird Festival (p222) in Cordova (www.cordovachamber.com) or the Kachemak Bay Shorebird Festival (p263) in Homer (www.homeralaska.org).

For a local bird listing or schedule of various field trips during the summer, birders can contact the **Anchorage Audubon Society** (☎ 907-338-2473; www.anchorageaudubon.org).

albatross, is to board the Alaska Marine Highway ferry for its special run along the Alaska Peninsula to Unalaska in the Aleutian Islands (p285).

An amazing variety of waterfowl also migrates to Alaska, including trumpeter swans. The trumpeter swan is the world's largest member of the waterfowl family and occasionally tips the scales at 30lb. Other waterfowl include Canada geese, of which more than 130,000 nest in Alaska; all four species of eider in the world; the colorful harlequin duck; and five species of loon (*Gavia*).

A puffin's beak is specially adapted to carry fish. Puffins can hold 10 fish at once, but one bird was observed carrying a record 62!

FLORA

The flora of Alaska, much like everything else in the state, is diverse, changing dramatically from one region to the next. In the coastal regions of Southeast and Southcentral Alaska, mild temperatures and frequent rains produce lush coniferous forests of giant Sitka spruce and western hemlock.

But the Interior, between the Alaska Range and the Brooks Range, is dominated by boreal forests: stands of scrawny cottonwood, paper birch and stunted black spruce. Continue north and the forests give way to the taiga zone, characterized by muskeg, willow thickets and more stunted spruce. Eventually you'll end up in the tundra, an Arctic coastal region where there are no trees at all.

Trees

There are 33 native species of trees, the fewest of any state in the USA, and only 12 of these are classified as large trees (more than 70ft high). Not surprisingly, nine of these species live in the coastal regions of Southeast and Southcentral Alaska.

Wild, Edible & Poisonous Plants of Alaska (1993), by University of Alaska-Fairbanks, is a handy guide if you plan to snack along the Alaskan trails.

Alaska's state tree, the Sitka spruce, thrives in the coastal regions of Southcentral and Southeast Alaska. The largest species of spruce in the USA, Sitka spruce grows quickly and can reach heights of 225ft and diameters of 8ft. The short, sharp needles are dark green on top, silvery blue underneath.

Sitka spruce lumber is strong and lightweight, making it ideal for constructing aircraft, gliders and boats. Alaska Natives use its roots for basket weaving. Commercially, it is the most valuable species in Alaska, though the recent devastation wrought by spruce bark beetles has changed this drastically.

Occupying the same regions as the Sitka spruce is the western hemlock. In Southeast Alaska, the western hemlock makes up more than 70% of the trees in coastal spruce/hemlock forests. Hemlocks can grow to 190ft high and 5ft in diameter, and live to be 500 years old. Their needles are short, soft and rounded at the tip. Like the Sitka spruce, hemlock is commercially harvested, with much of the wood used for construction.

The temperate rain forest of Tongass National Forest in Southeast Alaska has more biomass than the famous tropical rainforests of the Amazon.

Found primarily in Interior Alaska, white spruce is considerably smaller than the Sitka spruce, rarely exceeding 50ft in height and 1ft to 2ft in diameter. Needles are less than an inch long and yellow to blue-green in color. The subarctic species, black spruce, can withstand severe winds and extreme cold. Pockets of dwarfed black spruce exist in the Brooks Range, and in bogs, wetlands and tundra areas further south.

Paper birch is widely found in the Interior and Southcentral, and easily identified by its dull white, peeling bark. These trees reaches heights of 70ft and diameters of 1ft to 3ft. Their green, pointed leaves range from 1in to 4in long. Birches are an important food source for wildlife, as the twigs are cropped by moose and mountain goats, the seeds by songbirds and the inner bark by porcupines and beavers.

Ranging from the size of a shrub to a small tree, alder is found in the southern half of the state and is the most common broadleaf tree in the Southeast. Alder is a pioneer species, a rapid invader of bare soil that has been newly exposed by glaciers, avalanches or loggers clear-cutting a track of hemlock. The dark green leaves are 1in to 3in wide with serrated edges, and the gray bark is smooth.

Various species of willow can be found alongside alder in stream beds or in newly scarred areas. It's the tangle of willow and alder that makes cross-country trekking such a nightmare in many parts of Alaska. Willow has light, gray-green leaves that are 2in to 5in long, smooth and oblong. The telltale signs of willow are the caterpillar-shaped catkins that explode with white fluff in the spring.

Commonly found mixed with alder, the black cottonwood occurs throughout Southeast and Southcentral Alaska, most often in river valleys. It's one of the tallest of Alaska's broadleaf trees, often reaching a height of 80ft. Cottonwood leaves are dark green on top and silvery white beneath, with smooth edges (unlike the alder's toothed leaves).

Wild Berries

From a hiker's perspective, Alaska's wild berries may be the most interesting kind of flora. Blueberries, which grow throughout much of the state, can reach heights of 6ft in the Southeast. Thickets of salmonberries thrive in moist woods and lower mountain slopes from the Alaskan Peninsula to Southcentral and Southeast Alaska. A cousin of the raspberry, the fruit looks similar but can range in color from red to yellow to orange.

You'll encounter raspberries in fields and thickets in the Interior, and Southcentral and Southeast regions. Wild strawberries grow in scattered clumps throughout Southeast and Southcentral Alaska and the Aleutian Islands, particularly on beaches. Other edible species worth learning to identify include red huckleberries, lowbush and highbush cranberries and red currants or gooseberries, which have an excellent flavor without the skunklike smell associated with many species of currants.

If you plan to feast on wild berries, take the time to learn which ones are inedible. The most common poisonous variety is the baneberry, which often appears as a white berry in the Southeast and the Interior.

Wildflowers

Alaska's state flower is the forget-me-not, a delicate, sky-blue flower with a yellow eye. It grows 6in to 20in high. Blue-violet wild lupine can reach heights of up to 4ft; it thrives along coastal shores and in alpine areas. Even more impressive is fireweed, whose pink blossoms can be found throughout much of subarctic Alaska, in open areas such as meadows, riverbanks and clear-cuts. If conditions are right, fireweed can grow up to 7ft tall.

In the bogs and wetlands of Southeast and Southcentral Alaska, you'll most likely see – and definitely smell – skunk cabbage. The yellow-brown flower often appears while snow is still on the ground, and the leaves soon follow. The prickly wild rose features five pink petals, which you may see anywhere from Sitka north to the Alaska Range and as far west as Unalaska. Its fruits, rosehips, are often collected in the fall and are an excellent source of vitamin C.

Other common types of wildflower in Alaska are the pink-and-red primrose, the yellow mountain marigold, the blue mountain harebell, the white Arctic daisy and the dark blue monkshood, a member of the buttercup family.

Alaska's state tree, the Sitka spruce, is the largest species of spruce in the USA and it is a popular tonewood that is used for making guitar bodies.

Global warming has brought unusual species to Alaska. Hard-shelled turtles, great white sharks and jumbo squid are now north of Oregon.

www.adfg.state.ak.us /pubs/notebook/note home.php – The Alaska Dept of Fish and Game's excellent *Wildlife Notebook* covers Alaska's major types of animals and birds.

Tundra

The Arctic tundra is a bizarre world, a treeless area except for a few small stands on gravel flood plains of rivers. Plant life hugs the ground – even willow trees that only grow 6in high still produce pussy willows. Other plants, including grasses, mosses and a variety of tiny flowers, provide a carpet of life for a short period in July and August despite little precipitation and a harsh climate.

Tundra can make for tough hiking for those who travel this far north in Alaska. Wet and moistened tundra sits on top of permanently frozen ground known as permafrost. The tundra thaws in the summer but remains waterlogged because the permafrost prevents drainage. The caribou can navigate these soggy conditions because their dew claws and spreading cleft hooves help support their weight on the soft ground. Hikers are not so lucky.

Alaska Outdoors

Alaskans love to play outdoors, and the season when they play the most is summer. Lucky you. That's also the tourist season and you can play with them. Whether your passion is hiking, mountain biking, climbing a mountain or catching a curl on a surfboard, Alaska is the USA's biggest playground. Go outside and play.

For multiday wilderness adventures that involve backpacking, kayaking, canoeing or rafting see p64; for birding see p54.

CAMPING

www.kck.org – the website of Knik Canoeists & Kayakers, based in Anchorage, is helpful to visiting paddlers when planning wilderness trips in Alaska.

Camping is not just cheap accommodations in Alaska; it's a reason to be outside, soaking up the scenery while watching that trout you just caught sizzling on an open campfire. Camping is such a popular activity that many communities have set up facilities on the edge of town with Homer's Karen Hornday Memorial Campground (p264) and Wrangell's City Park (p116) being particularly scenic spots to pitch a tent.

But the best camping experience is away from towns at one of the public campgrounds operated by the Alaska Division of Parks, the US Forest Service (USFS) or the Bureau of Land Management (BLM) in northern Alaska. The state park systems maintains the most, more than 70 rustic campgrounds scattered throughout Alaska, with fees from free to $15 a night in the more popular ones. The majority do no take reservations.

If you are planning to camp in Alaska, here are five campgrounds you should not pass up:

Mendenhall Lake Campground (p144) Near Juneau, it's one of Alaska's most beautiful USFS campgrounds with a view of the famous glacier from many sites.

Blueberry Lake State Recreation Area (p351) Ten sites in a scenic alpine setting north of Valdez.

Ninilchik View State Campground (p256) Lots of sites overlooking Cook Inlet, Old Ninilchik, and great clamming beaches.

Marion Creek Campground (p389) Camp north of the Arctic Circle with stunning views of the Brooks Range at this BLM facility along the Dalton Hwy.

Fort Abercrombie State Historical Park (p281) Near Kodiak; wooded sites, interesting WWII artifacts and intriguing tidal pools to explore.

CABINS

Every agency overseeing public land in Alaska, from the BLM and the National Park Service (NPS) to the Alaska Division of Parks, maintains rustic cabins in remote areas. The cabins are not expensive ($25 to $50 per night) but they are not easy to reach either. Most of them are accessed via a floatplane charter. Others are reached on foot, by boat or by paddling. Very few can be driven to. But by arranging a charter and reserving a cabin in advance you can sneak away into the wilderness without half the effort or time backpackers or paddlers put in to reach a remote corner of Alaska.

Tongass National Forest has the most cabins available, almost 150 (opposite). Alaska Division of Parks has more than 40 cabins scattered from Point Bridget State Park near Juneau to Chena River State Recreation Area east of Fairbanks. You can get a list of cabins and reserve them six months in advance through the **DNR Public Information Center** (☎ 907-269-8400; www.alaskastateparks.org).

The BLM manages 10 cabins in the **White Mountain National Recreation Area** (☎ 907-474-2251, 800-437-7021; aurora.ak.blm.gov; per night $20-25) north of Fairbanks, and the US Fish & Wildlife Service has eight in the **Kodiak National Wildlife**

ALASKA'S FOREST SERVICE CABINS

Of all the backcountry cabins available in Alaska the US Forest Service (USFS) has the most, including the more popular ones. These small structures offer more than shelter in the mountains or cheap lodging in this land of high prices. When you rent a USFS cabin ($25 to $50 a night), you're renting a personal wilderness.

Although some cabins can be reached on foot or by boat, the majority require a flight on a floatplane, ensuring that your party will be the only one in the area until the next group is flown in. The fishing can be outstanding, the chances of seeing wildlife excellent and your wilderness solitude guaranteed.

This is Alaskan wilderness at its easiest and cheapest; but remember that a USFS cabin is not a suite at the Hilton. The cabin provides security from the weather, a wood-burning stove, an outhouse and, often, a small rowboat, but you need to pack sleeping bags, food, a water filter and a cooking stove.

Of the 190 USFS cabins, 150 of those are in Tongass National Forest, which covers most of Southeast Alaska, and the other 40 are in Chugach National Forest, most of them in the Prince William Sound area. To see what each cabin offers check the websites for **Tongass National Forest** (www.fs.fed.us/r10/tongass) or **Chugach National Forest** (www.fs.fed.us/r10/chugach). Cabins can be reserved 180 days in advance through the **National Recreation Reservation Service** (NRRS; ☎ 877-444-6777, 518-885-3639; www.reserveusa.com).

In addition to the nightly fee, you need to budget the cost of the floatplane, paying a bush pilot for both a drop-off and a pickup. For cabins within 15 to 20 minutes of major towns such as Juneau or Ketchikan, expect to pay $300 to $400 for a party of two or three.

Refuge (☎ 907-487-2600; kodiak.fws.gov; per night $30) on Kodiak Island. In **Kenai Fjords National Park** (☎ 907-224-3175; www.nps.gov/kefj; per night $50), the NPS maintains four cabins that are reached by floatplane or water taxi and are reserved through the **Alaska Public Lands Information Center** (☎ 907-271-2737) after January 1 for that summer.

FISHING

Many people cling to a 'fish-per-cast' vision of angling in Alaska. They expect every river, stream and lake, no matter how close to the road, to be bountiful, but often go home disappointed when their fishing efforts produce little to brag about. Serious anglers visiting Alaska carefully research the areas to be fished and are equipped with the right gear and tackle. They often pay for guides or book a room at remote camps or lodges where rivers are not 'fished out' by every passing motorist.

If you plan to camp away from towns or, even better, undertake a wilderness trip, by all means pack a rod and reel. A backpacking rod that breaks down into five sections and has a light reel is ideal and in the Southeast and Southcentral will allow you to cast for cutthroat trout, rainbow trout and Dolly Varden (another type of trout). Further north, especially around Fairbanks, you'll get grayling, with its sail-like dorsal fin, and arctic char; during August, salmon seem to be everywhere.

An open-face spinning reel with light line, something in the 4lb to 6lb range, and a small selection of spinners and spoons will allow you to fish a wide range of waters from streams and rivers to lakes. After you arrive you can always purchase the lures used locally, but in most wilderness streams, we've rarely had a problem catching fish on Mepps spinners, sizes No 1 to No 3. For fly fishing, a No 5 or No 6 rod with a matching floating line or sinking tip is well suited for Dolly Vardens, rainbows and grayling. For salmon, a No 7 or No 8 rod and line are better choices. For ease of travel, rods should also break down and be carried in a case.

www.akflyfishers.com – Alaska Fly Fishers has great information for visiting anglers, including what flies to bring, when to fish, where to go to catch what.

You also need a fishing license. A nonresident's fishing license costs $100 a year, but you can purchase a 7- to 14-day license for $30/$50; every bait shop in the state sells them. You can also order a license online or obtain other information through the **Alaska Department of Fish & Game** (☎ 907-465-4100; www.state.ak.us/adfg).

The most comprehensive angler's guide to the state is the 450-page *Alaska Fishing* by Gunnar Pedersen & Rene Limeres. The authors begin with a detailed look at all 17 of the major species and then follow with a review of each region and major river system throughout the state. Equally good for fly fishing is *Flyfishing Alaska* by Anthony Route.

The Alaska River Guide (1998), by Karen Jettmar, is the most complete river guide for Alaska, covering more than 100 possible trips, from the Chilkat in the Southeast to Colville on the Arctic slope.

Serious anglers should consider a fishing charter. Joining a captain on his boat is $150 to $250 per person for four to six hours on the water but the local knowledge is the best investment you can make to put a trophy fish on your line. Communities with large fleets of charter captains include Homers, Seward, Petersburg, Kodiak and Ketchikan, with halibut most in demand among visitors (see p262). Head to Soldotna to land a 50lb king salmon from a driftboat in the Kenai River.

If money is no option, fly-in fishing adventures are available in cities such as Anchorage and Fairbanks. These outings use small charter planes to reach wilderness lakes and rivers for a day of salmon and steelhead fishing. In Anchorage, **Regal Air** (☎ 907-243-8535) will take you on a nine-hour, guided fly-in fishing trip to a river in Lake Clark National Park for $329. It's an expensive day trip but the fishing is legendary, sometimes even a catch per cast.

MOUNTAIN BIKING

The mountain bike's durable design, knobby tires and suspension may have been invented in California but it was made for Alaska. With such a bike you can explore an almost endless number of dirt roads, miner's two-tracks and even hiking trails that you would never consider with a road bike. For many, the versatile mountain bike is the key, and 4WD

WHO CONTROLS WHAT

With almost three-quarters of Alaska owned by federal or state agencies, it's good to know who administers the land on which you plan to hike, paddle or camp. Almost all of the recreational areas, parks and forests, including the campgrounds and trails in them, are controlled by one of five agencies:

Alaska Division of Parks (☎ 907-269-8400; www.alaskastateparks.org) Includes 121 units, from the country's largest state park (Wood-Tikchik) to many small wayside parks and campgrounds along the highway. The state areas often feature trails, campgrounds, rental cabins, wilderness areas and historic sites.

Bureau of Land Management (BLM; ☎ 907-474-2200; www.ak.blm.gov) This is the federal agency that maintains much of the wilderness around and north of Fairbanks. It has developed almost 30 camping areas and a dozen public-use cabins in the Interior, and two popular trails (Pinnell Mountain and White Mountain) off the highways north of Fairbanks.

National Park Service (NPS; ☎ 907-257-2687; www.nps.gov/parks.html) Administers 15 national parks in Alaska including such popular units as Denali National Park & Preserve, Glacier Bay National Park & Preserve, Kenai Fjords National Park and Klondike Gold Rush National Historical Park.

US Fish & Wildlife Service (UFWS; ☎ 907-786-3309; www.r7.fws.gov) Administers 16 federal wildlife refuges in Alaska, covering more than 120,312 sq miles. Many of the refuges are in remote areas of the Bush with few, if any, developed facilities. The one exception is Kenai National Wildlife Refuge, which can be reached by road from Anchorage.

US Forest Service (USFS; ☎ 907-586-8806; www.fs.fed.us/r10) Oversees the Tongass and Chugach National Forests, which cover nearly all of Southeast Alaska, the eastern Kenai Peninsula, and Prince William Sound.

PANNING FOR A FORTUNE

After all the gold rushes that have been staged in Alaska, can there possibly be any gold left for recreational gold panners? You bet! Although more than 30 million ounces of placer gold have been mined in Alaska since 1880, some geologists estimate that this amount represents only 5% of what the state contains.

Suddenly interested? Alaska has more than 150 public prospecting sites where you can recreationally pan for gold without staking a claim or filing for a permit. The best choices are in the Interior region of the state. They include the Jack Wade Dredge, at Mile 86 Taylor Hwy, and American Creek, at Mile 151; the Petersville State Recreation Mining Area, on Petersville Rd off the George Parks Hwy at Trapper Creek; and Caribou Creek, at Mile 106.8 Glenn Hwy, and Nelchina River, at Mile 137.5.

When panning for gold, you must have one essential piece of equipment: a gravity-trap pan, one that measures 10in to 20in in diameter. It can usually be bought at any good Alaskan hardware or general store. Those who have panned for a while also show up with rubber boots and gloves to protect feet and hands from icy waters; a garden trowel to dig up loose rock; a pair of tweezers to pick up gold flakes; and a small bottle to hold their find.

Panning techniques are based on the notion that gold is heavier than the gravel it lies in. Fill your pan with loose material from cracks and crevices in streams, where gold might have washed down and become lodged. Add water to the pan, rinse and discard larger rocks, keeping the rinsing in the pan. Continue to shake the contents toward the bottom by swirling the pan in a circular motion and wash off the excess sand and gravel by dipping the front into the stream.

You should be left with heavy black mud, sand and, if you are lucky, a few flakes of gold. Use tweezers or your fingernails to transfer the flakes into a bottle filled with water.

---

tracks are the avenue to escaping roads and RVers for the scenery and wildlife of the backcountry.

Just remember to pick your route carefully before heading out. Make sure the length of the route and the ruggedness of the terrain are within your capability, and that you have appropriate equipment. Always pack a lightweight, wind-and-water-resistant jacket and for all-day rides an insulating layer because the weather changes quickly in Alaska and so can the terrain. Even when renting a bike, make sure you can repair a flat with the proper spare tube and tools. Water, best carried in a hydration pack, is a must and so is energy food.

Alaska has room to ride but near cities such as Anchorage and Juneau there is still conflict between mountain bikers and hikers. Always give way to walkers and stay away from trails and areas where bikes are banned. If you choose a route already dedicated to vehicle use, such as an All-Terrain Vehicle (ATV) trail, your trip is unlikely to contribute to erosion.

There is much mountain bike activity around Anchorage, and several places to rent bikes (p182). Within the city, mountain bikers head to Kincaid Park and Far North Bicentennial Park (p179) for their fill of rugged single track. In surrounding Chugach State Park, the Powerline Pass Trail (p182) is an 11-mile round-trip adventure into the mountains while rentals are available for the 13.5-mile Lakeside Trail (p202) a popular leisurely ride that skirts Eklutna Lake.

The Resurrection Pass Trail, Russian River Trail and Johnson Pass Trails in the Chugach National Forest have become popular among off-road cyclists on the Kenai Peninsula. North of Anchorage Hatcher Pass is a haven of mountain biking activity with riders following Archangel Rd (also known as the Archangel Valley), Craggie Creek Trail and Gold Mint Trail (p206) to glaciers and old mines in the Talkeetna Mountains.

www.dnr.state.ak.us /parks/aktrails – the Alaska Department of Natural Resources website has details on trails in every corner of the state.

The most popular area for riders in Fairbanks is the Chena River State Recreation Area (p369), while in Juneau mountain bikers head to Perseverance Trail (p139), near downtown, and Montana Creek Trail (p140) out Egan Drive near the Mendenhall Glacier.

If you are able to travel with equipment on your bike (sleeping bag, food and tent), you can partake in a variety of overnight trips or longer bicycle journeys. The 92-mile Denali Park Rd (p313) is off limits to vehicles, but you can explore it on a mountain bike. Another excellent dirt road for such an adventure is the 135-mile Denali Hwy (p330) from Passon to Cantwell.

The state's most unusual mountain bike event is the Fat Tire Festival at the end of July, a 60-mile ride from Chitina to McCarthy on a Saturday and chainless downhill races on Sunday. For registration information or a list of other cycling events contact **Arctic Bicycle Club** (☎ 907-566-0177; www.arcticbike.org). There isn't a statewide guidebook to off-road riding in Alaska but there's *Mountain Bike Anchorage*, by Rosemary Austin, that covers trails and two-tracks from Girdwood to Eklutna.

If you need a guide and a set of wheels, **Alaska Backcountry Bike Tours** (☎ 2745-5014, 866-354-2453; www.mountainbikealaska.com) is a great little company that offers bike adventures from Anchorage, both day outings and multiday trips. Single day rides include the Eklutna Lakeside Trail ($109) and a 20-mile ride along Johnson Pass Trail in the Kenai Peninsula ($129). The Alaskan Epic ($995) is six days and 90 miles of single track with lodging for two nights, camping for three nights and most meals.

ROCK CLIMBING & MOUNTAINEERING

Rock climbing has been growing in popularity in Alaska. On almost any summer weekend, you can watch climbers working bolt-protected sport routes just above Seward Hwy along Turnagain Arm. Canyons in nearby Portage are also capturing the attention of rock climbers. Off Byron Glacier, several routes grace a slab of black rock polished smooth by the glacier. Not far from Portage Lake, a short hike leads to the magnificent slate walls of Middle Canyon.

Fairbanks climbers head north of town to the limestone formations known as Grapefruit Rocks, or else pack a tent and sleeping bag for the Granite Tors Trail (p369) off the Chena Hot Springs Rd. A 7-mile hike from the trailhead brings them to the tors, a series of 100ft granite spires in a wilderness setting.

For climbing equipment and more information in Anchorage, contact **Alaska Mountaineering & Hiking** (☎ 907-272-1811; www.alaskamountaineering.com). In Fairbanks, contact **Beaver Sports** (☎ 907-479-2494) for equipment. An excellent outfitter specializing in rock climbing in the Girdwood/Portage area is **The Ascending Path** (☎ 783-0505; www.theascendingpath.com).

Mt McKinley and the other high peaks in Alaska also draw the attention of mountain climbers from around the world. For information on scaling the state's loftiest peaks start with Anchorage-based **Mountaineering Club of Alaska** (☎ 907-272-1811; www.mcak.org). The FAQ section on its website is a solid introduction for visiting climbers. The best mountaineering guidebook to the state is *Alaska: A Climbing Guide* by Michael Wood and Colby Coombs.

Among the best mountaineering outfitters are **Alaska Mountaineering School** (☎ 907-733-1016; www.climbalaska.org) of Talkeetna, which specializes in Mt McKinley ($4500), and **St Elias Alpine Guides** (☎ 907-544-4445, 888-933-5427; www.steliasguides.com) which tackles Mt Blackburn and other peaks in Wrangell-St Elias National Park from McCarthy.

By linking Resurrection Pass to both Russian Lakes and Resurrection River Trails in Chugach National Forest, you can hike 71 miles from Seward to Hope crossing only one road.

55 Ways to the Wilderness in Southcentral Alaska (1994), by Helen Nienhueser & John Wolfe, guides you to the popular trails around the Kenai Peninsula, the Anchorage area and from Palmer to Valdez.

SURFING

Surfin' USA? Alaska has more coastline than any other state in the USA, but the last thing most people associate with the frozen north is surfing. Until now.

In recent years a growing number of hardy surfers have been showing up with their boards at a handful of beaches. In 1995, *Surfer* magazine wrote a cover story on surfing in Alaska and four years later the **Icy Waves Surf Shop** (☎ 907-784-3226; www.icywaves.com) opened in Yakutat. That caught the attention of CBS News which sent a camera crew to the remote town for three days. Yakutat's 20-minute segment on the news show *Sunday Morning* with Charles Osgood propelled it into the limelight of the surfing world.

50 Hikes in Alaska's Chugach State Park (2001), by Shane Shepherd & Owen Wozniak, covers the state park's best trails and routes near Anchorage.

Due to its big waves and uncrowded beaches, Yakutat was named one of the five best surf towns in the USA by *Outside Magazine* in 2005. Today more than 100 surfers from all over the world will visit the surf capital of Alaska every summer to join 20 to 30 locals for 'surfing under St Elias,' the 18,000ft peak that overshadows the town. The best waves occur from mid-April to mid-June and mid-August through September.

Surfers have also hit the beaches of Sitka and Kodiak, home of the **Kodiak Island Surf Shop** (☎ 907-486-4995), where visitors can call for a loaner board. Alaska's 'Big Island' has an almost endless number of places to surf, but the majority of surfers head to the beaches clustered around Pasagshak Point, 40 miles south of town.

A surfin' safari, Alaskan style, means packing as warm a wet suit as you can find and often wearing a helmet. You also need to watch out for the brown bears, which often roam the beaches in search of washed up crabs, salmon and other meals. Surfers have been known to encounter gray whales, sea otters, and even chunks of ice if they hit the waves too soon after spring breakup.

Wilderness Hikes & Paddles

Alaska is many things, but firstly it is the great outdoors. Travelers head straight here for the mountains, the trails, the wildlife, the camping and the adventure of combining all these experiences. Encounters with wildlife such as bears, moose, deer and bald eagles can become the highlight of a trip to Alaska, particularly when a traveler can inconspicuously watch an animal casually move about its natural environment.

The best way to enter the state's wilderness is to begin with a day hike the minute you step off the ferry or depart from the Alcan Hwy. After the initial taste of the woods, many travelers reorganize their plans by forgoing the cities and spending the rest of their trip on multiday adventures into the backcountry to enjoy of Alaska's immense surroundings. The trails are all maintained by the United States Forest Service (USFS), and a night spent in one of the USFS cabins lends itself to a great wilderness experience.

Kayakers can enjoy the truly awesome sight of the glaciers from sea level. They can also escape into the wilderness, away from motor boats and cruise ships. Watching whales and seals can be spectacular from this proximity. The range of paddling opportunities in these regions means that novice canoeists can find calm river waters while more experienced paddlers can tackle the coast and tidal fluctuations.

HIGHLIGHTS

- **Chilkoot Trail** (p221) – follow the trail of the Klondike stampeders and then return by train that put the trail out of business
- **Chena Dome Trail** (p222) – a three-day alpine hike with views of Mt McKinley during the day and the midnight sun and in the evening
- **Iditarod National Historic Trail** (p212) – the best way to bypass Anchorage, a threee-day hike from Eagle to Girdwood
- **Tracy Arm Kayak Route** (p228) – this is an easy kayak route with glaciers, icebergs and marine life.
- **Swan Lake Canoe Route** (p215) – calm water, beautiful lakes, moose, fishing makes this the perfect canoe trip.

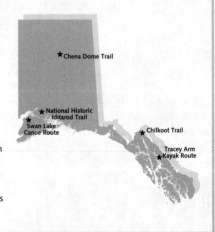

Chena Dome Trail

National Historic
Iditarod Trail

Swan Lake
Canoe Route

Chilkoot Trail

Tracey Arm
Kayak Route

| AREA CODE: ☎ 907 | POPULATION: 7,500 | ELEVATION: MT BARCUS BAKER 13,176FT |

This chapter covers 18 trips, which are popular wilderness excursions. They are either maintained trails by the United States Forest Service (USFS) or natural paddling routes – that backpackers can embark on as an unguided journey if they have the proper equipment and have sufficient outdoor experience. Some hiking or paddling excursions cannot provide an authentic 'wilderness experience,' because they are too popular with travelers and locals alike during the summer. However, many of them are located in isolated areas and they provide at least a glimpse of pristine backcountry.

The range of hikes also offer different scenery, such as coastlines, rain forests, glaciers, wildlife, depending on your interests as well as different levels of difficulty.

BACKPACKING

The following hikes are those trails that occur along routes that are popular and well developed. Backpackers still require the appropriate gear and knowledge to be totally self-reliant in the wilderness, which is a foreign experience for most city dwellers. Always confirm with the relevant authorities or park headquarters for current trail conditions. For more detailed descriptions of the hiking trails, it's best to refer to Lonely Planet's *Hiking in Alaska*.

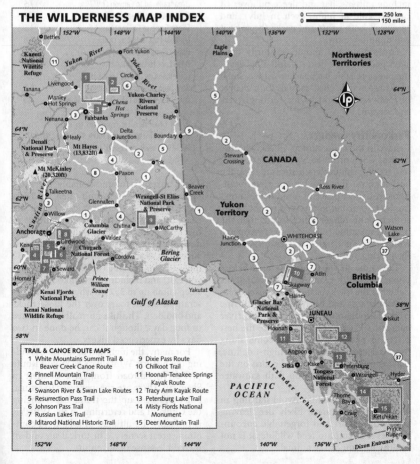

THE WILDERNESS MAP INDEX

TRAIL & CANOE ROUTE MAPS
1 White Mountains Summit Trail & Beaver Creek Canoe Route
2 Pinnell Mountain Trail
3 Chena Dome Trail
4 Swanson River & Swan Lake Routes
5 Resurrection Pass Trail
6 Johnson Pass Trail
7 Russian Lakes Trail
8 Iditarod National Historic Trail
9 Dixie Pass Route
10 Chilkoot Trail
11 Hoonah-Tenakee Springs Kayak Route
12 Tracy Arm Kayak Route
13 Petersburg Lake Trail
14 Misty Fiords National Monument
15 Deer Mountain Trail

Backpacking Gear

Double-check your equipment before leaving home. Most towns in Alaska will have at least one store with a wall full of camping supplies, but prices will be high and by mid- to late summer certain items will be out of stock.

For the backpacker the absolute essential equipment, aside from a backpack, includes a lightweight tent with rain fly and bug netting, a three-season sleeping bag with a temperature range of –10°F to 40°F, hiking boots that are broken in before you arrive in Alaska, a water filter, a compass or GPS unit and the corresponding US Geological Survey (USGS) map for the area (see p404). Your clothing bag should include mittens, hat and fleece pullover (it can get cold at night, even in July), and rain gear, both pants and parka (because it will definitely rain).

Equipment you should seriously consider packing include a self-inflating sleeping pad, a reliable backpacker's stove, small cooking kit and sports sandals for a change of footwear at night or for fording rivers and streams.

Backcountry Conduct

Behave in the backcountry! Check with the nearest USFS office or National Park Service (NPS) headquarters before entering the backcountry. By telling them your intentions, you'll get peace of mind from knowing that someone knows you're out there. If there is no ranger office in the area, the best organization to leave your travel plans with is the air charter service responsible for picking you up.

Take time to check out the area before unpacking your gear. Avoid animal trails (whether the tracks be moose or bear), areas with bear scat and berry patches with ripe fruit. Throughout much of Alaska, river bars and old glacier outwashes are the best places to pitch a tent. If you come along the coast stay well above the high-tide line, that last ridge of seaweed and debris on the shore, to avoid waking up with saltwater flooding your tent.

Do not harass wildlife. Avoid startling an animal, as it will most likely flee, leaving you with a short and forgettable encounter. Never attempt to feed wildlife; it is not healthy for you or the animal.

Finally, be thoughtful when in the wilderness. It is a delicate environment. Carry in your supplies and carry out your trash. Never litter or leave garbage smoldering in a fire pit. Better still, don't light a fire in heavily traveled areas because numerous fire pits are an eyesore. Use biodegradable soap and do all washing away from water sources. In short, leave no evidence of your stay. Only then can an area remain a true wilderness.

CHILKOOT TRAIL

CHILKOOT TRAIL

Section	Miles
Dyea trailhead to Canyon City	7.5
Canyon City to Sheep Camp	4.3
Sheep Camp to Chilkoot Pass	3.5
Chilkoot Pass to Happy Camp	4.0
Happy Camp to Deep Lake	2.5
Deep Lake to Lindeman City	3.0
Lindeman City to Bare Loon Lake	3.0
Bare Loon Lake to the log cabin	6.0
Bare Loon Lake to Lake Bennett trailhead	4.0

Level of difficulty: medium to hard
Information: **National Park Service** (☎ 907-983-2921; www.nps.gov/klgo)

The Chilkoot is unquestionably the most famous trail in Alaska and often the most popular during the summer. It was the route used by the Klondike gold miners in the 1898 gold rush, and walking the well-developed trail is not so much a wilderness adventure as a history lesson. The trip is 32 miles to 34 miles long (depending on where you exit) and includes the Chilkoot Pass – a steep climb up to 3525ft, where most hikers scramble on all fours over the loose rocks and boulders. The hike normally takes three to four days, though it can be done in two days by experienced hikers.

For many, the highlight of the hike is riding the historic White Pass & Yukon Route (WP&YR) railroad from Lake Bennett to Skagway. There are cheaper ways to return, but don't pass up the train. Experiencing the Chilkoot and returning on the WP&YR is probably the ultimate Alaska trek, combining great scenery, a historical site and an incredible sense of adventure.

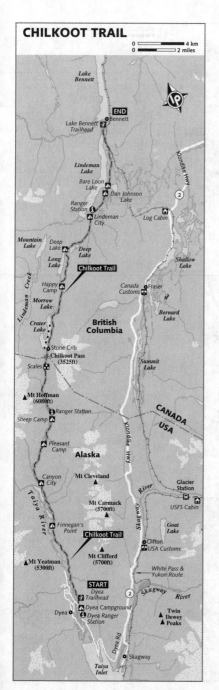

CHILKOOT TRAIL

Getting Started

The Chilkoot trail can be hiked from either direction but it is actually less difficult and safer when you commence from Dyea in the south and climb up the loose scree of the Chilkoot Pass rather than down. Additionally, following the footsteps of the Klondike miners makes this a special adventure.

From Skagway, make your way 8 miles northwest to Dyea trailhead. Mile 0 of the Chilkoot is just before the Taiya River crossing. **Frontier Excursions** (☎ 877-983-2512, 907-983-2512; www.frontierexcursions.com) charges $10 for a ride to the trailhead from Skagway.

In Skagway, stop at the **Chilkoot Trail Center** (☎ 907-983-3655), across from the WP&YR depot on Broadway St, to obtain backpacking permits. The US permit is adult/child $20/10, while the **Parks Canada** (☎ 867-667-3910, 800-661-0486; parkscan.harbour.ca) permit is adult/child C$35/17.50. Parks Canada allows only 50 hikers per day on the trail so reserve your permits in advance if walking in July or early August.

Getting Back

At the northern end of the trail, hikers can catch the train on the **White Pass & Yukon Route** (☎ 800-343-7373; www.whitepassrailroad.com) from June through August. The train departs from the Lake Bennett Depot at 1pm from Friday to Sunday. The one-way fare to Skagway is $65 on Fridays and Sundays and $80 on Saturdays.

There are two alternative ways to leave the trail at the northern end: you can hike 6 miles south from Bare Loon Lake Campground to the log cabin on Klondike Hwy or alight the WP&YR train from Bennett and travel to Fraser ($30 one way) where you can catch a bus in either direction. Frontier Excursions operates services to the log cabin and provides a drop-off and pickup ticket for $25 per person (minimum two people). It also offers combination tickets for a drop-off at Dyea and a pickup at log cabin for $30.

RESURRECTION PASS TRAIL

Located in the Chugach National Forest, this 39-mile trail was carved by prospectors in the late 1800s and today is the most popular hiking route on the Kenai Peninsula. A strong hiker can do the whole trip

WILDERNESS HIKES & PADDLES

RESURRECTION PASS TRAIL

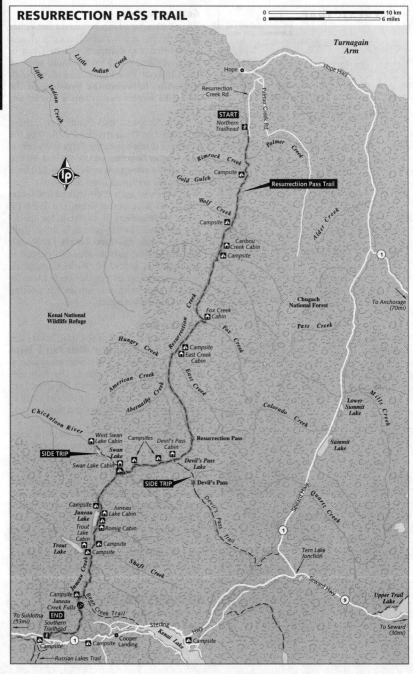

0 — 10 km
0 — 6 miles

Turnagain Arm

Little Indian Creek

Little Indian Creek

Hope

Hope Hwy

Resurrection Creek Rd

Palmer Creek Rd

START
Northern Trailhead

Rimrock Creek

Palmer Creek

Gold Gulch

Campsite

Resurrectiion Pass Trail

Wolf Creek

Campsite

Alder Creek

Caribou Creek Cabin

Campsite

Resurrection Creek

Fox Creek Cabin

Chugach National Forest

Pass Creek

Kenai National Wildlife Refuge

Fox Creek

Hungry Creek

Campsite
East Creek Cabin

American Creek

East Creek

Abernathy Creek

Chickaloon River

Lower Summit Lake

Colorado Creek

Mills Creek

West Swan Lake Cabin

Campsites

Devil's Pass Cabin

Resurrection Pass

Summit Lake

SIDE TRIP

Swan Lake

Devil's Pass Lake

Swan Lake Cabin

SIDE TRIP

Devil's Pass

Seward Hwy

Quartz Creek

Campsite

Juneau Lake Cabin

Juneau Lake

Romig Cabin

Trout Lake Cabin

Devil's Pass Trail

1

Tern Lake Junction

Seward Hwy

Campsite

Trout Lake

Campsite

Shaft Creek

Upper Trail Lake

Campsite
Juneau Creek Falls

Juneau Creek

Bear Creek Trail

END
Southern Trailhead

To Soldotna (53mi)

1

Campsite

Cooper Landing

Sterling

Kenai Hwy

Kenai Lake

Campsite

9

To Seward (30mi)

Campsite

Russian Lakes Trail

To Anchorage (70mi)

1

in three days, but most people prefer four to five days.

Eight USFS cabins are along the route ($35 to $45 per night). They must be reserved in advance through the NRRS and, being quite popular, are fully booked for most of the summer.

Getting Started

The northern trailhead is 20 miles from the Seward Hwy and 4 miles south of Hope on Resurrection Creek Rd. Hope, a historic mining community founded in 1896 by gold seekers, is a charming, out-of-the-way place to visit, but Hope Hwy is not an easy road for hitchhiking.

From Hope Hwy, turn south at the Resurrection Pass trail signs onto Resurrection Creek Rd, passing the fork to Palmer Creek Rd. The southern trailhead is on the Sterling Hwy, near Cooper Landing, 53 miles east of Soldotna.

An alternate route that avoids traveling to the remote northern trailhead is the Devil's Pass trail, which is posted at Mile 39 of Seward Hwy, 88 miles south of Anchorage. The 10-mile path climbs to Devil's Pass at 2400ft, where it joins the Resurrection Pass trail. By using the Devil's Pass trail and the lower portion of Resurrection Pass trail, you can hike from the Seward Hwy to the Sterling Hwy in two days.

RESURRECTION PASS TRAIL

Section	Miles
Resurrection Creek Rd to Caribou Creek cabin	6.9
Caribou Creek cabin to Fox Creek cabin	4.7
Fox Creek cabin to East Creek cabin	2.8
East Creek cabin to Resurrection Pass	4.9
Resurrection Pass to Devil's Pass cabin	2.1
Devil's Pass cabin to Swan Lake cabin	4.4
Swan Lake cabin to Juneau Lake cabin	3.3
Juneau Lake cabin to Trout Lake cabin	2.7
Trout Lake cabin to Juneau Creek Falls	2.3
Juneau Creek Falls to Sterling Hwy	4.4

Level of difficulty: easy
Information: **USFS Seward Ranger District** (☎ 907-224-3374; www.fs.fed.us/r10/chugach);
National Recreation Reservation Service (NRRS; ☎ 877-444-6777, 518-885-3639; www.reserveusa.com)

RUSSIAN LAKES TRAIL

RUSSIAN LAKES TRAIL

Section	Miles
Cooper Lake trailhead to junction of Resurrection River trail	5.0
Trail junction to Upper Russian Lake cabin	4.0
Upper Russian Lake to Aspen Flats	3.0
Aspen Flats to Lower Russian Lake	6.0
Lower Russian Lake to Russian River USFS Campground	3.0

Level of difficulty: easy
Information: **USFS Seward Ranger District** (☎ 907-224-3374; www.fs.fed.us/r10/chugach); **National Recreation Reservation Service** (NRRS; ☎ 877-444-6777, 518-885-3639; www.reserveusa.com)

This 21-mile, two-day trek is ideal for hikers who do not want to overextend themselves in Chugach National Forest. The trail is well maintained and well marked and most of the hike is a pleasant forest walk broken up by patches of wildflowers, ripe berries, lakes and streams.

Highlights include possibly seeing moose or bears, the impressive glaciated mountains across from Upper Russian Lake and the chance to catch your own dinner. The trek offers good fishing for Dolly Varden, rainbow trout and salmon in the upper portions of the Russian River; rainbow trout in Lower Russian Lake, Aspen Flats and Upper Russian Lake; and Dolly Varden in Cooper Lake near the Cooper Lake trailhead.

Three USFS cabins are on the trail ($35 to $45 per night); on Upper Russian Lake (9 miles from the Cooper Lake trailhead); Aspen Flats (12 miles from the Cooper Lake trailhead) and Barber Cabin (3 miles from the western trailhead).

Getting Started

It is easiest to begin this trek from the Cooper Lake trailhead, the higher end of the trail. To get there, turn off at Mile 47.8 Sterling Hwy onto Snug Harbor Rd; the road leads south 12 miles to Cooper Lake and ends at a marked parking lot and the trailhead.

The western trailhead is on a side road marked 'Russian River USFS Campground'

WILDERNESS HIKES
& PADDLES

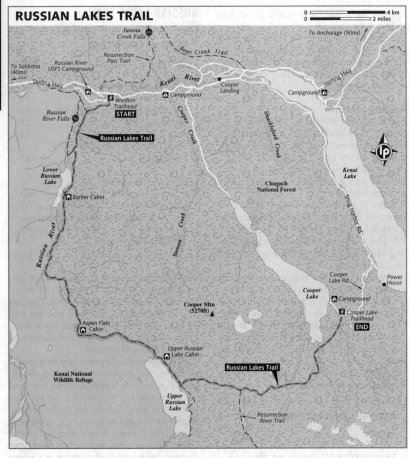

at Mile 52.7 Sterling Hwy. From there it's just under a mile's hike to the parking lot at the end of the campground road – the beginning of the trail. There is a small fee if you leave a car here. If you're planning to camp at Russian River the night before starting the hike, keep in mind that the campground is extremely popular during the salmon season in June and July.

JOHNSON PASS TRAIL

In the same area as the Resurrection Pass and Russian Lakes trails, and nearly as popular, is the Johnson Pass trail, a two-day, 23-mile hike over a 1550ft alpine pass. The trail was originally part of the original Iditarod trail blazed by prospectors on their

way from Seward to the golden beaches of Nome.

Most of the trail is fairly level, which makes for easy hiking and explains the growing numbers of mountain bikers on it. Anglers will find arctic grayling in Bench Lake and rainbow trout in Johnson Lake. Plan to camp at either Johnson Lake or Johnson Pass; these places are above the tree line, making a small stove necessary.

Getting Started

The trail can be hiked from either direction. The northern trailhead is at Mile 64 of the Seward Hwy, 96 miles south of Anchorage and reached from a gravel road marked 'Forest Service trail No 10.' The trail goes south

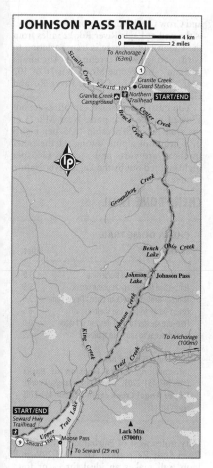

JOHNSON PASS TRAIL

Section	Miles
Northern trailhead to Bench Creek Bridge	3.8
Bench Creek Bridge to Bench Lake	5.5
Bench Lake to Johnson Pass	0.7
Johnson Pass to Johnson Lake	0.6
Johnson Lake to Johnson Creek Bridge	5.1
Johnson Creek Bridge to Upper Trail Lake	3.7
Upper Trail Lake to Seward Hwy trailhead	3.6

Level of difficulty: medium
Information: **USFS Seward Ranger District**
(☎ 907-224-3374; www.fs.fed.us/r10/chugach)

over Johnson Pass and then to the shore of Upper Trail Lake before reaching the Seward Hwy again at Mile 32.5, just northwest of the small hamlet of Moose Pass. Hitchhiking from either end of the trail is easy during the summer, or arrangements can be made with Seward Bus Lines (p194).

IDITAROD NATIONAL HISTORIC TRAIL

Section	Miles
Crow Creek Rd to Crow Pass	4.0
Crow Pass to Eagle River Ford	9.0
Eagle River Ford to Icicle Creek	7.3
Icicle Creek to Eagle River Nature Center	5.7

Level of difficulty: medium
Information: **Eagle River Nature Center** (☎ 907-694-2108; www.ernc.org); **USFS Glacier Ranger District** (☎ 783-3242; www.fs.fed.us/r10/chugach); **National Recreation Reservation Service** (NRRS; ☎ 877-444-6777, 518-885-3639; www.reserveusa.com)

The best backpacking adventure near Anchorage is the historic Iditarod trail, a 26-mile route once used by gold miners and mushers. This classic alpine crossing begins in Chugach National Forest near Girdwood, 37 miles east of Anchorage, climbs Crow Pass and wanders past Raven Glacier. You then enter Chugach State Park and descend Eagle River Valley, ending north of Anchorage at the Eagle River Nature Center. The trail is well maintained and well marked but does require fording Eagle River which can be tricky if it has been raining.

With a light pack and good weather you could cover this trail in one long Alaskan summer day. Heck, they stage a mountain race here every summer with the winner covering it in less than 3½ hours. But why rush? The alpine scenery is remarkable, the mining ruins along the trail interesting and the hike reasonably challenging. Plan two days or even three because this is why you come to Alaska – to wander in the mountains.

Getting Started
The Crow Pass trailhead is reached 7 miles from Mile 90 Seward Hwy via Alyeska Hwy

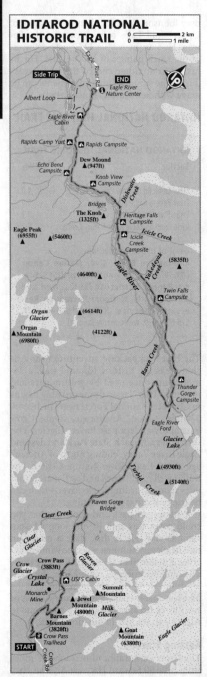

IDITAROD NATIONAL HISTORIC TRAIL

and Crow Creek Rd. The northern trailhead is the end of Eagle River Rd, 12 miles from the Glenn Hwy. There is transportation to Girdwood (p194). To return to Anchorage you can catch People Mover bus 76 or 102 near the junction of Eagle River Rd and Glenn Hwy.

You must have a stove; campfires are not allowed in the state park. Near Mile 3 of the trail is a USFS cabin ($35 per night) in a beautiful alpine setting. At the other trailhead are yurts and a cabin ($65 per night) rented out by the Eagle River Nature Center.

CHENA DOME TRAIL

CHENA DOME TRAIL

Section	Miles
Northern trailhead to timberline	3.0
Timberline to military airplane wreck	5.5
Military airplane wreck to Chena Dome summit	2.0
Chena Dome to free-use shelter	6.5
Free-use shelter to final descent off ridge	10.0
Final descent to southern trailhead	2.5

Level of difficulty: hard
Information: **Alaska Division of Parks**
(☎ 907-451-2705; www.alaskastateparks.org);
Upper Angel Creek cabin (☎ 907-451-2705 reservations)

Fifty miles west of Fairbanks in the Chena River State Recreation Area, this 29½-mile loop trail makes an ideal three- or four-day backpacking trip for people who enjoy alpine romping. The trail circles the Angel Creek drainage area, with the vast majority of it along tundra ridgetops above the treeline. Highlights of the hike are views from Chena Dome, a 4421ft, flat-topped ridge, picking blueberries in August and a free-use shelter.

Getting Started
It's easier to hike the loop by beginning at the northern trailhead at Mile 50.5 Chena Hot Springs Rd. The trailhead is to the west, 0.7 miles past Angel Creek Bridge on the left side of the road. The southern trailhead is at Mile 49. You can hitch or call **Chena Hot Springs Resort** (☎ 907-451-8104, 800-478-4681;

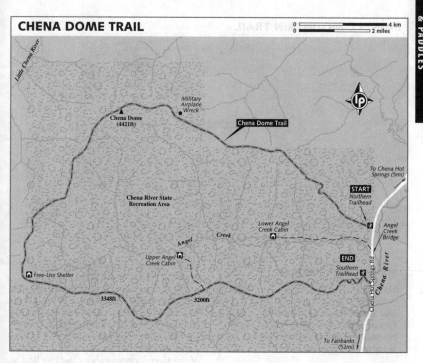

CHENA DOME TRAIL

www.chenahotsprings.com) which will provide round-trip van transportation for $45 per person (minimum two people).

Pack a stove – open fires are not permitted in the area – and carry at least 3 quarts (3 liters) of water per person. Replenish your water bottles from small pools in the tundra. There is a free-use shelter at Mile 17, while a 1½-mile and 1500ft descent from the main trail will bring you to Upper Angel Creek cabin ($25 per night) which can be reserved as a place to stay on the third night.

PINNELL MOUNTAIN TRAIL

The outstanding sight on this trail is the midnight sun. The trail is a 27.3-mile trek, 85 miles northeast of Fairbanks on the Steese Hwy, and from June 18 to 25, the sun doesn't set on the trail. You can view the sun sitting above the horizon at midnight from several high points on the trail, including the Eagle Summit trailhead.

The route is mostly tundra ridge tops that lie above 3500ft and can be steep and rugged. But the tundra wildflowers are un-

matched in most of the state and the views from the ridge tops are spectacular, with the Alaska Range visible to the south and the Yukon Flats to the north. Water is scarce in the alpine sections, so bring plenty.

Getting Started

This is a three-day trek, covering 8 to 10 miles a day. Most hikers start at the Eagle Summit trailhead on Mile 107.3 Steese Hwy, the higher end of the trail. The Twelvemile Summit trailhead is closer to Fairbanks, at Mile 85 Steese Hwy. Two free-use shelters (North Fork shelter and Ptarmigan Creek shelter) along the trail are great places to wait out a storm or cook a meal, but bring a tent with good bug netting. Take at least 2 quarts (2 liters) of water per person and refill your supply at snow patches, springs or tundra pools at every opportunity.

Traffic on the Steese Hwy this far out of Fairbanks is a steady trickle. Hitchhiking is possible if you are willing to give up a day getting there. Even those who bring a car will end up hitchhiking back to the trailhead where they began.

WILDERNESS HIKES & PADDLES

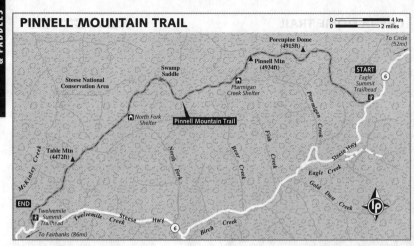

PINNELL MOUNTAIN TRAIL

Section	Miles
Eagle Summit trailhead to Porcupine Dome	6.0
Porcupine Dome to Ptarmigan Creek shelter	4.0
Ptarmigan Creek shelter to North Fork shelter	8.0
Second shelter to Twelvemile Summit	9.5

Level of difficulty: medium to hard
Information: **Bureau of Land Management**
(BLM; ☎ 907-474-2200; www.ak.blm.gov)

Check with the **Fairbanks Visitors Bureau**
(☎ 907-456-5774; www.explorefairbanks.com) to see
if anyone is running a van service up the
Steese Hwy. Otherwise, the best alternative
to hitchhiking is to rent a car and take the
opportunity to drive to Circle Hot Springs
or the wilderness town of Circle on the
Yukon River. **Rent-A-Wreck** (☎ 907-452-1606,
800-478-1606) in Fairbanks has small cars for
$39 a day.

WHITE MOUNTAINS SUMMIT TRAIL

The Bureau of Land Management (BLM),
which maintains the Pinnell Mountain
trail, also administers the White Mountains
National Recreation Area, including the
Summit trail. This 20-mile, one-way route
was built for summer use and has boardwalks over the wettest areas. The trail winds
through dense spruce forest, traverses scenic alpine ridge tops and Arctic tundra, and
ends at Beaver Creek, in the foothills of the
majestic White Mountains.

On the opposite bank of the creek from
the trail is the Borealis-Le Fevre cabin,
which can be reserved, but you must bring
a tent, as Beaver Creek is rarely low enough
to ford safely. The grayling fishing is outstanding here, but most parties stop short
of the river, camping above the tree line so
they don't have to deal with swamps near
the end.

Hiking in for a day of fishing is a five-
day adventure. Even if hikers stop short
of Beaver Creek, they still require two or
three days to camp near the highest point
along the route. The Summit trailhead is
at Mile 28 Elliott Hwy, 31 miles north of
Fairbanks. Bring water: it is scarce in the
alpine sections.

Getting Started

Hitchhiking is generally more difficult on
the Elliott Hwy than the Steese Hwy. Contact **Dalton Highway Express** (☎ 907-474-3555;
www.daltonhighwayexpress.com) about possible
drop-off or pick up at the trailhead. The
company runs vans to Prudhoe Bay and
will try to accommodate a White Mountain
request if possible.

Once you get there, don't confuse the
White Mountains Summit trail (also called
Summer trail), which was made for hikers,
with the Wickersham Creek trail. The Wickersham Creek, or winter trail, departs from
the same trailhead but was cut primarily

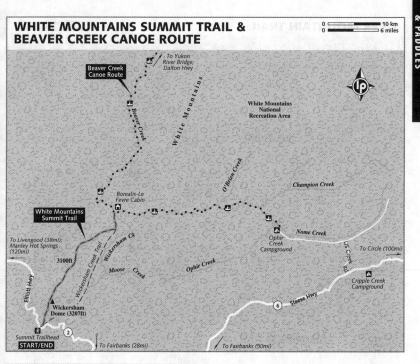

WHITE MOUNTAINS SUMMIT TRAIL & BEAVER CREEK CANOE ROUTE

0 ━━━━ 10 km
0 ━━━━ 6 miles

To Yukon River Bridge; Dalton Hwy

Beaver Creek Canoe Route

Beaver Creek

White Mountains

White Mountains National Recreation Area

O'Brien Creek

Champion Creek

Borealis-Le Fevre Cabin

White Mountains Summit Trail

Wickersham Creek Trail

Wickersham Ck

Nome Creek

Ophir Creek Campground

US Creek Rd

To Livengood (38mi); Manley Hot Springs (120mi)

Elliott Hwy

3100ft

Moose Creek

Ophir Creek

To Circle (100mi)

Cripple Creek Campground

Wickersham Dome (3207ft)

Steese Hwy

6

Summit Trailhead
START/END

To Fairbanks (28mi)

To Fairbanks (50mi)

WHITE MOUNTAINS SUMMIT TRAIL

Section	Miles
Summit trailhead to Wickersham Dome	4.0
Wickersham Dome to 3100ft high point	4.0
3100ft high point to Wickersham Creek	6.0
Trail junction to Borealis-Le Fevre cabin	2.0

Level of difficulty: hard
Information: **Bureau of Land Management** (BLM; ☎ 907-474-2200; www.ak.blm.gov); **Borealis-Le Fevre cabin** (☎ 800-437-7021 reservations)

for snow machines, cross-country skiers and people using snowshoes.

DEER MOUNTAIN TRAIL

Located in Ketchikan, the Deer Mountain trail is part of a challenging, overnight alpine trail system incorporating three trails. It's an 11-mile trip, beginning with the 3-mile Deer Mountain trail that leads into the Blue Lake trail. This path follows a natural

route along an alpine ridge that extends 4 miles north to John Mountain. From here, hikers can return to the Ketchikan road system by taking the John Mountain trail for 2 miles to Upper Silvis Lake and then following an old service road from the hydroelectric plant on Lower Silvis Lake to a parking lot off the S Tongass Hwy.

A quarter of a mile before reaching the Deer Mountain summit, you pass the junction with Blue Lake trail and the posted trail to the Deer Mountain cabin, a free-use shelter above the tree line. Within 2 miles the Blue Lake trail reaches Blue Lake, a popular camping area that, at 2700ft, is above the tree line in a scenic alpine setting.

Getting Started

The trailhead for the Deer Mountain trail can be reached by following a road from the corner of Fair and Deermount Sts in Ketchikan. Just before a landfill, a side road posted 'Deer Mountain' leads you a short ways to the trailhead.

To get to the start of the John Mountain trail, head east on S Tongass Hwy for 12.9

WILDERNESS HIKES
& PADDLES

DEER MOUNTAIN TRAIL

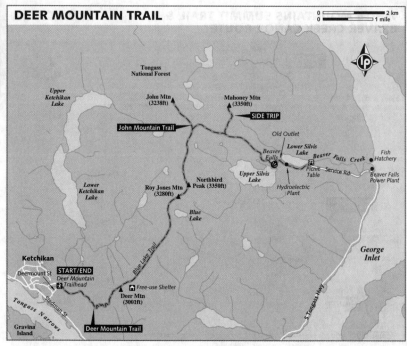

Tongass
National Forest

Upper
Ketchikan
Lake

John Mtn
(3238ft)

Mahoney Mtn
(3350ft)

SIDE TRIP

John Mountain Trail

Old Outlet

Beaver
Falls

Lower Silvis
Lake

Beaver Falls Creek

Fish
Hatchery

Picnic
Table

Service Rd

Beaver Falls
Power Plant

Upper Silvis
Lake

Hydroelectric
Plant

Northbird
Peak (3350ft)

Roy Jones Mtn
(3280ft)

Lower
Ketchikan
Lake

Blue
Lake

George
Inlet

Ketchikan

Deermount St

START/END
Deer Mountain
Trailhead

Free-use Shelter

Deer Mtn
(3001ft)

Blue Lake Trail

Stedman St

Tongass Narrows

Gravina
Island

Deer Mountain Trail

S Tongass Hwy

0   2 km
0   1 mile

miles to its end at the Beaver Falls Power
Plant. From here there is a 2-mile hike along
an old access road from the Beaver Falls
Power Plant at the tidewater to the hydroelectric plant on the south side of Lower Silvis
Lake. From the road you'll find the start of
a trail that climbs steeply to the upper lake.
The John Mountain trail begins at the old
outlet at the western end of the upper lake.

DEER MOUNTAIN TRAIL

Section	Miles
Deer Mountain trailhead to Deer Mountain summit	3.1
Deer Mountain summit to Blue Lake	2.2
Blue Lake to John Mountain	2.0
John Mountain to Upper Silvis Lake	2.0
Upper Silvis Lake to S Tongass Hwy	2.0

Level of difficulty: medium to hard
Information: **Southeast Alaska Discovery
Center** (☎ 907-228-6220; www.fs.fed.us/r10
/tongass; 50 Main St; ⏱ 8am-5pm)

PETERSBURG LAKE TRAIL

Across the Wrangell Narrows from the fishing community of Petersburg is the Petersburg Lake trail, the first segment of a trail
system collectively known as the Portage
Mountain Loop. The Petersburg Lake trail
is well planked and allows backpackers access to the Petersburg Lake cabin in the
wilderness without the expense of bush-
plane travel. To hike further to Portage Bay
or Salt Chuck along the Portage Mountain
Loop, however, requires wilderness experience, and map and compass skills as the
trails are not planked or maintained, and
only lightly marked.

Bring a fishing rod, as there are good
spots for catching Dolly Varden and rainbow
trout. In August and early September large
coho and sockeye salmon runs throughout
the area, attracting anglers and bears.

The trek begins at the Kupreanof Island
public dock. From the dock a partial boardwalk leads southwest for a mile past a handful
of cabins, then turns northwest up the tidewater arm of the creek almost directly across
Wrangell Narrows from the ferry terminal. A

PETERSBURG LAKE TRAIL

Section	Miles
Kupreanof Island dock to saltwater arm	1.0
Saltwater arm to Petersburg Creek	2.5
Trail by creek to Petersburg Lake cabin	3.5
Petersburg Lake cabin to Portage Bay	7.0
Portage Bay to Salt Chuck East cabin	4.5

Level of difficulty: medium
Information: **USFS Petersburg Ranger District** (☎ 907-772-3871; www.fs.fed.us/r10 /tongass); (NRRS; ☎ 877-444-6777, 518-885-3639; www.reserveusa.com)

well-planked trail begins at the saltwater arm and continues along the northern side of Petersburg creek to the Petersburg Lake USFS cabin. From the cabin, Portage Mountain Loop continues north to Portage Bay.

Getting Started

The only hitch to this trip is getting across Wrangell Narrows to the public dock on Kupreanof Island. Either hitch a ride at the North Boat Harbor or call **Tongass Kayak Adventures** (☎ 907-772-4600; www.tongasskayak.com), which runs hikers across the channel for $25 per person.

This is one trip where you'll need good waterproof clothing as well as rubber boots. Bring a tent or plan to reserve the cabins at least two months in advance.

DIXIE PASS ROUTE

Even by Alaskan standards, Wrangell-St Elias National Park is a large tract of wilderness. At 20,625 sq miles, it's the largest US national park, contains the most peaks over 14,500ft in North America and has the greatest concentration of glaciers on the continent.

Within this huge, remote park, Dixie Pass provides the best wilderness adventure that doesn't require a bush-plane charter. The trek from the trailhead up to Dixie Pass and the return journey is 24 miles. Plan to camp there at least one or two additional days to take in the alpine beauty and investigate the nearby ridges. Such an itinerary requires three or four days and is moderately hard.

To get to the Dixie Pass trailhead, hike 2½ miles up Kotsina Rd and then another 1.3 miles along Kotsina Rd after Nugget Creek trail splits off to the northeast. The trailhead is on the right-hand side of Kotsina Rd; look for a marker, usually a pile of rocks with a stick in it.

The route begins as a level path to Strelna Creek for 3 miles, and then continues along the west side of the creek for another 3 miles to the first major confluence. After fording the creek, it's 5 to 6 miles to the pass; along the way you cross two more confluences and hike through an interesting gorge. The ascent to Dixie Pass is fairly easy to spot, and once there you'll find superb scenery, and alpine ridges to explore.

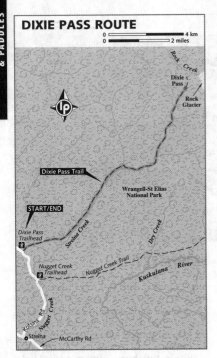

DIXIE PASS ROUTE

DIXIE PASS

Section	Miles
McCarthy Rd to Dixie Pass trailhead	3.8
Dixie Pass trailhead to Strelna Creek	3.0
Strelna Creek to Dixie Pass	8.5

Level of difficulty: moderately hard
Information: **Wrangell-St Elias National Park** (☎ 907-822-5234; www.nps.gov/wrst)

Getting Started

Collect supplies in Copper Center, then stop at the park headquarters to complete a backcountry trip itinerary and get your USGS quadrangle maps (Valdez C-1 and McCarthy C-8). To arrange to be dropped off from Glennallen or Chitina and collected at Nugget Creek/Kotsina Rd, 14½ miles east of Chitina, call **Backcountry Connection** (☎ 907-822-5292; www.alaska-backcountry-tours.com), which runs a daily bus to McCarthy. The one-way fare from Glennallen to McCarthy, with a drop-off and pickup at Kotsina Rd, is $70.

PADDLING

Alaskan paddling adventures range from open-water sea kayaking and rafting the white water of rivers to portaging a canoe through a chain of calm lakes. No matter your skill level or how wild you like your water, there are many opportunities for an extended paddle in the Far North.

Blue-Water Paddling

In Alaska, 'blue water' refers to the coastal areas of the state, which are characterized by extreme tidal fluctuations, cold water, and the possibility of high winds and waves. Throughout Southeast and Southcentral Alaska, the open canoe is replaced with the kayak, and blue-water paddling is the means of escape into coastal areas such as Muir Inlet in Glacier Bay National Park or Tracy Arm Fjord, south of Juneau.

Tidal fluctuations are the main concern in blue-water areas. Paddlers should always pull their boats above the high-tide mark and keep a tide book in the same pouch as their topographic map. Cold coastal water, rarely above 45°F in the summer, makes capsizing worse than unpleasant. With a life jacket, survival time in the water is less than two hours; without one there is no time. If your kayak flips, stay with the boat and attempt to right it and crawl back in. Trying to swim to shore in Arctic water is risky at best.

Framed backpacks are useless in kayaks; gear is best stowed in duffel bags or small day packs. Carry a large supply of assorted plastic bags, including several garbage bags. All gear, especially sleeping bags and clothing, should be stowed in plastic bags, as water tends to seep in even when you seal yourself in with a cockpit skirt. Over-the-calf rubber boots are the best footwear for getting in and out of kayaks

White-Water Paddling

Throughout Alaska's history, rivers have been the traditional travel routes through the rugged terrain. Many rivers can be paddled in canoes; others, due to extensive stretches of white water, are better handled in rafts or kayaks.

Alaska's rivers vary, but they share characteristics not found on many rivers in the Lower 48: water levels tend to change rapidly while many rivers are heavily braided and boulder-strewn. Take care in picking out the right channel to avoid spending most of the day pulling your boat off gravel. You can survive flipping your canoe in an Alaskan river, but you'll definitely want a plan of action if you do.

Much of the equipment for white-water canoeists is the same as it is for blue-water paddlers. Tie everything into the canoe; you never know when you might hit a whirlpool or a series of standing waves. Wear a life jacket at all times. Many paddlers stock their life jacket with insect repellent, waterproof matches and other survival gear in case they flip and get separated from their boat.

Research the river you want to run and make sure you can handle the level of difficulty. The class categories are:

Class I – easy Mostly flat water with occasional series of mild rapids.

Class II – medium Frequent stretches of rapids with waves up to 3ft high and easy chutes, ledges and falls. The best route is easy to identify, and the entire river can be run in open canoes.

Class III – difficult Features numerous rapids with high, irregular waves and difficult chutes and falls that often require scouting. These rivers are for experienced paddlers who use kayaks or rafts, or have a spray cover for their canoe.

Class IV – very difficult Long stretches of irregular waves, powerful eddies and even constricted canyons. Scouting is mandatory, and rescues can be difficult in many places. Suitable for rafts or white-water kayaks, and paddlers must wear helmets.

Class V – extremely difficult Continuous violent rapids, powerful rollers and high, unavoidable waves and haystacks. These rivers are only for paddlers with white-water kayaks who are proficient in the Eskimo roll.

Class VI – highest level of difficulty Rarely run except by very experienced kayakers under ideal conditions.

MISTY FIORDS NATIONAL MONUMENT

The Misty Fiords National Monument encompasses 3594 sq miles of wilderness and lies between two impressive fjords – Behm Canal (117 miles long) and Portland Canal (72 miles long). The two natural canals give the preserve its extraordinarily deep and long fjords with sheer granite walls that rise thousands of feet out of the water. Misty Fiords is well named; annual rainfall is 14ft.

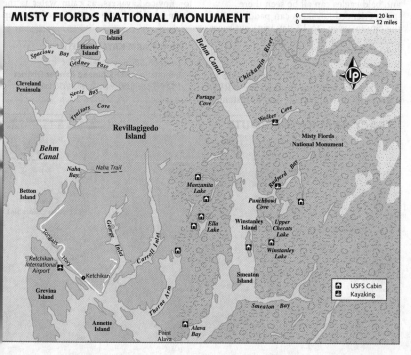

MISTY FIORDS NATIONAL MONUMENT

0   20 km
0   12 miles

Bell Island
Spacious Bay
Hassler Island
Gedney Pass
Cleveland Peninsula
Neets Bay
Traitors Cove
Behm Canal
Chickamin River
Portage Cove
Walker Cove
Revillagigedo Island
Misty Fiords National Monument
Behm Canal
Naha Bay
Naha Trail
Rudyerd Bay
Betton Island
Manzanita Lake
Punchbowl Cove
George Inlet
Ella Lake
Winstanley Island
Upper Checats Lake
Tongass Hwy
Carroll Inlet
Winstanley Lake
Ketchikan International Airport
Ketchikan
Smeaton Island
Grevina Island
Thorne Arm
Smeaton Bay
Annette Island
Point Alava
Alava Bay

USFS Cabin
Kayaking

MISTY FIORDS NATIONAL MONUMENT

Section	Miles
Ketchikan to Thorne Arm	13.0
Thorne Arm to Point Alava	9.0
Point Alava to Winstanley Island	21.0
Winstanley Island to Rudyerd Bay	9.0
Rudyerd Bay to Walker Cove	10.0

Level of difficulty: Open water
Information: **Southeast Alaska Discovery Center** (☎ 907-228-6220; www.fs.fed.us/r10 /tongass); **National Recreation Reservation Service** (NRRS; ☎ 877-444-6777, 518-885-3639; www.reserveusa.com)

The destinations for many kayakers are the smaller but equally impressive fjords of Walker Cove and Punchbowl Cove in Rudyerd Bay, off Behm Canal. Dense spruce-hemlock rain forest is the most common vegetation throughout the monument, and sea lions, harbor seals, killer whales, brown and black bears, mountain goats, moose and bald eagles can all be seen there.

Experienced kayakers can paddle out of the city (a seven- to 12-day trip) but most paddlers arrange to be dropped off deep in Behm Canal near the protected water of Rudyerd Bay.

Misty Fiords has 15 USFS cabins ($25 to $45) that are reserved through the NRRS. Two paddles – Alava Bay and Winstanley Island in Behm Canal – allow kayakers to end the day at the doorstep of a cabin.

Getting Started

Southeast Sea Kayaks (☎ 907-225-1258, 800-287-1607; www.kayakketchikan.com), right on the Ketchikan waterfront, has single/double kayaks for $45/60 per day and discounts for longer rentals. This wonderful outfitter can assist in all aspects of a self-guided trip including boat transportation to Behm Canal. The round-trip cost is $250 to $300 per person depending on where they drop you off. It's best to reserve kayaks well before the summer season.

You cannot do this trip without good rain gear and a backpacker's stove – wood in the monument is often too wet for campfires. Be prepared for extended periods of rain and have all gear sealed in plastic bags.

TRACY ARM KAYAK ROUTE

Tracy Arm is a Southeast Alaskan fjord that features tidewater glaciers and 2000ft granite walls that rise straight out of the water. This 30-mile arm is an ideal choice for novice kayakers, as calm water is the norm here due to the protection of the steep

TRACY ARM KAYAK ROUTE

Level of difficulty: Open water
Information: **USFS Juneau Ranger District** (☎ 907-586-8790; www.fs.fed.us/r10/tongass)

TRACY ARM KAYAK ROUTE

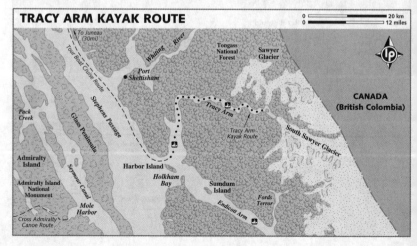

and narrow fjord walls. But keep in mind that the arm has become a major attraction for cruise ships and tour boats.

If you are an experienced kayaker, consider exploring the other fjords that adjoin Tracy Arm at Holkham Bay. Just to the south is Endicott Arm, another 30-mile fjord that was carved by the Dawes and North Dawes Glaciers. Endicott Arm also has considerably more places to pitch a tent than Tracy Arm. The only camping spots in the first half of Tracy Arm are two valleys almost across from each other, 8 miles north along the fjord, and a small island at the head of the fjord.

Getting Started

The departure point for Tracy Arm-Fords Terror Wilderness Area is Juneau. Kayaks can be rented in Auke Bay from **Alaska Boat & Kayak** (☎ 907-789-6886; www.juneaukayak.com) for $40/55 per day for a single/double kayak. **Adventure Bound Alaska** (☎ 800-228-3875, 907-463-2509; www.adventureboundalaska.com) charges $150 per person for drop-off and pickup in Tracy Arm. Drop-offs and pickups make the trip considerably easier; otherwise it's a two- or three-day paddle in open water.

HOONAH–TENAKEE SPRINGS KAYAK ROUTE

> **HOONAH–TENAKEE SPRINGS KAYAK ROUTE**
>
> Level of difficulty: Open water
> Information: **USFS Juneau Ranger District**
> (☎ 907-586-8790; www.fs.fed.us/r10/tongass)

This 40-mile paddle follows the shorelines of Port Frederick and Tenakee Inlet from Hoonah to Tenakee Springs and includes a short portage of 100 yards or so. You pass a depressing number of clear-cuts around Hoonah and up Port Frederick, but there are few other signs of civilization once you are beyond the two villages. The area that lies in the Tongass National Forest consists of rugged and densely forested terrain populated by brown bears, often seen feeding along the shoreline.

Carry a tide book, and reach the portage at high tide. There's boot-sucking mud along the portage, but take heart, it's just a short

HOONAH–TENAKEE SPRINGS KAYAK ROUTE

0 _____ 10 km
0 _____ 6 miles

walk over a low ridge to the next inlet. After the paddle Tenakee Springs has natural hot springs to melt away those sore muscles.

Getting Started

This adventure is good for those on a budget but with lots of time as the Alaska Marine ferry connects both Hoonah and Tenakee Springs to Juneau. The one-way fare from Juneau to Hoonah/Tenakee Springs with a kayak is $45/50.

It's best to start the paddle from Hoonah, in order to end the trip in Tenakee Springs, a charming village. However, this has to be planned carefully, as there is only one ferry every three to five days from Tenakee Springs. Kayaks can be rented in Juneau from **Alaska Boat & Kayak** (left).

GLACIER BAY – MUIR INLET

Glacier Bay is a kayaker's paradise. With stunning alpine scenery of the Fairweather Mountains, views of many glaciers and the marine wildlife, it's easy to realize the park's attraction to blue-water paddlers. The drawbacks are the cost of getting there, the cost of getting up the bay with a kayak and the armada of cruise ships that visit. But by utilizing the tour boat within the park, you can put together a paddle that stays totally in Muir Inlet (East Arm), Glacier Bay's designated wilderness area where motorized vessels are banned.

The tour boat will drop you off near the entrance of the inlet, allowing you to avoid

GLACIER BAY – MUIR INLET	
Section	**Miles**
Mt Wright to Wachusett Inlet	16.0
Wachusett Inlet to Riggs Glacier	9.0
Riggs Glacier to Muir Glacier	.0
Muir Glacier to Mt Wright	33.0

Level of difficulty: Open water
Information: **Glacier Bay National Park**
(☎ 907-697-2230; www.nps.gov/glba)

the long paddle from Bartlett Cove, the park headquarters. Many kayakers then travel the length of the inlet to McBride, Riggs and Muir Glaciers at the north end before returning for a pickup. Such a trip would require four or six days of paddling and would be roughly a $600 to $800 per person sidetrip from Juneau. Those with more time but less money can book just a drop-off and then paddle back to Bartlett Cove, an eight- to 10-day trip. A round-trip paddle out of Bartlett Cove to the glaciers of Muir Inlet is a two-week adventure for most people.

Getting Started
It's best to arrange both kayak rental and tour-boat passage in advance. Within the park **Glacier Bay Sea Kayaks** (☎ 907-697-2257; www.glacierbayseakayaks.com) rents single/double kayaks for $40/50 a day, or $35/40 a day for three days or longer. The **Baranof Wind** (☎ 907-264-4600, 800-229-8687; www.visitglacierbay .com), which departs daily at 7:30am, provides drop-off and pickup near Mt Wright at the mouth of Muir Inlet from mid-May to late September. The round-trip is $203 per person. Glacier Bay Sea Kayaks will also book the drop-off for you.

See p152 for general information about Glacier Bay National Park and a map of the park.

SWANSON RIVER & SWAN LAKE CANOE ROUTES
In the northern lowlands of the Kenai National Wildlife Refuge, there is a chain of rivers, lakes, streams and portages that make up the Swanson River and Swan Lake canoe routes. The trips are perfect for novice canoeists, as rough water is rarely a problem and portages do not exceed half a

mile on the Swan Lake system or a mile in the Swanson River area.

Fishing for rainbow trout is good in many lakes, and wildlife is plentiful; a trip on either route could result in sightings of moose, bears, beavers or a variety of waterfowl.

The Swanson River system links more than 40 lakes and 46 miles of river, and a one-way trip is 80 miles, beginning at Swan Lake Rd and ending at Cook Inlet in Captain Cook State Park. It's a more challenging trip than the Swan Lake paddle, especially when the water is low, but also a more popular one. The easier Swan Lake route connects 30 lakes with forks in the Moose River; the one-way trip is 60 miles. A common four-day trip on the Swan Lake route begins at the west entrance of the canoe route on Swan Lake Rd and ends at Moose River Bridge on the Sterling Hwy.

Getting Started
To reach the Swan Lake or Swanson River canoe routes, travel to Mile 84 Sterling Hwy east of Soldotna and turn north on Robinson Lake Rd, just west of Moose River Bridge. Robinson Lake Rd turns into Swanson River Rd, which leads to Swan Lake Rd 17 miles north of the Sterling Hwy. East on Swan Lake Rd are the entrances to both canoe systems. The Swanson River route begins at the end of the road. The west entrance for the Swan Lake route is at Canoe Lake, and the east is another 6 miles beyond, at Portage Lake.

During the summer, **Alaska Canoe & Campground** (☎ 907-262-2331; www.alaskacanoetrips.com) rents canoes and runs a shuttle service to the Swan Lake and Swanson River canoe routes. It's $40 per day for a canoe rental three days or longer, $40 for a drop-off and pickup for up to four boats for the Swan Lake route, and $50 to the Swanson River trailhead. Alaska Canoe's campground (campsites $10) is near the takeout along Sterling Hwy and makes a nice place to stay if you come in late on the last day.

SWANSON RIVER & SWAN LAKE CANOE ROUTES

Level of difficulty: Class I
Information: **Kenai National Wildlife Refuge** (☎ 907-262-7021; kenai.fws.gov)

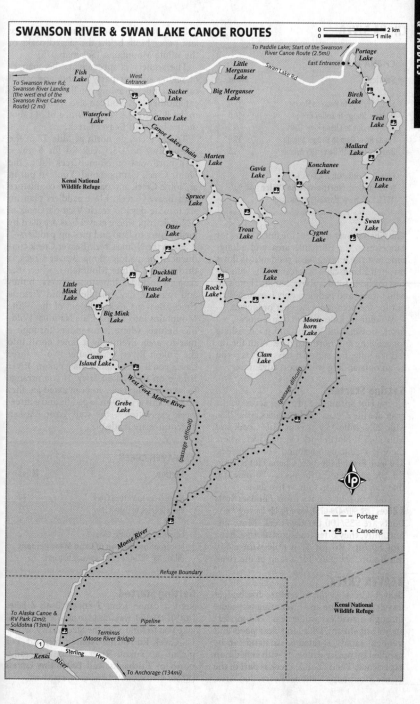

SWANSON RIVER & SWAN LAKE CANOE ROUTES

0   2 km
0   1 mile

To Paddle Lake; Start of the Swanson
River Canoe Route (2.5mi)

Portage
Lake

East Entrance

Swan Lake Rd

Fish
Lake

West
Entrance

Little
Merganser
Lake

Big Merganser
Lake

To Swanson River Rd;
Swanson River Landing
(the west end of the
Swanson River Canoe
Route) (2 mi)

Sucker
Lake

Birch
Lake

Waterfowl
Lake

Canoe Lake

Teal
Lake

Canoe Lakes Chain

Mallard
Lake

Marten
Lake

Gavia
Lake

Konchanee
Lake

Raven
Lake

Kenai National
Wildlife Refuge

Spruce
Lake

Otter
Lake

Trout
Lake

Cygnet
Lake

Swan
Lake

Duckbill
Lake

Weasel
Lake

Rock
Lake

Loon
Lake

Little
Mink
Lake

Big Mink
Lake

Moose-
horn
Lake

Camp
Island Lake

West Fork Moose River

Clam
Lake

Grebe
Lake

(passage difficult)

(passage difficult)

Portage

Canoeing

Moose River

Refuge Boundary

Kenai National
Wildlife Refuge

To Alaska Canoe &
RV Park (2mi);
Soldotna (13mi)

Pipeline

Terminus
(Moose River Bridge)

Sterling Hwy

Kenai River

To Anchorage (134mi)

CHENA RIVER

CHENA RIVER	
Section	**Miles**
Second Bridge to Hodgins Slough	15.0
Hodgins Slough to Bailey Bridge	16.0
Bailey Bridge to Chena River Dam	8.5
Chena River Dam to Badger Slough	19.0
Badger Slough to University Avenue	15.5

Level of difficulty: Class I–II
Information: **Northern Area Office** (☎ 907-451-2659; www.alaskastateparks.org)

The Chena River is one of the finest rivers for canoeing in the Fairbanks area, and a long-time favorite among local residents. It flows through a landscape of forested hills with access to alpine tundra above 2800ft. There's no white water and paddlers only have to watch out for the occasional sweeper or logjam.

Wildlife includes brown bears, moose, red foxes, beavers and otters, and good fishing for grayling and northern pike. With the Interior's long, hot summer days, this trip can be an outstanding wilderness adventure.

Getting Started

Chena Hot Springs Rd provides access to the river at Mile 27.9 east of Fairbanks, Mile 28.6, Mile 29.4, Mile 33.9 at Four Mile Creek and Mile 39.6 at North Fork Chena River, where there is a state campground (20 campsites, $10 fee). From Mile 39.6, Chena Hot Springs Rd, the paddle to Fairbanks is a 70-mile trip that can be done in four to five days.

You can rent canoes from **7 Bridges Boats & Bikes** (☎ 907-479-0751; www.7gablesinn.com/7bbb). Boats are $35/100 per day/week. More importantly, they offer transport along Chena Hot Springs Rd for $2 a mile with a $10 minimum. See p369 for a map of the river.

BEAVER CREEK

Beaver Creek is *the* adventure for budget travelers with time and a yearning to paddle through a roadless wilderness. The moderately swift stream, with long clear pools and frequent rapids, is rated Class I and can be handled by novice canoeists with expedition experience. The 111-mile creek is part of the White Mountains National Recreation Area;

it flows past hills forested in white spruce and paper birch below the jagged peaks of the White Mountains. (See map p75)

The scenery is spectacular, the chances of seeing another party remote and you'll catch so much grayling you'll never want to eat another one. You can also spend a night in the Borealis-Le Fevre cabin, a BLM cabin on the banks of Beaver Creek.

To get there, go north at Mile 57 of the Steese Hwy on US Creek Rd for 6 miles; then northwest on Nome Creek Rd to the Ophir Creek Campground. You can put in at Nome Creek and paddle to its confluence with Beaver Creek. Most paddlers plan on six to nine days to reach Victoria Creek, a 127-mile trip, where gravel bars are used by bush planes to land and pick up paddlers.

From the Nome Creek/Beaver Creek confluence, the paddle along Beaver Creek is through the White Mountains, where the scenery includes limestone towers, buttes and spires. A day's paddle beyond Victoria Creek, Beaver Creek spills out of the White Mountains into Yukon Flats National Wildlife Refuge, where it meanders through a marshy area. Eventually it flows north into the Yukon River, where after two or three days, you'll pass under the Yukon River Bridge on the Dalton Hwy. If you arrange to be picked up here, you can avoid another airfare. This is a 399-mile paddle and a three-week expedition – the stuff great Alaskan adventures are made of.

BEAVER CREEK	
Section	**Miles**
Nome Creek to Victoria Creek	127
Victoria Creek to Dalton Hwy	272

Level of Difficulty: Class I
Information: **Bureau of Land Management** (BLM; ☎ 907-474-2200; www.ak.blm.gov)

Getting Started

Rent a canoe from **7 Bridges Boats & Bikes** (☎ 907-479-0751; www.7gablesinn.com/7bbb). They'll take you to Mile 57 of the Steese Hwy, where US Creek Rd reaches Nome Creek Rd. For pickup at Yukon River Bridge 175 miles north of Fairbanks, call **Dalton Hwy Express** (☎ 907-474-3555; www.daltonhighwayexpress.com).

RALPH LEE HOPKINS

Tlingit totem pole, Sitka National Historic Park (p126)

An Alaska Native performs a traditional dance, Alaskan Native Heritage Center (p179), Anchorage

BRENT WINEBRENNER

LEE FOSTER

An indigenous woman proudly displays a traditional mask (p126)

Native clan house, Saxman Totem Park (p105)

EMILY RIDDELL

MARK NE

Humpback whale breaching in Southeast Alaska (p120)

ERNEST MANEWAL

Hoary Marmot, Denali National Park (p312)

Moon jellyfish on display for those prepared to brave cold waters (p227)

RALPH LEE HO

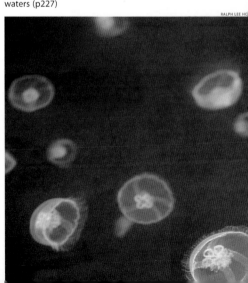

MARK NEWMAN

Grey wolf in Alaskan winter snow (p52), a rare sight for the traveler

The ever-watchful bald eagle (p54) thrives in Alaska despite being on the nation's endangered species list

MARK NEWMAN

Brown bear and cubs, Mikfik Creek (p292)

MARK NEWMAN

Polar bears, found predominantly around Barrow (p394), won't shy away from a wrestling match

ERNEST MANEWAL

Thunderbird Falls (p201), Chugach
State Park

A blanketing Alaskan winter frost (p12)

Sitka Sound (p123), where the
Russians first arrived in 1741

Facing page:
Arrowhead Peak looms over Alaska
Pioneers' Home (p124), Sitka
ERNEST MANEWAL

Autumn colors shimmer beneath the Chugach Mountains (p346)

MARK NE

BRENT WINEBRE[

Hikers take in the vista over Exit Glacier and Harding Ice Field (p243)

MARK NEWMAN

Snowmobiles (p31) are a well-suited transport option in some rural parts of Alaska

Kayaking along the Kenai Peninsula (p239)

ERNEST MANE

Ice climbing (p215) in Prince William Sound region

MARK NEWMAN

BRENT WINEBRENNER

Ship Creek Viewing Platform (p178) is a great spot to watch the salmon run battle in action

Parasail skiing over Alyeska Ski Resort, Girdwood (p197)

MARK NEWMAN

Border town, Hyder (p106), located between Canada and Alaska

Historic buildings along Creek Street, Ketchikan (p96)

Old Russian Orthodox Church
(p255), Ninilchik

Anchorage (p175)

Southeast Alaska

The North Country starts in Southeast Alaska, as do the summer adventures of many visitors to the state. It is the closest slice of Alaska to the Lower 48 and travel around the region is easy due an expanding system of ferries. Its climate, though rainy at times, is Alaska's mildest.

The best reason to top and tail your trip here is its scenery and rare spectacular views. Rugged snowcapped mountains rise steeply from the water to form sheersided fjords embellished by cascading waterfalls. Ice-blue glaciers among the highest peaks fan out into valleys of dark green Sitka spruce and melt into waters with whales, sea lions, harbor seals and salmon.

Once, the Southeast was Alaska's heart and soul, and Juneau was the capital plus the state's major city. However, WWII and the Alcan (Alaska Hwy) made Anchorage and Fairbanks grow. Now the state's Panhandle is characterized by big trees, mainly lying within Tongass National Forest, and small towns. Each community in Southeast has its own character, color and past: from Norwegian-influenced Petersburg to Russian-tinted Sitka. You can feel the gold fever in Skagway, see lumberjacks in Ketchikan, or glaciers near Juneau.

The best way to see the Panhandle is with an Alaska Marine Hwy ferry ticket from Bellingham to Skagway and stop at a handful of towns. To rush from the Lower 48 to Juneau and then fly to Anchorage is to miss some of the best that Alaska has to offer.

HIGHLIGHTS

- **Best lumberjack show** (p104) – watching them chop wood, roll logs and climb poles at Ketchikan's Great Alaskan Lumberjack Show

- **Best bear watching** (p113) – spotting brown *and* black bears at Anan Creek Wildlife Observatory

- **Best hot tub** (p132) – soaking away your worries and sore muscles at Tenakee Springs' bathhouse

- **Alaska's most affordable accommodations** (p143) – marveling at the location and price ($10 a night) of the Juneau International Hostel

- **Steepest train ride in Alaska** (p168) – going from sea level to the alpine in one afternoon on the White Pass & Yukon Railroad

★ Skagway

★ Juneau

★ Tenakee Springs

Anan Creek ★

Ketchikan ★

■ AREA CODE: ☎ 907   ■ POPULATION: 69,315   ■ ELEVATION: MT FAIRWEATHER 15,300FT

Climate

The Southeast has Alaska's most mild climate. Greatly affected by warm ocean currents, the region offers warm summer temperatures averaging 69°F, with an occasional heat wave that sends temperatures to 80°F. The winters are equally mild, and subzero days are rare. Residents, who have learned to live with an annual rainfall of 60in to 200in, call the frequent rain 'liquid sunshine.' The heavy precipitation creates the dense, lush rain forests and numerous waterfalls most travelers come to cherish.

History

Petroglyphs lying along the shoreline in Wrangell, Petersburg and other locations indicate human habitation in Southeast Alaska dates back at least 8000 to 10,000 years and probably longer. The Russians arrived in 1741, entered Sitka Sound and sent two longboats ashore in search of fresh water. The boats never returned, and the Russians wisely departed.

What the unfortunate shore party encountered were members of the Tlingit tribes, who over time had developed the most advanced culture of any group of Alaska Natives. The Tlingits were still there in 1799 when the Russians returned and established the Southeast's first nonindigenous settlement. Aleksandr Baranov built a Russian fort near the present ferry terminal to continue the rich sea-otter fur trade. He was in Kodiak three years later

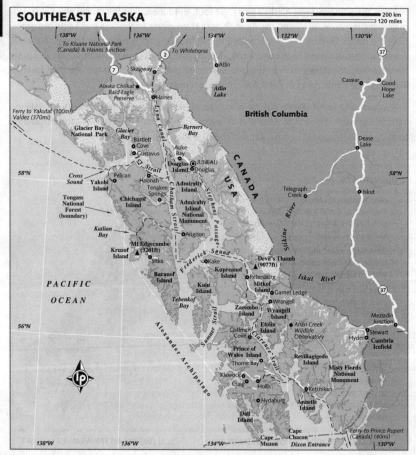

SOUTHEAST ALASKA

when Tlingits, armed with guns from British and American traders, overwhelmed the fort, burned it to the ground and killed most of its inhabitants.

Baranov returned in 1804, this time with an imperial Russian warship, and after destroying the Tlingit fort, established the headquarters of the Russian-American Company at the present site of Sitka. Originally called New Archangel, Sitka flourished both economically and culturally on the strength of the fur trade and in its golden era was known as the 'Paris of the Pacific.'

In an effort to strengthen their grip on the region and protect their fur-trading interests, the Russians built a stockade near the mouth of the Stikine River in 1834. They named it Redoubt St Dionysius but in 1840 the political winds shifted and the Russians leased the entire Southeast coastline to the British, who renamed the new outpost Fort Stikine. After purchasing Alaska from the Russians, the Americans formally took control of the territory in Sitka in 1867. A year later Wrangell was renamed and raising its third national flag in less than 30 years.

In 1880, at the insistence of a Tlingit chief, Joe Juneau and Dick Harris returned to Gastineau Channel to prospect for gold again. This time they hacked their way through the thick forest to the head of Gold Creek. They found, in the words of Harris, 'little lumps as large as peas and beans.' The news spurred the state's first major gold strike, and within a year a small town named Juneau appeared, the first to be founded after Alaska's purchase from the Russians. After the decline in the whaling and fur trades reduced Sitka's importance, the Alaska capital was moved to Juneau in 1906.

The main gold rush, the turning point in Alaska's history, occurred in Skagway when more than 40,000 gold-rush stampeders descended on the town at the turn of the century as part of the fabled Klondike Gold Rush. Most made their way to the Yukon goldfields by way of the Chilkoot Trail until the White Pass & Yukon Railroad was completed in 1900.

In 1887 the population of Skagway was two; 10 years later, 20,000 people lived there and the gold-rush town was Alaska's largest city. A center for saloons, hotels and brothels, Skagway became infamous for its lawlessness. For a time, the town was held under the tight control of Jefferson Randolph 'Soapy' Smith and his gang, who conned and swindled naive newcomers out of their money and stampeders out of their gold dust. Soapy Smith was finally removed from power by a mob of angry citizens. In a gunfight between Smith and city engineer Frank Reid, both men died, and Smith's reign as the 'uncrowned prince of Skagway' ended after only nine months.

At the time Wrangell was also booming as the supply point for prospectors heading up the Stikine River to the Cassiar Gold District of British Columbia in 1861 and 1874, and then using the river again to reach the Klondike fields in 1897. Wrangell was as ruthless and lawless as Skagway. With miners holding their own court, it was said 'that a man would be tried at 9am, found guilty of murder at 11:30am and hung by 2pm.'

Just as gold fever was dying out, the salmon industry was taking hold. One of the first canneries in Alaska was built in Klawock on Prince of Wales Island in 1878. Ketchikan was begun in 1885 as a cannery and in 1897 Peter Buschmann arrived from Norway and established Petersburg as a cannery site because of the fine harbor and a ready supply of ice from nearby LeConte Glacier.

After WWII, with the construction of the Alcan (Alaska Hwy) and large military bases around Anchorage and Fairbanks, Alaska sphere of influence shifted from Southeast to the mainland further north. In 1974 Alaskans voted to move the state capital again, this time to the small town of Willow, an hour's drive from Anchorage. The so-called 'capital move' issue hung over Juneau like a dark cloud, threatening to turn the place into a ghost town. The issue became a political tug-of-war between Anchorage and the Southeast, until voters, faced with a billion-dollar price tag to construct a new capital, defeated the funding in 1982.

Today Juneau is still the capital and the Panhandle a roadless, lightly populated area where residents make a living fishing, and catering to tourists and cruise ships.

Getting There & Around

Most of Southeast may be roadless but getting there and getting around is easy. Ketchikan is only 90 minutes away from Seattle by air on **Alaska Airlines** (☎ 800-426-0333; www.alaskaair.com) or 37 hours on the

Alaska Marine Highway (☎ 800-642-0066; www .ferryalaska.com) from Bellingham, WA. The state ferries, North America's longest public ferry system, also provide transportation between the regions, cities, towns and little fishing ports. Separate ferries link Prince of Wales Island with Ketchikan, Wrangell and Petersburg (p111), Haines with Skagway (p162), and Juneau and Glacier Bay (p149).

SOUTHERN PANHANDLE

KETCHIKAN
☎ 907 / pop 7922

Once known as the 'Canned Salmon Capital of the World,' today Ketchikan settles for 'First City', the initial port for Alaska Marine ferries and cruise ships coming up from the south. It could also be called the 'Thin City.' Just 90 miles north of Prince Rupert, Ketchikan hugs the bluffs that form the shoreline along the southwest corner of Revillagigedo Island. Space is so scarce here the airport had to be built on another island.

Founded as a cannery site in 1885, Ketchikan's mainstay for most of its existence was salmon, and then timber when the huge Ketchikan Pulp Mill was constructed at Ward Cove in 1954. But in the 1970s, strikes and changes in public policy began to mar the logging industry. Louisiana-Pacific closed the sawmill in the city center after a strike in 1983 and the pulp mill in 1997, resulting in hundreds of workers losing their high-paying jobs.

There is still commercial fishing in Ketchikan and the industry accounts for 30% of the local economy. What rings the local cash registers now is tourism. Beginning in the mid-1990s Ketchikan transformed itself into a cruise-ship capital with up to 10 ships visiting a day. Many Alaskans were appalled by the commercialism that took over downtown where many shops are owned by the cruise-ship companies and open only from May to October.

If you stay in Ketchikan longer than an hour, chances are good that it will rain at least once. The average annual rainfall is 162in, but in some years it has been known to be more than 200in. Local residents never use umbrellas or let the rain interfere with daily activities, even outdoor ones. If they stopped everything each time it drizzled, Ketchikan would cease to exist.

When the skies finally clear, the beauty of Ketchikan's setting becomes apparent. The town is backed by forested hills and faces a waterway humming with floatplanes, fishing boats, ferries and barges hauling freight to other Southeast ports.

Orientation

Several miles long but never more than 10 blocks wide, Ketchikan centers on the single main drag of Tongass Ave, which sticks to the shore of Tongass Narrows like a bathtub ring. On one side of Tongass, many businesses and homes are built on stilts out over the water, while on the other side they cling to the steep slopes and often have winding wooden staircases leading to their doors. North of town, Tongass Ave becomes the N Tongass Hwy. South of town it's the S Tongass Hwy.

Downtown is a two-block area for about two blocks inland from the cruise-ship docks. The area northwest of downtown along Tongass, known as the West End, has a commercial/industrial feel; here you'll find fish-processing plants and Plaza Mall. Southeast along Tongass it's more residential, and past Saxman Totem Park it's rural.

MAPS

The best map of the road system is in the *Ketchikan Area Guide* put out by the Ketchikan Visitors Bureau. The publication is free and available at the visitors bureau (see Tourist Information, p98).

Information
BOOKSTORES

Parnassus Books (Map p97; ☎ 225-7690; 5 Creek St; ⓨ 8am-6pm) Half hidden on Creek St but well worth searching for is this delightful bookstore filled with Alaskan books, cards and local art.

EMERGENCY
Ambulance, Fire, Police (☎ 911)

LAUNDRY

Highliner Laundromat (Map p97; ☎ 225-0628; 2701 Tongass Ave; ⓨ 7am-9pm) Out toward Plaza Mall; also has showers and storage lockers.

Thomas Wash Basin (Map p97; ☎ 225-9274; 124 Thomas St; ⓨ 8am-6pm Tue-Sat, to 4pm Sun) Convenient to downtown (and the Potlatch Bar, p103) is this cleverly named place, which has showers, an espresso bar, wi-fi and TV.

SOUTHEAST ALASKA

KETCHIKAN

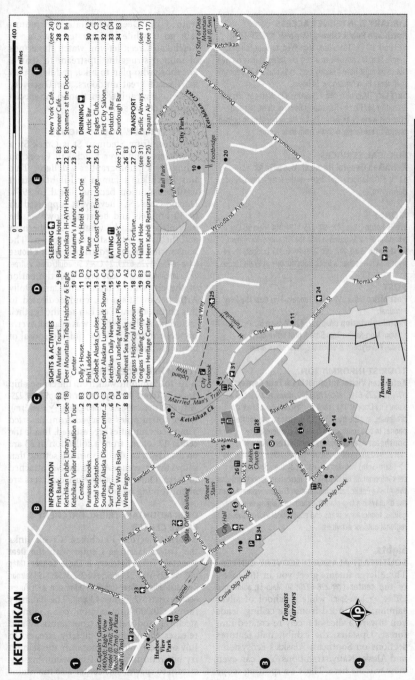

INFORMATION
First Bank..1 B3
Ketchikan Public Library...........(see 1B)
Ketchikan Visitor Information & Tour
Center...2 B3
Parnassus Books...............................3 C3
Postal Substation...............................4 C3
Southeast Alaska Discovery Center...5 C3
Surf City...6 A3
Thomas Wash Basin..........................7 D4
Wells Fargo......................................8 B3

SIGHTS & ACTIVITIES
Allen Marine Tours.............................9 B4
Deer Mountain Tribal Hatchery & Eagle
Center...10 E2
Dolly's House....................................11 D3
Fish Ladder.......................................12 C3
Goldbelt Alaska Cruises....................13 C4
Great Alaskan Lumberjack Show......14 C4
Ketchikan Daily News.......................15 C3
Salmon Landing Market Place..........16 C4
Southeast Historical Museum...........17 A2
Tongass Trading Company................18 C3
Totem Heritage Center......................20 E3

SLEEPING
Gilmore Hotel...................................21 B3
Ketchikan HI-AYH Hostel.................22 B2
Madame's Manor..............................23 A2
New York Hotel & That One
Place..24 D4
West Coast Cape Fox Lodge.............25 D2

EATING
Annabelle's...................................(see 21)
Chico's...26 B3
Good Fortune...................................27 C3
Halibut Hole................................(see 31)
Heen Kahidi Restaurant.................(see 25)

New York Café.............................(see 24)
Pioneer Café.....................................28 C3
Steamers at the Dock........................29 B4

DRINKING
Arctic Bar...30 A2
Eagles Club......................................31 C3
First City Saloon...............................32 A2
Potlatch Bar......................................33 D4
Sourdough Bar..................................34 B3

TRANSPORT
Pacific Airways.............................(see 17)
Taquan Air....................................(see 17)

To Captain's Quarters
(400yd); Eagle View
Hostel (0.7mi) & 8
Motel (0.7mi) & Plaza
Mall (0.3mi)

Harbor
View
Park

Schoenbar Rd

To Start of Deer
Mountain
Trail (0.5mi)

Tongass
Narrows

Cruise Ship Dock

Cruise Ship Dock

Thomas
Basin

Revilla St

Water St

Main St

Grant St

Pine St

Carlanna St

Edmond St

Bawden St

Park Ave

Ketchikan Ck

Married Man's Trail

City
Overlook

Upland Way

Venetia Way

Funicular

Creek St

Stedman St

Thomas St

Woodland Ave

Ball Park

Park Ave

City Park

Ketchikan Creek

Footbridge

Fair St

Deermount Ave

Lotus St

E 5th

Dermount St

Married Man's Trail

Dock St

Front St

Mill St

Mission St

Dock St

Street of
Stairs

Post Office Building

State Office Building

City Hall

St John's
Church

Tunnel

0   400 m
0   0.2 miles

LIBRARY & INTERNET ACCESS

Ketchikan Public Library (Map p97; ☎ 225-3331; 629 Dock St; ☻ 10am-8pm Mon-Wed, to 6pm Thu-Sat, 1-5pm Sun) It's possible to access the Internet here for free but users must have a library card, ($5) plus a $20 deposit that won't be refunded for 24 hours.

Surf City (Map p97; ☎ 225-5475; 425 Water St; per 20min/hr $5/10; ☻ 8am-4pm) Rows of terminals and Ethernet wires (30minutes $5) for those needing to upload photos to the family website from their laptop.

MEDICAL SERVICES

Ketchikan General Hospital (Map p99; ☎ 225-5171; 3100 Tongass Ave) Between the ferry terminal and downtown.

MONEY

Wells Fargo (Map p97; ☎ 225-2184; 306 Main St) One of a handful of banks mixed in with the gift shops downtown.

First Bank (Map p97; ☎ 228-4474; 331 Dock St) Its 24-hour ATM is less than a block from the one at Wells Fargo.

POST

Post office (Map p99; 3609 Tongass Ave) Near the ferry terminal.

Postal substation (Map p97; 422 Mission St; ☻ 9am-5:30pm Mon-Sat, to 3pm Sun) A post office open on Sunday? Everybody is when the cruise ships are in.

TOURIST INFORMATION

Ketchikan Visitor Information & Tour Center (Map p97; ☎ 225-6166, 800-770-3300; www.visit-ketchikan .com; City Dock at 131 Front St; ☻ 7am-5pm) Pick up brochures, ask the friendly staff questions, use courtesy phones to find room, even book tours offered here.

Southeast Alaska Discovery Center (Map p97; ☎ 228-6220; www.fs.fed.us/r10/ketchikan; 50 Main St; ☻ 8am-5pm) You don't need to pay the admission to seek information on Ketchikan's recreation opportunities at this Alaska Public Lands Information Center. Separate from the displays is a trip-planning room containing reference guides, topographic maps and educational videos about regional outdoor activities.

Sights

SOUTHEAST ALASKA DISCOVERY CENTER

Three large totems greet you in the lobby of the **center** (☎ 228-6220; 50 Main St; adult/child $5/free; ☻ 8am-5pm) while a school of silver salmon, suspended from the ceiling, leads you toward a slice of nicely re-created rain forest. Upstairs, the exhibit hall features sections on Southeast Alaska's ecosystems and Alaska Native traditions. You can even view wildlife here. There's a spotting scope

trained on Deer Mountain for mountain goats while underwater cameras in Ketchikan Creek let you watch thousands of salmon struggling upstream to spawn. For those who plan to hike, paddle or play in Alaska's great outdoors, the Discovery Center is a great introduction to the special qualities of this state.

CREEK STREET & DOLLY'S HOUSE

Departing from Stedman St is Creek St, a boardwalk built over Ketchikan Creek on pilings – a photographer's delight. This was Ketchikan's famed red-light district until prostitution became illegal in 1954. During Creek St's heyday, it supported up to 30 brothels and became known as the only place in Alaska where 'the fishermen and the fish went upstream to spawn.' The house with bright red trim is **Dolly's House** (Map p97; ☎ 225-6329; 24 Creek St; adult/child $5/free; ☻ 8am-5pm or when cruise ships are in), the parlor of the city's most famous madam, Dolly Arthur. Now it's a museum dedicated to this notorious era. You can see the brothel, including its bar, which was placed over a trapdoor to the creek for quick disposal of bootleg whiskey.

TOTEM HERITAGE CENTER

A 10- to 15-minute walk from the cruise-ship docks is **Totem Heritage Center** (Map p97; ☎ 225-5900; 601 Deermount St; adult/child $5/free; ☻ 8am-5pm), where totem poles salvaged from deserted Tlingit communities are restored. Inside the center 17 totems from a collection of 33 are on display in an almost spiritual setting that shows the reverence Alaska Natives attached to them. Outside Alaska Native carvers are often working on one.

DEER MOUNTAIN TRIBAL HATCHERY & EAGLE CENTER

A bridge across Ketchikan Creek links the Totem Heritage Center with the **Deer Mountain Tribal Hatchery & Eagle Center** (Map p97; ☎ 225-5158, 225-6767, 800-252-5158; 1158 Salmon Rd; adult/child $9/free, combined admission with Totem Heritage Center $12; ☻ 8am-4:30pm). The hatchery raises 350,000 king salmon, coho salmon, steelhead and rainbow trout annually and releases them into the nearby stream. In July or later, you'll see not only the salmon fry but returning adult fish swimming upstream to spawn. The center also maintains

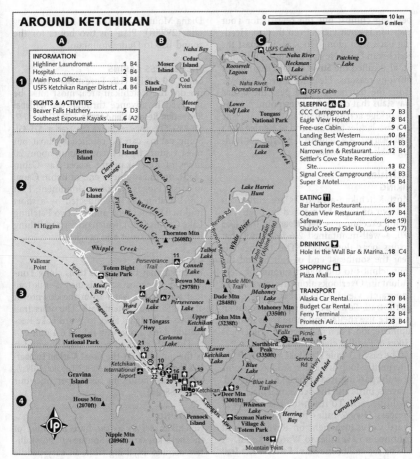

AROUND KETCHIKAN

0   10 km
0   6 miles

INFORMATION
Highliner Laundromat...............**1** B4
Hospital................................**2** B4
Main Post Office....................**3** B4
USFS Ketchikan Ranger District ..**4** B4

SIGHTS & ACTIVITIES
Beaver Falls Hatchery..............**5** D3
Southeast Exposure Kayaks **6** A2

SLEEPING
CCC Campground...................**7** B3
Eagle View Hostel..................**8** B4
Free-use Cabin......................**9** C4
Landing Best Western.............**10** B4
Last Change Campground........**11** B3
Narrows Inn & Restaurant........**12** B4
Settler's Cove State Recreation
  Site................................**13** B2
Signal Creek Campground........**14** B3
Super 8 Motel......................**15** B4

EATING
Bar Harbor Restaurant............**16** B4
Ocean View Restaurant...........**17** B4
Safeway............................(see **19**)
SharJo's Sunny Side Up...........(see **17**)

DRINKING
Hole In the Wall Bar & Marina...**18** C4

SHOPPING
Plaza Mall..........................**19** B4

TRANSPORT
Alaska Car Rental..................**20** B4
Budget Car Rental.................**21** B4
Ferry Terminal......................**22** B4
Promech Air........................**23** B4

SOUTHEAST ALASKA

an eagle pavilion, home to a pair of eagles who were injured and can no longer fly. Thus the 25-minute tours are dubbed 'Live Eagles & Salmon,' providing an interesting lesson in the salmon's life cycle and an opportunity to get close and personal to our national symbol.

TONGASS HISTORICAL MUSEUM

Sharing a building with the Ketchikan Public Library is the **Tongass Historical Museum** (Map p97; ☎ 225-5600; 629 Dock St; adult/child $2/free; ☺ 8am-5pm), which houses a small collection of local historical and Alaska Native artifacts, many dealing with Ketchikan's fishing industry. Outside the museum you'll find the impressive Raven Stealing the Sun

totem and an observation platform overlooking the Ketchikan Creek falls.

THOMAS BASIN

If you thought Creek St was photogenic, cross Stedman St and be ready to burn some film (or megapixels). **Thomas Basin** (Map p97) is home to Ketchikan's fishing fleet and the city's most picturesque harbor. When the boats come in you can photograph them unloading their catch and then follow the crews to the colorful **Potlatch Bar** (p103) nearby, a classic fisherman's pub.

CITY STAIRWAYS

All over Ketchikan there are stairways leading somewhere higher. Sure, they're knee-bending climbs, but the reward for your exertion is great views from the top. Heading back west along Dock St, just past the Ketchikan Daily News Building, is Edmond St, also called the **Street of Stairs** (Map p97) for obvious reasons. Heading down Park Ave from the hatchery, you'll pass the **Upland Way stairs** that climb to a viewpoint. Nearby is a bridge across Ketchikan Creek, the site of a fish ladder and one end of **Married Man's Trail** (Map p97) – a delightful boardwalk leading back to Creek St.

Activities

HIKING

Most Ketchikan-area trails are either out of town or must be reached by boat. The major exception is **Deer Mountain Trail** (Map p97), a well-maintained 2½-mile trail that begins near downtown. The trailhead is near the southeast end of Fair St and the route climbs to the 3000ft summit of Deer Mountain. Overlooks along the way provide panoramic views – the first is about a mile up the trail. Toward the top of the mountain is a free-use shelter and more trails into the alpine region. For a map, see the Wilderness Hikes & Paddles chapter (p75).

The easy 1.3-mile **Ward Lake Nature Walk**, an interpretive loop around Ward Lake, begins near the parking area at the lake's north end. Beavers, birds and the occasional black bear might be seen. To reach the lake, follow N Tongass Hwy 7 miles from downtown to Ward Cove; turn right on Revilla Rd and continue up 1½ miles to Ward Lake Rd.

The 2.3-mile (one way) **Perseverance Trail** from Ward Lake to Perseverance Lake passes through mature coastal forest and muskeg. The view of Perseverance Lake with its mountainous backdrop is spectacular, and the hiking is moderately easy. The trailhead is on Ward Lake's east side just past 3C's Campground.

Ketchikan's other alpine trek is **Dude Mountain Trail**, reached from Revilla Rd by turning right on Brown Mountain Rd, 5 miles from N Tongass Hwy. At the end of Brown Mountain Rd is the trailhead for Dude Mountain Trail, which begins as a boardwalk through stands of old-growth spruce then becomes a trail as you follow a narrow ridge to the 2848ft peak. It's a mile's trek and a gain of 1200ft to the top, but once there you're in open alpine and can easily ridge-walk to

Diana Mountain (3014ft) or Brown Mountain (2978ft). Plan on two hours for the round-trip to Dude Mountain.

WILDERNESS CABINS

Some 30 USFS (US Forest Service) cabins dot the Ketchikan area; most must be reserved in advance through the **National Recreation Reservation Service** (☎ 877-444-6777, 518-885-3639; www.reserveusa.com; cabins $25-45). Some cabins can be reached by boat but most visitors fly to them. Within about 20 miles of Ketchikan are Alava Bay Cabin ($35), on the southern end of Behm Canal in Misty Fiords National Monument; Fish Creek Cabin ($45), connected by a short trail to Thorne Arm; and the two Patching Lake Cabins ($25), which offer good fishing for cutthroat trout and grayling.

CYCLING

Ketchikan has two bicycle trails along Tongass Ave. The most scenic is the 2½-mile trail that follows the water from the downtown area to Saxman Totem Park. The other trail follows N Tongass Hwy to Ward Lake Recreation Area, a one-way ride of 6.4 miles.

The only place to rent a bike downtown is the gift shop at the **Great Alaskan Lumberjack Show** (Map p97; ☎ 225-9050; 330 Spruce Mill Way), which has mountain bikes (per one/four hours $8/25).

PADDLING

Ketchikan serves as the base for some of the best kayaking in Southeast. Possibilities include anything from an easy paddle around the waterfront to a weeklong trip in Misty Fiords National Monument (p79). Pick up charts and topographic maps from the Southeast Alaska Discovery Center and outdoor supplies from **Tongass Trading Company** (Map p97; ☎ 225-5101, 201 Dock St), across from the Gilmore Hotel.

Southeast Sea Kayaks (Map p97; ☎ 225-1258, 800-287-1607; www.kayakketchikan.com; 1007 Water St; kayaks per day single/double $45/60), behind the Taquan Air office, also offers tours including a 2½-hour paddle of Ketchikan's waterfront (adult/child $79/59). A much better paddling experience, however, is its Orcas Cove trip (adult/child $149/99), a four-hour adventure that begins with a boat ride across the Tongass Narrows and then paddling among protected islands looking for sea lions, orcas and seals.

Also renting kayaks is **Southeast Exposure Kayaks** (Map p97; ☎ 225-8829; www.southeastexposure.com; 37 Potter St; single/double $45/55), 14 miles north of town, convenient if you're paddling out of Settler's Cove State Park, a logistic headache if you're not.

Betton Island
Due west of Settler's Cove State Park at the north end (Mile 18.2) of N Tongass Hwy is this island and several smaller islands nearby, making it an excellent day paddle if you're staying at the campground. Although Clover Pass is a highly trafficked area, the backside of Betton Island offers a more wildernesslike setting. Pack a tent and sleeping bag and you can turn this into an overnight excursion by camping on the great beaches of Tatoosh Islands on the west side of Betton Island.

Naha Bay
Also from Settler's Cove State Park, it's an 8-mile paddle to Naha Bay, the destination of an excellent three- or four-day adventure. At the head of the bay is a floating dock where you can leave your kayak and set off down the Naha River National Recreation Trail. The scenic 5.4-mile trail follows the river up to Jordan and Heckman Lakes, both of which have **USFS cabins** (NRRS; ☎ 877-444-6777, 518-885-3639; www.reserveusa.com; cabins $35). The fishing here is good and black bears are plentiful – in August you might see them catching salmon at a small waterfall 2 miles up the trail from Roosevelt Lagoon.

A narrow outlet connects Naha Bay with Roosevelt Lagoon. You don't have to enter the lagoon to access the trail. Kayakers wishing to paddle into the lagoon must either portage around the outlet or enter it at high slack tide, as the narrow pass becomes a frothy, roaring chute when the tide is moving in or out.

George & Carroll Inlets
From Hole In The Wall Bar & Marina (p105), 7½ miles southeast of Ketchikan down the S Tongass Hwy, you can start an easy one- to four-day paddle north into George or Carroll Inlets or both. Each inlet is protected from the area's prevailing southwesterlies, so the water is usually calm (although north winds occasionally whip down George Inlet). From Hole in the Wall to the top of George Inlet is a 26-mile paddle.

While not on the same dramatic scale as Misty Fiords, the two inlets are scenic. Highlights include Herring Bay, a mile north of Hole in the Wall, which attracts lots of salmon and seagulls; and Mahoney Inlet, 8 miles north, which has beautiful waterfalls.

Tours
Being the cruise-ship port that it is, Ketchikan can be seen in a short period of time thanks to a large number of tour companies operating here. The best place to see what's available and to sign up is the **Ketchikan Visitor Information & Tour Center** (☎ 225-6166) building on City Dock, where a whole wing is devoted to a gauntlet of tour providers touting their services.

Alaska Amphibious Tours (☎ 225-9899, 866-341-3825; www.akduck.com; per person $35) Using three amphibian vehicles that double as a bus and a boat to provide 90-minute tours of the downtown area and the harbor. The top-heavy vehicle puts you 8ft above anything on the road for a great view, but sharp turns have you gripping the seat in front.

Alaska Dive & Snorkel Tours (☎ 225-4667, 866-333-7749; www.alaskadeepsix.com; per person $89) Takes out groups no larger than six people for a snorkeling encounters with the marine life on the bottom of the Narrows: sea anemones, starfish and whatever happens to come swimming along. The three-hour snorkel tours include all the equipment, most importantly a wetsuit to stay warm in Alaska's frigid waters.

Alaska Undersea Tours (☎ 225-9899, 866-341-3825; www.akduck.com; adult/child $49/29) From top of the water to below it, this 90-minute tour puts you in a semisubmersible vessel with underwater viewing windows so you can see the marine life and seascapes in the Ketchikan harbors.

Northern Tours (☎ 247-6457; www.northerntoursofalaska.com) Offers the standard city tour, which is a two-hour outing in vans or minibuses and includes Saxman Native Village, Creek St, Dolly's House and the boat harbors for $30.

Rainbird Deluxe Tours (☎ 888-505-8810) Offers the same tour.

Festivals & Events
Ketchikan's **Fourth of July** celebration includes a parade, contests, softball games, an impressive display of fireworks and a logging show. The smaller **Blueberry Festival**, held at the State Office Building and the Main Street Theater on the first weekend in August, consists of arts and crafts, singers, musicians, and food stalls serving blueberries every possible way.

Sleeping

Ketchikan charges 13% on lodging in city and bed taxes.

BUDGET

There are no public campgrounds close to town. The closest campgrounds are 4½ miles north of the ferry terminal at Ward Lake Recreation Area (p105).

Ketchikan HI-AYH Hostel (Map p97; ☎ 225-3319; 400 Main St; dm members/nonmembers $12/15; ☼ 7am-9am & 6-11pm Jun-Aug; ✗) Right downtown; in the Methodist church, provides kitchen facilities, showers and separate-sex dorm rooms. The friendly hostel is spotlessly clean, has comfortable common areas, and offers free hot drinks and cookies. If you're arriving at night, call first to make sure space is available.

Eagle View Hostel (Map p99; ☎ 225-5461; www.eagleviewhostel.com; 2303 Fifth Ave; per person $25; ☼ April-Oct; ✗) This hostel is well named. From a deck outside or the breakfast table inside you gaze down at the boat traffic in Tongass Narrows, the mountains beyond and float planes that are almost at eye level. Keep that in mind when you first arrive in town and realize you have to carry your luggage up five steep blocks from the bus stop at Plaza Mall. The house has dorms for men and women. There is no curfew or lockout.

MIDRANGE

New York Hotel (Map p97; ☎ 225-0246, 866-225-0246; www.thenewyorkhotel.com; 207 Stedman St; s/d $109/119; ✗ ▯) This has a great downtown location near Creek St and Thomas Basin but is just far enough away from the cruise-ship crowds for a quiet setting. It's an older hotel, modernized and furnished with antiques. All rooms have private bath, cable TV and small refrigerators. Some have harbor views. There's shuttle service to/from the ferry/airport and a $10 per night discount if you stay two nights or longer.

Madame's Manor (Map p97; ☎ 247-2774; www.madamesmanor.com; 324 Cedar St; r $115-169; ✗ ▯) The only thing better than the gourmet breakfast served at this B&B on Nob Hill is the view Tongass Narrows that lies below you. Lodging is offered in three lavishly furnished rooms in the Victorian home and a separate apartment.

Gilmore Hotel (Map p97; ☎ 225-9423, 800-275-9423; www.gilmorehotel.com; 326 Front St; r $115-155; ✗ ▯)

Built in 1927 as a hotel and renovated several times since, the Gilmore has 38 rooms that still retain a historical flavor. The rooms are 'historically proportioned' (ie small) but very comfortable with cable TV, coffeemakers and hair dryers. The entire 2nd floor is nonsmoking.

Captain's Quarters (Map p97; ☎ 225-4912; www.ptialaska.net/~captbnb; 325 Lund St; r$90-95) There are three rooms, one with a full kitchen.

Super 8 Motel (Map p99; ☎ 225-9088; 800-800-8000; 2151 Sea Level Dr; r $109-121) Eighty-two rooms are lined along the waterfront behind Plaza Mall. Pay the token extra money for one of the Narrows-view rooms, as the area surrounding the motel is aesthetically challenged. Shuttle service to/from the ferry/airport is available.

TOP END

West Coast Cape Fox Lodge (Map p97; ☎ 225-8001, 866-225-8001; www.westcoasthotels.com/capefox; 800 Venetia Way; r $190-200, ste $251; ▯) This is Ketchikan's splashiest lodging. Perched atop the hill behind Creek St, it offers the best views in town and can be reached by a high-tech funicular tram from the Creek St boardwalk. The opulent lodge has 72 amenity-filled rooms and suites, and an acclaimed restaurant overlooking the city. It's an extra $10 for a room with a view of the Tongass Narrows, but well worth it.

Landing Best Western (Map p97; ☎ 225-5166, 800-428-8304; www.landinghotel.com; 3434 Tongass Ave; s/d from $155/165; ▯) Across the street from the ferry terminal is this spiffy place with large rooms that feature cable TV, microwaves, coffeemakers and small refrigerators. Both a pub and restaurant are on-site, and a courtesy shuttle van that will take you anywhere downtown.

Narrows Inn (Map p97; ☎ 247-2600, 888-686-2600; www.narrowsinn.com; 4871 N Tongass Hwy; s $125-135, d $135-145; ✗ ▯) A mile north of the airport ferry on the waterfront, it offers 44 standard rooms that are well kept and very clean. You pay extra for the ocean-view rooms despite the fact that the view from most of them is the airport runway on the other side of the Narrows.

Eating

Ketchikan has many places to eat, but the expensive Alaskan prices usually send the newly arrived visitor into a two-day fast. If this is your first Alaskan city, don't fret – it only gets worse as you go north!

RESTAURANTS

Bar Harbor Restaurant (Map p97; 2813 Tongass Ave; lunch $9-12, dinner $15-19; 11am-2:30pm & 4:30-9pm Mon-Sat; ✗) A small cozy place between downtown and the ferry terminal. The menu is intriguingly eclectic – from coconut prawns with a marmalade-cream sauce to home-style pot roast just like Mom used to make it – all enjoyed to superb views of the Narrows. Beer and wine are available, and so is a back deck for outdoor dining when the sun is out.

Heen Kahidi Restaurant (Map p97; ☎ 225-8001; 800 Venetia Way; breakfast $7-10, lunch $10-18, dinner $18-40; 7am-2pm & 5:30-10pm Mon-Sat, 5:30-9pm Sun; ✗) Generally regarded as Ketchikan's best dining experience, the West Coast Cape Fox Lodge restaurant offers hilltop dining with city views and a menu that is not dominated by seafood.

Steamers at the Dock (Map p97; 76 Front St; lunch $9-13, dinner $15-30; 10am-9pm) The view from this waterfront restaurant's 3rd-floor perch is wonderful if there's not a cruise ship docked in front of it, which is usually the case during the summer. The menu features many unusual seafood dishes – crab-stuffed oysters among them – while at the bar they pour an excellent selection of microbrews.

Narrows Restaurant (Map p99; ☎ 247-2600; 4871 N Tongass Hwy; lunch $7-11, dinner $13-30; 6am-2pm & 5-9pm; ✗) At the Narrows Inn, a mile northwest of the airport ferry, is this local favorite for upscale dining. There are lots of seafood dishes, but also pasta and steaks.

Ocean View Restaurant (Map p99; 1831 Tongass Ave; lunch specials $7-9, dinner $9-17; 11am-11pm). Ketchikan's best Mexican restaurant offers 10 types of burritos, seven sizzling fajita dishes and, in that great Alaskan tradition, pasta and pizza. Come early and grab one of the three tables with an unobstructed view of the Narrows.

Good Fortune (Map p97; 4 Creek St; lunch specials $6.25, dinner $8-14; 9am-9pm). Head upstairs in Ketchikan's best Chinese restaurant to feast on double mushroom pork while watching the cruise-ship crowds on Creek St.

CAFÉS

That One Place (Map p97; 207 Stedman St; breakfast $7-10, lunch $8-13; 8am-4pm; ✗) The owners of Bar Harbor Restaurant have turned the café at the New York Hotel into one of the best places for breakfast or lunch. Practically everything on the lunch menu is seafood related. Let's face it – if you're in Alaska long enough you'll eventually order halibut tacos. You might as well do it here, where the locals rave about them.

Annabelle's (Map p97; 326 Front St; chowders $6-9, salads $11-15; 10am-9:30pm) At the Gilmore Hotel, this is a chowder house with a 1920s decor. When the cruise-ship passengers arrive, this place packs 'em in tighter than a tin of sardines.

SharJo's Sunny Side Up (Map p99; 1630 Tongass Ave; lunch $7-10; 11am-8pm Mon-Tue, to 3pm Wed-Sat; ✗) A bright and funky eatery in a can't-miss yellow building. Inside three of the tables are lawn furniture complete with umbrellas. This is where you come for a milk shake and a salmon burger.

Chico's (Map p97; 435 Dock St; lunch special $6.50, dinner $9-14, medium pizza $11-14; 10am-11pm) From the minute you walk in you know this small downtown cantina serves good burritos and tacos by its colorful Mexican-themed interior. But when you open the menu you discover it also serves a decent pizza. Hey, they're just trying to make a living.

Pioneer Café (Map p97; 619 Mission St; breakfast $7-13, lunch $7-12, dinner $9-17; 24hr) One of the few downtown restaurants that was around when the lumber mills were. At $3 a bowl, its clam chowder is the best in the city.

GROCERIES

Safeway (Map p99; 2417 Tongass Ave; salad bar per lb $5; 5am-midnight) A grocery store on the side of Plaza Mall; has a salad bar, Starbucks, deli and ready-to-eat items including Chinese food. An informal inside dining area overlooks the boat traffic on Tongass Narrows.

Drinking

Potlatch Bar (Map p97; 126 Thomas St) Just above Thomas Basin, this is the town's longtime fisher's pub and is still a piece of the real Ketchikan, a setting with more locals than tourists.

Sourdough Bar (301 Front St) On the northwest end of City Dock; the walls are covered with photos of fishing boats – most beached, wrecked, sunk, listing wildly or even aflame. A ship's bell, ring floats and other fishing paraphernalia add to the decor.

Arctic Bar (Map p97; 509 Water St) Just past the tunnel on downtown's northwest side, this has a great back deck jutting out over the water. The deck is a sunny spot with great views of the Narrows if a cruise ship isn't tied up in front of it.

First City Saloon (Map p97; ☎ 225-1494; 830 Water St) This sprawling club, with giant TV screens, pool tables, dart boards, three bars and a small dancefloor, was renovated in 2005 but still has plenty of 'Ketchikan kharacter.' On most weekends during the summer there is live music (cover $3) and Edgar Winter once played here (obviously at the end of his career).

Eagles Club (Map p97; Creek St; pints/pitchers $3.50/5.50) For cheap beer without all the fixings, try this odd little oasis on touristy Creek St. On its narrow back deck that juts out over Ketchikan Creek is Halibut Hole for good fish-and-chips.

Entertainment

Great Alaskan Lumberjack Show (Map p97; ☎ 225-9050, 888-320-9049; www.lumberjacksports.com; adult/child $29/14.50) Who knew that chopping wood could be so entertaining? When the lumberjacks are at the peak of their axe-and-saw battles you can hear the crowd cheering all the way to the cruise-ship docks. One of the main cruise ship–oriented attractions, the hourlong show features 'rugged woodsmen' using handsaws and axes, climbing poles, log rolling and engaging in other activities that real loggers haven't engaged in since the invention of the chainsaw. There's also a gift shop where you can buy wide suspenders, red plaid woolies, frilly underwear and other lumberjack-themed necessities. There are three to four shows daily from May to September at the outdoor grandstand just off Spruce Mill Way.

Getting There & Away
AIR
Flights to Ketchikan from Seattle, Anchorage and major Southeast communities are possible with **Alaska Airlines** (☎ 225-2145, 800-252-7522; www.alaskaair.com).

Pacific Airways (Map p97; ☎ 225-3500, 877-360-3500; www.flypacificairways.com; 1007 Water St) offers scheduled floatplane flights between Ketchikan and Prince of Wales Island; Hollis (one way $92), Craig/Klawock ($106) and Thorne Bay ($92).

Ketchikan has many bush-plane operators, including **Taquan Air** (Map p97; ☎ 225-8800, 800-770-8800; www.taquanair.com; 1007 Water St) and **Promech Air** (Map p99; ☎ 225-3845, 800-860-3845; www.promechair.com; 1515 Tongass Ave).

BOAT
Northbound Alaska Marine Highway ferries leave almost daily in summer, heading north for Wrangell (six hours, $33), Petersburg ($52, nine hours), Sitka ($73, 20 hours), Juneau ($94, 29 hours) and Haines ($118, 33½ hours). Ferries leave Ketchikan twice a week (Sunday and Wednesday) and head south to Bellingham ($210, 37 hours). The MV *Lituya* provides service to Metlakatla ($21, 1½ hours) Thursday through Monday. For sailing times call the **ferry terminal** (☎ 225-6181; 3501 Tongass Ave).

The **Inter-Island Ferry Authority** (☎ 225-4838, 866-308-4848; www.interislandferry.com) runs the MV *Prince of Wales* to Hollis, on Prince of Wales Island (one way adult/child $30/18). The car-and-passenger ferry makes two round-trips daily in summer, starting in Hollis (at 7am and 2:30pm, departing from Ketchikan for the return trip at 10:45am and 6:15pm). Keep in mind that there is little to see in Hollis. Prince of Wales Island is a wonderful sidetrip but you need to spend at least a night there (p107).

Getting Around
TO/FROM THE AIRPORT
The Ketchikan airport is on one side of Tongass Narrows, the city is on the other. A small car-and-passenger ferry ($5 for walk-on passengers) runs between the airport and a landing off Tongass Ave, just northwest of the main ferry terminal. The **Airporter** (☎ 225-5429) bus meets all arriving Alaska Airlines flights at the terminal and will take you to/from downtown for $20, ferry fare included. There isn't a better way to arrive at the First City than **Tongass Water Taxi** (cell ☎ 209-8294). Richard Schuerger meets all flights at the baggage-claim area and then gives you a lift on his boat to the dock nearest to your destination. The cost depends on where he's dropping you off, but is usually less than half of what the Airporter charges.

BUS
Ketchikan Gateway Borough Transit (☎ 225-8726) buses operate along two routes. The green

line ($1.50) runs from the airport ferry to Thomas Basin, circling back by Totem Heritage Center and within a half-mile of Deer Mountain trailhead. The longer blue line ($2.25) runs to Saxman Totem Park in the southeast and also continues northwest past the airport ferry to North Tongass Shopping Center. The bus service runs from Monday to Saturday from 6am to 9pm and a reduced schedule on Sunday.

CAR
For two to four people, renting a car is a good way to spend a day seeing sights out of town. There's unlimited mileage with either of the following but a 16% tax:
Alaska Car Rental (☎ 225-2232, 800-662-0007; 2828 Tongass Ave; compacts $49)
Budget (☎ 800-527-0700; per day $53) Ketchikan Intl Airport (☎ 225-6004); Tongass Hwy (☎ 225-8383; 4950 N Tongass Hwy)

TAXI
Cab companies in town include **Alaska Cab** (☎ 225-2133) and **Yellow Taxi** (☎ 225-5555). The fare from the ferry terminal or the airport ferry dock to downtown is $9.

AROUND KETCHIKAN
South Tongass Highway
On S Tongass Hwy 2½ miles south of Ketchikan is **Saxman Native Village & Totem Park** (Map p99; ☎ 225-4421; www.capefoxtours.com; village tour adult/child $35/17; ☼ 8am-5pm), an incorporated Tlingit village of 431 residents. The village is best known for its **Saxman Totem Park**, which holds 24 totem poles brought here from abandoned villages around the Southeast and restored or recarved in the 1930s. Among the collection is a replica of the Lincoln Pole (the original is in the Alaska State Museum in Juneau), which was carved in 1883, using a picture of Abraham Lincoln, to commemorate the first sighting of white people.

You can wander around the Totem Park at no charge, but most visitors take a Alaska Native–led village tour that includes a Tlingit language lesson, traditional drum-and-dance performance, narrated tour of the totems and a visit to the carving shed. Independent travelers can join this tour by prebooking at the Ketchikan visitors bureau or by calling the village (☎ 225-4421), a day in advance.

From Saxman, S Tongass Hwy continues another 12 miles, bending around Mountain Point and heading back north to George Inlet. This route is more scenic than N Tongass Hwy, but holds little in the way of stores, restaurants or campgrounds. One exception is **Hole in the Wall Bar & Marina** (Map p99; ☎ 247-2296; 7500 S Tongass Hwy; ☼ noon-2pm), a funky little hangout run by the affable John Jackson, who's lived here for almost 40 years. Hole in the Wall feels light years away from the tourist madness of Ketchikan in summer, and it enjoys a beautiful isolated spot near Herring Bay. A small community of boaters and fishers hangs out in the cozy little bar and if you can find a flat place to pitch a tent, you're welcome to camp.

The S Tongass Hwy ends at Beaver Falls Hatchery, where the Silvis Lake Trail begins nearby.

North Tongass Highway
The closest campgrounds to Ketchikan are in Ward Lake Recreation Area; take N Tongass Hwy 4½ miles north of the ferry terminal and turn right onto Revilla Rd, then continue 1½ miles to Ward Lake Rd. **CCC Campground** (Map p99; sites $10), basically an overflow area, is on Ward Lake's east shore while **Signal Creek Campground** (Map p99; sites $10) has 24 sites on the south shore. **Last Chance Campground** (Map p99; Revilla Rd; sites $10) is in a beautiful area with four scenic lakes, 19 sites and three trails that depart into the lush rain forest.

Ten miles northwest of Ketchikan is **Totem Bight State Park** (Map p99; ☎ 247-8574; 9883 N Tongass Hwy; sites free), which contains 14 restored or recarved totems and a colorful community house. Just as impressive as the totems are the park's coastline and wooded setting. A viewing deck overlooks Tongass Narrows.

Tongass Hwy ends 18 miles north of Ketchikan at **Settler's Cove Recreation Site** (Map p99; sites $10), a scenic coastal area with a lush rain forest bordering a gravel beach and rocky coastline. Its campground has 14 sites, a quarter-mile trail to a waterfall and observation deck, and is rarely overflowing like those at Ward Lake.

Misty Fiords National Monument
This spectacular, 3570-sq-mile national **monument** (Map p79), lying just 22 miles east of Ketchikan, is a natural mosaic of sea cliffs, steep fjords and rock walls jutting 3000ft

straight out of the ocean. Brown and black bears, mountain goats, Sitka deer, bald eagles and a multitude of marine mammals inhabit this drizzly realm. The monument receives 150in of rainfall annually but many people think Misty Fiords is at its most beautiful when the granite walls and tumbling waterfalls are veiled in fog and mist. Walker Cove, Rudyerd Bay and Punchbowl Cove – the preserve's most picturesque areas – are reached via Behm Canal, the long inlet separating Revillagigedo Island from the mainland.

Kayaking is *the* best way to experience the preserve (see p79). Ketchikan's **Southeast Sea Kayaks** (☎ 225-1258, 800-287-1607; www .kayakketchikan.com; 1007 Water St) offers a one-day guided paddle in which small groups and their kayaks are transported by boat to the fjords and back ($389 per person). It also has a five-day guided tour ($1399) and rents kayaks (see Paddling, p100).

You can also view the area on sightseeing flights or day cruises. Flightseeing may be the only option if you're in a hurry and most

---

DETOUR: HYDER

On the eastern fringe of Misty Fiords National Monument, at the head of Portland Canal, is Hyder (Map p94; population 83), a misplaced town if there ever was one. It was founded in 1896 when Captain DD Gailland explored Portland Canal for the US Army Corps of Engineers and built four stone storehouses, the first masonry buildings erected in Alaska, which still stand today. Hyder and its British Columbian neighbor Stewart boomed after major gold and silver mines were opened in 1919. Hyder became the supply center for more than 10,000 residents. It's been going downhill ever since, the reason it now calls itself 'the friendliest ghost town in Alaska.'

A floatplane or a long drive from Prince Rupert are the only options for getting here. Because of Hyder's isolation from the rest of the state it's almost totally dependent on larger Stewart (population 600, optimistically), just across the Canadian border. Hyder's residents use Canadian money, set their watches to Pacific time (not Alaska time), use a British Columbia area code and send their children to Canadian schools. All this can make a sidetrip here a little confusing.

The most famous thing to do in Hyder is drink at one of its 'friendly saloons.' The historic **Glacier Inn** (☎ 250-636-9092) is the best known and features an interior papered in signed bills, creating the '$20,000 Walls' of Hyder. Next door is First and Last Chance Saloon, and both bars hop at night.

But a better reason to find your way to this out-of-the-way place is for bear watching. From late July to September, you can head 6 miles north of town to **Fish Creek Bridge** and watch brown and black bears feed on chum salmon runs. The USFS has constructed a viewing platform here and there are interpreters on-site during summer. Continue along the road and you cross back into British Columbia at Mile 11. At Mile 23 is a point from which to view the impressive **Bear River Glacier**, Canada's fifth largest. If you don't have wheels **Seaport Limousine** (☎ 250-636-2622; 516 Railway St) picks up at Stewart hotels every evening for a trip out to observation area (per person C$10).

The venerable family-run **Grandview Inn** (☎ 250-636-9174; www.grandviewinn.net; s/d $55/60) has 10 rooms with private bath and TV, and is on the main drag about a quarter-mile from downtown Hyder. On the Canadian side there's **King Edward Hotel & Motel** (☎ 250-636-2244, 800-663-3126; www .kingedwardhotel.com; 5th & Columbia Sts; hotel s C$59-79, d C$69-89, motel s/d C$99/109). A mile from Stewart is **Bear River RV Park** (☎ 250-636-9205; www.stewartbc.com/rvpark; Hwy 37A, Stewart; campsites/RV sites C$12/21) with 55 sites along the Bear River. In Stewart your room rate will be jacked skyward by Canada's 7.5% Goods & Services Tax (GST) and another 10% in BC provincial taxes.

Unfortunately if you're in Ketchikan, the only way to reach Hyder is to fly with **Taquan Air** (Map p97; ☎ 225-8800, 800-770-8800; www.taquanair.com) making the run twice a week on Monday and Thursday ($330 round-trip). That may seem expensive but consider that a day trip to Admiralty Island to see brown bears at Pack Creek is around $500. If you're in Terrace, BC, with nowhere to go, **Seaport Limousine** (☎ 250-636-2622; 516 Railway St, Stewart) offers scheduled buses to Stewart that depart at 5pm Monday to Friday (C$32 one way).

For information on either town, contact the **Stewart/Hyder International Chamber of Commerce** (☎ 250-636-9224, 888-366-5999; www.stewart-hyder.com; 222 5th Ave, Stewart).

tours include landing on a lake and a short walk in the rain forest. But keep in mind that this is a big seller on the cruise ships and when the weather is nice it is an endless stream of floatplanes flying to the same area: Rudyerd Bay and Walker Cove. Throw in the tour boats and one local likened such days to 'the Allie invasion of Omaha Beach.'

For more on the monument, contact the **USFS Ketchikan Ranger District** (☎ 225-2148; www .fs.fed.us/r10/tongass; 3031 Tongass Ave).

SLEEPING

If you plan ahead, you can rent one of 13 **USFS cabins** (NRRS; ☎ 877-444-6777, 515-885-3639; www.reserveusa.com; per night $25-45) in the area. The cabins must be reserved in advance, usually several months. A 14th cabin, at Big Goat Lake, is free and available on a first-come, first-served basis, as are four Adirondack shelters (three-sided free-use shelters) in the preserve.

GETTING THERE & AROUND

There isn't an air charter in Ketchikan that doesn't do Misty Fiords. The standard offering is a two-hour flight with a lake landing for $199, easily booked at the visitors center. Among them are **Island Wings** (☎ 225-2444, 888-845-2444; www.islandwings .com), a one-plane, one-pilot company run by Michelle Masden, and **Carlin Air** (☎ 225-3036, 888-594-3036; www.carlinair.com), with Jeff Carlin serving as pilot and owner. Both will do cabin drop-offs.

Cruises on speedy catamarans is another option. **Goldbelt Alaska Cruises** (Map p97; ☎ 225-6044, 800-228-1905; www.mistyfjord.net; 29 Main St, Suite 205) offers a 6½-hour tour (adult/child $125/100) through the monument that includes a light meal and narration. **Allen Marine Tours** (Map p97; ☎ 225-8100; www .mistyfjordwildlifequest.com; 50 Front St) has a four-hour version of the same tour (adult/child $139/89). Goldbelt's quickie special is a four-hour cruise-and-flight option (adult/child $250/210) with a boat cruise one way to Rudyerd Bay and a 30-minute floatplane sightseeing flight on the other leg.

PRINCE OF WALES ISLAND

☎ 907 /pop 3411

For some tourists, the Alaska they come looking for is only a three-hour ferry ride away from the crowds of cruise-ship tourists they experienced in Ketchikan. At 135 miles long and covering more than 2230 sq miles, Prince of Wales Island (POW) is the USA's third-largest island, after Alaska's Kodiak and Hawaii's Big Island.

This vast, rugged island is a destination for the adventurous at heart, loaded with hiking trails and canoe routes, Forest Service cabins and fishing opportunities.

The 990-mile coastline of POW meanders around numerous bays, coves, saltwater straits and protective islands, making it a kayaker's delight. And for someone carrying a mountain bike through Alaska, a week on the island is worth all the trouble of bringing the bike north. The island has the most extensive road system in the Southeast, 1300 miles of paved or maintained gravel roads that lead to small villages and several hundred miles more of shot-rock logging roads that lead to who-knows-where.

Presently tourism is relatively light but is bound to increase due to the expanding service of the Inter-Island Ferry Authority. The Authority launched its first vessel, MV *Prince of Wales*, in 2002 replacing the Alaska Marine Highway service between Ketchikan and Hollis. In mid-2006 the Authority will launch MV *Stikine*. From Coffman Cove the new ferry will make runs to Wrangell and Petersburg, eliminating the need to backtrack to Ketchikan if you want to visit POW.

There are no cruise ships on POW but there are clear-cuts and you must be prepared for them. Blanketing the island is a patchwork quilt of lush spruce-hemlock forest and fields of stumps where a forest used to be. They are a sign that you have reached real Alaska, a resource-based state where people make a living fishing, mining and cutting down trees.

Orientation & Information

Hollis (population 165), where the ferry from Ketchikan lands, has few visitor facilities and no stores or restaurants. The towns best set up for tourism are Craig (population 1127) and Klawock (population 848), only 7 miles apart and a 31-mile drive across the island along the paved Hollis–Klawock Hwy. Founded as a salmon-canning and cold-storage site in 1907, Craig is the island's largest and most interesting community, with its mix of commercial fishermen and loggers.

SOUTHEAST ALASKA

Also supporting lodging, restaurants, small grocery stores and other visitor amenities are Thorne Bay (population 497), 38 miles northeast from Klawock, and Coffman Cove (population 177), 55 miles north of Klawock. By 2008 all five of these towns are scheduled to be connected to one another by paved roads.

For a quick visit, the map found inside the free *Prince of Wales Island Guide* is sufficient. For an extended stay or if you're planning to explore the logging roads, purchase the *Prince of Wales Island Road Guide* ($4) published by the USFS. Either is available at the POW Chamber of Commerce or USFS Ranger Station.

Alicia Roberts Medical Center (☎ 755-4800; Hollis-Klawock Hwy, Klawock) Is the main medical facility on the island.

Craig Library (☎ 826-3281; 504 3rd St; ☺ 10am-noon & 1-5pm Tue-Fri, 7-9pm Mon-Thu, noon-4pm Sat) Has used books for sale and free Internet access.

Emergency (ambulance, fire, police ☎ 911)

TLC Laundry & Rooms (☎ 826-2488; 333 Cold Storage Rd; ☺ 7am-9pm) Laundromat in Craig with showers.

Prince of Wales Chamber of Commerce (☎ 755-2626; www.princeofwalescoc.org; Klawock Bell Tower Mall, Hollis-Klawock Hwy; ☺ 10am-3pm Mon-Fri) Operates a visitors center in Klawock.

Post office (Craig-Klawock Hwy, Craig) Next to Thompson House Supermarket.

USFS office (☺ 8am-5pm Mon-Fri) Craig (☎ 826-3271; 900 9th St); Thorne Bay (☎ 828-3304; 1312 Federal Way) In Craig, head here for information on trails, cabins and paddling adventures.

Voyageur Bookstore & Coffee Company (☎ 826-2333; 801 Water St; ☺ 7am-6pm Mon-Fri, from 8am Sat, 10am-4pm Sun) A wonderful bookstore in Craig with espresso bar and Internet access (per 15mins/hour $4/10).

Wells Fargo (☎ 826-3040; 301 Thompson Rd, Craig) Next to the post office and equipped with a 24-hour ATM.

Sights & Activities

Of the three totem parks on POW, the **Klawock Totem Park** (Bayview Blvd) is by far the most impressive and obviously a great source of community pride. Situated on a hill overlooking the town's cannery and harbor, Klawock's 21 totems are the largest collection in Alaska and make for a scenic, almost dramatic setting. The totems are either originals from the former village of Tukekan or replicas.

The **Prince of Wales Hatchery** (☎ 755-2231; Mile 9 Hollis-Klawock Hwy; ☺ 7am-7pm) was established in 1897 and today is the second-oldest one

in Alaska. The present facility was built in 1976 and raises coho, king and sockeye salmon as well as steelhead trout. On site is a visitors center, aquarium and gift shop where fresh coho is often for sale. You can explore the operations on a self-guided tour or join a free guided tour from 1pm to 6pm Monday to Saturday.

On the island's southern half, you can watch salmon attempt to negotiate a couple of **fish ladders** during the summer spawning season. Both **Cable Creek Fish Pass** and **Dog Salmon Fish Pass** have viewing platforms, from which you might also see hungry black bears.

The USFS maintains more than 20 hiking trails on POW with the vast majority of them short walks to rental cabins, rivers or lakes. In the south, a good hike can be made to **One Duck Shelter** from a trailhead on the road to Hydaburg, 2 miles south of Hollis junction. The trail is steep, climbing 1400ft in 1.2 miles, but it ends at a three-sided, free-use shelter that sleeps four. To spend the night in the open alpine area with panoramic views of the Klawock Mountains is worth the knee-bending climb. To the north the **Balls Lake Trail** begins in the Balls Lake Picnic Area just east of Eagle Nest Campground and winds 2.2 miles around the lake.

Mountain bikers have even more opportunities than hikers. Bikes can be rented in Klawock from **Alaska Kustom Kayaks** (☎ 907-755-2800; www.alaskakustomkayaks.com; Klawock Bell Tower Mall, Hollis-Klawock Hwy; per day $20; ☺ 9am-5pm) and then taken on any road to explore the island. One of the most scenic roads to bike is South Beach Rd (also known as Forest Rd 30) from Thorne Bay to Coffman Cove. It's a 37-mile ride along the narrow, winding dirt road that is often skirting Clarence Strait. Along the way is **Sandy Beach Picnic Area** (Mile 6 Sandy Beach Rd), an excellent place to see humpback whales, orcas and harbor seals offshore or examine intriguing tidal pools at low tides.

Opportunities for paddlers are almost as limitless as they are for mountain bikers. At the north end of POW off Forest Rd 20 is the **Sarkar Lakes Canoe Route**, a 15-mile loop of five major lakes and portages along with a USFS cabin and excellent fishing. For a day of kayaking depart from Klawock and paddle into **Big Salt Lake**, where the water is calm and the birding is excellent. Alaska Kustom Kayaks rents kayaks (per day single/double $60/70) as well as canoes (per day $45). It

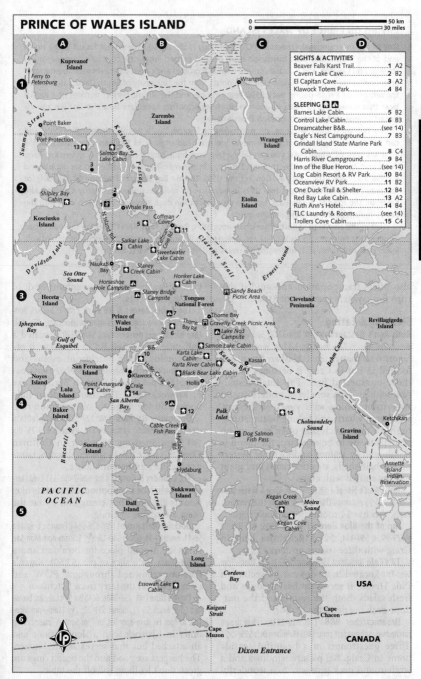

PRINCE OF WALES ISLAND

0   50 km
0   30 miles

SIGHTS & ACTIVITIES
Beaver Falls Karst Trail.....................1 A2
Cavern Lake Cave............................2 B2
El Capitan Cave..............................3 A2
Klawock Totem Park.........................4 B4

SLEEPING
Barnes Lake Cabin...........................5 B2
Control Lake Cabin..........................6 B3
Dreamcatcher B&B....................(see 14)
Eagle's Nest Campground.................7 B3
Grindall Island State Marine Park
Cabin......................................8 C4
Harris River Campground.................9 B4
Inn of the Blue Heron................(see 14)
Log Cabin Resort & RV Park..........10 B4
Oceanview RV Park........................11 B2
One Duck Trail & Shelter................12 B4
Red Bay Lake Cabin.......................13 A2
Ruth Ann's Hotel...........................14 B4
TLC Laundry & Rooms..............(see 14)
Trollers Cove Cabin........................15 C4

SOUTHEAST ALASKA

Kupreanof Island
Ferry to Petersburg
Wrangell
Zarembo Island
Wrangell Island
Point Baker
Port Protection
13
Salmon Bay Lake Cabin
3
Kashevarof Passage
Shipley Bay Cabin
2
1
Whale Pass
Coffman Cove
5
11
Etolin Island
Kosciusko Island
Sarkar Lake Cabin
Coffman Cove Rd
Sweetwater Lake Cabin
Davidson Inlet
Naukati Bay
Staney Creek Cabin
Honker Lake Cabin
Clarence Strait
Ernest Sound
Sea Otter Sound
Horseshoe Hole Campsite
Staney Bridge Campsite
Sandy Beach Picnic Area
Cleveland Peninsula
Heceta Island
Tongass National Forest
7
Iphegenia Bay
Prince of Wales Island
Thorne Bay
Gravelly Creek Picnic Area
Revillagigedo Island
Gulf of Esquibel
Thorne Bay Rd
6
Lake No3 Campsite
Salmon Lake Cabin
Behm Canal
10
Karta Lake Cabin
Kasaan
San Fernando Island
Karta River Cabin
Kasaan Bay
Noyes Island
4
Klawock
Black Bear Lake Cabin
Point Amargura Cabin
Craig
14
Hollis
8
Ketchikan
Lulu Island
San Alberto Bay
9
12
15
Baker Island
Polk Inlet
Cholmondeley Sound
Gravina Island
Suemez Island
Cable Creek Fish Pass
Dog Salmon Fish Pass
Annette Island Indian Reservation
PACIFIC OCEAN
Hydaburg
Dall Island
Sukkwan Island
Kegan Creek Cabin
Moira Sound
Kegan Cove Cabin
Tlevak Strait
Long Island
Cordova Bay
USA
Essowah Lake Cabin
Kaigani Strait
Cape Chacon
Cape Muzon
CANADA
Dixon Entrance

SOUTHEAST ALASKA

CAVING ON PRINCE OF WALES ISLAND

One of the most unusual aspects of POW's geology is the broad cave system found in the north end of the island. The karst formation is an area of eroded limestone concealing underground streams and caverns, and it includes more than 850 grottos and caves. The caves received national attention in the mid-1990s when paleontologists from the University of South Dakota discovered the remains of a man dating back 9500 years in one, and the almost perfect remains of a brown bear that dated 45,000 years in another. Both let scientists speculate how the last ice age affected animal and human migration from Asia.

The two most popular caves are northwest of Thorne Bay, a 94-mile drive from Hollis, and can be easily viewed even if you've never worn a headlamp. At **El Capitan Cave** (Forest Rd 15), 11 miles west of Whale Pass, you can take a free, two-hour, ranger-led cave tour offered at 9am, noon and 2pm from Thursday through Saturday in summer. Tours are limited to six people and involve a 370-step stairway trail. Contact the USFS **Thorne Bay Ranger Station** (☎ 828-3304) for reservations (required at least two days in advance; no children under 7). Nearby **Cavern Lake Cave**, on the road to Whale Pass, features an observation deck allowing visitors to peer into the cave's mouth at the gushing stream inside.

Also in the area is the short, wheelchair-accessible **Beaver Falls Karst Trail**, on the main road between the two turnoffs for Whale Pass, which offers an aboveground experience as its boardwalk leads past sinkholes, pits, underground rivers and other typical karst features.

---

also offers transportation and guided day trips for kayakers (per person $160).

Sleeping & Eating

Ruth Ann's Restaurant (☎ 826-3377; 300 Front St; dinner $19-43; ⏱ 7am-9pm; ✗) This would be a favorite no matter what Alaskan city it was located in but in Craig it becomes one of those unexpected joys. The small restaurant with an even smaller bar offers quaint waterfront dining with views of the bay, weathered wharfs and fishing boats returning with their catch that often ends up on your plate. As to be expected, the menu is dominated by seafood and includes oysters on the half-shells, steamer clams and giant prawns stuffed with crab.

Ruth Ann's Hotel (☎ 826-3378; Main & Water Sts; r $90-125; ✗) Across the street from the restaurant, this has 14 rooms in two buildings.

Inn of the Blue Heron (☎ 826-3606; 406 9th St; s $79-99, d $94-114; ✗) A delightful B&B in Craig with three rooms upstairs.

TK's Café (breakfast $5-8, lunch $5-11; ⏱ 10am-3pm Mon-Fri) Located in the downstairs section of Blue Heron, it serves up hearty soups and fresh salads. Both the rooms and the outdoor deck overlook the harbor.

Dreamcatcher B&B (☎ 826-2238; www.dream catcherbedandbreakfast.com; 1405 Hamilton Dr; r $95; ✗) Three guestrooms in a beautiful seaside home in Craig. Big picture windows and a wraparound deck give way to a wonderful view of water, islands, mountains and, of course, clear-cuts.

Log Cabin Resort & RV Park (☎ 755-2205, 800-544-2205; www.logcabinresortandrvpark.com; Big Salt Lake Rd; sites per person/cabins $8/65-120) Located a half-mile up Big Salt Rd in Klawock, it offers condos, rustic beachfront cabins and tent space with showers. It also rents canoes ($25 per day) for use on Big Salt Lake or Klawock Lake. The resort is often fully booked during August's silver salmon run.

Oceanview RV Park (☎ 329-2226; www.coffman cove.org/rvpark.html; campsites $15, RV sites $23-25; dm $20) Positioned on the water in Coffman Cove, this place has 14 spaces, showers, laundry facilities and a bunkhouse.

TLC Laundry & Rooms (☎ 826-2488, 331 Cold Storage Rd; r $40), Not the flophouse it sounds like. Rooms are small but clean, and by far the most affordable in Craig.

Dockside Restaurant (☎ 826-5544; Front St; breakfast $6-11, lunch $9-11, dinner $10-18; ⏱ 5:30am-8pm Mon-Sat, to 3pm Sun) A good place for breakfast and a great place for a slice of pie ($3.50). Karen's Pies are renowned throughout POW and even served on the ferry from Ketchikan.

Dave's Dine (☎ 755-2986; 6648 Big Salt Lake Rd; breakfast $5-9, lunch $6-11, dinner $11-20; ⏱ 11am-7pm Mon-Thu, to 8pm Fri, 8am-8pm Sat, to 7pm Sun) A rambling diner in Klawock with a sloping floor and an attached bus that serves as the kitchen. The burgers are good and the onion rings are great; don't let them roll off the table.

CABINS & CAMPING
There are 18 **USFS cabins** (NRRS; ☎ 877-444-6777; www.reserveusa.com; cabins $35-45), one Adirondack shelter and two campgrounds on the island (see map p109). Two cabins can be reached by rowing across a lake, thus eliminating the floatplane expense required with many others. Control Lake Cabin is reached from State Hwy 929, where a dock and rowboat are kept on the west end of the lake. Red Bay Lake Cabin is at the north end of the POW, off Forest Rd 20, and reached with a half-mile hike to a boat and then a 1½-mile row across the lake.

The Alaska Division of Parks has a cabin at Grindall Island State Marine Park, at the end of the Kasaan Peninsula on POW's east-central coast. This cabin is managed by **Ketchikan Ranger Station** (☎ 247-8574; 9883 N Tongass Hwy, Ketchikan; per night $25).

Harris River Campground (sites $8) This is near the Hollis Rd junction. The 14-site USFS campground has fire rings, BBQ grills and picnic tables; seven sites have tent pads.

Eagle's Nest Campground (sites $8) This 11-site campground, 18 miles west of Thorne Bay, overlooks a pair of lakes. It has a canoe-launching site and a half-mile shoreline boardwalk.

Getting There & Away
The **Inter-Island Ferry Authority** (Craig ☎ 866-308-4848, Klawock ☎ 826-4848, Hollis ☎ 530-4848, Ketchikan ☎ 225-4838; www.interislandferry.com) operates the MV *Prince of Wales* between Ketchikan and Hollis daily (one way adult/child $30/18) with two round-trips daily in summer, departing from Hollis at 7am and 2:30pm, and departing from Ketchikan at 10:55am and 6:15pm.

In mid-2006 the Authority's new MV *Stikine* began service between Coffman Cove, Wrangell and Petersburg.

Getting Around
BICYCLE
The one-way fare to carry a bike over on the ferry is $11, or you can rent one in Klawock (p108).

CAR
Another option is to rent a car in Ketchikan and take it over on the ferry. Rates for the ferry are based on vehicle length; a subcompact one way is $34. You can also rent a car on the island through **Wilderness Rent-A-Car** (☎ 800-949-2205, Craig ☎ 826-5200, Klawock ☎ 755-2691) for $89 a day with unlimited mileage.

TAXI
POW Ferry Shuttle (☎ 957-2224) connects with ferries in Hollis but you will want to give them a call from Ketchikan to reserve a seat. One-way fare to Craig is $20. There are several other taxi companies on POW, including **Jackson Cab** (☎ 755-2557) in Klawock.

WRANGELL & AROUND
☎ 907 / pop 2023
Strategically located near the mouth of the Stikine River, Wrangell is one of the oldest towns in Alaska and the only one to have existed under three flags and ruled by four nations – Tlingit, Russia, Britain and America.

Wrangell's heyday was as a jumping-off point for three major gold rushes up the Stikine River from 1861 to the late 1890s. Back then Wrangell was as lawless and ruthless as Skagway and at one point Wyatt Earp, the famous Arizona lawman, filled in as a volunteer marshal for 10 days before moving on to Nome. Wrangell's most famous visitor, however, was John Muir, who came in 1879 and again in 1880. Muir wrote that 'Wrangell village was a rough place. It was a lawless draggle of wooden huts and houses, built in crooked lines, wrangling around the boggy shore of the island for a mile or so.'

Eventually Wrangell became a fishing and lumber town typical of Southeast Alaska and when the timber industry crashed in the early 1990s the town was hit harder than most others. Some pin a brighter future on an emerging dive fishery as more than 60 divers already harvest sea urchins, sea cucumbers and geoducks. Others see Wrangell's salvation in the proposed Bradfield Rd and ferry that would connect the town to Canada's mainland roads.

Of all the Alaska Marine Highway's major stops, Wrangell is the least gentrified. Cruise ships are only a once-a-week occurrence here, so the town is rarely inundated and isn't ritzy. You don't come to Wrangell for posh luxury hotels or well-developed tourist attractions. Instead, use Wrangell as a home base for explorations of the surrounding wilds.

The island offers great mountain-biking and bike-camping opportunities; kayakers

SOUTHEAST ALASKA

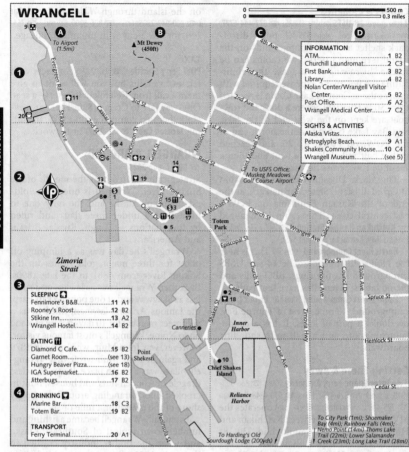

WRANGELL

SOUTHEAST ALASKA

INFORMATION	
ATM..............................1	B2
Churchill Laundromat...........2	C3
First Bank.......................3	B2
Library..........................4	B2
Nolan Center/Wrangell Visitor	
Center........................5	B2
Post Office......................6	A2
Wrangell Medical Center........7	C2

SIGHTS & ACTIVITIES	
Alaska Vistas....................8	A2
Petroglyphs Beach..............9	A1
Shakes Community House.....10	C4
Wrangell Museum...........(see 5)	

SLEEPING	
Fennimore's B&B.................11	A1
Rooney's Roost..................12	B2
Stikine Inn.......................13	A2
Wrangell Hostel..................14	B2

EATING	
Diamond C Cafe..................15	B2
Garnet Room..................(see 13)	
Hungry Beaver Pizza...........(see 18)	
IGA Supermarket.................16	B2
Jitterbugs.........................17	B2

DRINKING	
Marine Bar........................18	C3
Totem Bar........................19	B2

TRANSPORT	
Ferry Terminal....................20	A1

can explore the Stikine River or myriad
islands and waterways around the river's
mouth; and local guides lead boat trips to
Anan Creek bear observatory and other
places of interest.

Orientation & Information

Wrangell is blessed with a ferry terminal
downtown, so even if you're not planning
to spend the night here, you can still disem-
bark for a brief look around or a (quick!)
hike to the petroglyphs.

Churchill Laundromat (☎ 874-874-3954; Shakes St;
☉ 8am-8pm) Next to the Marine Bar (how convenient!)
with showers and a sign that reads 'No Pets Allowed In
Showers!'

Emergency (ambulance, fire, police ☎ 911)

First Bank (☎ 874-3333; 224 Brueger St) Across from
IGA Supermarket, also maintains a 24-hour ATM on Front St.

Irene Ingle Public Library (☎ 874-3535; 124 2nd St;
☉ 10am-noon & 1-5pm Mon & Fri, 1-5pm & 7-9pm Tue-
Thu, 9am-5pm Sat) A wonderful facility for such a small
town and includes free Internet access on four computers.

Post office (112 Federal Way) At the town's north end.

USFS Office (☎ 874-2323; 525 Bennett St; ☉ 8am-
4:30pm Mon-Fri) Located 0.75 miles north of town; has
information on regional USFS cabins, trails and campgrounds.

Wrangell Medical Center (☎ 874-7000; 310 Bennett
St) For anything from Aspirin to Zoloft.

Wrangell Visitor Center (☎ 874-3699, 800-367-9745;
www.wrangell.com; 296 Outer Dr; ☉ 9am-4pm Mon-Fri) In
the new Nolan Center, stocks the free *Wrangell Visitors Guide*
and shows a 10-minute film on the area in a small theater.

Sights

WRANGELL MUSEUM

This **museum** (☎ 874-3770; 296 Outer Dr; adult/child/family $5/3/12; ⊙ 10am-5pm Mon-Sat) was completely renovated in 2004 when it moved into the new Nolan Center. Now Wrangell has a museum worthy of its extensive and colorful history. As you stroll through the many rooms an audio narrator automatically comes on and explains that chapter of Wrangell's history, from Tlingit culture and the gold-rush era to the time Hollywood arrived in 1972 to film the movie *Timber Tramps*. You can marvel at a collection of Alaskan art that includes a Sidney Laurence painting or be amused that this rugged little town has had two presidential visits (Warren Harding and Ronald Reagan).

CHIEF SHAKES ISLAND

This **island** (Shakes St) is the most enchanting spot in Wrangell. It is a small grassy islet in the middle of the boat harbor, reached by a pedestrian bridge just before you descend to the docks. The tiny island with its totems, tall pines and the half-dozen eagles usually perched in the branches is a quiet oasis compared to the hum of the fishing fleet that surrounds it. In the middle is **Shakes Community House**, an excellent example of a high-caste tribal house that contains tools, blankets and other cultural items. It's open only to accommodate cruise ships (call the Wrangell Museum for the tour schedule). Just as impressive are the six totems surrounding the tribal house, all duplicates of originals carved in the late 1930s.

PETROGLYPH BEACH

Located on the town's north side is a state historic park where you can see primitive rock carvings believed to be 8000 years old. The best set lies three-quarters of a mile from the ferry terminal and can be reached by heading north on Evergreen Ave or, as the locals call it, Old Airport Rd. Walk past Stough's Trailer Court and proceed to a marked boardwalk on the left that features interpretive displays. Follow the boardwalk to the beach and then turn right and walk north about 50yd. With your back to the water, look for the carvings on the large rocks, many of them resembling spirals and faces.

There are almost 50 in the area, but most are submerged at high tide. Check a tide book before you leave. Remember that to walk there and back, and to have a good look around, you'll want an hour or two – too long for the ferry stopover (though some fast walkers manage a quick trip).

ANAN CREEK WILDLIFE OBSERVATORY

This is the perfect place to view one of Southeast Alaska's largest pink salmon runs, which enters Anan Bay and heads up Anan Creek, southeast of Wrangell on the mainland in late July and early August. From the observatory and photography platform, you can safely watch eagles, harbor seals, black bears and a few brown bears chowing down gluttonously on the spawning humpies. This is one of the few places in Alaska where black and brown bears coexist at the same run or at least put up with each. In 2004 a permit system was instituted here. Permits ($10) are required from early July through August, or basically when the bears are there, and are reserved online or by calling the USFS Office (opposite) in Wrangell. Almost half of the daily 64 permits go to local tour operators. Another 18 are available from March 1 for that particular year and 12 permits are issued three days in advance.

Anan Creek is a 20-minute floatplane flight or 31-mile kayak trip from Wrangell and almost every tour operator in town offers a trip there. Alaska Vistas (see p114) uses a jet boat for a guided eight-hour trip ($186). **Alaska Waters Inc** (☎ 874-2378, 800-347-4462; www.alaskawaters.com), at the Stikine Inn, has a six-hour boat tour ($198), while **Sunrise Aviation** (☎ 874-2319; www.sunriseflights.com) will fly you in for $260 for up to four passengers each way.

The best way to see the bears, if you have the time and can plan ahead, is to book the USFS **Anan Bay Cabin** (reserve ☎ 877-444-6777; www.reserveusa.com; cabins $35), which comes with four permits and is a mile hike from the observation area. This cabin can be reserved six months in advance and during the bear-watching season it pretty much has to be.

Activities

HIKING

Other than the climb up Mt Dewey, all of Wrangell's trails are off the road and often include muskeg. You'll need a car for the roads and a pair of rubber boots for the trails.

SOUTHEAST ALASKA

Mt Dewey Trail is a half-mile climb up a hill to a small clearing in the trees, overlooking Wrangell and the surrounding waterways. From Mission St, walk a block and turn left at 3rd St. Follow the street past the houses to the posted stairway on the right. The hike to the top takes 15 minutes or so, but the trail is often muddy. John Muir fanatics will appreciate the fact that the great naturalist climbed the mountain in 1879 and built a bonfire on top, alarming the Tlingit people living in the village below. Ironically, the only signs on top now say 'No Campfires.'

Signposted 4.7 miles south of the ferry terminal on the Zimovia Hwy is the **Rainbow Falls Trail**. The trail begins directly across from Shoemaker Bay Recreation Area. It's a mile hike to the waterfalls and then another 2½ miles to an observation point overlooking Shoemaker Bay on Institute Ridge, where there is a three-sided shelter. The lower section of the trail can be soggy at times, the upper sections steep. The views are worth the hike, and a pleasant evening can be spent on the ridge. A round-trip takes four to six hours.

A 1.4-mile path to the lake, **Thoms Lake Trail** is reached by following Zimovia Hwy to its paved end and then turning east on Forest Rd 6265. About halfway across the island, just before crossing Upper Salamander Creek, turn right on Forest Rd 6290 and follow it 4 miles to the trailhead. The first half-mile of the trail is planked, but the rest cuts through muskeg and can get extremely

muddy during wet weather. There's an old ragged but still usable cabin on the lake.

Long Lake Trail begins 28 miles southeast of Wrangell on Forest Rd 6270 and is a pleasant 0.6-mile hike. The planked trail leads to a shelter, skiffs and outhouses on the shores of the lake. Plan on an hour round-trip for the trek.

PADDLING
One look at a nautical chart of Wrangell will have kayakers drooling and dreaming. Islands and protected waterways abound, though many are across the vast Stikine River flats, where experience is a prerequisite due to strong tides and currents. Novices can enjoy paddling around the harbor, over to Petroglyph Beach or to Dead Man's Island.

Alaska Vistas (☎ 874-2997, 866-874-3006; http://alaskavistas.com/Vistas; 106 Front St; ⏰ 7am-6pm), inside the Java Junkies espresso shed, a wi-fi hot spot at City Dock, rents kayaks (per 24 hours single/double $45/55) and offers discounts for longer rental. The company also runs guided kayak tours including a full-day paddle to Aaron Creek ($190) on the well-protected east side of Wrangell Island. Vans are used to transport you to the east shore and a jet boat returns you to Wrangell at the end of the day.

Rainwalker Expeditions (☎ 874-2549; www.rainwalkerexpeditions.com) also rents kayaks (per day single/double $40/60) and offers a kayaker drop-off service ($25) to the easy-to-explore back side of the island and other areas.

CELEBRATING SPRING IN WRANGELL

On the third week of April, eagles can be seen gathering around Wrangell and people can be seen gathering garnets. Thus the reason for the town's annual Garnet Festival.

The weeklong event is a celebration of the arrival of spring with residents staging an art fair, fish-fry dinners and even a golf tournament at Muskeg Meadows (opposite). But the festival's main attractions take place on the nearby Stikine River.

The largest spring concentration of bald eagles in Southeast Alaska occurs along the river. They are viewed by hundreds of birders during the festival in specially arranged boat cruises. The other popular tour is to travel 8 miles upriver to gather garnets at Garnet Ledge.

Garnets are the result of crystallization created by heat and pressure, and Wrangell garnets have long been recognized for their faceted, luminous, green and red beauty. But they are not gemstones because garnets' structure makes them difficult to cut and polish for jewelry. Still, they have become a very popular souvenir.

Even if you're not in Wrangell for the Garnet Festival, local boys and girls meet most cruise ships and ferries during the summer, selling single garnets ($2 to $20) and garnets still lodged in a piece of schist ($5 to $50). Many Stikine River tours will stop at the ledge and allow you to `mine' a few garnets if you have purchased a permit from the Wrangell Museum.

Stikine River

A narrow, rugged shoreline and surrounding mountains and glaciers characterize the beautiful, wild Stikine River, which begins in the high peaks of interior British Columbia and ends some 400 miles later in a delta called the Stikine Flats, just north of Wrangell. The Stikine is North America's fastest navigable river, and its most spectacular sight is the Grand Canyon of the Stikine, a steep-walled gorge where violently churning white water makes river travel impossible. John Muir called this stretch of the Stikine 'a Yosemite 100 miles long.'

Trips from below the canyon are common among rafters and kayakers. They begin with a charter flight to Telegraph Creek in British Columbia and end with a 160-mile float back to Wrangell.

Travelers arriving in Wrangell with a kayak but insufficient funds to charter a bush plane can paddle from the town's harbor across the Stikine Flats (where there are several USFS cabins) and up one of the Stikine River's three arms. By keeping close to shore and taking advantage of eddies and sloughs, experienced paddlers can make their way 30 miles up the river to the Canadian border, or even farther, passing 12 USFS cabins (see p100), the two bathing huts at **Chief Shakes Hot Springs** and the Garnet Ledge (see the boxed text, opposite) along the way. But you must know how to line a boat upstream and navigate a highly braided river and, while in the lower reaches, accept the fact that you'll encounter a lot of jet-boat traffic.

Wrangell's USFS office can provide information on the Stikine River, including two helpful publications: *Stikine River Canoe/Kayak Routes* ($4) and *Lower Stikine River Map* ($3), the latter covering the river up to Telegraph Creek.

Several Wrangell guide services run trips on the Stikine or offer drop-off service for kayakers. **Breakaway Adventures** (☎ 874-2488, 888-385-2488; www.breakawayadventures.com) uses a jet boat for a day trip up the river that includes Shakes Glacier and the hot springs ($140). Alaska Vistas (see opposite) provides a water-taxi service for kayakers and rafter, charging $160 per hour for up to six passengers or $140 if you rent kayaks from it. Also providing tours or transport up the Stikine River is **Alaska Waters Inc** (☎ 874-2378,

> ### MUSKEG MEADOWS
>
> Built in 1998 atop the sawdust and wood chips left behind by local sawmill operations, Wrangell's **Muskeg Meadows Golf Course** (☎ 874-4653; www.wrangellalaskagolf.com; Ishiyama Dr; per round $20), 0.5 miles east of Bennet Dr, may be a US Golf Association–certified nine-hole, par 36 course, but it's uniquely Alaskan. Surrounded by wilderness, members are rarely alarmed when a bear comes bounding across a fairway. Then there is the club's Raven Rule; if a raven steals your ball you may replace it with no penalty provided you have a witness. Finally, the course's narrow fairways and tangled roughs of spruce and muskeg have resulted in this warning posted in the clubhouse: 'You got to have a lot of balls to play Muskeg Meadows.'

800-347-4462; www.alaskawaters.com) and **Alaska Peaks & Seas** (☎ 874-2454; www.wedoalaska.com).

Festivals & Events

The summer's biggest event is the **Fourth of July** celebration. All of Wrangell gets involved in the festival, which features a parade, fireworks, live music, a logging show, street games, food booths and a salmon bake.

In the third week of April, Wrangell has its **Garnet Festival** (see the boxed text, opposite).

Sleeping

Wrangell has a half-dozen B&Bs (complete list available at the visitors center) but no top-end hotels. The city levies a 7% sales tax and a flat $4 per room bed tax on all lodging.

Harding's Old Sourdough Lodge (☎ 874-3613, 800-874-3613; www.akgetaway.com; 1104 Peninsula St; s/d $89/99; ✗ 🖳) After a pleasant 10-minute walk south of town around the harbor, you'll reach this place with 16 rooms, a sauna, steam bath and free transportation to/from the ferry or airport. Home-style meals, often including local seafood, are available. Attentive hosts and a spotless facility make this Wrangell's nicest place to stay.

Rooney's Roost (☎ 874-2026; www.rooneysroost.com; 206 McKinnon St; r incl breakfast $75-95; ✗ 🖳) Within easy walking distance from the ferry, just a short way up 2nd St, is this antique-filled B&B. There are five guestrooms with queen-size beds and TV, and two with

SOUTHEAST ALASKA

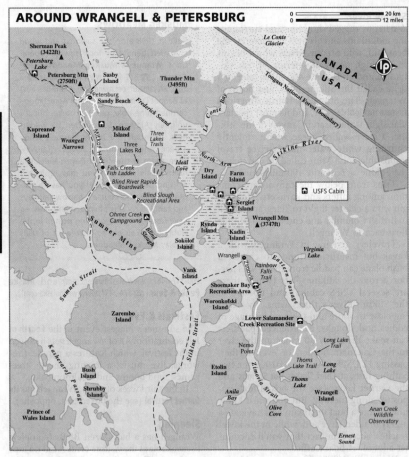

AROUND WRANGELL & PETERSBURG

0 ——— 20 km
0 ——— 12 miles

Le Conte Glacier

CANADA
USA

Sherman Peak (3422ft) ▲
Petersburg Lake
Petersburg Mtn (2750ft) ▲
Sasby Island
Thunder Mtn (3495ft) ▲
Tongass National Forest (boundary)
Petersburg
Sandy Beach
Frederick Sound
Le Conte Bay
Kupreanof Island
Mitkof Island
Three Lakes Trails
Wrangell Narrows
Three Lakes Rd
North Arm
Stikine River
Duncan Canal
Falls Creek Fish Ladder
Ideal Cove
Dry Island
Farm Island
Blind River Rapids Boardwalk
Blind Slough Recreational Area
Ohmer Creek Campground
Blind Slough
Sergief Island
Wrangell Mtn ▲ (3747ft)
USFS Cabin
Sumner Mtns
Rynda Island
Kadin Island
Sokolof Island
Virginia Lake
Wrangell
Rainbow Falls Trail
Eastern Passage
Vank Island
Shoemaker Bay Recreation Area
Sumner Strait
Zarembo Island
Woronkofski Island
Stikine Strait
Lower Salamander Creek Recreation Site
Nemo Point
Long Lake Trail
Long Lake
Kashevarof Passage
Bush Island
Etolin Island
Zimovia Strait
Thoms Lake Trail
Thoms Lake
Wrangell Island
Shrubby Island
Anila Bay
Olive Cove
Anan Creek Wildlife Observatory
Prince of Wales Island
Ernest Sound

---

private bath. In the morning you enjoy a full breakfast, and in the afternoon you can relax on the deck with view of Wrangell.

Stikine Inn (☎ 874-3388; www.stikine.com; 107 Stikine Ave; s $85-95, d $95-105; 🖳) Near the ferry dock and convenient to the Front St business district is Wrangell's largest motel. All 33 rooms have private bath and there's a restaurant on-site. Rooms with a view of the water are $10 extra.

Fennimore's B&B (☎ 874-3012; www.fennimores bbb.com; 321 Stikine Ave; s/d $65/70; ✗) The easiest lodging for late-night ferry passengers to reach, as it's a five-minute walk across the street from the ferry terminal. Three rooms on the 1st floor have private bath and private entrances. All have cable TV, a refriger-

ator, microwave and queen-size bed. The coffeepot is always on and there are bikes for guests to tool around town on.

Wrangell Hostel (☎ 874-3534; 220 Church St; dm $15; ✗) In the First Presbyterian Church, this basic place has separate-sex dorm rooms with well-used foam-rubber pads on the floor, as well as kitchen facilities, shared bath and showers. It has no lockout hours, but an 11pm curfew is requested.

CAMPING

City Park (☎ 874-2444; Mile 1.7 Zimovia Hwy; campsites free) For those with a tent, the closest campground is this delightful waterfront park, a mile south of town and immediately south of an historic cemetery. Within the pleasant wooded setting are eight sites, shelters and rest rooms. Camping is free, but for tents only. There's a one-night limit if you have a car, but that's overlooked if you arrive on foot.

Shoemaker Bay Recreation Area (☎ 874-2444; Mile 4.5 Zimovia Hwy; campsites limited to 5 days free, RV sites limited to 10 days $15-25) This is across from the Rainbow Falls trailhead in a wooded area near a creek. There are 25 sites, 15 with hook-ups, for RVers (recreation vehicles) and a tent-camping area for everybody sleeping in ripstop nylon. All sites have a good view of Zimovia Strait. Note the time limit for site hire.

Nemo Point (☎ 874-2323; Forest Rd 6267; sites free) This offers the best camping on Wrangell Island, but unfortunately it is 14 miles from town. Each of the six free wheelchair-accessible sites has a picnic table, outhouse and a stunning view of Zimovia Strait. Take Zimovia Hwy/Forest Hwy 16 south to Forest Rd 6267. The sites stretch along 4 miles of Forest Rd 6267.

Lower Salamander Creek Recreation Site (☎ 874-2323; Forest Rd 50050; campsites free) East of Nemo Point is where this campground is located and you're allowed three free campsites along beautiful Salamander Creek. Take Zimovia Hwy 23 miles south of town to Forest Rds 6265 and 50050.

Eating

Harding's Old Sourdough Lodge (☎ 874-3613; 1104 Peninsula St; dinner $19-24) If you call ahead, it allows you to join its guests for home-style meals that include a salad bar and often crab, halibut and salmon during the summer.

Garnet Room (☎ 874-4388; 107 Stikine Ave; breakfast $5-10, dinner $11-25; ☽ 6am-9pm) Located on the ground floor of the Stikine Inn, it serves beef, poultry, pasta and seafood with excellent harbor views. Its seafood-mix grill is pricey ($20) but good.

Jitterbugs (☎ 874-3350; 309 Front St; ☽ 5am-4pm Mon-Fri, from 6am Sat) An early-opening espresso stand with an attitude and tables outside, proffering lattes, cappuccinos and Italian sodas. On one side of the building a sign says 'We Support Resources Development Jobs – Timber & Fisheries'; on the other 'Jitterbugs parking only. Violators will be decaffeinated.'

Diamond C Café (☎ 874-3677; 223 Front St; breakfast $4-10, lunch $7-10; ☽ 6am-3pm) The only place

hopping on a Sunday morning in this otherwise quiet town. This is where locals come to satisfy their deep-sea, deep-fried fix.

Hungry Beaver Pizza (☎ 874-3005; Shakes St; pizza $10-20; ☽ 4-10pm) It's in the same building as the Marine Bar but if you can't handle the smoke, there's an outdoor deck with tables. Wrangell's favorite pizza is a taco pizza with seasoned hamburger and refried beans. It comes with the fantasy of spending the winter in Mexico.

IGA Supermarket (223 Brueger St; ☽ 8am-6pm Mon-Sat) It has an in-store bakery, espresso and a deli with ready-to-eat items. You can grab a sandwich and take it outside to benches overlooking the water.

Drinking

Totem Bar (Front St) Right downtown, this is the biggest scene. If a cruise ship is in, make sure you're there, front row, for the local troupe of cancan dancers.

Marine Bar (Shakes St) Fishing industry folks hang out at this place, near the harbor.

Getting There & Around

Daily northbound and southbound flights are available with **Alaska Airlines** (☎ 874-3308, 800-426-0333). Many claim the flight north to Petersburg is the 'world's shortest jet flight,' since the six- to 11-minute trip is little more than a takeoff and landing.

Alaska Marine Ferries (☎ 874-3711) run almost daily both northbound and southbound from Wrangell in summer. To the north is Petersburg ($28, three hours) via the scenic, winding Wrangell Narrows, to the south Ketchikan ($33, six hours). In 2006 the new MV *Stikine* is slated to be operating between Coffman Cove on Prince of Wales Island and Wrangell. Contact the **Inter-Island Ferry Authority** (☎ 866-308-4848; www.interislandferry.com) for schedule and rates.

Practical Rent-A-Car (☎ 874-3975), at the airport, rents compacts for $47 per day plus a 17% rental tax. **Rainwalker Expeditions** (☎ 874-2549; www.rainwalkerexpeditions.com) rents mountain bikes for $25 per day.

PETERSBURG

☎ 907 / pop 3123

When the ferry heads north from Wrangell, it begins one of the Inside Passage's most scenic sections. After crossing over from Wrangell Island to Mitkof Island, the ferry

SOUTHEAST ALASKA

threads through the 46 turns of Wrangell Narrows, a 22-mile channel that is only 300ft wide and 19ft deep in places. At one point, the sides of the ship are so close to shore you can almost gather firewood for the evening.

At the other end of this breathtaking journey lies Norwegian-influenced Petersburg, one of Southeast Alaska's hidden gems. Peter Buschmann arrived in 1897 and found a fine harbor, abundant fish and a ready supply of ice from nearby LeConte Glacier. He built a cannery in the area, enticed his Norwegian friends to follow him here, and gave his first name to the resulting town. Today, a peek into the local phone book reveals the strong Norwegian heritage that unifies Petersburg.

The waterfront of this busy little fishing port is decorated with working boats and weathered boathouses, while tidy homes and businesses – many done up with distinctive Norwegian rosemaling, a flowery Norwegian art form – line the quiet streets. Petersburg boasts the largest home-based halibut fleet in Alaska and processes more than $20 million worth of seafood annually in its four canneries and two cold-storage plants. The canneries sit above the water on pilings, overlooking boat harbors bulging with vessels, barges, ferries and seaplanes. Even at night, you can see small boats trolling the nearby waters for somebody's dinner.

The town lies across Frederick Sound from a spectacular glaciated wall of alpine peaks – including the distinctive Devil's Thumb – that form a skyline of jagged snowcapped summits. Nearby LeConte Glacier discharges icebergs to the delight of visitors.

Without a dependency on timber, Petersburg enjoys a healthier economy than Wrangell or Ketchikan, so it doesn't need to pander to tourists. That makes Petersburg a joy for independent travelers, who will quickly discover the locals are friendly and their stories interesting.

Orientation

The ferry terminal is a mile north from downtown Petersburg; the airport is a mile east. Either is an enjoyable walk, unless you're hauling too many bags or it's the middle of the night. The main road out of town is the Mitkof Hwy, which heads 34 miles south to Sumner Strait with the

first half paved to Blind Slough. The best map for downtown and the road system is Petersburg Chamber of Commerce's *Petersburg Map*, handed out free all over town.

Information

Emergency (ambulance, fire, police ☎ 911)

First Bank (☎ 772-4277; 103 N Nordic Dr) Has a 24-hour ATM.

Glacier Laundry (☎ 772-4144; 313 Nordic Dr; ☺ 8am-9pm Sat-Thu, 24hr Fri) This place doesn't close on Friday so all the cannery workers can jump in the shower ($2) and be ready for the weekend.

Petersburg Medical Center (☎ 772-4299; 103 Fram St; ☺ 9am-5pm Mon-Fri, to 1pm Sat) Has a 24-hour emergency room, while on Saturday operates as a drop-in health clinic.

Petersburg Public Library (☎ 772-3349; 12 S Nordic Dr at Haugen; ☺ noon-9pm Mon-Thu, 10am-4pm Fri & Sat) Upstairs in the Municipal Building. There's free Internet, but its two terminals are only marginally faster than LeConte Glacier.

Sing Lee Alley Books (☎ 772-4440; 11 Sing Lee Alley; ☺ 9:30am-5:30pm) In a former boardinghouse built in 1929, this delightful bookstore has five rooms of books including an impressive selection of Alaska-based material.

Stick Dog (☎ 772-4800; www.stickdog.alaska.com; 110 Harbor Way; per hr $10; ☺ 8am-8pm) A tour operator with an Internet room.

Petersburg Visitor Center (☎ 772-4636, 772-3646; www.petersburg.org; Fram & 1st Sts; ☺ 9am-5pm Mon-Sat, noon-4pm Sun) A good first stop, with both tourist and USFS information.

Post office (1201 Haugen Dr; ☺ 9am-5:30pm Mon-Fri, 11am-2pm Sat) Located 0.5 miles east of downtown on the way to the airport.

USFS Petersburg Ranger District (☎ 772-3871; 12 N Nordic Dr; ☺ 8am-5pm Mon-Fri) For information about hiking trails, paddling, camping or reserving cabins.

Sights

Clausen Memorial Museum (☎ 772-3598; 203 Fram St; adult/child $3/free; ☺ 10am-5pm Mon-Sat) holds an interesting collection of artifacts and relics, mostly related to local fishing history. Exhibits include the largest king salmon ever caught (126lb) and a giant lens from the old Cape Decision lighthouse. Outside is *Fisk*, the intriguing fish sculpture that was commissioned in 1967 to honor the Alaska Centennial.

Heading south, Harbor Way passes Middle Boat Harbor and turns into **Sing Lee Alley**. This was the center of old Petersburg, and much of the street is built on pilings over

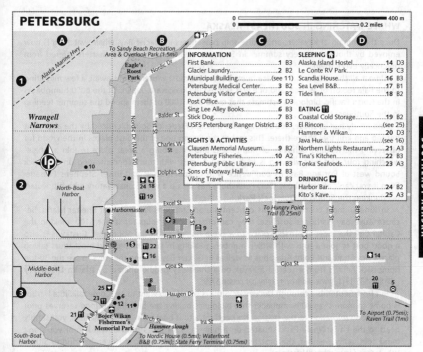

PETERSBURG

INFORMATION
First Bank..1 B3
Glacier Laundry................................2 B2
Municipal Building...................(see 11)
Petersburg Medical Center...........3 B2
Petersburg Visitor Center.............4 B2
Post Office..5 D3
Sing Lee Alley Books.......................6 B3
Stick Dog..7 B3
USFS Petersburg Ranger District..8 B3

SIGHTS & ACTIVITIES
Clausen Memorial Museum...........9 B2
Petersburg Fisheries.....................10 A2
Petersburg Public Library............11 B3
Sons of Norway Hall......................12 B3
Viking Travel..................................13 B3

SLEEPING
Alaska Island Hostel......................14 D3
Le Conte RV Park...........................15 C3
Scandia House................................16 B3
Sea Level B&B..................................17 B1
Tides Inn..18 B2

EATING
Coastal Cold Storage.....................19 B2
El Rincon..................................(see 25)
Hammer & Wikan............................20 D3
Java Hus....................................(see 16)
Northern Lights Restaurant..........21 A3
Tina's Kitchen................................22 B3
Tonka Seafoods..............................23 A3

DRINKING
Harbor Bar.......................................24 B2
Kito's Kave.......................................25 A3

SOUTHEAST ALASKA

Hammer Slough. On the alley, **Sons of Norway Hall** is the large white building with the colorful rosemaling built in 1912 and the center for Petersburg's Norwegian culture. Come on down and play bingo at 7pm on Saturday; 'O-32,' ja shore you betcha.

Also along Sing Lee Alley is **Bojer Wikan Fishermen's Memorial Park**. This deck of a park is built on pilings over Hammer Slough and is a monument honoring local fishers lost at sea. Also on display is the *Valhalla*, a replica of a Viking ship that was built in 1976 and purchased by Petersburg two years later.

The **North Boat Harbor** (Excel St at Harbor Way), is the best one for wandering the docks, talking to crews and possibly even scoring some fresh fish. Begin at the Harbormaster Office where a wooden deck provides a picturesque overview of the commercial fleet and has a series of interpretive panels that will teach you the difference between purse seine and a long-liner. Continue north along the waterfront to see **Petersburg Fisheries** (Dolphin St at Nordic Dr), the original outfit founded by Peter Buschmann in 1900; today it's a subsidiary of Seattle's Icicle Seafoods.

From downtown, Nordic Dr heads north on a scenic route that ends at **Sandy Beach Recreation Area**, 2 miles from downtown. This beautiful day-use area features Tlingit petroglyphs, visible at low tide.

Activities
HIKING
Within town is the 0.7-mile **Hungry Point Trail** that begins at the ball field at the end of Excel St and cuts across muskeg. The gravel path keeps your feet dry, but surrounding you are stunted trees so short you have a clear view of Petersburg's mountainous skyline. The trail ends at Sandy Beach Rd and by heading right a quarter-mile you reach **Outlook Park**, a whale observatory with free binoculars to search Frederick Sound for humpbacks, orcas and sea lions.

The 4-mile **Raven Trail** begins at the water tower on the airport's southeast side (accessible from Haugen Dr). It crosses muskeg areas on a boardwalk, then climbs to beautiful open alpine areas at 2000ft. Some sections are steep and require a little scrambling. The trail eventually leads to the

WHALE WATCHING IN SOUTHEAST ALASKA

Once the domain of kayakers and cruise-ship passengers in Glacier Bay, whale watching is now enjoyed by thousands every summer in Southeast Alaska, with wildlife charters offered from practically every town.

Almost all the whales sighted are humpbacks with most wintering in Hawaii, a few migrating to the Baja region of Mexico, and one was sighted in Ogasawara, Japan. Of the 6000 humpbacks in the North Pacific, biologists estimate that more than 1000 of them spend the summer feeding in the Southeast.

And nearly half of those, 500 strong, pass through Frederick Sound, enticed by the abundant herring and krill that thrive there. This makes the Sound one of the best places in the world for observing the feeding behavior of humpbacks and Petersburg a great place to join a whale-watching tour. The best viewing is in July and August with tours concentrating on Frederick Sound west of Portage Bay, its confluence with Chatham Strait and lower Stephens Passage. Even if you can't afford a boat tour, Petersburg has set up a whale observatory with binoculars overlooking the Sound at **Overlook Park**.

In Juneau, most charter captains concentrate on Stephens Passage near Shelter Island. Because Auke Bay Harbor is so close, they can offer half-day tours for under $100, making the Capital City the most affordable place to a see a humpback in the Southeast. Gustavus is also a good port to join a tour with whale numbers peaking in late summer and most tours taking place in Icy Strait and Point Adolphus as well as in Glacier Bay. Among the ways to see the 30-ton humpback here is from a seat of a kayak on a three-day paddle offered by **Alaska Discovery** (☎ 800-586-1911; www.akdiscovery.com; per person $799).

But from September through December, Sitka is where you want to be. Come fall Sitka Harbor is home to more than 80 humpbacks that biologists believe are building up food reserves prior to their long migration to the tropics. No need for a tour boat then. To watch them, you simply head to the city's Whale Park, situated on a high bluff six miles from downtown. If you don't mind cold, rainy weather, the best time to arrive is the first week of November during Sitka's **Whalefest** (www.sitkawhalefest.org).

Even travelers counting their coins can enjoy a little whale watching by riding the MV *LeConte* when it makes its run between Sitka and Juneau (one way $39). Whales are often spotted on board along this route, particularly at the mouth of Port Frederick on Icy Strait where the ferry heads in for Hoonah.

USFS **Raven's Roost Cabin** (per night $35), which requires reservations (see p100). The cabin is above the tree line, providing easy access to good alpine hiking and spectacular views of Petersburg, Frederick Sound and Wrangell Narrows.

On Kupreanof Island, the 3½-mile **Petersburg Mountain Trail** climbs to the top of Petersburg Mountain (2750ft), which offers views of Petersburg, the Coast Mountains, glaciers and Wrangell Narrows. Plan on five hours for the round-trip. To get across the channel, go to the skiff float at the North Boat Harbor and hitch a ride with somebody who lives on Kupreanof Island. On the Kupreanof side, head right on the overgrown road toward Sasby Island. You can also call **Tongass Kayak Adventures** (☎ 772-4600; www.tongasskayak.com), which runs hikers across the channel for $25 per person.

Petersburg Lake Trail is a 10½-mile trail in the Petersburg Creek–Duncan Salt Chuck Wilderness on Kupreanof Island leading to the USFS **Petersburg Lake Cabin** (NRRS; ☎ 877-444-6777, 515-885-3639; www.reserveusa.com; cabin $35). See p76 for details.

At Mile 14.5 of the Mitkof Hwy is the mile-long **Blind River Rapids Boardwalk** that winds through muskeg to the rapids, a scenic area and busy in June for king salmon fishing.

Along Three Lakes Rd, a USFS road heading east off Mitkof Hwy at Mile 13.6 and returning at Mile 23.8, are **Three Lakes Loop Trails**, a series of four short trails that total 4.5 miles. At Mile 14.2 is a 3-mile loop with boardwalks leading to Sand, Crane and Hill Lakes, all known for good trout fishing. Sand Lake has a free-use shelter. From the Sand Lake Trail, a 1½-mile trail leads to Ideal Cove on Frederick Sound.

PADDLING

Petersburg offers interesting possibilities for kayakers, LeConte Glacier and Tebenkof Bay Wilderness among them, but many of the trips require a week or more. Kayak rentals are available from **Tongass Kayak Adventures** (☎ 772-4600; www.tongasskayak.com; s/d $55/65, weeklong discounts available), which also offers kayak transfers and guided tours, including a four-hour paddle up Petersburg Creek ($70). Its best outing, however, begins with boat transport to LeConte Glacier for a day spent whale watching and paddling among the icebergs ($200).

LeConte Glacier

The most spectacular paddle in the region is to LeConte Glacier, 25 miles east of Petersburg. It's North America's southernmost tidewater glacier. From town, it takes three to four days to reach the frozen monument, including crossing Frederick Sound north of Coney Island. The crossing should be done at slack tide, as winds and tides can cause choppy conditions. If the tides are judged right, and the ice is not too thick, it's possible to paddle far enough into LeConte Bay to camp within view of the glacier.

Thomas Bay

Almost as impressive as LeConte Glacier is Thomas Bay, 20 miles from Petersburg and north of LeConte Bay on Frederick Sound's east side. The bay has a pair of glaciers, including Baird Glacier, where many paddlers go on day hikes. The mountain scenery around the bay is spectacular, and the area has three USFS cabins: **Swan Lake Cabin** (per night $35), **Spurt Cove Cabin** (per night $25) and **Cascade Creek Cabin** (per night $35). All need reservations. Paddlers should allow four to seven days for the round-trip out of Petersburg.

Kake to Petersburg

Kayakers can take the ferry to the Alaska Native village of Kake and paddle back to Petersburg. This 90-mile route follows Kupreanof Island's west side through Keku Strait, Sumner Strait and up the Wrangell Narrows to Petersburg. The highlight of the trip is Rocky Pass, a remote and narrow winding waterway in Keku Strait that has almost no boat traffic other than the occasional kayaker. Caution has to be used in Sumner Strait, which lies only 40 miles away from open ocean and has

its share of strong winds and waves. Plan on seven to 10 days for the trip.

WHALE WATCHING

In recent years, whale watching has become a popular trip out of Petersburg. From mid-May to mid-September humpback whales migrate through and feed in Frederick Sound 45 miles northwest of Petersburg (see the boxed text, opposite) with the peak feeding period in July and August. Other wildlife that can be spotted includes Steller's sea lions, orcas and seals.

Most charter-boat operators in town offer a full-day, eight-hour whale-watching tour that costs $200 per person. Among them are **Kaleidoscope Cruises** (☎ 772-3736, 800-868-4373; www.petersburglodgingandtours.com), run by Barry Bracken, a marine biologist who focuses on eco-education, and **Whale Song Cruises** (☎ 772-9393, 772-3724; captainron389@yahoo.com which is equipped with a hydrophone so you can listen to the whales as well as see them.

Tours

For a large selection of area tours, head to **Viking Travel** (☎ 772-3818, 800-327-2571; 101 N Nordic Dr), which acts as a clearinghouse for just about every tour in town. Possibilities include an easy four-hour kayak trip around the harbor ($70), a four-hour boat tour to LeConte Glacier ($110), an eight-hour whale-watching tour ($175) and a helicopter flightseeing tour with a glacier walk ($225).

To see the rest of Mitkof Island and enjoy a little freshwater fishing and possibly even catch a 20lb salmon, contact **Stick Dog Tours** (cell ☎ 512-554-5677; www.stickdogalaska.com). On its four-hour fishing adventure ($150 per person) you travel by van to the guide's favorite streams and fishing holes off the road. All equipment is provided.

Most of the charter operators who do whale watching also have sightseeing trips to view LeConte Glacier and that includes Kaleidoscope Cruises (see above), whose five-hour tour is $145 per person. **Pacific Wing Air Charters** (☎ 772-4258; www.pacificwing.com) offers a 45-minute flightseeing trip to the glacier for $240 for two people.

Also available, either through Viking or directly, is a combination rain forest hike and LeConte Glacier cruise with **Tongass Kayak Adventures** (☎ 772-4600; www.tongasskayak.com; per person $160). The full-day outing begins with a hike along Three Lakes Loop Rd and then another to Ideal Cove where a charter boat picks you up for an afternoon at the glacier.

Festivals & Events

The community's best event, famous around the Southeast, is the **Little Norway Festival**, held the third full weekend in May. The festival celebrates Norwegian Independence Day (May 17). The locals dress in old costumes, there's a foot race in the morning, Nordic Dr is filled with a string of booths, games and beer tents in the afternoon, and several dances are staged in the evenings. Best of all are the fish and shrimp feeds, all-you-can-manage-to-eat affairs that are held on various nights.

Sleeping

The city adds 11% sales and bed tax on accommodations.

BUDGET

Alaska Island Hostel (☎ 907-772-3632; 877-772-3632; www.alaskaislandhostel.com; 805 Gjoa St; dm $22; ☺ May-Sep; ☒ ▣) This is Petersburg's excellent budget-lodging alternative. The nine-bunk hostel, a short walk from downtown, is comfortable, casual and fun. Amenities include free high-speed Internet access, coffee in the morning and use of laundry facilities, kitchen and the BBQ outside. It's best to reserve your space in advance.

Le Conte RV Park (☎ 772-3022, 772-4144; 4th St at Haugen Dr; campsites $7, RV sites $10-15) Right in town, but it isn't the most attractive spot and the tent area is extremely small. Still, the price is right, the location ideal and the amenities include laundry and shower facilities.

Ohmer Creek Campground (☎ 772-3871 for information; Mile 22 Mitkof Hwy; sites $6) The USFS campground is 21 miles southeast of town, but it's cheap. It has 15 sites (for tents or RVs), an interpretive trail, fishing in the creek and a scenic setting. If you need transport, Stick Dog Tours (see p121) runs a van out to the campground ($10 per person).

MIDRANGE

Scandia House (☎ 772-4281, 800-722-5006; www.scandiahousehotel.com; 110 Nordic Dr; s $90-110, d $100-110, ste $185; ▣) The brightest and shiniest place in town, this 33-room motel has one suite and rooms with kitchenettes. Rates include courtesy shuttle service from the

airport/ferry and muffins and coffee in the morning, though it's hard to pass up the espresso in the adjoining Java Hus.

Sea Level B&B (☎ 772-3240; 913 N Nordic Drive; r $70-110; ☒) This elegant B&B is built on pilings over the Wrangell Narrows, making it look more like a boathouse than a home. Two guestrooms have private bath and large picture windows filled with the view of eagles, sea lions and boat traffic cruising past Mt Petersburg. On the outside deck there are chairs and rod holders so you can catch your dinner when the tides are in. Highly recommended.

Waterfront B&B (☎ 772-9300; 866-772-9301; www.waterfrontbedandbreakfast.com; 1004 S Nordic Dr; r $95-105; ☒ ▣) The closest place to the ferry terminal – it's practically right next door. It has a hot tub overlooking the harbor where you can soak while watching the ferry depart. Five bright and comfortable rooms have private bath and share a living room that overlooks the Petersburg Shipwrights. For many guests, watching a boat being repaired on dry dock is far more interesting than whatever is on TV.

Nordic House (☎ 772-3620; www.nordichouse.net; 806 S Nordic Dr; s/d/ste $77/99/120; ☒ ▣) Also near the ferry terminal, but this place does not have quite the high standards of the Waterfront B&B. Still, the rooms are large and clean and you have the use of a kitchen and a common area that overlooks the boat harbor. There are five rooms along with an on-site dentist in case you need a root canal. Rental bikes ($10) are available.

Tides Inn (☎ 772-4288, 800-665-8433; www.tidesinnalaska.com; 307 1st St; s/d $75/95; ▣) The largest motel in town with 46 rooms, some with kitchenettes. Rates include a light (very light) continental breakfast.

Eating

Tina's Kitchen (☎ 772-2090; Nordic Dr next to Scandia House; sandwiches $6-7, dinner $7-8; ☺ 10am-7pm Mon-Sat, 11am-7pm Sun) From this small shack comes some good food and great prices. Tina's Korean beef sticks are wonderful: marinated, grilled slices of steak served with steamed rice and kimchi. Also burritos, hamburgers and outdoor tables.

Northern Lights Restaurant (☎ 772-2900; 203 Sing Lee Alley; breakfast $4-10; sandwiches $7-12, dinner $15-30; ☺ 6am-10pm; ☒) Near Sons of Norway Hall, this reliable standby offers steak, chicken, seafood and pasta, which can be enjoyed to a view of the busy boat harbor. The seafood platter has halibut, crab cakes and a half-pound of shrimp, all of it locally caught, none of it deep-fried.

Coastal Cold Storage (☎ 772-4177; 306 N Nordic Dr; breakfast $3-6, lunch $6-9; ☯ 6am-5:30pm Mon-Sat, 7-2pm Sun) You're in Petersburg, you have to indulge in what they catch. At the very least, stop at this processor/seafood store/carryout restaurant for a shrimp burger, a plate of crab claws and coleslaw or the local specialty; halibut beer bits. It's the most affordable seafood in town, plus there are usually a couple of king crabs in a tank inside. Man, they're big!

Java Hus (☎ 772-2626; Nordic Dr next to Scandia House; ☯ 6am-5pm Mon-Sat, 7am-4pm Sun; ☒) It's where Petersburg gets buzzed first thing in the morning.

El Rincon (☎ 772-2255; Sing Lee Alley in Kino's Kave; dinner $9-11; ☯ 11am-7:45pm Mon-Thu, to 10pm Fri & Sat) If you don't mind eating in a bar, this is Petersburg's best Mexican.

Tonka Seafoods (☎ 772-3662; 22 Sing Lee Alley; ☯ 8am-5pm Mon-Sat) A boutique processor that sells fresh salmon (9lb for $6), delightful smoked fish (24lb for $12) and ready-to-eat Petersburg shrimp (per pound $5.50). If you're really intrigued about seafood processing there's also an hour-long tour of its small cannery operation ($5 per person at 1:30pm Monday to Saturday) that ends with a seafood sampling.

Hammer & Wikan (1300 Howkan; ☯ 7am-8pm Mon-Sat, 8am-7pm Sun) Off Haugen Dr on the way to the airport, this is Petersburg's main supermarket.

Drinking

Harbor Bar (310 Nordic Dr) The classic place of fishers and cannery workers, with pool tables and an excellent beer selection.

Kito's Kave (Sing Lee Alley) This has regular live music and dancing and when the cruise ships are in, it can be a rowdy place that hops well after midnight.

Getting There & Around

There are daily northbound and southbound flights with **Alaska Airlines** (☎ 772-4255, 800-426-0333). The airport is on Haugen Dr, a mile east of the post office.

The Alaska Marine Highway **ferry terminal** (☎ 772-3855) is about a mile south of downtown. Travelers heading north to Juneau might consider taking the MV *Le Conte* if it suits their schedule. This ship sails from Petersburg to Juneau ($58, 27 hours, one weekly) but stops at Kake, Angoon and Hoonah and Tenakee Springs along the way.

In 2006, the new MV *Stikine* (☎ 866-308-4848; www.interislandferry.com) is slated to be in operation, connecting Coffman Cove on Prince of Wales Island with Wrangell and Petersburg.

Scandia House (☎ 772-4281, 800-722-5006; www.scandiahousehotel.com; 110 Nordic Dr) rents midsize cars for $52 a day and boats for $160. **Nordic House** (☎ 772-3620; www.nordichouse.net; 806 S Nordic Dr) rents bicycles for $10 a day.

NORTHERN PANHANDLE

SITKA
☎ 907 / pop 8805

Fronting the Pacific Ocean on Baranof Island's west shore, Sitka is a gem in a beautiful setting. Looming on the western horizon, across Sitka Sound, is the impressive Mt Edgecumbe, an extinct volcano with a graceful cone similar to Japan's Mt Fuji. Closer in, a myriad of small, forested islands out in the Sound turns into beautiful ragged silhouettes at sunset, competing for attention with the snowcapped mountains and sharp granite peaks flanking Sitka on the east. And in town, picturesque remnants of the Sitka's Russian heritage lurk around every corner.

Sitka is the heart of the Russian influence in Southeast Alaska. The Russians may have landed here as early as 1741 and stayed for more than a century until the Americans finally arrived in 1867 after purchasing Alaska from them. Today Sitka's Russian history, the main attraction for tourists, is as interesting and as well preserved as the Klondike Gold Rush era is in Skagway.

Orientation

The heart of Sitka's downtown is St Michael's Cathedral, the city's beloved Russian Orthodox church, with Lincoln St serving as Main St. From here you're within easy walking distance of almost all of Sitka's attractions. To head out the road, follow either Halibut Point Rd north to the ferry terminal and Starrigavan Campground or Sawmill Creek Rd southeast. Harbor Dr will lead you across O'Connell Bridge and to the airport.

BOOKSTORES

Old Harbor Books (☎ 747-8808; 201 Lincoln St; ⊙ 9am-6pm Mon-Fri, 10am-5pm Sat, to 3pm Sun) A fine bookstore with a large Alaska section.

EMERGENCY & MEDICAL SERVICES

Ambulance, Fire, Police (☎ 911)

Sitka Community Hospital (☎ 747-3241; 209 Moller Dr) By the intersection of Halibut Point Rd and Brady St.

LAUNDRY

Sitka Laundry Center (☎ 747-7284; 906 Halibut Point Rd) For clean clothes or a hot shower near the hostel.

LIBRARY & INTERNET ACCESS

Kettleson Memorial Library (☎ 747-8708; 320 Harbor Dr; ⊙ 10am-9pm Mon-Thu, to 6pm Fri, 1-5pm Sat & Sun) Next door to the Centennial Building is the city's impressive library with free Internet access.

Seaport Cyber (☎ 747-9849; 407 Lincoln St; per hr $5; ⊙ 9am-5pm) Rows of computers for high-speed Internet access upstairs in the MacDonald Bayview Trading Company.

MONEY

First National Bank of Anchorage (☎ 747-3272; 318 Lincoln St) Downtown with a 24-hour ATM.

POST

Post office (1207 Sawmill Creek Rd) Main center is a mile east of town.

Pioneer substation (336 Lincoln St; ⊙ 8:30am-5:30pm Mon-Sat) Conveniently located downtown.

TOURIST INFORMATION

Sitka Convention & Visitors Bureau (☎ 747-5940; www.sitka.org; 303 Lincoln St, Suite 4; ⊙ 8am-5pm Mon-Fri) Across the street from the cathedral. The bureau also staffs a visitor-information desk in the Centennial Building next to Crescent Harbor when the cruise ships are in.

USFS Sitka Ranger District Office (☎ 747-6671, recorded information ☎ 747-6685; 204 Siginaka Way at Katlian St; ⊙ 8am-4:30pm Mon-Fri) Has information about local trails, camping and USFS cabins.

Sights

ISABEL MILLER MUSEUM

Within the Centennial Building is this **museum** (☎ 747-6455; 330 Harbor Dr; admission by donation; ⊙ 8am-5pm Mon-Sat), which is one room with a good portion of it a gift shop. The rest is crammed with a collection of relics, a model of the town as it appeared in 1867 and displays on Russian Alaska. Outside between the museum and the library is an

impressive handcarved Tlingit canoe, made from a single log.

ST MICHAEL'S CATHEDRAL

Two blocks west of the Centennial Building is the **cathedral** (☎ 747-8120; Lincoln St; donation $2; ⊙ 9am-4pm Mon-Fri). Built between 1844 and 1848, the church stood for over 100 years as Alaska's finest Russian Orthodox cathedral. When fire destroyed it in 1966 along with much of downtown Sitka, the church was the oldest religious structure from the Russian era in Alaska. Luckily the priceless treasures and icons inside were saved by Sitka's residents, who immediately built a replica of their beloved church.

CASTLE HILL & TOTEM SQUARE

Continue west on Lincoln St for the walkway to Castle Hill. Kiksadi clan houses once covered the hilltop site, but in 1836 the Russians built 'Baranov's Castle' atop the hill to house the governor of Russian America. It was here, on October 18, 1867, that the official transfer of Alaska from Russia to the USA took place. The castle burned down in 1894.

More Russian cannons and a totem pole can be seen in **Totem Square**, near the end of Lincoln St. Across Katlian St from the square is the prominent, yellow **Alaska Pioneers Home**. Built in 1934 on the old Russian Parade Ground, the home is for elderly Alaskans. The 13ft-tall bronze prospector statue in front of the state home is modeled on longtime Alaska resident William 'Skagway Bill' Fonda.

BLOCKHOUSE & PRINCESS MAKSOUTOFF'S GRAVE

Still more of Sitka's Russian background guards the hill north of the Alaska Pioneers Home. The **blockhouse** (cnr Kogwanton & Marine Sts) is a replica of what the Russians used to protect their stockade from the Indian village.

Across Marine St, at the top of Princess St, is **Princess Maksoutoff's Grave**, marking the spot where the wife of Alaska's last Russian governor is buried. But for a strategically placed chain-link fence, the grave would be in the Russian Cemetery. But a bright and shiny sign proclaims this tiny three-grave site as the **Lutheran Cemetery**. Cynics might postulate that the princess probably lost her

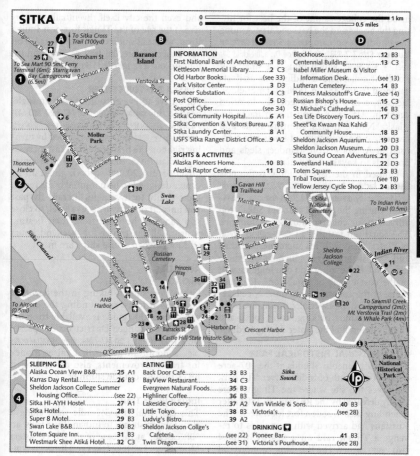

SITKA

SOUTHEAST ALASKA

status as a bona fide Lutheran when she married the Russian Orthodox governor, but now that she's a bona fide tourist attraction, the Lutherans want her back.

More old headstones and Russian Orthodox crosses can be found in the overgrown and quintessentially creepy **Russian Cemetery** (located at the north end of Observatory St, or just squeak through the gap in the chain-link fence behind the princess' grave), where the drippy verdure seems poised to swallow up the decaying graves, like something out of a Stephen King novel.

RUSSIAN BISHOP'S HOUSE

East of downtown along Lincoln St, the **Russian Bishop's House** (☎ 747-6281; Lincoln St at Monastery St; adult/child $4/free; 🕙 9am-5pm) is the oldest intact Russian building in Sitka. Built in 1843 out of Sitka spruce, the two-story log house is one of the few surviving examples of Russian colonial architecture in North America. The National Park Service (NPS) has renovated the building to its condition in 1853, when it served as a school, Bishop's residence and chapel. Tours are on the hour and half-hour until 4:30pm.

SHELDON JACKSON COLLEGE

Farther east along Lincoln St is the beautiful 17-acre campus of Sheldon Jackson College. James Michener stayed and worked here for much of the three summers he spent in Alaska and in 2003 *Outside Magazine* listed the college as one of the best for hitting the books and the backcountry. Among the buildings on campus is **Sheldon Jackson Museum** (☎ 747-8981; 104 College Dr; adult/child $4/free; ☼ 9am-5pm), which houses a small but excellent collection of indigenous artifacts gathered from 1888 to 1898 by Dr Sheldon Jackson, a minister and federal education agent in Alaska. Among the artifacts are Alaska Native masks, hunting tools and baskets, and a collection of boats and sleds used in Alaska – from reindeer sleds and dogsleds to kayaks and umiaks.

Housed in the Sage Building is the new **Sheldon Jackson Aquarium** (☎ 747-5220; 801 Lincoln St; admission by donation; ☼ 8:30am-4pm), a classroom during the school year but Sitka's top attraction for children during the summer. The aquarium features an 800-gallon 'Wall of Water' filled with sea anemones, rockfish and starfish and three touch tanks where kids can feel the spiny skin of a huge starfish or the coarse shell of an abalone. It is also home of the country's only on-site, college-run hatchery, an especially impressive sight when thousands of king, coho, pink and chum salmon boil the water during feeding.

SITKA NATIONAL HISTORICAL PARK

To the east Lincoln St ends at the 107-acre park at the mouth of Indian River. The park preserves the site where the Tlingits were finally defeated by the Russians in 1804 after defending their wooden fort for a week. The Russians had arrived with four ships to revenge a Tlingit raid on a nearby outpost two years earlier. The Russians' cannons did little damage to the walls of the Tlingit fort and, when the Russian soldiers stormed the structure with the help of Aleuts, they were repulsed in a bloody battle. It was only when the Tlingits ran out of gunpowder and flint, and slipped away at night, that the Russians were able to enter the deserted fort.

Begin at the park's **visitors center** (☎ 747-0110; adult/child $4/free; ☼ 8am-5pm), where Russian and indigenous artifacts are displayed and carvers demonstrate traditional arts. Outside, a mile-long trail leads you past 18 totems that were first displayed at the 1904 Louisiana Exposition in St Louis and then moved to the newly created park. It is these intriguing totems, standing in a beautiful forest setting by the sea and often enveloped in mist, that have become synonymous with the national park

and even the city itself. Eventually you arrive at the site of the Tlingit fort near Indian River, where its outline can still be seen. You can either explore the trail as a self-guided tour or join a ranger-led 'Battle Walk.'

ALASKA RAPTOR CENTER

For an eye-to-eye encounter with an eagle, head to this **raptor center** (☎ 747-8662, 800-643-9425; www.alaskaraptor.org; 1101 Sawmill Creek Rd; adult/child $12/6; ☼ 8am-4pm Mon-Fri), reached by turning right on the first gravel road after crossing Indian River. In 2003 the 17-acre center unveiled its 20,000-sq-ft flight-training center designed to help injured birds regain their ability to fly. Eagles literary fly past you only 2ft or 3ft away at eye level, so close you can feel the wind from their beating wings. Call the center for weekend hours and tours when cruise ships are in.

Activities
HIKING

Sitka offers superb hiking in the beautiful but tangled forest surrounding the city. A complete hiking guide is available from the USFS Sitka Ranger District office (p124). **Sitka Trail Works** (☎ 747-7244; www.sitkatrailworks .org), a nonprofit group that raises money for trail improvements, also offers guided hikes throughout the summer.

Indian River Trail

This easy trail is a 5½-mile walk along a clear salmon stream to Indian River Falls, an 80ft cascade at the base of the Three Sisters Mountains. The hike takes you through typical Southeast rain forest, and offers the opportunity to view brown bears, deer and bald eagles. The trailhead, a short walk from the town center, is off Sawmill Creek Rd, just east of Sitka National Cemetery. Pass the driveway leading to the Public Safety Academy parking lot and turn up the gated dirt road. This leads back to the city water plant, where the trail begins left of the pump house. Plan on four to five hours round-trip to the falls.

Gavan Hill Trail

Also close to town is this trail, which ascends almost 2500ft over 3 miles to Gavan Hill peak. The trail offers excellent views of Sitka and the surrounding area. From the trail's end, the adventurous hiker can continue to the peaks of the Three Sisters Mountains.

Gavan Hill is also linked to Harbor Mountain Trail. Halfway across the alpine ridge is a free-use USFS shelter available on a first-come, first-served basis; it's 3½ miles from the Gavan Hill trailhead, a hike of three to four hours.

From Lincoln St, head north up Baranof St for six blocks. The trailhead and a small parking area is reached just before the cemetery gate at the end of Baranof St. Camping is good in the trail's alpine regions, but bring water as drinking water is unavailable above the tree line.

Sitka Cross Trail

Rather than leading up out of town, this easy, well-used 2.2-mile trail runs roughly parallel to civilization, from one end of town to the other. The west end starts by the water tower at the intersection of Charteris St and Georgeson Loop, but you can pick it up behind the baseball field at the end of Kimsham St, beside the hostel. The trail leads east from there, crossing Gavan Hill Trail and ending at Indian River Trail. Along the way you'll pass peat bogs and old-growth forests.

Harbor Mountain Trail

This trail is reached from Harbor Mountain Rd, one of the few roads in the Southeast providing access to a subalpine area. Head 4 miles northwest from Sitka on Halibut Point Rd to the junction with Harbor Mountain Rd. A parking area and picnic shelter are 4½ miles up the rough dirt road.

Another half-mile further is the parking lot at road's end, where an unmarked trail begins on the lot's east side. The trail ascends 1½ miles to alpine meadows, knobs and ridges with spectacular views. From here a trail follows the tundra ridge to the free-use shelter on the saddle between Harbor Mountain and Gavan Hill, where you can pick up Gavan Hill Trail. Plan on spending two to four hours if you are just scrambling through the alpine area above Harbor Mountain Rd.

Mosquito Cove Trail

At the northwest end of Halibut Point Rd, 0.7 miles past the ferry terminal, Starrigavan Recreation Area offers a number of short but scenic trails. One of them, Mosquito Cove Trail, is an easy and scenic 1¼-mile loop over gravel and boardwalk.

Mt Verstovia Trail

This 2½-mile trail is a challenging climb of 2550ft to the 'shoulder,' a compact summit that is the final destination for most hikers, although it is possible to continue climbing to the peak of Mt Verstovia (3349ft). The panorama from the shoulder on clear days is spectacular, undoubtedly the area's best.

The trailhead is 2 miles east of Sitka, along Sawmill Creek Rd; look for a large sign for the trailhead near a lone restaurant (which changes names so frequently that it shall here remain nameless). The Russian charcoal pits (signposted) are reached within a quarter-mile, and shortly after that the trail begins a series of switchbacks. It's a four-hour round-trip to the shoulder, from where a ridgeline leads north to the peak (another hour each way).

Beaver Lake Hike

This short trail starts from Sawmill Creek Campground, which is reached from Sawmill Creek Rd, 5½ miles east of Sitka. Across from the former pulp mill on Sawmill Creek Rd, turn left onto Blue Lake Rd for the campground; the trailhead is on the campground's south side.

Although initially steep, the 0.8-mile trail levels out and ends up as a scenic walk through open forest, muskeg and marsh areas to Beaver Lake, which is surrounded by mountains. Plan on an hour round-trip.

Mt Edgecumbe Trail

The 6.7-mile trail begins at the USFS **Fred's Creek Cabin** (cabin $35), reservations required (see p100), and ascends to the crater of this extinct volcano. Views from the summit are spectacular on a clear day. About 3 miles up the trail is a free-use shelter (no reservations required).

Mt Edgecumbe (3201ft) is on Kruzof Island, 10 miles west of Sitka, and can only be reached by boat because large swells from the ocean prevent floatplanes from landing. Stop at the Sitka Convention & Visitors Bureau (p124) for a list of local operators who will drop off and pick up hikers (around $125 per party one way). Actual hiking time is five to six hours one-way, but by securing Fred's Creek Cabin, you can turn the adventure into a pleasant three-day trip, with two nights spent in shelters.

PADDLING

Sitka also serves as the departure point for numerous blue-water trips along the protected shorelines of Baranof and Chichagof Islands. You can rent kayaks in town at **Sitka Sound Ocean Adventures** (☎ 747-6375; www.ssocean adventures.com), which operates from a blue bus in the parking lot near the main harbor. Kayaks are available (per day single/double $50/60) with discounts for multiday rentals. Guided trips are also available, indicated by the company motto on the side of the bus, 'Tip Your Guide, Not Your Kayak!'

Katlian Bay

This 45-mile round-trip from Sitka Harbor to scenic Katlian Bay (on Kruzof Island's north end) and back is one of the area's most popular paddles. The route follows narrow straits and well-protected shorelines in marine traffic channels, making it an ideal trip for less experienced blue-water paddlers who will never be far from help.

A scenic sidetrip is to hike the sandy beach from Katlian Bay around Cape Georgiana to Sea Lion Cove on the Pacific Ocean. Catch the tides to paddle the Olga and Neva Straits on the way north and return along Sukot Inlet, staying night at the USFS **Brent's Beach Cabin** (cabin $35); reservations required (see p100). Plan on four to six days for the paddle.

Shelikof Bay

You can combine a 10-mile paddle to Kruzof Island with a 6-mile hike across the island from Mud Bay to Shelikof Bay along an old logging road and trail. Once on the Pacific Ocean side, you'll find a beautiful sandy beach for beachcombing and the USFS **Shelikof Cabin** (cabin $35); reservations required (see p100).

West Chichagof

Chichagof Island's western shoreline is one of Southeast Alaska's best blue-water destinations for experienced kayakers. Unfortunately, the trip often requires other transportation, because few paddlers have the experience necessary to paddle the open ocean around Khaz Peninsula (which forms a barrier between Kruzof Island's north end and Slocum Arm, the south end of the West Chichagof–Yakobi Wilderness). Either rent a folding kayak and then book a floatplane or hire a water-taxi service to take you there.

The arm is the southern end of a series of straits, coves and protected waterways that shield paddlers from the ocean's swells and extend over 30 miles north to Lisianski Strait. With all its hidden coves and inlets, the trip is a good two-week paddle. Travelers with even more time and a sense of adventure could continue another 25 miles through Lisianski Strait to the fishing village of Pelican, where the ferry stops twice a month in summer. Such an expedition would require at least two to three weeks.

WHALE WATCHING

Since the late 1990s, Sitka has replaced Glacier Bay (p152) as the center of whale watching in Southeast Alaska. Over a dozen companies in Sitka offer boat tours to view whales and other marine wildlife.

Sea Life Discovery Tours (☎ 966-2301, 877-966-2301; www.sealifediscoverytours.com) operates a glass-bottomed boat that gives visitors views of the area's underwater marine life from 10ft below the surface. The narrated two-hour tours (adult/child $79/59) leave from Crescent Harbor dock.

Sitka Wildlife Quest/Allen Marine Tours (☎ 747-8100, 888-747-8101; www.allenmarinetours.com) offers a two-hour cruise (adult/child $59/30) on Tuesday and Thursday at 6pm to view whales, sea otters, puffins and other wildlife and a three-hour tour (adult/child $79/40) on Saturday and Sunday at 8:30am. All tours depart from Crescent Harbor dock and are narrated by a naturalist.

Sitka's Secrets (☎ 747-5089; www.sitkasecret.com) runs its 27ft boat to St Lazaria Island National Wildlife Refuge on a four-hour cruise (per person $100) to view seabirds galore and any other marine wildlife that happens along the way – usually a lot. The operators are a married couple, both degreed biologists and former national wildlife refuge managers.

If you can't afford a wildlife cruise, try **Whale Park** (Sawmill Creek Rd), 4 miles south of town, which has a boardwalk and spotting scopes overlooking the ocean. Fall is the best time to sight cetaceans; as many as 80 whales – mostly humpbacks – have been known to gather in the waters off Sitka from mid-September to the end of the year.

WILDERNESS CABINS

A number of USFS cabins lie within 30 minutes flying time of Sitka. Among the most popular cabins are **Redoubt Lake Cabin**, at the northern end of Redoubt Lake, about 10 miles south of Sitka; **Baranof Lake Cabin**, which enjoys a scenic (though reportedly buggy) mountainous setting on the island's east side; barrier-free **Lake Eva Cabin**, also on Baranof Island's east shore, north of the Baranof Lake Cabin; and **White Sulphur Springs Cabin**, on the west shore of Chichagof Island, which is popular with locals because of the adjacent hot-springs bathhouse.

All cost $35 per night and should be reserved in advance through the National Recreation Reservation Service (see p100). For air-taxi service, try **Harris Aircraft Services** (☎ 966-3050; www.harrisaircraft.com).

Tours

Harbor Mountain Tours (☎ 747-8294) Offers a 90-minute van tour of town (adult/child $15/10).

Sitka Tours (☎ 747-8443) If you're only in Sitka for as long as the ferry stopover, don't despair: Sitka Tours runs a bus tour (two/three hours adult $12/16, child $6/8) just for you. The tour picks up and returns passengers to the ferry terminal, making brief visits to Sitka National Historical Park and St Michael's Cathedral. Time is allotted for the obligatory T-shirt-shopping experience.

Sitka Wildlife Tours (☎ 752-0006; http://sitkawildlife tours.com) offers 1½-hour (per person $40) van tours and hourlong floatplane tours (per person $140) emphasizing local wildlife watching.

Tribal Tours (☎ 747-7290, 888-270-8687; www .sitkatribe.org) A wide array of local tours, from simple walks around the harbor to VIP tour (per person $125) that includes hors d'oeuvres, beverages and preferential seating at local performances. In-between there is its 2½-hour bus tour (adult/child $44/34) that includes Sitka National Historical Park, Sheldon Jackson College and a Tlingit Native dance performance.

Festivals & Events

Sitka Summer Music Festival (☎ 747-6774; www .sitkamusicfestival.org) For three weeks in June, extending Sitka's reputation as the Southeast's cultural center is this bringing together professional musicians for chamber-music concerts and workshops. The evening concerts are truly a treat to the senses; classical music filling Centennial Hall where the glass backdrop of the stage gives way to views of the harbor, snow-covered mountains and eagles soaring in the air. The highly acclaimed event is so popular you should purchase tickets in advance of your trip.

Alaska Day Festival On the weekend nearest October 18, the city reenacts, in costumes (and even beard styles) of the 1860s, the transfer of the state from Russia to the USA.

WhaleFest! (☎ 747-7964; www.sitkawhalefest.org) The city stages this festival during the first weekend of November to celebrate the large fall gathering of humpbacks with whale-watching cruises, lectures, craft shows and more.

Sleeping

Sitka levies a 12% city and bed tax on all lodging.

BUDGET

Sitka HI-AYH Hostel (☎ 747-8661; 303 Kimsham St; dm $19; ☺ Jun-Aug) Located in the Methodist church and reached from Halibut Point Rd, northwest out of downtown, by turning right onto Peterson Ave then veering left onto Kimsham St. Facilities include cots, a kitchen, lounge and eating area. Buses from the ferry will drop you at the doorstep, and the hostel will open for late-night ferry arrivals (advance notification appreciated). Lockout is from 8am to 6pm.

Camping

Two USFS campgrounds are in the area, but neither is close to town.

Starrigavan Bay Campground (Mile 7.8 Halibut Point Rd; sites $12-30) Recently rebuilt, this 35-site campground has three loops for three types of campers: RVers, car-and-tent campers, and backpackers and cyclists' walk-in sites. You're 7 miles from town but the coastal scenery is beautiful and nearby is Old Sitka State Historic Site, which features trails and interpretive displays dedicated to the site of the original Russian settlement. Most of the new amenities – bird and salmon viewing decks, boardwalks and vault toilets – are wheelchair accessible.

Sawmill Creek Campground (Blue Lake Rd) In the opposite direction from town from Starrigavan Bay, via Sawmill Creek Rd and Blue Lake Rd, is this free 11-site campground that features mountain scenery, the Beaver Lake Trail and fishing opportunities in nearby lakes.

MIDRANGE

Sitka Hotel (☎ 747-3288; fax 747-8499; www.sitka hotel.com; 118 Lincoln St; s/d with bath $80/85, without bath $60/65; ▢) This venerable hotel dates from 1939, but its 60 rooms have been upgraded long since then. The rooms are small but well kept and all have cable TV and a few even have kitchenettes. The hotel also offers laundry and luggage storage to

SOUTHEAST ALASKA

guests. In Sitka it's hard to beat the price or the location of this hotel.

Karras Day Rental (☎ 747-3978; 230 Kogwanton St; s/d $55/80) There are four rooms with shared bath in a private home overlooking the colorful Katlian St–harbor area just a few blocks from downtown. The rooms have their own common areas and entrance.

Swan Lake B&B (☎ 747-5764; 206½ Lakeview Dr; r $85; ✗) A 10-minute walk from downtown, this B&B offers three rooms, two of them with their own entrance and a common area that overlooks Swan Lake and the mountains that surround Sitka. In the morning you can sip your coffee while watching the sunrise spread across the peaks.

Sheldon Jackson College (☎ 747-5252; www.sj-alaska.edu; 801 Lincoln St; s/d $80/100; ☯ mid-May–early Aug) Rents out its dorm rooms to travelers in summer. Big groups usually book most rooms, leaving few available for walk-ins. If you're interested, make reservations well in advance.

Super 8 Motel (☎ 747-8804, 800-800-8000; fax 747-6101; 404 Sawmill Creek Rd; s/d from $102/108) This is Super 8 Motel, Anywhere, USA: the rooms look the same here as they do in Dallas or Detroit. Along with 35 rooms there is an indoor hot tub, free continental breakfast and 24-hour Laundromat.

TOP END

Westmark Sitka Hotel (☎ 747-6241, 800-544-0970; www.westmarkhotels.com; 330 Seward St; r from $159; ▣) The business traveler's favorite. It has a central location, a restaurant with a view of the harbor and room service, and is the first stop of every tour company in town.

Shee Atika Totem Square Inn (☎ 747-3693; 866-300-1353; www.sheeatika.com; 201 Katlian St; r $119; ✗ ▣) Extensively renovated in 2005, the inn has 66 rooms, free continental breakfast and a full kitchen on the fourth floor. Its best feature, however, is still the views from the rooms, overlooking either the historic square or the ocean.

Alaska Ocean View B&B (☎ 747-8310, 888-811-6870; www.sitka-alaska-lodging.com; 1101 Edgecumbe Dr; r $109-209; ✗ ▣) A three-level cedar home within walking distance of downtown. It has three rooms, all with private bath, refrigerator, microwave, phone, cable TV and VCR. Outside is a hot tub where you can soak away those hiking sores while watching eagles fly overhead.

Eating

RESTAURANTS

Ludvig's Bistro (☎ 966-3663; 256 Katlian St; dinner $19-30; ☯ 2-10pm; ✗) Sitka's newest restaurant is also its best. Inside Ludvig's is as colorful as the commercial fishing district that surrounds it and European-quaint. There are only seven tables and a handful of stools at a brass-and-blue-tile bar. The women who run it describe their menu as 'rustic Mediterranean fare' and it is by far the most innovative cooking in Sitka. Their Katlian Special is whatever the local boats catch that day then pan-seared with a hint of smoke from Sitka alder. Reservations, possibly a day or two in advance, are a must for summer weekends.

Van Winkle & Sons (205 Harbor Dr; lunch $13-17, pizza $11-17, dinner $18-30; ☯ 11:30am-1:45pm Mon-Fri, 5pm-9:30pm Mon-Sat) Sitka's longtime proprietor of seafood serves up such specialties as Dungeness crab cakes, seafood soufflé and even a pizza covered with shrimp and scallops. Its 2nd-floor location and wall of windows allows you to dine to a view of Sitka's island-studded harbor.

Twin Dragon (201 Katlian St; lunch $6.50-8, dinner $11-13; ☯ 11:30am-3 & 5-9:30pm Mon-Sat, noon-9pm Sun; ✗) Located in the back of the Totem Square Inn, the Chinese dishes – Mandarin, Szechwan and Cantonese – are good; the view of the bustling boat harbor is outstanding.

BayView Restaurant (407 Lincoln St; breakfast $6-10, lunch $8-11, dinner mains $16-27; ☯ 5am-9pm Mon-Sat, to 3pm Sun; ✗) A casual place upstairs in the MacDonald Bayview Trading Company Building that serves large portions, keeps the coffee cup filled and has 14 different types of hamburgers on the menu, even one called Basic Burger.

CAFÉS

Back Door Café (104 Barracks St; light fare under $5; ☯ 6:30am-5pm Mon-Sat, 9am-2pm Sun; ✗) The town's best coffeehouse; accessed through either Old Harbor Books on Lincoln St or through the...you guessed it...which is off Barracks St. The cruise-ship hordes parading endlessly down Lincoln St can't immediately see it so they go elsewhere. As a result, the small place is full but not packed, and it's as local as it gets. The pleasant young staff members serve an eclectic clientele with a menu that includes great baked goods, bagel sandwiches and excellent high-octane espresso drinks.

Little Tokyo (315 Lincoln St; lunch $8-10; fish & tempura rolls $6-12; 🕙 11am-9pm Mon-Fri, from noon Sat & Sun; ✗) Even crewmembers from the commercial fleet, who know a thing or two about raw fish, say Sitka's only sushi bar is a good catch.

Highliner Coffee (327 Seward St, Seward Square Mall; meals under $5; 🕙 5:30am-5pm Mon-Sat, 8am-4pm Sun; ✗) This is a bustling coffee emporium that roasts its own coffee and serves bagels, croissants and homebaked goodies. Among the sofas and tables are computers for Internet access (per 20/60 minutes $3.18/10.60).

Victoria's (118 Lincoln St; breakfast $8-11, lunch $9-13, dinner $14-16; 🕙 4:30am-9pm; ✗) Have a fishing charter to catch at the break of dawn? Then this is where you'll want to come for breakfast, the reason the busy café next to the Sitka Hotel opens at 4:30am. Most likely you'll see your charter captain eating here as well. For lunch try the halibut wraps.

Sheldon Jackson College's cafeteria (Sweetland Hall; breakfast $5, lunch $7.50, Sunday brunch & dinner $10; 🕙 breakfast 6:30-8am, lunch 11:30am-1pm & dinner 5-6:30pm Mon-Sat, brunch 11:30am-1pm Sun; ✗) A budget find on campus. Since it's a cafeteria, you'll save money on tips, too.

GROCERIES

Sea Mart (1867 Halibut Point Rd) Sitka's largest supermarket is northwest of town and features a bakery, deli, ready-to-eat items and a dining area overlooking Mt Edgecumbe.

Lakeside Grocery (705 Halibut Point Rd) It's closer to town, near the hostel, and it has sandwiches, soups and a salad bar.

Evergreen Natural Foods (2A-1 Lincoln St) Near the municipal building, practically underneath the O'Connell Bridge, is this shop that sells a variety of vitamins, juices and other natural goodies.

Drinking

Pioneer Bar (212 Katlian St) Known locally as the 'P-Bar,' this is the most interesting place to have a beer in Sitka and one of Alaska's classic bars. The walls are covered with photos of fishing boats, their crews and big fish and a blackboard where occasionally a captain advertises for a crew. Don't ring the big brass ship's bell over the bar unless you're ready to buy a round.

Victoria's Pourhouse (118 Lincoln St) A friendly pub inside the Sitka Hotel with the largest TV screen in Sitka.

Entertainment

New Archangel Russian Dancers (☎ 747-5516; adult/child $7/5) Whenever a cruise ship is in port, this troupe of more than 30 dancers in Russian costumes takes the stage at Centennial Hall for a half-hour show. A schedule is posted at the hall.

Sheet'ka Kwaan Naa Kahidi Dancers (☎ 747-7290; www.sitkatribe.com; 200 Katlian St; adult/child $7/5) Not to be outdone, these dancers perform traditional Tlingit dances at the eponymous Tlingit Clan House, next to the Pioneers' Home.

Getting There & Away

AIR

Sitka is served by **Alaska Airlines** (☎ 966-2422, 800-426-0333; www.alaskaair.com) and its airport is on Japonski Island, 1.8 miles west of downtown. On a nice day it's a scenic 20-minute walk from the airport terminal over O'Connell Bridge to downtown Sitka. The white **Airport Shuttle** (☎ 747-8443) minibus meets all jet flights in summer and charges $6 one way to the city hotels (or $8 for a return ride to your choice of the airport or ferry).

Floatplane air-taxi service to small communities and USFS cabins is provided by **Harris Aircraft Services** (☎ 966-3050, within Alaska ☎ 877-966-3050; www.harrisaircraft.com).

BOAT

The Alaska Marine Highway **ferry terminal** (☎ 747-8737) is 6.5 miles northwest of town; ferries depart in both directions almost daily to Juneau ($39, nine hours), Angoon ($31, six hours), Petersburg ($39, 11 hours) and Tenakee Springs ($31, nine hours).

Ferry Transit Bus (☎ 747-8443; one way/round-trip $6/8), operated by Sitka Tours, meets all ferries year-round for the trip into town. You also catch the bus out to the ferry terminal from anywhere downtown – just call in advance.

Getting Around

BICYCLE

Yellow Jersey Cycle Shop (☎ 747-6317; 329 Harbor Dr; per 2hr/day $15/25), across the street from the library, rents quality mountain bikes.

BUS

Sitka doesn't yet have a public bus system, but in summer it runs a **transit shuttle** (☎ 747-7290), which operates only when cruise ships

The shuttle makes a loop past the city's major attractions, stopping every 30 minutes at Crescent Harbor shelter, Sheldon Jackson Museum, Sitka National Historical Park and Alaska Raptor Center. The fare is $7 per day for unlimited use, or $5 for a one-way trip.

CAR
At the airport, **Northstar Rent-A-Car** (☎ 966-2552, 800-722-6927) rents compacts for $50 per day with unlimited mileage (as if you needed that in Sitka).

TAXI
For a ride around Sitka, try 24-hour-on-the-go **Alaska Classic Taxi** (☎ 752-7020).

WATER-TAXI
The going rate for water-taxi service from **Esther G Sea Taxi** (☎ 747-6481, cell ☎ 738-6481) or **EZC Transfer Co** (☎ 747-5044) is $80 to $100 per hour.

SECONDARY PORTS
On the ferry runs between Sitka and Juneau, you can stop at a handful of secondary ports to escape the cruise ships and tourists found at the larger towns. Some stops are scenic, others are not; all are a cultural experience in rural Alaska.

Kake
☎ 907 / pop 710

Kake is an Indian beachfront community on the northwest coast of Kupreanof Island, the traditional home of the Kake tribe of the Tlingit Indians. Today the community maintains subsistence rights and also runs commercial fishing and fish processing to supplement its economy. Kake is known for having the tallest totem pole in Alaska (and some say the world), a 132ft carving that was first raised at Alaska's pavilion in the 1970 World's Fair in Osaka, Japan.

Within town, 1½ miles from the ferry terminal, are three general stores, a Laundromat, restaurant and **Waterfront Lodge** (☎ 785-3472; 222 Keku Rd; s/d $75/95).

The Alaska Marine Highway ferry MV *Le Conte* stops twice weekly at Kake on its run between Petersburg ($31, four hours) and Sitka ($33, 10 hours). **LAB Flying Service** (☎ 785-6435; www.labflying.com) has regularly scheduled flights. The one-way fare to Juneau is $138.

TEBENKOF BAY WILDERNESS
Kake is the departure point for blue-water kayak trips into Tebenkof Bay Wilderness, a remote bay system composed of hundreds of islands, small inner bays and coves. The return paddle is a scenic 10-day adventure that can offer sightings of bald eagles, black bears and various marine mammals. Paddlers should have ocean-touring experience and be prepared to handle a number of portages. Kayaks can be rented in either Juneau or Sitka and then carried on the ferry to Kake or contact **Island Excursions** (in Kake ☎ 785-3369; www.kayak-islandexcursions.com), which offers three- to seven-day guided kayak trips.

The most common route is to paddle south from Kake through Keku Strait into Port Camden, at the western end of which is a 1.3-mile portage trail to the Bay of Pillars. From the Bay of Pillars, you encounter the only stretch of open water, a 3-mile paddle around Point Ellis into Tebenkof Bay. The return east follows Alecks Creek from Tebenkof Bay into Alecks Lake, where a 2.3-mile portage trail leads to No Name Bay. From here paddlers can reach Keku Strait and paddle north to Kake via scenic Rocky Pass.

Tenakee Springs
☎ 907 / pop 105

Since its period in the late 1800s as a winter retreat for fishers and prospectors, Tenakee Springs has evolved into a rustic village known for its slow and relaxed pace of life. On the east side of Tenakee Inlet, the settlement is little more than a ferry dock, a row of houses on pilings and the hot springs – the town's main attraction – which bubble out of the ground at 108°F.

Tenakee's alternative lifestyle centers around the free public bathhouse at the end of the ferry dock. The building encloses the principal spring, which flows through the concrete bath at 7 gallons per minute. Bath hours, separate for men and women, are posted, and most locals take at least one good soak per day, if not two.

While you're in the area, always keep an eye out for marine mammals, such as humpback whales (commonly seen in Tenakee Inlet), killer whales and harbor porpoises. You may also see brown bears, as Chichagof Island is second only to Admiralty Island in the Southeast for the density of its bear population.

SLEEPING & EATING

Opposite the bathhouse, at the foot of the ferry dock, is **Snyder Mercantile Co** (☎ 736-2205; 9am-5pm Mon-Sat, 10am-2pm Sun). Founded by Ed Snyder, who arrived in a rowboat full of groceries in 1899, the store has been in business ever since. It sells limited supplies and groceries, and also rents a cabin ($85).

Other rental places in town include **Cabin 37** (☎ 789-9668 in Juneau; cabin $60) and **Tenakee Log Cabin Rental** (☎ 736-2262; per day/week $125/500), which sleeps six and is a stairway climb of 60 steps from the main street. Or you can pitch a tent at the rustic campground a mile east of town, at the mouth of the Indian River.

For food, there's **Rosie's Blue Moon Café** (10am-6pm) and the **Bakery & Giftshop** (☎ 736-2274; 8am-2pm Tue-Sat), both on Tenakee Ave.

GETTING THERE & AWAY

The ferry MV *Le Conte* stops at Tenakee Springs roughly once a week, connecting it to Hoonah and Juneau northbound and to Angoon and Sitka (and occasionally Kake and Petersburg) southbound. Study the ferry schedule carefully to make sure you don't have to stay in town longer than you want. The one-way fare from Tenakee Springs to Juneau or Sitka is $31.

Wings of Alaska (Juneau ☎ 789-0790, Tenakee Springs ☎ 736-2247; www.wingsofalaska.com) flies daily to/from Juneau (one way/round-trip $90/170). **Alaska Seaplane Service** (☎ 789-3331 in Juneau, ☎ 888-350-8277; www.akseaplanes.com) has scheduled service six days a week (each way $90).

Hoonah
☎ 907 / pop 841

Hoonah is the largest Tlingit village in Southeast Alaska. The Huna, a Tlingit tribe, have lived in the Icy Strait area for hundreds of years, and legend tells of them being forced out of Glacier Bay by an advancing glacier. A store was built on the site of Hoonah in 1883, and an established community has been here ever since.

The town lacks the charm and friendliness (as well as the public bathhouse) of Tenakee Springs, and even much coastal beauty due to intense logging of Port Frederick.

The **City of Hoonah** (☎ 945-3663; PO Box 360, Hoonah) can tell you more about the town, and the USFS **Hoonah Ranger District** (☎ 945-3631) has information about hiking and paddling in the area.

GETTING THERE & AWAY

Alaska Marine Highway's MV *Le Conte* docks in Hoonah three days a week from Sitka ($33, seven hours) and Juneau ($29, four hours). The **ferry terminal** (☎ 945-3292) is half a mile from town.

Pelican
☎ 907 / pop 118

If you time it right, you can catch the twice-a-month state ferry to Pelican, a lively little fishing town on Chichagof Island's northwest coast. The cruise through Icy Straits is scenic, with a good possibility of seeing humpback whales, and the two hours in port is more than enough time to walk the length of town, and even have a beer, in one of Southeast Alaska's last true boardwalk communities.

The town was established in 1938 by a fish packer and named after his boat. Fishing is Pelican's raison d'être. It has the closest harbor to Fairweather's salmon grounds; its population swells from June to mid-September, when commercial fishers and cold-storage workers come for the trolling season.

INFORMATION

The website of the **Pelican Visitors Association** (www.pelican.net) has lodging and charter fishing information. Pelican has a small library, several bars, a café, Laundromat/Internet café, general store, and a liquor store with adjoining steam baths and showers.

SIGHTS & ACTIVITIES

Pelican is a photographer's delight. Most of it is built on pilings over tidelands, and its main street, dubbed Salmon Way, is a mile-long wooden boardwalk. Only a very short gravel road runs beyond that.

The kayaking is excellent out of Pelican and at **Highliner Lodge** (☎ 735-2476) you can rent singles/doubles for $50/75 a day. For kayak drop-offs, fishing, or whale watching, contact **Lisianaki Inlet Charters** (☎ 735-2282).

SLEEPING & EATING

Highliner Lodge (☎ 735-2476, 877-386-0397; www.highlinerlodge.com; s $65-75, d $80-100;) This is surprisingly nice, in view of being in Pelican; it has rooms, condos, a café and a sauna.

Rose's Bar & Grill (☎ 735-2288) A classic Alaskan fisherman's bar where you can mingle with trollers, long-liners and Pelican Seafood workers.

GETTING THERE & AWAY

Alaska Marine Highway's MV *Le Conte* runs from Juneau to Pelican and back twice a month, providing a unique day trip for $88 round-trip.

If you miss the ferry, call **Alaska Seaplane Service** (Juneau ☎ 735-2244, Pelican ☎ 789-3331, toll-free ☎ 888-350-8277; www.akseaplanes.com), which offers scheduled flights to/from Juneau Monday to Saturday (one way $125).

JUNEAU

☎ 907 / pop 30,966

So where's Juneau? is something of a rallying cry among disenchanted visitors departing the state ferry expecting a domed capitol and instead are told they are 14 miles from the city center. When they learn there's no bus or shuttle service into town, not even high-priced taxis waiting for them, they mumble something else.

Welcome to Juneau, Alaska's strange little capital. In the winter it's a beehive of legislators, their loyal aides and lobbyists locked in political struggles. They no more leave, than in May the cruise ships arrive with swarms of passengers. It's the most geographically secluded state capital in the country, the only one that cannot be reached by car, only boat or plane.

But Juneau is also the most beautiful city in Alaska, described by many of its residents as a 'little San Francisco' while others proudly claim it as the nation's most scenic capital. On that point it's hard to argue with them.

The city center, which hugs the side of Mt Juneau and Mt Roberts, has many narrow streets running past a mix of new structures, old storefronts and slanted houses, all held together by a network of staircases. The waterfront is bustling with cruise ships, fishing boats and floatplanes buzzing in and out. High above the city is the Juneau Ice Field, covering the Coastal Range and sending glaciers down between the mountains like chocolate syrup on a sundae.

The state's first major gold strike and the first town to be founded after Alaska's purchase from the Russians, Juneau became the territorial capital in 1906. Juneau's darkest hour occurred in the late 1970s after Alaskans voted to move the state capital again. The so-called 'capital move' issue became a political tug-of-war between Anchorage and the Southeast, until voters, faced with a billion-

dollar price tag of a new capital, defeated the funding in 1982. The statewide vote gave Juneau new life, and the town burst at its seams, booming in typical Alaskan fashion.

Considering it's still a state capital, Juneau isn't the hive of cultural activity you might expect. Entertainment venues are minimal and good restaurants are rare. But many find it a refreshing haven of liberalism in a state that is steadily marching to the right. Spend a morning eavesdropping in cafés and coffeehouses, and you'll hear the environmental and social conscience of Alaska.

For visitors who come to Alaska for outdoor adventure, what really distinguishes the state capital from other Alaskan towns – and certainly other state capitals – is the superb hiking. Dozens of great trails surround the city; some begin downtown, just blocks from the capitol. Juneau also serves as the departure point for several wilderness attractions, including Glacier Bay National Park, Tracy Arm-Fords Terror Wilderness and Admiralty Island National Monument.

So where's Juneau? Ask any hiker and they'll tell you at the end of the trail.

Orientation

While the downtown area clings to a mountainside, the rest of the city 'officially' sprawls over 3100 sq miles to the Canadian border, making it one of the largest cities (in area) in the USA.

The city center is the busiest and most popular area among visitors in summer. From there, Egan Dr, Southeast's only four-lane highway, heads northwest to Mendenhall Valley. Known to locals as simply 'the Valley,' this area contains a growing residential section, much of Juneau's business district and world-famous Mendenhall Glacier. In the Valley, Egan Dr turns into Glacier Hwy, a two-lane road that leads to Auke Bay, site of the Alaska Marine Highway terminal, and ends at Echo Cove.

Across Gastineau Channel is Douglas, a small town that was once the major city in the area.

MAPS

At the visitors centers (see p136) you can obtain a free map of Juneau with the downtown area on one side and the Juneau road system on the other. Also available is *Guide to Historic Downtown Juneau,* a walking

JUNEAU

SOUTHEAST ALASKA

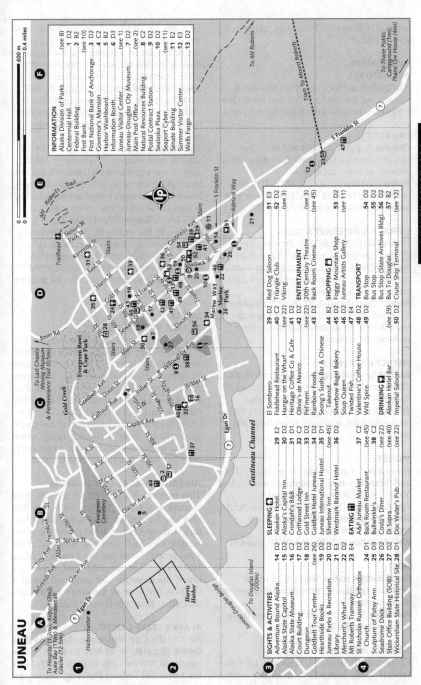

INFORMATION
Alaska Division of Parks	(see 8)
Centennial Hall	1 D2
Federal Building	2 B2
First Bank	(see 10)
First National Bank of Anchorage	3 D2
Governor's Mansion	4 C2
Harbor Washboard	5 B2
Information Booth	6 D3
Juneau Visitor Center	(see 1)
Juneau-Douglas City Museum	7 D2
Main Post Office	(see 2)
Natural Resources Building	8 C2
Postal Contract Station	9 D2
Sealaska Plaza	10 D2
Seaport Cyber	(see 11)
Senate Building	11 E2
Summer Visitor Center	12 E3
Wells Fargo	13 D2

SIGHTS & ACTIVITIES
Adventure Bound Alaska	14 D2
Alaska State Capitol	15 D2
Alaska State Museum	16 C2
Court Building	17 D2
Dungeon	18 D2
Goldbelt Tour Center	(see 26)
Hearthside Books	19 D2
Juneau Parks & Recreation	20 D2
Library	21 D2
Merchant's Wharf	22 D2
Mt Roberts Tramway	23 E4
St Nicholas Russian Orthodox Church	24 D1
Sculpture of Patsy Ann	25 D3
Seadrome Dock	26 D2
State Office Building (SOB)	27 C2
Wickersham State Historical Site	28 D1

SLEEPING
Alaskan Hotel	29 E2
Alaska's Capital Inn	30 D1
Crondahl's B&B	31 D1
Driftwood Lodge	32 C2
Gold Street Inn	33 D2
Goldbelt Hotel Juneau	34 D2
Juneau International Hostel	35 D1
Silverbow Inn	(see 45)
Westmark Baranof Hotel	36 D2

EATING
A&P Juneau Market	37 C2
Back Room Restaurant	(see 45)
Bullwinkle's	38 D2
Costa's Diner	(see 40)
Di Sopra	(see 22)
Doc Water's Pub	(see 22)
El Sombrero	39 D2
Fiddlehead Restaurant	40 C2
Hangar on the Wharf	(see 22)
Heritage Coffee Co & Cafe	41 D2
Olivia's de Mexico	42 D2
Pel'meni	(see 22)
Rainbow Foods	43 D2
Seong's Sushi Bar & Chinese Takeout	44 B2
Silverbow Bagel Bakery	45 D2
Soup Queen	46 D2
Twisted Fish	47 E4
Valentine's Coffee House	48 D2
Wild Spice	49 D2

DRINKING
Alaskan Hotel Bar	(see 29)
Imperial Saloon	50 D2
Red Dog Saloon	51 E3
Triangle Club	52 D2
Viking	(see 3)

ENTERTAINMENT
20th Century Theatre	(see 3)
Back Room Cinema	(see 45)

SHOPPING
Foggy Mountain Shop	53 D2
Juneau Artists Gallery	(see 11)

TRANSPORT
Bus Stop	54 D2
Bus Stop	55 D2
Bus Stop (State Archives Bldg)	56 D2
Bus To Douglas	57 B2
Cruise Ship Terminal	(see 12)

tour to 38 historical buildings, totem poles and public art.

Information

BOOKSTORES
Hearthside Books (Map p135; ☎ 586-1726; www.hearth sidesbooks.com; 254 Front St; ☺ 9am-9pm) Juneau's best bookstore also has a store in the Nugget Mall in the Valley.

LAUNDRY
Dungeon (Map p135; 4th & N Franklin Sts; ☺ 8am-6pm) In the basement of the Mendenhall Building with no attendant, no showers and no phone.
Harbor Washboard (Map p135; ☎ 586-1133; 1114 Glacier Ave; ☺ 8am-9pm) Across Egan Dr from the small boat harbor; also has showers. Entrance is on F St.

LIBRARY & INTERNET ACCESS
Library (Map p135; ☎ 586-5249; 292 Marine Way; ☺ 11am-9pm Mon-Thu, noon-5pm Fri-Sun) Juneau's main public library sits atop a four-story parking structure and offers free Internet access and wi-fi. It's worth a stop here just for the views of downtown Juneau.
Seaport Cyber (Map p135; ☎ 463-9865; 175 S Franklin St; ☺ 9am-7pm; per hr $5) From the 2nd floor of the Senate Building, you can access email, purchase phone-cards, even rent a cell phone.

MEDICAL SERVICES
Bartlett Regional Hospital (Map p135; ☎ 796-8900; 3260 Hospital Dr) Southeast Alaska's largest hospital is off Glacier Hwy between downtown and Lemon Creek.
Juneau Urgent Care (Map p135; ☎ 790-4111; 8505 Old Dairy Rd) A walk-in medical clinic near Nugget Mall in the Valley.

MONEY
Juneau has many banks. Most have ATMs and branches both downtown and in the Valley. Some downtown offices:
First Bank (Map p135; ☎ 586-8801; 1 Sealaska Plaza)
First National Bank of Anchorage (Map p135; ☎ 586-5400; 238 Front St)
Wells Fargo (Map p135; ☎ 586-3324; 123 Seward St)

POST
Postal contract station (Map p135; 225 Front St; ☺ 9:30am-6pm Mon-Fri, 10am-5:30pm Sat) Conveniently located downtown.
Post office (Map p135; cnr 9th St & Glacier Ave) On the 1st floor of the Federal Building.

TOURIST INFORMATION
Conveniently lumped together in Centennial Hall, Juneau's convention center complex, is all the information you need to explore Juneau, find a trail or get out of town. The center's Alaska Marine Highway desk is staffed Monday to Friday and can make reservations and sell tickets.
Alaska Division of Parks (Map p135; ☎ 465-4563; 400 Willoughby Ave; ☺ 8am-4:30pm Mon-Fri) Head to the 5th floor of the Natural Resources Building for state park information or the availability of cabins at Point Bridget State Park (p150).
Juneau Visitor Center (Map p135; ☎ 586-2201, 888-581-2201; www.juneau.com; 101 Egan Dr; ☺ 8:30am-5pm) The main visitors center is in Centennial Hall and has loads of printed information. The center also maintains smaller information booths at the airport, the marine ferry terminal and two of them where the cruise ships dock.
USFS Juneau Ranger District Office (Map p140; ☎ 586-8790; 8461 Old Dairy Rd; ☺ 8am-5pm Mon-Fri) This USFS office is in Mendenhall Valley and can answer questions about cabins, area trails, kayaking and Pack Creek bear viewing permits. There is also an unstaffed counter at the central visitors center with a free phone link to this office.

Sights

ALASKA STATE MUSEUM
The outstanding **Alaska State Museum** (Map p135; ☎ 465-2901; www.museums.state.ak.us; 395 Whittier St; adult/child $5/free; ☺ 8:30am-5:30pm) is near Centennial Hall and houses artifacts from Alaska's major indigenous groups, including the famous Lincoln totem, Aleut baskets and birdskin parkas. There are also displays relating to the state's Russian period and major gold strikes, while a circular ramp winds around an impressive diorama: a two-story-high tree holding a full-size eagle's nest.

JUNEAU-DOUGLAS CITY MUSEUM
This **museum** (Map p135; ☎ 586-3572; 114 W 4th St; adult/child $4/free; ☺ 9am-5pm Mon-Fri, from 10am Sat & Sun) focuses on local goldmining history with interesting displays and the video *Juneau: City Built On Gold*. Booklets on the Perseverance Trail and the Treadwell Mine Historic Trail are available and, if you're a hiker, the museum's 7ft-long relief map is the best overview of the area's rugged terrain other than a helicopter ride.

ALASKA STATE CAPITOL
Next to the City Museum is the **Alaska State Capitol** (Map p135; ☎ 465-3800; 120 4th St; ☺ 9am-5pm Mon-Fri, from noon Sat). Built in 1929–31 as the territorial Federal Building, the capitol

A ROAD TO SOMEWHERE ELSE

Juneau is not only one of the most nerve-racking airline approaches in the USA – jumbo jets must search for a runway planted between two tree-topped ridges – but it's the only capital in North America you can't reach by road. Alaska's state capital has more than 100 miles of pavement around it, but none of it goes anywhere.

Meanwhile, every year 200 scheduled flights never make it into the city because of bad weather. That's fuel for the long-running debate on whether a road should be built along the Lynn Canal to connect Juneau to the rest of the state highway system.

The idea was first proposed in 1994 and has since been the focus of several Draft Environmental Impact Statements (EIS), all concluding that a 65-mile highway could be punched through to Skagway. From there – via the Alcan (Alaska Hwy) – it's only 832 miles to Anchorage and 710 miles to Fairbanks. The estimated cost to carve a two-lane road along the east side of Lynn Canal is now at $265 million or $4 million per mile.

The biggest concern, however, may not be the money but the 58 known avalanche areas the road would traverse. Engineers estimate avalanches would close the road a dozen times each winter for two days or longer. The fear of a motorist dying in a snowslide is the reason half of the road's proposed $1.5-million maintenance budget would be for avalanche control.

Building such a road has much of Alaska in an uproar. That's why after originally supporting the project in 2000, Governor Tony Knowles shelved it in favor of high-speed ferries. But road-building is the personal crusade of current Gov Frank Murkowski and shortly after taking office he placed a budget request before US Congress. If funding is approved a road could be open as early as 2008.

Road supporters cite increased opportunity for Alaskans to travel to their state's capital, lower out-of-pocket cost for travelers, a better emergency evacuation route in case of disaster and increased economic development from opening this region of Southeast to more recreation, tourism and mining.

Ironically, those most set against it are from the Southeast. In Skagway, residents resent a road cutting through their beloved Lower Dewey Lakes recreation area, one of the few places to escape the cruise-ship masses during the summer. Other Southeast communities fear that the project will siphon away much-needed funds for maintaining and improving the state ferry system.

And in Juneau the proposed road renews the old conflict about what Alaska is and what people were looking for when they moved there. Build a road and a little more of that unique remoteness will be lost. Some residents imagine with horror the scene when the hoard of RVs meets the wave of tourists off the cruise ships.

'This is the only place where we'd be having this discussion: should we build a road to our town,' said the city manager. 'But if it's built, Juneau is going to be the end of it. The question is, what are we going to do with all those buses and trailers and Winnebagos once they get here?'

looks like an overgrown high school. Stuffed inside are legislative chambers, the governor's office, and offices for the hundreds of staff members who arrive in Juneau for the winter legislative session. Free 30-minute tours are held every half-hour and start from the visitor desk in the lobby; a self-guided tour pamphlet is also available.

LAST CHANCE MINING MUSEUM

Amble out to the end of Basin Rd, a beautiful half-mile walk from the north end of Gastineau Ave, to the intriguing **Last Chance Mining Museum** (Map p135; ☎ 586-5338; 1001 Basin Rd; adult/child $4/free; ⏲ 9:30am-12:30pm & 3:30-6:30pm).

The former Alaska-Juneau Gold Mining Company complex is now a museum where you can view the remains of the compressor house and examine tools of what was once the world's largest hard-rock goldmine. There is an impressive 3-D glass map of shafts that shows just how large it was. Nearby is the Perseverance Trail (p139), and combining the museum with a hike to more mining ruins is a great way to spend an afternoon.

MT ROBERTS TRAMWAY

As far as trams go this **tramway** (Map p135; ☎ 463-3412, 888-461-8726; 490 S Franklin St; www .goldbelttours.com; adult/child $24/12.50; ⏲ 9am-9pm) is rather expensive for a relatively short, five-minute ride. But from a marketing point of view, its location couldn't be better. It whisks passengers right from the cruise-ship dock up 1800ft to the tree line of Mt Roberts, where they'll find a restaurant, gift shops and a small theater with a film on Tlingit culture. Or skip all that and just use the tram for access to day hikes in the alpine area (right).

WATERFRONT AREA & S FRANKLIN ST

Between the cruise ships and Willoughby Ave, **Marine Park** (Map p135) is an open space where kids practice their skateboard tricks, state workers enjoy a sack lunch and tired tourists occasionally take a nap in the sun. Free binoculars let you search Mt Juneau for mountain goats while on the dock is a **sculpture of Patsy Ann** (Map p135), the late faithful Fido who became known as the 'Official Greeter of Juneau' for her tendency to rush down to the docks to meet arriving cruise ships. A block inland from the waterfront is **S Franklin St**, a refurbished historical district where many buildings date from the early 1900s and have since been turned into bars, gift shops and restaurants.

OTHER MUSEUMS & HISTORICAL SITES

Overlooking downtown Juneau is **Wickersham State Historical Site** (Map p135; ☎ 586-9001; 213 7th St; adult/child $3.50/free; ☽ 8:30am-10am & 1-5pm Tue-Mon) which preserves the 1898 home of pioneer judge and statesman James Wickersham. Inside are photographs, books and other memorabilia from the judge's colorful career.

Two blocks downhill is **St Nicholas Russian Orthodox Church** (Map p135; ☎ 586-1023; 326 5th St; adult/child $2/free; ☽ noon-5pm Mon, 9am-5pm Tue-Thu, to noon Fri, 11am-1pm Sat, 1-3pm Sun). Built in 1894 against the backdrop of Mt Juneau, the onion-domed church is a photographer's delight. Inside are Russian icons, original vestments and religious relics, while adjacent to the church is a small gift shop filled with books, *matreshkas* (nestling dolls) and other handcrafted items from Russia.

Across from the Juneau-Douglas City Museum is the **State Office Building** (Map p135; 400 Willoughby Ave), known locally as the SOB. From the outdoor court on the 8th floor there is a spectacular view of the channel and Douglas Island, while in the lobby is a massive Kimball organ dating back to 1928. Every Friday at noon a performance is given, a good reason

to join state workers for a brown-bag lunch. West of the SOB along 4th Ave is the pillared **Governor's Mansion** (Map p135; 716 Calhoun Ave). Built and furnished in 1912 at a cost of $44,000, the mansion is not open to the public.

Activities
GOLD PANNING

What's in them thar hills? Many visitors passing through the Southeast are fascinated with gold-rush history. Two of the Juneau area's most successful historic mines were the **Alaska-Juneau Mine**, on the side of Mt Roberts, and the **Treadwell Mine**, across Gastineau Channel near Douglas. The Alaska-Juneau Mine closed in 1944 after producing more than $80 million in gold, then valued at $20 to $35 an ounce. The Treadwell Mine closed in 1922 after a 1917 cave-in caused the company's financial collapse. During its heyday at the turn of the 20th century, the Treadwell made Douglas the channel's major city, with a population of 15,000. For more information about these mines and what you can see of them today, stop by the Juneau-Douglas City Museum (p136).

Alaska Travel Adventures (☎ 789-0052, 800-791-2673; adult/child $$45/30) Offers a 1½-hour tour to Last Chance Mining Museum with gold panning in Gold Creek but you don't have to join a tour to pan, not even in Gold Creek. Recreational panning is easy and any hardware store in Juneau will sell you a gold pan for far less (black plastic ones are the cheapest and easiest to see the flecks of gold). The best public creeks to pan are Bullion Creek in the Treadwell Mine area, Gold Creek up by the Last Chance Basin, Sheep Creek on Thane Rd, and Salmon, Nugget and Eagle Creeks off Egan Dr and Glacier Hwy north of downtown.

HIKING

Few cities in Alaska have such a diversity of hiking trails as Juneau. A handful of these trails are near the city centre, the rest are out the road and shown on the Around Juneau map in this chapter. All five hike-in USFS cabins (NRRS ☎ 877-444-6777; www.reserveusa .com; $35) should be reserved.

GUIDED WALKS

Juneau Parks & Recreation (☎ 586-5226, for recorded information ☎ 586-0428; www.juneau.lib.ak.us/parksrec /hike; 155 S Seward St) offers volunteer-led hikes every Wednesday (adults) and Saturday (kids OK). Call or check the website for a schedule and the trails. **Gastineau Guiding** (☎ 586-2666; www.stepintoalaska.com) offers a number of guided hikes that include snacks, ponchos if needed and transportation. Its Guide's Choice Adventure Hike (adult/child $79/48) is a four-hour trek with an elevation gain of between 600ft and 1000ft.

City Center Trails

Perseverance Trail (Map p135) off Basin Rd is Juneau's most popular and provides access to two other popular treks: **Mt Juneau Trail** and **Granite Creek Trail**. Together, this system of trails can be combined into a rugged 10-hour walk for hardy hikers, or an overnight excursion into the mountains surrounding Alaska's capital city.

To reach Perseverance Trail, take 6th St one block southwest to Gold St, which turns into Basin Rd, a dirt road that curves away from the city into the mountains as it follows Gold Creek. The trailhead is at the road's end, at the parking lot for Last Chance Mining Museum. The trail leads into Silverbow Basin, an old mining area that still has many hidden and unmarked adits and mine shafts; be safe and stay on the trail.

From the Perseverance Trail, you can pick up Granite Creek Trail and follow it to the creek's headwaters basin, a beautiful spot to spend the night. From there, you can reach Mt Juneau by climbing the ridge and staying left of Mt Olds, the huge rocky mountain. Once atop Mt Juneau, you can complete the loop by descending along the Mt Juneau Trail, which joins Perseverance Trail a mile from its beginning. The hike to the 3576ft peak of Mt Juneau along the ridge from Granite Creek is an easier but longer trek than the ascent from the Mt Juneau Trail. The alpine sections of the ridge are serene, and on a clear summer day you'll have outstanding views. From the trailhead for the Perseverance Trail to the upper basin of Granite Creek is 3.3 miles one way. Then it's another 3 miles along the ridge to reach Mt Juneau.

Mt Roberts Trail is a 4-mile climb up Mt Roberts that begins at a marked wooden staircase at the northeast end of 6th St. It starts with a series of switchbacks, then breaks out of the trees at Gastineau Peak and comes to the tram station. From here

it's a half-mile to the Cross, where you'll have good views of Juneau, Douglas and the entire Gastineau Channel. The Mt Roberts summit (3819ft) is still a steep climb away through the alpine brush. If you hike up, you can ride down the Mt Roberts Tramway to S Franklin St for only $5. And if you purchase $5 worth of food or drink at the visitors center on top, the ride down is free.

Dan Moller Trail is a 3.3-mile trail leads to an alpine bowl at the crest of Douglas Island, where you'll find the **Dan Moller Cabin**. Just across the channel in West Juneau, the public bus conveniently stops at Cordova St in West Juneau and from there, you turn left onto Pioneer Ave and follow it to the end of the pavement to the trailhead. Plan on six hours for the round-trip.

Treadwell Ditch Trail can be picked up either a mile up the Dan Moller Trail or just above D St in Douglas. The trail stretches 12 miles north from Douglas to Eagle Crest, although most people begin in Douglas and hike to the Dan Moller Trail and then return to the road, a 5-mile trip. The path is rated as easy and provides views of Gastineau Channel as it winds through scenic muskeg meadows.

Mendenhall Glacier Trails

East Glacier Loop is one of many trails near Mendenhall Glacier, a 3-mile round-trip providing good views of the glacier from a scenic lookout at the halfway point. Pick up the loop along the **Trail of Time**, a half-mile nature walk that starts at the Mendenhall Glacier Visitor Center.

Nugget Creek Trail begins just beyond the East Glacier Loop's scenic lookout. The 2½-mile trail climbs 500ft to Vista Creek Shelter, a free-use shelter that doesn't require reservations, making the round-trip to the shelter from the Mendenhall Glacier Visitor Center an 8-mile trek. Hikers who plan to spend the night at the shelter can continue along the creek toward Nugget Glacier, though the route is hard to follow at times.

West Glacier Trail is one of the most spectacular hikes in the Juneau area. The 3.4-mile trail begins off Montana Creek Rd past Mendenhall Lake Campground and hugs the mountainside along the glacier, providing exceptional views of the icefalls and other glacial features. It ends at a rocky outcropping, but a rough route continues

SOUTHEAST ALASKA

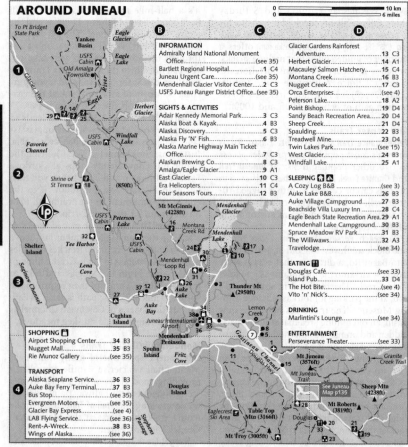

AROUND JUNEAU

INFORMATION
Admiralty Island National Monument
Office..(see 35)
Bartlett Regional Hospital.....................1 C4
Juneau Urgent Care...........................(see 35)
Mendenhall Glacier Visitor Center.......2 C3
USFS Juneau Ranger District Office..(see 35)

SIGHTS & ACTIVITIES
Adair Kennedy Memorial Park.............3 C3
Alaska Boat & Kayak............................4 B3
Alaska Discovery..................................5 C3
Alaska Fly 'N' Fish...............................6 B3
Alaska Marine Highway Main Ticket
Office..7 C3
Alaskan Brewing Co.............................8 C3
Amalga/Eagle Glacier..........................9 A1
East Glacier...10 C3
Era Helicopters....................................11 C4
Four Seasons Tours..............................12 B3

Glacier Gardens Rainforest
Adventure..13 C3
Herbert Glacier...................................14 A1
Macaulay Salmon Hatchery................15 C4
Montana Creek....................................16 B3
Nugget Creek......................................17 C3
Orca Enterprises...............................(see 4)
Peterson Lake......................................18 A2
Point Bishop.......................................19 D4
Sandy Beach Recreation Area.............20 D4
Sheep Creek..21 D4
Spaulding..22 B3
Treadwell Mine...................................23 D4
Twin Lakes Park...............................(see 15)
West Glacier..24 B3
Windfall Lake.....................................25 A1

SLEEPING
A Cozy Log B&B................................(see 3)
Auke Lake B&B...................................26 B3
Auke Village Campground..................27 B3
Beachside Villa Luxury Inn 28 C4
Eagle Beach State Recreation Area.....29 A1
Mendenhall Lake Campground...........30 B3
Spruce Meadow RV Park.....................31 B3
The Williwaws.....................................32 A3
Travelodge...(see 34)

EATING
Douglas Café.....................................(see 33)
Island Pub...33 D4
The Hot Bite.......................................(see 4)
Vito 'n' Nick's...................................(see 34)

DRINKING
Marlintini's Lounge...........................(see 34)

ENTERTAINMENT
Perseverance Theater.......................(see 33)

SHOPPING
Airport Shopping Center........34 B3
Nugget Mall............................35 B3
Rie Munoz Gallery ....(see 35)

TRANSPORT
Alaska Seaplane Service...........36 B3
Auke Bay Ferry Terminal.........37 B3
Bus Stop................................(see 35)
Evergreen Motors.................(see 35)
Glacier Bay Express................(see 4)
LAB Flying Service.................(see 36)
Rent-A-Wreck.........................38 B3
Wings of Alaska...................(see 36)

See Juneau Map p135

from there to the summit of Mt McGinnis (4228ft), another 2 miles away. Allow five hours for the West Glacier Trail, or plan on a long day if you want to tackle the difficult Mt McGinnis route.

Juneau Area Trails
Sheep Creek Trail, southeast of Juneau along Thane Rd, is a scenic 3-mile walk into the valley south of Mt Roberts. The trailhead is 4 miles from Juneau, at a staircase on the gravel spur to a Snettisham Power Plant substation. The trail is fairly flat in the Valley, from where you scramble up forested hillsides to the alpine zone. Once above tree line, many hikers follow the power line to reach the ridge to Sheep Mountain (4238ft).

You can continue from Sheep Mountain over Mt Roberts, returning to Juneau along the Mt Roberts Trail. This is a 10- to 12-hour day hike.

Point Bishop Trail is at the end of Thane Rd, 7½ miles southeast of Juneau. This 8-mile trail leads to Point Bishop, a scenic spot overlooking the junction of Stephens Passage and Taku Inlet. The trail is flat but can be wet in many spots, making waterproof boots the preferred footwear. The hike makes for an ideal overnight trip, as there is good camping at Point Bishop.

Montana Creek Trail and **Windfall Lake Trail** connect at Windfall Lake and can be combined for an interesting 11½-mile overnight hiking trip. It is easier to begin at the trailhead at Montana Creek and follow the Windfall Lake Trail out to the Glacier Hwy.

The 8-mile Montana Creek Trail, known for its high concentration of bears, begins near the end of Montana Creek Rd, 2 miles from its junction with Mendenhall Loop Rd. The 3½-mile Windfall Lake Trail begins off a gravel spur that leaves the Glacier Hwy just before it crosses Herbert River, 27 miles northwest of Juneau. The trail has been improved considerably in recent years and now features the newest USFS cabin in the Juneau area. **Windfall Lake Cabin** sleeps six and is open as a warming shelter during the day.

Spaulding Trail is primary use for cross-country skiing, but can be hiked in the summer. The 3-mile route provides access to the Auke Nu Trail, which leads to the **John Muir Cabin**. The trailhead is off Glacier Hwy just past and opposite Auke Bay Post Office, 12.3 miles northwest of Juneau.

Peterson Lake Trail is a 4-mile route along Peterson Creek to its namesake lake, a favorite among hike-in anglers for the good Dolly Varden fishing. The trailhead is 20ft before the Mile 24 marker on Glacier Hwy, north of the Shrine of St Terese. Wear rubber boots, as it can be muddy during the summer. The **Peterson Lake Cabin** turns this trail into a delightful overnight adventure.

Herbert Glacier Trail extends 4.6 miles along the Herbert River to Herbert Glacier, a round-trip of four to five hours. The trail is easy with little climbing, though wet in places, and begins just past the bridge over Herbert River at Mile 28 of Glacier Hwy.

Amalga Trail, also known as the Eagle Glacier Trail, is a level route that winds 7½ miles to the lake formed by Eagle Glacier and the **Eagle Glacier Cabin**. Less than a mile from the glacier's face, the view from the cabin is well worth the effort of reserving it in advance. The trailhead is beyond the Glacier Hwy bridge, across Eagle River, 0.4 miles past the trailhead for the Herbert Glacier Trail. Plan on a round-trip of seven to eight hours to reach the impressive Eagle Glacier and return to the trailhead, a round-trip of 15 miles.

WILDERNESS CABINS

Numerous **USFS cabins** (NRRS ☎ 877-444-6777, 518-885-3639; www.reserveusa.com) are accessible from Juneau, but all are heavily used, requiring advance reservations. If you're just passing through, check with the **USFS Juneau Ranger District Office** (☎ 586-8790; Old Dairy Rd; ☺ 8am-5pm Mon-Fri) for a list of what's available.

The following cabins are within 30 minutes' flying time from Juneau; air charters will cost around $500 round-trip from Juneau, split among a planeload of up to five passengers. **Alaska Seaplane Service** (Map p135; ☎ 789-3331, 888-350-8277; www.akseaplanes.com) and **Wings of Alaska** (Map p135; ☎ 789-0790; www.wingsofalaska.com) can provide flights on short notice.

West Turner Lake Cabin (r $35) is one of the most scenic and is by far the Juneau area's most popular cabin. It's 18 miles east of Juneau on the west end of Turner Lake, where the fishing is good for trout, Dolly Varden and salmon. A skiff is provided.

Admiralty Island's north end has three popular cabins, all $35 a night. **Admiralty Cove Cabin** is on a scenic bay and has access to Young Lake along a rough 4½-mile trail. Brown bears frequent the area. The two **Young Lake Cabins** have skiffs to access a lake with good fishing for cutthroat trout and landlocked salmon. A lakeshore trail connects the two cabins.

There are also three rental cabins in Point Bridget State Park (cabins $35). **Cowee Meadow Cabin** is a 2½-mile hike into the park, **Blue Mussel Cabin** is a 3.4-mile walk and **Camping Cove Cabin** a 4-mile trek. Both Blue Mussel and Camping Cove overlook the shoreline and would make a great destination for kayakers. Reserve them through the **DNR Public Information Center** (☎ 269-8400; www.dnr.state.ak.us/parks/cabins).

PADDLING

Both day trips and extended paddles are possible out of the Juneau area in sea kayaks. Rentals are available from **Alaska Boat & Kayak** (☎ 789-6886; www.juneaukayak.com; 11521 Glacier Hwy; single/double $45/60; ☺ 9am-6pm), which is based in the Auke Bay Harbor and offers transport service and multiday discounts.

Guided Tours

Alaska Boat & Kayak also offers half-day guided paddles ($89) and full-day outings ($149). For something more adventurous **Alaska Discovery** (☎ 780-6226, 800-586-1911; www.akdiscovery.com) offers three-day paddles in Berners Bay ($495). Tours include transportation from downtown Juneau.

Auke Bay

The easiest trip is to paddle out and around the islands of Auke Bay. You can even camp on the islands to turn the adventure into an overnight trip.

Taku Inlet

This waterway is an excellent four- to five-day trip with close views of Taku Glacier. Total paddling distance is 30 to 40 miles, depending on how far you travel up the inlet. It does not require any major crossing, though rounding Point Bishop can be rough at times. It is possible to camp at Point Bishop and along the grassy area southwest of the glacier, where brown bears are occasionally seen.

Berners Bay

At the western end of Glacier Hwy, 40 miles from Juneau, is Echo Cove, where kayakers put in for paddles in the protected waters of Berners Bay. The bay, which extends 12 miles north to the outlets of the Antler, Lace and Berners Rivers, is ideal for an overnight trip or longer excursions up Berners River. The delightful USFS **Berners Bay Cabin** (NRRS ☎ 877-444-6777; www.reserveusa.com; cabin $35) is an 8-mile paddle from Echo Cove. Alaska Boat & Kayak (p141) charges $120 for kayak transportation out to Echo Cove.

Oliver Inlet

On Admiralty Island's northeast coast is Oliver Inlet State Marine Park. A 0.8-mile portage tramway links the inlet to scenic Seymour Canal, known for one of the world's greatest locations for nesting bald eagles and a large population of brown bears. Seals, sea lions and whales spend the summer feeding in the canal. The paddle to Oliver Inlet is 18 miles and involves crossing Stephens Passage, a challenging open-water crossing (for experienced kayakers only). At the south end of the portage tram from Oliver Inlet is the state's Seymour Canal Cabin, which rents for $25 a night and can be reserved through the DNR Public Information Center (p141). To avoid the open-water crossing, Alaska Boat & Kayak (p141) will take you and your kayak to Oliver Inlet for $250.

CYCLING

Bike paths run between Auke Bay, Mendenhall Glacier and downtown, and from the Juneau-Douglas Bridge to Douglas. Pick up a route guide at the Centennial Hall's main visitors center. Because most of Juneau's trails are steep, mountain biking is limited, but the Windfall Lake and Peterson Lake trails are popular with off-road cyclists.

Driftwood Lodge (Map p135; ☎ 586-2280; 435 W Willoughby Ave; incl helmet & lock per 8hr/day$15/25) rents basic mountain bikes.

Juneau for Children

The best attraction for kids visiting Juneau is the **Macauley Salmon Hatchery** (☎ 463-4810, 877-463-2486; www.dipac.net; 2697 Channel Dr; adult/child $3.25/1.75; ☼ 10am-6pm Mon-Fri, to 5pm Sat & Sun), 3 miles northwest of downtown. Just don't tell them it's educational. The hatchery has huge seawater aquariums loaded with local marine life, from tanner crabs to octopus, while the interpretive displays explaining the life cycle of salmon are museum quality. Underwater viewing windows and a 450ft fish ladder allow children to witness, from July to September, the amazing sight of thousands of salmon fighting their way upstream to spawn. You can also wander the outside grounds and pier to watch people catching lunker salmon. Or rent a rod and reel at the adjacent Catch-A-Bunch shack and try your luck.

The City of Juneau maintains a wonderful system of parks, offering more than just playscapes. **Twin Lakes Park** (Old Glacier Hwy), just past the hospital, is stocked with king salmon and equipped with a fishing pier. There's also a solar-system trail around the lake that provides a realistic idea how far each planet is from the sun. If your young climbers are not ready for Mt Mckinley yet, take them to **Adair Kennedy Memorial Park** (3800 Mendenhall Loop Rd at Floyd Dryden Middle School) to scale the 'Boldr,' a 9ft-tall climbing rock with handholds and a layer of rubber chips around the base for any mishaps.

Tours

The easiest way to book a tour in Juneau is to head to the cruise ship terminal, near the Mt Roberts Tram, where most of the operators will be hawking their wares from a line of booths like sideshow barkers at a carnival.

CITY/GLACIER

Gray Line (☎ 586-3773, 800-544-2206; www.grayline ofalaska.com) Has several tours including the standard city-Macauley Salmon Hatchery-Mendenhall Glacier tour. The three-hour tour occurs twice daily at 8am and 2pm for $39.

Juneau Trolley Car Company (☎ 586-7433; www
.juneautrolley.com) Runs a narrated 30-minute loop past
12 popular visitor attractions, including Franklin St Historic
District, St Nicholas Russian Orthodox Church, the capitol,
Juneau-Douglas City Museum, the Governor's Mansion
and Alaska State Museum but nothing in the Valley. The
adult/child $14/10 fare covers unlimited rides for the day.

Mendenhall Glacier Transport/Mighty Great Trips
(☎ 789-5460; www.mightygreattrips.com) Offers a city-
and-glacier tour for only $20.

Princess Tours (☎ 463-3900) Offers a 1½-hour tour to
Mendenhall Glacier ($19) and a three-hour Mendenhall Gla-
cier & Salmon Hatchery Tour (adult/child $37/27). Another
offering from Princess is its unique Historic Juneau Gold
Mine Tour, which visits the remains of the Alaska Gastineau
Mine and its mill (adult/child $59/35). The three-hour tour
heads underground via a conveyer tunnel to explore the mill
ruins and ends with a little gold panning.

JUNEAU ICE FIELD
The hottest tour in Juneau is a helicopter
ride to the Juneau Ice Field for a 20-minute
ride in the basket of a dogsled. These tours
last less than two hours and are $400 a
pop but when the weather is nice people –
primarily cruise-ship passengers – are waiting to hand over their money.

Era Helicopters (☎ 586-2030, 800-843-1947; www
.era-aviation.com) You spend an hour on Middle Branch
Glacier as part of its glacier dogsled adventure ($410). For
something more affordable, book its hourlong, four-glacier
tour ($229) that includes a 20-minute glacier landing.

NorthStar Trekking (☎ 790-4530; www.glaciertrek
king.com) Skip the dogsled and strap on the crampons.
NorthStar offers several glacier treks that first begin with
a helicopter ride and includes all equipment and training.
On its four-hour glacier trek ($339), you cross two miles of
frozen landscape riddled with crevasses and the hike is as
stunning as it gets.

Temsco Helicopters (☎ 789-9501, 877-789-9501;
www.temscoair.com) Its mushing and glacier flightseeing tour ($410) lasts 1½ hours and lands at a dog camp
on Denver Glacier. The company also has a 55-minute
Mendenhall Glacier tour ($199) that includes 25 minutes'
walking around high up on the glacier.

Wings of Alaska (☎ 789-0790; www.wingsofalaska
.com) It's 40-minute glacier flightseeing adventure (adult/
child $148/120) is the most affordable way to get into the
air for a peek at the ice field.

TRACY ARM
This steepsided fjord, 50 miles southeast
of Juneau, has a pair of tidewater glaciers
and a gallery of icebergs floating down its
length. Tracy Arm makes an interesting day

trip, far less expensive and perhaps even
more satisfying than a visit to Glacier Bay.
You're almost guaranteed to see seals inside
the arm, and you might spot whales on the
way there. The full-day cruises leave from
the Juneau waterfront.

Adventure Bound Alaska (☎ 463-2509, 800-228-
3875; www.adventureboundalaska.com) Offers a more
intimate and personal trip. It charges adult/child $115/75
to the general public or $105 to hostel members. You need
to bring your own lunch or buy food onboard.

Goldbelt Tours (☎ 586-8687, 800-820-2628; www
.goldbelttours.com) Offers the trip four days a week on a
large catamaran for adult/child $139/90, including lunch.

WHALE WATCHING
The whale watching in nearby Stephens
Passage is so good that some tour opera-
tors will refund your money if you don't see
at least one. The boats depart from Auke
Bay and most tours last three to four hours.
Some operators offer courtesy transport
from downtown.

Four Seasons Tours (Map p140; ☎ 790-6671,
877-774-8687; www.4seasonsmarine.com; adult/child
$119/59) Combines whale watching with a stop at its
remote Orca Point Lodge for a salmon feast.

Orca Enterprises (Map p140; ☎ 789-6801, 888-733-
6722; www.alaskawhalewatching.com; adult/child $105/49)
Uses a 42ft jet boat to cruise the passage and look at sea
lions, orcas and harbor seals as well as humpback whales.

Festivals & Events
Alaska Folk Festival (☎ 463-3316; www.juneau
.com/aff) Attracts musicians from around the state for a
week of performances, workshops and dances at Centennial Hall in mid-April.

Juneau Jazz & Classics festival (☎ 463-3378; www
.jazzandclassics.org; tickets $20-60) Brings jazz and classi-
cal music concerts and workshops during the third week in
May. Similar to the Alaska Folk Festival.

Gold Rush Days (☎ 780-6075; www.juneaugoldrush
.com) A late-June festival of logging and mining events.

Fourth of July Celebrations include a parade, carnival,
fireworks and a lot of outdoor meals – from Sandy Beach
in Douglas to Juneau's city center.

Sleeping
Juneau tacks on 12% in bed and sales taxes
to the price of lodging.

BUDGET
Juneau International Hostel (Map p135; ☎ 586-
9559; www.juneauhostel.org; 614 Harris St, Juneau; dm
$10; ✗ 🖳) One of Alaska's best hostels. The

large yellow house has an ideal location – only a few blocks from the Mt Roberts Trail and Basin Rd and the beginning of the scenic Gold Creek area. Amenities include cooking and laundry facilities, showers, and a common room with a fireplace and free Internet access. Reservations are a must during the summer and are best done on the phone, using a credit card. Lockout is from 9am to 5pm.

Camping

Thane Public Campground (Map p135; ☎ 463-4463; 1585 Thane Rd; sites $5) Located about a mile south of downtown on Thane Rd is the city-operated place for tents only.

Mendenhall Lake Campground (Map p135; Montana Creek Rd; campsites/RV sites $10/26-29) One of Alaska's most beautiful USFS campgrounds. The 68-site area (18 sites with hookups) is on Montana Creek Rd, off Mendenhall Loop Rd, and has a separate seven-site walk-in backpacking unit. The campsites are alongside a lake, and many have spectacular views of the nearby glacier. It's first-come, first-served.

Spruce Meadow RV Park (Map p140; ☎ 789-1990; www.juneaurv.com; 10200 Mendenhall Loop Rd; campsites/ RV sites $20/25-27) If Mendenhall Lake Campground is full, this full-service campground is practically next door. Spruce Meadows has all the amenities, from a Laundromat and cable TV to a modem station to check email, plus it's right on the city bus route.

Auke Village Campground (Map p140; Glacier Hwy; sites $8) Located 2 miles from the ferry terminal on Glacier Hwy, this is a 12-site USFS campground with shelters, tables, firewood and a nice beach. It's first-come, first-served.

Eagle Beach State Recreation Area (Map p140; ☎ 586-2506; Mile 28 Glacier Hwy; sites $10) This is 15 miles from the ferry terminal and 28 miles from downtown Juneau. Renovated in 2003, the state recreation area now includes a ranger station and day-use parking area and 17 wooded campsites with fire rings and vault toilets; ideal for tenters.

MIDRANGE

Silverbow Inn (Map p135; ☎ 586-4146, 800-586-4146; www.silverbowinn.com; 120 2nd St; r $129-149; ✕) An artsy six-room inn on top of the best bakery downtown. How convenient! Rooms have private bath, phone, cable TV and come with

a full breakfast in the morning and coffee, tea and fresh-baked cookies in the afternoon.

Crondahls B&B (Map p135; ☎ 586-1464; www .juneaucrondahls.com; 626 5th St; s/d $70/80) Accessed by one of Juneau's picturesque stairways, this art-filled home offers two guestrooms with shared bath in the historic Starr Hill neighborhood. From the wraparound deck outside, you can prop your feet up to the view of downtown Juneau and Douglas Island.

A Cozy Log B&B (Map p140; ☎ 789-2582; www .cozylog.net; 8668 Dudley St; r $95) Offers two rooms with shared bath in a beautiful log house in the Valley. Author Sydney Sheldon used the home as a setting in his novel *The Sky Is Falling*. A full breakfast in the morning might include such local delicacies as just-picked blueberries or smoked salmon.

Auke Lake B&B (Map p140; ☎ 790-3253, 800-790-3253; www.admiraltytours.com; 11595 Mendenhall Loop Rd; r $115-135) It's blessed with a great lakefront location between the airport and ferry, a short distance from Mendenhall Glacier. The three B&B rooms have their own entry, and each room has a private bath, phone, TV/VCR, refrigerator and coffeemaker. A big back deck with hot tub overlooks the lake, where guests can paddle about in the B&B's paddleboat, canoes or kayak.

Driftwood Lodge (Map p135; ☎ 586-2280, 800-544-2239; www.driftwoodalaska.com; 435 Willoughby Ave; r $89-97, ste $119; ✕ ▯) Near the Alaska State Museum, this is a convenient place to stay downtown. The 63 rooms are clean, the motel offers courtesy transportation to the airport/ferry and it's hard to top the location unless you're willing to spend twice as much.

Alaskan Hotel (Map p135; ☎ 586-1000, 800-327-9347; www.ptialaska.net/~akhotel; 167 S Franklin St; r with/without bath $80/60, ste $90) The historical decor in its lobby makes you feel like you're just in time for the gold rush. The smallish rooms, some dating back to 1913, are more than adequate. Great rates for this town but avoid rooms overlooking Franklin St unless you plan to join the revelry below.

Gold Street Inn (☎ 586-9863; www.goldstreetinn .com; 303 Gold St; s/d/ste $95/110/155) This dates back to 1914, when it consisted of two cabins and a horse barn. Eventually the buildings were combined into a five-room inn. It's not plush, but each room has a private bath, kitchenette, telephone and TV, and rates include continental breakfast. The living-room view on the top floor makes the two-bedroom suite a bargain.

Travelodge (Map p140; ☎ 789-9700, 888-660-2327; 9200 Glacier Hwy; s/d $139; 🖥 🕭) For a late-night flight this is one of a handful of chain motels clustered around the airport with courtesy phones in the terminal to call for a 24-hour pickup. During the day the motel provides transport downtown for guests.

Williwaws (Map p140; ☎ 789-2803, 888-837-9617; www.williwaws.com; 19100 Willow Way; s/d/cabins $55/110/175) For those who truly want to escape. Located on North Tee Harbor, 10 miles north of the airport, is this pair of log cabins at the tip of a wooded peninsula. You can book a room or the entire Cedar Bungalow. Either rent a car and drive out or, for the adventurous, rent a kayak in Auke Bay and spend a day paddling to your shoreline cabin.

TOP END

Alaska's Capital Inn (Map p135; ☎ 907-586-6507, 888-588-6507; www.alaskacapitalinn.com; 113 W 5th St; r $125-219, attic ste $275; ✕ 🖥) In the gorgeously restored 1906 downtown home of wealthy gold rush–era miner John Olds. All seven rooms have private bath, phone and TV/VCR, and feature hardwood floors covered by colorful Persian rugs. The attic suite, with its Jacuzzi, fireplace and rocking chair, is a quiet sanctuary from the hustle and bustle just a few blocks away. Outside there's a clothing-optional hot tub out on the big back deck, which overlooks the city. Kicking back on the deck – sipping a glass of port or sherry and watching the city lights appear – you'll understand why Olds chose this spot for his opulent abode.

Beachside Villa Luxury Inn (Map p140; ☎ 463-5531, 888-879-0858; www.beachsidevilla.com; 3120 Douglas Hwy; r $159-229; ✕ 🖥) On Douglas Island, just a half-mile south of the bridge, this immense, three-story home offers five guestrooms on the edge of the Channel. Rooms have a private entrance, bath, microwave and a stocked refrigerator. Four rooms have picture-window views of Juneau, three have a two-person, in-room Jacuzzi, one a small outside deck; pampering is found everywhere.

Goldbelt Hotel Juneau (Map p135; ☎ 586-6900, 888-478-6909; www.goldbelttours.com; 51 Egan Dr; r $169-179; 🖥) Alaska Native–owned and centrally located downtown, the hotel has big rooms and

big, comfortable beds with such amenities as room service, cable TV and courtesy pickup from the airport. Half the rooms face the waterfront where you can watch the cruise ships unload and the floatplanes take off.

Westmark Baranof Hotel (Map p135; ☎ 586-2660, 800-544-0970; www.westmarkhotels.com; 127 N Franklin St; r $169-189, ste $209-249; ✕ 🖥) The grand dame of Juneau's luxury hotels. The Baranof has been anchoring Franklin St since 1939 and during the legislative session a lot of political posturing takes place at the back tables of its lounge and restaurant. Rooms tend to be small and not overly impressive considering what you're paying. But snag one on the 8th or 9th floor and it's almost worth it.

Eating

Juneau's restaurant scene is a mixed bag. On one hand, many feel it's missing the fine cuisine deserving of a state capital. On the other, for a city of more than 30,000 the lack of fast-food chains is refreshing; basically you have just two McDonald's and a Subway.

SALMON BAKES

Juneau has several salmon bakes. Though aimed primarily at tourists, they provide great food (hard to go wrong with fresh salmon) with an experience conveying the flavor of frontier Alaska.

Thane Ore House (Map p135; ☎ 586-3442; 4400 Thane Rd; dinner $23; ✕) Found 4 miles south of town, this is the best. The all-you-can-eat dinner of grilled salmon, halibut and ribs includes a salad bar, corn, baked beans and more. There is a courtesy bus that departs nightly from the downtown area.

Taku Glacier Lodge (☎ 586-8258; www.takuglacier lodge.com; adult/child $210/145) Reached via a 15-minute floatplane flight up Taku Inlet, and allows you to combine flightseeing, glacier viewing and a salmon bake in one excursion. The tour lasts three hours and is a little pricey for a salmon dinner, but a much better experience and cheaper than taking a helicopter to the ice field. Sign up at the lodge's booth on Juneau's waterfront, behind Merchant's Wharf.

RESTAURANTS

Fiddlehead Restaurant (Map p135; ☎ 586-3150; 429 W Willoughby Ave; breakfast $9-13, lunch $9-12, dinner $17-24; 🕑 7am-9:30pm; ✕) Juneau's longtime favorite has excellent food, a healthy variety of vegetarian and a fresh-and-creative 'California cuisine' approach to every dish – like breakfast offering 'Sylvia's Mom's Favorite': two eggs, cheddar cheese, guacamole and sour cream over brown rice.

Wild Spice (Map p135; ☎ 523-0344; 140 Seward St; lunch $7.50, dinner $10.50; ⌚ 11am-9pm; ✗) Adventure cuisine arrived in Juneau in 2005 in the form of a Mongolian BBQ . Either fill your own plate with fresh veggies, meats, seafood and species and watch a chef cook it on an open grill or choose mains such as Mango Mojo chicken or coconut catfish from a set menu.

Twisted Fish (Map p135; ☎ 463-5033; 550 S Franklin St; dinner $15-22; ⌚ 11am-10pm; ✗) Sure you can order a burger here, but why? Located between Taku Smokeries and a wharf where commercial fishermen unload their catch, this restaurant is all about seafood. Indulge yourself by ordering wild salmon baked in puff pastry topped with crab, shrimp and cream cheese. So rich it'll have you thinking, This comes from the sea?

Di Sopra (Map p135; ☎ 586-3150; 429 W Willoughby Ave; pastas $16-25, mains $18-28; ⌚ 5:30-9:30pm; ✗) The Fiddlehead's upstairs dining room is Juneau's best upscale effort. The Italian restaurant features white-linen tablecloths, Mediterranean-mustard walls, a Chianti-colored carpet and a wine list that has been honored by *Wine Spectator* magazine. Most of the tables are along a wall of windows with a view of bustling Juneau below.

Island Pub (Map p140; ☎ 364-1595; 1102 2nd St; pizza $13-16; ⌚ 4-10pm Sun-Thu, to midnight Fri & Sat) The Capital City's newest restaurant opened up across the channel in Douglas in 2005, serving firebrick-oven focaccia and gourmet pizza to a mountainous view. Have a sweet tooth? Indulge in its apple-pie pizza.

Hangar on the Wharf (Map p135; ☎ 586-5018; 2 Marine Way, dinner $15-30; ⌚ 11am-10pm) A waterfront restaurant in Merchant's Wharf with tables perched right over a seaplane dock. The view of the channel and all the activity buzzing and floating around greatly improves whatever you ordered. Better than the food is the restaurant's large selection of imported beers and microbrews.

Doc Water's Pub (Map p135; ☎ 586-3627; Merchant's Wharf on Marine Way; sandwiches $8-10, dinner $15-30; ⌚ 10:30am-1am) If the Hangar doesn't put you close enough to the water head next door where you can grab an outside table complete with seagulls. Dinner is served until 1am, but this is a better place to linger in the late afternoon sun drinking beer and devouring the pub's Big Island burger (teriyaki sauce, pineapple salsa and Swiss cheese).

Olivia's de Mexico (Map p135; ☎ 586-6870; 222 Seward St; lunch $7-10, dinner $9-16; ⌚ 11am-9pm Mon-Fri, from 5pm Sat; ✗) A friendly family-run *cocina* since 1974 that pipes Mexican music onto the street to entice you into its brightly colored restaurant downstairs. No halibut burritos here; the food is authentic as well as tasty.

Seong's Sushi Bar & Chinese Takeout (Map p135; ☎ 586-4778; 740 W 9th St; sushi $4-6, Chinese lunch $7-9, dinner $11-13; ⌚ 10am-8pm Mon-Thu, to 9pm Fri, 4-9pm Sat; ✗) Across from the Federal Building, this little hole-in-the-wall is bright, airy and at lunchtime it's filled with government workers who know how to save a buck. The sushi menu is extensive and loved by locals.

Bullwinkle's (Map p135; ☎ 586-8988; 318 Willoughby Ave; med pizza $11-16; ⌚ 11am-11pm Mon-Thu, to midnight Fri & Sat, noon-11pm Sun) Okay, they have this strange fascination with a moose and his friend, Rocky the flying squirrel. But they're doing something right at Bullwinkle's – it's Juneau's oldest pizza parlor. No doubt it's the cheap pitchers of beer ($7.50 to $13.75).

CAFÉS

Hot Bite (Map p140; ☎ 790-2483; 11465 Auke Bay Harbor Dr; hamburgers $8-11; ⌚ 11am-7pm; ✗) You have to drive out to the Auke Bay Harbor for the best milk shakes and burgers in Juneau. The cheesecake shakes are pricey ($5.25) but worth every scoop of ice cream they put in 'em. While sitting outside feasting on a Big Bite buffalo burger you can watch the state ferry sail out of Auke Bay.

Costa's Diner (Map p135; Merchant's Wharf on Marine Way; breakfast $5-7; ⌚ 6am-noon Mon-Sat, 8am-2pm Sun; ✗) A bizarre little breakfast nook with a counter and stools inside and three tables in the hallway of the Merchant's Wharf. The food is good, the portions huge and there's no cash register. After finishing off a plate of eggs and smoked-salmon hash, you merely toss your money into a huge brass bucket on the counter and wave goodbye.

Douglas Café (Map p140; ☎ 364-3307; 916 3rd St; breakfast $6-8, hamburgers $7-10; ⌚ 11am-230pm Tue, 11am-8:30pm Wed-Fri, 9am-8:30pm Sat, to 1:30pm Sun; ✗) One of two good restaurants in Douglas worth waiting for the bus for. Serves almost 20 different types of burgers, each weighing in at a third of a pound. Can't make up your mind? Go with the local favorite, the Douglas Burger (ham, sautéed mushrooms and Swiss cheese).

Silverbow Bagel Bakery (Map p135; ☎ 586-4146; 120 2nd St; bagel sandwiches $5-8; ⏰ 7am-6pm; ✗) Downtown, this place bakes bagels daily, serving them au naturel, with a variety of spreads and toppings, or using them as bookends for breakfast and lunch sandwiches. Join the locals for the Two On Tuesday special when they double your order for free, whether it's one bagel or a dozen.

Heritage Coffee Co & Café (Map p135; ☎ 586-1087; 174 S Franklin; 6am-7pm Mon-Fri, from 7am Sat, 7am-6pm Sun; ✗) Juneau's most popular coffeehouse, for good reason. The coffee is great, the sofas comfortable and with the purchase of an espresso drink you get free Internet. The company also has several other cafés, including another one downtown at 216 2nd St.

Valentine's Coffee House (Map p135; ☎ 463-5144; 111 Seward St; sandwiches $5-7; ⏰ 7am-6pm Mon-Fri, 9am-4pm Sat & Sun; ✗) Nearby, it serves espresso drinks and fresh baked goods in the morning and makes excellent sandwiches for lunch.

QUICK EATS

Soup Queen (Map p135; Merchant's Wharf on Marine Way; soup $3.50-6; ⏰ 11:30am-4pm) You'll find hot-dog vendors all over downtown Juneau but pass them up for the Soup Queen, holding court in a small shack-on-wheels on the dock at the edge of Merchant's Wharf. Soups – like Thai fish chowder and andouille lentil – are made nightly and explode with flavor by the time the queen ladles them out the next day.

Pel'Meni (Map p135; Merchant's Wharf on Marine Way; dumplings $5; ⏰ 11:30am-1:30am Sun-Thu, to 3:30am Fri & Sat) It serves one thing and one thing only – a bowl of authentic homemade Russian dumplings, filled with either potato or sirloin. Night owls will like the hours, record buffs will be amazed by the wallful of LPs (remember those?) and a turntable, providing music while you wait for your order.

Vito 'n' Nick's (Map p140; ☎ 789-7070; 9342 Glacier Hwy; med pizza $11-17; ⏰ 11am-2pm & 4-10pm Mon-Sat) A small pizzeria just north of the airport that makes 22 different varieties of pizza, as well as calzones, lasagna, wings and hot

subs. For lunch you can buy pizza by the slice and it's like getting a quarter of a pizza on a paper plate.

GROCERIES

Rainbow Foods (Map p135; ☎ 586-6476; 224 4th St; ⏰ 9am-7pm Mon-Sat, to 6pm Sun) Practically right next door to the state capitol, a bastion of conservative politicians, is this natural food store, a haven of liberal thinkers. Only in Alaska. Along with a large selection of fresh produce and bulk goods, the store has a hot-and-cold food bar ($6.50 per pound) for lunch, espresso and a bulletin board with the latest cultural happenings.

A&P Juneau Market (Map p135; ☎ 586-3101; 615 W Willoughby Ave; ⏰ 6am-10pm) It has a good selection of local seafood, an espresso counter, salad bar ($5 per pound), deli and small seating area near the Federal Building.

Drinking

Nightlife centers on S Franklin St, a quaint (but not quiet) narrow main drag attracting locals and tourists alike.

Red Dog Saloon (Map p135; 200 Admiral Way at S Franklin St) A sign at the door says it all – Booze, Antiques, Sawdust Floor, Community Singing – and the cruise-ship passengers love it! Most don't realize, much less care, that this Red Dog is but a replica of the original, a famous Alaskan drinking hole that was across the street until 1987. Now that was a bar. The duplicate is interesting, but the fact that it has a gift shop should tell you who the clientele is during the summer.

Alaskan Hotel bar (Map p135; 167 S Franklin St) Tucked away in the back of the hotel and frequented by locals. It has historical decor, a cigar room and regular live music.

Viking (Map p135; 218 Front St) In this classic tin-ceiling building are actually three bars. At street level is a sports pub with four giant TV screens and almost 200 beers on tap, while in the back is a cozy martini lounge complete with sofas and easy chairs. Upstairs is a billiards hall with 17 tables.

Imperial Saloon (Map p135; 241 Front St) This is where the local softball teams come after the game. Inside are pool tables, darts and a dancefloor with a DJ Thursday to Saturday. Some tables open up to busy Front St, making them prime pickings for people-watchers.

Triangle Club (Map p135; 251 Front St at S Franklin St) Friendly, and is a nicer place than its nondescript exterior might suggest. One row of barstools looks onto the street through a big plate-glass window, making this a good place to chill out and people-watch. Or check your email; Seaport Cyber maintains an Internet terminal right on the bar.

Marlintini's Lounge (Map p140; 9121 Glacier Hwy) Out in the Valley in the Airport Shopping Center is Juneau's sole entry as a happening dance bar. There's DJs Thursday to Saturday, Karaoke Sunday to Wednesday and live music on only the rarest occasions.

Entertainment

THEATER

Perseverance Theater (Map p140; ☎ 364-2421; www.perseverancetheatre.org; 914 3rd St, Douglas) Founded in 1979, this is Alaska's only genuine full-time professional theater company. Sadly the theatre season begins in September and ends in May: during the summer locals are too busy playing outside to attend plays.

CINEMAS

Back Room Cinema (Map p135; ☎ 586-4146; 120 2nd St) Located in the Silverbow Inn, it screens art films and classics one to three nights a week. The seating is at tables where you can enjoy a beer, dessert or even dinner while watching the movie.

20th Century Theatre (☎ 463-3549; www.juneaumovies.com; 222 Front St) Shows two current releases (or current by Alaskan standards) a night.

Shopping

Like most cruise-ship ports, Juneau is overrun with many of the same gift shops and jewelry stores that you'll see in Ketchikan or Skagway, begging the question, 'Who comes to Alaska to shop at a Caribbean jewelers?' Avoid them like the plague.

Instead search out the shops and havens of local artists to take home something that is truly unique. One of the best downtown is the **Juneau Artists Gallery** (Map p135; ☎ 586-9891; www.juneauartistsgallery.com; Senate Bldg at 175 S Franklin St; ☉ 9am-9pm), a co-op of 26 local artists who have filled the store with paintings, etchings, glass work, jewelry, pottery and quilts. The person behind the counter ready to help you is that day's 'Artist On Duty.' Out in the Valley, near Nugget Mall, is the **Rie Munoz Gallery** (Map p140; ☎ 789-7411; 2101 Jordan Ave; ☉ 9am-5:30pm) featuring a large selection of Rie Munoz prints as well as Dale DeArmond, Byron Birdsall and several other noted Alaskan artists.

For packs, outdoorwear, USGS topo maps and anything else you need for backcountry trips stop at **Foggy Mountain Shop** (Map p135; ☎ 586-6780; www.foggymountainshop.com; 134 N Franklin St; ☉ 9:30am-6pm Mon-Fri, 10am-5:30pm Sat). This is the only outdoor shop in town with top-of-the-line equipment and the prices reflect that.

Getting There & Away

AIR

Alaska Airlines (Map p140; ☎ 800-252-7522; www.alaskaair.com) offers scheduled jet service to Seattle, all major Southeast cities, Glacier Bay, Anchorage and Cordova daily in summer.

Alaska Seaplane Service (Map p140; ☎ 789-3331, 888-350-8277; www.akseaplanes.com), at the airport, flies floatplanes from Juneau to Angoon ($90), Elfin Cove ($125), Pelican ($125) and Tenakee Springs ($90).

LAB Flying Service (Map p140; ☎ 789-9160; www.labflying.com), at the airport, has regular scheduled flights from Juneau to Gustavus ($87), Haines ($105), Hoonah ($61), Kake ($138) and Skagway ($116).

Wings of Alaska (Map p140; ☎ 789-0790; www.wingsofalaska.com; 8421 Livingston Way) flies to Angoon ($90), Gustavus ($82), Haines ($90), Hoonah ($58), Skagway ($100) and Tenakee Springs ($88).

BOAT

Alaska Marine Highway (☎ 465-3941, 800-642-0066; www.ferryalaska.com) ferries dock at Auke Bay Ferry Terminal, 14 miles from downtown. In summer, the mainline ferries traversing the Inside Passage depart daily southbound for Sitka (nine hours; $39), Petersburg ($58, eight hours) and Ketchikan ($94, 18 hours), and northbound for Haines ($33, 4½ hours) and Skagway ($44, 5 ½ hours).

Several shorter routes also operate in summer. The high-speed MV *Fairweather* makes a nonstop run to Haines and then another Skagway Thursday to Sunday. The smaller MV *Le Conte* regularly connects Juneau to the secondary ports of Hoonah ($29, four hours), Tenakee Springs ($31, eight hours) and Angoon ($33, 12 hours). Two to three times a month, the MV *Kennicott* departs Juneau for a trip to Yakutat ($81, 15½ hours) then across the Gulf of Alaska to

Valdez ($119, 32 hours) and Whittier ($194, 39 hours); reservations strongly suggested.

No state ferries run to Glacier Bay, but **Glacier Bay Express** (☎ 789-0081, 888-289-0081; www.glacierbayexpress.com) runs a catamaran to Glacier Bay's Bartlett Cove visitors center daily from Auke Bay. Round-trip fare is $159 but includes an hour of whale watching. A kayak is an additional $54.

Getting Around

Good luck.

TO/FROM THE AIRPORT & FERRY

A taxi to/from the airport costs around $20. The city bus express route runs to the airport, but only from 7:30am to 5:30pm Monday to Friday. On weekends and in the evening, if you want a bus you'll need to walk 10 minutes to the nearest 'regular route' stop on the backside of Nugget Mall. The regular route headed downtown stops here regularly from 7:15am until 10:45pm Monday to Saturday, and from 9:15am until 5:45pm Sunday. The fare on either route is adult/child $1.50/1.

Unbelievable but true: no buses or regularly scheduled shuttles go to the ferry terminal; an ungodly long 14 mile distance from downtown in Auke Bay. Some of the hotels and B&Bs offer courtesy transportation by prebooking – try to line up one of these if possible, as it will make your life much easier. You'll have to either take a cab (about $30), stick out your thumb (hitchhiking is commonplace) or take the city bus to/from the end of the line, which is almost 2 miles south of the ferry terminal at DeHart's Store in Auke Bay. One way to save a few dollars out to the ferry is to take the bus to the airport, where there are usually cabs stationed, and then catch a taxi for the rest of the way.

BUS

Juneau's sadistic public bus system, **Capital Transit** (☎ 789-6901), stops well short of the ferry terminal and a mile short of the Mendenhall Glacier Visitor Center. Even getting to/from the airport can be problematic: only the 'express' route goes right to the terminal, and it only runs during business hours on weekdays. At other times, you'll have to schlep your bags between the airport and the 'regular' route's stop at Nugget Mall, which is a 10-minute walk.

The 'regular' route buses start around 7am and stop just before midnight, running every half-hour after 8am and before 6:30pm. The main route circles downtown then heads out to the Valley and Auke Bay Boat Harbor via Mendenhall Loop Rd, where it travels close to Mendenhall Lake Campground. Routes 3 & 4 make stops in the Mendenhall Valley either from downtown or Auke Bay while a bus runs every hour from city stops to Douglas. Fares are adult/child $1.50/1 each way, and exact change is required. Major stops downtown include the Federal Building and on Main St, a block from Egan Hwy.

CAR

Juneau has many car-rental places, and renting a car is a great way for two or three people to see the sights out of the city or to reach a trailhead. For a $35 special, call **Rent-A-Wreck** (Map p140; ☎ 789-4111; 2450 Industrial Blvd), a mile from the airport, which provides pickup and drop-off service. **Evergreen Motors** (Map p140; ☎ 789-9386; www.evergreenmotors .com; 8895 Mallard St) has compacts for around $48 a day. It offers pickup and drop-off in the Valley and out to the ferry, but not downtown. You can also rent a car at the airport, but will have to stomach a 26% tax as opposed to a 15% tax elsewhere.

AROUND JUNEAU
Alaskan Brewing Company

Alaska's largest **brewery** (Map p140; ☎ 780-5866; www.alaskanbeer.com; 5429 Shaune Dr; 11am-5pm) also makes some of its best beer. Established in 1986, the brewery is in the Lemon Creek area and reached from Anka St, where the city bus will drop you off, by turning right on Shaune Dr. The tour includes viewing the small brewery, sampling lagers and ales plus an opportunity to purchase beer in the gift shop, even five-gallon party kegs ($45). The brewery's beer-bottle collection from around the world is amazing. So many beers, so little time to drink them.

Glacier Gardens Rainforest Adventure

This 50-acre **garden** (Map p140; ☎ 790-3377; 7600 Glacier Hwy; www.glaciergardens.com; adult/child $20/16; 9am-6pm), near the brewery, includes ponds, waterfalls and lots of ferns and flowers on the side of Thunder Mountain. You hop on electric carts for a guided tour of the gardens that ends at a viewing point almost 600ft up the mountain.

Mendenhall Glacier

The most famous of Juneau's ice floes, and the city's most popular attraction, is Mendenhall Glacier, Alaska's famous drive-in glacier. The river of ice is 13 miles from downtown, at the end of Glacier Spur Rd. From Egan Dr at Mile 9 turn right onto Mendenhall Loop Rd, staying on Glacier Spur Rd when the loop curves back toward Auke Bay.

The Mendenhall Glacier flows 12 miles from its source, the Juneau Ice Field, and has a 1½-mile-wide face. On a sunny day it's beautiful, with blue skies and snow-capped mountains in the background. On a cloudy and drizzly afternoon, it can be even more impressive, as the ice turns shades of deep blue.

Near the face of the glacier is the USFS **Mendenhall Glacier Visitor Center** (Map p140; ☎ 789-0097; adult/child $3/free; ☉ 8am-7:30pm), which houses various glaciology exhibits, a large relief map of the ice field, an observatory with telescopes and a theater that shows the film *Magnificent Mendenhall.*

Outside you'll find a salmon-viewing platform overlooking Steep Creek, as well as six hiking trails, ranging from a 0.3-mile photo-overlook trail to a trek of several miles up the glacier's west side (p138).

The cheapest way to see the glacier is to hop on a Capital Transit bus (p149) but that leaves you a mile short of it. It's easier to jump on a bus from either **Mendenhall Glacier Transport** (☎ 789-5460; www.mightygreatrips.com) or **Last Frontier Tours** (☎ 321-8687, 888-396-8687; www.lastfrontiertours.com). Both pick up passengers from the cruise-ship docks downtown (one way/round-trip $5/10) to the glacier. The tickets are also interchangeable so you can come and go whenever a bus is ready to leave.

GLACIER TREKKING
One of the most unusual outdoor activities in Juneau is glacier trekking: stepping into crampons, grabbing an ice axe and roping up to walk on ice 1000 years or older. The scenery and the adventure is like nothing you've experienced before as a hiker. The most affordable outing is offered by **Above & Beyond Alaska** (☎ 364-2333; www.beyondak.com).

Utilizing a trail to access Mendenhall Glacier, it avoids expensive helicopter fees on its guided six-hour outing. The cost is $150 per person and includes all mountaineering equipment, lunch and transportation.

Shrine of St Terese
At Mile 23.3 Glacier Hwy is the Shrine of St Terese, a natural stone chapel on an island connected to the shore by a stone causeway. As well as being the site of numerous weddings, the island lies along the Breadline, a well-known salmon-fishing area in Juneau. The island is perhaps the best place to fish for salmon from the shore.

Point Bridget State Park
Juneau's only state park is 2850-acre **Point Bridget State Park** (Mile 39 Glacier Hwy), which overlooks Berners Bay and Lynn Canal; salmon fishing is excellent off the Berners Bay beaches and in Cowee Creek. Hiking trails wander through rain forest, along the park's rugged shoreline and past three rental cabins (p141). The most popular hike is Point Bridget Trail, a 3½-mile, one-way walk from the trailhead on Glacier Hwy to Blue Mussel Cabin at the point, where often you can spot sea lions and seals playing the surf. Plan on six to seven hours for a round-trip with lunch at the cabin.

ADMIRALTY ISLAND
Only 15 miles southeast of Juneau is Admiralty Island National Monument, a 1493-sq-mile preserve, of which 90% is designated wilderness. The Tlingit Indians, who know Admiralty Island as Kootznoowoo, 'the Fortress of Bears,' have lived on the 96-mile-long island for more than 1000 years.

Admiralty Island has a wide variety of wildlife. Bays such as Mitchell, Hood, Whitewater and Chaik contain harbor seals, porpoises and sea lions. Seymour Canal, the island's largest inlet, has one of the highest densities of nesting eagles in the world, and humpback whales often feed in the waterway. Sitka black-tailed deer are plentiful, and the streams choke with spawning salmon during August.

But more than anything else, Admiralty Island is known for its bears. The island has one of the highest populations of bears in Alaska, with an estimated 1500 to 1700 living there, enjoying a good life roaming the drainages for sedges, roots and berries much of the year, but feasting on salmon in August before settling into dens on the upper slopes to sleep away most of the winter.

Admiralty is a rugged island, with mountains that rise to 4650ft and covered by tundra and even permanent ice fields. Numerous lakes, rivers and open areas of muskeg break up the coastal rain forest of Sitka spruce and western hemlock.

You can fly in for a stay at a USFS cabin, spend time kayaking Seymour Inlet and Mitchell Bay (p141) or arrange a bear-watching trip to Pack Creek. The most unusual adventure on the island is the Cross Admiralty Island canoe route, a 32-mile paddle that spans the center of the island from the village of Angoon to Mole Harbor. Although the majority of the route consists of calm lakes connected by streams and portages, the 10-mile paddle from Angoon to Mitchell Bay is subject to strong tides that challenge even experienced paddlers.

Most visitors arrive from Juneau where they secure supplies and obtain information from the **Admiralty Island National Monument office** (Map p140; ☎ 586-8790; www.fs.fed.us /r10/tongass/districts/admiralty; 8461 Old Dairy Rd) in Mendenhall Valley.

Angoon

☎ 907 / pop 481

The lone settlement on Admiralty Island is Angoon, a predominantly Tlingit community. Tlingit tribes occupied the site for centuries, but the original village was wiped out in 1882 when the US Navy, sailing out of Sitka, bombarded the indigenous people after they staged an uprising against a local whaling company. In 1973 Angoon won a $90,000 out-of-court settlement from the Federal government for the bombardment.

Today the economy is a mixture of commercial fishing and subsistence, and in town the strong indigenous heritage is evident in the painted fronts of the 16 tribal community houses. The old lifestyle is still apparent in this remote community, and time in Angoon can be spent observing and gaining some understanding of the Tlingit culture. Tourism seems to be tolerated only because the village is a port of call for the ferry. It's also a dry community, so you'll find no bars.

The village is perched on a strip of land between Chatham Strait on Admiralty Island's west coast and turbulent Kootznahoo Inlet, which leads into the national monument's interior. The community serves as the departure point for many kayak and canoe trips into the heart of the monument, including the 32-mile Cross Admiralty canoe.

Many people are content to just spend a few days paddling and fishing Mitchell Bay and Salt Lake. To rent a canoe or kayak in Angoon, call **Favorite Bay Inn** (☎ 788-3123, 800-423-3123), which charges $60 a day, less for a rental of six days or longer. The tides here are among the strongest in the world; the walk between the airport and the town allows you to view the turbulent waters at mid-tide. Before undertaking any paddling adventures, stop at the **USFS office** (☎ 788-3182) in Angoon's Community Services Building for information on the tides in Kootznahoo Inlet and Mitchell Bay.

SLEEPING

Favorite Bay Inn (☎ 788-3123, 800-423-3123; www .favoritebayinn.com; s/d $99/139; ✕) This is a large, rambling log home 2 miles from the ferry terminal, and it's by far the best place to stay in Angoon. Here, you can get a bed and a hearty breakfast.

GETTING THERE & AWAY

Approximately three southbound and two northbound ferries a week stop at Angoon on the run from Sitka to Juneau in summer. The one-way fare to Angoon is $33 from Juneau, $31 from Sitka. The ferry terminal is 3 miles from town.

Wings of Alaska (Angoon ☎ 788-3530; www.wings ofalaska.com) and **Alaska Seaplane Service** (☎ 888-350-8277, in Juneau 789-3331, ; www.akseaplanes.com) offer scheduled flights between Juneau and Angoon (around $90 one way).

Pack Creek

From 4000ft in the mountains, Pack Creek flows down Admiralty Island's east side before spilling into Seymour Canal. The extensive tide flats at the mouth of the creek draw a large number of bears to feed on salmon, making the spot a favorite for observing and photographing the animals.

Within this area is **Stan Price State Wildlife Sanctuary**, named for an Alaskan woodsman who lived on a float house here for almost 40 years. The sanctuary includes an area that has been closed to hunting since the mid-1930s, and due largely to the former presence of Price and his visitors, the bears here have become used to humans. The bears are most abundant in July and August, when the salmon are running.

Most visitors to Pack Creek are day-trippers who arrive and depart on floatplanes. Upon arrival, all visitors are met by a ranger who explains the rules. You must leave all food in a cache provided near the south sand spit. You may not leave the viewing sand spit to get closer to the bears, although you may use a small observation tower – reached by a mile-long trail – that overlooks the creek. No camping is allowed at Pack Creek. The only nearby camping is on the east side of Windfall Island (permit required), a half-mile away and accessible only by boat.

Pack Creek has become so popular that the area buzzes with planes and boats every morning from early July to late August. Anticipating this daily rush hour, most resident bears escape into the forest, but a few bears hang around to feed on salmon, having long since been habituated to the human visitors. Seeing five or six bears would be a good viewing day at Pack Creek. You might see big boars during the mating season from May to mid-June, otherwise it's sows and cubs the rest of the summer.

PERMITS

From June to mid-September, the USFS and Alaska Department of Fish and Game operate a permit system to limit visitors. Only 24 people are allowed per day from July to the end of August. One- to three-day permits should be reserved in advance and cost $50 per adult per day. Guiding and tour companies receive half the permits, leaving 12 for individuals who want to visit Pack Creek on their own. Note that only one tour company has permits for any given day, so if your schedule is critical, you'll need to shop around and find out who has the guide permits for the day you need to go; a complete list of guide companies is on the USFS website.

Permits are available starting March 1, and most are snapped up quickly. But four permits per day are available on a walk-in basis, up to three days in advance at the USFS **Juneau Ranger District** (☎ 586-8800; 8465 Old Dairy Rd).

GETTING THERE & AWAY

Experienced kayakers can rent a boat from in Juneau and paddle to the refuge – a two-day trip (30 to 35 miles) that uses a tram at Oliver Inlet to portage into Seymour Canal. The run down Gastineau Channel and around Douglas Island isn't bad, but the Stephens Passage crossing to reach Oliver Inlet has to be done with extreme care and a close eye on the weather. **Alaska Boat & Kayak** (☎ 789-6886; www.juneaukayak.com; single/double $45/60) will rent you a kayak and also arrange a drop-off at Oliver Inlet (see p142).

Alaska Discovery (p141) offers a one-day tour ($550 per person) that includes a flight from Juneau and then kayaking to Pack Creek for a day of watching bears before returning. A three-day, two-night trip costs $1050. **Alaska Fly 'N' Fish** (☎ 790-2120; www.alaskabyair.com; 9604 Kelly Ct, Juneau) also holds permits and offers a 5½-hour, fly-in tour ($475) or will transport you ($250 per person, minimum two) if you're lucky enough to snare a permit.

GLACIER BAY NATIONAL PARK & PRESERVE

Eleven tidewater glaciers that spill out of the mountains and fill the sea with icebergs of all shapes, sizes and shades of blue have made Glacier Bay National Park and Preserve an icy wilderness renowned worldwide.

When Captain George Vancouver sailed through the ice-choked waters of Icy Strait in 1794, Glacier Bay was little more than a dent in a mountain of ice. In 1879 John Muir made his legendary discovery of Glacier Bay and found that the end of the bay had retreated 20 miles from Icy Strait. Today, the glacier that bears his name is more than 60 miles from Icy Strait, and its rapid retreat has revealed plants and animals that continue to fascinate modern-day naturalists.

Apart from its high concentration of tidewater glaciers, Glacier Bay is the habitat for a variety of marine life, including whales. The humpbacks are by far the most impressive and acrobatic, as they heave their massive bodies in spectacular leaps (called 'breaching') from the water. Adult humpbacks often grow to 50ft and weigh up to 40 tons. Other marine life seen at Glacier Bay includes harbor seals, porpoises, killer whales and sea otters, and other wildlife includes brown and black bears, wolves, moose, mountain goats and over 200 bird species.

Glacier Bay is also where the cruise-ship industry and environmentalists have squared off. After the number of whales seen in the park dropped dramatically in 1978, the NPS reduced ship visits to 79 during the three-month season. But the cruise-ship industry lobbied the US Congress and in 1996 Alaska's Republican senators pushed through a 30% increase in vessels allowed in the bay – almost 200 cruise ships a season – based on a NPS environmental assessment. Environmentalists sued the park service, calling the assessment flawed, and in 2001 won, sending the park service back to the drawing board. The new regulations will allow 139 cruise ships into the park from June through August beginning 2006.

But the whales aren't the only area of concern here. Glacier Bay's ice, like glaciers all over Alaska, is rapidly melting. This is particularly true in Muir Inlet, or the East Arm as it's commonly called. Twenty years ago it was home to three active tidewater glaciers, but now there is only one, McBride. Only two glaciers in the park are advancing; Johns Hopkins and Lamplugh. The rest are receding and thinning.

Still, Glacier Bay is the crowning jewel in the itinerary of most cruise ships and the dreamy destination for anybody who has ever paddled a kayak. The park is an expensive sidetrip, even by Alaskan standards. Plan on spending at least $400 for a trip from Juneau, but remember that the cost per day drops quickly after you've arrived. Of the more than 300,000 annual visitors, over 90% arrive aboard a ship and never leave the boat. The rest are a mixture of tour-group members who head straight for the lodge and backpackers who wander toward the free campground.

Orientation & Information

'Civilization' around the park is focused in two areas. **Bartlett Cove** is the park headquarters and the site of visitors centers, hiking trails and Glacier Bay Lodge. This is where the ferry from Juneau ties up, paddlers rent kayaks and visitors hop on the tour boat for a cruise to the glaciers 40 miles up the bay.

About 9 miles away is the small settlement of **Gustavus** (gus-*tay*-vus), an interesting backcountry community. The town's 400 citizens include a mix of professional people – doctors, lawyers, former government workers and artists – who decided to drop out of the rat race and live on their own in the middle of the woods. Electricity only arrived in the early 1980s and in some homes you still must pump the water at the sink or build a fire before you can have a hot shower. Gustavus has no downtown. It's little more than an airstrip left over from WWII and a road to Bartlett Cove, known to most locals as 'the Road.' Along the Road there is little to see, as most cabins and homes are tucked away behind a shield of trees.

The best source of information is from the NPS in Bartlett Cove. Campers, kayakers and boaters can stop at the the the park's **Visitor Information Station** (☎ 697-2627; 🕑 7am-9pm) at the foot of the public dock for backcountry permits, logistical information and a 20-minute orientation video. The **Glacier Bay Visitor Center** (☎ 697-2661; www.nps.gov/glba; 🕑 noon-8:45pm) is on the second floor of Glacier Bay Lodge and has exhibits, a bookshop and an information deck.

Sights & Activities
GLACIERS

The glaciers are 40 miles up the bay from Bartlett Cove. If you're not on a cruise ship or don't want to spend a week or two kayaking, the only way to see them is onboard the *Baranof Wind* operated by **Glacier Bay Lodge & Tours** (☎ 264-4600, 800-229-8687; www .visitglacierbay.com). The high-speed catamaran departs at 7:30am for an eight-hour tour into the West Arm and returns by 4pm, when a waiting bus will whisk you away in time to catch the Alaska Airlines flight back to Juneau. The tour costs adult/child $159/80 and includes lunch and narration by an onboard park naturalist.

The *Baranof Wind* also drops off and picks up campers and kayakers, which is by far the best way to experience the park.

HIKING

Glacier Bay has few trails, and in the backcountry, foot travel is done along riverbanks, on ridges or across ice remnants of glaciers. The only developed trails are in Bartlett Cove.

The mile-long **Forest Trail** is a nature walk that begins and ends near the Bartlett Cove dock and winds through the pond-studded spruce and hemlock forest near the campground. Rangers lead walks on this trail daily in summer; inquire at the Glacier Bay Visitor Center.

Bartlett River Trail, a 1½-mile trail, begins just up the road to Gustavus, where there is a posted trailhead, and ends at the Bartlett River estuary. Along the way, it meanders along a tidal lagoon and passes through a few wet spots. Plan on two to four hours for the 3-mile round-trip.

The **Point Gustavus Beach Walk**, along the shoreline south of Bartlett Cove to Point Gustavus and Gustavus, provides the only overnight trek from the park headquarters. The total distance is 12 miles, and the walk to Point Gustavus, an excellent spot to camp, is 6 miles. Plan on hiking the stretch from Point Gustavus to Gustavus at low tide, which will allow you to ford the Salmon River, as opposed to swimming across it. Point Gustavus is an excellent place to sight orcas in Icy Strait.

PADDLING

Glacier Bay offers an excellent opportunity for people who have some experience on the water but not a lot as kayakers. By using the tour boat, you can skip the long and open paddle up the bay and enjoy only the well-protected arms and inlets where the glaciers are located. Transportation is on the high-speed catamaran, *Baranof Wind,* which departs at 7:30am daily and will put you ashore at one of several spots up the bay, where the landing sites are changed periodically. The most dramatic glaciers are in the West Arm, but the upper areas of the arm are often closed to campers and kayakers due to seal-pupping and brown bear activity. For more detailed information on kayaking the bay, see p81.

Paddlers who want to avoid the tour-boat fares but still long for a kayak adventure should try the Beardslee Islands. While there are no glaciers to view, the islands (a day's paddle from Bartlett Cove) offer calm water, protected channels and pleasant beach camping. Wildlife includes black bears, seals and bald eagles, and the tidal pools burst with activity at low tide. The islands make for an easy three-day paddle, including getting there and back, and a day paddling around the islands.

Both **Glacier Bay Sea Kayaks** (☎ 697-2257; www.glacierbayseakayaks.com; per day single/double $40/50, 3 days or longer $35/40) and **Sea Otter Kayak** (☎ 697-3007; www.he.net/~seaotter; single/double per day $40/50) rent kayaks.

Alaska Discovery (p141) leads single-day trips around the Beardslee Islands that begin and end at Bartlett Cove. The company supplies kayaks and all equipment; you supply $135. It also has a five-day adventure that includes the first night in a lodge, transportation up the bay and three days of camping and kayaking among the glaciers. The cost is $1895 per person.

Spirit Walker Expeditions (☎ 697-2266, 800-529-2537; www.seakayakalaska.com) has paddling trips to nearby Pleasant Island for half-/two days $75/$487.

WHALE WATCHING

Cross Sound Express (☎ 697-2726, 888-698-2726; www.visitglacierbay.com) operates the 47ft MV *Taz* that carries up to 23 passengers and departs the Gustavus dock daily during the summer at 8:30am and 1pm for a 3½-hour whale-watching tour. The cost is $85 per person.

Tours

You can see Glacier Bay in a hurry, though you have to ask yourself if that is a wise use of your travel funds. For a quicky flightseeing tour Haines is the closest community and thus offers cheaper flights (see p159).

Alaska Discovery (Map p141; www.akdiscovery.com) Has a two-day package (s/d $195/295) that includes a night at its lodge in Gustavus and a day of kayaking to the Beardslee Islands. But there's no glaciers and you still have to pay for transportation to Gustavus.

Glacier Bay Lodge & Tours (☎ 264-4600, 888-229-8687; www. visitglacierbay.com) offers an eight-hour tour ($199) that includes the transfer from Gustavus Airport and a trip on the *Baranof Wind;* you have to get to Gustavus from Juneau. Turn it into a two-day trip with a night at its lodge in Bartlett Cove and it's a $299 sidetrip.

Sleeping & Eating

Most of the accommodations are in Gustavus, which adds a 4% bed tax to lodging.

BARTLETT COVE

NPS campground (0.25 miles south of Glacier Bay Lodge) This is set in a lush forest just off the shoreline, and camping is free. There's no need for reservations, there always seems to be space for another tent. It provides a bear cache, eating shelter and pleasant surroundings. Coin-operated showers are available in the park, but there aren't any places selling groceries or camping supplies.

Glacier Bay Lodge (☎ 697-2225, 888-229-8687; www.visitglacierbay.com; 199 Bartlett Cove Rd; r $180-205; ✗) This is the only hotel and restaurant in Bartlett Cove. The lodge has 55 rooms, a crackling fire in a huge stone fireplace and a dining room that usually hums in the evening with an interesting mixture of park employees, backpackers and locals from Gustavus. Nightly slide presentations, ranger talks and movies held upstairs cover the park's natural history.

GUSTAVUS

Gustavus Inn (☎ 697-2254, 800-649-5220; www.gustavusinn.com; 1 Mile Gustavus Rd; d per person $165; ✗) This wonderful place is a charming family homestead lodge mentioned in every travel book and brochure on Alaska, with good reason. It's thoroughly modern and comfortable, but without being sterile, ostentatious or losing its folksy touch. The inn is well known for its gourmet dinners, which feature homegrown vegetables (the big backyard garden is a work of horticultural art) and fresh local seafood served family style. Guests have free use of bicycles, and courtesy transportation to/from Bartlett Cove and the airport is cheerfully provided.

Blue Heron B&B (☎ 697-2293; www.blueheronbnb.net; Dock Rd; s/d/cottages $105/130/160) Another comfortable option, offering two regular rooms and two cottages with kitchenettes. All are modern, bright and clean, and each has a TV/VCR and private bath. The friendly B&B sits on a beautiful 10-acre spread near the Salmon River. Outside there are picnic tables, BBQ and a huge garden filled with oversized cabbages and other vegetables, fragrant herbs, and flowers. Inside every morning begins with a gourmet breakfast in a sunroom. Bikes are available.

Good River B&B (☎ 697-224; fax 697-2269; www.goodriver.com; s/d/cabins $80/95/85) A beautiful, three-story log home with four guestrooms, shared bath and free bicycles. Tucked away in the woods is the Honeymoon Cabin, no running water and an outhouse. Now that's a honeymoon only an Alaskan could love.

Bear's Nest Café & Cabin Rentals (☎ 697-2440; 2 White Dr; r $125, cabins $99-125; ☺ 11am-8pm; ✗)

Located north of Gustavus Rd off Wilson/Rink Creek Rd, this place offers good food and lodging in the form of two cabins and a room above the café. The cabins come with a basket of food so you can whip up sourdough pancakes, fruit and freshly brewed coffee for breakfast. The restaurant features organic produce and local seafood with vegetarian offerings always available.

Beartrack Mercantile (☎ 697-2358; Dock Rd; ☺ 9am-7pm Mon-Sat, 10:30am-6pm Sun) It's a quarter-mile south of Gustavus Rd on the way to the dock. It makes good deli sandwiches and has a range of expensive groceries – it's best to purchase supplies in Juneau, before you arrive.

Getting There & Away
AIR

Alaska Airlines (☎ 800-252-7522; www.alaaskaair.com) offers the cheapest fares, departing from Juneau daily for the 25-minute trip to Gustavus for a round-trip of $150 to $165. Smaller **Wings of Alaska** (Juneau ☎ 789-0790, Gustavus ☎ 697-2201; www.wingsofalaska.com) offers scheduled flights for one way/round-trip $82/164. Charter services include **Air Excursions** (☎ 697-2375; www.airexcursions.com) and **Fjord Flying Service** (☎ 697-2377; www.fjordflyingservice.com).

BOAT

Glacier Bay Express (☎ 789-0081, 888-289-0081; www.glacierbayexpress.com) operates a catamaran ferry that departs Auke Bay Harbor in Juneau at 11am daily except Wednesday, reaches Bartlett Cove at 3pm and departs at 5pm for the return trip. On the way over, you enjoy an hour of whale watching. The round-trip fare is adult/child $149/99. Bringing a kayak over is an additional $27 each way.

Getting Around

If you arrive at the Gustavus airport, you're still 9 miles from Bartlett Cove. The Glacier Bay Lodge bus meets all Alaska Airline flights and charges $12 for the ride. So does **TLC Taxi** (☎ 697-2239).

HAINES
☎ 907 / pop 2245

Heading north of Juneau on the state ferry takes you up Lynn Canal, North America's longest and deepest fjord. Along the way, Eldred Rock Lighthouse stands as a picturesque sentinel, waterfalls pour down off the Chilkoot Range to the east, and the Davidson and Rainbow Glaciers draw 'oohs' and 'aahs' as they snake down out of the jagged Chilkat Mountains to the west. You end up in Haines, a scenic departure point for Southeast Alaska and a crucial link to the Alaska Hwy. Every summer thousands of travelers, particularly RVers, pass through this slice in the mountains on their way to Canada's Yukon Territory and Interior Alaska.

Haines is 75 miles north of Juneau on a wooded peninsula between the Chilkat and Chilkoot Inlets. Originally a stronghold of the wealthy Chilkat Tlingit Indians, it was a gun-toting entrepreneur named Jack Dalton who put Haines on the map. In 1897 Dalton turned an old Indian trade route into a toll road for miners seeking an easier way to reach the Klondike. The Dalton Trail quickly became such a heavily used pack route to mining districts north of Whitehorse that the army arrived in 1903 and established Fort William H Seward, Alaska's first permanent post. For the next 20 years it was Alaska's only army post and then was used as a rest camp during WWII.

WWII led to the construction of the Haines Hwy, the 159-mile link between the Southeast and the Alcan. Built in 1942 as a possible evacuation route in case of a Japanese invasion, the route followed the Dalton Trail and was so rugged it would be 20 years before US and Canadian crews even attempted to keep it open in winter. By the 1980s, the 'Haines Cut-off Rd' had become the paved Haines Hwy and now more than 50,000 travelers in cars and RVs follow it annually.

After logging fell on hard times in the 1970s, Haines swung its economy towards tourism and it's still surviving. And it should. Haines has spectacular scenery, quick access to the rivers and mountains where people like to play and is comparatively dry (only 53in of rain annually). All of this prompted *Outside* magazine to plaster a photo of Haines on its cover in 2004 and call it one of the country's '20 best places to live and play.'

You'll immediately notice that this town is different from what you've experienced elsewhere in Southeast. Maybe it's the relative lack of cruise-ship traffic, which gives

Haines a tangible sense of peace and tranquility. As a port Haines receives less than 40,000 cruise-ship passengers in a season – it is lucky to reach the number that Juneau sees in a good weekend. Or maybe it's the fact that there isn't a restaurant, gift shop or tour operator along Main Street that is owned by a corporate conglomerate. Haines' businesses are uniquely Haines and most likely the person behind the counter is one who owns the store. The town isn't especially well developed for tourism: you won't find a salmon bake here and, no doubt for many travelers, that's part of its charm.

Orientation & Information

Most of the sights and businesses are spread between downtown Haines – Main St – and Fort Seward, all within easy walking distances of each other.

BOOKSTORES
Babbling Book (☎ 766-3356; 223 Main St; ⌚ 10:30am-5:30pm Mon-Sat, noon-5pm Sun) Stocks a great selection of Alaska books, cards and calendars while its walls serve as the notice board for Haines' cultural scene.

EMERGENCY & MEDICAL SERVICES
Haines Medical Clinic (☎ 766-2521; 131 1st Ave S) For whatever ails you.
Ambulance, Fire, Police (☎ 911)

LAUNDRY
Haines Quick Laundry (☎ 766-2330; Mile 0 Haines Hwy; ⌚ 7am-9pm) At the foot of Mud Bay Rd, behind the Quick Mart. Showers are 25¢ a minute. Wash fast.

MONEY
First National Bank of Anchorage (☎ 766-6100; 123 Main St) For all your presidential-portrait needs.

LIBRARY & INTERNET ACCESS
Haines Borough Public Library (☎ 766-2545; 111 S 3rd Ave; ⌚ 10am-9pm Mon-Tue, from noon Wed & Thu, 10am-6:30pm Fri, 12:30-4:30pm Sat & Sun) Opened in 2003 and is the jewel of the community. The impressive facility has used books for sale, seven computers for Internet access (donation), a beautiful reading area with rocking chairs and a two-story window overlooking the mountains. Curl up and read to the majestic view.

POST
Post office (near cnr Haines Hwy & Mud Bay Rd) Close to Fort Seward.

TOURIST INFORMATION

Alaska Division of Parks (☎ 766-2292; Ste 25, 219 Main St; ☻ 8am-5pm Mon-Fri) For information on state parks and hiking.

Haines Convention & Visitors Bureau (☎ 766-2234, 800-458-3579; www.haines.ak.us; 122 2nd Ave; ☻ 8am-7pm Mon-Fri, 9am-6pm Sat & Sun) Has rest rooms and racks of free information for tourists. There is also a lot of information on Canada's Yukon for those heading up the Alcan.

Sights

Sheldon Museum (☎ 766-2366; 11 Main St; adult/child $3/free; ☻ 10am-5pm Mon-Fri, from 2pm Sat & Sun) This houses a collection of indigenous artifacts upstairs with an interesting display on Chilkat blankets. Downstairs is devoted

to Haines' pioneer and gold-rush days and includes the sawn-off shotgun that Jack Dalton used to convince travelers to pay his toll.

American Bald Eagle Foundation (☎ 766-3094; www.baldeagles.org; adult/child $3/1; ☻ 10am-6pm) A impressive wildlife diorama is featured here, displaying more than 180 specimens and almost two dozen eagles. A highlight is the live video feed from a remote camera trained on an active eagle's nest.

Fort Seward, reached by heading uphill (east) at the Front St–Haines Hwy junction, was Alaska's first permanent army post. Built in 1903 and decommissioned after WWII, the fort is now a national historical site with an increasing number of

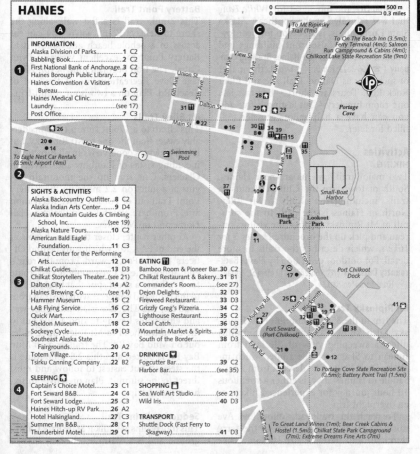

HAINES

0 — 500 m
0 — 0.3 miles

INFORMATION
Alaska Division of Parks	**1** C2
Babbling Book	**2** C2
First National Bank of Anchorage	**3** C2
Haines Borough Public Library	**4** C2
Haines Convention & Visitors Bureau	**5** C2
Haines Medical Clinic	**6** C2
Laundry	(see 17)
Post Office	**7** C3

SIGHTS & ACTIVITIES
Alaska Backcountry Outfitter	**8** C2
Alaska Indian Arts Center	**9** D4
Alaska Mountain Guides & Climbing School, Inc.	(see 19)
Alaska Nature Tours	**10** C2
American Bald Eagle Foundation	**11** C3
Chilkat Center for the Performing Arts	**12** D4
Chilkat Guides	**13** D3
Chilkat Storytellers Theater	(see 21)
Dalton City	**14** A2
Haines Brewing Co	(see 14)
Hammer Museum	**15** C2
LAB Flying Service	**16** C2
Quick Mart	**17** C2
Sheldon Museum	**18** C2
Sockeye Cycle	**19** C2
Southeast Alaska State Fairgrounds	**20** A2
Totem Village	**21** C4
Tsirku Canning Company	**22** A2

SLEEPING
Captain's Choice Motel	**23** C1
Fort Seward B&B	**24** C4
Fort Seward Lodge	**25** C1
Haines Hitch-up RV Park	**26** A2
Hotel Halsingland	**27** C4
Summer Inn B&B	**28** C1
Thunderbird Motel	**29** C1

EATING
Bamboo Room & Pioneer Bar	**30** C2
Chilkat Restaurant & Bakery	**31** B1
Commander's Room	(see 27)
Dejon Delights	**32** D3
Fireweed Restaurant	**33** D3
Grizzly Greg's Pizzeria	**34** C2
Lighthouse Restaurant	**35** C2
Local Catch	**36** D3
Mountain Market & Spirits	**37** C2
South of the Border	**38** D3

DRINKING
Fogcutter Bar	**39** C2
Harbor Bar	(see 35)

SHOPPING
Sea Wolf Art Studio	(see 21)
Wild Iris	**40** D3

TRANSPORT
Shuttle Dock (Fast Ferry to Skagway)	**41** D3

SOUTHEAST ALASKA

restaurants, lodges and art galleries utilizing the original buildings. A walking-tour map of the fort is available at the visitors center, or you can just read the historical panels that have been erected there. Within the parade ground is **Totem Village**. Although not part of the original fort, it includes two tribal houses and totem poles and is the home of the **Chilkat Storytellers Theater Show** (☎ 766-2540; adult/child $10/5; ☉ 4:30pm Mon-Fri), an hourlong performance of Alaska Native dramatization.

Alaska Indian Arts Center (☎ 766-2160; www .alaskaindianarts.com; ☉ 9am-5pm Mon-Fri) More indigenous culture can be seen in Fort Seward at this location, in the former post hospital, where indigenous artists carve totems or weave Chilkat blankets.

Dalton City, the movie set for *White Fang* that was relocated at the Southeast Alaska State Fairgrounds, is a beacon for beer lovers. Among the false-front buildings and wooden sidewalks is the **Haines Brewing Company** (☎ 766-3823; Fair Dr; ☉ 1-7pm), the maker of such beer as Dalton Trail Ale and Elder Rock Red. Tours are short – hey this is a one-room brewery – but tasting is free and you can have a half-gallon growler ($8) filled for later.

Activities
HIKING

Two major trail systems are near Haines. South of town are the Chilkat Peninsula trails, including the climb to Mt Riley. North of Haines is the path to the summit of Mt Ripinsky. Stop at the visitors bureau and pick up the brochure *Haines is for Hikers*, which describes the trails in more detail. For outdoor gear, stop by **Alaska Backcountry Outfitter** (☎ 766-2876; 210 Main St, upstairs; ☉ 10am-5pm Mon-Sat).

Mt Ripinsky Trail

The trip to the 3563ft summit of Mt Ripinsky (also known as the South Summit) offers a sweeping view of the land from Juneau to Skagway. The route, which includes Peak 3920 and a descent from 7 Mile Saddle to Haines Hwy, is either a strenuous 10-hour journey for experienced hikers or an overnight trip.

To reach the trailhead, follow 2nd Ave north to Lutak Rd (the road to the ferry terminal) and past the fire station. Leave Lutak Rd when it curves right and head up the hill on Young St. Turn right along an old, buried pipeline and follow it for a mile to the start of the trail, just as the pipeline heads downhill to the tank farm.

The North Summit has a benchmark and a high wooden surveyor's platform. You can camp in the alpine area between the two peaks and then continue the next day by descending the North Summit and hiking west along the ridge to Peak 3920. From here you can descend to 7 Mile Saddle and then to the Haines Hwy, putting you 7 miles northwest of town. This is a 10-mile loop and a challenging overnight hike; the trail is steep in places and easily lost. The views, however, are spectacular.

Battery Point Trail

This 2-mile trail is a flat walk along the shore to Kelgaya Point, where you can cut across to a pebble beach and follow it to Battery Point for excellent views of Lynn Canal. The trail begins a mile beyond Portage Cove Recreation Site at the end of Beach Rd. Plan on a two-hour round-trip.

Mt Riley Trails

This climb to a 1760ft summit is considerably easier than the one to Mt Ripinsky, but it still provides good views in all directions, including vistas of Rainbow and Davidson Glaciers. One trail up the mountain begins at a junction 2.2 miles up the Battery Point Trail out of Portage Cove Recreation Site. From here, you hike 3 miles over Half Dome and up Mt Riley.

Another route, closer to town, begins at the end of FAA Rd, which runs behind Officers' Row in Fort Seward. From the road's end, follow the water-supply access route for 2 miles to a short spur that branches off to the right and connects with the trail from Mud Bay Rd. The hike is 3.9 miles one way and eliminates having to find a ride out to the third trailhead to Mt Riley, three miles out on Mud Bay Rd. The trailhead off Mud Bay Rd is posted and this 2.8-mile route is the steepest but easiest to follow and most direct to the summit. Plan on a five- to six-hour round-trip.

Seduction Point Trail

This trail begins at Chilkat State Park Campground and is a 6½-mile, one-way hike to the point separating Chilkoot and Chilkat Inlets. The trail swings between forest and beaches, and provides excellent views of Davidson Glacier.

If you have the equipment, this trail can be turned into an excellent overnight hike by setting up camp at the cove east of Seduction Point. Carry in water and check the tides before departing, as the final stretch along the beach after David's Cove should be walked at low- or midtide. The entire round-trip takes nine to 10 hours.

RIVER RUNNING

Haines is also a departure point for numerous raft trips. **Chilkat Guides** (☎ 766-2491; adult/child $79/62; www.raftalaska.com) offers a four-hour float down the Chilkat River through the bald-eagle preserve, with opportunities to view eagles and possibly brown bears; there is little or no white water. The company runs the trip twice daily, beginning from its shop on Beach Rd by the Port Chilkoot dock.

On a much grander scale of adventure is the exciting nine- to 10-day raft trip down the Tatshenshini/Alsek River system, from Yukon Territory to the coast of Glacier Bay. This river trip is unmatched for its scenic mix of rugged mountain ranges and dozens of glaciers. Chilkat Guides and **Alaska Discovery** (☎ 780-6226, 800-586-1911; www.akdiscovery .com) both run the trip, which costs between $2500 and $2900 per person.

CYCLING

You can discover some great road trips or what little single-track mountain biking there is in Haines by visiting **Sockeye Cycle** (☎ 766-2869; www.cyclealaska.com; 24 Portage St; ⏱ 10am-6pm Tue-Fri, to 4pm Sat), which rents a variety of top-of-the-line bicycles (per two/four/eight hours $12/20/38). The most popular road trip is the scenic 22-mile ride out to Chilkoot Lake. The shop also offers bike tours, with its best being an eight-hour ride on dirt roads through the alpine of the newly created Tatshenshini/Alsek Provincial Park. The cost is $120 per person and includes mountain bikes, guide, transport and lunch.

Quirky Haines

Hammer Museum (☎ 766-2374; 108 Main St; adult/child $3/free; ⏱ 10am-5pm Mon-Fri) This is a monument to Dave Pahl's obsession with hammers. He's got a zillion of them, well actually 1400 on display and another 300 waiting to be displayed. In Pahl's museum you learn world history through the development of the hammer, from one less than ¼oz to another weighing more than 40lb. The national press this place has generated is amazing.

Great Land Wines (☎ 766-2698; www.great landwines.com; 1817 Small Tract Rd; ⏱ 1-5pm) They can't grow grapes in Alaska but that doesn't mean they can't make wine. Maybe Haines isn't quite Napa Valley but you can still stop at this winery's tasting room, and sip and purchase wines made from rhubarb, strawberries, blueberries, fireweed flower or anything else they find growing outside. The most unusual is its onion wine that has a definite hint of, well, onions.

Tsirku Canning Company (☎ 766-3474; Main St at 5th Ave; www.cannerytour.com; tour adult/child $10/free; ⏱ Mon-Sat) If historic salmon canning is your passion, you're in luck. This cannery has the only three-piece can-reform line left in existence. You can watch the antique equipment clank along during the hourlong tour, shaping flat metal into cans and then filling them with salmon. Afterwards you can visit the gift shop and purchase a 'Friends Don't Let Friends Eat Farmed Fish' bumper sticker.

Tours

Other than Gustavus, Haines is the closest community to Glacier Bay National Park, making flightseeing tours much more reasonable than Skagway or Juneau.

Alaska Nature Tours (☎ 766-2876; www.kcd.com /aknature; 130 2nd Ave S) Offers excellent environmentally focused tours with knowledgeable guides for activities that range from birding and bear-watching to easy hikes to Battery Point. Its Twilight Wildlife Watch is a 2½-hour tour (adult/child $50/35) that departs at 6:15pm and heads up the Chilkoot River, stopping along the way to look for eagles, mountain goats and brown bears who emerge at dusk to feed on spawning salmon.

Alaska Mountain Guides & Climbing School, Inc (☎ 766-3366, 800-766-3396; www.alaskamountain guides.com; Portage St) Behind Sockeye Cycle, can get you out into the awesome local wilds for some fine adventure – be it sea kayaking, white-water rafting, alpine hiking, mountaineering, rock and ice climbing, or glacier skiing. Classes and trips are offered for all levels of ability.

Mountain Flying Service (☎ 766-3007, 800-954-8747; www.flyglacierbay.com) Offers an hourlong tour of the Glacier Bay's East Arm for $129 per person and an 80-minute tour of the more dramatic West Arm for $169. On a clear day, it's money well spent.

Festivals & Events

Great Alaska Craft Beer & Home Brew Festival
Haines stages this festival (third week of May) when most of the state's microbrews compete for the honors of being named top suds.

Fourth of July Like every other Alaskan town, Haines has a celebration.

Southeast Alaska State Fair Haines' biggest festival is in mid-August. Includes parades, dances, livestock shows and exhibits, and the famous pig races that draw participants from all Southeast communities.

Bald Eagle Music Festival (☎ 766-3094; www .baldeaglefestival.org)Coincides with the state fair in mid-August; brings together more than 50 musicians for five days of blues and bluegrass music.

Alaska Bald Eagle Festival Mid-November. See the boxed text, opposite.

Sleeping

Haines tacks 9.5% tax onto the price of lodging.

BUDGET

Bear Creek Cabins & Hostel (☎ 766-2259; www .bearcreekcabinsalaska.com; 1.5 Small Tract Rd; 2-person site/dm/d cabins $14/18/48) A 20-minute walk outside town – follow Mud Bay Rd near Fort Seward and when it veers right, continue straight onto Small Tract Rd for 1½ miles – this hostel has no lockout or curfew. A number of cabins surround a well-kept, grassy common area. Two of the cabins are used as the hostel dorms. A rest-room/shower building also has laundry facilities and there is a common kitchen area.

Salmon Run Campground & Cabins (☎ 766-3240; www.salmonrunadventures.com; 6.5 Mile Lutak Rd; cabins $45-65) Situated near the campground are two small cabins that come with heating and bunks but no indoor plumbing or kitchen facilities.

Camping

Portage Cove State Recreation Site (Beach Rd; sites $5) Half a mile southeast of Fort Seward or a 2-mile walk from downtown, this scenic campground overlooks the water and has nine sites that are for backpackers and cyclists only. Follow Front St south; it becomes Beach Rd near Fort Seward.

Chilkoot Lake State Recreation Site (Lutak Rd; sites $10) Five miles north of the ferry terminal. The campground has 32 sites and picnic shelters. The fishing for Dolly Varden is good on Chilkoot Lake, a turquoise blue body of water surrounded by mountains.

Chilkat State Park Campground (Mud Bay Rd; sites $10) Found 7 miles southeast of Haines toward the end of Chilkat Peninsula; this campground has good views of Davidson and Rainbow Glaciers spilling out of the mountains into the Lynn canal. There are 15 woodsy campsites and a beach to explore at low tide.

Haines Hitch-up RV Park (☎ 766-2882; www .hitchuprv.com; 851 Main St; RV sites $26-34; 🖳) A plain but beautifully tended park open to RVs only, no tents. It has 92 sites with hookups, some with cable TV, as well as laundry and shower facilities.

MIDRANGE

Fort Seward Bed & Breakfast (☎ 766-2856, 800-615-6676; www.fortsewardbnb.com; r $85-135; ✗) This occupies the restored former home of the army's surgeon; the three-story Victorian house has seven guestrooms, five with shared bath, two with private bath. A wide porch overlooks the parade grounds and Lynn Canal beyond. If the view alone isn't worth the room rate then innkeeper Norm Smith's wonderful sourdough pancakes are. Guests also enjoy free use of bikes.

On the Beach Inn (☎ 907-766-2131, 800-766-3992; www.onthebeachinn.com; 6.5 Mile Lutak Rd; r $75-125, cabins $65; ✗) Near the ferry terminal, this B&B has a great view of Lynn Canal and a long porch to sit and soak up the scenery. Accommodations range from two rooms with shared bath and two suites with private bath to two small cabins. For the caffeine-addicted, there's an espresso drive-thru right in front of the inn.

Hotel Halsingland (☎ 766-2000, 800-542-6363; www.hotelhalsingland.com; 13 Fort Seward Dr; r $69-109; ✗) Housed in the bachelor officers' quarters and overlooking the fort's parade ground is this hotel that is gradually getting renovated. Some rooms still have fireplaces and classic claw-foot bathtubs; many now have new carpeting and beds. Four economy rooms, with shared bath, are $69 a night.

Summer Inn B&B (☎ 766-2970; www.summerinn bnb.com; 117 2nd Ave; s/d $70/80; ✗) This has five bedrooms with shared bath in the heart of town, along with an enclosed porch where you can watch life in Haines come and go. Rates include a full breakfast.

ALASKA BALD EAGLE FESTIVAL

Why would anybody want to travel to Haines in mid-November when it is drizzly, cold and generally gloomy? To see bald eagles by the thousands. The annual gathering of 4000 eagles in only three sq miles along the Chilkat River (see p163) is the basis for the Alaska Bald Eagle Festival.

The five-day event attracts hundreds of visitors from around the country to Haines in the second week of November for speakers and presentations at the Sheldon Museum and the American Bald Eagle Foundation Center. Entertainment takes place at the Chilkat Center for the Arts, there are photo workshops and the release of an injured eagle that has been rehabilitated.

But the basis of the festival is trooping out to the Chilkat River and (in the rain, snow and sleet) encountering eagles like you cannot anywhere else in the country at anytime of the year. Twenty or 30 whiteheads perched in a single tree is standard. The festival organizes 'expedition buses' with noted naturalists on board who provide a fully narrated journey to the sightings 21 miles north of Haines.

The timing of the festival is ideal. Not only is it during the peak migration period of the eagles but it immediately follows Sitka's **Whalefest!** (☎ 747-7964; www.sitkawhalefest.org), held in the first week of November. For wildlife enthusiasts, it's the ultimate Alaskan vacation; two weeks of watching eagles and whales in a cold drizzle. Just don't forget the long underwear.

SOUTHEAST ALASKA

Fort Seward Lodge (☎ 800-478-7772; www.ftsewardlodge.com; 39 Mud Bay Rd; s/d $70/80, without bath $50/60; ✗) Features a large restaurant, cocktail lounge and 10 rooms, plain but some of the most affordable you'll find in Haines.

Thunderbird Motel (☎ 766-2131, 800-327-2556; www.thunderbird-motel.com; 216 Dalton St; s/d $70/80) Somehow a TV, microwave and refrigerator are squeezed into tiny rooms. What, no dishwasher!

TOP END

Captain's Choice Motel (☎ 766-3111, 800-478-2345; www.capchoice.com; 108 2nd Ave N; s/d $107/117; ✗ 🖳) The captain chose well. This is by far the town's nicest lodging. The motel's big flower-ringed sundeck overlooking Lynn Canal is a great place to whittle away the day watching boats and whales plying the waters. Courtesy transportation to the ferries is available.

Eating

RESTAURANTS

Fireweed Restaurant (☎ 766-3838; 37 Blacksmith St; sandwiches $8-13, pastas $13-19, pizza $10-20; ✦ 11am-10pm; ✗) This clean, bright and laid-back bistro bills its fare as 'fine organic world cuisine,' though someone also once summed it up as 'an oasis in a sea of grease.' There's grilled halibut burgers, hero sandwiches and baked veggie *ziti*, but the clear favorites are organic salads and pizza made with a sourdough-herb crust. Don't be in a hurry; you'll most likely have to wait for a table

and then your order. Just signal the bartender for a local beer, served in an icy mug, and relax to the view of Lynn Canal.

Commander's Room (☎ 766-2000; 13 Fort Seward Dr; dinner $19-28; ✦ 5:30-9pm; ✗) Located in Hotel Halsingland in Fort Seward is Haines' most upscale restaurant. There's white tablecloths, a fine wine list and a chef who has a herb garden out back. Begin the evening with a drink in its cozy Officer's Club Lounge. Tired of seafood? Try the butternut-squash ravioli served with hazelnut brown butter and sage sauce.

Lighthouse Restaurant (☎ 766-2442; 2 Front St; lunch $9-12, dinner $17-23; ✦ 11am-9pm; ✗) Major renovation in 2005 included bay windows to highlight the restaurant's best asset, a table overlooking a bustling boat harbor. The seafood-laden menu has also been upgraded with mains such as buttery, rich ginger sable fish with a coconut-wasabi sauce and blackened sockeye salmon that was netted by the local fleet in Lynn Canal.

South of the Border (☎ 766-2840; 31 Tower Rd; dinner $10-17; ✦ 5-10pm Wed-Sat; ✗) A small Mexican restaurant that serves decent tamales, chile relleno and, of course, a Nacho Supreme. If only they had a license to serve beer.

CAFÉS

Chilkat Restaurant & Bakery (Dalton St at 5th Ave; breakfast $5-8, sandwiches $6-8; ✦ 7am-3pm Mon-Sat; ✗) A popular local place that has been baking goodies and serving breakfast for 25 years. For a nice break from eggs and toast, try the homemade granola with blueberries and peaches…but first you have to get past that display case filled with the daily offering of doughnuts, muffins and pastries.

Bamboo Room (2nd Ave; breakfast $5-10, lunch $8-12, dinner $14-25; 6am-midnight) Another longtime Haines survivor with a footnote in history: CBS newsman Charles Kuralt once ate here. The blueberry hotcakes come smothered in whipped cream and syrup, and will kickstart your day with a sugar buzz that will last until noon. For dinner, mingle with locals in the adjoining Pioneer Bar for a beer and then indulge in a plate of steamed Dungeness crabs served whole.

QUICK EATS

Grizzly Greg's Pizzeria (766-3622; 126 Main St; medium pizza $14-25; 11am-9pm Mon-Sat, noon-9pm Sun;) This place is multifaceted; it serves pizza but also offers sandwiches, fried chicken, nachos and ice cream. If you just climbed Mt Riley, try the Grizzly Combo calzone stuffed with eight toppings. Big enough to feed a grizzly.

Local Catch (766-3557; Portage St; breakfast $4-6; 6:30am-4pm Mon-Fri) Near Fort Seward is this small shed with a big deck and outdoor tables. Here you'll find your morning latte, as well as interesting Thai, vegetarian and breakfast fare like the popular Big 'O' Burrito, a tortilla overflowing with eggs, potatoes, cheese and homemade salsa.

GROCERIES

Mountain Market & Spirits (766-3340; 3rd Ave at Haines Hwy; 7am-7pm Mon-Fri, to 6pm Sat & Sun, wine store 11am-8pm) has health foods and stocks local specialities like Birch Boy syrup, made by tapping birch instead of maple trees. Its deli is loaded with vegetarian options, the espresso bar serves great coffee and now adjoining the store is Mountain Spirits, the best wine shop in town. No doubt about it, this is the center of Haines hipness.

Dejon Delights (766-2505; 37 Portage St; 9am-6pm) A shop in Fort Seward that turns out some of the best smoked salmon and halibut in Southeast. If camping at Portage Bay pick up a fillet of just-caught king salmon ($8 per pound) and grill it on your campfire to the view of mountainous Lynn Canal. That is Alaska.

QuickMart (Mud Bay Rd) A convenience store that offers basic supplies.

Drinking

Fogcutter Bar (Main St) Haines is a hard-drinking town and this is where a lot of them belly up to the bar and spout off.

Harbor Bar (2 Front St) Dates back to the turn of the century when it opened in Skagway before being moved to Haines in the early 1900s. Doesn't look like it's been updated since. Still, this place is hopping when the band takes over Wednesday to Sunday and the dancefloor gets crowded.

Shopping

Despite a lack of cruise-ship traffic, or maybe because of it, Haines supports an impressive number of artists and has enough galleries to fill an afternoon.

Sea Wolf Art Studio (766-2558; www.tresham .com; Ft Seward Parade Ground; 9am-6pm), Housed in a log cabin is Tresham Gregg's gallery, one of Haines' best-known indigenous artists. Gregg combines spiritism, animism and shamanism of Northwest Coast Indians to create woodcarvings, totem poles, masks, bronze sculpture and talismanic silver jewelry.

Extreme Dreams Fine Arts (766-2097; www .extremedreams.com; Mile 6.5 Mud Bay Rd; noon-6pm) Out of town, near the entrance of Chilkat State Park, is this gallery packed with the work of 20 local artists, from watercolors and tapestry to handblown glass, cast silver and beautiful beads. The gallery also has a climbing wall because it's the studio of artist John Svenson, a renowned mountain climber who has scaled the highest peak on every continent except Mt Everest.

Wild Iris (766-2300; Portage St; 9am-7pm) Just one of a growing number of galleries on the edge of Fort Seward. Outside the home is a beautiful Alaskan garden, inside a fine selection of original jewelry, silkscreen prints, cards, pastels and other local art.

Getting There & Around

AIR

There is no jet service to Haines, but several charter companies run scheduled flights. Try **Wings of Alaska** (766-2030; www.wingsofalaska .com) or **LAB Flying Service** (766-2222; 390 Main St; www.labflying.com), both offering daily flights to Juneau. One-way fare is $90 to $105.

BOAT

State ferries, including the high-speed catamaran MV *Fairweather*, arrive and depart daily from the **ferry terminal** (☎766-2111; 2012 Lutak Rd) north of town for Skagway ($27, one hour) and Juneau ($33, 5½ hours;). **Haines Shuttle** (☎766-3138) meets all ferries and charges $10 for the 4-mile run into town. It also departs Haines 30 minutes before each ferry arrival, after stopping at various hotels around town.

Chilkat Cruises & Tours (☎766-3395, 888-766-2103; adult/child round-trip $45/23) operates the Fast Ferry, which streaks down Taiya Inlet to Skagway in 35 minutes. The 80ft cat departs Haines from the Port Chilkoot shuttle dock at 6:30am, 11am and 5pm Monday through Thursday and more often if cruise ships are packing Skagway.

BUS
Since 2002 no buses have served Haines. You'll need to either thumb it north or take the ferry to Skagway and get a bus north from there.

CAR
To visit Alaska Chilkat Bald Eagle Preserve on your own, you can rent a car at **Captain's Choice Motel** (☎766-3111, 800-478-2345), which has compacts for $69 a day with unlimited mileage. There is also **Eagle Nest Car Rentals** (☎907-766-2891, 800-354-6009; 1183 Haines Hwy), in the Eagle Nest Motel, which has cars for $45 to $50 with 100 miles included.

AROUND HAINES
Alaska Chilkat Bald Eagle Preserve
In 1982 the state reserved 48,000 acres along the Chilkat, Klehini and Tsirku Rivers to protect the largest known gathering of bald eagles in the world. Each year from October to February, more than 4000 eagles congregate here to feed on spawning salmon. They come because an upwelling of warm water prevents the river from freezing, thus encouraging the late salmon run. It's a remarkable sight – hundreds of birds sitting in the bare trees lining the river, often six or more birds to a branch.

The eagles can be seen from the Haines Hwy, where turnouts allow motorists to park and view the birds. The best view is between Mile 18 and Mile 22, where you'll find telescopes, interpretive displays and paved walkways along the river. You really have to be here after November to enjoy the birds in their greatest numbers, but many

of the 200 to 400 eagles that live here year-round can be spotted throughout summer.

The state park office in Haines can provide a list of state-authorized guides who conduct preserve tours. Among them is **Alaska Nature Tours** (☎766-2876; http://kcd.com/aknature; 103 2nd Ave S), which conducts three-hour tours (adult/child $55/40) daily in summer. The tours cover much of the scenery around the Haines area but often concentrate on the river flats and river mouths, where you usually see up to 40 eagles, many of them nesting.

You can camp in the area at **Mosquito Lake State Recreation Site** (Mile 27.2 Haines Hwy; campsites $5), a primitive five-site campground with drinking water, toilets and a boat launch.

SKAGWAY
☎907 / pop 862
Lying at the head of Lynn Canal is Skagway, one of the driest places in an otherwise soggy Southeast. While Petersburg averages over 100in of rain a year and Ketchikan a drenching 154in, Skagway gets only 26in annually.

Much of Skagway is within Klondike Gold Rush National Historical Park, which comprises downtown Skagway, the Chilkoot Trail, the White Pass Trail corridor and a Seattle visitors center. Beginning in 1897, Skagway and the nearby ghost town of Dyea were the starting places for more than 40,000 gold-rush stampeders who headed to the Yukon primarily by way of the Chilkoot Trail. The actual stamped lasted only a few years but it produced one of the most colorful periods in Alaskan history, that of a lawless frontier town controlled by villainous 'Soapy' Smith who was finally removed from power in gun fight by town hero Frank Reid.

At the height of the gold rush, Michael J Heney, an Irish contractor, convinced a group of English investors that he could build a railroad over the White Pass Trail to Whitehorse. The construction of the White Pass & Yukon Route was nothing short of a superhuman feat, and the railroad became the focal point of the town's economy after the gold rush and during the military buildup of WWII.

The line was shut down in 1982 but was revived in 1988, to the delight of cruise-ship tourists and backpackers walking the

Chilkoot Trail. Although the train hauls no freight, its rebirth was important to Skagway as a tourist attraction. Today Skagway survives almost entirely on tourism, as bus tours and more than 400 cruise ships a year turn this village into a boomtown again every summer. Up to five ships a day stop here and, on the busiest days, over 8000 tourists – 10 times the town's resident population – march off the ships and turn Broadway into something of an anthill. It's the modern-day version of the Klondike Gold Rush and the fact that one gift shop is called the 'Alaska Fleece Company' probably has Soapy Smith smiling in his grave.

The best day to be here is Saturday, when only one cruise ship is in port. But even if there are 2000 tourists in town (two ships' worth), Skagway can still be a pleasant place. To totally escape these crowds you have to skip Skagway and depart Southeast through much quieter Haines.

Orientation & Information

Unlike most Southeast towns, Skagway is a delightful place to arrive aboard the ferry. Cruise-ship and state-ferry passengers alike step off their boats and are funneled to Broadway St, Skagway's main avenue and the heart of Klondike Gold Rush National Park Historic District. Suddenly you're in a bustling town, where many people are dressed as if they are trying to relive the gold-rush days and the rest are obviously tourists off the luxury liners.

BOOKSTORES
Skaguay News Depot (☎ 983-3354; 264 Broadway St; ☽ 9am-6pm) A small bookstore with an excellent selection on the Klondike Gold Rush.

EMERGENCY & MEDICAL SERVICES
Ambulance, Fire, Police (☎ 911)
Skagway Medical Clinic (☎ 983-2255; 340 11th Ave; ☽ 9am-5pm) If gold fever strikes, head to this clinic.

LAUNDRY
Garden City RV Park (☎ 983-2378; 15th Ave at State St) Has a Laundromat with showers at the campground.
Services Unlimited (☎ 983-2595; 170 State St; ☽ 7am-8pm) Has a Laundromat.

LIBRARY & INTERNET ACCESS
Alaska Cruise Services (☎ 983-3398; 2nd Ave at State St; per 15 min/hr $1/4; ☽ 9am-8pm) Makes a living, and

probably a decent one, selling cruise-ship workers high-speed Internet access on 20 computers and phone cards.
Skagway Library (☎ 983-2665; 8th Ave at State St; ☽ noon-9pm Mon-Fri, 1-5pm Sat & Sun) Internet access is free but its one computer is so heavily used, people sign up for it the night before.

MONEY
Wells Fargo (☎ 983-2264; Broadway St at 6th Ave) Occupies the original office of National Bank of Alaska.

POST
Post office (☎ 983-2330; 641 Broadway St) Next door to Wells Fargo bank.

TOURIST INFORMATION
Klondike Gold Rush National Historical Park Visitor Center (☎ 983-9223; www.nps.gov/klgo; Broadway St at 2nd Ave; ☽ 8am-6pm) For everything outdoors – local trails, public campgrounds, National Park Service programs – head to the NPS' center.
Skagway Convention & Visitors Bureau (☎ 983-2854, 888-762-1898; www.skagway.com; Broadway St at 2nd Ave; ☽ 8am-6pm) For information on lodging, tours or what's new, visit this bureau housed in the can't-miss Arctic Brotherhood Hall (think driftwood).
Trail Center (☎ 983-3655, 800-661-0486; Broadway at 2nd Ave; ☽ 8am-6pm) If you're stampeding to the Chilkoot Trail, first stop here in the restored Martin Itjen House at the foot of Broadway. The center is a clearinghouse for information on permits and transportation. The Chilkoot Trail hike is covered in detail on p66.

Sights

KLONDIKE GOLD RUSH NATIONAL HISTORICAL PARK VISITOR CENTER
The first stop of the day should be this **NPS center** (☎ 983-2854; Broadway St at 2nd Ave; ☽ 8am-6pm) in the original 1898 White Pass & Yukon Route depot. The center features displays, ranger talks and the 30-minute film *Days of Adventure, Dreams of Gold*, an excellent introduction to the gold rush, which is shown on the hour. The center's rangers also lead a 45-minute walking tour of the historic district five times a day and offer talks on various topics related to the park. Everything is free.

SKAGWAY MUSEUM
Skagway celebrated its centennial in 2000 by expanding the venerable century-old McCabe Building and moving the city offices and jail into the new addition. Now the **city museum** (☎ 983-2420; 7th Ave at Spring St;

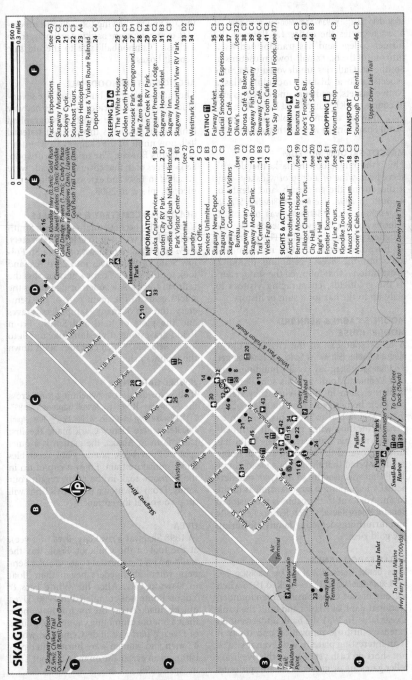

SKAGWAY

SOUTHEAST ALASKA

0 ————— 500 m
0 ————— 0.3 miles

INFORMATION
Alaska Cruise Services.......................1 B3
Garden City RV Park..........................2 D1
Klondike Gold Rush National Historical
  Park Visitor Center.......................3 B3
Laundromat...............................(see 2)
Laundry..4 D1
Post Office......................................5 C3
Services Unlimited............................6 B3
Skagway News Depot.......................7 C3
Skagway Tour Co.............................8 C3
Skagway Convention & Visitors
  Bureau..................................(see 13)
Skagway Library...............................9 C2
Skagway Medical Clinic...................10 D2
Trail Center...................................11 B3
Wells Fargo...................................12 C3

SIGHTS & ACTIVITIES
Arctic Brotherhood Hall...................13 C3
Bernard Moore House...................(see 19)
Chilkoot Charters & Tours...............14 C2
City Hall....................................(see 20)
Eagle's Hall..................................15 C3
Frontier Excursions.........................16 E1
Gray Line Tours..........................(see 34)
Klondike Tours.............................17 C3
Mascot Saloon Museum..................18 C3
Moore's Cabin...............................19 C3

Packers Expeditions....................(see 45)
Skagway Museum...........................20 C3
Sockeye Cycle..............................21 C3
Southeast Tours.............................22 C3
Temsco Helicopters.........................23 A4
White Pass & Yukon Route Railroad
  Depot..24 C4

SLEEPING
At The White House.......................25 C2
Golden North Hotel........................26 C3
Hanousek Park Campground............27 D1
Mile Zero B&B..............................28 C2
Pullen Creek RV Park......................29 B4
Sergeant Preston's Lodge.................30 C3
Skagway Home Hostel.....................31 B3
Skagway Inn..................................32 C3
Skagway Mountain View RV Park......33 D2
Westmark Inn................................34 C3

EATING
Fairway Market..............................35 C3
Glacial Smoothies & Espresso...........36 C3
Haven Café...................................37 C2
Olivia's....................................(see 32)
Sabrosa Café & Bakery....................38 C3
Skagway Fish Company....................39 C4
Stowaway Café..............................40 C4
Sweet Tooth Café..........................41 C3
You Say Tomato Natural Foods......(see 37)

DRINKING
Bonanza Bar & Grill........................42 C3
Moe's Frontier Bar..........................43 C3
Red Onion Saloon..........................44 B3

SHOPPING
Mountain Shop..............................45 C3

TRANSPORT
Sourdough Car Rental.....................46 C3

adult/child $2/1; ◷ 9am-5pm Mon-Fri, noon-4pm Sat & Sun) occupies the entire 1st floor of the former college and has transformed itself into one of the best small-town museums in Southeast. Galleries are devoted to various aspects of local history, including Alaska Native baskets, beadwork and carvings and of course the Klondike Gold Rush. The display drawing the most looks is the small pistol Soapy Smith kept up his sleeve.

MASCOT SALOON MUSEUM

This is the only saloon in Alaska that doesn't serve beer, wine or a drop of whiskey – but it did during the gold rush, and plenty of it. Built in 1898, the **Mascot** (Broadway St at 3rd Ave; admission free; ◷ 8am-6pm) was one of 70 saloons during Skagway's heyday as 'the roughest place in the world.' The park service has since turned it into a museum that looks into the vices – gambling, drinking, prostitution – that followed the stampeders to the goldfields, encouraging visitors to belly up to the bar for a shot of history.

MOORE'S CABIN & BERNARD MOORE HOUSE

A block southeast of the city museum is **Moore's Cabin** (5th Ave at Spring St; admission free; ◷ 10am-5pm), Skagway's oldest building. Captain William Moore and his son, Bernard, built the cabin in 1887, when they staked out their homestead as the founders of the town. Moore had to move his home to its present location when gold-rush stampeders overran his homestead. The NPS has since renovated the building and, in doing so, discovered that the famous Dead Horse Trail that was used by so many stampeders actually began in the large lawn next to the cabin. Adjacent to the cabin is the restored **Bernard Moore House**, which features exhibits and furnishings depicting family life during the gold rush.

WELLS FARGO BANKS

This **bank** (Broadway St at 6th Ave; admission free; ◷ 9:30am-5pm Mon-Fri) dates back to 1916 when a group of East Coast businessmen founded National Bank of Alaska and built the bank a year later. In 1981 the bank underwent an extensive historic renovation and today it is an interesting place to visit even if you're not short on cash yet. Two of the five brass teller gates are originals, there are spittoons

in case you're chewing tobacco and on display everywhere are banking artifacts, from a classic 'Cannonball' safe to the old safe deposit boxes.

ARCTIC BROTHERHOOD HALL

The most outlandish building of the seven-block historical corridor along Broadway St and possibly the most photographed building in Alaska is this defunct **fraternal hall**, now home of the Skagway Convention & Visitors Bureau. The original driftwood, 8833 pieces of it, that covers the façade were attached in 1899 and extensively renovated, piece-by-piece, in 2005.

GOLD RUSH CEMETERY & REID FALLS

Visitors who become infatuated with Smith and Reid can walk out to **Gold Rush Cemetery**, a 2½-mile stroll northeast on State St. Follow State until it curves into 23rd Ave and look for the sign to Soapy's grave across the railroad tracks. A wooden bridge along the tracks leads to the main part of the cemetery, the site of many stampeders' graves and the plots of Reid and Smith. From Reid's gravestone, it's a short hike uphill to lovely **Reid Falls**, which cascades 300ft down the mountainside.

JEWELL GARDENS

If the crowds are overwhelming you, cross the Skagway River to **Jewell Gardens** (☎ 983-2111; Klondike Hwy; adult/child $8.50/4.25; ◷ 10am-4pm). Located where Henry Clark made the first truck farm in Alaska, the garden is a quiet spot of flowerbeds, ponds, giant vegetables and a miniature train. Enjoy a cup of tea in the tearoom, soak in the color, regain your sanity. From downtown the SMART bus will drop you off at the entrance.

DYEA

In 1898 Skagway's rival city, **Dyea** (*die-yee*), at the foot of the Chilkoot Trail, was the trailhead for the shortest route to Lake Bennett, where stampeders began their float to Dawson City. After the White Pass & Yukon Route was completed in 1900, Dyea quickly died. Today the town is little more than a few old crumbling cabins, the pilings of Dyea Wharf and Slide Cemetery, where 47 men and women were buried after perishing in an avalanche on the Chilkoot Trail in April 1898.

The ghost town is a 9-mile drive along winding Dyea Rd, whose numerous hairpin turns are not for timid RVers. But it's very scenic drive especially at **Skagway Overlook**, a turnoff with a viewing platform 2½ miles from Skagway. The overlook offers an excellent view of Skagway, its waterfront and the peaks above the town. Just before crossing the bridge over the Taiya River, you pass the Dyea Camping Area (p169) where an NPS ranger is stationed in the summer to assist hikers on the Chilkoot Trail.

Activities

HIKING

The 33-mile Chilkoot Trail (p66) is Southeast Alaska's most popular hike, but other good trails surround Skagway. There is no USFS office in Skagway, but the NPS Visitor Center has a free brochure entitled *Skagway Trail Map*. You can also get backcountry information and any outdoor gear you need (including rentals) at the excellent **Mountain Shop** (☎ 983-2544; www.packerexpeditions .com; 355 4th Ave).

Dewey Lakes Trail System

This series of trails leads east of Skagway to a handful of alpine and subalpine lakes, waterfalls and historic sites. From Broadway, follow 3rd Ave southeast to the railroad tracks. On the east side of the tracks are the trailheads to Lower Dewey Lake (0.7 miles), Icy Lake (2½ miles), Upper Reid Falls (3½ miles) and Sturgill's Landing (4½ miles).

Plan on taking an hour round-trip for the hike to Lower Dewey Lake, where there are picnic tables, camping spots and a trail circling the lake. At the lake's north end is an alpine trail that ascends steeply to Upper Dewey Lake, 3½ miles from town, and Devil's Punchbowl, another 1.25 miles south of the upper lake.

The hike to Devil's Punchbowl is an all-day trip or an ideal overnight excursion, as the views are excellent and there is a free-use shelter on Upper Dewey Lake that is in rough condition but does not require reservations. There are also campsites at Sturgill's Landing.

Yakutania Point & AB Mountain Trails

The Skagway River footbridge, reached by following 1st Ave west around the airport runway, leads to two trails of opposite caliber. For an easy hike to escape the cruise-ship crowds turn left from the bridge and follow the mile-long trail to picnic areas and lovely views at Yakutania Point and Smugglers Cove.

Nearby on Dyea Rd is AB Mountain Trail, also known as the Skyline Trail, This route ascends 5½ miles to the 5100ft summit of AB Mountain, named for the 'AB' that appears on its south side when the snow melts every spring. The first 30 minutes is along a well-defined trail through a hemlock forest to a view of Skagway. After that the trail is considerably more challenging, especially above the tree line, and requires a full day to reach the summit.

Denver Glacier Trail

This trail begins at Mile 6 of the White Pass & Yukon Route, where the USFS has renovated a White Pass & Yukon caboose into the **Denver Caboose** (reserve ☎ 877-444-6777; www.reserveusa.com; r $35), a rental cabin of sorts. Hikers need to make arrangements with the White Pass & Yukon Route to be dropped off at the caboose. The trailheads up the east fork of Skagway River for 2 miles, then swings south and continues another 1½ miles up the glacial outwash to Denver Glacier. Most of the trail is overgrown with brush, and the second half is particularly tough hiking.

Laughton Glacier Trail

At Mile 14 of the White Pass & Yukon Route is a 1½-mile hike to the USFS **Laughton Glacier Cabin** (NRRS ☎ 877-444-6777; www.reserveusa .com; cabins $35). The cabin overlooks the river from Warm Pass but is only a mile from Laughton Glacier, an impressive hanging glacier between the 3000ft walls of the Sawtooth Range. The alpine scenery and ridge walks in this area are worth the $54 ticket White Pass & Yukon Route charges to drop off and pick up hikers. There are two excursion trains from Skagway, so this could be a possible day hike. But it's far better to carry a tent and spend a night in the area.

CYCLING

Sockeye Cycle (☎ 983-2851; 381 5th Ave; bikes per 2/4/8hr $12/20/30) rents hybrids and mountain bikes and offers several bike tours out of Skagway that include all equipment. Its 2½-hour Klondike Tour ($72) begins with van

SOUTHEAST ALASKA

transportation to Klondike Pass (elevation 3295ft) on the Klondike Hwy. From there it's a 15-mile downhill ride back to town, with plenty of stops to view waterfalls and the White Pass & Yukon Route.

RAFTING

Skagway Float Tours (☎ 983-3688; www.skagway float.com) offers a three-hour tour of Dyea that includes a 45-minute float down the placid Taiya River (adult/child $70/50). Its Hike & Float Tour (adult/child $80/60) is a four-hour outing that includes the beginning of the Chilkoot Trail then some floating back.

Tours

WHITE PASS & YUKON ROUTE RAILROAD

Without a doubt the most spectacular tour from Skagway is a ride aboard the historic railway of the **White Pass & Yukon Route** (☎ 983-2217, 800-343-7373; www.whitepassrailroad .com; depot on 2nd Ave). Two different narrated sightseeing tours are available; reservations are required for both.

The premier daylong Lake Bennett Adventure (8½ hours, 80 miles round-trip) begins at Skagway's railroad depot, where you board parlor cars for the trip to White Pass on the narrow-gauge line built during the 1898 Klondike Gold Rush. This segment is only a small portion of the 110-mile route to Whitehorse, but it contains the most spectacular scenery, including crossing Glacier Gorge and Dead Horse Gulch, viewing Bridal Veil Falls and then making the steep 2885ft climb to White Pass, only 20 miles from Skagway. At the end of the trip you arrive at the historic 1903 Lake Bennett Railroad Depot, where there is a two-hour layover for lunch and time to explore this beautiful area. The Lake Bennett trip departs from Skagway at 8am Saturday from mid-June to late August and the fare is adult/child $160/80. Note that Lake Bennett is across the border in British Columbia, Canada, so passengers will need to carry passports or other proof of citizenship.

The Summit Excursion (three to 3½ hours, 40 miles round-trip) is a shorter tour to White Pass Summit and back. The tour is offered at 8:15am and 12:45pm daily mid-May to mid-September, and also at 4:30pm on Monday through Thursday until early

September. Tickets are adult/child $89/45 and can be purchased at the depot.

SUMMIT & CITY TOUR

This is the standard tour in Skagway and includes Gold Rush Cemetery, White Pass Summit and Skagway Overlook, including a lively narration that might be historically accurate. The cost ranges from around $35 to $65 per person for a two- to three-hour outing. Companies offering such a tour and others:

Chilkoot Charters & Tours (☎ 983-3400, 877-983-3400; www.skagwaysbesttour.com; 340 7th Ave)

Frontier Excursions (☎ 983-2512, 877-983-2512; www.frontierexcursions.com; 1602 State St)

Gray Line (☎ 983-2241, 800-544-2206) At the Westmark Inn.

Klondike Tours (☎ 983-2075, 866-983-2075; www .klondiketours.com; 5th Ave at Broadway St)

Skagway Tour Co (☎ 983-2168, 866-983-2168; www .skagwaytourco.com; 7th Ave btwn Broadway & Spring)

Southeast Tours (☎ 983-2990; www.southeasttours .com; 2990 French Alley)

OTHER TOURS

A couple of cruise tourist–oriented attractions lie out along the Klondike Hwy a short way.

Alaska Fjordlines (☎ 800-320-0146; www.alaskafjord lines.com) Offers a day cruise to Juneau aboard the fast *Fjordland*, a 65ft catamaran. Continental breakfast is served on the way down, and on arrival in Juneau, passengers transfer to a bus for a tour of Mendenhall Glacier and the city. You're on your own there for lunch, then a light dinner is served onboard during the return trip. The tour is $129.

Klondike Gold Dredge Tours (☎ 983-3176, 877-983-3175; www.klondikegolddredge.com; Mile 1.7 Klondike Hwy; adult/child $35/24) Runs tours of a former working gold dredge that was in Dawson before being moved to Skagway where it has hit the mother lode. A Gold Dredge van will provide a ride for $5 per person.

Liarsville Gold Rush Trail Camp (☎ 983-3000; Mile 3 Klondike Hwy; $51) Offers a miner's show, a turn at gold panning and Skagway's salmon bake.

Temsco Helicopters Inc (☎ 983-2900; www.temsco air.com; waterfront end of Terminal Way) And if you have money to burn, Temsco offers a helicopter flight to a dogsledding opportunity for $399.

Festivals & Events

Skagway's **Fourth of July** celebrations feature a footrace, parade and fish feed. But the town's most unusual celebration is **Soapy Smith's Wake**, on July 8. Locals and the cast of the *Days of '98 Show* celebrate with a hike out to the grave and a champagne toast, with champagne often sent up by Smith's great-grandson from California.

Sleeping

Alas the Golden North Hotel, Alaska's oldest hotel, is no longer a place of lodging. The sign is still up because it's a historical structure, but now its rooms are simply storage areas for the gift shops on the first floor. Skagway levies a 8% sales and bed tax on all lodging.

BUDGET

Skagway Home Hostel (☎ 983-2131; www.skagway hostel.com; 456 3rd Ave; PO Box 231, Skagway, AK 99840; dm/r $15/40; ✕ ▭) This lies in a quiet residential neighborhood a half-mile from the ferry terminal. It's a relaxed if somewhat cluttered hostel with kitchen and laundry facilities but small dorm rooms and common areas.

Skagway Mountain View RV Park (☎ 983-3333, 888-778-7700; 12th Ave at Broadway St; campsites $15, RV sites $18-26) The town's best campground for tenters. Has 65 RV sites and a limited number of campsites. Amenities include firepits, laundry facilities, showers, restaurants and dump stations for both humans and RVs. It's easy walking distance from downtown, but you won't feel trampled by tourists.

Pullen Creek RV Park (☎ 983-2768, 800-936-3731; sites/with car/with electricity & water $14/18/25) Located in a busy location near the ferry terminal and cruise ships. It has 46 sites with hookups, as well as rest rooms and showers.

Dyea Campground (☎ 983-2921; sites $6) Located near the Chilkoot trailhead in Dyea, about 9 miles north of Skagway, this used to be a free, 22-site campground operated by the NPS on a first-come, first-served basis. But even at $6 a night it's still the cheapest spot to pitch a tent. There are vault toilets and tables but there's no water.

MIDRANGE

Cindy's Place (☎ 983-2674, 800-831-8095; www .alaska.net/~croland; Mile 1 Dyea Rd; cabins $49-110) Two miles from town are Cindy's cabins, three log units tucked away into the forest, each with refrigerator, microwave and coffeemaker. At night you can soak in a hot tub among the towering pines. Aaaah!

Skagway Bungalows (☎ 983-2986; www.apt alaska.net/~saldi; Mile 1 Dyea Rd; cabins $99) Right next door to Cindy's Place are four more classic log cabins, situated among the trees and on top of rock outcroppings as if Frank Lloyd Wright was here for the summer. Each cabin has a bath, a king-size bed, a kitchenette and a small porch overlooking the forest. In the morning a basket of baked goods magically appears at your door.

Sergeant Preston's Lodge (☎ 983-2521, 866-983-2521; www.sgt-prestonslodgeskagway.com; 370 6th Ave; s $70-108, d $80-118; ✕ ▭) A tidy motel in the heart of Skagway offering 37 rooms, all with TV, phone and private bath. Other amenities include free Internet access, courtesy transportation and rental cars. Budgeteers should ask about the four economy rooms (single/double $70/80).

TOP END

At the White House (☎ 983-9000; www.atthewhite house.com; 475 8th Ave at Main St; r $120-145; ✕) An elegant 10-room inn that knows how to keep the cookie jar filled. All rooms have private bath, cable TV and phone. In the morning you wake up to a breakfast of fresh baked goods and fruit served in a sundrenched dining room.

Chilkoot Trail Outpost (☎ 983-3799; www.chil koottrailoutpost.com; Mile 8.5 Dyea Rd; cabins $90-140) Hitting the 'Koot? Start the big adventure with a good night's sleep at this resort located a half-mile from the trailhead. The cabins are very comfortable and equipped with microwaves, refrigerators and coffeemakers. The screened-in gazebo is strategically located at a waterfall.

Mile Zero B&B (☎ 983-3045; www.mile-zero.com; 901 Main St; r $125; ✕ ▭) This B&B has six large rooms, each with private bath and its own entrance on the wraparound porch. If you hook the fish of your dreams there's a BBQ area where you can grill it for dinner.

Skagway Inn (☎ 983-2289, 888-752-4929; www .skagwayinn.com; Broadway St at 7th Ave; r with/without bath $169/119; ✕ ▭) In a restored 1897 Victorian that was originally one of the town's brothels. The 10-room inn is downtown, filled with antiques and provides a breakfast buffet in its on-site restaurant, Olivia's.

Westmark Inn (☎ 983-6000, 800-544-0970; 3rd Ave at Spring St; r $119) Skagway's largest hotel is more of a sprawling complex with 250 rooms on both sides of 3rd Ave.

SOUTHEAST ALASKA

Eating

Skagway has more than 20 restaurants operating during the summer and some would say better ones than what you find in that Capital City just to the south. You decide.

RESTAURANTS

Skagway Fish Company (☎ 983-3474; Congress Way; salad & sandwiches $10-14, dinner $17-35; ☣ 11am-10pm) Located next to the Stowaway Café, Skagway's newest restaurant is arguably its best. In a large room overlooking the harbor, with a horseshoe bar in the middle and crab traps on the ceiling, you feast on stuffed halibut or coconut-curry prawns. Surprisingly what many locals rave about are its baby back ribs, great BBQ even if you weren't in Alaska.

Stowaway Café (☎ 983-3463; 205 Congress Way; dinner mains $16-21; ☣ 4pm-10pm; ✗) Just past the harbormaster's office, this place is fun, funky and fantastic. Outside, is a beautiful mermaid and the restaurant's artfully cluttered front and back yards. The small café has a handful of tables, a view of the boat harbor, and excellent fish, seafood gumbo and Cajun-style steak dinners.

Olivia's (☎ 983-3287; Broadway St at 7th Ave; lunch $16, dinner $18-26; ☣ 11:30am-1:30pm & 5-9pm; ✗) The extensive garden outside the Skagway Inn is a good indication of how fresh the mains are inside. Staff members don't waste time cooking fish-and-chips at this bistro; lunch is a fixed-priced meal, dinner is a choice of four mains. The chicken pot pie sounds plain but it's delicious.

CAFÉS

Sabrosa Café & Bakery (600 Broadway St; breakfast $5-6, soups, salads & sandwiches $5-8, Mexican dishes $7-9; ☣ 6am-4pm; ✗) Tucked away just off Broadway St, this small café – four tables outside, four inside – is easy to miss but shouldn't be. Its vegetarian choices, from Rockin' Vegetarian Chili to spicy veggie tacos, are extensive and its King Ranch Casserole (layers of corn tortillas, roasted chicken and cheese) will give you the get-up-and-go to face five cruise ships at once.

Haven Café (☎ 983-3553; 9th Ave at State St; breakfast $3-7, salads $7.50, panini $8; ☣ 6am-8pm; ✗) The aptly named coffeehouse is removed from the heart of the fray and makes a great place to kick back and plan your next move. Inside, a sofa and wooden floorboards create a warm ambience, while soft music plays on the sound system. A bulletin board in the foyer provides insight into local life, and the café often hosts special events (live music, poetry reading etc). Oh yeah, the espresso is potent and the panini sandwiches and salads are large.

Glacial Smoothies & Espresso (☎ 907-983-3223; 336 3rd Ave; ☣ 6am-6pm; breakfast $4-7; ✗) For great Belgian waffles, smoothies named Blueberry Blues and Summer Solstice or just a place where you can sip a latte while surfing the Internet (per 20 minutes/hour $3/5).

Sweet Tooth Café (☎ 983-2405; 315 Broadway; breakfast $4-8, lunch $5-8; ☣ 6am-2pm) This longtime café is the place for that pile of pancakes first thing in the morning.

GROCERIES

Fairway Market (4th Ave at State St) This is Skagway's grocer, a place where a gallon of milk is $5. Check the produce carefully here; you don't know when the barge came in.

You Say Tomato Natural Foods (☎ 9th Ave at State St) Located in the same building as Haven Café is this small store with natural foods and fresh produce.

Drinking & Entertainment

Red Onion Saloon (☎ 983-2222; Broadway St at 2nd Ave) If there's any dancing in town, it'll be here in this former brothel built in 1898. The 'RO' is now done up as a gold-rush saloon, complete with mannequins leering down at you from the 2nd story to depict pioneer-era working girls. When bands are playing here, it'll be packed, noisy and rowdy.

Moe's Frontier Bar (☎ 983-2238; Broadway St) The locals' dive of choice is this agreeable bar between 4th and 5th Aves. It opens at 9am and makes a mean Bloody Mary. Wild Bill plays country on Friday night.

Bonanza Bar & Grill (☎ 983-6214; Broadway St) With Guinness, Newcastle and many other excellent beers on tap and TVs on the wall, this is the closest thing Skagway has to a sports bar.

THEATER

Skagway has Southeast Alaska's best and longest-running melodrama. The entertaining and lively **Days of '98 Show with Soapy Smith** (☎ 983-2545; Eagle's Hall; 598 Broadway at 6th Ave; adult/child matinee $14/7, evening show $16/8) covers the

---

DETOUR: YAKUTAT

Isolated on the strand that connects Southeast to the rest of Alaska, Yakutat – of all places – is now experiencing something of a minor tourism boom. The main reason is improved transportation. You still can't drive to the most northern Southeast town but in 1998 it became a port for the **Alaska Marine Highway** (☎ 800-642-0066; www.ferryalaska.com) when the MV *Kennicott* began its Cross-Gulf trips. Now the ferry stops fives times a month during the summer, headed to either Juneau or Valdez, while **Alaska Airlines** (☎ 800-252-7522; www.alaskaair.com) stops daily both northbound and southbound.

What does Yakutat have to offer curious tourists? Big waves, a big and very active glacier and a lot of USFS cabins next to rivers with big salmon.

The waves rolling in from the Gulf of Alaska have made Yakutat the Surf Capital of the far north (p63). This town of 700 even has its own surf shop, the **Icy Waves Surf Shop** (☎ 907-784-3226; www.icywaves.com).

Just 30 miles north of Yakutat is **Hubbard Glacier**, the longest tidewater glacier in the world. The 70-mile-long glacier captured national attention by galloping across Russell Fjord in the mid-1980s, turning the long inlet into a lake. Eventually Hubbard receded to reopen the fjord, but did it again in 2002. To this day the 8-mile-wide glacier remains one of Alaska's most active. The rip tides and currents that flow between Gilberts Point and the face of the glacier, a mere 1000ft away, are so strong that they cause Hubbard to calve almost continuously at peak tides. The entire area, part of the 545-sq-mile Russell Fjord Wilderness, is one of the most interesting places in Alaska and usually visited through flightseeing or boat tours. The **Yakutat Charter Boat Co** (☎ 888-317-4987; www.alaska-charter.com) runs a four-hour tour of the area for $125 per person. The last outfitter to run kayaking trips in the area was **Alaska Discovery** (☎ 800-586-1911; www.akdiscovery.com).

There are also 12 **USFS cabins** (NRRS ☎ 877-444-6777; www.reserveusa.com; per night $25-35) in the area with five of them accessible via Forest Hwy 10, which extends east from Yakutat. Many are near rivers and lakes that are renowned, even by Alaskan standards, for sport fishing of salmon, steelhead trout and Dolly Varden.

Yakutat has a dozen lodges and B&Bs including the **Mooring Lodge** (☎ 888-551-2836; www.mooringlodge.com; 1-4 persons $350) and the **Glacier Bear Lodge** (☎ 866-425-6343; www.glacierbear.lodge.com; s/d $110/150; ☐), which also has a restaurant. For more information contact the **Yakutat Chamber of Commerce** (www.yakutatalaska.com) or the USFS **Yakutat Ranger Station** (☎ 784-3359).

---

town's gold-rush days and the full story of Soapy and his gang. Four shows are offered daily in summer; the evening show is preceded by an hour of 'mock gambling.'

Getting There & Away

AIR

Regularly scheduled flights from Skagway to Juneau, Haines and Glacier Bay are available from **LAB Flying Service** (☎ 983-2471; www.labflying.com), **Wings of Alaska** (☎ 983-2442; www.wingsofalaska.com) and **Skagway Air Service** (☎ 983-2218; www.skagwayair.com), which generally offers the cheapest fares. Expect to pay about $100 one way to Juneau, $65 to Haines and $150 $190 to Gustavus.

BOAT

Six vessels of the **Alaska Marine Highway** (☎ 983-2941, 800-642-0066; www.ferryalaska.com)

stop at Skagway but the best one to catch is the MV *Fairweather*, the state's high-speed catamaran. During the summer it offers nearly daily service between Skagway, Haines and Juneau, including a direct run to Skagway that leaves the Capital City at 12:30pm and departs at 3:30pm for a return trip. It's only a 2½-hour trip between the two towns and the one-way fare is adult/child $44/22. In Skagway, the ferry departs from the terminal and dock at the southwest end of Broadway St.

Chilkat Cruises & Tours (☎ 983-2143, 888-766-2103; www.chilkatcruises.com) operates the Fast Ferry to Haines. Its speedy 80-passenger catamaran, the MV *Fairweather Express*, makes the run in 35 minutes. The boat departs from the Skagway small boat harbor at 8am, noon and 6pm Monday through Thursday in summer with additional trips if needed by the cruise ships. The round-trip/one-way fare is $45/25; purchase tickets onboard.

BUS

Alaska Direct Bus Line (☎ 800-770-6652, in Whitehorse 867-668-4833) runs a bus between Skagway and Whitehorse on Monday, Tuesday, Thursday and Saturday when there is demand, and there usually is during the summer. But you must call the Whitehorse office in advance. The bus departs from 509 Main St in Whitehorse at noon Yukon time, arriving in Skagway at 2pm Alaska time. It then departs from the Skagway ferry terminal at 3pm, arriving in Whitehorse at 7pm Yukon time. The one-way fare is $80. On Sunday, Wednesday and Friday, an Alaska Direct bus departs from Whitehorse for either Anchorage ($208) or Fairbanks ($180).

Yukon-Alaska Tourist Tours (☎ 866-626-7383, in Whitehorse 867-668-5944; www.yukonalaskatourist tours.com) offers a minibus service three times daily to Whitehorse, departing the train depot in Skagway at 8:45pm, 1:15pm and 3:30pm. One way is $30.

HITCHHIKING

Hitchhiking is possible along the Klondike Hwy just after a ferry pulls in. But backpackers thumbing north would do better buying a $27 ferry ticket to Haines and trying the Haines Hwy instead, as it has considerably more traffic.

TRAIN

It's possible to travel part-way to Whitehorse, Yukon Territory, on the trains of the **White Pass & Yukon Route** (☎ 983-2217, 800-343-7373; www.whitepassrailroad.com) then complete the trip with a bus connection at Fraser,

British Columbia. The northbound train departs from the Skagway depot at 8am daily in summer, and passengers arrive in Whitehorse by bus at 1pm Yukon time. The southbound bus departs from Whitehorse at 1:30pm Yukon time, and passengers arrive in Skagway on the train at 4:30pm Alaska time. The one-way fare is adult/child $95/48, more than taking the Alaska Direct bus, however the ride on the historic, narrow-gauge railroad is worth it.

Getting Around

BICYCLE

Several places in town rent bikes including Sockeye Cycle (p167). And Sourdough Car Rental (below), which rents better bikes for $10 a day.

BUS

From May 1 to September 30, the city runs the SMART bus on two different routes. The regular route ($1) runs from the docks up to 8th Ave; the long route ($2) runs from 8th Ave to 23rd Ave. Buses come along about every 10 minutes from 7am to 9pm.

CAR

Sourdough Car Rental (☎ 983-2523; 6th Ave at Broadway St) has compacts for $50 a day with unlimited miles. In Skagway, there's a 14% tax on rental cars.

TAXI

Just about every taxi and tour company in Skagway will run you out to Dyea and the trailhead for the Chilkoot Trail, and the price hasn't gone up in years – $10 a head. **Frontier Excursions** (☎ 983-2512, 877-983-2512; www.frontierexcursions.com; Broadway St at 7th Ave) has trips daily.

Anchorage & Around

Almost in the center of Alaska but on the edge of the wilderness, is Anchorage, the Big Apple of the Far North. There is no other city like it. On the same latitude as Helsinki, Finland, Anchorage is a place with city amenities and city problems. It officially has 42% of the state's population but bedroom communities (residential towns) such as Eagle River push it closer to half.

Anchorage is young (the average age is 32 years old) and active, the reason for all the parks and bike paths. Office workers go salmon fishing during lunchtime; people climb Flattop Mountain (3500ft) on a whim; families head to a carnival in the middle of winter.

Their slogan is 'Anchorage is only 30 minutes from Alaska' because embracing the city on one side are the salmon-rich waters of Cook Inlet. On the other are the 5000ft-plus peaks of Chugach State Park, the third-largest US state park. Within an hour's drive are wilderness adventures galore. Almost any type of adventure is possible within a short plane ride.

If you're a tourist, you'll probably pass through Anchorage at least once. It's an almost essential travel hub in Alaska. But while you're in Anchorage don't limit yourself to reprovisioning or plotting your escape. Dedicate some time to exploring this city, and spend a day climbing the alpine in the morning and listening to a local blues band at happy hour.

HIGHLIGHTS

- **Best Alaska Native attraction** (p179) – watching Alaska Natives dance to ancient songs, carve a totem or dry a salmon at Greater Anchorage's Alaska Native Heritage Center

- **Best salmon viewing** (p178) – seeing salmon-as-art along downtown Anchorage streets (p184) or real ones swimming up Ship Creek

- **Best bike ride** (p198) – looking for beluga whales and bore tides while pedaling the Indian–Girdwood Trail, starting from Indian Valley

- **Best glacier** (p200) – cruising Portage Glacier or checking out the ice and ice worms at Begich-Boggs Visitor Center

- **Best state fair** (p205) – joining locals to cheer on greased pigs at the Alaska State Fair in Palmer

★ Best State Fair

★ Best Native Attraction
★ Best Salmon Viewing

Best Bike Ride
★

★ Best Glacier

▪ AREA CODE: ☎ 907   ▪ POPULATION: 227,498   ▪ ELEVATION: MT BASHFUL 8005FT

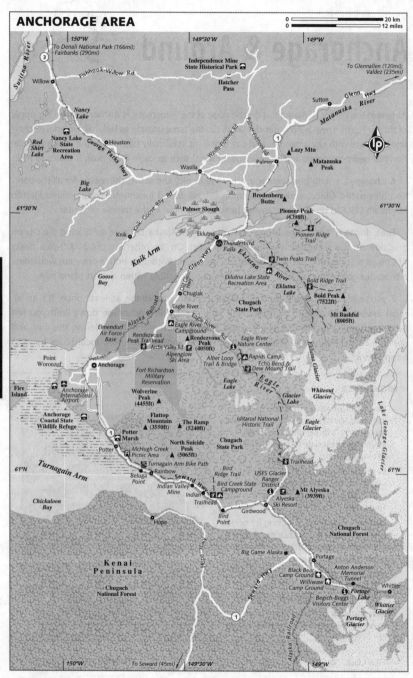

ANCHORAGE AREA

| 0 | 20 km |
| 0 | 12 miles |

To Denali National Park (166mi);
Fairbanks (290mi)

Susitna River

Willow

Fishhook-Willow Rd

Independence Mine
State Historical Park

Hatcher
Pass

To Glennallen (120mi);
Valdez (235mi)

Sutton

Glenn Hwy

Matanuska River

Nancy
Lake

Red
Shirt
Lake

Nancy Lake
State
Recreation
Area

Houston

George Parks Hwy

Wasilla-Fishhook Rd

Palmer-Fishhook Rd

Lazy Mtn

Matanuska
Peak

Big
Lake

Wasilla

Palmer

61°30'N

Knik

Knik-Goose Bay Rd

Palmer Slough

Brodenberg
Butte

Pioneer Peak
(6398ft)

61°30'N

Eklutna

Pioneer Ridge
Trail

Goose
Bay

Knik Arm

Old Glenn Hwy

Thunderbird
Falls

Eklutna River

Twin Peaks Trail

Bold Ridge Trail

Chugiak

Eklutna Lake State
Recreation Area

Eklutna
Lake

Bold Peak
(7522ft)

Alaska Railroad

Eagle River

Chugach
State Park

Mt Bashful
(8005ft)

Elmendorf
Air Force
Base

Rendezvous
Peak Trailhead

Eagle River Rd

Eagle River
Campground

Rendezvous
Peak
(4050ft)

Eagle River
Nature Center

Eklutna Glacier

Point
Woronzof

Anchorage

Arctic Valley Rd

Alpenglow
Ski Area

Alder Loop
Trail & Bridge

Rapids Camp
Echo Bend &
Dew Mound Trail

Eagle River

Glacier
Lake

Whiteout
Glacier

Lake George Glacier

Fire
Island

Anchorage
International
Airport

Fort Richardson
Military
Reservation

Eagle
Lake

Eagle
Glacier

Anchorage
Coastal State
Wildlife Refuge

Potter
Marsh

Wolverine
Peak
(4455ft)

Flattop
Mountain
(3550ft)

The Ramp
(5240ft)

Iditarod National
Historic Trail

61°N

Potter

McHugh Creek
Picnic Area

North Suicide
Peak
(5065ft)

Chugach
State Park

61°N

Turnagain Arm

Turnagain Arm Bike Path

Rainbow

Seward Hwy

Bird
Ridge Trail

Trailhead

Beluga
Point

Indian Valley
Mine

Indian

Trailhead

Bird Creek State
Campground

USFS Glacier
Ranger
District

Mt Alyeska
(3939ft)

Alyeska
Ski Resort

Chickaloon
Bay

Bird
Point

Girdwood

Chugach
National Forest

Kenai
Peninsula

Hope

Hope Hwy

Big Game Alaska

Portage

Anton Anderson
Memorial
Tunnel

Whittier

Chugach
National Forest

Black Bear
Camp Ground

Williwaw
Camp Ground

Portage
Lake

Whittier
Glacier

Begich-Boggs
Visitors Center

Portage Glacier

Seward Hwy

Alaska Railroad

To Seward (45mi)

150°W

149°30'W

149°W

ANCHORAGE

HISTORY

British explorer Captain James Cook sailed past the site in 1778 searching for the elusive Northwest Passage and hopeful gold prospectors had been stepping ashore at Ship Creek since the 1880s. But Anchorage wasn't founded until 1915, the year the Alaska Railroad decided to call this area home and the 'Great Anchorage Lot Sale' was held. In no time at all there was a tent city of 2000 people.

Anchorage soon became the epicenter for Alaska's fledgling rail, air and highway systems. Folks here built up the Depression-era settlement in the Matanuska Valley by way of military activities during WWII and developing Cook Inlet oil, discovered during the late 1950s.

Growth was explosive during these years: Anchorage's population, 8000 before WWII, jumped to 43,000 afterward. After the 1964 Good Friday Earthquake, which dumped more than 100 homes into Knik Arm, the city was rebuilding itself when another opportunity arose, the discovery of a $10 billion oil reserve in Prudhoe Bay.

Though the Trans-Alaska Pipeline doesn't come within 300 miles of Anchorage, the city took its share of the wealth, growing another 47% between 1970 and 1976. As headquarters of various petroleum and service companies, Anchorage still gushes with oil money.

This city of stage plays and snowy peaks has serious pork-barrel power. Nine of the 20 state senators and 17 of 40 state representatives come from the municipality of Anchorage. During the late 1970s, when a barrel of crude oil jumped more than $20 and Alaska couldn't spend its tax revenue fast enough, Anchorage received the lion's share. It used its political muscle to revitalize downtown Anchorage with the Sullivan Arena (p192), Egan Civic Center (p192) and stunning Alaska Center for the Performing Arts (p192).

Despite sagging oil prices throughout the late 1980s and early '90s, Anchorage continues to grow as the business center of Alaska and what remains of the last boom. But it prays and lobbies for the next one. While there are plenty of folks who were disenchanted with plans to drill oil in the scenic Arctic National Wildlife Refuge (ANWR, see p30), few of them live in Anchorage, which would love nothing more than another black-gold rush.

ORIENTATION

Anchorage sprawls across a broad peninsula that divides Cook Inlet into Knik Arm to the north and Turnagain Arm to the south. Chugach State Park and lands occupied by Elmendorf Air Force Base and Fort Richardson Military Reservation make up the city's eastern border. The airport is in the southwest of the city center; the train station is downtown.

The pedestrian-friendly downtown is arranged in a regular grid: numbered avenues run east–west and lettered streets north–south. East of A St, street names continue alphabetically, beginning with Barrow. Many streets are irritatingly one way. The grid begins to break down as you leave downtown, but numbered streets remain reliable.

As it heads northeast from downtown, 5th Ave becomes Glenn Hwy, the route to Fairbanks and Valdez; south from the city center, C St becomes New Seward Hwy with service to the Kenai Peninsula. Heading due south, L St becomes Spenard Rd, which runs through the interesting neighborhoods of Midtown and Spenard en route to the airport.

Maps

At the start of the tourist season, free city maps pop up in Anchorage like wildflowers in the spring. The Anchorage Convention & Visitors Bureau has one, but the best is the *Alaska Activities Map* published by Alaska Channel. Any of them are more than adequate to navigate you through the downtown area. For something more detailed, where all the streets have a name, there's Rand McNally's *Anchorage* ($4). The best map for hikers interested in area trails is *Chugach State Park,* published by Imus Geographics ($8).

The best place to purchase maps is the Cook Inlet Book Company (p176) or the Alaska Publics Land Information Center (APLIC, p178). At the APLIC there's a National Geographic Map Machine where you can create your own custom, waterproof topographic maps for $8 a sheet.

INFORMATION

Bookstores

Cook Inlet Book Company (Map p177; ☎ 258-4544; www.cookinlet.com; 415 W 5th Ave; ☻ 8:30am-10pm) Practically the entire store is Alaskan titles, with many of them autographed.

Title Wave Books (Map p177; ☎ 277-5127; 1360 W Northern Lights Blvd; ☻ 9am-9pm Mon-Thu, to 10pm Fri & Sat, 11am-7pm Sun) A huge, fabulous, (mostly) used bookstore, with lots of books on Alaska and everything else at about half the price you'd pay new.

Emergency

Ambulance, Fire, Police (☎ 911)

Laundry

Cleaning World II (Map p177; ☎ 561-7406; 2494 E Tudor Rd; ☻ 9am-9pm) Offers a self-serve and drop-off service.

K-Speed Wash (Map pp180-1; ☎ 279-0731; 600 E 6th Ave; ☻ 7am-8pm Mon-Sat) To clean your clothes at the speed of 'K,' whatever that means, try this place.

Left Luggage

In town many hotels and hostels will store excessive luggage for you either free or for a small fee.

Anchorage International Baggage Storage

(☎ 248-0373; Baggage Area, Domestic Terminal; per bag per day $7; ☻ 5am-2am) A bit pricey, but it's conveniently located at the Anchorage International Airport.

Library & Internet Access

Internet access and wi-fi are widely available all over Anchorage at hotels, restaurants, bars, even gift shops.

Cyber City (Map p177; ☎ 277-7601; 1441 W Northern Lights Blvd; per hr $4; ☻ 11am-2am Mon-Thu, to 3am Fri & Sat, noon-2am Sun) Midtown for late-night gamers.

Kaladi Bros Internet Cafe (Map p177; ☎ 277-5127; 1360 W Northern Lights Blvd; per hr $7; ☻ 9am-9pm Mon-Thu, to 10pm Fri & Sat, 11am-9pm Sun) Attached to Title Wave Books.

ZJ Loussac Public Library (Map p177; ☎ 343-2975; Denali St at W 36th Ave; ☻ 10am-8pm Mon-Thu, to 6pm Fri & Sat) For free Internet access and topo maps for the state. Take bus No 2, 36 or 75.

Media

Tourist freebies are available everywhere: the *Official Anchorage Visitors Guide* and Anchorage Daily News' *Alaska Visitor's Guide* are all packed with useful information.

ANCHORAGE IN...

One Day

Begin with breakfast at **Snow City Café** (p189), with the healthiest menu and hippest people downtown. Head over to the **Anchorage Museum of History & Art** (p178) and soak in Sydney Laurence's Mt McKinley masterpiece. Catch the free shuttle from the museum to the **Alaska Native Heritage Center** (p179) for an intriguing look at Alaska Native culture. In the evening stroll to the **Ship Creek Viewing Platform** (p178) to see thousands of salmon, then settle into one of many gourmet eating spots downtown.

Two Days

Follow the one-day itinerary and begin your second day with a hike up **Flattop Mountain** (p182), Alaska's most scaled peak. Idle away the afternoon at the **Alaska Zoo** (p183) because you won't get to Barrow to see a polar bear. Finish the day by joining Alaskans making fun of themselves and Spam in the *Whale-Fat Follies* at **Mr Whitekeys Fly by Nite Club** (p193).

Four Days

After the two previous days' activities, spend your third day driving scenic Seward Hwy. Look for beluga whales in Turnagain Arm and stop at **Portage Glacier** for a cruise to the retreating ice floe (p200). Spend the afternoon in funky **Girdwood** (p197) and take a ride on the **Alyeska Resort tram** (p197) to wander in the alpine above the town. Before heading back, enjoy a glass of wine and the views from on top of the mountain at **Seven Glaciers Lounge** (p199).

If it's Saturday or Sunday head over to the **Saturday Market** (p193) downtown for live music, cheap food and great souvenirs. Then rent a bicycle from **Downtown Bicycle Rental** (p182) and pedal the **Tony Knowles Coastal Trail** (p182). Finish your stay in Anchorage that evening listening to locals jam at **Humpy's** (p192).

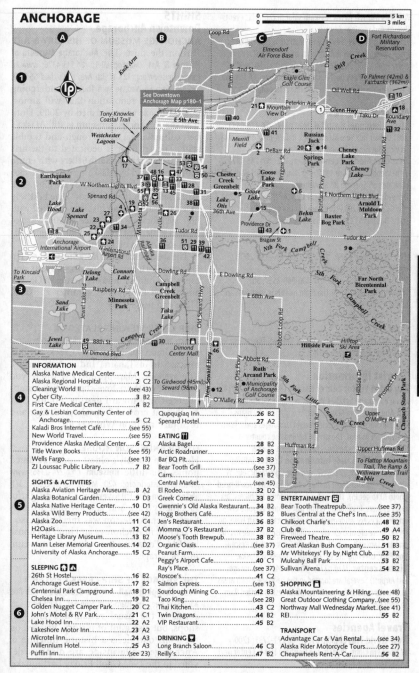

ANCHORAGE

See Downtown Anchorage Map p180–1

ANCHORAGE & AROUND

INFORMATION
Alaska Native Medical Center....................1 C2
Alaska Regional Hospital..........................2 C2
Cleaning World II...............................(see 43)
Cyber City..3 B2
First Care Medical Center.........................4 B2
Gay & Lesbian Community Center of
  Anchorage...5 C2
Kaladi Bros Internet Café....................(see 55)
New World Travel................................(see 55)
Providence Alaska Medical Center..........6 C2
Title Wave Books................................(see 55)
Wells Fargo.......................................(see 13)
ZJ Loussac Public Library.........................7 B2

SIGHTS & ACTIVITIES
Alaska Aviation Heritage Museum....8 A2
Alaska Botanical Garden...........................9 D3
Alaska Native Heritage Center.............10 D1
Alaska Wild Berry Products.............(see 42)
Alaska Zoo...11 C4
H2Oasis..12 C4
Heritage Library Museum....................13 B2
Mann Leiser Memorial Greenhouses..14 D2
University of Alaska Anchorage..........15 C2

SLEEPING
26th St Hostel.....................................16 A2
Anchorage Guest House.......................17 B2
Centennial Park Campground..............18 D1
Chelsea Inn..19 B2
Golden Nugget Camper Park...............20 C2
John's Motel & RV Park.......................21 C1
Lake Hood Inn....................................22 A2
Lakeshore Motor Inn...........................23 A2
Microtel Inn..24 A3
Millennium Hotel................................25 A3
Puffin Inn.......................................(see 23)

Qupqugiaq Inn...................................26 B2
Spenard Hostel...................................27 A2

EATING
Alaska Bagel.......................................28 B2
Arctic Roadrunner...............................29 B3
Bar BQ Pit..30 B3
Bear Tooth Grill..............................(see 37)
Carrs..31 B2
Central Market................................(see 45)
El Rodeo...32 D2
Greek Corner......................................33 B2
Gwennie's Old Alaska Restaurant.......34 B2
Hogg Brothers Café.............................35 B2
Jen's Restaurant.................................36 B3
Momma O's Restaurant...................(see 37)
Moose's Tooth Brewpub......................38 B3
Organic Oasis.................................(see 37)
Peanut Farm.......................................39 B3
Peggy's Airport Cafe...........................40 C1
Ray's Place....................................(see 37)
Roscoe's...41 C2
Salmon Express...............................(see 13)
Sourdough Mining Co.........................42 B3
Taco King.......................................(see 28)
Thai Kitchen.......................................43 C2
Twin Dragons.....................................44 B2
VIP Restaurant....................................45 B2

DRINKING
Long Branch Saloon.............................46 C3
Reilly's...47 B2

ENTERTAINMENT
Bear Tooth Theatrepub.....................(see 37)
Blues Central at the Chef's Inn.........(see 35)
Chilkoot Charlie's................................48 B2
Club @..49 A4
Fireweed Theatre................................50 B2
Great Alaskan Bush Company..............51 B3
Mr Whitekeys' Fly by Night Club........52 B2
Mulcahy Ball Park...............................53 B2
Sullivan Arena....................................54 B2

SHOPPING
Alaska Mountaineering & Hiking....(see 48)
Great Outdoor Clothing Company...(see 55)
Northway Mall Wednesday Market..(see 41)
REI...55 B2

TRANSPORT
Advantage Car & Van Rental.........(see 34)
Alaska Rider Motorcycle Tours......(see 27)
Cheapwheels Rent-A-Car....................56 B2

AK This Month (www.alaskathismonth.com) Has events listings and music reviews.

Anchorage Daily News (www.adn.com) This Pulitzer Prize–winning paper publishes an entertainment section, 8, every Friday, and an excellent outdoor section on Sunday.

Anchorage Press (www.anchoragepress.com) A fabulous free weekly with events listings and social commentary.

Medical Services

Alaska Regional Hospital (Map p177; ☎ 276-1131; 2801 DeBarr Rd) Near Merrill Field; has 24-hour emergency service. Bus Nos 8, 11 and 12 go there.

First Care Medical Center (Map p177; ☎ 248-1122; 3710 Woodland Dr, ste 1100; ☼ 7am-midnight) Walk-in clinic just off Spenard Rd in Midtown.

Providence Alaska Medical Center (Map p177; ☎ 562-2211; 3200 Providence Dr) The largest in the state. Bus Nos 1, 3, 4, 8, 1 and 45 go there.

Money

Key Bank (Map p177; ☎ 257-5500, 800-539-2968; 601 W 5th Ave) Downtown.

Wells Fargo (Map p177; ☎ 800-869-3557; 301 W Northern Lights Blvd) The main bank is in midtown and one of 12 in the city.

Post

Post office (Map pp180-1; 344 W 4th Ave) Downtown in the Village at Ship Creek Center.

Tourist Information

Log Cabin Visitor Center (Map pp180-1; ☎ 257-2342; www.anchorage.net; 524 W 4th Ave; ☼ 7:30am-7pm Jun-Aug, 8am-6pm May & Sept) Has pamphlets, maps, bus schedules, city guides in several languages and a lawn growing on its roof. The person behind the counter is a local volunteer who loves talking about Alaska.

Alaska Public Lands Information Center (APLIC; Map pp180-1; ☎ 271-2737; www.nps.gov/aplic; 605 W 4th Ave; ☼ 9am-5pm) In the Federal Building (you'll need photo ID to get in). The center has handouts for hikers, bikers, kayakers, fossil hunters and just about everyone else, on almost every wilderness area of the state. Start here, go there. There are also excellent wildlife displays, free movies and at 11am daily a guided Captain Cook walk to Resolution Park, covering the sea captain's travels in Alaska.

Visitors center (Map p177; ☎ 266-2437; Anchorage Intl Airport) Several are located in the baggage-claim areas of both terminals; the south-terminal desk is staffed 9am to 4pm daily in summer.

Travel Agencies

New World Travel (Map p177; ☎ 271-2737; 1200 W Northern Lights Blvd) In the Northern Lights Center next to REI (see boxed text, p193).

SIGHTS
Downtown Anchorage

ANCHORAGE MUSEUM OF HISTORY & ART
Pardon the dust. The **Anchorage Museum of History & Art** (Map pp180-1; ☎ 343-4326; www.anchoragemuseum.org; 121 W 7th Ave; adult/child $6.50/2; ☼ 9am-6pm Fri-Wed, to 9pm Thu) is undergoing a $75 million renovation that will almost double its size when finished by 2009. Until then the Anchorage museum is still Alaska's best cultural jewel in this rough-and-tumble state. The 1st floor is dedicated to the arts and has the **Art of the North Gallery** with entire rooms occupied by Alaskan masters Eustace Ziegler and Sydney Laurence (see p38). The **Alaska Gallery** on the 2nd floor – the best way to learn your Alaskan history – is filled with life-size dioramas that trace 10,000 years of human settlement from early subsistence villages to modern oil dependency.

The spacious, atrium **Marx Bros Café** (☎ 343-6190; lunch $8-11) serves lunches, desserts and espresso. Guided tours of the Alaska Gallery are offered throughout summer at 10am, 11am and noon daily.

SHIP CREEK VIEWING PLATFORM
From mid- to late summer, king, coho and pink salmon spawn up Ship Creek, the historical site of Tanaina Indian fish camps. The **overlook** (Map pp180-1) is where you can cheer on those love-starved fish humping their way toward destiny. Follow C St north as it crosses Ship Creek Bridge and then turn right on Whitney Rd.

OSCAR ANDERSON HOUSE
Housed in the city's oldest wooden-framed home, this little **museum** (☎ 274-2336; www.anchoragehistoric.org; 420 M St; adult/child $3/1; ☼ noon-5pm Mon-Fri) overlooks the delightful Elderberry Park and is open June to mid-September. Anderson was the 18th person to set foot in Anchorage and built his house in 1915. Today it's the only home museum in Anchorage.

THE VILLAGE OF SHIP CREEK CENTER
This **shopping mall** (☎ 278-3263; 333 W 4th Ave; admission free; ☼ 10am-9pm Mon-Sat, 11am-6pm Sun) contains the usual restaurants and gift shops, but also a lot of history. Painted on the walls outside is a historic timeline of Anchorage while inside are displays devoted to the 1964 Good Friday Earthquake.

An Alaska Native dance show is staged at 1pm daily and, if you're intrigued by the dancing, there's a shuttle-van service to the Alaska Native Heritage Center.

RESOLUTION PARK

At the west end of 3rd Ave, this small park is home to the **Captain Cook Monument** (Map p177), built to mark the 200th anniversary of the English captain's 'discovery' of Cook Inlet. If not overrun by tour-bus passengers, this observation deck has an excellent view of the surrounding mountains. Nearby, on 2nd Ave, is the **Alaska Statehood Monument**, marking the original 1915 town site with a bust of oft-ignored President Ike Eisenhower.

DELANEY PARK

Known locally as the **Park Strip** (Map pp180–1), this narrow slice of well-tended grass stretches from A to P Sts between W 9th and W 10th Aves; there's an impressive playground near the corner of E St. It was the site of the 50-ton bonfire celebrating statehood in 1959 and Pope John Paul II's 1981 outdoor mass. Today it hosts festivals like Summer Solstice and Pridefest, not to mention Frisbee games any time the weather's nice.

Midtown Anchorage & Spenard

HERITAGE LIBRARY MUSEUM

Inside the Midtown Wells Fargo bank, the **Heritage Library Museum** (Map p177; ☎ 265-2834; 301 W Northern Lights Blvd; admission free; ☷ noon-5pm Mon-Fri) is home to one of the largest collections of Alaska Native artifacts in the city and includes costumes, baskets and hunting weapons. There are also original paintings covering walls, including several by Sydney Laurence and lots of scrimshaw. The museum's collection is so large that there are displays in the elevator lobbies throughout the bank.

ALASKA AVIATION HERITAGE MUSEUM

Ideally located on the south shore of Lake Hood, the world's busiest floatplane lake, is the **Alaska Aviation Heritage Museum** (Map p177; ☎ 248-5325; www.alaskaairmuseum.com; 4721 Aircraft Dr; adult/child $5/3; ☷ 10am-6pm Wed-Mon), a tribute to Alaska's colorful bush pilots plus their faithful planes. Housed within are 25 planes along with historic photos and displays of pilots' achievements, from the first flight to Fairbanks (1913) to the

early history of Alaska Airlines. You can view early footage of bush planes in the museum's theater or step outside to its large observation deck and watch today's pilots begin their own quest for adventure with a roar on Lake Hood.

THE ALASKA NATIVE MEDICAL CENTER

This **hospital** (Map p177; ☎ 800-478-1636; 4315 Diplomacy Dr; admission free) has a fantastic collection of Alaska Native art and artifacts: take the elevator to the top floor and wind down the staircase past dolls, basketry and tools from all over Alaska.

EARTHQUAKE PARK

For decades after the 1964 earthquake, this **park** (Map p177) remained a barren moonscape revealing the tectonic power that destroyed nearby Turnagain Heights. Today Earthquake Park, at the west end of Northern Lights Blvd on the Knik Arm, is being reclaimed by nature; you'll have to poke around the bushes to see evidence of tectonic upheaval. The rippled land is now a favorite of mountain bikers.

UNIVERSITY OF ALASKA ANCHORAGE

UA-Anchorage (Map p177; ☎ 786-1800; www.uaa.alaska.edu; Providence Dr; bus Nos 3, 13 & 45) is the largest college campus in the state, but there is far less to do here than at its sister school UA Fairbanks. The Campus Center is home to a small art gallery and the bookstore, which has a good selection of Alaskana, clothing that says 'Alaska' on it and used microbiology texts. There are trails from the campus that connect UA to Goose Lake, Chester Creek Greenbelt and Earthquake Park.

GOOSE LAKE

You'll stop complaining about global warming once you experience an 85°F Anchorage afternoon at **Goose Lake** (Map p177; UA Dr). Just off Northern Lights Blvd (bus Nos 3 and 45), this is the city's most developed lake for swimming with lifeguards, paddleboat rentals and a small café, which serves hot dogs and pizza.

Greater Anchorage

ALASKA NATIVE HERITAGE CENTER

Experiencing Alaska Native culture firsthand in the Bush is logistically complicated and expensive. Instead, come to this 26-acre

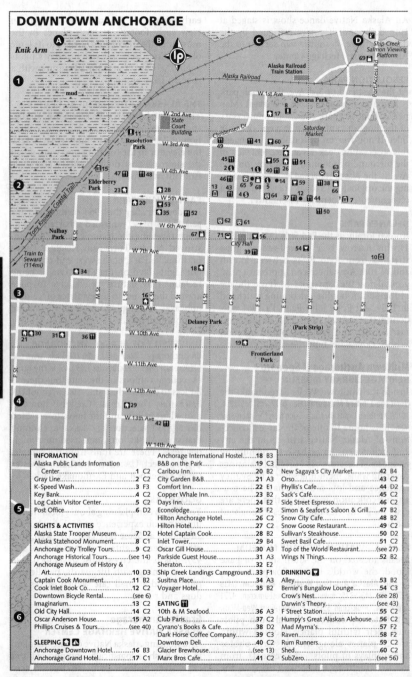

DOWNTOWN ANCHORAGE

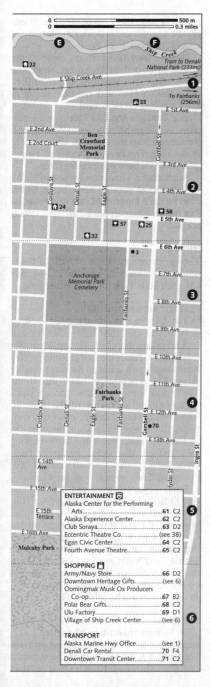

center (Map p177; ☎ 330-8000, 800-315-6608; www
.alaskanative.net; 8800 Heritage Center Dr; adult/child $21/16;
⏱ 9am-6pm) and see how humans survived –
and thrived – before central heating.

The main building houses meandering
exhibits on traditional arts and sciences –
including kayaks and rain gear that rival
outdoors department store REI's best offerings. It also features various performances, among them, the staccato Alaghanak
song, lost for 50 years: the center collected
bits and pieces of the traditional song from
different tribal elders and reconstructed
it. Outside, examples of typical structures
from the Aleut, Yupik, Tlingit and other
tribes are arranged around a picturesque
lake. Docents explain the ancient architects'
cunning technology: check out wooden
panels that shrink in the dry summers (allowing light and air inside) but expand to
seal out the cold during the wet winter.

This is much more than just a museum;
it represents a knowledge bank of language,
art and culture that will survive no matter
how many sitcoms are crackling through
the Alaskan stratosphere. It's a labor of love,
and of incalculable value.

The center runs a free shuttle bus that
picks up from five places downtown, including the Log Cabin Visitors Center
(p178) and the Anchorage Museum of History & Art (p178).

ALASKA BOTANICAL GARDEN
The garden (Map p177; ☎ 770-3692; Campbell Airstrip
Rd; adult/family $5/10; ⏱ 9am-9pm) is a colorful
showcase for native species, where gentle
paths lead you through groomed herb, rock
and perennial gardens in a wooded setting.
The mile-long Lowenfels Family Nature
Trail, built for tanks during WWII, is a great
place to learn your basic Alaskan botany
or just watch the bald eagles pluck salmon
from Campbell Creek.

RUSSIAN JACK SPRINGS PARK
Named after the original homesteader of the
site, this 300-acre park (Map p177) is south of
Glenn Hwy on Boniface Parkway and can be
reached by bus Nos 3 and 12. The park has
tennis courts, hiking and biking trails, and
a picnic area. Near the DeBarr Rd entrance
you'll find the Mann Leiser Memorial Greenhouses
(☎ 343-4717; ⏱ 8am-3pm), a toasty oasis of tropical plants, exotic birds and fish.

ANCHORAGE & AROUND

FAR NORTH BICENTENNIAL PARK

Comprising 4000 acres of forest and muskeg in east central Anchorage, this **park** (Map p177) features 20 miles of trails. In the center of the park is Bureau of Land Management's (BLM's) **Campbell Tract**, a 700-acre wildlife preserve where it's possible to see moose and bears in the spring and brilliant fall colors in mid-September. Take O'Malley Rd east to Hillside Dr and follow the signs.

KINCAID PARK

At the western 'nose' of the peninsula and southern terminus of the Tony Knowles Coastal Trail is a beloved 1400-acre **park** (Map p177) populated by hikers and cyclists all summer long. Trails wind through a rolling terrain of forested hills where there are views of Mt Susitna, Mt McKinley on a clear day and fiery sunsets in the evening. Follow Raspberry Rd west to the parking lot and trailheads.

ACTIVITIES
Cycling

Anchorage has 122 miles of paved paths that parallel major roads or wind through the greenbelts, making a bicycle the easiest and cheapest way to explore the downtown and Midtown areas of the city. If you run out of gas before the end of the ride, all People Mover buses (p195) are equipped with bike racks.

Downtown Bicycle Rental (Map pp180-1; ☎ 279-5293; www.alaska-bike-rentals.com; 333 W 4th Ave; per 3/24hr $15/29; ☼ 8am-8pm) has road, hybrid and mountain bikes as well as tandems, trailers and even clip-in pedals and shoes. Locks, helmets and bike maps are free.

Pablo's Bicycle Rentals (☎ 250-2871; 5th & L St; per 4/24hr $15/20; ☼ 7am-7pm Mon-Fri, from 8am Sat & Sun) is next to Copper Whale Inn downtown.

BIKE TRAILS

Anchorage's favorite trail is the **Tony Knowles Coastal Trail** (Map pp180-1), 11 scenic miles that begins at the west end of 2nd Ave downtown and reaches Elderberry Park a mile away. From there, it winds through Earthquake Park, around Point Woronzof (Map p174) and finally to Point Campbell in Kincaid Park. There are good views of Knik Arm and the Alaska Range along the way.

Chester Creek Trail is a scenic 6-mile path through the Chester Creek Greenbelt that connects with the Coastal Trail at Westchester Lagoon and follows a mountain-fed stream to Goose Lake Park.

Campbell Creek Trail features some of the newest paved path in Anchorage, stretching 8 miles from Far North Bicentennial Park to the Seward Hwy with most of the ride in the Campbell Creek Greenbelt.

The **Turnagain Arm Bike Path** is a 14-mile paved bicycle path that begins at Potter Marsh Refuge and hugs the shoreline all the way to Bird Creek. The sweeping views of Turnagain Arm will have you pausing often.

Anchorage is a haven for mountain biking with the most popular areas being **Kincaid Park**, **Far North Bicentennial Park** and **Powerline Pass Trail** in Chugach State Park. For details see p61.

Hiking

Though there are dozens of trails in town, outdoors enthusiasts head to 773-sq-mile Chugach State Park for the mother lode.

FLATTOP MOUNTAIN TRAIL

In Los Angeles, you cruise the Sunset Strip; in Paris, you stroll the Champs-Elysées; and in Anchorage, you climb Flattop Mountain (Map p177). This is the first mountain every Anchorage youth scales on the way to higher things. The very popular 3-mile hike to the 3550ft peak is easy to follow, though you'll be scrambling a bit toward the summit. Allow three to five hours. Another trail continues three more miles along the ridgeline to Flaketop Peak. From the same parking area, you can also access the 2-mile Blueberry Loop (perfect for kids) and 11-mile Powerline Trail, popular with bicyclists.

From Seward Hwy, head 4 miles east on O'Malley Dr and make a right on Hillside Rd; after 1 mile make a left on Upper Huffman Rd and follow the signs to the Glen Alps park entrance. Parking is $5. For transportation there's **Flattop Mountain Shuttle** (☎ 279-3334; round-trip adult/child $29/15) that leaves various locations downtown at 10:30am, 1pm, 3:30pm and 6:30pm daily. Round-trip is adult/child $29/15.

THE RAMP

This 14-mile round-trip **hike** (Map p177) starts close to the Flattop Mountain trailhead and it takes you past alpine summits and through tranquil tundra. Rather than following the upper trail to Flattop Mountain, hike half a mile to Powerline Trail. Turn right and follow the power line for 2 miles, where an old jeep trail crosses over from the left and heads downhill to the south fork of Campbell Creek.

The trail then crosses the creek and continues to a valley on the other side. Hike up the alpine valley to Ship Lake Pass, which lies between the 5240ft Ramp and the 4660ft Wedge, with great camping and climbing. Allow eight to 10 hours.

WILLIWAW LAKES TRAIL

This easy 13-mile **hike** (Map p177) also begins close to the Flattop Mountain trailhead, leading to the handful of alpine lakes at the base of Mt Williwaw. The trail makes a pleasant overnight hike and many consider it the most scenic outing in the Hillside area of Chugach State Park.

Walk half a mile to the Powerline Pass Trail and then turn right, continuing 300yd to Middle Fork Loop Trail. Follow it down and across the south fork of Campbell Creek, then north for 1½ miles to the middle fork of the creek. Here you reach a junction; make a right on Williwaw Lakes Trail. You can make this an overnight trek or a seven- to nine-hour day hike.

WOLVERINE PEAK TRAIL

This strenuous but rewarding 14-mile round-trip ascends the 4455ft triangular peak, visible from Anchorage. The marked trail begins at an old homesteader road that crosses the south fork of Campbell Creek. Keep heading east and the road will become a footpath that ascends above the tree line and eventually fades out (mark it for the return trip). From there, it's 3 miles to Wolverine Peak.

From Seward Hwy, head 4 miles east on O'Malley Rd and make a left on Hillside Dr and follow the signs to the Prospect Heights entrance of Chugach State Park. Parking costs $5.

RENDEZVOUS PEAK ROUTE

The 4-mile trek to this 4050ft peak is an easy three- to five-hour trip, rewarding hikers with incredible views of Mt McKinley, Cook Inlet, Turnagain and Knik Arms, and the city far below. From the parking lot, a short trail leads along the right-hand side of the stream up the valley to the northwest. It

ends at a pass where a short ascent to Rendezvous Peak is easily seen and climbed.

From Glenn Hwy, exit Arctic Valley Rd (Fort Richardson) and follow signs to Arctic Valley; a 7-mile gravel road leads to the Alpenglow Ski Area parking lot. Parking costs $5.

MCHUGH LAKE TRAIL

This 13-mile trail originates at McHugh Creek Picnic Area, 15 miles south of Anchorage at Mile 111.8 of the Seward Hwy. The route follows the McHugh Creek valley, and in 7 miles reaches Rabbit and McHugh Lakes, two beautiful alpine pools reflecting the 5000ft Suicide Peaks.

The first 3 miles feature some good climbs, and the round-trip trek makes for a long day. It's better to haul in a tent and then spend the afternoon exploring the open tundra country and nearby ridges.

ANCHORAGE FOR CHILDREN

Anchorage is exceptionally kid-friendly – more than 40 city parks boast playscapes. Close to downtown, **Frontierland Park** (10th Ave & E St) is a local favorite while **Valley of the Moon Park** (Arctic Blvd & W 17th St) makes a delightful picnic spot. Entice your family to the **Anchorage Museum of History & Art** (p178) by promising to first explore the hands-on exhibits of its Children's Gallery.

Alaska Zoo

The unique wildlife of the Arctic is on display at the **Alaska Zoo** (Map p177; ☎ 346-3242; 4731 O'Malley Rd; adult/child $9/5; ♥ 9am-6pm Wed-Thu & Sat-Mon, to 9pm Tue & Fri), the only zoo in North America that specializes in northern animals, including snow leopards, Amur tigers and Tibetan yaks. Alaska Native species, from wolverines and moose to caribou and Dall sheep, are abundant. What kids will love watching, however, are the bears. The zoo has all four Alaskan species (brown, black, glacier and polar) but Ahpun, the polar bear, is clearly the star attraction. New exhibits for black bears, otters and seals have made the zoo a much more realistic setting to view wildlife.

Imaginarium

Whoever thought science could be so much fun? At the **Imaginarium Science Discovery Center** (Map pp180-1; ☎ 276-3179; 725 W 5th Ave; adult/child

---

OFFBEAT ANCHORAGE

The wildest salmon in Anchorage are nowhere near Ship Creek. They're found spawning along downtown streets as part of the **Wild Salmon on Parade**, an annual event in which local artists turn fiberglass fish into anything but fish. Modeled after Chicago's 'Cows on Parade,' the art competition has resulted in an Elvis Presley salmon; a salmon turned into a floatplane; 'Uncle Salmon' painted in red-white-and-blue stripes; and 'Fish & Chips,' a poker-playing halibut. The 30 or so colorful fish appear on the streets in early June just when the king salmon begin spawning in Ship Creek and stick around until September when the tourists are fleeing the state. To see them all, pick up a fish tour map at the Log Cabin Visitors Center (p178).

Most of us would rather avoid the police. But who can resist the **Alaska State Trooper Museum** (Map pp180-1; ☎ 279-5050; www.alaskatroopermuseum.com; 245 W 5th Ave; admission free; ☺ 10am-4pm Mon-Fri, from noon Sun)? Dedicated to law enforcement starting when Alaska was a territory, the storefront museum has a 1952 Hudson Hornet cop car, state-issued sealskin cop boots and a tribute to Fran Howard, the nation's first unrestricted (ie on the beat and carrying a gun) female cop. In the gift shop you can stay one step ahead of the TV networks with its 'CSI: Alaska' T-shirt.

$5.50/5; ☺ 10am-6pm Mon-Fri, noon-5pm Sun) kids can hug a life-size *Tyrannosaurus rex*, stand inside a giant bubble, pick up a sea star from a touch tank or become a human gyroscope. Far from being bored, parents will also love this award-winning center of hands-on fun and everybody will leave with a better understanding of uniquely Alaskan topics.

H²Oasis

Qualifying as surreal, Anchorage's original **waterpark** (☎ 344-8610; www.h2oasiswaterpark.com; 1520 O'Malley Rd; adult/child $20/15; ☺ 10am-10pm) is a $7 million, three-level amusement zone with palm trees, water slides, a wave pool and the 505ft Master Blaster, one very wet roller coaster. Feel free to just watch from the grown-ups-only hot tubs.

Alaska Wild Berry Products

If the Flattop Mountain hike is overly ambitious for your kids, head to this giant **jam and gift shop with chocolate falls** (☎ 907-562-8858; 5525 Juneau St; admission free; ☺ 10am-11pm). Inside the sprawling store is the falls, outside there's a short nature trail that leads to a handful of reindeer that kids can feed and pet.

TOURS
City Tours

Anchorage City Trolley Tours (Map pp180-1; ☎ 276-5603; 612 W 4th Ave; adult/child $10/5; ☺ tours on the hour 9am-5pm) One-hour rides in a bright ride trolley past Lake Hood, Earthquake Park and Cook Inlet among other sights.

Anchorage Historical Tours (Map pp180-1; ☎ 274-3600; 524 W 4th Ave; adult/child $5/1) Starting at the Old

City Hall, its hour-long downtown walking tour begins at 1pm Monday to Friday.

Gray Line (Map pp180-1; ☎ 277-5581, 800-478-6388; www.graylineofalaska.com; 745 W 4th Ave) Three-hour bus downtown tours and the Alaska Native Heritage Center ($46).

Flightseeing Tours

They're costly and never as long as you wish, but they're a stunning way to spend an hour or two. If you've got the cash – lots of it – flightseeing tours provide an eagle-eye view of the wilderness and mountains, imparting a sense of scale that's difficult to appreciate from the ground.

Alaska Air Taxi (☎ 243-3944, 800-789-5232; www .alaskaairtaxi.com) Has a 1½-hour tour over the Chugach Mountains to Knik Glacier ($195) and another the same length and price to Blackstone Glacier in Prince William Sound.

Regal Air (☎ 243-8535) Flying out of Lake Hood, this has some of the best rates for flightseeing. Its Mt McKinley tour is only $239, a 1½-hour tour of Knik Glacier is $179.

Rust's Flying Service (☎ 243-1595, 800-544-2299; www.flyrusts.com) Offers a three-hour Mt McKinley flight that includes flying the length of Ruth Glacier ($269) and a three-hour Columbia Glacier tour ($259).

Day Tours

Have a leftover day? Have an adventure. There are few places in Alaska that somebody in Anchorage isn't willing to whisk you off to in a day. Gray Line (left) offers a one-day trip to Barrow ($643) with four hours in the village itself and the rest of the day spent flying. Pray for clear weather

Alaska Railroad (Map pp180-1; ☎ 265-2494, 800-544-0552; www.akrr.com; 411 W 1st Ave) Has a number of one-day tours from Anchorage that begin with a train ride. Its nine-hour Spencer Glacier Adventure (per person $159) includes a ride to Spencer Lake and a gentle raft trip among the glacier's icebergs. The Kenai National Park Cruise ($221) is a train ride to Seward and a six-hour wildlife cruise.

K2 Aviation (☎ 733-2291, 800-764-2291; www.flyk2 .com) Has an affordable day tour to Talkeetna (adult/child $115/55). It departs Anchorage at 7:35am and returns by 5:30pm to give you four hours in a quaint frontier town. That's enough time to even squeeze in a Mt McKinley flightseeing tour.

Phillips Cruises & Tours (Map pp180-1; ☎ 276-8023, 800-544-0529; www.26glaciers.com; 519 W 4th Ave) Takes you on bus to Whittier and then on a boat past 26 glaciers in Prince William Sound. The eight-hour tour (adult/child $138/78) is offered daily and includes lunch.

Ring of Fire Pedal & Paddle Tours (☎ 332-0225; www.ringoffiretours.com) Its one-day, guided kayak adventure in Seward's Resurrection Bay ($110) includes transport from Anchorage, equipment and lunch.

Rust's Flying Service (☎ 243-1595, 800-544-2299; www.flyrusts.com) One of many air charters that will zip you off to Katmai National Park to view brown bears feeding on salmon at Brooks Falls. The 10-hour tour is $599 per person.

FESTIVALS & EVENTS

These are just a few of Anchorage's more popular events; contact the **Anchorage Convention & Visitors Bureau** (☎ 276-3200; www.anchorage .net) to see what's on while you're here.

Anchorage Fur Rendezvous (☎ 274-1177; www .furrondy.net) The place to get fresh-trapped furs is still the 'Rondy,' but most folks prefer to sculpt ice, taste local microbrews or ride the Ferris wheel in freezing late-February temperatures. When the Rondy ends the famed 1100-mile National Historic Iditarod Trail begins. Better stay another week.

Blues on the Green Is there a better way to spend a mid-June day than listening to blues and jazz at Kincaid Park? Musicians range from locals to legends like John Lee Hooker, Jr.

Mayor's Midnight Sun Marathon (☎ 786-1230; www.mayorsmarathon.com) You know it's going to be a long day when you start this on the Summer Solstice in late June.

SLEEPING

Sleeping in Anchorage is expensive no matter what type of accommodations you choose. In Anchorage, we've listed budget places as under $100, midrange $100 to $180 and top end from $180 and up. To make matters even worse, the city raised its sales-and-bed tax to 12% in 2006 (not included in prices given below).

Budget
HOSTELS

Anchorage Guest House (Map p177; ☎ 907-274-0408; www.akhouse.com; 2001 Hillcrest Dr; dm $28, r from $78; ☒ ▣) This beautiful place feels more like a B&B than a hostel, and the prices reflect that. Rent a bike ($2.50 per hour) for the nearby Tony Knowles Coastal trail or soak up the midnight sun in the sunroom. The location is a little isolated but Bus Nos 3, 7 and 36 cruise within easy walking distance; exit at West High School.

Spenard Hostel (Map p177; ☎ 248-5036; www .alaskahostel.org; 2845 W 42nd Pl; campsite/dm/r $18/18/72; ☒ ▣) Two blocks from Spenard Rd, near Gwennie's Old Alaska Restaurant, is this clean and relaxed hostel, with laundry, no lockout and three kitchens to avoid meal-time madness. Guests can rent mountain

ANCHORAGE & AROUND

GAY & LESBIAN ANCHORAGE

It's not West Hollywood, but Anchorage does have a handful of gay- and lesbian-friendly bars (see p192) and lodgings (see p186). The city's not particularly gay- and lesbian-friendly, so consider the situation carefully before revealing your sexual orientation.

The weeklong **Pridefest** (mid-June) is a gay-pride celebration that includes a Queer Film Festival, Drag Queen Bingo, a parade through downtown and a party at Delaney Park.

The **Gay & Lesbian Community Center of Anchorage** (GLCCA; ☎ 929-4528; 2110 E Northern Lights Blvd; ☺ 3-9pm Mon-Fri, noon-6pm Sat-Sun) has a community bulletin board and lots of personal advice. It also helps organize Anchorage Pridefest and carries two good newsletters, *North View*, an Anchorage-based monthly, and the *Klondyke Kontact*, a bimonthly women's journal.

Alaska GLBT News (alaskaglbtnews@yahoo.com) and **Anchorage Pride** (www.egroups.com/subscribe /anchoragepride) both provide news and events listings via email.

The **Gay & Lesbian Helpline** (☎ 258-4777, toll-free across Alaska ☎ 888-901-9876; ☺ 6-11pm) is operated by Identity, Inc.

ANCHORAGE & AROUND

THE AUTHOR'S CHOICE

If you're thinking of splurging on accommodations in Anchorage, think small. This is ine of two boutique hotels conveniently located downtown that combine luxurious rooms with the personal attention and gracious service that only small hotels can deliver.

The **Historic Anchorage Hotel** (Map pp180-1; ☎ 272-4553, 800-544-0988; www .historicanchoragehotel.com; 330 E St; r $209-249; ✕ ▣) has 26 rooms and suites with lots of history. Established in 1916 (a year after the city was) the current hotel was built in 1936 and somehow survived the 1964 earthquake that destroyed most of the buildings around it. The hotel once housed the studio of painter Sydney Laurence while pilots Will Rogers and Wiley Post stayed there two days before their fateful flight to Barrow in 1935.

---

bikes ($3 per hour) or use old beaters for free and store bags (per day/month $1/15). Its message board is a good place to find a ride or a temporary job. Reservations are highly recommended for July and August. Take bus No 7 or 36.

26 Street Hostel (Map p177; ☎ 274-1252; 1037 W 26th St; dm $22; ✕ ▣) Anchorage's newest hostel is in Midtown and trying hard with clean rooms, free Internet and Continental breakfast plus a TV room with loads of videos. If you catch a whopper in Ship Creek, there is a BBQ area with a covered picnic table outside.

Anchorage International Hostel (Map pp180-1; ☎ 276-3635; www.anchorageinternationalhostel.org; 700 H St; dm/r $20/50) No longer affiliated with HI, this hostel is still somewhat regimented with lockout times (9am to 5pm) and curfews (1am). But its location is hard to beat; downtown practically across from the bus terminal. There's laundry facilities, common areas, luggage storage and beater bikes to toll around town on.

MOTELS
Anchorage Downtown Hotel (Map pp180-1; ☎ 258-7669; www.anchoragedowntownhotel.com; 826 K St; r $92-105; ✕ ▣) Although not exactly downtown, this small hotel was renovated and renamed in 2005. Now it's a pleasant place to stay with 17 rooms that feature private baths,

coffeemakers, small refrigerators and microwaves. Among its many amenities is an airport-shuttle service.

Chelsea Inn (Map p177; ☎ 276-5002; 3836 Spenard Rd; s/d with bath $79/89, without bath $69/79; ▣) This European-style inn has comfortable rooms with a community kitchen, Internet access, Continental breakfast and free transport from the airport. What more could you want?

Caribou Inn (Map pp180-1; ☎ 272-0444; 800-272-5878; www.cariboubnb.com; 501 L St; s/d with bath $99/109, without bath $89/99; ✕) The downtown location is perfect and the 14 rooms, though sort of run-down, are acceptable and come with a full breakfast. Among the amenities are free bikes and airport/train shuttle service.

Qupqugiaq Inn (Map p177; ☎ 563-5633; www.qupq .com; 640 W 36th Ave; s/d with bath $70/82, without bath $50/62; ✕ ▣) Rooms are small but clean and well kept, and amazingly include cable TV.

John's Motel & RV Park (Map p177; ☎ 277-4332, 800-478-4332; www.johnsmotel.com; 3543 Mountain View Dr; RV sites $25, s/d $55/60) It's more RV park than motel. Only thing smaller than the 18 rooms is the price.

CAMPING
Chugach State Park has several public campgrounds, but none is close to town.

Ship Creek Landings (Map pp180-1; ☎ 277-0877; alaskarv.com; 150 Ingra St; campsites/RV sites $15/30; ▣) It isn't exactly pristine wilderness and there's the train rumbling by, but it does provide laundry facilities, Internet access and a convenient location.

Centennial Park Campground (Map p177; ☎ 343-6986; 8300 Glenn Hwy; sites $17) Located 5 miles from downtown but is pleasant and People Mover buses (No 3 or 75) stop nearby.

Golden Nugget Camper Park (Map p177; ☎ 333-5311, 800-449-2012; 4100 DeBarr Rd; campsites/RV sites $17/27) Located near Russian Jack Springs Park, it can be accessed via bus No 3. It caters to the RV crowd but accepts tents.

Midrange
B&BS
Lake Hood Inn (Map p177; ☎ 258-9321; www.lake hoodinn.com; 4702 Lake Spenard Dr; r $119-139; ✕ ▣) If you're infatuated with floatplanes and bush pilots, book a room here. This upscale home, with four guest rooms, is adorned with airplane artifacts, from a Piper propeller that doubles as a ceiling fan to a row of seats from a Russian airline. Outside are

two decks, one with a hot tub, where you can watch a parade of floatplanes lift off the lake like an impromptu air show.

B&B on the Park (Map pp180-1; ☎ 277-0878, 800-353-0878; www.bedandbreakfastonthepark.net; 602 W 10th Ave; r $125; ✖) All five rooms in this beautifully restored 1946 log church have a private bath. Family-style breakfast is served at 8am sharp, so no lollygagging in bed!

Oscar Gill House (Map pp180-1; ☎ 279-1344; www.oscargill.com; 1344 W 10th Ave; r $99-125; ✖) This historic clapboard home was built in 1913 in Knik and later moved to its Midtown location. The B&B offers three guest rooms (two that share a bath), a fantastic breakfast and free bikes.

City Garden B&B (Map pp180-1; ☎ 276-8686; www.citygarden.biz; 1352 W 10th Ave; r $100-150; ✖ 🖥) One of several B&Bs located on a two-block stretch of 10th Ave, this is an open, sunny, gay-and-lesbian-friendly place with more cutting-edge art than antiques. The nicest of the three rooms has a private bath.

MOTELS

Puffin Inn (Map p177; ☎ 243-4044, 800-478-3346; www.puffininn.net; 4400 Spenard Rd; s $110-190, d $120-200; ✖ 🖥) It has three tiers of fine rooms, from 26 sardine can–economy rooms to full suites, all accessible via free 24-hour airport shuttle.

Comfort Inn (Map pp180-1; ☎ 277-6887; 111 W Ship Creek Ave; r $174; 🖥 🐾) Right by the train station and so close to Ship Creek you can watch anglers hook salmon from your room. This is a rather elegant branch of the chain, and comes complete with an indoor pool and kitchenettes.

Microtel Inn (Map p177; ☎ 245-5002; 5205 Northwood Dr; r $129-139; 🖥) Unphotogenic and inconvenient unless you're catching an early flight, but it has huge rooms and is excellent value.

Lakeshore Motor Inn (Map p177; ☎ 248-3485, 800-770-3000; www.lakeshoremotorinn.com; 3009 Lakeshore Dr; s/d $129/139) Older and more worn than neighboring Puffin Inn, but it has laundry facilities, kitchenettes and its own airport shuttle. This is the kind of place that needs to post in the lobby: 'Hunters – no racks or meat in the rooms.'

Days Inn (Map pp180-1; ☎ 276-7226; www.daysinnalaska.com; 321 E 5th Ave; r $169; 🖥) Clean, utilitarian and staff members give you a voucher for breakfast at the restaurant across the

street. Plus there's a free shuttle to the train station or airport.

Econolodge (Map pp180-1; ☎ 274-1515; 642 E 5th Ave; r $115) Shabby but adequate, with a guest kitchen and free airport shuttle to sweeten the deal.

HOTELS

Voyager Hotel (Map pp180-1; ☎ 277-9501, 800-247-9070; www.voyagerhotel.com; 501 K St; r $179; ✖ 🖥) A 40-room hotel with a great location downtown. It was renovated in 2005, making it conveniently clean.

Inlet Tower (Map pp180-1; ☎ 276-0110, 800-544-0786; www.inlettower.com; 1200 L St; s/d $189/229; 🖥) Fifteen floors of spacious suites with kitchenettes, gourmet coffee for the coffeemaker, large TVs with in-room movies. Could use a little TLC, but the views are amazing.

Top End
B&BS

Susitna Place (Map pp180-1; ☎ 274-3344; www.susitnaplace.com; 727 N St; r $95-150, ste $175; 🖥 ✖) On the edge of downtown, this 4000-sq-ft home sits on a bluff overlooking Cook Inlet and Mt Susitna in the distance. You can enjoy the spectacular view from any of the nine guest rooms, from a number of decks outside or through the floor-to-ceiling windows in the living room. Four rooms have shared baths while the Susitna suite comes with a fireplace, Jacuzzi and a private deck.

Copper Whale Inn (Map pp180-1; ☎ 258-7999; www.copperwhale.com; W 5th Ave & L St; r $145-185; ✖) Just blocks from the city center, the 15 rooms are no-frills but tidy, and your view of Cook Inlet and the Alaska Range is the highlight of breakfast.

Parkside Guest House (Map pp180-1; ☎ 683-2290; www.campdenali.com; 1302 W 10 Ave; r $150-175; ✖) The Cole family that runs Camp Denali inside Denali National Park also operates this luxurious B&B. The four rooms are large and lead out to spacious, 2nd-floor sitting area with a fireplace, rocking chairs and a view of the city skyline and Cook Inlet.

HOTELS

Anchorage Grand Hotel (Map pp180-1; ☎ 929-8888, 888-800-0640; www.anchoragegrandhotel.com; 505 W 2nd Ave; r $169; ✖ 🖥) Less than two blocks away from Anchorage Heritage Hotel is this hotel with 30 spacious suites that include full kitchens and separate living and

188 ANCHORAGE •• Eating

bedroom areas. Many overlook Ship Creek and Cook Inlet and its downtown location is convenient to everything.

Hilton Anchorage (☎ 272-7411, 800-245-2527; www.hiltonanchorage.com; 500 W 3rd Ave; s/d $289/309; ✗ ⬜ ⬛) The Hilton has the best location of any of the luxury hotels, right in the heart of the downtown scene. Three restaurants, a fitness center with a pool, two 1000lb bears in the lobby, lots of elegance. If you're going to pay this much ask for a room with a view of Cook Inlet.

Hotel Captain Cook (☎ 276-6000, 800-843-1950; www.captaincook.com; cnr 4th Ave & K St; s/d $245/255; ✗ ⬜ ⬛) The grand dame of Anchorage accommodations still has an air of an Alaskan aristocrat right down to the doormen with top hats. Plenty of plush services and upscale shops: Jacuzzis, fitness clubs, beauty salon, jewelry store, four restaurants including the famed Crow's Nest Bar on the top floor.

Sheraton (Map pp180-1; ☎ 276-8700; www.sheraton anchoragehotel.com; 401 E 6th Ave; r $279; ⬜) Sixteen floors, 375 rooms, amenities galore including a fitness center. The art collection and Alaskan jade staircase are impressive, while its Ptarmigan Bar can be a relaxing end to a long day of sightseeing.

Millennium Hotel (Map p177; ☎ 243-2300, 800-544-0553; 4800 Spenard Rd; r $239; ✗ ⬜) A large, 246-room resort with a woodsy log-cabin theme overlooking Lake Spenard. PETA members take note; there are stuffed animals, trophy mounts and large fish everywhere, including the obligatory 1500lb Kodiak brown bear. All rooms are large with king or queen beds and recently renovated.

EATING

Anchorage has plenty of fast food, espresso stands every five blocks and, of course, more fried halibut and smoked salmon than you can shake a rod and reel at. But the bustling city also boasts a variety of international cuisines, from Polynesian to Mexican to Vietnamese, that you'll be hard-pressed to find in the Bush. Take advantage of this savory melting pot while you can.

Downtown
RESTAURANTS

Sack's Cafe (Map pp180-1; ☎ 274-4022; 328 G St; lunch $9-12, dinner $18-35; ⏲ 11am-2:30pm & 5-9:30pm Mon-Thu, 11am-2:30pm & 5-10:30pm Fri & Sat, 10:30am-3pm & 5-9:30pm Sun; ✗) A bright, colorful restaurant

serving light American fare that is consistently creative. It is always bustling (reservations recommended) with patrons feasting on ravioli filled with roasted butternut squash or free-range chicken stuffed with spinach, caramelized onions and prosciutto.

Marx Bros Cafe (Map pp180-1; ☎ 278-2133; 627 W 3rd Ave; dinner $28-50; ⏲ 5:30-10pm Tue-Sat; ✗) They woo you into this historic (1916) home promising views of Cook Inlet but let's face it, you're looking at fuel tanks along Ship Creek. Some of Anchorage's most innovative cooking and a 500-bottle wine list are the real reasons this 12-table restaurant is so popular. There's more meat than seafood on the menu here, with mains like Misty Island Ranch steak that has been crusted in peppercorns and topped with caramelized onions and Stilton cheese. In the summer a table needs to be booked a week in advance.

Humpy's Great Alaskan Alehouse (Map p177; ☎ 276-2337; 610 W 6th Ave; dinner $12-30; ⏲ 11am-2am) Anchorage's most beloved beer place with 44 draughts on tap. There's also ale-battered halibut, gourmet pizzas and outdoor tables.

Glacier Brewhouse (Map pp180-1; ☎ 274-2739; 737 5th Ave; lunch $8-16, dinner $10-34; ⏲ 11am-9:30pm Mon, to 10pm Tue-Thu, to 11pm Fri & Sat, noon-4pm Sun) Grab a table overlooking the three giant copper brewing tanks and enjoy wood-fired pizzas and rotisserie-grilled ribs and chops with a pint of oatmeal stout.

THE AUTHOR'S CHOICE

Orso (Map pp180-1; ☎ 222-3232; 737 W 5th Ave; lunch $9-16, dinner $16-27; ⏲ 11am-10:30pm; ✗) The boldest restaurant in town. With smoked salmon walls and wooden floors covered with oriental rugs, it's like a stepping into a Tuscany country inn – only there's modern art all around and soft jazz floating into both dining levels and the bar. Its mains are Mediterranean grill with an Alaskan twist, its pasta is made fresh daily and everything is served by wait staff members that know how the chef prepares it. Break that Alaskan seafood rut you're in by ordering osso buco, lamb shanks braised in sweet-and-sour onions, kalamata olives and plum tomatoes, and served with creamy polenta.

Simon & Seafort's Saloon & Grill (☎ 274-3502; 420 L St; lunch $8-16, dinner $19-40; ☺ 11:15am-2:30pm Mon-Fri, 4:30-10pm daily) Lets you watch the sun set behind Mt Susitna while you enjoy surf-and-turf or halibut stuffed with crab and macadamias, in a century-old saloon. Check out Anchorage's largest offering of single-malt Scotch.

Snow Goose Restaurant (Map pp180-1; ☎ 277-7727; 717 W 3rd Ave; medium pizza $13-14; ☺ 11:30am-11:30pm) The outdoor deck on the 2nd floor is positioned to lookout onto Cook Inlet, Mt Susitna and the sunsets whenever they occur. That alone is worth a $5 pint of the microbrew beer.

Club Paris (Map pp180-1; ☎ 277-6332; 417 W 5th Ave; lunch $7-20, dinner $17-42; ☺ 11am-2:30pm Mon-Sat, 5-10pm daily; ☒) This longtime restaurant – it survived the 1964 earthquake – serves the best steaks in Anchorage. If there's room on your credit card try the 4in-thick filet mignon.

Sullivan's Steakhouse (Map pp180-1; ☎ 258-2882; 320 W 5th Ave; lunch $9-18, dinner $20-32; ☺ 11:30am-2pm & 5:30pm-11pm Mon-Fri, 5:30-11pm Sat, 5-11pm Sun; ☒) Another longtime steakhouse with a wood-paneled, 'old boys' club' atmosphere and giant photos of the boxer on the walls. A piano player (but not Billy Joel) performs nightly in the bar.

Twin Dragons (Map p177; ☎ 276-7535; 612 E 15th Ave; ☺ 11am-10pm Mon-Thu, to 10:30pm Fri & Sat, noon-9:30pm Sun; ☒) The all-you-can-eat Mongolian BBQ buffet is a bargain at lunch/dinner $9/12. If that wasn't enough, there is also a Chinese buffet.

CAFÉS

Snow City Café (Map pp180-1; ☎ 272-2489; 1034 W 4th Ave; breakfast $7-12; lunch $7-9; ☺ 7am-3pm Mon-Fri, 7am-4pm Sat & Sun; ☒) Consistently voted best breakfast by Anchorage Press readers, this café serves healthy grub to a mix of clientele that ranges from the tattooed to the up-and-coming. For breakfast skip the usual eggs-and-toast and try a bowl of Snow City granola with dried fruit, honey and nuts.

Downtown Deli (Map pp180-1; ☎ 276-7716; 525 W 4th Ave; breakfast $8-10, sandwiches $7-9; ☺ 6am-10pm; ☒) Owned by former governor Tony Knowles, this fabulous deli offers more than just thick sandwiches. Try its famed reindeer stew or bouillabaisse with salmon, halibut, shrimp, mussels and whatever else lives in the sea.

Cyrano's Books & Cafe (Map pp180-1; ☎ 274-2599; 413 4th Ave; light meals $5-8; ☺ noon-10pm Tue-Sun) An offbeat bookstore where you can lose yourself in a paperback over tempting sweets, soups and salads.

Sweet Basil Café (Map pp180-1; ☎ 274-0070; 335 E St; breakfast $4-6; sandwiches $7; ☺ 8am-3pm Mon-Fri, 9am-4pm Sat; ☒) It does inexpensive, healthy cuisine (as well as decidedly unhealthy but recommended desserts), fruit smoothies and coffee in the heart of the tourist quarter.

Phyllis' Café (Map pp180-1; ☎ 274-6576; 436 D St; dinner $17-38; ☺ 11am-10pm; ☒) Happy tourists head here for a salmon bake that can even be enjoyed outdoors beneath a circus tent.

QUICK EATS

Scattered among the gift shops on 4th Ave downtown are hot-dog vendors where $3 to $4 gets you a dog or a reindeer sausage smothered in sauerkraut.

Wings N Things (Map pp180-1; ☎ 277-9464; 529 I St; fast food $4-10; ☺ 8:30am-3pm Mon-Wed, to 10pm Thu-Sat) Introduced Anchorage to thermonuclear chicken wings in 1983 and serves them, along with subs and excellent cheesecake.

Side Street Espresso (Map pp180-1; ☎ 258-9055; 412 G St; ☺ 7am-3pm Mon-Sat; ☒) It serves espresso, bagels and muffins in what feels like your best pal's living room.

Dark Horse Coffee Company (Map pp180-1; ☎ 279-0647; 646 F St; ☺ 6:45am-6pm Mon-Fri, 8am-4pm Sat, 9am-4pm Sun; ☒) It has lots of lattes, big pastries, even bigger waffles, and savory quiches and sandwiches. For $6 you can get 30 minutes of Internet access and an espresso drink of your choice. Surf and sip.

GROCERIES

New Sagaya City Market (Map pp180-1; ☎ 274-6173; 3900 W 13th Ave; ☺ 6am-10pm Mon-Sat, 8am-9pm Sun) Eclectic and upscale, this is a grocery store with lots of organic goodies, a great deli specializing in Asian fare and seating indoors and outdoors.

10th & M Seafood (Map pp180-1; ☎ 272-FISH; 1020 M St; ☺ 8am-6pm Mon-Fri, from 9am Sat) Sells the freshest seafood in a city that loves its seafood fresh. Staff will also butcher and ship your freshly killed moose or 200lb halibut.

Midtown
RESTAURANTS

Jen's Restaurant (Map pp180-1; ☎ 561-5367; 701 W 36th Ave; lunch $10-22, dinner $18-37; ☺ 11am-2pm

Mon-Fri, 6-10pm Tue-Sat; ✗) The finest restaurant in Midtown has dazzled the critics with innovative, Scandinavian-accented cuisine emphasizing fresh ingredients and elaborate presentation. There's also a wine bar that stays open to midnight with music and a menu of tapas.

Moose's Tooth Brewpub (☎ 258-2537; 3300 Old Seward Hwy; medium pizza $12-21; 🕙 11am-11pm Mon-Thu, to midnight Fri & Sat, noon-11pm Sun; ✗) An Anchorage institution serving 18 custom-brewed beers including monthly specials. There are also 50 gourmet pizzas on the menu and an outdoor eating area totally enclosed by plastic and canvas. Hey, this is Alaska, it could snow any minute.

Bear Tooth Grill (Map p177; ☎ 276-4200; 1230 W 27th St; sandwiches $8-12, dinner $10-20; 🕙 4-11pm; ✗) A popular hangout with an adjacent theatre (p192), that serves excellent Mexican, pasta and seafood alongside fresh microbrews. Try the chicken with orange-habanero sauce.

Roscoe's (☎ 276-5879; 3001 Penland Parkway; sandwiches lunch $7-9, dinner $12-17; 🕙 11am-9pm Mon-Thu, to 10pm Fri & Sat, noon-7pm Sun) The guy in the back of Roscoe's smoking the ribs is Roscoe, the reason this new restaurant next to Northway Mall is already challenging for Anchorage's best BBQ. He claims he wanted to bring the best of the south to the rest of the north with dishes like fried catfish and jambalaya.

El Rodeo (Map p177; ☎ 338-5393; 385 Muldoon Rd; 🕙 11am-9:30pm Mon-Thu, to 10pm Fri, 11:30am-10pm Sat, to 9pm Sun; lunch & dinner $7-15; ✗) This little Mexican restaurant gets packed at night but the wait for a table is well worth it. For more than 10 years this has been the best and most affordable Tex-Mex in Anchorage.

Thai Kitchen (Map p177; ☎ 907-561-0082; 3405 Tudor Rd; dinner $8-12; 🕙 11am-3pm & 5pm-9pm; ✗) This kid-friendly place comes highly recommended, with more than 100 items on the menu, dozens of which are vegetarian.

Greek Corner (Map p177; ☎ 276-2820; 302 W Fireweed; lunch $6-10, dinner $11-20; 🕙 11am-10pm Mon-Fri, from noon Sat, from 4pm Sun; ✗) Best moussaka and stuffed grape leaves in Alaska. So what are they doing serving pizza and pasta? Trying to make a living.

VIP Restaurant (Map p177; ☎ 279-8514; 555 W Northern Lights Blvd; lunch $8-10, dinner $9-17; 🕙 11am-11pm Mon-Sat, from noon Sun; ✗) Have a hankering for *nakjiboggeum* (stirfried baby octopus) or other Korean dishes? You know this place

is good, it's next door to the largest Asian market in Anchorage.

Ray's Place (Map p177; ☎ 279-2932; 32412 Spenard Rd; dinner $7-13; 🕙 10am-3pm & 5-8pm Mon-Thu, 10am-3pm & 5-9pm Sat; ✗) Leave Chilkoot Charlies (opposite) early and cross the street to this Vietnamese restaurant that does great soups and stirfries and stocks Vietnamese beer.

CAFÉS

Organic Oasis (Map p177; ☎ 277-7882; 2610 Spenard Rd; mains $7-12; 🕙 11am-7pm Mon, to 9pm Tue-Thu, to 10pm Fri & Sat) Anchorage's hippest juice bar. Not into puréed carrots? It also serves beer, wine, wraps, pasta and burgers with loads of veggie choices.

Hogg Brothers Café (Map p177; ☎ 276-9649; 1049 W Northern Lights Blvd; breakfast $4-9, lunch $6-10; 🕙 6:30am-4pm; ✗) The breakfasts are so big and the omelets so varied – 22 types – most diners never realize there are burgers and sandwiches on the other side of the menu. The piggy theme has made this café a lovable local institution.

Gwennie's Old Alaska Restaurant (Map p177; ☎ 243-2090; 4333 Spenard Rd; breakfast $6-11, dinner $15-25; 🕙 6am-10pm Mon-Sat, from 8am Sun) Alaska at its best; lots to look at – totems, stuffed bears and a gurgling stream – and big portions. Non-Alaskans can probably share a reindeer sausage omelet and not be hungry for two days.

Peggy's Airport Café (Map p177; ☎ 258-7599; 1675 E 5th Ave; breakfast $5-14, dinner $8-16; 🕙 6:30am-10pm; ✗) This café across from Merrill Airfield has been serving great breakfasts and large dinner portions since 1944. But most locals know it for the 21 types of pie baked daily, with the 6in-high cream pies the best of the bunch.

Alaska Bagel (Map p177; ☎ 276-3900; 113 W Northern Lights Blvd; breakfast $5-9, bagels $7-9; 🕙 6am-3:30pm Mon-Fri, from 7am Sat, from 8am Sun; ✗) Two dozen types of bagels and lots of shmears to spread on top of them, from avocado and blueberry cream cheese to hummus.

QUICK EATS

Momma O's Seafood Restaurant (Map p177; ☎ 278-2216; 2636 Spenard Rd; mains $7-13; 🕙 11am-8pm Mon-Fri; ✗) The place for a halibut fix – have it fried or, better, Cajun style – but don't discount the excellent onion rings or *udon* noodles.

Salmon Express (Map p177; ☎ 336-7657; 606 W Northern Lights Blvd; fast food $4-8; 🕙 10:30am-6pm

Mon-Fri) It serves salmon chowder, salmon kabobs and the recommended salmon quesadillas from the most ramshackle little drive-through stand imaginable.

Taco King (Map p177; ☎ 276-7387; 113 W Northern Lights Blvd; dinner $7-8; ⊙ 10:30am-11pm Mon-Sat, noon-10pm Sun) It does authentic street-style Mexican cuisine, including chicken enchiladas and *carne asada*. The five salsas are made fresh daily.

GROCERIES

Carrs (Map p177; ☎ 339-0500; 1650 W Northern Lights Blvd; ⊙ 24hr) It's always open.

Central Market (Map p177; ☎ 277-1170; 555 W Northern Lights Blvd; ⊙ 9am-9pm) A touch of Asia in the heart of Anchorage.

South Anchorage

Peanut Farm (Map p177; ☎ 523-3683; 5227 Old Seward Hwy; breakfast $7-11; sandwiches $7-9; ⊙ 6am-2am) What was once a small, funky bar is now a shockingly large restaurant and sports bar complex. Thank goodness the beer is cheap and the burgers big. This is the place for an evening of hot wings and cold, 25oz brews.

Bar BQ Pit (Map p177; ☎ 349-2450; 1160 W Dimond Blvd; dinner $8-19; ⊙ 11am-9pm Mon-Thu, to 10pm Fri & Sat, noon-8pm Sun; ✗) Great for homesick Southerners: kick-ass ribs, country music and catfish imported from Arkansas will bring out the drawl in anyone.

Sourdough Mining Company (Map p177; ☎ 563-2272; 5200 Juneau St; lunch $9-20, dinner $13-40; ⊙ 11am-11pm Mon-Sat, from 10am Sun; ✗) An amazingly rustic place no tourist-trap connoisseur should miss. Dine on burgers, seafood and steak 'in a gold mine' while enjoying house musician and workaholic Dusty Sourdough, who really does put on a good show. There is a free shuttle from any Anchorage hotel.

Arctic Roadrunner (Map p177; ☎ 561-1245; 5300 Old Seward Hwy; burgers $4-5; ⊙ 10:30am-9pm Mon-Sat; ✗) Since 1964 this place has been turning out beefy burgers and great onion pieces and rings. If your timing is right you can eat outdoors while watching salmon spawn up Campbell Creek.

DRINKING

With its young and lively population, Anchorage has a lot to do after the midnight sun finally sets. The free *Anchorage Press* and Friday *Anchorage Daily News* both have events listings.

SubZero (Map pp180-1; 610 6th Ave) Slick, silver and smoke-free, this wi-fi hot spot, downstairs from Humpy's, has an ice bar and lots of upscale beverages, including more than 100 Belgian beers.

Darwin's Theory (Map pp180-1; 426 G St) Something of an institution and a testosterone-fueled hangout in the middle tourist central. After visiting the bar while on tour in 1995, Amy Ray of the Indigo Girls wrote the song 'Cut It Out.'

Bernie's Bungalow Lounge (Map pp180-1; 626 D St) Absolutely fabulous, dahlings, with pink flamingoes, colorful leather couches and extravagant, brightly colored mixed drinks. On Thursdays bands play on the tiki torch–lit patio, on the weekends it's DJs.

Reilly's (Map p177; 317 W Fireweed) A friendly Irish pub with the goodness of Ireland on tap: Guinness Extra Stout, Murphy's Irish Stout and Harp Irish Ale.

F Street Station (Map pp180-1; 325 F St) This is the place where everybody knows your name. The only thing missing in this friendly, music-free drinking hole is Norm sitting at the end of the bar.

There's upscale dining at the **Crow's Nest** (Map pp180-1; 5th Ave & K St), at the top of the Hotel Captain Cook, and **Top of the World** (Map pp180-1; ☎ 272-7411; 500 W 3rd Ave), on the top of the Hilton, but most people come for a drink and a million-dollar view of Cook Inlet.

ENTERTAINMENT
Clubs

Chilkoot Charlie's (Map p177; ☎ 272-1010; 2435 Spenard Rd) More than Anchorage's favorite meat market, 'Koots', as the locals call it, is a landmark. The sprawling, wooden edifice has 22 beers on tap, 10 bars, four dancefloors and a couple of stages where basically every band touring Alaska ends up. It's newest addition is a replica of the legendary Bird House. The original was a log-cabin bar on Seward Hwy that was still standing but drunkenly slanted after the 1964 earthquake before burning down in 2002. Its slogan 'Come in. Have a beer. Leave your undies' is the reason for all the bras and briefs pinned to the ceiling of the replica at Koots.

Rumrunners (Map pp180-1; 445 W 4th Ave) Is packed when DJs are spinning after 10pm Friday and Saturday.

Club Soroya (Map pp180-1; 333 W 4th Ave; cover $3-10) A huge Latin dance place. If you can't salsa, cha cha or merengue, Latin dance lessons are on offer from 8pm to 10pm on Friday and Saturday followed by live music, tango is on Wed.

Club @ (Map p177; 8801 Jewel Lake Rd; Sat cover $5) On Friday its Anchorage's other Latin hot spot with lessons followed by open dancing. On Saturday DJs spin Euro, garage, soul. Start the evening with a bomb; order an Atomic Fusion.

Shed (Map pp180-1; 535 W 3rd Ave; Fri & Sat cover $5) It's karaoke seven days a week and they'll cut a CD of your performance. DJs take over after 10pm Thursday through Saturday.

Gay & Lesbian Venues
Several straight bars are regarded as gay-and-lesbian-friendly: try the Alley (below), Bernie's Bungalow Lounge (see p191) and the Moose's Tooth Brewpub (p189).

Mad Myrna's (Map pp180-1; 530 E 5th Ave; cover Sat & Sun $5-10) A fun, cruisy bar with line dancing on Thursday, Drag Divas shows on Friday and dance music most nights after 9pm.

Raven (Map pp180-1; 708 E 4th Ave) The other gay and lesbian bar in town.

Live Music
JAZZ & BLUES
Blues Central at the Chef's Inn (Map p177; ☎ 272-1341; 825 W Northern Lights Blvd) An intimate venue with live blues and jazz nightly.

Alley (Map pp180-1; 900 W 5th Ave; cover $3-5) Has a dancefloor, but on Wednesday it's jazz jams while blues and jazz groups often visit on the weekends.

For free jazz head to Cyrano's Books & Cafe (p189) while Organic Oasis (p189), has live jazz, bluegrass or acoustic alternative music most evenings. On the third Thursday of every month there's more live jazz at Bear Tooth Grill (p188).

Anchorage Museum of History & Art (p178) offers Jazz After Hours at 7pm on Thursday, free with the cost of museum admission ($6.50).

OTHER MUSIC
Long Branch Saloon (Map p177; 1737 E Dimond Blvd) It has pool tables, stiff drinks and live country and western music almost nightly.

Humpy's Great Alaskan Alehouse (p188) features live music Monday to Saturday at around 9pm with a mix of acoustic, bluegrass and blues throughout the summer. If you're packing your six-string, Monday is open-mic night.

Cinemas
Bear Tooth Theatrepub (Map p177; ☎ 276-4200; www.beartooththeatre.net; 1230 W 27th Ave) Cruise into this very cool venue where you can enjoy great microbrews, wine or even dinner while watching first-run movies ($3). It's also an awesome place to see eclectic live music (covers vary widely).

Alaska Experience Center (Map p177; ☎ 276-3730; 705 W 6th Ave; adult/child movie $8/4, earthquake $6/4, combined ticket $10/7; ☯ 9am-9pm) More a tourist trap than movie house, with IMAX nature films and a theatrical simulation of the 1964 Good Friday Earthquake.

Fireweed Theatre (☎ 800-326-3264, ext 101; cnr Fireweed & Gambell Rd) and **Dimond Center** (☎ 800-326-3264, ext 100; 800 E Dimond Rd), in the Dimond Center Mall, are both fine places for a flick. Take bus No 1, 2 or 9.

Theater & Performing Arts
Anchorage had an orchestra before it had paved roads, which says a lot about priorities around here.

Egan Civic Center (Map pp180-1; ☎ 263-2800; www.egancenter.com; 555 W 5th Ave) Try this place for top-drawer musical groups and other big events.

Sullivan Arena (Map pp180-1; ☎ 279-0618; www.sullivanarena.com; 1600 Gambell St) It also hosts musical events.

Alaska Center for the Performing Arts (Map pp180-1; ☎ 263-2900, tickets 263-2787; www.alaskapac.org; 621 W 6th Ave) impresses tourists with the film *Aurora: Alaska's Great Northern Lights* (adult/child $9/$6.50; ☯ on the hour 9am-9pm) during summer in its Sydney Laurence Theatre. It's also home to the **Anchorage Opera** (☎ 279-2557; www.anchorageopera.org), **Anchorage Symphony Orchestra** (☎ 274-8668; www.anchoragesymphony.org), **Anchorage Concert Association** (☎ 272-1471; www.anchorageconcerts.org) and **Alaska Dance Theatre** (☎ 277-9501; www.alaskadancetheatre.com).

Eccentric Theatre Company (Map pp180-1; ☎ 274-2599; 413 D St; tickets $12-15) Adjacent to Cyrano's Books & Cafe, this may be the best live theater in town, staging everything from Hamlet to *archy and mehitabel* (comic characters of a cockroach and a cat), Mel Brooks' jazz musical based on the poetry of Don Marquis. Only in Anchorage…

Other Entertainment

Mr Whitekeys' Fly by Night Club (Map p177; ☎ 279-7726; 3300 Spenard Rd; admission $13-21; ☽ shows 8pm Tue-Sat) Bookings are a must at this place, home to the *Whale-Fat Follies*, a raunchy musical about duct tape, spawning salmon and Alaska's official state fossil, the woolly mammoth. Surprisingly the dinner theater serves good food, but try the coconut-and-beer-battered Spam or Spam nachos instead.

Fourth Avenue Theatre (Map pp180-1; ☎ 257-5609; 630 W 4th Ave; adult/child $15/8) An Alaska-themed musical comedy that is cleaner than what Mr Whitekeys does (but not nearly as funny) in a historic 1947 cinema house, Anchorage's first $1 million building.

Anchorage Bucs (Map p177; ☎ 561-2827; www.anchoragebucs.com) and **Anchorage Glacier Pilots** (☎ 274-3627; www.glacierpilots.com) This team plays semi-pro baseball at Mulcahy Ball Park, where living legend Mark McGuire slammed a few homers. General admission is around $5.

Great Alaskan Bush Company (Map pp180-1; ☎ 561-2609; 631 E International Airport Rd) It's about as beloved as a strip club gets. The cozy landmark is woman-owned and -operated, and everyone agrees that the truly moral thing to do is tip well.

SHOPPING
Souvenirs

Moose-dropping jewelry and thin T-shirts are available downtown at a variety of cheesy tourist shops.

Saturday Market (Map pp180-1; ☎ 272-5634; www.anchoragemarkets.com; W 3rd Ave & E St; ☽ 10am-6pm Sat & Sun) Now open on Sunday at the height of tourist season, a fantastic open market with live music and almost 100 booths stocked with cheap food, Mat-Su Valley veggies and souvenirs from birch steins to birch syrup.

Ulu Factory (Map pp180-1; ☎ 276-3119; 211 W Ship Creek Ave; ☽ 8am-7pm) The *ulu* (oo-loo) is to Alaska what the rubber alligator is to Florida: everybody sells them. Still, this shop is interesting with demonstrations that will teach you how to use the cutting tool.

Polar Bear Gifts (Map pp180-1; ☎ 274-4387; 442 W 5th Ave; ☽ 8am-midnight) It sells the cheapest stuff. It's open until the midnight sun sets.

Northway Mall Wednesday Market (Map pp180-1; 3101 Penland Parkway; ☽ 11am-6pm Wed) Many vendors head to this market on Wednesday; take bus No 8 or 45.

Alaska Native Arts & Crafts

Alaska Native Heritage Center (Map p177; ☎ 330-8000, 800-315-6608; www.alaskanative.net; 8800 Heritage Center Dr; ☽ 9am-6pm) It has a gift shop packed with artifacts of questionable authenticity, but also features booths where craftspeople make fresh knickknacks while you watch.

Downtown Heritage Gifts (Map pp180-1; ☎ 272-5048; 333 4th Ave; ☽ 8am-10pm) The Alaska Native Heritage Center also has a downtown store in the Ship Creek Center with a larger selection and longer hours than its gift shop.

GEARING UP

With so much wilderness at its doorstep you'd expect Anchorage to have a wide variety of outdoor shops – and it does. The largest is **REI** (Map p177; ☎ 272-4565; 1200 W Northern Lights Blvd; ☽ 10am-9pm Mon-Sat, 10am-6pm Sun), which extends over two floors in Midtown crammed with backpacks, kayaks, climbing gear and stuff for camping. This is the best place in the state to come to replace high-priced equipment like a backpacker's stove. The store also rents canoes, kayaks, tents, stoves and bear containers.

Nearby is **Alaska Mountaineering & Hiking** (Map p177; ☎ 272-1811; www.alaskamountaineering.com; 2633 Spenard Rd; ☽ 9am-7pm Mon-Fri, to 6pm Sat, noon- 5pm Sun) a smaller shop that carters to the serious adventurer, selling top-of-the-line climbing, paddling and other outdoor gear. Even better is expedition advice because the staff members here either have been there or know somebody who has.

Next door to REI in the same mall is **Great Outdoor Clothing Company** (Map p177; ☎ 277-6664; 1200 W Northern Lights Blvd; ☽ 10am-8pm Mon-Fri, to 6pm Sat & Sun) A manufacturer's outlet with better prices on clothing, Gore-Tex parkas and hiking boots.

For a pair of those Alaskan-loving Carhartt overalls there's **Army/Navy Store** (Map p177; ☎ 279-2401; 320 W 4th St; ☽ 9am-7pm Mon-Fri, to 6pm Sat & Sun), a downtown shop that also stocks US military gear and some outdoor equipment.

ANC Auxiliary Craft Shop (Map p177; ☎ 729-1122; 4315 Diplomacy Dr; ⏱ 10am-2pm Mon-Fri, from 11am 1st & 3rd Sat of month) Located on the 1st floor of the Alaska Native Medical Center, it has some of the finest Alaska Native arts and crafts available to the public. It does not accept credit cards.

Oomingmak Musk Ox Producers Co-op (Map pp180-1; ☎ 272-9225; www.qiviut.com; 604 H St; ⏱ 10am-6pm Mon-Sat) Handles a variety of very soft, very warm and very expensive garments made of arctic musk-ox wool, hand-knitted in isolated Inupiaq villages.

GETTING THERE & AWAY
Air

Ted Stevens Anchorage International Airport, 6½ miles west of the city center, is the largest airport in the state, handling 130 domestic and international flights daily from more than a dozen major airlines.

Alaska Airlines (☎ 800-426-0333; www.alaskaair .com) provides the most intrastate routes to travelers, generally through its contract carrier, ERA Aviation, which operates services to Valdez, Homer, Cordova, Kenai, Iliamna and Kodiak. You can book tickets either online or at the airport, but no longer downtown as Alaska Airlines closed its office in the Hotel Captain Cook in 2005.

PenAir (☎ 800-448-4226; www.penair.com) flies smaller planes to 27 difficult-to-pronounce destinations in Southwest Alaska, including Unalakleet, Aniak and Igiugig.

Boat

The **Alaska Marine Highway** (Map pp180-1; ☎ 272-4482; 605 W 4th Ave; ⏱ 8am-5pm Mon-Fri) doesn't service Anchorage but does have an office in the Old Federal Courthouse.

Bus

Anchorage is a hub for various small passenger and freight lines that make daily runs between specific cities. Always call first; the turnover in Alaska's volatile bus industry is unbelievable.

Alaska Direct Busline, Inc (☎ 277-6652, 800-770-6652) has regular services between Anchorage and Glennallen ($50), Tok ($75), Fairbanks ($85) and Whitehorse ($180) and points in-between.

Homer Stage Line (☎ 868-3914; www.homerstage line.com) runs daily in the summer between Anchorage and Cooper Landing ($40), Soldotna ($45), Homer ($55).

Seward Bus Line (☎ 563-0800; www.sewardbuslines .net) runs between Anchorage and Seward ($40) twice daily in summer.

Talkeetna Shuttle Service (☎ 733-1725; 888-288-6008; www.denalicentral.com) runs between Anchorage and Talkeetna ($55) twice daily in summer.

Alaska Yukon Trails (☎ 888-600-6001) runs a bus up the George Parks Hwy to Talkeetna Junction ($66), Denali National Park ($76) and Fairbanks ($91). The next day it will transport you from Fairbanks to Dawson City, Canada ($162), passing through Tok along the way.

Alaska Park Connection (☎ 277-2757, 888-277-2757; www.alaskacoach.com) offers daily service from Anchorage to Denali National Park ($69) and Seward ($49) as well as between Seward and Denali ($118).

Train

From its downtown depot, the **Alaska Railroad** (Map pp180-1; ☎ 265-2494, 800-544-0552; www.akrr .com; 411 W 1st Ave) sends its *Denali Star* north daily to Talkeetna (adult/child $80/40), Denali National Park (adult/child $129/65) and Fairbanks (adult/child $179/90). The *Coastal Classic* stops in Girdwood (adult/child $49/25) and Seward (adult/child $59/30) while the *Glacial Discovery* connects to Whittier (adult/child $52/26). You can save 20% to 30% traveling in May and September.

GETTING AROUND
To/From the Airport

Unlike Juneau, public buses in Anchorage do stop at the airport. People Mover bus No 7 ($1.50, running 6:45am to 10:55pm Monday to Friday, 8:20am to 8:20pm Saturday, 10:20am to 6pm Sunday) offers hourly service between downtown and the airport from picking up at both the international and domestic terminals.

You can call **Alaska Shuttle Service** (☎ 338-8888, 694-8888) for door-to-door service to downtown ($10), South Anchorage ($20) or Eagle River ($30). Plenty of the hotels and B&Bs also provide a courtesy-van service. Finally, an endless line of taxis will be eager to take your bags and your money. Plan on a $16 to $18 fare to the downtown area.

RIDING THE ALASKA RAILROAD

In a remote corner of the Alaskan wilderness, you stand along a railroad track when suddenly a small train appears. You wave a white flag in the air – actually yesterday's dirty T-shirt – and the engineer acknowledges you with a sound of his whistle and then stops. You hop onboard to join others fresh from the bush; fly fishermen, backpackers, a hunter with his dead moose, locals whose homestead cabin can be reached only after a ride on the *Hurricane Turn*, one of America's last flag-stop trains.

This unusual service between Talkeetna and Hurricane along the Susitna River is only one aspect that makes the Alaska Railroad so unique. At the other end of the rainbow of luxury is the railroad's Gold Star Service, two lavishly appointed cars that in 2005 joined the *Denali Star* train as part of the Anchorage–Fairbanks run. The 89ft double-decked dome cars include a glass observation area on the second level with 360-degree views and a bartender in the back serving your favorite libations. Sit back, sip a chardonnay and soak in the grandeur of Mt McKinley.

Take your pick, rustic or relaxing, but don't pass up the Alaska Railroad. There's not another train like it.

The railroad was born on March 12, 1914, when the US Congress passed the Alaska Railroad Act, authorizing the US President to construct and operate the line. With the exception of the train used at the Panama Canal, the US government had never before owned and operated a railroad.

President Woodrow Wilson chose the more mild grades found along the Susitna River and a route that swung by the Healy and Matanuska coalfields. When the Alaska Engineering Commission set up a camp on the muddy banks of Ship Creek in 1915 to begin surveying the line, Anchorage was born.

It took eight years and 4500 men to build a 470-mile railroad from the ice-free port of Seward to the boomtown of Fairbanks, a wilderness line that was cut over what was thought to be impenetrable mountains and across raging rivers. On a warm Sunday afternoon in 1923, President Warren Harding – the first US president to visit Alaska – tapped in the golden spike at Nenana and then immediately pounded in its iron replacement.

The Alaska Railroad has been running ever since. Within 15 years it was making a profit and during WWII the Army's demands were so great it increased tonnage fourfold on the railroad, straining the line's infrastructure to the breaking point. In 1985, 70 years after the route was chosen, the federal government transferred the Alaska Railroad to the state of Alaska.

The classic trip is to ride the railroad from Anchorage to Fairbanks, with a stop at Denali National Park. Many believe the most scenic portion, however, is the 114-mile run from Anchorage to Seward, which begins by skirting the 60-mile-long Turnagain Arm, climbs an alpine pass and then comes within a half-mile of three glaciers. There are cheaper ways to reach Seward, Fairbanks or points in-between. But in the spirit of adventure, which is why many of us come to Alaska, a van or bus pales in comparison to riding the Alaska Railroad.

Bus

Anchorage's excellent bus system, **People Mover** (☎ 343-6543; www.peoplemover.org; Downtown Transit Center, 700 W 6th Ave; ☷ 8am-5pm Mon-Fri), runs from 6am to 11pm Monday to Friday, 8am to 8pm Saturday and 9:30am to 6:30pm Sunday. Pick up a schedule at the Downtown Transit Center ($1) or call for specific route information. One-way fares are adult/child $1.50/0.75 and an unlimited day pass ($3) is available at the transit center.

MASCOT (Map pp180-1; ☎ 376-5000; www.matsutransit.com), the Mat-Su Community Transit, began service in 2004 between Anchorage and Wasilla and Palmer, with three runs a day that depart from the Downtown Transit Center Monday through Friday (one way/day pass $2.50/5).

Ship Creek Shuttle (☎ 562-8448), is a free bus service that connects downtown with the Ship Creek area. The minibuses run every 30 minutes from 8am to 5pm daily in summer.

Car & Motorcycle

If at all possible rent your car in the city where you'll be hit with an 18% rental tax. At the airport they'll also add an airport tax that pushes it up to 32% on all rentals.

Ouch! That's highway robbery before you even get to the highway. All the national concerns (Avis, Budget, Hertz, Payless, National etc) have counters in the airport's south terminal.

Denali Car Rental (Map pp180-1; ☎ 276-1230, 800-757-1230; 1209 Gambell St) has subcompacts for daily/weekly $45/270 with 150 daily miles included.

Cheapwheels Rent-A-Car (Map p177; ☎ 561-8627; 3811 Spenard Rd) is one of several discount rental places on Spenard Rd and has compacts for daily/weekly $45/270. Rent three days or more and you get unlimited mileage.

Advantage Car & Van Rental (Map p177; ☎ 243-8806, 888-877-3585; 4211 Spenard Rd) is another Spenard cheapie with subcompacts for daily/weekly $40/240.

Alaska Rider Motorcycle Tours (Map p177; ☎ 272-2777; www.akrider.com; 4346 Spenard Rd) rents Harley Davidsons ($250 per day) and Kawasakis ($150 per day) and offers both guided and self-guided tours. It's pricey, but still much better value than traditional psychotherapy.

Taxi

If you need to call a cab, try **Anchorage Yellow Cab** (☎ 272-2422) or **Anchorage Checker Cab** (☎ 276-1234).

SOUTH OF ANCHORAGE

Sure, you can fly from Anchorage anywhere on the Kenai Peninsula, probably more cheaply, and certainly more quickly, than traveling by road or rail. But stay on the ground, feel the bore tide roar through Turnagain Arm and be in awe of the Chugach's mountain majesty.

SEWARD HIGHWAY

Starting at the corner of Gambell St and 10th Ave in Anchorage, Seward Hwy parallels the Alaska Railroad south 127 miles to Seward. Expect lots of traffic, a frightening percentage of which involves folks who have (1) never seen a Dall sheep before and (2) never driven an RV before; it's a frustrating and sometimes deadly combination. Mile markers measure the distance from Seward.

Try to catch the **bore tide**, a neat trick of geography that concentrates the incoming tide into a wall of water up to 6ft tall, which

rushes along Turnagain Arm at 15mph daily. Schedules are available at any Anchorage visitors center; note that the most intense waves occur around a new or full moon. Top spots for viewing this satisfyingly loud phenomenon include **Beluga Point** (Mile 110) and **Bird Point** (Mile 96).

Potter Marsh (Mile 117) was created in 1916, when railroad construction dammed several streams; it's currently in the process of filling with eroded earth. You can stretch your legs along the 1500ft boardwalk while spying on ducks, songbirds, grebes and gulls.

Chugach State Park Headquarters (☎ 345-5014; Mile 115; 10am-4:30pm Mon-Fri) is housed in the **Potter Section House**, a historic railroad workers' dorm that also includes a free museum with a snowplow train and other era artifacts.

Turnagain Arm Trail, an easy 11-mile, hike, begins at Mile 115. Originally used by Alaska Natives, the convenient route has since been used by Russian trappers, gold miners and happy hikers. The trail, with a mountain goat's view of Turnagain Arm, alpine meadows and beluga whales, can also be accessed at the **McHugh Picnic Area** (Mile 112), **Rainbow** (Mile 108) and **Windy Corner** (Mile 107).

Indian Valley Mine (☎ 653-1120; www.indianvalleymine.com; Mile 104; admission $1; 9am-9pm Jun-Aug), a lode mine originally blasted out in 1901, still produces gold. You can buy bags of ore ($3 to $50) and see for yourself. The wonderful proprietors are extremely knowledgeable on the history and science of Alaskan gold mining; ask about the potato retort.

Indian Valley Trail (Mile 103) is an easy 6-mile path that starts 1.3 miles along the gravel road behind Turnagain House. You can also access Powerline Trail (p182) for a much longer hiking or biking. Nearby is the **Brown Bear Motel** (☎ 653-7000; www.brownbearmotel.com; Mile 103 Seward Hwy; s/d $52/57) with clean rooms and cheap beer in the adjoining **Brown Bear Saloon** that can get hopping at night.

The **Bird Ridge Trail** (Mile 102) starts with a wheelchair-accessible loop, then continues with a steep, popular and well-marked path that reaches a 3500ft overlook at Mile 2; this is a traditional turnaround point for folks in a hurry. Or you can continue another 4 miles to higher peaks and even better views from sunny Bird Ridge, a top spot for rock climbing.

Bird Creek State Campground (Mile 101; sites $10) is popular for fishing, hiking and, best of all, the sound of the bore tide rushing by your tent. Remind children and morons to stay off the deadly mud flats.

GIRDWOOD
☎ 907/pop 1850

Best known for its luxurious Alyeska Ski Resort and the fabled **Girdwood Forest Fair** (www.gird woodforestfair.com) – a much-anticipated romp that occurs on the first weekend of July near town, featuring food, crafts and music aplenty – Girdwood is grand. Enfolded in mighty peaks famed for skiing, and overlooking the beauty of Turnagain Arm, the town is a magnet for epicurean urbanites, artists and hippies successful in spite of themselves. It has fine restaurants, great hiking, a colorful town center and not one but two trams.

Orientation

Girdwood lies 37 miles south of Anchorage at Mile 90 Seward Hwy. There's a strip mall at the junction with Alyeska Hwy, which runs 3 miles east to the junction with gravel Crow Creek Rd, the start of the town center and ski resort.

Information

There are ATMs at the Tesoro Station, Alyeska Resort and Crow Creek Mercantile.

Emergency (ambulance, fire, police ☎ 911)

Gerrish Library (☎ 783-2565; end of Hightower Rd; ☽ 1-6pm Tue & Thu, to 8pm Wed, 10am-6pm Fri & Sat) Offers Internet access.

Girdwood Chamber of Commerce (☎ 222-7682; www.girdwoodalaska.com) No visitors center but a great web site for pretrip planning.

Girdwood Clinic (☎ 783-1355; Hightower Rd; ☽ 10am-6:30pm Tue-Fri, to 5:30pm Sat) Offers limited medical care.

Girdwood Community Needs Center (☎ 783-3883; Limblad Ave; ☽ 9am-10pm Mon-Sat) The cleanest Laundromat you'll ever clean in. Also has Internet access (per 10 min $1), showers ($3.50) and even a dog wash ($15).

Post office (cnr Limblad Ave & Hightower Rd) Girdwood's new post office is the pride of the community.

USFS Glacier Ranger Station (☎ 783-3242; Ranger Station Rd; ☽ 8am-5pm Mon-Fri) Has maps and information on area hikes, campgrounds and public-use cabins.

Sights

Girdwood was named for James Girdwood, who staked the first claim on Crow Creek in 1896. Two years later the **Crow Creek Mine** (☎ 278-8060; Mile 3.5 Crow Creek Rd; adult/child $3/free; ☽ 9am-6pm) was built and today you can still see some original buildings and sluices at this working mine. You can even learn how to pan for gold and then give it a try yourself (adult/child $5/4) or pitch the tent and spend the night ($5).

In town the **Girdwood Center for Visual Arts** (☎ 783-3209; Hightower Rd; ☽ 11am-6pm) serves as an artisan cooperative during the summer and is filled with the work of those locals who get inspired by the majestic scenery that surrounds them.

The **Alyeska Ski Resort Tram** (☎ 754-1111; hotel guests/nonguests $15/16; ☽ 10:30am-9:30pm) offers the easiest route to the alpine during the summer. At the top you can dine at Seven Glaciers Restaurant (p199) or just wander above the tree line, soaking up the incredible views.

Activities
HIKING

Take the Alyeska resort tram to this easy, 1-mile **Alyeska Glacier View Trail** via an alpine area with views of the tiny Alyeska Glacier. You can continue up the ridge to climb the so-called summit of Mt Alyeska, a high point of 3939ft. The true summit lies farther to the south, but is not a climb for casual hikers.

Winner Creek Gorge is an easy and pleasant hike that winds 5½ miles through lush (and sometimes muddy) forest, ending in the gorge itself, where Winner Creek becomes a series of small cascades. You can also connect to the National Historic Iditarod Trail for a 7.7-mile loop. Either way, you'll cross the gorge on an ultrafun **hand-tram**. The most popular trailhead is near Arlberg Rd: walk along the bike path past the Alyeska Prince Hotel, toward the bottom of the tram. Look for the footpath heading into the forest.

The highly recommended **Crow Pass Trail** is a short but beautiful alpine hike that has gold-mining relics, an alpine lake and often there are Dall sheep on the slopes above. It's 4 miles to Raven Glacier, the traditional turnaround point of the trail and 3 miles to a **USFS cabin** (NRRS ☎ 877-444-6777, 518-885-3639; www.reserveusa.com; cabins $35). Or you can continue on the three-day, 26-mile route along the Iditarod Trail to the Eagle River Nature Center (p71). The trailhead is 5.8 miles north of Alyeska Hwy on Crow Creek Rd.

ANCHORAGE & AROUND

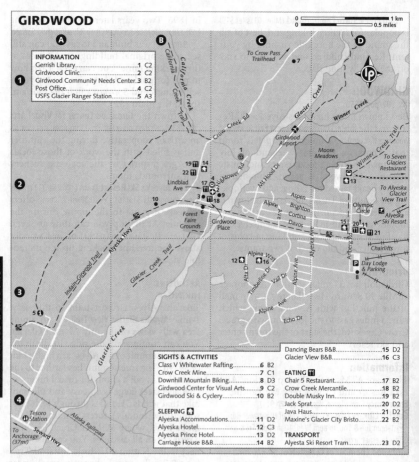

GIRDWOOD

0 — 1 km
0 — 0.5 miles

INFORMATION
Gerrish Library...............................1 C2
Girdwood Clinic..............................2 C2
Girdwood Community Needs Center.3 B2
Post Office....................................4 C2
USFS Glacier Ranger Station.............5 A3

SIGHTS & ACTIVITIES
Class V Whitewater Rafting..............6 B2
Crow Creek Mine...........................7 C1
Downhill Mountain Biking................8 D3
Girdwood Center for Visual Arts.......9 C2
Girdwood Ski & Cyclery..................10 B2

SLEEPING
Alyeska Accommodations...............11 D2
Alyeska Hostel.............................12 C3
Alyeska Prince Hotel.....................13 D2
Carriage House B&B......................14 B2
Dancing Bears B&B.......................15 D2
Glacier View B&B.........................16 C3

EATING
Chair 5 Restaurant.......................17 B2
Crow Creek Mercantile..................18 B2
Double Musky Inn.........................19 B2
Jack Sprat...................................20 D2
Java Haus...................................21 D2
Maxine's Glacier City Bristo...........22 B2

TRANSPORT
Alyesta Ski Resort Tram.................23 D2

CYCLING

The most scenic ride is the **Indian–Girdwood Trail**, a paved path that leads out of the valley and along the Seward Hwy above Turnagain Arm. A new segment built in 2005 has extended the route to Mile 103 of the highway, linking Alyeska Resort with Indian Creek 17 miles away. **Girdwood Ski & Cyclery** (754-2453; www.girdwoodskicyclery.com; bikes per 3hr/day $15/25; 10am-7pm Wed-Sun) will rent you the bikes to enjoy it.

For some hair-rising biking go to the Alyeska Resort day lodge where **Downhill Mountain Biking** (230-3437; noon-8pm Sat & Sun) will send you up on the chairlift for a wild ride down one of four trails. Lift tickets are $29 per person and bike rentals are available.

Tours

Alpine Air (783-2360; www.alaska.net/~alpineair; airport) Has a two-hour glacier tour that includes a helicopter landing on the ice and an opportunity to drive a sled dog team (adult/child $349/299).

Alyeska Prince Hotel (754-2111, www.alyeska resort.com; 1000 Arlberg Ave) Whether you want to golf, paraglide or photograph brown bears, this has the (expensive) tour for you.

Ascending Path (783-0505; www.theascending path.com) A climbing-guide service that has a three-hour glacier hike on Alyeska Glacier ($139), including a midnight-sun glacier trek from mid-June to mid-July that begins at 9pm. The company also offers a three-hour rock-climbing outing designed for beginners ($129).

Class V Whitewater (783-2004, 877-783-2004; www.alaskanrafting.com) Offers guided raft trips through some of the whitest water in Alaska, the class V canyons of Sixmile River ($130). If you can't handle that icy roller coaster, trips through class III rapids ($75 to $95) are available.

Sleeping

B&Bs make up the bulk of Girdwood's lodging and are the only midrange option. The **Alyeska/Girdwood Accommodations Association** (☎ 222-3226; www.agaa.biz) can find last-minute rooms. Girdwood has an 8% bed tax.

Alyeska Prince Hotel (☎ 754-2111, www.alyeskaresort.com; 1000 Arlberg Ave; d $275-299, ste $420-960; ✗ 🖳 🕿) This place earned four stars from AAA because it deserved them – from the whirlpool with a view to bathrobes and slippers in every room, this place is swanky. For something less swanky you can park your RV in the day lodge for $10 a night and then ride the resort shuttle to use the pool or take a shower.

Glacier View B&B (☎ 783-1160, 350-0674; www.glacierviewbnb.com; Alpina Way; r $125-175; ✗ 🖳) The most upscale B&B in the area with three guest rooms on the 2nd floor along with a common area where you can view the mountains and see six glaciers. Rooms come with full breakfast and use of an outdoor hot tub.

Carriage House B&B (☎ 783-9464, 888-961-9464; www.thecarriagehousebandb.com; Mile 0.2 Crow Creek Rd; r $115-90) This is a stunning cedar house where breakfast is served in a vaulted-ceiling common room that overlooks the mountains, is furnished in antiques and warmed on nippy mornings by a fieldstone fireplace.

Dancing Bears B&B (☎ 783-2481, 866-727-2481; www.dancingbearsbb.com; cnr Arlberg Ave & Cortina Dr; r $80-100; ✗ 🖳) Operated by one of the local artists, this B&B has three rooms, a private kitchen for the guests, hot tub and a lot of art on the walls.

Alyeska Hostel (☎ 783-2222; www.alyeskahostel.com; Alta Dr; dm/r $15/40; ✗) A small but charming guesthouse with great mountain views, a woodfired sauna and eight bunks.

Alyeska Accommodations (☎ 783-2000, 888-783-2001; www.alyeskaaccommodations.com; r $110-172) At the Alyeska Ski Area; sublets massive, privately owned (and decorated) condos, most with full kitchens, hot tubs and saunas.

Eating

For such a tiny place, Girdwood has amazing selection of restaurants that often pull their patrons in from Anchorage.

Double Musky Inn (☎ 783-2822; Crow Creek Rd; dinner $20-44; ☯ 5pm-10pm Tue-Thu; ✗) One of the most honored restaurants in the Anchorage bowl, the reason you have to wait (reservations are not accepted) two hours on weekends. The cuisine is Cajun accented and it specializes in steaks, like its New York strips crusted in cracked peppercorns and served with a burgundy sauce.

Seven Glaciers Restaurant (☎ 754-2237; dinner $28-52; ☯ 5:30pm-9:30pm; ✗) Sitting on top of Mt Alyeska, 2300ft above sea level, is the best of Alyeska Resort's six restaurants and bars. The hotel tram will take you to an evening of gourmet dining and absolutely stunning views that include Turnagain Arm and, yes, seven glaciers. The menu is dominated by seafood; even the meat mains are offered with a side of king crab.

Jack Sprat (☎ 783-5225; Olympic Circle Dr; brunch $7-11, dinner $9-23; ☯ 4-9pm Mon-Fri, 10am-10pm Sat-Sun; ✗) Creative, inspired cuisine at the base of the ski hill. Its salads are wonderful, dark chocolate torte sinful, and it's recommended.

Maxine's Glacier City Bristol (☎ 783-2888; Crow Creek Rd; dinner $14-20; ☯ 5pm-midnight; ✗) What use to be Max's is now Maxine's, a burger-and-beer bar that has been transformed into a dining experience. The cooking has a Mediterranean theme and the menu includes spinach ravioli, roasted leg of lamb and seared ahi tuna. The rock–and-roll bands have been replaced by acoustic music on Friday and Saturday nights.

Chair 5 Restaurant (☎ 783-2500; 5 Lindblad Ave; medium pizza $12-16, dinner $17-23; ☯ 11am-2am, food served until 11pm) The kind of bar and restaurant skiers love after a long day on the slopes. It features more than 60 beers, including a dozen on tap, gourmet pizzas, big burgers and a lot of blackened dishes like blackened halibut tacos.

Java Haus (☎ 783-2827; Olympic Circle Dr; breakfast $4-6; ☯ 6am-3pm Mon-Fri, from 7am-3pm Sat & Sun; ✗) The place to go for espresso drinks, cheap egg sandwiches and Internet access.

Crow Creek Mercantile (☎ 783-3900; Hightower Rd; ☯ 8am-midnight) Girdwood's small grocery store with some ready-to-eat items.

Getting There & Away

Although the fare is steep, you could hop on the **Alaska Railroad** (☎ 265-2494; www.akrr.com) in Anchorage for a day trip to Girdwood (one way adult/child $49/25). On its way to Seward, the Coastal Classic train arrives at Girdwood at 8am daily during the summer and again at 9pm for the return journey to Anchorage.

Seward Bus Lines (☎ 563-0800; www.sewardbus lines.net) can arrange transport to Seward and Anchorage, while **Homer Stage Line** (☎ 868-3914; www.homerstageline.com) can arrange transportation throughout the Kenai Peninsula. You might also call **Magic Bus** (☎ 268-6311; www .themagicbus.com), an accommodating charter-bus service that will handle groups as small as four and always will take independents on any booked run to Girdwood.

SOUTH OF GIRDWOOD

Seward Hwy continues southeast past Girdwood and a few nifty tourist attractions to what's left of Portage, which was destroyed by the 1964 Good Friday Earthquake basically a few structures sinking into the nearby mud flats.

The **Wetland Observation Platform** (Mile 81) features interpretive plaques on the ducks, arctic terns, bald eagles and other wildlife inhabiting the area.

Alaska Wildlife Conservation Center (☎ 783-2025; 866-773-2025; www.alaskawildlife.org; Mile 79; adult/child $7.50/5; ☼ 8am-8pm) is a nonprofit wildlife center where injured and rescued animals are on display; you can see most of them from your car.

PORTAGE GLACIER

Portage Glacier Access Rd leaves Seward Hwy at Mile 79, continuing 5.4 miles to the **Begich-Boggs Visitors Center** (☎ 783-2326; ☼ 9am-6pm) en route to Whittier (see p224), on the other side of the Anton Memorial Tunnel.

The building, with its observation decks and telescopes, was designed to provide great views of Portage Glacier. But ironically (and to the dismay of thousands of tourists) the glacier has retreated so fast you can no longer see it from the center. Still, inside are neat high-tech wildlife displays and the excellent movie, *Voices from the Ice* (admission $1, shown every 30 minutes).

Most people view the glacier through **Gray Line** (☎ 277-5581) whose cruise boat, MV *Ptarmigan*, departs from a dock near the Begich-Boggs Center five times daily in June to September for a trip to the face of

it. It's a costly one-hour cruise; adult/child $26/13 or $67 with transportation from Anchorage. If you have a pair of hiking boots, **Portage Pass Trail**, a mile-long trek to the pass, will provide a good view of Portage Glacier. The trail begins near the tunnel on the Whittier side so it's a $12-per-car fare to drive through and then return. The only free way to see the glacier is to stop at a pullover on the Portage side of the tunnel where you can view a small corner of it.

Another interesting hike is **Byron Glacier View Trail**, a single, flat mile to an unusually ice worm–infested snowfield and grand glacier views.

To pitch a tent, there's two USFS campgrounds. **Black Bear Campground** (Mile 3.7 Portage Glacier Access Rd; sites $10) is pleasant and woodsy while **Williwaw Campground** (Mile 4.3 Portage Glacier Access Rd; s/d $13/20) is stunningly located beneath Explorer Glacier. Both campgrounds are extremely popular although sites at Williwaw can be reserved in advance through **National Recreation Reservation Service** (NRRS; ☎ 877-444-6777, 518-885-3639; www .reserveusa.com).

NORTH OF ANCHORAGE

GLENN HIGHWAY

In Anchorage, 5th Ave becomes Glenn Hwy, running 189 miles through Palmer, where it makes a junction with the George Parks Hwy, to Glennallen and the Richardson Hwy. Milepost distances are measured from Anchorage.

At Mile 11.5 of Glenn Hwy is **Eagle River State Campground** (☎ 694-7982; Hiland Rd exit; sites $15), with beautiful walk-in sites. The river runs closest to the shady sites in the 'Rapids' section. Keep in mind this is one of the most popular campsites in the state and half the sites can be reserved up to a year in advance.

Eagle River
☎ 907/pop 22,000
At Mile 13.4 of Glenn Hwy is the exit to Old Glenn Hwy, which takes you through the bedroom communities of Eagle River and Chugiak. Eagle River has a couple of plazas and just about every business you'll need. The **Bear Paw Festival**, held here in July, is worth the trip just for the 'Slippery Salmon

Olympics,' which involves racing with a hula hoop, serving tray and, of course, a large dead fish. Most people, however, come here for the drive down Eagle River Rd.

INFORMATION
Acute Family Medicine Clinic (☎ 622-4325; 11470 Business Blvd; ☯ 9am-7pm Mon-Fri, 9am-5pm Sat-Sun) Offers walk-in service.

Chugiak-Eagle River Chamber of Commerce (☎ 694-4702; www.cer.org; 11401 Old Glenn Hwy; ☯ 9am-4pm) Is located in the Eagle River Shopping Mall and has lots of pamphlets and free maps of town.

Emergency (ambulance, fire, police ☎ 911)

Key Bank (☎ 694-4464; 10928 Eagle River Rd) Also has an ATM.

Laundry Basket (☎ 694-8670; 12110 Business Blvd; ☯ 7am-10pm Mon-Sat, 8am-9pm Sun) Located in the Regional Park Plaza.

SIGHTS & ACTIVITIES
Eagle River Road
This stunning sidetrip into the heart of the Chugach Mountains follows the Eagle River for 13 miles. The road is paved and winding, and paralleled by a well-maintained bicycle trail. At Mile 7.4 there is a put-in for rafts to float the Class I & II section of the river. Class III & IV rapids are located upstream: put in at Echo Bend, which is accessed by the 3-mile footpath from the Eagle River Nature Center. The traditional pullout point is at Eagle Creek Loop Bridge. **Lifetime Adventures** (☎ 746-4644, 694-7982; Eagle River Campground) guides rafts down the Class III portions of Eagle River ($30 per person).

The road ends at the **Eagle River Nature Center** (☎ 694-2108; www.ernc.org; 32750 Eagle River Rd; admission per vehicle $5; ☯ 10am-5pm Sun-Thu, to 7pm Fri & Sat). The log-cabin center offers wildlife displays, telescopes for finding Dall sheep and guided hikes on most Saturday and Sundays.

Hiking
Several trails depart from the Eagle River Nature Center with **Rodak Nature Trail** being the easiest. Kids will love the mile-long interpretive path, as it swings by an impressive overlook straddling a salmon stream and a huge beaver dam. **Albert Loop Trail** is a slightly more challenging 3-mile hike through boreal forest and along Eagle River.

The **National Historic Iditarod Trail** is a 26-mile trek used by gold miners and sled-dog teams until 1918, when the Alaska Railroad was finished. It's a three-day hike through superb mountain scenery to Girdwood and the region's best backpack adventure. For details see Wilderness Hikes & Paddles (p71).

For a shorter outing you can turn around at the Perch, a very large rock in the middle of wonderland, then backtrack to the **Dew Mound Trail** at Echo Bend and loop back to the Nature Center, making this a scenic 8-mile trip. Pitch a tent at **Rapids Camp** (Mile 1.7) or **Echo Bend** (Mile 3), or rent one of two **yurts** (per night $65) close by.

Thunderbird Falls, closer to Eklutna, is a rewarding 2-mile walk with a gorgeous little waterfall for the grand finale. Anchorage's People Mover bus Nos 76 and 102 stop at the trailhead, off Thunderbird Falls exit of Glenn Hwy.

SLEEPING
Eagle River has an 8% bed tax.

Eagle River Motel (☎ 694-5000, 866-256-6835; www.eaglerivermotel.com; 11111 Old Eagle River Rd; s $89-139, d $94-143; ▢) It has much nicer (and bigger) rooms, all equipped with microwaves and refrigerators, than you'd get at this price in Anchorage.

Randy's Valley B&B (☎ 694-8266; 10131 Chandalar St; r $65-85; ✗ ▢) It's in the center of town and has three rooms, and the host speaks German.

Alaska Chalet B&B (☎ 694-1528, 877-694-1528; www.alaskachaletbb.com; 11031 Gulkana Cr; r/ste $55/95; ✗) In a small neighborhood within walking distance of downtown Eagle River with three rooms and a view of the Alaskan Range from the deck.

EATING
Haute Quarter Grill (☎ 622-4745; 11221 Old Glenn Hwy; lunch $8-15, dinner $16-30; ☯ 11:30am-2pm Tue-Fri, 5-9:30pm Tue-Sat; ✗) A highly recommended splurge, it offers a lot of gourmet for your dollar – try the giant scallops that are grilled in a roasted walnut marinade

Garcia's Cantina & Cafe (☎ 694-8600; 11901 Business Blvd; lunch $7-10, dinner $9-15; ☯ 11am-11pm Mon-Thu, to midnight Fri, noon-midnight Sat, to 11pm Sun; ✗) It has good burgers and better fajita quesadillas, plus a full bar. Even people not crazy about Mexican flock here. Be prepared to wait for a table.

North Slope Saloon (☎ 694-9120; 11501 Old Glenn Hwy; breakfast $5-13, dinner $9-24; ☯ 6am-10pm

Sun-Thu, to 11pm Fri & Sat) It claims to be the first brewpub in Alaska; true or not, its Copper River Amber blows Alaska Amber away. There's live music Thursday through Saturday with often a blues group on stage.

Sleepy Dog Coffee Company (☎ 694-8565; 11525 Old Glenn Hwy; ☑ 6am-9pm Mon-Thu, to 10pm Fri & Sat, 7am-7pm Sun; ☒) A newly remodeled coffeehouse that serves espresso and baked goods and has live entertainment almost nightly.

Eklutna

☎ 907 / pop 371

This 350-year-old Alaska Native village is just west of the Eklutna Lake Rd exit, Mile 26.5 of Glenn Hwy. One of the most interesting anthropological sites in the region is preserved at **Eklutna Village Historical Park** (☎ 688-6026; tour adult/child $5/2.50; ☑ 10am-6pm Mon-Fri, to 4pm Sat, 1-4pm Sun), where the uneasy marriage of the Athabascan and Russian Orthodox cultures is enshrined. The interior of St Nicholas Church is modeled after Noah's arc while outside, outdoor altars abound, including a heartfelt lean-to for St Herman, patron saint of Alaska. The most revealing structures, however, are the 80 brightly colored spirit boxes in the nearby Denáina Athabascans cemetery. Invest your time in one of the half-hour tours.

Eklutna Lake State Recreation Area (sites $10) is 10 long, bumpy miles east on Eklutna Lake Rd. It's worth every minute once the sky suddenly opens, unveiling a stunning valley with glacier-and-peak-ringed Eklutna Lake, the largest body of water in Chugach State Park, at its center.

Rochelle's Ice Cream & Cheely's General Store (☎ 688-6201, 800-764-6201; goalaskan.com; Eklutna Lake Rd; cabin/r $40/50; ☑ 9am-9pm Mon-Thu, 8am-10pm Fri & Sat, to 9pm Sun summer) has laundry, showers, groceries and lovely accommodations not far from the lake.

ACTIVITIES

Eklutna Lake State Recreation Area in Chugach State Park is a recreational paradise, including more than 27 miles of hiking and mountain-biking trails that can be accessed from the campground.

Lakeside Trail is a relaxing 13-mile walk to the other end of the lake, with two excellent free campsites: **Eklutna Alex Campground** (Mile 9) and **Kanchee Campground** (Mile 11). **East Fork Trail** diverts from the main trail at Mile 10.5 and

it runs another 5½ miles to a great view of Mt Bashful, the tallest mountain (8005ft) in the park. You could hike an easy 1 mile past the Lakeside Trail terminus to **Eklutna Glacier**. ATVs can use the trails Sunday through Wednesday, hikers and bikers anytime.

Bold Ridge Trail is a steep 3½-mile spur hike that begins 5 miles along the Lakeshore Trail and continues to the alpine area below Bold Peak (7522ft) for views of the valley, Eklutna Glacier and even Knik Arm. People with the energy can scramble up nearby ridges. Plan on two hours to climb the trail and an hour for the return. To actually climb Bold Peak requires serious equipment.

Twin Peaks Trail is shorter (3½ miles from the parking lot), but just as steep. It takes you through lush forest into alpine meadows presided over by the imposing eponymous peaks. Berries, wildlife and great lake views make scrambling toward the top downright enjoyable.

The lake makes for great paddling. **Lifetime Adventures** (☎ 746-4644, www.lifetimeadventures.net; Eklutna Lake State Recreation Area) rents single kayaks (half-/full day $30/50) and doubles for $5 more. It also rents mountain bikes (half-/full day $20/30) and offers a fun Paddle & Pedal rental where you kayak down the lake and then ride a mountain bike back ($70 per person).

PALMER

☎ 907 / pop 5197

From Eklutna Lake Rd, Glenn Hwy continues north, crossing Knik and Matanuska Rivers at the northern end of Cook Inlet, and at Mile 35.3 reaching a major junction with the George Parks Hwy. At this point, Glenn Hwy curves sharply to the east and heads into Palmer, 7 miles away. If you're driving, a much more scenic way to reach Palmer is to leave Glenn Hwy just before it crosses Knik River and follow Old Glenn Hwy into town.

Born during President Roosevelt's New Deal, Palmer was one of the great social experiments in an era when human nature was believed infinitely flexible. The mission was to transplant 200 farming families, who were refugees from the Depression-era dustbowl (the worst agricultural disaster in US history), to Alaska where they would cultivate a new agricultural economy.

Trainloads of Midwesterners and their Sears & Roebuck furniture were dropped off in the Matanuska and Susitna valleys, deemed suitable by the government for such endeavors. Soil rich by Alaskan standards enjoyed a growing season just long enough for cool-weather grains and certain vegetables. There was little margin for error, however, and any unexpected frost could destroy an entire year of seed and sweat.

The farmers' perseverance paid off, however, and today the Mat-Su Valley is Alaska's breadbasket, producing 75% of the state's total agricultural output. Palmer is famed for its 90lb cabbages and monster root vegetables but what is grown commercially, from potatoes and peas to carrots and broccoli, is the same size found in markets in every other state. To Alaskans the attraction of Mat-Su veggies is not their size but their freshness: produce that comes from just up the road, not 2000 miles across the country.

The attraction of Palmer to tourists is that of a small farming community with a Midwestern appearance but almost encircled by mountains. For those who want to skip the city hassles and high prices of Anchorage, Palmer is an excellent option

with just enough choices in lodging, restaurants and sights to keep you satisfied for a day or two.

Information

Alaskana Bookstore (☎ 745-8695; 564 S Denali St; ☾ noon-5:30pm Fri-Sun) Huge selection of used and rare, state-related tomes.

Emergency (ambulance, fire, police ☎ 911)

Fireside Books (☎ 745-2665; 720 S Alaska St; ☾ 10am-7pm Mon-Sat, noon-4pm Sun) New and used books and a good selection of maps.

Laundry Depot (☎ 745-3008; 127 S Alaska St; ☾ 8am-10pm) Shower ($4) or access the Internet (per 30 minutes $3.50) while you launder.

Palmer Library (☎ 745-4690; 655 S Valley Way; ☾ noon-6pm Mon-Fri, 10am-2pm Sat) An excellent library with free Internet access.

Palmer Visitor Center (☎ 745-2880; www.palmer chamber.org; 723 S Valley Way; ☾ 9am-6pm) In the log cabin downtown; has pamphlets, maps of the town, free coffee and a small collection of colonial-era tools and other artifacts.

Post office (cnr S Cobb St & W Cedar Ave)

Valley Hospital (☎ 746-8600; 515 E Dahlia Ave) East of the library.

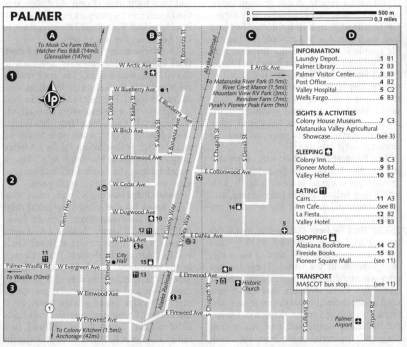

PALMER

INFORMATION	
Laundry Depot	1 B1
Palmer Library	2 B3
Palmer Visitor Center	3 B3
Post Office	4 B3
Valley Hospital	5 C2
Wells Fargo	6 B3

SIGHTS & ACTIVITIES	
Colony House Museum	7 C3
Matanuska Valley Agricultural Showcase	(see 3)

SLEEPING	
Colony Inn	8 C3
Pioneer Motel	9 B1
Valley Hotel	10 B2

EATING	
Carrs	11 A3
Inn Cafe	(see 8)
La Fiesta	12 B2
Valley Hotel	13 B3

SHOPPING	
Alaskana Bookstore	14 C2
Fireside Books	15 B3
Pioneer Square Mall	(see 11)

TRANSPORT	
MASCOT bus stop	(see 11)

ANCHORAGE & AROUND

Wells Fargo (☎ 745-2161; 705 S Bailey St) Lets you drain that account.

Sights & Activities

Outside the visitors center is **Matanuska Valley Agricultural Showcase** (open 8am to 7pm June to August), a garden featuring flowers and the area's famous oversized vegetables. But you have to be passing through in August if you want to see a cabbage bigger than a basketball. Every Friday during summer is **Friday Fling** (from 11am to 6pm June to August), an open-air market with local produce, art, crafts, food and live music.

The thought-provoking **Colony House Museum** (☎ 745-1935; 316 E Elmwood Ave; adult/child $2/1; 🕑 10am-4pm Tue-Sun) was a home built in 1935 during the original settlement of Palmer and its eight rooms are still furnished with artifacts and stories from that era. To bring the living-room piano to Alaska, members of one pioneer family left behind their luggage and stuffed their clothes in it, the only way to make their weight allotment.

FARMS

If you have a vehicle, cruise through Palmer's back roads past original colony farms. Go northeast 9 miles on Glenn Hwy and hop on Farm Loop Rd; look for vegetable stands if you're passing through here from mid- to late summer. South of Palmer **Pyrah's Pioneer Peak Farm** (☎ 745-4511; Mile 2.8 Bodenberg Loop Rd; 🕑 9am-5pm Mon, to 9pm Tue-Sat) is the largest pick-your-own-vegetables place in the Mat-Su Valley with would-be farmers in the fields from July to early October picking everything from peas and potatoes to carrots and cabbage.

The **Reindeer Farm** (☎ 745-4000; www.reindeerfarm.com; Mile 11.5 Old Glenn Hwy; adult/child $5/3; 🕑 10am-6pm) is a great place to bring the kids where they will be able to pet and feed, and are encouraged to think the reindeer are connected to Santa.

The **Musk Ox Farm** (☎ 745-4151; www.muskoxfarm.org; Mile 50 Glenn Hwy; adult/child $8.50/5.50; 🕑 10am-6pm) is the only domestic herd of these big, shaggy beasts in the world. These Ice-Age critters are intelligent enough to have evolved a complex social structure that allows survival under incredibly harsh conditions. Yes, you'll probably get to pet them, too. Qiviut, the incredibly warm, soft and pricey ($60 per ounce) material made from the musk

ox's soft undercoat, is harvested here; fine sweaters and hats are for sale in the gift shop. Tours are given every half-hour.

KNIK GLACIER

Trekkies take note: Knik Glacier is best known as the setting where a portion of *Star Trek VI* was filmed. You can get a partial view of the ice floe at Mile 7 of Knik River Rd off Old Glenn Hwy but the best way to experience it is on an airboat ride up the Knik River. Several outfitters offer such a trip, including **Knik Glacier Adventures** (☎ 746-5133; www.knikglacieradventures.com; Mile 8.5 Knik River Rd; adult/child $65/35) whose four-hour tours depart at 10am and 3pm daily and include a cookout within view of the ice.

HIKING

The best hike near Palmer is the berry-lined climb to the top of 3720ft **Lazy Mountain**. The 2½-mile trail is steep at times, but makes for a pleasant trek that ends in an alpine setting with good views of Matanuska Valley farms. Take Old Glenn Hwy across the Matanuska River, turn left onto Clark–Wolverine Rd and then right onto Huntly Rd; follow it to the Equestrian Center parking lot and trailhead, marked 'Foot Trail.' Plan on three to five hours for the round-trip.

The backcountry hike up the **McRoberts Creek Valley** provides an easy approach to 6119ft Matanuska Peak. The trail reaches the tree line in 2½ miles and 3880ft Summit Ridge in 9 miles. The trek to Matanuska Peak is a serious 18-mile endeavor. To reach the trailhead, take Old Glenn Hwy from Palmer toward Butte and turn left onto Smith Rd at Mile 15.5. Follow Smith Rd for 1.4 miles, until it curves into Harmony Ave. There is no parking at the South Fork trailhead, so leave the car at the bend in the road.

Pioneer Ridge Trail is a 5.7-mile route from Knik River Rd that climbs the main ridge extending southeast from Pioneer Peaks (6400ft). You'll climb through forest until you reach the alpine tundra at 3200ft. Once on the ridge, South Pioneer Peak is a mile to the northwest, North Pioneer Peak is 2 miles. Scaling either requires rock-climbing experience and equipment. To the southeast, the ridge leads toward Bold Peak, the Hunter Creek drainage and eventually Eklutna Lake. To reach the trailhead, turn onto Knik River Rd, just before crossing the river on Old Glenn Hwy, and follow it for almost 4 miles.

Festivals & Events

Palmer becomes the state's hottest ticket during the **Alaska State Fair** (☎ 800-850-3247; www.alaskastatefair.org; per day adult/child $10/6), a rollicking 12-day event that ends on Labor Day, the first Monday in September. The fair features live music and prized livestock from the surrounding area, as well as horse shows, a rodeo, a carnival and, of course, the giant cabbage weigh-off to see who grew the biggest one in the valley (2004 winner weighed in at 90 lbs). If greased pigs, Spam-sponsored recipe contests and the Great Alaskan Husband Holler contest aren't enough to get you here, try this: berry pie cook-offs.

The fairground is also home to the **Mat-Su Miners** (☎ 745-6401; www.matsuminers.org; adult/child $4/2) another semipro team of the Alaska Baseball League that plays against clubs like Fairbanks Goldpanners and the Anchorage Bucs. Until 1980 the Palmer players were the Valley Green Giants but changed their name for obvious reasons.

Sleeping

If you arrive late, outside the Palmer Visitor Center is a courtesy phone with direct lines connected to area accommodations. Palmer has an 8% bed tax.

Colony Inn (☎ 745-3330; 325 E Elmwood; s/d $80/100; ✗) What was constructed in 1935 as the Matanuska Colony Teacher's Dorm has become Palmer's nicest lodge. The 12 rooms are spacious, especially the corner rooms, well kept and equipped with TVs and whirlpool tubs. Register at the Valley Hotel.

Valley Hotel (☎ 745-3330, 800-478-7666 Alaska only; 606 S Alaska St; r $79-110) This is a step up from the Gold Miner's Hotel. The rooms are smaller but recently renovated while its Caboose Lounge is a friendly pub to end a day.

River Crest Manor (☎ 746-6214; www.rivercrestmanor.com; 2655 Old Glenn Hwy; r $85-95; ✗) A beautiful home that provides three guest rooms on the Mantanuska River 1½ miles from downtown Palmer.

Hatcher Pass B&B (☎ 745-6788; www.hatcherpassbb.com; Mile 6.6 Palmer-Fishhook Rd; cabin s/d $79/89; ✗) If you have wheels you can rent a cabin at several places on the way to Hatcher Pass. This B&B, 14 miles from Palmer, offers four button-cute, one-room log cabins with bath, kitchenette and TV.

Pioneer Motel (☎ 745-3425; 124 W Arctic Ave; r $59-69) Your best budget option. The rooms are nicer than the outside appearance indicates and come with microwaves, coffeemakers and refrigerators.

Matanuska River Park (☎ 745-9631; Mile 17.5 Old Glenn Hwy; campsites/RV sites $10/15) Less than a half-mile east of town, this place lets you pitch a tent or park a trailer. Some sites are wooded and there is a series of trails that winds around ponds and along the Matanuska River.

Mountain View RV Park (☎ 745-5747, 800-264-4582; Mile 42 Glenn Hwy; campsites/RV sites $18/22) It has laundry facilities, showers and a rather gravelly camping area located almost 3 miles south of Palmer.

Eating

Inn Café (☎ 745-3330; 325 E Elmwood; sandwiches $8-9, brunch $15, dinner $18; ☺ 11am-3pm Mon-Thu, 11am-3pm & 5-9pm Fri, 9am-2pm Sun; ✗) What was once the Colony Inn where teachers dined is now a pleasant restaurant with sandwiches and salads most of the week, dinner and live jazz on Friday evenings and brunch on Sunday.

Colony Kitchen (☎ 746-4600; 1890 Glenn Hwy; breakfast $6-12, dinner $11-20; ☺ 6am-10pm; ✗) It serves the best breakfasts in town and serves it all day. Diner dinners include fried chicken, meat loaf and chicken fried steak. You'll eat beneath stuffed birds suspended from the ceiling (hence the 'Noisy Goose Cafe' nickname).

Vagabond Blues (☎ 745-2233; 642 S Alaska St; light meals $4-7; ☺ 7am-9pm Mon-Thu, 7am-10pm Fri & Sat, 8am-6pm Sun; ✗) A cozy, gay-friendly coffee shop, with local art on the walls and often live music at night. It has healthy, homemade quiches, soups and salads.

La Fiesta (☎ 746-3335; 132 W Evergreen; lunch $8-10, dinner $10-15; ☺ 11am-9pm Mon-Fri, from noon Sat & Sun; ✗) Palmer has this lively and affordable Mexican restaurant that fills up fast with locals.

Carrs (☎ 745-7505; 535 W Evergreen; ☺ 24hr) It has groceries, a deli and a salad bar stocked in late summer with Mat-Su's finest.

Getting There & Around

MASCOT (☎ 376-5000; www.matsutransit.com; single ride/day pass $2/5) Created in 1999, the Mat-Su Community Transit system makes six trips daily

DETOUR: HATCHER PASS

A sidetrip from either Glenn or George Parks Hwys and a wonderful way to spend a spare day is Hatcher Pass. This photogenic alpine passage cuts through the Talkeetna Mountains and leads to meadows, ridges and a beautiful body of water known as Summit Lake. Gold was the first treasure people found here; today it's footpaths, abandoned mines and popular climbs that outshine the precious metal. You can drive here from Wasilla, Willow or Palmer, but the latter is the shortest and most scenic route, with Hatcher Pass Rd following Little Susitna River through a steep-walled gorge.

The main attraction of Hatcher Pass is 272-acre **Independence Mine State Historical Park** (Mile 18 Hatcher Pass Rd; admission per vehicle $5), a huge, abandoned gold mine sprawled out in a beautiful alpine valley. The 1930s facility, built by the Alaska-Pacific Mining Company (APC), was for 10 years the second-most-productive hardrock goldmine in Alaska. At its peak, in 1941, APC employed 204 workers, blasted almost 12 miles of tunnels and recovered 34,416oz of gold, today worth almost $18 million. The mine was finally abandoned in 1955.

Today you can explore the structures, hike several trails and take in one of the most stunning views in the state at Hatcher Pass. The **visitors center** (☎ 745-2827; ⏲ 11am-7pm) has a map of the park, a simulated mining tunnel, displays on the ways to mine gold (panning, placer mining and hardrock) and **guided tours** ($5 per person, 1pm and 3pm). From the center, follow Hardrock Trail past the dilapidated buildings, which include bunkhouses and a mill complex that is built into the side of the mountain and looks like an avalanche of falling timber. Make an effort to climb up the trail to the water tunnel portal, where there is a great view of the entire complex and a blast of cold air pouring out of the mountain.

Hatcher Pass also offers some of the best alpine hiking in the Mat-Su areas. The easy, beautiful **Gold Mint Trail** begins at a parking lot across from Motherlode Lodge, at Mile 14 Fishhook–Willow Rd. The trail follows the Little Susitna River into a gently sloping mountain valley and within 3 miles you spot the ruins of Lonesome Mine. Keep hiking and you'll eventually reach Mint Glacier.

With two alpine lakes, lots of waterfalls, glaciers and towering walls of granite, the 7-mile **Reed Lakes Trail** (9 miles to the upper lake) is worth the climb, which includes some serious scrambling. A mile past Motherlode Lodge, a road to Archangel Valley splits off from Fishhook–Willow Rd and leads to the trailhead of Reed Lakes; a wide road. If you've got a 4WD, you can (theoretically) drive the first 3 miles of the **Craigie Creek Trail**, posted along the Fishhook-Willow Rd just west of Hatcher Pass. It's better, however, to walk the gently climbing old road up a valley and past several abandoned mining operations to the head of the creek. It then becomes a very steep trail for 3 miles to Dogsled Pass, where you can access several wilderness trails into the Talkeetna Mountains.

If the weather is nice and you have the funds it's hard to pass up spending the night at the pass. **Motherlode Lodge** (☎ 745-6171, 877-745-6171; www.motherlodelodge.com; Mile 14 Hatcher Pass Rd; r $129; ✗) was originally built in the 1930s as part of the local mining operation. It has since been renovated into an inn with a restaurant and bar where every stool gives way to views of the mountains. **Hatcher Pass Lodge** (☎ 745-5897; www.hatcherpasslodge.com; Mile 17.5 Hatcher Pass Rd; s/d $95/110, cabins $145; ✗), inside the state park, is a highly recommended splurge. Aside from spectacular views at 30,000ft, the lodge has nine cabins, three rooms, a (pricey) restaurant and bar and a sauna built over a rushing mountain stream.

between Wasilla and Palmer and three commuter runs from the Valley to the Transit Center in Anchorage. If staying in Anchorage you can use the bus for a cheap day trip to Palmer. All buses stop at Carrs.

Alaska Cab (☎ 746-2727) and **Mat-Su Taxi** (☎ 373-5861) both provide service around town, as well as to Wasilla ($20) and Anchorage ($70).

WASILLA
☎ 907 / pop 6109

Just seven miles north of the Glenn Hwy/ George Parks Hwy junction, Wasilla was a sleepy little town in the 1970s that served local farmers. Then urban sprawl reached it. From 1980 to 1983 the population of Wasilla doubled as Alaskans who wanted to work in Anchorage but live elsewhere began moving in. Today it's a full-fledged bedroom community of the big city to the south. Shopping centers and businesses – including the ubiquitous Wal-Mart – have mushroomed along the highway, and this is one of the few places in Alaska where you'll notice rush-hour traffic. If you need services – banks, auto mechanics etc – you'll find them here and should take advantage of them, as things get sketchier and more expensive between here and Fairbanks.

Information

Dorothy Page Museum & Visitor Center (☎ 373-9071; 323 Main St; museum adult/child $3/free; 9am-5pm Tue-Sat) In town is this three-room museum named after the woman known as 'the Mother of the Iditarod.'

iCafé (☎ 357-6622; 991 N Hermon Rd; per hr $5; 8am-6pm Mon-Sat) In the Hunter Plaza next to Lowe's, check your email, surf the Internet or sip a cup Kaladi coffee.

Matanuska-Susitna Visitors Center (☎ 746-5000; www.alaskavisit.com; Mile 35.5 George Parks Hwy; 8:30am- 6:30pm) Near the junction of the Parks and Glenn Hwys is this large log lodge with a great view of the mountains surrounding Knik Inlet from its outdoor deck. Inside are racks of area information.

Sights & Activities

The **Iditarod**, a famous 1100-mile dogsled race to Nome, begins in Anchorage – but only for the sake of appearances. At the end of a short run in Anchorage, the teams wave goodbye to the cameras, pack up their dogs and sleds, and drive to snowier country up north for the 'restart.' Wasilla serves as the second official starting point for the race, though the lack of snow often pushes the restart north to Willow.

Near Wasilla, **Knik** boasts a rich sled-dog history, since it's the home of many Alaskan mushers and checkpoint No 4 on the route. For more information about this uniquely Alaskan race, stop in at **Iditarod Trail Headquarters** (☎ 376-5155; www.iditarod.com; Mile 2.2 Knik Rd; admission free; 8am-7pm). The log-cabin museum's most unusual exhibit is Togo, the famous sled dog that led his team across trackless Norton Sound to deliver serum to diphtheria-threatened Nome in 1925 – a journey that gave rise to today's Iditarod. He's been stuffed and is now on display. Outside, you can get a short **sled-dog ride** ($10, from 9am to 5pm) on a wheeled dogsled.

Sleeping & Eating

Wasilla adds 7.5% in bed and sales tax to lodging.

Alaska Kozey Cabins (☎ 376-3190; 351 E Spruce Ave; d $129;) For a night in the woods, just five minutes north of downtown, are these six *kozey* log cabins on five private acres. The cabins sleep up to six ($20 for each additional person) and are equipped with wi-fi, a kitchen, cable TV and a private bath.

Windbreak Hotel (☎ 376-4209; 2201 E George Parks Hwy; s/d $65/70;) A mile south of town, this is Wasilla's most affordable accommodations with 10 rooms, private baths, a friendly pub and a good café.

Lake Lucille Park (☎ 745-9631; Mile 2.4 Knik Rd; sites $10) The nearest place to camp, the park's 64-site campground has rest rooms, a shelter and a network of trails.

Great Bear Brewing Co (☎ 373-4782; 238 N Boundary St; burgers $8-11, dinner $16-22; 11am-midnight) Wasilla's eatery of choice with great home-brewed ales, tasty food and a dozen creative burgers.

Getting There & Around

BUS

MASCOT (Mat-Su Community Transit; ☎ 376-5000; www .matsutransit.com; single ride/day pass $2/5) makes six trips daily to Palmer with buses in Wasilla departing from both the Wal-Mart and Carrs. There are also three commuter runs to Transit Center in Anchorage that depart Wasilla Carrs at 5:40am, 8:28am and 3:32pm.

CAR

A rental car in Wasilla is cheaper than Anchorage because the city adds *only* a 12.5% tax; it's the best way to reach Hatcher Pass (opposite) **Valley Car Rental** (☎ 775-2880; 435 S Knik St) is in downtown Wasilla and has compacts for $45 a day with unlimited mileage.

TRAIN

The **Alaska Railroad** (☎ 265-2494 in Anchorage, 800-544-0552; www.alaskarailroad.com) from Anchorage stops at Wasilla at 9:45am daily in summer *if* there are paid reservations (otherwise it just blows on by). Fare is $129 to Denali and $179 to Fairbanks. The train from Fairbanks arrives at 6:05pm; the fare to Anchorage is $43. Any of the bus services to Denali (see p194) will drop you off in town en route far cheaper than the train.

Prince William Sound

Prince William Sound, the Gulf of Alaska northernmost extent, rivals the Southeast for the steepest fjords, stunning coastlines and glaciers, the earthiest, saltiest fisherfolk and the most rain. It's flanked by the Kenai Mountains and the Chugach Mountains, the region covers 15,000 sq miles. The sea is a paddlers' paradise of steepsided coves, islands and channels; the land is mountains and rainforest. Wildlife abounds: whales, sea lions, harbor seals, otters, eagles, Dall sheep, mountain goats and, of course, bears.

There are three wildly different towns here. Valdez, the region's hub, boasts stellar scenery, radical skiing, and the chance of paddling near the face of the massive Columbia Glacier, which calves so frantically its fjord is often blocked by bergs. Valdez is about oil, which flows by the millions of gallons from the Trans-Alaska Pipeline into tankers waiting at the city's port.

Valdez people are prosperous and proud, and think of the Sound's second-largest town, Cordova, as a depressed fishing village isolated from roads. Cordovans say they're doing fine in their seaside place, oriented toward the salmon-rich ocean. When they want to drive, they hit the Copper River Hwy, through a wondrous wetland to a glacier that rivals the Columbia.

There's also Whittier, accessed by the US's longest highway tunnel. Like Alice falling down the rabbit hole, visitors who pass through this tunnel experience an alternate universe, with Soviet-style architecture and lovable oddballs, and dotted by waterfalls and peaks.

HIGHLIGHTS

■ **Most gobsmacking glaciers** (p221) – admiring supergiant Columbia Glacier (p214), near Valdez, and superactive Childs Glacier, near Cordova

■ **Best place to flock to** (p222) – being at Cordova's Copper River Delta during the annual Copper River Delta Shorebird Festival

■ **Biggest shake-up** (p212) – checking out the legacy of the Good Friday Earthquake of 1964, which measured a whopping 9.2 on the Richter scale, is etched on the foundations of Old Valdez

■ **Best journey to the center of the earth** (p228) – driving to Whittier through the Anton Anderson Memorial Tunnel

■ **Slipperiest slopes** (p215) – taking on the near-vertical Chugach Mountains around Valdez, where extreme skiing is all downhill

■ AREA CODE: ☎ 907   ■ POPULATION: 7,500   ■ ELEVATION: MT BARCUS BAKER 13,176FT

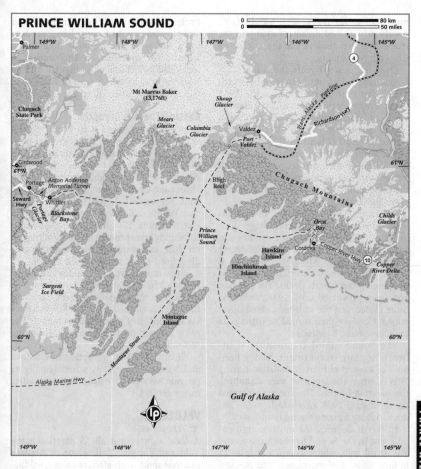

PRINCE WILLIAM SOUND

0 _____ 80 km
0 _____ 50 miles

Palmer — 149°W — 148°W — 147°W — 146°W — 145°W

4

Mt Marcus Baker
(13,176ft)

Shoup
Glacier

Chugach
State Park

Mears
Glacier

Columbia
Glacier

Valdez
Port
Valdez

Trans-Alaska Pipeline

Richardson Hwy

Girdwood
61°N

Portage   Anton Anderson
Memorial Tunnel

Bligh
Reef

Chugach Mountains

Seward
Hwy

Whittier

Portage Glacier

Blackstone
Bay

61°N

Childs
Glacier

Prince
William
Sound

Orca
Bay

Cordova   Copper River Hwy   10

Hawkins
Island

Hinchinbrook
Island

Copper
River Delta

Sargent
Ice Field

60°N

Montague
Island

60°N

Montague Strait

Alaska Marine Hwy

Gulf of Alaska

149°W — 148°W — 147°W — 146°W — 145°W

PRINCE WILLIAM SOUND

Climate

It's wet here – except in the winter, when it's snowy. That's right, precipitation is the norm in Prince William Sound, where clouds, bloated with moisture from crossing the Pacific, crash into the Chugach Mountains and dump their watery burden. In summer, Valdez is the driest of the towns; Whittier is by far the wettest. In all communities, average July high temperatures are barely above 60°F. So no matter what your travel plans are, pack your fleece and some bombproof wet-weather gear. And as the raindrops fall, just remember that if it wasn't for precipitation, this place wouldn't be the glacier-carved, snowcapped, forest-clad Eden that it is.

History

Prince William Sound was long a crossroads of Alaska Native cultures; the region has been inhabited at various times by coastal Chugach Inuit people, Athabascans originally from the Interior, and Tlingits who traveled up from Alaska's panhandle. The first European to arrive was Vitus Bering, a Danish navigator sailing for the tsar of Russia, who anchored his ship near Kayak Island, east of Copper River, in 1741.

The Sound's three major towns have rather divergent modern histories. Valdez was settled in 1897, when 4000 gold prospectors took what had been billed as the 'All-American Route' to the Klondike goldfields. It turned out to be one of the most dangerous trails, with hundreds of poorly provisioned dreamers dying on the trek across two glaciers and the uncharted Chugach Mountains.

Over the next 60 years the community largely languished until catastrophe struck again, this time in the form of the 1964 Good Friday Earthquake, which killed 37 locals and forced the wholesale relocation of the town. However, Valdez' fortunes turned in the 1970s when it was selected as the terminus of the Trans-Alaska Pipeline. The $9 billion project was a windfall beyond those early miners' wildest dreams; the population grew by 320% and the town never looked back.

Cordova's past is somewhat less fraught with catastrophe. A cannery village since the late 1800s, it was chosen a century ago as the port for a railway from the Kennecott copper mines near McCarthy. By 1916 it was a boomtown, with millions worth of ore passing through its docks. The railroad and town prospered until 1938, when the mine closed and the railroad ceased operations. Cordova then turned to fishing, its main economic base today.

The Sound's third community, Whittier, is of more recent origin, having been built as a secret military installation during WWII, when the Japanese were assaulting the Aleutian Islands. The army maintained the town until 1968, after which, as in Cordova, fishing became the main industry.

In recent decades, the most monumental event in the Sound has been the *Exxon Valdez* oil spill, which dumped at least 11 million gallons of petroleum into the sea, killing countless birds and marine mammals, and devastating the fishing industry for several years. Though fishing – and the environment – has largely rebounded, oil is still easy to find beneath the surface of beaches, and certain species are expected never to recover.

Dangers & Annoyances
By definition, glaciers move at a glacial pace, so you'd think they'd be harmless. In glacier-strewn Prince William Sound, however, they can be a real hazard. Not only have trekkers and mountaineers been killed when they've plunged into crevasses in the ice, but glaciers can also wreak havoc when they calve. In 1993, a football field–sized berg broke off from Cordova's Childs Glacier and plunged into the Copper River, producing a 40ft wave that seriously injured two women. The same year, an Anchorage man was killed by a chunk of ice that fell on him while he was kayaking around Blackstone Glacier near Whittier. Keep your distance.

Getting There & Around
Prince William Sound is all about the sea, and by far the best way to get around is on water. The **Alaska Marine Highway** (☎ 800-642-0066; www.ferryalaska.com) provides a fairly convenient, fairly affordable service, linking Valdez and Cordova daily and making three runs per week between Valdez, Cordova and Whittier. But the ferry is more than just transport: it's an experience. There's something transcendent about bundling up on deck and watching the mountain-riddled, fjord-riven, watery world unfurl.

If you must drive, both Valdez and Whittier are highway accessible; the former is the beginning of the Richardson Hwy, and the latter is connected to the Seward Hwy via the continent's longest auto tunnel. The route between the two towns is a whopping 368 miles.

Finally, planes are an option in Cordova and Valdez, where daily scheduled flights provide service to Anchorage and other major centers.

VALDEZ
☎ 907 / pop 4454
A local sign says it all: 'Switzerland: the Valdez of Europe.' This is one of Alaska's prettiest spots, with glaciers galore, wildlife running amok and a Norman Rockwell–style harbor cradled by some of the highest coastal mountains (topping 7000ft) in the world. The city offers excellent paddling, hiking and other outdoor adventures, plus some quality restaurants, accommodations and museums, as befits a city blessed by the biggest boom Alaska has ever known.

Despite its attractions, Valdez is not primarily a tourist mecca. Nor, despite its proximity to the Sound, is it mainly a fishing village. On August 1, 1977, when the first tanker of oil issued forth from Trans-Alaska Pipeline Terminal across the bay, Valdez became an oil town.

The drive into town along the Richardson Hwy overlooks the pipeline, snaking its silvery way from the northern oil fields to this (in)famous port. If you arrive by ferry, no mountain and no glacier dominates the scenery like the massive storage tanks, which seem so precariously perched above shore. And no matter how many precautions you know the oil companies have taken, no matter how much you appreciate their bounty (not many folks walk to Alaska), these views remain…unsettling. Visitors who remember the 1989 *Exxon Valdez* oil spill (p213) will have a difficult time relaxing into the wonder of this place. Those awful images of birds thickly coated with oil come unbidden, even as you kayak peacefully through one of nature's most inspiring creations.

Orientation
Valdez is on a flat slip of land on the north shore of Port Valdez, a gray green inlet ringed by glaciated peaks and linked to Prince William Sound via Valdez Narrows. To take in the view, visitors gravitate to the waterfront along Fidalgo and North Harbor Drs; from there, the town stretches about a dozen walkable blocks back toward the mountains and Mineral Creek Canyon. At the west end of the waterfront is the ferry terminal. East of town, Egan Dr turns into the Richardson Hwy, passes the airport, crests Thompson Pass and runs 366 miles to Fairbanks.

Information
Crooked Creek Information Site (☎ 835-4680; Mile 0.9 Richardson Hwy) Staffed by US Forest Service (USFS) naturalists offering great advice about outdoorsy activities. The nearby viewing platform is a good place to watch chum and pink salmon spawn in July and August.
Emergency (ambulance, fire, police ☎ 911)
Harbormaster's office (☎ 835-4981; 300 N Harbor Dr) Has showers ($4).
Like Home Laundromat (☎ 831-0567; 121 Egan Dr; showers per 10 min $4; ☼ 8am-8pm Mon-Fri, from 10am Sat & Sun) In the Valdez Mall; has showers and laundry machines.
Post office (cnr Galena Dr & Tatitlek Ave) Sells phonecards.
Valdez Community Hospital (☎ 835-2249; 911 Meals Ave) Has an emergency room.
Valdez Consortium Library (☎ 835-4632; 212 Fairbanks Dr; ☼ 10am-6pm Mon & Fri, 10am-8pm Tue-Thu, to 5pm Sat; 🖳) Head here for free Internet access.
Valdez Medical Clinic (☎ 835-4811; 912 Meals Ave) Provides walk-in care.

Visitor Information Center (☎ 835-2984; www.valdezalaska.com; 200 Fairbanks Dr; ☼ 8am-8pm Mon-Sat, 9am-6pm Sun) Has free maps and can book accommodations. There's an unstaffed information booth at the airport with a direct line to the downtown visitors center.
Wells Fargo (☎ 835-4381; 101 337 Egan Dr) This bank can probably handle extremely large accounts considering the presence of the local oil fields.

Sights
VALDEZ MUSEUM
This fairly gargantuan **museum** (☎ 835-2764; www.valdezmuseum.org; 217 Egan Dr; adult/child $5/free; ☼ 9am-6pm) includes a hand-cranked antique fire engine, a 19th-century saloon bar and the ceremonial first barrel of oil to flow from the Trans-Alaska Pipeline. There are arresting photos of the six minutes when Valdez was shaken to pieces by the 1964 Good Friday Earthquake, and an exhibit featuring correspondence from stampeders attempting the grueling All-American Route from Valdez to the inland goldfields. Wrote one goldseeker, 'I wash at least once a month, whether I need it or not.'

'REMEMBERING OLD VALDEZ' ANNEX
Operated by the Valdez Museum, this **annex** (☎ 835-5407; 436 Hazelet Ave; admission free; ☼ 9am-6pm) is dominated by a scale model of the Old Valdez township. Each home destroyed in the Good Friday Earthquake has been restored in miniature, with the family's name in front. Other exhibits on the earthquake and subsequent tsunamis and fires are moving, but none are as heartwrenching as the recordings of ham-radio operators communicating across the Sound as the quake wore on. This is a fitting memorial to the lives and countless memories lost on Valdez' darkest day.

MAXINE & JESSE WHITNEY MUSEUM
This high-quality **museum** (☎ 834-1612; 300 Airport Rd; adult/child $5/3; ☼ 9am-8pm), located near the airport, is well worth the trip. Opened by Prince William Sound Community College in 1999, the center is devoted to Alaska Native culture and Alaskan wildlife, and features ivory and baleen artwork, historical photographs and natural-history displays, including some very creative taxidermy.

SMALL-BOAT HARBOR
Valdez' harbor is a classic: raucous with gulls and eagles, reeking of fish guts and

sea salt and creosote, and home to all manner of vessels – even a Chinese junk. The benches and long boardwalk are ideal for watching lucky anglers weighing in 100lb or 200lb halibut, and for taking in the fairytale mountainscape in the background. Nearby is the **civic center** (Fidalgo Dr), which has more picnic tables and panoramic vistas.

OLD VALDEZ

Valdez has been unduly blessed by nature, but 5:46pm, March 27, 1964, was payback time. Some 45 miles west of town and 14 miles underground, a fault ruptured, triggering a magnitude-9.2 earthquake – the most powerful in American history. The land rippled like water as Valdez slid into

the harbor; tsunamis destroyed what was left. Thirty-seven people died.

After the quake, survivors labored to relocate and rebuild Valdez at its present site. But if you drive out the Richardson Hwy you can see the ghostly and overgrown foundations of Old Valdez. The **Earthquake Memorial**, listing the names of the dead, is reached by turning off the highway onto the unsigned gravel road just south of Mark's Repair. On the day of the quake, Valdez' post office was here; in mere moments the ground sank so far that nowadays high tides reach the spot.

TRANS-ALASKA PIPELINE TERMINAL

Across the inlet from town, Valdez' everpumping heart once welcomed visitors,

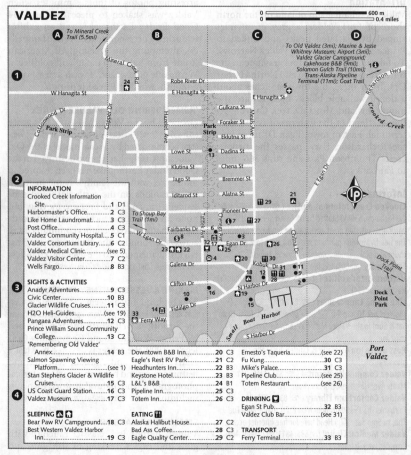

VALDEZ

0 ————— 600 m
0 ————— 0.4 miles

To Mineral Creek Trail (5.5mi)

To Old Valdez (3mi); Maxine & Jesse Whitney Museum; Airport (3mi); Valdez Glacier Campground; Lakehouse B&B (9mi); Solomon Gulch Trail (10mi); Trans-Alaska Pipeline Terminal (11mi); Goat Trail

To Shoup Bay Trail (1mi)

Port Valdez

Dock Point Park

Small Boat Harbor

INFORMATION	
Crooked Creek Information Site	1 D1
Harbormaster's Office	2 C3
Like Home Laundromat	3 C3
Post Office	4 C3
Valdez Community Hospital	5 C1
Valdez Consortium Library	6 C2
Valdez Medical Clinic	(see 5)
Valdez Visitor Center	7 C3
Wells Fargo	8 B3

SIGHTS & ACTIVITIES	
Anadyr Adventures	9 C3
Civic Center	10 B3
Glacier Wildlife Cruises	11 C3
H2O Heli-Guides	(see 19)
Pangaea Adventures	12 C3
Prince William Sound Community College	13 C2
'Remembering Old Valdez' Annex	14 B3
Salmon Spawning Viewing Platform	(see 1)
Stan Stephens Glacier & Wildlife Cruises	15 C3
US Coast Guard Station	16 C3
Valdez Museum	17 C3

SLEEPING	
Bear Paw RV Campground	18 C3
Best Western Valdez Harbor Inn	19 C3
Downtown B&B Inn	20 C3
Eagle's Rest RV Park	21 C2
Headhunters Inn	22 B3
Keystone Hotel	23 B3
L&L's B&B	24 B1
Pipeline Inn	25 C3
Totem Inn	26 C3

EATING	
Alaska Halibut House	27 C2
Bad Ass Coffee	28 C3
Eagle Quality Center	29 C2

Ernesto's Taqueria	(see 22)
Fu Kung	30 C3
Mike's Palace	31 C3
Pipeline Club	(see 25)
Totem Restaurant	(see 26)

DRINKING	
Egan St Pub	32 B3
Valdez Club Bar	(see 31)

TRANSPORT	
Ferry Terminal	33 B3

PRINCE WILLIAM SOUND

THE EXXON VALDEZ

It was the worst environmental disaster in modern American history: on March 23, 1989, the tanker *Exxon Valdez* left Valdez' Trans-Alaska Pipeline Terminal without the escorts regulations had once required and with its captain tippled. It sailed through Valdez Narrows, swung wide to avoid icebergs from Columbia Glacier, failed to return to its shipping lane, and grounded on Bligh Reef. At least 11 million gallons of oil spilled into Prince William Sound. By a trick of the storm the slick swept westward, fouling 1400 miles of coastline but missing its home port entirely. Within days, countless animals perished: perhaps 250,000 seabirds, 2800 otters, 250 bald eagles – and billions of salmon and herring eggs. Only about 8% of the slick was reclaimed by human efforts.

Nearly two decades later, it's still not over – ask anyone who lives here. Oil from the *Exxon Valdez* can be collected just beneath the surface of beaches throughout the Sound. While certain fisheries have rebounded, herring stocks haven't recovered at all, the Dungeness crab population remains low and many pink-salmon runs have been eliminated. Loons, harlequin ducks, otters and seals still suffer the effects of the spill. Moreover, $5 billion in fines awarded in a class-action lawsuit has yet to be paid out.

Thankfully, other legacies of the disaster are more inspiring. Long-recommended security measures have finally been enacted at oil-processing facilities across the nation. Double-hulled tankers, once a pipe dream of environmentalists, will be a pipeline requirement by 2015; some are already in service. Tugs must once again escort tankers passing through Prince William Sound. And the *Exxon Valdez* itself, now renamed the *SeaRiver Mediterranean*, has been banned from ever returning to Valdez.

but since September 11, 2001, stricter security protocols have closed it to the public. From the end of Dayville Rd you can still get a peek at the facility, including the storage tanks holding nine million barrels of oil apiece. But heed the dire warnings: plenty of septuagenarian RVers have been pulled over and interrogated for getting too close. Those truly interested in the terminal can learn more about it at **Prince William Sound Community College** (☎ 834-1600; 303 Lowe St), which for $5 offers a pipeline exhibit and thrice-daily 'video tour,' featuring great photography and a narrative that amounts to little more than Big Oil propaganda.

Activities

HIKING

Valdez has a number of scenic and historic trails to get you away from town and up into the surrounding slopes.

Dock Point Trail

Not so much a hike as an enjoyable stroll through Dock Point Park beside the small-boat harbor, this 1-mile loop offers views of the peaks and the port, proximity to eagle nests, as well as salmonberry and blueberry picking.

Mineral Creek Trail

A great walk away from town is the trek to the old Smith Stamping Mill. Built by WL Smith in 1913, the mill required only two men to operate it and used mercury to remove the gold from the ore.

To reach the trailhead, turn onto Mineral Creek Rd from Hanagita St. The marginal road bumps along for 5.5 miles and then turns into a mile-long trail to the old mill. Bears and mountain goats are often visible on this hike.

Shoup Bay Trail

This verdant stunner has views of Port Valdez, Shoup Glacier and the impressive Gold Creek delta. Turn around when you reach Gold Creek Bridge at Mile 3.5 to make this a somewhat challenging day, or go another seven steep, difficult and not always perfectly maintained miles along the water (and sometimes through it), bearing right to follow Shoup Bay to its tidewater glacier. A free campsite and two reservable **public-use cabins** (in Soldotna ☎ 907-262-5581; www.alaskastateparks.org; cabins $65), Kittiwake and Moraine, are at the end of the trail, near a noisy kittiwake rookery. **McAllister Creek Cabin** (cabins $65) is accessible by boat only. The trailhead is at a parking lot at the western terminus of Egan Dr.

Solomon Gulch Trail

A mile past the Solomon Gulch Fish Hatchery on Dayville Rd, this 1.7-mile trail is a steep, uphill hike that quickly leads to splendid views of Port Valdez and the city below. It ends at Solomon Lake, which is the source of 80% of Valdez' power.

Goat Trail

The oldest hike in the area is the Goat Trail, originally an Alaska Native trade route and later used by Captain Abercrombie in his search for safe passage to the Interior. Today, you can pick up the posted trailhead at Mile 13.5 of the Richardson Hwy, just past Horsetail Falls in Keystone Canyon. Best tackled in dry weather, the trail twists and turns for 2.5 miles as it follows the Lowe River, stopping at the original bridge over Bear Creek. The round-trip will take you half a day.

PADDLING

This is a kayaker's paradise, though folks sticking to the bay will be rewarded with views of seagulls fighting over cannery offal for the first hour or so. Independent kayakers should be aware of no-go zones around the pipeline terminal and moving tankers; contact the **US Coast Guard** (☎ 835-7222; 105 Clifton Dr) for current regulations.

Anadyr Adventures (☎ 835-2814, 800-865-2925; www.anadyradventures.com; 225 N Harbor Dr) rents kayaks to experienced paddlers (single/double $45/65, discounts for multiple days) and offers guided trips, ranging from a day at Columbia Glacier ($199) to a week on the water (from $2700).

Pangaea Adventures (☎ 835-8442, 800-660-9637; www.alaskasummer.com; 101 N Harbor Dr) has received great reader recommendations for its guided tours, costing from $55 for a three-hour trip on Duck Flats to $199 for a day trip to Columbia Glacier. It also does longer custom tours and rents kayaks (single/double $45/65).

Shoup Bay

Protected as a state marine park, this bay off Valdez Arm makes for a great overnight kayaking trip. The bay is home to a retreating glacier, which has two tidal basins and an underwater moraine that protects harbor seals and other sea life. It's about 10 miles to the bay and another 4 miles up

to the glacier. You must enter the bay two hours before the incoming tide to avoid swift tidal currents.

Columbia Glacier

A mile wide and rising 300ft from the waterline at its face, this is the largest tidewater glacier in Prince William Sound, and a spectacular spot to spend a few days kayaking and watching seals and other wildlife. In recent years the glacier has been in 'catastrophic retreat,' filling its fjord with so many calved bergs that it's difficult to get within miles of the face. Only experienced paddlers should attempt to paddle the open water from Valdez Arm to the glacier, a multiday trip. Others should arrange for a drop-off and pickup; Anadyr Adventures charges $300 for up to four people one way.

Lowe River

This glacial river, 12 miles from Valdez, cuts through impressive Keystone Canyon. The popular float features Class III rapids, sheer canyon walls and cascading waterfalls. The highlight is Bridal Veil Falls, which drops 900ft from the canyon walls.

Keystone Raft & Kayak Adventures (☎ 835-2606, 800-328-8460; www.alaskawhitewater.com; Mile 16.5 Richardson Hwy) provides 1½-hour trips ($40) along 6 miles of white water past the cascading waterfalls that have made the canyon famous. It also has half-day and day trips on the Class IV Tsaina and Tonsina Rivers.

Tours

Columbia Glacier is the second-largest tide-water glacier in North America, spilling forth from the Chugach Mountains and ending with a face as high as a football field. Several tour companies can take you into Columbia Bay, west of Port Valdez, but it's difficult for any boat to get close to the face as the water is too clogged with ice. You're more likely, therefore, to see calving further west in Unakwik Inlet, where the more accessible Mears Glacier, a smaller ice-tongue, dumps bergs from a snout just half the height of Columbia's.

Lu-Lu Belle Glacier Wildlife Cruises (☎ 835-5141, 800-411-0090; www.lulubelletours.com; Kobuk Dr) Takes the dainty and ornately appointed MV *Lu-Lu Belle* into Columbia Bay where, unless winds have cleared away the

---

EXTREME SKIING

To a certain set of unhinged individuals, Valdez is legendary not for its oil spill or its earthquake, but for being *the* place to strap on skis, slip from a helicopter and plunge into the snowy abyss. This is the Holy Land of extreme skiing.

Thanks to geography and climate, nowhere else do such steep slopes get so much sticky snow. At inland ski resorts in, say, Colorado, dry powder barely clings to 50-degree inclines; here in the coastal Chugaches, the sopping-wet flakes glue to angles of 60-plus-degrees, creating ski slopes where elsewhere there'd be cliffs. Factor in 1000in of snow per winter and mountains that descend 7000ft from peak to sea, and you've got a ski bum's version of Eden.

Since extreme skiing exploded here a decade ago, numerous companies have cropped up to capitalize. **Valdez Heli-Ski Guides** (☎ 835-4528; www.valdezheliskiguides.com) offers a day of heli-skiing (usually six runs) for $750; **H20 Heli-Guides** (☎ 835-8418; www.h2oguides.com; 100 N Harbor Dr) has three-day heli-skiing packages – including lodging – for $3124. Alas, the ski season lasts only from February to the end of April; after that, extremists will have to settle for H20's mellower summer offerings – for instance, spending a day with crampons and ice-axes, scaling a sheer blue-ice cliff on Worthington Glacier ($200).

---

ice, wildlife is more the attraction than glacier-calving. The tour departs at 2pm daily, costing $88.50.

Stan Stephens Glacier & Wildlife Cruises (☎ 835-4731, 866-867-1297; www.stanstephenscruises.com; 112 N Harbor Dr) The biggest tour operator in town, runs large vessels on seven-hour journeys to Columbia Glacier ($85) and nine-hour trips ($130) to both Columbia and Mears Glaciers. Lunch and lots of tummy-warming tea are included.

Festivals & Events

Fourth of July Valdez hosts a celebration.

Gold Rush Days A five-day festival in mid-August that includes a parade, bed races, dances, a free fish feed and a portable jailhouse that's pulled throughout town by locals, who arrest people without beards and other innocent bystanders.

Sleeping

Valdez no longer has a hostel; devout budgeteers will have to settle for a campsite. The town does have plenty of B&Bs and most belong to the **Valdez Bed & Breakfast Association** (www.valdezbnb.com). The visitors center has a 24-hour hotline outside, where you can book last-minute rooms. Valdez' 6% bed tax is above and beyond the rates quoted below.

BUDGET

Valdez Glacier Campground (☎ 835-2282; Airport Rd; sites $10) Located 6 miles out of town, this spot has 101 pleasant wooded sites and a nice waterfall. Though it's privately owned, it has a noncommercial feel.

Bear Paw RV Campground (☎ 835-2530; 101 N Harbor Dr; campsites/RV sites $17/30) Conveniently located right downtown, this campground has showers and a laundry – and a great little wooded glade just for tents!

Eagle's Rest RV Park (☎ 835-2373, 800-553-7275; www.eaglesrestrv.com; 631 E Pioneer Dr; campsites $20, RV sites $20-30, cabins $125) Also has showers and laundry, but the tent sites aren't quite as nice.

MIDRANGE

L&L's B&B (☎ 835-4447; www.alaskan.com/lnlbnb; 533 W Hanagita St; r with/without bath $75/65) Located in a bright, airy suburban home, this B&B has two bicycles at your disposal.

Headhunters Inn (☎ 835-2900; 328 Egan Dr; r $85) This B&B, upstairs from Ernesto's Taqueria, has cozy rooms with private baths.

Downtown B&B Inn (☎ 835-2791, 800-478-2791; www.alaskan.com/downtowninn; 113 Galena Dr; r with/without bath $100/85) More hotel than B&B, though you do get breakfast with your clean, basic room.

Pipeline Inn (☎ 835-4332; 112 Egan Dr; r $100) Here you'll find worn and aesthetically out-of-date rooms, but some hold four or five people, making this a good big-group option.

Keystone Hotel (☎ 835-3851, 888-835-0665; www.keystonehotel.com; 401 W Egan Dr; s/d summer $85/95) This modular relic of the pipeline boom years has lots of clean, cramped, prefab rooms.

TOP END

Lakehouse B&B (☎ 835-4752; Mile 6 Richardson Hwy; r $110-120) This snazzily decorated place has six rooms, all spacious and each with its own deck overlooking the absurdly pretty

Robe Lake. If you've got your own wheels, this is a good option.

Best Western Valdez Harbor Inn (☎ 835-4391, 888-222-3440; www.valdezharborinn.com; 100 N Harbor Dr; s/d $129/139) If you can swing it, the corner suite overlooking the ocean has the best view of any bedroom in town.

Totem Inn (☎ 835-4443; www.toteminn.com; 144 E Egan Dr; r $129) This clean, well-appointed motel has fridges and microwaves in each room.

Eating

RESTAURANTS

Pipeline Club (☎ 835-4332; 112 Egan Dr; dinner $17-30; ☽ 5:30-10pm Sun-Thu, to 11pm Fri & Sat) Lowlit with lots of leather, Valdez' classiest joint specializes in steak and seafood. Photos of Old Valdez adorn the walls.

Totem Inn Restaurant (☎ 835-4443; 144 E Egan Dr; breakfasts $6-10, lunches $8-10; ☽ 5am-10pm) In the morning, tourists and locals flock here for the excellent breakfasts and Alaska-sized mugs of coffee. Lunch is all about burgers and sandwiches, while dinner has decent seafood.

Fu Kung (☎ 835-5255; 207 Kobuk Dr; lunch $7-10; dinner $12-17; ☽ 11am-11pm Mon-Sat, from 4pm Sun) In a building that wonderfully fuses Asian and Alaskan themes, this restaurant has fantastic Chinese food. Lunch specials include egg rolls and quality wonton soup.

CAFÉS, QUICK EATS & GROCERIES

Alaska Halibut House (☎ 835-2788; 208 Meals Ave; fish $4-10; ☽ 6am-10pm) Frying up fresh local fish, this place is what every fast-food joint should be. The halibut basket is delish.

Bad Ass Coffee (☎ 835-2560; 201 N Harbor Dr; coffee $3-5; ☽ 6am-10pm Sun-Thu, to 11pm Fri & Sat) This coffee shop, in a cheery harbor-view location, pours good-ass coffee and serves fish tacos and deli sandwiches.

Mike's Palace (☎ 835-2365; 201 N Harbor Dr; mains $5-15; ☽ 11am-11pm) This dingy little waterfront diner has a menu that spans the continents, with everything from Rueben on rye to chicken cacciatore.

Ernesto's Taqueria (☎ 835-2519; 328 Egan Dr; meals $7-8; ☽ 5:30am-10pm) Locally loved, this place serves large portions of serviceable Mexican food on the cheap.

Eagle Quality Center (☎ 835-2100; 185 Meals Ave; ☽ 4:30am-midnight) With its impressive sandwich and salad bar, this grocery store is among Valdez' best places for a bite.

Drinking & Entertainment

Pipeline Club (☎ 835-2788; 112 Egan Dr) Valdez' favorite drinkery, this swanky lounge has occasional live music, plus karaoke, darts, pool and virtual golf. It's the watering hole where Captain Hazelwood had his famous scotch-on-the-rocks before running the *Exxon Valdez* aground. If only he'd played virtual golf instead…

Valdez Club Bar (201 N Harbor Dr) Fisherfolk swap stories of the sea at this smoky waterfront saloon.

Egan Street Pub (210 Egan Dr) This pub, at Glacier Sound Inn, keeps at least three microbrews on tap at all times.

Getting There & Around

AIR

There are flight services with **ERA Aviation** (☎ 835-2636, 800-843-1947; www.eraaviation.com) three times daily between Anchorage and Valdez; one-way tickets cost from $141 to $174, depending on how early you make reservations. The **Valdez Airport** (Airport Rd) is 3 miles from town, off the Richardson Hwy.

BICYCLE

Bikes can be rented through **Anadyr Adventures** (☎ 835-2814, 800-865-2925; www.anadyradventures.com; 225 N Harbor Dr; per half-/full day $20/30).

BOAT

Within Prince William Sound, the **Alaska Marine Highway** (☎ 835-4436, 800-642-0066; www.ferryalaska.com) provides daily services from Valdez to Cordova ($47, five hours) and thrice-weekly direct service to Whittier ($85, six hours). In 2005, plans for a fast ferry that would have halved those travel times were suspended, though they may eventually become reality.

Twice per month, the MV *Kennicott* departs Valdez, crosses the Gulf of Alaska and docks in Juneau ($130, 32 hours). The ferry terminal is at the southern end of Hazelet Ave.

CORDOVA
☎ 907 / pop 2298
Cut off from Alaska's road system (for now), Cordova is slightly inconvenient and somewhat expensive to get to. Perhaps that's why this picturesque outpost, spread thinly between Orca Inlet and Eyak Lake, and overshadowed by Mt Eccles, can still claim to be

one of the Alaskan coast's truly endangered species: a fishing village that hasn't sold its soul to tourism. That's all the more reason to visit.

Though not set in the same sort of mountain-thronged kingdom as Valdez, Cordova is more appealing: a quaint cluster of rainforest-rotted homes climbing up a pretty hillside overlooking the busy harbor. Populating the place are folks who, you can't help thinking, exemplify what's best about Alaska: ruggedly independent freethinkers, clad in rubber boots and driving rusted-out Subarus, unconcerned with image and pretense, and friendly as hell. They seem to revel in their isolation. In recent years, prodevelopment politicians have proposed connecting the community to the state highway system. Judging from the ubiquity of 'No Road' bumper stickers in town, it's a prospect locals abhor.

Visitors will also be enthralled by what lies beyond the town limits. Just outside the city along the Copper River Hwy is one of the largest wetlands in Alaska, with more than 40 miles of trails threading through spectacular glaciers, alpine meadows and the remarkable Copper River Delta. Into that delta run some of the world's finest salmon, and fishermen here turn them into what may be the fattest and finest fillets you'll ever enjoy.

Orientation

Cordova's main north–south drag is officially 1st St, but is often called Main St – the names are used interchangeably. Railroad Ave becomes the Copper River Hwy as it leaves town, connecting Cordova to the airport at Mile 12, continuing another 40 miles to Childs Glacier and Million Dollar Bridge. The village itself is easy to explore on foot, but seeing the Copper River Delta will require arranging transportation for all but the hardiest explorers.

Information

Bidarki Recreation Center (☎ 424-7282; cnr 2nd St & Council Ave; ☻ 9am-9:30pm Mon-Sat) For $5 you get a shower plus all-day use of the sauna and the fitness room.
Chamber of Commerce (☎ 424-7260; www.cordovachamber.com, www.cordovaalaska.com; 404 1st St; ☻ 10am-4pm Mon-Fri) If you find it open, you can get visitor info here.
Cordova Community Medical Center (☎ 424-8000; 602 Chase Rd) Provides emergency services.

Cordova Library (☎ 424-6667; 622 1st St; ☻ 10am-8pm Tue-Fri, 1-5pm Sat; 💻) In the same building as the Cordova Museum. Has the best lowdown on town: lots of pamphlets, plus B&B listings and free city maps. Internet access is free and very popular with the cannery crew; put your name on the list and *then* check out the museum.
Emergency (ambulance, fire, police ☎ 911)
First National Bank (☎ 424-3258; 515 Main St) Has fresh cash; so does the Wells Fargo branch across the street.
Harbormaster's office (☎ 424-6400; Nicholoff Way) Has $4 showers.
Orca Book & Sound (☎ 424-5305; 507 1st St; per 15 min $2.50; ☻ 7:30am-5pm Mon-Sat; 💻) If you can't wait for an Internet terminal at the library, head here. It's also your best source for locally oriented literature.
Post office (cnr Railroad & Council Aves) Near the small-boat harbor.
USFS Visitor Center (☎ 424-7661; 612 2nd St; ☻ 8am-5pm Mon-Fri) Has the latest on trails, campsites and wildlife in the Copper River basin.

Sights
CORDOVA MUSEUM
Adjacent to the Cordova Library, this **museum** (622 1st St; donation encouraged; ☻ 10am-6pm Mon-Sat, 2-4pm Sun) is a small, grassroots collection worth seeing. Displays cover local marine life, relics from the town's early history and from the nearby Kennecott mine, Russian artifacts and a three-seater *bidarka* (kayak) made from spruce pine and 12 sealskins.

Want your heart wrenched? Peruse the museum's coverage of the *Exxon Valdez* oil spill. The amateur photos and badly written local-newspaper articles revive the horror more vividly than any slick documentary. Then there's the jar of oily beach sand collected in nearby Sleepy Bay a decade after the spill.

ILANKA CULTURAL CENTER
This excellent **museum** (☎ 424-7903; 110 Nicholoff Way; admission free; ☻ 10am-4pm Mon-Fri), operated by local Eyaks, has a small but high-quality collection of Alaska Native art from all over the state. Especially cool are the swans'-feet pouches, sewn with bear hair and used for toting tobacco. Upstairs, don't miss the intact killer-whale skeleton – one of only five in the world – with flippers that could give you quite a slap. This place also has a wonderful gift shop and offers classes on such crafty subjects as scrimshaw and spruce-root weaving. Call for a schedule.

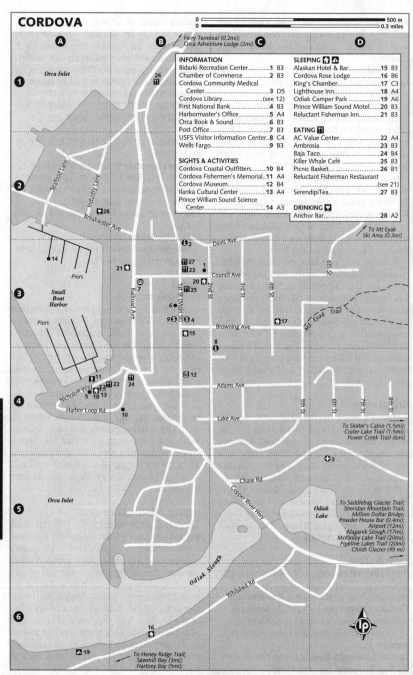

CORDOVA

0 ———— 500 m
0 ———— 0.3 miles

INFORMATION
Bidarki Recreation Center............**1** B3
Chamber of Commerce............**2** B3
Cordova Community Medical
  Center.................................**3** D5
Cordova Library.....................(see 12)
First National Bank.....................**4** B3
Harbormaster's Office...................**5** A4
Orca Book & Sound....................**6** B3
Post Office..............................**7** B3
USFS Visitor Information Center..**8** C4
Wells Fargo..............................**9** B3

SIGHTS & ACTIVITIES
Cordova Coastal Outfitters........**10** B4
Cordova Fishermen's Memorial..**11** A4
Cordova Museum......................**12** B4
Ilanka Cultural Center **13** A4
Prince William Sound Science
  Center...................................**14** A3

SLEEPING
Alaskan Hotel & Bar...................**15** B3
Cordova Rose Lodge.................**16** B6
King's Chamber.........................**17** C3
Lighthouse Inn..........................**18** A4
Odiak Camper Park **19** A6
Prince William Sound Motel......**20** B3
Reluctant Fisherman Inn............**21** B3

EATING
AC Value Center.......................**22** A4
Ambrosia..................................**23** B3
Baja Taco.................................**24** B4
Killer Whale Café **25** B3
Picnic Basket............................**26** B1
Reluctant Fisherman Restaurant
  ....(see 21)
SerendipiTea............................**27** B3

DRINKING
Anchor Bar..............................**28** A2

Orca Inlet

Ferry Terminal (0.2mi);
Orca Adventure Lodge (2mi)

To Mt Eyak
Ski Area (0.3mi)

Seafood Lane

Industry Lane

Breakwater Ave

Davis Ave

Council Ave

Browning Ave

Adams Ave

Lake Ave

Railroad Ave

1st St/Main St

2nd St

3rd St

4th St

5th St

6th St

7th St

8th St

Mt Eyak Trail

Small
Boat
Harbor

Piers

Piers

Nicholoff Way

Harbor Loop Rd

Chase Rd

Copper River Hwy

Odiak
Lake

Orca Inlet

To Skater's Cabin (1.5mi);
Crater Lake Trail (1.5mi);
Power Creek Trail (6mi)

To Saddlebag Glacier Trail;
Sheridan Mountain Trail;
Million Dollar Bridge;
Powder House Bar (0.4mi);
Airport (12mi);
Alaganik Slough (17mi);
McKinley Lake Trail (20mi);
Pipeline Lakes Trail (20mi);
Childs Glacier (49 mi)

Odiak Slough

Whitshed Rd

To Heney Ridge Trail;
Sawmill Bay (3mi);
Hartney Bay (5mi);

PRINCE WILLIAM SOUND

PRINCE WILLIAM SOUND SCIENCE CENTER
This dockside **research facility** (☎ 424-5800; www
.pwssc.gen.ak.us; 300 Breakwater Ave; admission free;
☒ 8:30am-5:30pm Mon-Fri) has a few interpretive
panels outside that, among other things,
will assist you in untangling the fisherfolk's
strange lingo, which is laced with words like
'openers,' 'IFQs' and 'sternpickers.' Inside
there's not much for visitors save for an
impressively enormous gray-whale skull
suspended from the ceiling.

SMALL-BOAT HARBOR
In Cordova, the standard greeting among
locals is 'Been fishing?' Unsurprisingly, the
harbor is the community's heart, humming
throughout the season as fishers frantically
try to meet their quota before the runs are
closed. The fishing fleet is composed primarily of seiners and gillnetters, with the
method used by the fishers determining the
species of salmon they pursue. The former
primarily target pink salmon, while the latter, generally one-person operations, go
for kings and reds early in the season and
silvers later on.

Watching over the hubbub is the **Cordova
Fisherman's Memorial**, a quiet place dominated by artist Joan Bugbee Jackson's sculpture *The Southeasterly* (1985).

SALMON CANNERIES
Every summer, Cordova's population swells
with youths hoping to make a mint canning
salmon on 30-hour shifts. Whether you're
curious about the effects of sleep depriva-
tion on adventurous teenagers or just want
to see how some of the finest salmon in the
world is processed, ask at the chamber of
commerce about canneries offering tours.
You can watch your *own* catch get processed at **Prime Select Seafoods** (☎ 424-7750,
888-870-7292; www.pssifish.com; 210 Seafood Lane), a
smaller-scale operation that packs salmon
and ships it to your home.

Activities
HIKING
More than 35 miles of trails are accessible
from Cordova roads. Several of these paths
lead to USFS cabins (p222). As in much
of the Southeast, the hiking in this area is
excellent, combining lush forest with alpine
terrain, great views and glaciers. See p223
for transportation options.

Heney Ridge Trail
Cordova's most popular trail – as it's accessible without a car – is this scenic, fairly
easy 3.7-mile route beginning at Mile 5.1
of Whitshed Rd. The first stretch winds
around Hartney Bay, followed by a mellow
2-mile climb through forests and wildflowers (and, in rainy weather, lots of mud –
rubber boots are recommended) to the tree
line. It's another steep mile up to the ridge,
where you'll enjoy a gorgeous view.

Crater Lake & Power Creek Trails
The 2.4-mile Crater Lake Trail begins on
Eyak Lake, about half a mile beyond the
municipal airport, across from Skater's
Cabin. The trail ascends steeply but is easy
to follow as it winds through lush forest. At
the top it offers panoramic views of both
the Copper River Delta and Prince William
Sound. Plan on two to four hours for the
round-trip.

Once at the lake you can continue with a
4.5-mile ridge route to Alice Smith Cutoff,
which descends to the Power Creek Trail.
The entire 12-mile loop makes for an ideal
overnight backpacking trip. Halfway along
the ridge is a free-use shelter, while at Mile
4.2 of the Power Creek Trail is the USFS
Power Creek Cabin (☎ 877-444-6777, 518-885-3639;
www.reserveusa.com; cabins $25). Arrange to be
dropped off at the Power Creek trailhead
and hike all the way back into town via the
Mt Eyak Trail.

McKinley Lake & Pipeline Lakes Trails
The 2.5-mile McKinley Lake Trail begins at
Mile 21.6 of the Copper River Hwy and leads
to the head of the lake and the remains of
the Lucky Strike gold mine. There are two
USFS cabins (☎ 877-444-6777, 518-885-3639; www
.reserveusa.com; cabins $35), McKinley Lake Cabin,
just past the trailhead, and McKinley Trail
Cabin, at Mile 2.4. The abandoned Lucky
Strike mine is accessible via an unmain-
tained trail behind McKinley Trail Cabin.

Departing from the midway point of the
McKinley Lake Trail is the Pipeline Lakes
Trail, which loops back to the Copper River
Hwy at Mile 21.4. Almost all of this marshy
2-mile trail has been boardwalked to provide easier access to several small lakes
packed with grayling and cutthroat trout,
but if it's rainy consider bringing rubber
boots.

PRINCE WILLIAM SOUND

Sheridan Mountain Trail

This trail starts near the picnic tables at the end of Sheridan Glacier Rd, which runs 4.3 miles from the turnoff at Mile 13 of Copper River Hwy. Most of the 2.9-mile route is a moderate climb, which passes through mature forests before breaking out into an alpine basin. From there, the view of mountains and the Sheridan and Sherman Glaciers is stunning, and it only gets better when you start climbing the surrounding rim. This trail isn't the best maintained, putting it into the 'difficult' category.

Saddlebag Glacier Trail

You reach this trail via a firewood-cutting road at Mile 25 of Copper River Hwy. It's an easy 3-mile walk through cottonwoods and spruce, emerging at Saddlebag Lake. Outstanding views of surrounding peaks and cliffs (and maybe mountain goats) are made even more fabulous by the namesake glacier, which litters the lake with icebergs.

BIKING

Most of Cordova's trails are too muddy and steep to ride; an exception is the **Saddlebag Glacier Trail**. However, if you have a few days, the Copper River Hwy itself is a remarkable mountain-bike route. Plan on at least three days if you ride out to the end of the road and back, or two days if you are dropped off at the end of the road and then ride the 48 miles back to town. For bicycle rentals and shuttles, see p223.

SKIING

The small but much-loved **Mt Eyak ski area** (☎ 424-7766; 6th St; ⏲ mid-Nov–mid-May), just a quick walk from town, features an 800ft drop, 118in of natural snow annually, and runs that accommodate everyone from novice snowboarders to world-class skiers. The most famous attraction is the vintage ski lift from Sun Valley, Idaho.

BIRDING

The Copper River Delta and the rich waters of Prince William Sound attract an astonishing number and variety of birds. Spring migration is the busiest, and that is when the town hosts the Copper River Delta Shorebird Festival (p222). Stop at the **USFS Visitor Center** (☎ 424-7661; 612 2nd St; ⏲ 8am-5pm Mon-Fri) for a birding checklist and advice about where to break out the binoculars.

A favorite birding area is **Hartney Bay**, six miles southwest of town along Whitshed Rd, where as many as 70,000 shorebirds congregate during spring migration. Bring rubber boots and plan to be there two hours before or after high tide for the best fall and spring viewing conditions. **Sawmill Bay**, at Mile 3 of Whitshed Rd, is also a prime bird-watching spot.

Another good place for bird and wildlife watching is **Alaganik Slough**. Turn south on Alaganik Slough Rd at Mile 17 of Copper River Hwy and travel 3 miles to the end, where a picnic area and boardwalk offer great views of dusky Canada geese, bald eagles and other feathered friends.

Also check out **Odiak Lake**, just southeast of town, and **Eyak Lake** on the Power Creek Trail.

PADDLING

The Copper River flows for 287 miles, beginning at Copper Glacier near Slana in the Interior and ending in the Gulf of Alaska, east of Cordova. Most of the river is for experienced rafters, as rapids, glaciers and narrow canyons give it a white-water rating of Class II–III much of the way. The 20-mile stretch between Million Dollar Bridge and Flag Point, at Mile 27 of the Copper River Hwy, is considerably wider and slower. Below Flag Point, the river becomes heavily braided, which inevitably means dragging your boat through shallow channels.

Alaska River Rafters (☎ 424-7238, 800-776-1864; www.alaskarafters.com; Mile 13 Copper River Hwy) operates rafting and kayaking trips at Sheridan Glacier, on the Copper River and elsewhere in the area; guided half-day trips start from $85 per person, ranging up to $4495 for multiday packages that include everything from hiking to flightseeing.

If the ocean is more your speed, **Cordova Coastal Outfitters** (☎ 424-7424, 800-357-5145; www.cdvcoastal.com; Harbor Loop Rd; kayaks per day single/double $35/50), in a cabin behind the AC Value Center, rents kayaks) and arranges guided tours in placid, pristine Orca Inlet north of town.

Tours

The Copper River Delta, right in Cordova's backyard, is a can't-miss experience. Guided

DETOUR: COPPER RIVER HWY

As if Cordova wasn't cool enough, there's something equally cool just out its back door: the Copper River Hwy. This 50-mile, mostly gravel road is the gateway to the Copper River Delta, a wildlife-rich wilderness with amazing opportunities for hiking, fishing and birding. Just as amazing are the twin wonders at the road's end: the improbable Million Dollar Bridge and the breathtaking Childs Glacier.

Constructed on the old railroad bed to the Kennecott mines, the highway was once destined to connect Cordova with Interior Alaska. Construction was interrupted after the 1964 Good Friday Earthquake knocked out the fourth span of the Million Dollar Bridge. Today, the road is gravel past Mile 13, difficult to hitchhike, pricey to arrange transportation, but worth every hassle. Before departing, visit the USFS Visitor Center in Cordova, which has maps and info on roadside attractions.

Copper River Delta

The Copper River Hwy begins as 1st St downtown. Barely 5 miles on, the mountains recede and you emerge, almost miraculously, into the 700,000-acre Copper River Delta, a 60-mile arc formed by six glacier-fed river systems.

Millions of birds and waterfowl stop here during the spring and fall, including seven million western sandpipers and the entire population of West Coast dunlins. Other species include Arctic terns, dusty Canada geese, trumpeter swans, great blue herons and bald eagles. There's also a chance you'll spot moose, brown bears, beavers and porcupines.

The delta has numerous hiking trails, some rafting opportunities as well as angling. There is sockeye-salmon fishing which begins in mid-June and peaks around July 4. Coho-salmon runs occur from August to September, and cutthroat trout and Dolly Varden can be caught throughout the summer and fall.

Childs Glacier

A common malaise affecting tourists in Alaska could be called 'glacier fatigue.' But no matter how jaded you've become, Childs will blow your mind.

For a warm-up, visit **Sheridan Glacier** at Mile 15 of the highway. Sheridan Glacier Access Rd leads to picnic tables with partial views of the ice floe and a 1-mile trail across the glacial moraine.

At the end of the Copper River Hwy, the 0.6-mile Copper River Trail takes you along the river to the observation deck for Childs Glacier. It's probable, however, that you'll hear the glacier before you see it. A rarity in Alaska, Childs is advancing some 500ft a year, perpetually dumping bergs into Copper River. The thunderous calvings are particularly frequent in late spring and summer, when the water's high. But heed the warnings: the glacier is a mere 1200ft away, and potentially deadly waves can reverberate quickly across the river when particularly big bergs break off the glacier.

Nearby, **Childs Glacier Recreation Area** (sites $5) has five wooded campsites that are a great place to awaken in the morning – if the calving doesn't keep you up.

Million Dollar Bridge

Just beyond the recreation area is this four-span trestle, created during the winter of 1909–10 but it was put out of commission by the 1964 earthquake. In 2004, fearing the damaged fourth span would fall into the river, the state spent $18 million to return the bridge to a passable condition.

You can now drive, bike or walk on to the bridge to take in the view. Downstream, close enough to hear it grumble, is Childs Glacier. Upstream, meanwhile, is the Miles Glacier – the source of those icebergs racing beneath you. In 1910, Miles' rapid advance threatened the newly constructed bridge, forcing workers to chisel at its face day and night. It stopped just feet from the struts. Now, it's four miles distant.

daylong driving tours of the delta are conducted by **Alaska River Rafters** (☎ 424-7238, 800-776-1864; www.alaskarafters.com; Mile 13, Copper River Hwy). The trips run to Million Dollar Bridge and Childs Glacier, and cost $85 per person with a six-person minimum. You can add a flightseeing excursion for another $100.

Festivals & Events

Iceworm Festival (☎ 424-3861; www.iceworm.org) Cordova's famous homegrown and tongue-in-cheek event is held on the second weekend of February. This draws mainly locals and their friends and families, who honor the miniscule glacier-dweller *Mesenchytraeus solifugus* by parading a 150ft-long puppet of him through the streets. There are also feasts, variety shows, tightly bundled-up beauty queens, and contests like the survival-suit races, in which competitors don buoyant, insulated jumpsuits and plunge into the frigid sea, racing to be the first to reach a buoy and return to shore.

Copper River Delta Shorebird Festival (☎ 424-7260) On the first weekend of May, this celebrates the largest migration in the USA, as some five million shorebirds throng the delta – the biggest continuous wetland on the Pacific coast – en route to their Arctic breeding grounds. The festival draws birders from the world over, and features presentations and workshops by international experts and field trips to the prime viewing areas. Nonbirders, don't scoff: this event fills every hotel room in town.

Sleeping

Cordova tacks on 12% in bed-and-sales tax to the rates listed below.

BUDGET

Skater's Cabin (☎ 424-7282; cabin 1st/2nd/3rd night $25/35/50) On Eyak Lake with a nice gravel beach and a woodstove, this place can be booked through the Bidarki Recreation Center. The escalating prices are to deter multiday use so more people can enjoy it.

Odiak Camper Park (☎ 424-7282; Whitshed Rd; campsites/RV sites $5/20) A half-mile from town, this is basically a gravel parking lot with a rest room and a view. Make reservations at the Bidarki Recreation Center.

Alaskan Hotel & Bar (☎ 424-3299; 1st St; r with/without bath $60/40) This downtown dive is tattered and reverberates with bar noise, but should be tolerable for the seasoned budget traveler.

Wilderness Cabins

There are 10 **USFS cabins** (☎ 877-444-6777, 518-885-3639; www.reserveusa.com; cabins $25-45) located in

the Cordova area, and they're much easier to reserve than those in other Southcentral Alaskan parts. Four are best accessible by boat or plane: Pete Dahl and Tideman Slough each bunk six in the wilderness of the Copper River flats; Softuk Bar sleeps six on a remote beach 40 miles southeast of Cordova; and popular Martin Lake, 30 minutes east of town by floatplane, has a boat that sleeps six people. Two others are along the McKinley Lake Trail (p219 and a third is on the Power Creek Trail (p219). Hinchinbrook Island, 20 minutes from Cordova by plane and at most two hours by boat, has three more cabins: Shelter Bay, Double Bay and Hook Point.

MIDRANGE & TOP END

Cordova Rose Lodge (☎ 424-7673; www.cordovarose.com; 1315 Whitshed Rd; r $85-125) This spot has rooms in a higgledy-piggledy assortment of structures, including a barge docked – sort of – on Odiak Slough. The more expensive rooms include a full breakfast.

Reluctant Fisherman Inn (☎ 424-3272, 800-770-3272; cnr Railroad & Council Aves; r $100-130) As close to luxurious as Cordova gets, this place overhangs Orca Inlet and has a restaurant and lounge.

Lighthouse Inn (☎ 424-7080; www.cordovalighthouseinn.com; 203 Nicholoff Way; r $115) This inn has brilliant views of the small-boat harbor from its small, plush rooms, all with baths.

Orca Adventure Lodge (☎ 424-7249, 866-424-6722; www.orcaadventurelodge.com; Railroad Ave; d full board with meals from $155) Housed in the historic Orca Cannery 2 miles north of downtown, this lodge caters to upscale adventurers with daily adventure-tour packages.

King's Chamber (☎ 424-3373; www.thekingschamber.com; cnr 4th St & Browning Ave; r from $85) At the top of downtown, King's Chamber has everything from an efficiency unit to a four-bedroom apartment.

Prince William Motel (☎ 424-3201, 888-796-6835; 501 2nd St; s/d $90/100) Though nothing fancy, it has huge, clean rooms, and for $20 extra you get a full kitchen.

Eating

RESTAURANTS

Ambrosia (☎ 424-7175; 413 1st St; dinner $10-17; ☼ 4-10pm) On the hillside downtown, Ambrosia serves Italian standards like veal parmigiana and chicken marsala, and has a not-too-shabby wine list.

Reluctant Fisherman Restaurant (☎ 424-3272, 800-770-3272; cnr Railroad & Council Aves; 6am-2pm Mon-Sat, from 9am Sun) At lunchtime this place fills with locals digging into hearty all-American fare and taking in the best harbor views in town.

CAFÉS

Killer Whale Café (☎ 424-7733; 1st St; breakfast $5-10, sandwiches & burgers $8-10; 7am-7pm Mon-Thu, to 8pm Fri & Sat) This café serves excellent breakfasts and fresh (sometimes organic) soups, salads and sandwiches. This is where the town's lefties hang out, plotting environmental strategy.

Picnic Basket (☎ 424-4337; Railroad Ave; meals $3-9; 8am-8pm) This spot does cheap, down-home cooking beloved by the cannery crowd – try the pork-chop sandwich or salmonberry pie.

Lighthouse Inn (☎ 424-7080; 203 Nicholoff Way; breakfast buffet $10; 6:30am-7pm Tue-Thu, to 8pm Fri-Sun) Overlooking the small-boat harbor, this establishment does a breakfast buffet and, later in the day, brick-oven pizzas. Who could pass up the Mt Eyak Supreme ($24)?

QUICK EATS & GROCERIES

Baja Taco (☎ 424-5599; Harbor Loop Rd; fast food $6-10; 8am-9pm Mon-Sat, from 10am Sun) Graft a bus onto a cabin, add flowers, cattle skulls and nautical implements, and what do you have? The best fish-taco stand north of San Diego. It also serves beer and espressos.

SerendipiTea (☎ 424-8327; 412 1st St; light meals $3-8; 10am-6pm) This spot has fresh-baked treats, soups and light lunches, and organic grocery items.

AC Value Center (☎ 424-7141; 106 Nicholoff Way; 7:30am-10pm Mon-Sat, 8am-9pm Sun) A supermarket with a deli, espresso bar, ATM and Western Union.

Drinking & Entertainment

There's not much of a formal entertainment scene in Cordova, but with scads of young cannery workers thronging the place in the summertime, there always seems to be a jam session going on *somewhere*.

Powder House Bar (Mile 2 Copper River Hwy; dinner $8-20; 10am-late Mon-Sat, from noon Sun) Overlooking Eyak Lake on the site of the original Copper River & Northwestern Railroad powder house, this is a fun place with live music; excellent beer, soup and sandwiches for lunch; and quality steak and seafood dinners. Friday is sushi night.

Alaskan Hotel & Bar (1st St) This raucous fishers' bar offers wine tastings from 5pm to 7pm Wednesday.

Anchor Bar (Breakwater Ave) Across from the small-boat harbor, this is your basic watering hole that's open 'as long as there are fish.'

Getting There & Around

Compact Cordova can be easily explored on foot, but the major problem for travelers exploring the outlying Copper River area is finding transportation. Hitchhiking along the Copper River Hwy is possible, though you might not encounter many passing motorists, even in the summer months.

AIR

ERA Aviation (☎ 800-866-8394) flies twice daily between Anchorage and Cordova's Merle K 'Mudhole' Smith Airport; an advance-purchase ticket is $145/290 one way/round-trip. **Alaska Airlines** (☎ 800-252-7522; www.alaskaair.com) comes here on a milk run from Anchorage to Yakutat and Juneau once per day. To Juneau, an advance-purchase ticket is $158/316 one way/round-trip.

BOAT

The **Alaska Marine Highway** (☎ 424-7333, 800-642-0066; www.ferryalaska.com) runs ferries daily to Valdez ($47, five hours). It goes to Whittier ($85, six hours) six times per week – three direct sailings and three via Valdez. The ferry terminal is on Railroad Ave, a half-mile north of town.

In 2005, the state's Republican administration put on hold plans for a Cordova-based fast ferry that would have halved travel times to Valdez and Whittier. Locals, who'd been eager to cash in on the day-traffic, were miffed, some believing it was a ploy to pressure Cordova into accepting a road link to the Interior.

BICYCLE

Cordova Coastal Outfitters (☎ 424-7424, 800-357-5145; www.cdvcoastal.com; Harbor Loop Rd) rents mountain bikes for $15 a day, including helmet, water bottles and a rack for gear. The company also provides drop-offs at the end of Copper River Hwy for $150 per trip for up to six people with gear.

CAR

Try **Cordova Auto Rental** (☎ 424-5982; www.ptiala ska.net/~cars) across from the airport. It hires out cars for $77 per day with unlimited mileage.

WHITTIER

☎ 907 / pop 172

You can see glaciers and brown bears, even mountains taller than Denali, without once visiting Alaska. But you will never, in a lifetime of searching, find another place like Whittier.

Shortly after the Japanese attack on the Aleutian Islands during WWII, the US began looking for a spot to build a secret military installation. The proposed base needed not to be only to be an ice-free port, but to be as inaccessible as possible, lost in visibility-reducing cloud cover and surrounded by impassable mountains. They found it all right here.

And so, in this place that would be considered uninhabitable by almost any standard, surrounded by 3500ft peaks and hung with sloppy gray clouds most of the year, Whittier was built. A supply tunnel was blasted out of solid granite, one of Alaska's true engineering marvels, and more than 1000 people were housed in a single tower, the Buckner Building. It wasn't picturesque, but it was efficient.

The army maintained Whittier until 1968, leaving behind not only the Buckner Building, now abandoned, but also the 14-story-tall Begich Towers, where, it seems, some 80% of Whittiots now reside. A labyrinth of underground tunnels connects the complex with schools and businesses, which certainly cuts down on snow-shoveling time. The structure has also given rise to a unique society, where 150-odd people, though virtually isolated from the outside world, live only a few cinder blocks away from one another. It's obviously a must-see attraction for cultural anthropologists.

The rest of us, however, come to Whittier for many of the reasons the military did. The impossibly remote location provides access to an almost unspoiled wilderness of water, ice and granite. Kayaking and scuba diving are superb, and the docks are packed with cruise ships and water-taxis waiting to take you out into the wildlife-rich waters. The town itself is rarely described as adorable, but then it's never really had the luxury of such pretensions.

But all this is changing. Until recently Whittier was accessible only by train or boat; though only 11 miles from the most traveled highway in Alaska, the hamlet was effectively isolated from the rest of the Kenai Peninsula. In 2000, however, the Anton Anderson Memorial Tunnel was overhauled for auto traffic (see The Road to Whittier, p228), opening one of the most abnormal places imaginable to increased tourism and slow normalization.

Orientation

Tucked in a pocket of mountains hard against the Sound, Whittier is famously compact. Still, it can be disorienting, because it doesn't so much have a streetscape as a variety of routes through its massive parking lot and rail yard. On the waterfront you'll find the Triangle, a colorful collection of restaurants, tour operators and gift shops located between the small-boat harbor and the new ferry terminal. The Anton Anderson Memorial Tunnel is west of town, while Begich Towers looms to the east. Most of the hiking trails and berry patches are farther east, on Salmon Run Rd.

Information

At the time of research, an information gazebo was under construction in the middle of the Triangle. The post office is in Begich Towers, along with the police and fire stations, a medical clinic – even a church.

Anchor Inn (☎ 472-2354; 100 Whittier St; www.an chorinnwhittier.com; ☼ 9am-9pm) Has an ATM, a coin-op laundry and $3 showers.

Emergency (ambulance, fire, police ☎ 911)

Harbor Store (☎ 472-2348; Harbor View Rd; ☼ 8am-8pm) Has an ATM.

Sportsman Inn (☎ 472-2354; Blackstone Rd; ☼ 3-11pm Wed-Sun; ▢) Beneath the looming Buckner Building ruin; offers Internet access at a single terminal set right on the beer-soaked bar.

USFS Information Yurt (☎ 242-8539; Herbor View Rd; ☼ 9am-5pm Fri-Sun) Has the best info on the town and on hiking, camping, public-use cabins and kayaking in Chugach National Forest.

Sights

Whittier's dystopian townscape is perversely intriguing, and thus well worth a stroll. Start at **Begich Towers**, visible from anywhere in town, where the 1st, 14th and 15th floors are open to nonresidents. Watching children playing in the cinder-block corridors, you can't help contemplating how much of your private business would be common knowledge if you'd grown up here.

From the southwest corner of Begich Towers, you can look west to Whittier Creek, while above it, falling from the ridge of a glacial cirque, is picturesque **Horsetail Falls**. Locals use the cascade to gauge the weather: if the tail is whipping upwards, it's too windy to go out in the boat. There are also great views of dozens of other waterfalls streaking from the snowfields to the Sound.

Heading back toward the waterfront along Eastern Ave, you'll come to the rather extravagantly named **Prince William Sound Museum** (100 Whittier St; adult/child $3/1.50; ☺ variable), which occupies an ill-lit room beside the Anchor Inn Grocery Store. The space has lots of displays about Whittier's military history, but the most striking exhibit is on the man who engineered the town's tunnel, Anton Anderson. A Swedish-Australian immigrant, Anderson discovered he had

a knack for carving holes through mountains, and then found he had a knack for politics, eventually becoming the mayor of Anchorage.

Climbing Blackstone Rd from the museum, **Buckner Building** dominates the otherwise picture-postcard view. Once the largest structure in Alaska, the 'city under one roof' looms dismal and abandoned above town; the use of asbestos in the structure has complicated attempts to remodel or tear down the eerie edifice.

From here, walk along the **Shotgun Cove Hiking Trail** (p226), which winds through blueberry and salmonberry thickets to First Salmon Run Picnic Area, and then head a quarter mile down the road to your right (northeast) to get to Smitty's Cove. At low tide you can comb the beach westward, following the water's edge past the ferry terminal to the Triangle

This growing group of restaurants, tour outfits and quirkier-than-average gift shops is fun; don't miss **Log Cabin Gifts** (☎ 472-2501; The Triangle; ☺ 10:30am-6pm), Whittier's best stab at adorable. The knickknacks include lots

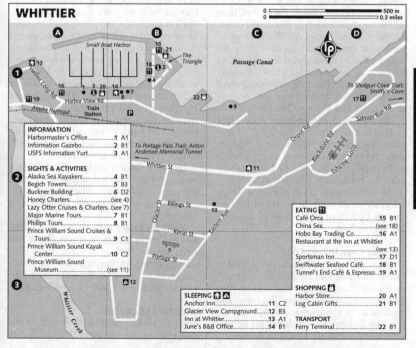

WHITTIER

INFORMATION	
Harbormaster's Office	1 A1
Information Gazebo	2 B1
USFS Information Yurt	3 A1

SIGHTS & ACTIVITIES	
Alaska Sea Kayakers	4 B1
Begich Towers	5 B3
Buckner Building	6 D2
Honey Charters	(see 4)
Lazy Otter Cruises & Charters	(see 7)
Major Marine Tours	7 B1
Phillips Tours	8 B1
Prince William Sound Cruises & Tours	9 C1
Prince William Sound Kayak Center	10 C2
Prince William Sound Museum	(see 11)

SLEEPING	
Anchor Inn	11 C2
Glacier View Campground	12 B3
Inn at Whittier	13 A1
June's B&B Office	14 B1

EATING	
Café Orca	15 B1
China Sea	(see 18)
Hobo Bay Trading Co.	16 A1
Restaurant at the Inn at Whittier	(see 13)
Sportsman Inn	17 D1
Swiftwater Seafood Café	18 B1
Tunnel's End Café & Espresso	19 A1

SHOPPING	
Harbor Store	20 A1
Log Cabin Gifts	21 B1

TRANSPORT	
Ferry Terminal	22 B1

Small Boat Harbor

The Triangle

Passage Canal

To Shotgun Cove Trail; Smitty's Cove

Harbor Loop Rd

Harbor View Rd

Alaska Railroad   Train Station

To Portage Pass Trail; Anton Anderson Memorial Tunnel

Whittier St

Billings St

Glacier St

Kenai St

Eastern Ave

Portage St

Depot Rd

Blackstone Rd

Etamy Loop

Salmon Run Rd

Whittier Creek

0   500 m
0   0.3 miles

PRINCE WILLIAM SOUND

of high-quality leatherwork, and they're handmade by owner Brenda Tolman, but the reindeer outside – Elizabeth and Violet, the day we were there – are the real crowd pleasers. If it's wet out, though, you won't see them. Apparently, they don't like rain – which makes it tough to live in Whittier.

Continue along the water to the **small-boat harbor**, where you'll find local commercial fishing boats and a whole lot of pleasure vessels owned by Anchorage-based weekenders. After checking out the fleet, finish up your tour with a meal at any of the good, inexpensive eateries lining the water.

Activities
HIKING
Portage Pass Trail

Whittier's sole USFS-maintained trail is a superb afternoon hike, providing good views of Portage Glacier, Passage Canal and the surrounding mountains and glaciers. Even better, hike up in the late afternoon and spend the evening camping at Divide Lake.

The Portage Pass Trail is along an old roadbed and is easy to follow. To reach it, head west of town toward the tunnel, then follow the signs leftward onto a road crossing the railroad tracks. You'll find a parking area at the trailhead. Proceed along the right fork as it begins to climb steeply along the flank of the mountain. There's a steady ascent for a mile, finishing at a promontory (elevation 750ft) that offers views of Portage Glacier and Passage Canal to the east.

The trail then descends for a half-mile to Divide Lake and Portage Pass. At this point the trail ends, and a route through alder trees continues to descend to a beach on Portage Lake. It's a 2-mile hike one way from the trailhead to the lake, and it's well worth bashing some brush at the end. There are great views from the shores of Portage Lake and plenty of places to set up camp on the alluvial flats.

Shotgun Cove Hiking Trail

This 0.8-mile walk along a dirt road leads to the First Salmon Run Picnic Area, so named because of the king and silver salmon runs during June and late August. The forest and mountains en route are scenic but, in true Whittier fashion, the roadsides are debris-strewn and the picnic area is in disrepair.

From the northeast corner of the Buckner Building, follow Salmon Run Rd up the mountain, staying to the right at the first fork and to the left at the second fork.

At the picnic area you can cross a bridge over the stream and continue another 3 miles to Second Salmon Run. This walk, along what is known as Shotgun Cove Rd, is exceptionally scenic, with views of Billings Glacier most of the way.

PADDLING

Whittier is a prime location for sea kayakers, as it's practically surrounded by glaciated fjords and inlets. The most common overnight trip from Whittier is Blackstone Bay, which contains a pair of tidewater glaciers, Blackstone and Beloit. Many kayakers utilize charter boats to access the dramatic fjords to the north, including Harriman Fjord, College Fjord and Unakwik Inlet.

Prince William Sound Kayak Center (☎ 472-2452, 877-472-2452; www.pwskayakcenter.com; Eastern Ave) is a well-run organization that rents kayaks (single/double $50/80, discounted for multiple days) and runs guided tours, including three-hour paddles to the kittiwake rookery (per person $160) and daylong excursions to Blackstone Bay (for two people $425; includes the water-taxi and lunch). It also has escorts for multiday trips. These aren't guided tours: while escorts will suggest camping spots and routes, you're in charge of your own trip, including food and gear. It's a neat option for independent-minded folks who don't have experience to feel comfortable spending a week on the water solo. The company will also let customers 'camp' and use the climbing wall inside its cavernous (but waterproof) facility. It rains a lot in Whittier.

Lazy Otter Charters (☎ 694-6887, 800-587-6887; www.lazyotter.com; Herbor View Rd; per person $195) offers guided day trips to Blackstone Bay for a minimum of four people. It also runs a water-taxi.

Alaska Sea Kayakers (☎ 472-2534, 877-472-2534; www.alaskaseakayakers.com; The Triangle; ⏲ 7am-7pm) rents kayaks ($40 to $75 per day), runs classes, arranges water-taxis and takes various multiday tours to places like Harriman Fjord, Nellie Juan Glacier and Whale Bay.

WILDERNESS CABINS

There are six **USFS cabins** (☎ 877-444-6777, 518-885-3639; www.reserveusa.com; cabins $35) accessible by boat from Whittier. Pigot Bay and Paulson Bay are the closest, with excellent salmon fishing and good views; Harrison Lagoon has the best access for mobility-impaired folks, plus some great tide pools; Shrode Lake comes with a boat; Coghill Lake is a scenic spot with good fishing and berry-picking; and South Culross Passage is on a picturesque cove on Culross Island.

DIVING

Whittier is a top spot for (involuntary shiver) Alaskan scuba diving – it's one of the wildest places easily accessible to human beings. The best time to dive is March through June.

Popular spots include the Dutch Group islands, known for the high visibility offshore, and the kittiwake rookery. There, a combination of steep cliffs and fresh fertilizer from the birds above has created a gently swaying rainbow of nudibranches. Good places to view Great Pacific octopuses, wolf eels and crabs the size of manhole covers are located in Esther and Culross Passages, close to **South Culross Passage cabin** (☎ 877-444-6777, 518-885-3639; www.reserveusa.com; cabins $35). Divers also often head to Smitty's Cove, which is east of the ferry terminal and is the only dive spot accessible by foot.

Lazy Otter Charters (☎ 694-6887, 800-587-6887; www.lazyotter.com; Herbor View Rd) can provide water-taxi service to the best underwater locations. It charges at least $100 for the boat plus additional fees based on mileage.

Tours

Various tour boats sail from the small-boat harbor into a rugged, icy world that's unbelievably rich in wildlife. On the way to Harriman Fjord, ships pass so close to a kittiwake rookery that you can see the eggs in the nests of the black-legged birds.

Honey Charters (☎ 888-477-2493; www.honeycharters.com; The Triangle) Offers tours of Blackstone Bay (per person $99) and Barry Arm ($149), both with a four-person minimum, as well as sightseeing trips to Cordova ($148) and Valdez ($138), which both have a 12-person minimum. It specializes in water-taxi transportation to public-use cabins and to remote hunting, fishing and hiking destinations. It's $7.50 per nautical mile for up to 30 people; rates are 40% cheaper if you can coordinate drop-offs and pickups with other groups.

Major Marine Tours (☎ 800-764-7300, 274-7300; www.majormarine.com; Herbor View Rd) Has a USFS ranger on every cruise. It does a five-hour tour of

glacier-riddled Blackstone Bay for $109/54 per adult/child.

Phillips Tours (☎ 472-2416, 800-544-0529; www.26glaciers.com; Herbor View Rd) Sends its speedy *Klondike Express* past 26 glaciers in one day for adult/child $129/69. Don't blink.

Prince William Sound Cruises & Tours (☎ 472-2410, 800-992-1297; www.princewilliamsound.com) Offers 'quality time' with the very active Surprise Glacier on its six-hour tour of Esther Passage (per adult/child $115/57).

Sleeping

Those wishing to stay overnight in Whittier face unappealing options: camping in puddles, flopping at a dive of a hotel, or paying through the nose for something nicer. There is a 3% sales tax added to Whittier accommodations.

BUDGET

You can (unofficially) pitch a tent close to the old oil tanks, to your right as you leave town on your way to the tunnel. That's a far better option than the horrid **Glacier View Campground** (Glacier St; sites $10), the town's only formal campground, which is basically a mud-soaked, clear-cut gravel quarry.

MIDRANGE & TOP END

Inn at Whittier (☎ 472-7000; www.innatwhittier.com; Harbor Loop Rd; r $179-389) Easily Whittier's poshest lodging, this new timber-frame hotel is a far cry from the decaying monoliths across town. It has 25 lavish rooms – many overlooking the small-boat harbor – plus a high-end restaurant.

June's B&B (☎ 472-2396, 888-472-2396; www.breadnbuttercharters.com; Lot 7, Harborside Dr; condos $98-140, with view $149-375) This business offers an insight into the local lifestyle, putting you up in swanky suites atop Begich Towers, or in economy rooms on the ground floor.

Anchor Inn (☎ 472-2354; www.anchorinnwhittier.com; 100 Whittier St; s/d $92/97) This multipurpose venue is pretty squalid but, as a last resort, it'll do. There's an attached restaurant, bar, laundry and grocery store.

Eating

RESTAURANTS

Restaurant at the Inn at Whittier (☎ 472-7000; lunch $10-13, dinner $23-30; 🕑 11am-10pm) This dining room has glorious views of the Sound and cooks up swell steaks and seafood, including grilled salmon with a honey-teriyaki glaze.

China Sea (☎ 472-2222; The Triangle; lunch $8-10, dinner $10-19; ☻ 11am-10pm summer) Serving up Chinese and Korean food, this place has a $10 lunch buffet featuring fresh *kung po* halibut.

CAFÉS & QUICK EATS

Hobo Bay Trading Co (☎ 472-2374; Herbor View Rd; mains $6-9; ☻ 10:30am-7pm Wed-Mon) When we visited, brassy old-timer Babs Reynolds had been serving up her exquisite burgers and nachos – with a heaping helping of local politics – for '27 years and tired of counting.' Alas, her place was for sale. No matter who buys it, it'll never be the same.

Café Orca (☎ 472-2450; The Triangle; light meals $8-12; ☻ 10am-7pm) The vegetable sandwiches,

lattes and homemade desserts here aren't cheap, but it's a restful place with remarkable views down the fjord.

Swiftwater Seafood Café (☎ 472-2550; The Triangle; mains $4-14; ☻ 11am-9pm Sun-Thu, 11:30am-10pm Fri & Sat) The fried halibut and homemade clam chowder hit the spot when it's raining horizontally outside. On the walls are photos of famous Alaskan shipwrecks, which you can peruse over your rhubarb crisp ($4.50).

Tunnel's End Café & Espresso (☎ 441-2248; 12 Harbor Loop Rd; mains $3-11; ☻ 9am-2pm Wed-Mon) This café has an extensive breakfast menu, served in what seems like someone's living room. For later, there are burgers, fried halibut and grilled salmon sandwiches.

THE ROAD TO WHITTIER

Reading about a human endeavor as willful and improbable as the Anton Anderson Memorial Tunnel is one thing; driving through 2.7 miles of ancient bedrock beneath the Chugach Mountains is another.

In the works for more than 20 years, plans for making this WWII-era tunnel accessible to autos finally leapt off the drawing board in 1993, when then-governor Wally Hickel convinced the Alaska legislature to appropriate $15 million for its construction. Ironically, the money came from the settlement Exxon paid the state after the 1989 oil spill; considering how much the road has undercut public transportation, the oil company may well make some of its money back.

Resistance to the road by area residents was formidable – many feared that Whittier would be engulfed in a relentless tide of wide-eyed Kenai sightseers, washing away all that was weird and wonderful about their town. But while trains ran daily all summer, winter snow and storms could trap locals for days at a time. Finally, cruise companies and other interested parties wore the resistance down. In 2000, with much fanfare, the Whittier Access Rd opened its gates.

Whittier is not yet entirely conjoined, either physically or psychologically, with the rest of the Kenai Peninsula. To be sure, the POW (Prisoner of Whittier) T-shirts are now collector's items rather than social statements, but the steep entry fee ($12 per car) and the potential hourlong wait at the tunnel still dissuade casual curiosity-seekers from making the effort. Whittier remains at its heart a part of Prince William Sound, not a bustling wilderness theme park on the other side of the mountain.

But more tourists are coming, bringing their RVs, jet skis and other noisy accoutrements to what used to be a primarily pedestrian destination. The once-quiet Sound is now alive with motorboats, an uncomfortable shock to the kayakers who've long made their way around these shores without internal combustion. There's a 650-spot parking lot in the center of town to accommodate what some estimate will eventually be 1.4 million tourists a year. Before the road, that number rarely broke 100,000.

Though there's more traffic, few businesses claim that they're finding any fabulous windfall. Several new restaurants and shops have popped up, many owners taking on serious debt in the hope that this undiscovered gem will become the next Exit Glacier. The pie may be a bit bigger, but there are more people at the table.

And there's another consequence that perhaps few anticipated. Even as the Kenai Peninsula is now passing through the tunnel to Whittier, Whittier is moving – literally – in the other direction. With sunnier, less claustrophobic environs on the far side of the mountain, and housing that's more appealing than derelict high-rise apartments, many locals now work *here* but live over *there*. Indeed, since the tunnel opened, the population has dwindled substantially – raising fears that one day, Alaska's strangest town may simply become one more place to commute to.

Sportsman Inn (☎ 472-2354; Blackstone Rd; pizza $6-16; 🕑 3-11pm Wed-Sun) A rugged little bar with pool tables and filling food.

GROCERIES
Harbor Store (☎ 472-2348; Herbor View Rd; 🕑 8am-8pm) This store has groceries and snacks for your hike.

Anchor Inn Grocery Store (☎ 472-2354; 100 Whittier St; 🕑 9am-10pm) A bigger grocery store across town.

Getting There & Around
Whittier is one of those places where getting there is half the fun. Sometimes, leaving can be even better.

BOAT
The **Alaska Marine Highway** (☎ 800-642-0066; www.ferryalaska.com) sails three times per week direct to Valdez ($85, seven hours), and another three times per week direct to Cordova for the same price. Both trips are superscenic – think Dall porpoises, Stellar sea lions and the kittiwake rookery. Twice per month a ferry departs Whittier, crosses the Gulf or Alaska and docks in Juneau (39 hours; $213). The ferry terminal is beside the Triangle.

BUS
Prince William Sound Cruises & Tours (☎ 472-2410, 877-777-2805; www.princewilliamsound.com) runs a daily shuttle between Anchorage and Whittier (one way/round-trip $26/52, 2½ hours). The bus leaves downtown Anchorage around 8am, and makes the return drive from Whittier at 5pm (or sometimes 6pm).

Magic Bus (☎ 230-6773; www.themagicbus.com) has a daily bus between Anchorage and Whittier (one way/round-trip $30/45, 1½ hours) that leaves Anchorage at 11am, and departs Whittier for the return trip at 6pm. On days when cruise ships are in Whittier, the bus makes a Anchorage–Whittier run at 3pm.

Every so often, **Homer Stage Line** (☎ 235-2252) has connections from Whittier to Seward and Homer.

CAR
Whittier Access Rd, also known as Portage Glacier Access Rd, leaves the Seward Hwy at Mile 79, continuing to Whittier through the claustrophobic Anton Anderson Memorial Tunnel, which at 2.7 miles long is the longest auto tunnel in North America (though Los Angeles, wouldn't you know, is planning a longer one). Negotiating the damp one-lane shaft as you skid across the train tracks is almost worth the steep price of admission (per car/RV $12/40), which is charged only if you're entering Whittier; if you bring your car into town on the Alaska Marine Hwy, you can exit through the tunnel for free. Eastbound and westbound traffic alternate every 15 minutes, with interruptions for the Alaska Railroad. Bring a magazine.

TRAIN
The **Alaska Railroad** (☎ 265-2494, 800-544-0552; www.akrr.com) operates the *Glacial Discovery* train between Anchorage and Whittier (one way/round-trip $55/68, 2½ hours) daily May through September.

Kenai Peninsula

Jutting into the Gulf of Alaska, the Kenai Peninsula is about the size of Belgium. Fewer than a tenth of Alaska's residents inhabit this southcentral extremity, and with mountains, glaciers, rivers, lakes, fjords, forests and fish galore, the area is an unparalleled recreational playground.

On the west coast is Cook Inlet, whose beaches offer razor clams, and whose waters support a vibrant fishing industry. You'll find the biggest salmon on the planet, which migrate each summer into the Kenai and Russian Rivers, attracting starry-eyed anglers by the tens of thousands.

On the rugged east coast, the Prince William Sound rains turn to snow among the jagged mountaintops, feeding North America's largest ice fields and sending glaciers toward the ocean. This sculpted seascape is a haven for marine creatures and heaven for kayakers, who could paddle for months among the berg-strewn fjords.

Down south, in Kachemak Bay, it's the best of all worlds, with islands and peaks, whales and trails, and plenty of succulent, barn door–sized halibut. There is the peninsula's fun-loving cruise-ship ports like Seward, dynamic hippie metropolises such as Homer, plus peaceful fishing villages the likes of Ninilchik and Seldovia.

The peninsula is largely well serviced, well developed and, being close to Anchorage, well frequented during the summer. Some trails are wildly popular and many campgrounds are filled to near-capacity, but if you hike a little further, you'll soon find only nature around you.

HIGHLIGHTS

- **Best clammy feeling** (p253) – digging, steaming and gorging on succulent razor clams on the beaches of Clam Gulch

- **Most urbane experience you can have in rubber boots** (p263) – patronizing the fine restaurants, wineries and galleries of Homer

- **Best way to feel the burn** (p238) – chasing 400 fiery-thighed racers up Seward's precipitous Mt Marathon

- **Best place to disappear for awhile** (p272) – enjoying the quiet coves and cool communities on the south side of Kachemak Bay

- **Most surreal splash** (p248) – watching (or wading into) 'combat fishing' on the legendary Kenai River

★ Kenai River

★ Clam Gulch

★ Mt Marathon

Homer
★ ★ Kachemak Bay

- AREA CODE: ☎ 907
- POPULATION: 51,000
- ELEVATION: TRUULI PEAK 6612FT

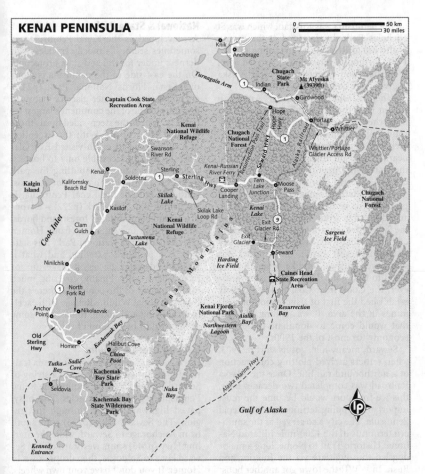

KENAI PENINSULA

0   50 km
0   30 miles

Climate

Weather-wise, the Kenai Peninsula is a compromise: drier than Prince William Sound, warmer than the Bush, wetter and cooler (in summer) than the Interior. Especially on the coast, extremes of heat and cold are unusual. Seward's normal daily high in July is 62°F; even in January most days barely drop below freezing. Inland, variations are only a bit more dramatic: Cooper Landing warms to around 68°F on midsummer days and falls to about 15°F during winter nights. Rainfall is quite high on the eastern coasts of the peninsula around Seward and Kenai Fjords National Park, moderate in the south near Homer and Seldovia, and somewhat less common on the west coast and inland around Soldotna and Cooper Landing.

History

For millennia, Dena'ina Indians made the Kenai Peninsula their home, as did Alutiiqs in the south and Chugaches in the east. They largely subsisted as many modern residents do: by pulling fish from the area's bountiful waterways. In 1741 Vitus Bering, a Dane sailing for the Russians, was the first European to lay eyes on the peninsula; in 1778, British explorer Captain James Cook sailed up the inlet that would bear his name, landing north of the present-day city of Kenai and claiming the area for England. Despite that, the first white settlement on the peninsula was Russian, which was St Nicholas Redoubt, founded at the mouth of the Kenai River as a fur trading post in 1791. Orthodox missionaries arrived soon thereafter, and many of the local Alaska Natives were converted to that faith.

When Alaska came under American rule in 1867 the US established Fort Kenay near where the redoubt had stood. The surrounding settlement endured as a commercial fishing village until 1957, when the nearby Swanson River became the site of the state's first major oil strike. Kenai has been an oil town ever since.

To the south, Homer was founded, and picked up its name, when Homer Pennock, an adventurer from Michigan, landed on the Spit with a crew of gold-seekers in 1896, convinced that Kachemak Bay was the key to their riches. It wasn't, and Pennock was soon lured to the Klondike, where he also failed to find gold. Three years later, however, the Cook Inlet Coal Field Company established the first of a succession of coal-mines in the area. It was fishing, though, that would come to dominate the town's economy for most of the 1900s.

Seward, meanwhile, got its start in 1903, when settlers arrived plotting construction of a northbound rail line. Once the Alaska Railroad was completed two decades later, this ice-free port would become the most important shipping terminal on the Kenai Peninsula. The city also served as the southern terminus of the 1200-mile Iditarod National Historic Trail to Nome, long a major dogsled thoroughfare via the Interior and Bush. In WWII the town got another boost when the US Army built Fort McGilvray at Caines Head, just south of town.

The 1964 Good Friday Earthquake hit Seward hard. After the earth finally stopped churning, oil tanks exploded and tsunamis rolled through, ravaging the town. With the bridges, railroad and boat harbor gone, Seward was suddenly cut off from the rest of the state. Homer suffered too: the quake dropped the Spit by 6ft and leveled most of the buildings. It took six years and almost $7 million to rebuild.

Since then tourism has boomed on the Kenai Peninsula, turning the region into Alaska's premier playground for visitors and locals, and becoming a key engine of the region's economy.

National & State Parks

As developed as the Kenai Peninsula can sometimes seem, it's mostly trackless wilderness under federal and state protection. On the east side of the peninsula is glorious Kenai Fjords National Park (p242), encompassing tidewater glaciers that pour down from one of the continent's largest ice fields, as well as the steep-sided fjords those glaciers have carved. With the exception of a single road to much-visited Exit Glacier, the park is accessible only to boaters, paddlers and alpinists. Abutting the park in places, and taking in much of the most southerly part of the Kenai Peninsula, is Kachemak Bay State Park (p272) – a wondrous land of mountains, forests and fjords, all accessible by water-taxi from Homer. Like Kenai Fjords National Park, this state park is a paddler's paradise, and what it lacks in tidewater glaciers it makes up for in excellent trails. Finally, covering much of the interior of the peninsula, there's the Kenai National Wildlife Refuge, with excellent canoeing and hiking routes, plus some of the world's best salmon fishing.

Getting There & Around

If you've ever been stuck in a Soldotna traffic jam or huffed fumes behind a string of Seward-bound RVs, you'll know: the Kenai Peninsula is a place of vehicles. Two busy, paved highways extend through this region. The Seward Hwy (p236) runs south from Anchorage to Seward, while the Sterling Hwy (p245) spurs westward off the Seward Hwy to Soldotna, then drops down to Homer. If you don't have your own wheels, you could either rent in Anchorage (p194). Alternatively, hop aboard a long-haul bus. **Homer Stage Line** (☎ 868-3914; www.homerstage line.com) operates daily between Anchorage, Homer and Seward; Seward is also connected to Anchorage by a couple of other operators (p242).

The best alternative to a road trip is to see this region from the water. The **Alaska Marine Highway** (800-642-0066; www.ferryalaska.com) hits three of the Kenai's most compelling communities – Seward, Homer and Seldovia. While it won't get you to the Resurrection Pass trailhead or the fishing grounds on the Russian River, it'll spare you from high-season automotive gridlock – and that might make all the difference.

A third transport possibility is rail; the southern terminus of the **Alaska Railroad** (☎ 265-2494, 800-544-0552; www.akrr.com) is at Seward, which is visited daily by trains from Anchorage.

Finally, as with everywhere in Alaska, there's always flying. Homer and the city of Kenai are served by **ERA Aviation** (☎ 235-7565, 800-426-0333; www.flyera.com); many of the peninsula's other towns also have airstrips and scheduled flights.

SEWARD HIGHWAY

The Seward Hwy is a stunner, running 127 mountain-flanked miles from Anchorage to Seward. When heading south, keep in mind that the mileposts along the highway show distances from Seward (Mile 0) to Anchorage (Mile 127). The first section of this road – from Anchorage to Portage Glacier (Mile 79) – is covered in the Anchorage chapter (p196).

TURNAGAIN PASS & AROUND

Having departed Turnagain Arm, Seward Hwy heads for the hills. Near Mile 68 it begins climbing into the alpine region of **Turnagain Pass**, where there's a roadside stop with garbage cans and toilets. In early summer, this area is a kaleidoscope of wildflowers.

Bertha Creek Campground (Mile 65 Seward Hwy; sites $10), just across the Bertha Creek Bridge, is understandably popular – site No 6 has its own waterfall. You can spend a day climbing the alpine slopes of the pass here, or head to Mile 64 and the northern trailhead of both the 23-mile **Johnson Pass Trail** (p70) and the paved **Sixmile Bike Trail**, which runs 8 miles – not six – along the highway.

Granite Creek Campground (Mile 63 Seward Hwy; sites $10) is reminiscent of Yosemite Valley: wildflower meadows, dramatic mountains…the works. Also similar to Yosemite, the sites here fill up fast.

The Hope Hwy junction and south trailhead for the Sixmile Bike Trail are both at Mile 56.7. From here, the Hope Hwy heads 16 miles north to the small hamlet of Hope (right).

The Seward Hwy continues south of this junction to Upper Summit Lake, surrounded by neck-craning peaks. The lakeside **Tenderfoot Creek Campground** (Mile 46 Seward Hwy; sites $10) has 27 sites that are open enough to catch the view but wooded enough for privacy.

Within walking distance of the campground is **Summit Lake Lodge** (☎ 244-2031; www.summitlakelodge.com; Mile 45.8 Seward Hwy; d $80), with basic rooms, an espresso shop and a decent **restaurant** (lunch $6-14, dinner $11-20; ☻ 8am-11pm).

The **Devil's Pass Trail** (Mile 39.4 Seward Hwy) is a well-signed, difficult, 10-mile hike over a 2400ft gap to the Resurrection Pass Trail (p67).

At **Tern Lake Junction** (Mile 37 Seward Hwy) is the turnoff for the Sterling Hwy (p245), running 143 miles to Homer.

HOPE

☎ 907/pop 165

Hope has beautiful views of Turnagain Arm surrounded by snowcapped mountains; a quaint and historic downtown; wonderful restaurants and gold rush–era relics; such incredible camping and hiking opportunities within easy access from Anchorage by car! With all this great stuff to distract you, it might take a minute to figure out what's missing. Give up? Here's a hint: just try to find one lame tourist trap. See? Even the gift shops around here are cool.

Somehow, the moose-nugget jewelry purveyors have passed this place by, perhaps missing the turnoff at Mile 56.7 of the Seward Hwy, or failing to follow the winding Hope Hwy the 16½ miles necessary to reach this rustic hamlet. Don't make the same mistake.

Orientation & Information

Driving along the Hope Hwy you'll encounter a few roadside stores and lodges at Mile 15.9. Just beyond, at Mile 16.2, Palmer Rd leaves the highway heading west and then forks; you need to take the right-hand fork, Resurrection Creek Rd, which runs 5 miles to the Resurrection Pass trailhead (p67), but if you stay left you'll wind six miles to Cour d'Alene Campground. Hope itself lies at Mile 16.5 of the Hope Hwy. What's best described as 'downtown Hope' is just east of the highway along Old Hope Rd.

Davidson Liquors (☎ 782-3418; Mile 17.8 Hope Hwy; ☻ 'we're usually here') Has snacks and the only gas in town, in an antique- (or perhaps just junk-) strewn homestead near the end of the Hope Hwy.

Hope Library (☎ 782-3740; Old Hope Rd; donation per hr $4; ☺ 11am-3pm Mon & Tue, noon-4pm Thu, to 3pm Sat; ▣) In a one-room 1938 schoolhouse. Don't miss its gift shop, next door, which sells locally made crafts to help support the grassroots facility.

Emergency (ambulance, fire, police ☎ 911)

Post office (Old Hope Rd) Opposite the museum.

Sights & Activities
HOPE-SUNRISE MINING MUSEUM
This small **log cabin** (☎ 782-3740; Old Hope Rd; admission free; ☺ noon-4pm) is packed with displays recalling the Turnagain Arm gold rush of 1894–9, with revealing historical photos of booming Hope and Sunrise. Relics from early miners and homesteaders are preserved here with a great deal of respect; a quick guided tour is worth the tip for history buffs and anyone with a little extra time.

GOLD PANNING
There are about 125 mining claims throughout the Chugach National Forest. Some of the more serious prospectors actually make money, but most are happy to take home a bottle with a few flakes of gold in it.

The Hope area provides numerous opportunities for the amateur panner, including a 20-acre claim that the US Forest Service (USFS) has set aside near the Resurrection Pass trailhead for recreational mining. Out there usually are some regulars who don't mind showing newcomers how to swirl the pan. Other panning areas are Sixmile Creek, between Mile 1.5 and Mile 5.5 of the Hope Hwy, and many of the creeks along the Resurrection Pass Trail.

HIKING
The northern trailhead of the legendary 39-mile Resurrection Pass Trail (p67) is near the end of Resurrection Creek Rd. From Porcupine Campground (right), two fine trails lead to scenic points overlooking Turnagain Arm.

The **Gull Rock Trail** is an easy 5-mile, four-to six-hour walk to Gull Rock, a rocky point 140ft above the Turnagain shoreline. The trail follows an old wagon road built at the turn of the 19th century, and along the way you can explore the remains of a cabin and a sawmill. You can camp at Gull Rock, but dead spruce trees are a serious fire hazard; stick with a stove.

Hope Point is steeper and a bit more difficult, following an alpine ridge 5 miles for incredible views of Turnagain Arm. Begin at an unmarked trail along the righthand side of the small Porcupine Creek. After 0.3 miles, the trail leaves the side of the creek and begins to ascend an outcrop with good views. From here, you can follow the ridge above the tree line to Hope Point (elevation 3708ft). Except for an early-summer snowfield, you'll find no water after Porcupine Creek.

PADDLING
Sixmile Creek is serious white water, with thrilling – and dangerous – rapids through deep gorges that survivors describe as 'the best roller coaster in Alaska.' The first two canyons are rated Class IV; the third canyon is a big, bad Class V.

Chugach Outdoor Center (☎ 277-7238; www.chugachoutdoorcenter.com; Mile 7.5 Hope Hwy) guides trips down Sixmile twice daily during summer. The two-canyon run is $95 per person; if you want to defy death on all three canyons it's $145 per person.

Nova River Runners (☎ 800-746-5753; www.novalaska.com) also does twice-daily trips down the river, at $90 for the Class IV canyons, and $130 for the Class V.

Sleeping
Near the end of Resurrection Creek Rd, just before and just after the Resurrection Pass trailhead, are many underdeveloped camping spots beneath a verdant canopy. The nearby creek is popular with gold panners.

Bear Creek Lodge (☎ 782-3141; www.bowmansbearcreeklodge.com; Mile 15.9 Hope Hwy; cabins $125) This place has five handhewn, shag-carpeted, sunny log cabins in a beautiful setting along a burbling creek.

Hope Gold Rush B&B (☎ 782-3436; Old Hope Rd; r from $95) It offers plush accommodations and wild-berry pancakes, all inside a 1916 log cabin built entirely with trees killed by spruce bark beetles almost a century ago. Well, almost entirely – the new addition is built with beetle-killed trees from just a few years back.

Porcupine Campground (Mile 17.8 Hope Hwy; sites $10) Popular for a reason: it's the trailhead for Hope Point and Gull Rock (left) and has transcendent views (especially from sites 4, 6, 8 and 10) of Turnagain Arm. Highly recommended.

KENAI PENINSULA

Seaview Café (☎ 782-3300; B St; campsites/RV sites $10/15, cabins $50) Rents sites that aren't very private, but the waterfront location and spectacular fishing make up for it. The cabins, however, are dilapidated and charmless.

Coeur d'Alene Campground (Mile 6.4 Palmer Rd; sites free) This is a gorgeous informal campground at the end of a narrow, winding back road.

Eating

Tito's Discovery Café (☎ 782-3275; Mile 16.5 Hope Hwy; breakfasts $6-9, wraps $11-12, dinners $12-18; ⊙ 8am-8pm) This is Hope's most popular eatery, with locals and visitors alike lining up out the door. It has excellent halibut wraps and unorthodox offerings like smoked-salmon corn chowder and Hungarian mushroom soup.

Bear Creek Lodge (☎ 782-3141; Mile 15.9 Hope Hwy; breakfasts $6-9, lunches $8-13, dinners $16; ⊙ 11am-9pm Wed & Thu, from 9am Fri-Sun) In the sunny café, the staff will serve you a chorizo, egg and potato burrito for breakfast, and a whole mess of halibut for dinner.

Seaview Café (☎ 782-3300; B St; mains $6-13; ⊙ noon-9pm Sun-Wed, to 11pm Thu-Sat) Specializes in seafood and serves up good beer with views of the Arm. There's often live music on weekends.

Alaska Dacha (☎ 782-3222; Mile 15.8 Hope Hwy; ⊙ 9am-7pm) Has the only pay phone between here and Moose Pass, plus groceries, showers and laundry.

Getting There & Away

Hope remains idyllic in part because of its isolation. Though the **Seward Bus Line** (☎ 224-3608) and **Homer Stage Line** (☎ 224-3608; www.homerstageline.com) will drop you off at the junction of the Hope and Seward Highways, the only way to get to the town proper is by driving, hitching, pedaling or plodding.

MOOSE PASS & AROUND

☎ 907/pop 220

Four miles south of Tern Lake Junction on the Seward Hwy is the trailhead for the **Carter Lake Trail** (Mile 33 Seward Hwy), a steep 1.9-mile Jeep track providing quick access to subalpine terrain and Carter Lake, where you can continue another mile to some excellent campsites and Crescent Lake.

Sturdy hikers can press on another 4 miles to **Crescent Lake Cabin** (☎ 877-444-6777; www.reserveusa.com; cabin $45). If you're not driving, Seward-bound buses can drop you off here (see p242).

At Mile 29.4, the village of **Moose Pass** relaxes along the banks of Upper Trail Lake. Founded during the Hope-Sunrise gold rush of the late 19th century, Moose Pass (which was named by a mail carrier who couldn't get past one of the critters) came into its own when the original Iditarod National Historic Trail was cut around the lake in 1910–11. Today the small town is known for its lively **Summer Solstice Festival**.

Estes Brothers Grocery (☎ 288-3151; ⊙ 8am-7pm Mon-Sat, from 10am Sun) has a deli, a small information booth and a gold rush–era waterwheel.

Across the highway from Estes Brothers Grocery, **Trail Lake Lodge** (☎ 288-3103; www.traillakelodge.com; Mile 29.5 Seward Hwy; r $89-105) has good, basic accommodations and a quality **restaurant** (breakfast & lunch $7-9, dinner $9-18; ⊙ 7am-9pm).

Moose Pass RV Park (☎ 288-5624; Mile 28.9 Seward Hwy; campsites/RV sites $10/12-17) has much more picturesque tent sites than the average RV park. Look for the chainsaw sculpture of the moose wearing Carhartts coveralls at the entrance.

Midnight Sun Log Cabins (☎ 288-3627; www.midnightsunlogcabins.com; Mile 30 Seward Hwy; cabins $100), hugging a hillside with stunning views, has luxurious cabins and outdoor fire pits.

Another five miles south is the USFS's **Trail River Campground** (Mile 24 Seward Hwy; sites $10), with 63 exceptionally lovely sites among tall spruce trees along Kenai Lake and Lower Trail River.

Ptarmigan Creek Campground (Mile 23 Seward Hwy; sites $10), with 16 shady sites, has great fishing. The **Ptarmigan Creek Trail** leads 3½ miles from the campground to Ptarmigan Lake, lazily reflecting the mountains that cradle its trout-filled waters. A 4-mile trail continues around the north side of the lake. This route is brushy in places and wet in others; plan on five hours for the round-trip.

The **Victor Creek Trail** (Mile 19.7 Seward Hwy), on the east side of the highway, is a fairly difficult path that ascends 3 miles to good views of the surrounding mountains.

Even if Seward is booked solid, there's often space at the **Primrose Landing Campground**

KENAI PENINSULA

(Mile 17.2 Seward Hwy; sites $10), a quiet and wooded spot with wonderful views of Kenai Lake and Andy Simon Mountain, named for a guide with a great philosophy: 'You never know what a man is until you've eaten a sack of flour with him.' It's also where the Primrose Trail (p239) begins.

The **Grayling Lake Trail**, accessed from a parking lot at Mile 13.2, leads 2 pleasant miles to Grayling Lake, a beautiful spot with views of Snow River and (surprise) excellent fishing for grayling. Side trails connect Grayling Lake with Meridian and Leech Lakes.

SEWARD
☎ 907/pop 2540

Flanked by rugged mountains and sparkling Resurrection Bay, Seward is so scenic that it hurts. The city serves as the gateway to Kenai Fjords National Park, and marks the intersection of the Alaska Railroad, Iditarod National Historic Trail, Alaska Marine Hwy and Seward Hwy – avoiding this place would take effort. But why would you want to? Though touristy, people throng here for good reason: fantastic hiking trails, an adorable downtown and rollicking tourist quarter, the awesome Alaska SeaLife Center, excellent in-town camping – and it's *the* place to be on the Fourth of July. Today most residents work in the fishing, shipping and tourist industries, but it's all just an excuse to live in this wilderness wonderland.

Orientation & Information
Seward is long and skinny, squeezed between Mt Marathon to the west and Resurrection Bay to the east. The Seward Hwy approaches from the north; many businesses are along this stretch or on Exit Glacier Rd, which spurs off the highway at Mile 3.7. Once in town, the highway becomes the town's main drag, 3rd Ave. For visitors, the town effectively has two cores: the vast summertime cluster of tourist shops and facilities around the small-boat harbor, and the more permanent downtown area at the end of 3rd Ave.

EMERGENCY
Ambulance, Fire, Police (☎ 911)

INTERNET ACCESS
Grant Electronics (☎ 224-7015; 222 4th Ave; per hr $8; ☺ 9am-6pm; 💻) Has Internet access and burns digital photos onto CDs.

Kayak Adventures Worldwide (☎ 224-3960; 328 3rd Ave; per 15 min $2; ☺ 8am-7pm; 💻) Gets you online.
Seward Library (☎ 224-3646; 238 5th Ave; access free; ☺ 10am-9pm Mon-Fri, to 7pm Sat; 💻) Also sells used books and displays what it claims is Benny Benson's first signed flag.

MONEY
First National Bank of Anchorage (☎ 224-4200; 303 4th Ave) One of two banks in town.

LAUNDRY
Seward Laundry & Dry Cleaning (☎ 224-5727; 806 4th Ave; ☺ 8am-8pm Mon-Sat, noon-6pm Sun) Has coin-op laundry and showers for $5.

MEDICAL SERVICES
Seward Medical Center (☎ 224-5205; 417 1st Ave) At the west end of Jefferson St.

POST
Post office (cnr 5th Ave & Madison St) Also sells phonecards.

TOURIST INFORMATION
Chamber of Commerce (☎ 224-8051; www.sewardak .org; 2001 Seward Hwy/3rd Ave; ☺ 8am-6pm Mon-Thu, to 8pm Fri, 9am-5pm Sat, 10am-3pm Sun) At the entrance to town, this helpful place provides everything from trail maps to local menus, plus lots of good advice.
Harbormaster's Office (Small-boat harbor; ☺ 8am-5pm, showers 24hr) Has showers for $2.
Kenai Fjords National Park Visitor Center (☎ 224-3175; ☺ 8am-6pm) Beside the small-boat harbor.
Seward Parks and Recreation (☎ 224-4054; 519 4th Ave; adult/child $4/2; ☺ 10am-10pm Mon-Fri) Has a gym and sauna as well as showers.
USFS Ranger Station (☎ 224-3378; 334 4th Ave; ☺ 8am-5pm Mon-Fri) Has maps and information about Seward's outstanding selection of trails, cabins and campgrounds.

Sights
ALASKA SEALIFE CENTER
A fitting legacy of the *Exxon Valdez* oil spill settlement, this $56-million **marine center** (☎ 224-6300, 800-224-2525; www.alaskasealife.org; 301 Railway Ave; adult/child $14/11; ☺ 8am-7pm) is more than just one of Alaska's finest attractions. As the only coldwater marine-science facility in the Western Hemisphere, it serves as a research and educational center and provides rehabilitation for injured marine animals; for $6 more you can tour the labs at 9am and 12:30pm daily.

KENAI PENINSULA

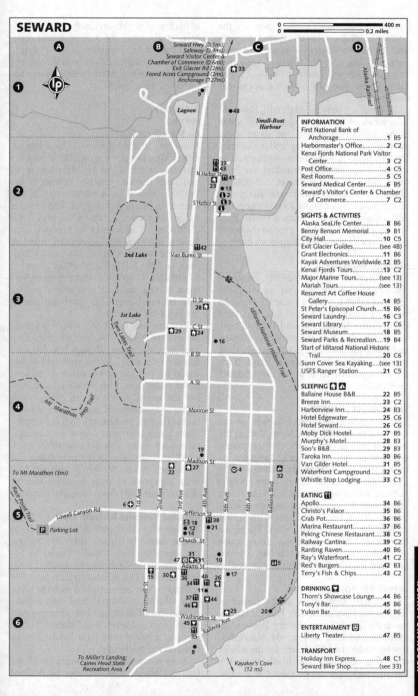

SEWARD

| 0 | | 400 m |
| 0 | | 0.2 miles |

INFORMATION
First National Bank of
  Anchorage......................................1 B5
Harbormaster's Office...................2 C2
Kenai Fjords National Park Visitor
  Center..3 C2
Post Office..4 C5
Rest Rooms.......................................5 C5
Seward Medical Center...................6 B5
Seward's Visitor's Center & Chamber
  of Commerce..................................7 C2

SIGHTS & ACTIVITIES
Alaska SeaLife Center....................8 B6
Benny Benson Memorial...............9 B1
City Hall..10 C5
Exit Glacier Guides....................(see 48)
Grant Electronics...........................11 B6
Kayak Adventures Worldwide..12 B5
Kenai Fjords Tours.........................13 C2
Major Marine Tours................(see 13)
Mariah Tours.............................(see 13)
Resurrect Art Coffee House
  Gallery...14 B5
St Peter's Episcopal Church.......15 B6
Seward Laundry.............................16 C3
Seward Library...............................17 C6
Seward Museum.............................18 B5
Seward Parks & Recreation.........19 B4
Start of Iditarod National Historic
  Trail..20 C6
Sunn Cover Sea Kayaking.....(see 13)
USFS Ranger Station.....................21 C5

SLEEPING
Ballaine House B&B.......................22 B5
Breeze Inn......................................23 C2
Harborview Inn..............................24 B3
Hotel Edgewater............................25 C6
Hotel Seward.................................26 C6
Moby Dick Hostel..........................27 B5
Murphy's Motel..............................28 B3
Soo's B&B.......................................29 B3
Taroka Inn.......................................30 B6
Van Gilder Hotel............................31 B5
Waterfront Campground..............32 C6
Whistle Stop Lodging...................33 C1

EATING
Apollo...34 B6
Christo's Palace.............................35 B6
Crab Pot..36 B6
Marina Restaurant.........................37 B3
Peking Chinese Restaurant.........38 C5
Railway Cantina.............................39 C2
Ranting Raven................................40 B6
Ray's Waterfront...........................41 C2
Red's Burgers.................................42 B3
Terry's Fish & Chips.......................43 C2

DRINKING
Thorn's Showcase Lounge.........44 B6
Tony's Bar.......................................45 B6
Yukon Bar.......................................46 B6

ENTERTAINMENT
Liberty Theater..............................47 B5

TRANSPORT
Holiday Inn Express......................48 C1
Seward Bike Shop.....................(see 33)

Seward Hwy (0.1mi);
Safeway (0.4mi);
Seward Visitor Center &
Chamber of Commerce (0.6mi);
Exit Glacier Rd (2mi);
Forest Acres Campground (2mi);
Anchorage (127mi)

Lagoon

Small-Boat
Harbour

Alaska Railroad

N Harbor St

S Harbor St

2nd Lake

Van Buren St

1st Lake

Two Lakes Trail

D St

C St

B St

A St

Mt Marathon Jeep Trail

Monroe St

To Mt Marathon (3mi)

Race Point Trail

Lowell Canyon Rd

Parking Lot

Iditarod National Historic Trail

Madison St

1st Ave
2nd Ave
3rd Ave
4th Ave
5th Ave
6th Ave
Ballaine Blvd

Jefferson St

Church St

Adams St

Bromwell St

Washington St

Railway Ave

To Miller's Landing;
Caines Head State
Recreation Area

Kayaker's Cove
(12 mi)

KENAI PENINSULA

Amazing enough for most folks are the regular exhibits, such as oil-spill displays and the Alaska Waters Gallery, with aquariums holding colorful fish and gossamer jellyfish. Kids will love the tidepool touch tank, where you can hold sea anemones and starfish.

Without a doubt the highlight, however, is a series of two story–deep, glass-sided tanks: upstairs you get the above-water view of seabird rookeries and recuperating harbor seals, while below deck you'll be eyeball-to-eyeball with prowling sea lions and puffins diving for dinner. An outdoor observation platform offers a fabulous view of the mountains ringing Resurrection Bay and a chance to watch salmon thrash their way up a fish ladder. Plan to spend the better part of one of your best afternoons here.

SEWARD MUSEUM
This eclectic **museum** (☎ 224-3902; 336 3rd Ave; adult/child $3/1; ☺ 9am-5pm) has an excellent Iditarod exhibit, a rare 49-star US flag, and relics of Seward's Russian era, the 1964 Good Friday Earthquake and 1989 oil spill. There are also lots of amusing antiques, including an ancient electric hair-curling machine and a 'cow raincoat' designed for the oft-drenched cattle at the now-defunct Seward dairy.

SMALL-BOAT HARBOR
The interesting small-boat harbor, at the northern end of 4th Ave, hums during the summer with fishing boats, charter vessels, cruise ships and a number of sailboats. At its heart is the **harbormaster's office** (☎ 224-3183; ☺ 8am-5pm). Look for the huge anchors outside. Radiating outward from the docks are seasonal restaurants, espresso bars, tourist offices, hotels and almost any other service the visitor might want. There are also picnic tables and a free sighting scope overlooking the harbor and the bay. A paved bike trail leads to the (other) city center.

BENNY BENSON MEMORIAL
This humble monument at the corner of the Seward Hwy and Dairy Hill Ln honors Seward's favorite son, Benny Benson. In 1926 the orphaned 13-year-old Alaska Native boy submitted his design for the Alaska state flag, arguably the loveliest in the Union. His stellar design (you can see one of his first at the library) includes the North Star, symbolizing the northernmost state, the Great Bear constellation for strength, and a blue background for both the sky and the forget-me-not, Alaska's state flower. Seward will never forget.

Activities
HIKING
Mt Marathon Trail
According to (rather suspect) local legend, grocer Gus Borgan wagered $100 in 1909 that no-one could run Mt Marathon in an hour, and the race was on. Winner James Walters clocked in at 62 minutes, losing the bet but becoming a legend. The 3.1-mile suffer-fest quickly became a celebrated 4th of July event and today is Alaska's most famous footrace, pitting runners from all over the world against the 3022ft-high peak. In 1981 Bill Spencer set the record at 43 minutes, 23 seconds. Many runners take twice as long, and each year several end up with broken bones after tumbling during the hell-bent descent.

You can trek to the top several ways. At the end of Monroe St, the so-called Jeep Trail provides easier (though not drivable) access to the peak. At the west end of Jefferson St, you can access either a trailhead at the picnic area, with switchbacks to mellow the ascent, or the official route, which begins at a nearby cliff face behind the water tanks. Though the runner's trail is painful – think Stairmaster with a view – its accomplishment earns you serious street cred, which is really the reason you're doing this to yourself. No matter which path you take to the high point, however, be sure to hike (or slide on your butt) down the gully's scree.

Iditarod National Historic Trail
Though the celebrated Iditarod Race to Nome currently departs from Anchorage, the legendary trail actually begins in Seward. In 1995 Mitch Seavey mushed from Seward along this well-worn path into Anchorage, where he continued with the regularly scheduled Iditarod; he finished 20th. At the foot of Ballaine Blvd, an unprepossessing sign and lonely dogsled mark Mile 0. Nearby, a paved bike path heads 2 miles north along the beach.

A far more interesting segment of the trail for hikers, however, can be reached by heading east 2 miles on Nash Rd, which intersects the Seward Hwy at Mile 3.2. From here you can follow the Iditarod National Historic Trail through woods and thick brush for a 4-mile hike to Bear Lake. Nearby is the trailhead for the **Mt Alice Trail**, a fairly difficult and highly recommended 2½-mile climb to the alpine summit. Bald eagles, blueberries and stunning views can be had elsewhere, but it's the solitude – this trail is relatively unused – that makes Mt Alice great. Back at Bear Lake, you can either backtrack to town or forge on another 11 miles to rejoin the Seward Hwy. For more details, see p71.

Two Lakes Trail

This easy 1-mile loop circumnavigates pleasant Two Lakes Park (cnr 2nd Ave & C St), through woods and picnic grounds, across a salmon-spawning creek and around the two promised lakes at the base of Mt Marathon. Unsatisfied hikers can access the Jeep Trail nearby, which climbs Mt Marathon, for a much more intense climb.

Lost Lake Trail

This challenging 7-mile trail to an alpine lake is one of the most scenic hikes the Kenai Peninsula has to offer in midsummer. The trailhead is in Lost Lake subdivision, at Mile 5.3 of the Seward Hwy. After 3 miles you come to the summer trail that winds 1½ miles south to the **Clemens Memorial Cabin** (right). The final 2 miles are above the tree line, making the shores of Lost Lake a wondrous place to pitch a tent.

If you'd rather not return the same way, continue around the east side of Lost Lake to the **Primrose Trail**, an 8-mile alpine trek ending at Primrose Campground at Mile 17.2 of the Seward Hwy (see Seward Highway earlier, p233). Plan on seven to 10 hours for the round-trip to Lost Lake, and bring a camp stove, as wood is hard to come by.

Caines Head State Recreation Area

This 6000-acre preserve, 5½ miles south of Seward on Resurrection Bay, contains WWII military facilities (bring a flashlight for exploring), a 650ft headland, the Coastal Trail, and two public-use cabins (p240). There's a $5 day-use fee for the recreation area, paid at the trailhead. If you're not up

for an overnight backpacking excursion, the hike to Tonsina Point is an easy 3-mile round-trip. Beyond that you will need to time your passage with low tide; hikers have gotten stranded and even drowned after being caught by the rising waters.

PADDLING

Though the best and most impressive paddling in the region is within Kenai Fjords National Park (p244), getting there requires a costly water-taxi. If you're looking to save money and don't mind foregoing the park's tidewater glaciers and more ample wildlife, kayaking right outside Seward in Resurrection Bay can still make for a stunning day on the water. Both **Sunny Cove Sea Kayaking** (☎ 224-8810, 800-770-9119; www.sunnycove.com; Small-Boat Harbor) and **Kayak Adventures Worldwide** (☎ 224-3960; www.kayakak.com; 328 3rd Ave) guide half- and full-day trips in the bay (see p244). The latter, as well as **Miller's Landing** (☎ 224-5739, 866-541-5739; www.millerslandingak.com; cnr Lowell Rd & Beach St), also rents kayaks.

WILDERNESS CABINS

Seward is a great place for a cabin-getaway in the wilderness. You can paddle, fly and even hike to a remote, rustic lodging administered by the Alaska Division of Parks, USFS and even the National Park Service as Kenai Fjords National Park has several boat-accessible public-use cabins (p245).

Orca Island Cabins (☎ 224-5846; cabins d $100, yurts d $150) In Humpy Cove 9 miles southeast of Seward by kayak or water-taxi; has a floating cabin with private bath and kitchen, plus two onshore yurts with similar facilities. All have propane-powered ranges and water-heaters but no electricity.

Clemens Memorial Cabin (☎ 877-444-6677, 518-885-3639; www.reserveusa.com; cabin $45) Located 4½ miles up the Lost Lake Trail (left), sleeps eight. The cabin is located at the tree line, providing spectacular views.

Resurrection River Cabin (☎ 877-444-6677, 518-885-3639; www.reserveusa.com; cabin $35) This is 6½ miles from the southern trailhead of the Resurrection River Trail (p244).

Derby Cove Cabin (www.alaskastateparks.org; cabin $65) Just off the tidal trail between Tonsina Point and North Beach in Caines Head State Recreation Area, 4 miles from the Lowell Point trailhead. It can be accessed on foot at low tide, or by kayak anytime.

KENAI PENINSULA

Callisto Canyon Cabin (www.alaskastateparks.org; cabin $65) Also located just off the tidal trail, a half-mile before you reach Derby Cove. It can be reached on foot or by kayak.

SLED-DOG MUSHING

Hey, this is where the Iditarod started. Why not meet the dogs?

IdidaRide (☎ 800-478-8607; Exit Glacier Rd; adult/child $49/24) is cheesy, but it's more like Stilton than Velveeta: after touring Iditarod veteran Mitch Seavey's kennels and hearing junior mushers discuss their experiences with subzero sleep deprivation, delicate doggy feet and cutthroat competition, you'll be strapped in for a 20-minute training run in a cart hitched behind a team of huskies.

Godwin Glacier Dog Sled Tours (☎ 224-8239; 888-989-8239; www.alaskadogsled.com; adult/child $390/355) goes one better, transporting you by helicopter to an alpine glacier, where you'll be met by lots of dogs and a genuine snow-sledding adventure, even in July.

BIKING

Popular with hikers, the **Lost Lake Trail** (p239) makes for sometimes steep and technical, but highly rewarding, single-track riding. Local cyclists say the **Iditarod National Historic Trail** (p238) and the **Resurrection River Trail** (p244) are also good rides.

For bike rentals, see p242.

GLACIER TREKKING

For those not satisfied with merely gazing up at Seward's backyard glacier, **Exit Glacier Guides** (☎ 224-5569; www.exitglacierguides.com) gives you the chance to tread upon it. Its five-hour ice-hiking trip costs $100 per person, gears you up with ice-axes and crampons, ascends part-way up the Harding Ice Field Trail and then heads out onto the glacier for crevasse exploration and interpretive glaciology. By the time you read this, Exit'll likely offer overnight treks as well.

Festivals & Events

Seward knows how to party, and these are just a few of the more popular events.

Polar Bear Jumpoff Festival A favorite of costumed masochists who plunge into frigid Resurrection Bay with a smile in mid-January.

Mt Marathon Race This July 4 race attracts runners who like to test themselves and fans who like to drink beer and yell.

Silver Salmon Derby An event held in mid-August that gets even bigger crowds, all vying for prizes in excess of $150,000.

Sleeping

Above and beyond the listed rates you have to add 11% in Seward sales and bed taxes to lodging.

BUDGET
Camping

Near Exit Glacier, Kenai Fjords National Park maintains one drive-up campground (p245). There are lots of informal campsites along Exit Glacier Rd.

Waterfront Campground (☎ 224-3331; Ballaine Blvd; campsites/RV sites $8/12-25) Perfectly situated between the city center and boat harbor. Most of it is open gravel parking for RVers, but there are grassy campsites, as well as a compact skateboard park, volleyball nets and a paved bicycle path running through.

Forest Acres Campground (☎ 224-4055; cnr Hemlock St & Seward Hwy; tent/RV sites $8/12) Located 2 miles north of town just off the Seward Hwy on Hemlock St; has quiet sites shaded by towering spruce.

Miller's Landing (☎ 224-5739; 866-541-5739; www.millerslandingak.com; cnr Lowell Rd & Beach St; campsites/RV sites $23/$28-30, cabin camping $45-59, modern $79-250) This touristplex – offering everything from campsites to kayak rentals to fishing charters – may not be the most clean or organized place, but the waterfront location is hard to beat.

Hostels

Snow River Hostel (☎ 440-1907; Mile 16 Seward Hwy; dm/d/cabins $15/40/40) Nestled beside the forest and a burbling creek, this place is some distance from town, but worth the trip for the idyllic atmosphere and easy access to challenging Lost Lake Trail.

Moby Dick Hostel (☎ 224-7072; www.mobydickhostel.com; 430 3rd Ave; dm/r $17/50) Is friendly, well located and popular, though it's overdue for a fresh coat of paint and new carpeting.

Kayaker's Cove (☎ 224-8662; www.geocities.com/kayakerscove_99664; dm/cabins $20/60) Located 12 miles southeast of Seward near Fox Island; is accessible by kayak or water-taxi only. There's a shared kitchen, and you'll need to bring your own food. It rents single/double kayaks for $20/30.

MIDRANGE

Among Seward's midrange places, dozens are B&Bs; you can book through **Alaska's Point of View** (☎ 224-2323, 800-844-2424) even at the last minute.

Creekside Cabins (☎ 224-1996; 11886 Old Exit Glacier Rd; sites $20, cabin $55-85) Beautiful and secluded, with a fantastic sauna next to a deliciously icy-cold salmon stream.

Ballaine House B&B (☎ 224-2362; 437 3rd Ave; s/d $68/90) Raved about by readers, this place does cook-to-order breakfasts and offers a wealth of advice on what to do in Seward.

Taroka Inn (☎ 224-8687; www.alaskaone.com/tar okainn; 235 3rd Ave; r $135-175) This place, which served as officers' quarters during WWII, has huge, unpretentious, kitchenette-equipped suites. If you've got a big group, this would be a great deal.

Hotel Seward (☎ 224-2378; 221 5th Ave; r $79-224) The old side has fairly scroungy but affordable shared-bath rooms; the new wing makes for an excellent splurge with grand views of Resurrection Bay.

TOP END

Van Gilder Hotel (☎ 800-204-6835; www.vangilder hotel.com; 307 Adams St; d $109-219) Gossips say poltergeists plague the 1st floor of this landmark, which dates from 1916. If you dare to spend the night, however, you'll find elegant suites with antique furnishings, plus some affordable European pensions with shared baths.

Soo's B&B (☎ 224-3207, 888-967-7667; www.seward alaska.com/soos; 810 2nd Ave; r $110-125) Has four rooms, each with private bath, and serves up full breakfasts.

Whistle Stop Lodging (☎ 224-5252; www.seward .net/seward/whistlestop; 411 Port Ave; d $127) Has two waterfront rooms aboard a plush WWII-era railroad car.

Murphy's Motel (☎ 224-8090; 911 4th Ave; r $104-154) Better harbor views are found at this clean and professional place.

Harborview Inn (☎ 224-3217; www.sewardhotel .com; 804 3rd Ave; s/d from $179/189) Has small, pleasant rooms but no real view of the harbor.

Breeze Inn (☎ 224-5237; www.sewardalaskamotel .com; 1306 Seward Hwy; s/d from $129/139) Has great basic rooms, and for $60 more, even nicer Jacuzzi-equipped ones in the newer annex.

Seward Windsong Lodge (☎ 224-7116; www .sewardwindsong.com; Exit Glacier Rd; d $189-239) This Alaska Native corporation–owned place is immaculate, modern and snazzy, but devoid of good views – and soul.

Hotel Edgewater (☎ 224-2700; 200 5th Ave; www .hoteledgewater.com; d $110-225) Has everything from balcony-bedecked ocean-view suites to cheaper rooms devoid of windows.

Eating

RESTAURANTS

Ray's Waterfront (☎ 224-5606; breakfast & lunch $10-16, dinner $19-31; ☷ 11am-11pm) Hands down, this is Seward's culinary high point, with attentive service, picture-postcard views and the finest seafood above water.

Crab Pot (☎ 224-2200; 303 Adams St; dinner $12-25; ☷ 4pm-midnight) All the locals will tell you: If it's crab you crave, nestle into the red-leather booths of this low-lit restaurant. The 1lb of king crab will set you back $43.

Exit Glacier Salmon Bake (☎ 224-2204; Exit Glacier Rd; lunch $6-10, dinner $18-22; ☷ 4:30-10pm) Its motto – 'cheap beer and lousy food' – is wrong on the second count. Both tourists and locals adore this steak-and-seafood place.

Apollo (☎ 224-3092; 229 4th Ave; lunch $8-15, dinner $15-25; ☷ 11am-11pm) A wildly popular and slightly overpriced restaurant with plenty of pasta-and-seafood dishes. It'll cook up your cleaned, filleted fish to order for $10.

Christo's Palace (☎ 224-5255; 133 4th Ave; dinner $19-25; ☷ 11am-midnight) Has a gorgeous dining room dominated by a 1950s Brunswick bar (featuring a great selection of beer on tap). The pizza and seafood get raves.

Resurrection Roadhouse (☎ 224-7116; Exit Glacier Rd; lunch $9-14, dinner $18-46; ☷ 6am-10pm) This local favorite is home to 'halibut tsunami,' Thai seafood cakes and the best nachos in town. It also has a vast range of on-tap brews.

Le Barn Appetit (☎ 224-3462; Eagle Lane; mains $5-16; ☷ 7am-2pm, 4-9pm) In this unorthodox eatery off Exit Glacier Rd there's not really a fixed menu – except for crepes, which are so sinful that, as chef Yvon Van Driessche says, 'you must go to confession.'

Peking Chinese Restaurant (☎ 224-5444; 338 4th Ave; lunch specials $8-9, dinner $12-20; ☷ 11am-11pm) Does Korean and Chinese well, with local flavors like halibut thrown in.

CAFÉS

Marina Restaurant (☎ 224-7991; 203 4th Ave; breakfast $6-11, lunch $6-7, dinner $10-23; ☷ 6am-8pm) With burnt coffee, smoking locals, gossip, lots of

KENAI PENINSULA

Formica and great breakfasts, this place has the hallmarks of a classic smalltown diner.

Terry's Fish & Chips (☎ 224-8807; cnr 4th Ave & North Harbor St; mains $8-13; 🕙 10am-midnight) If it swims, Terry's batter-fries it, throws it in a basket and serves it with fries.

QUICK EATS

Resurrect Art Coffee House Gallery (☎ 224-7161; 320 3rd Ave; 🕙 7am-7pm) In an old high-ceilinged church; serves espressos, Italian sodas and bagels, displays great local art and hosts live jazz on Tuesday nights.

Ranting Raven (☎ 224-2228; 224 4th Ave; light meals $3-6; 🕙 9am-5pm) The best place to pore over the newspaper, sip an espresso and nibble on scones, muffins or coffee cake.

Railway Cantina (☎ 224-8226; light meals $4-8; 🕙 11am-8pm) Near the small-boat harbor; offers unorthodox quesadillas, burritos and tacos. Try the 'black-n-blue' quesadilla, with blackened chicken and blue cheese.

Red's Burgers (cnr 3rd Ave & Van Buren St; fast food $6-12; 🕙 11am-9pm) In a converted school bus; does quality burgers, hot dogs, and, needless to say, fried halibut.

GROCERIES

Safeway (☎ 224-3698; Mile 1.5 Seward Hwy; 🕙 24hr) Has sushi, espressos, a sandwich bar and all the groceries you need.

Drinking & Entertainment

Seward has no shortage of welcoming watering holes, most featuring a mix of young and old, locals and tourists. Almost all the bars are downtown.

Yukon Bar (☎ 224-3063; 201 4th Ave) There are hundreds of dollars pinned to this bar's ceiling and almost nightly live music, including Hobo Jim, Alaska's official balladeer. It's festive.

Tony's Bar (☎ 224-3045; 135 4th Ave) It's not quite as festive (there are maybe seven dollars pinned to the ceiling), but locals consider it the best place just to hang out.

Thorn's Showcase Lounge (☎ 224-3700; 208 4th St; mains $14-18) This cozy saloon serves lots of liquor and what locals say is the best fried halibut in town.

Pit Bar (☎ 224-3006; Mile 3.5 Seward Hwy) Just past Exit Glacier Rd; this bar's interior has color to spare and good grub, plus pool tables, a horseshoe pit and the second-oldest shuffleboard court in Alaska. Closing time is late.

Liberty Theatre (☎ 224-5418; 304 4th Ave; admission $7) A delightful little WWII-era cinema showing first-run flicks daily.

Getting There & Around

BICYCLE

Bikes can be rented through **Seward Bike Shop** (☎ 224-2448; 411 Port Ave; per half/full day cruisers $14/23, mountain bikes $21/38; 🕙 9:30am-6:30pm Mon-Sat, 11am-4pm Sun), in a WWII-era railroad car, which has the latest details on local biking trails, and **Kayak Adventures Worldwide** (☎ 224-3960; www.kayakak.com; 328 3rd Ave; bikes per half/full day $10/15).

Hotel Seward (☎ 224-2378; 221 5th Ave; per hr $15-25) rents four-seat surrey bikes.

BOAT

The Alaska Marine Highway **ferry terminal** (☎ 224-5485; www.ferryalaska.com; 913 Port Ave) is by the Alaska Railroad dock, north of the small-boat harbor. The MV *Tustumena* provides direct service to Kodiak ($80, 13 hours), with onward connections to Homer ($139, 23 hours) and the Aleutian Islands.

BUS

The **Seward Bus Line** (☎ 224-3608) departs at 9:30am daily en route to Anchorage ($40).

Homer Stage Line (☎ 224-3608; www.homerstageline.com) runs daily from Seward to Homer ($45) and Anchorage ($45).

The **Park Connection** (☎ 800-266-8625; www.alaskacoach.com) has a daily service from Seward to Denali Park (one way $118) via Anchorage (one way $49).

TRAIN

From May to September, the **Alaska Railroad** (☎ 265-2631, 800-544-0552; www.akrr.com; 408 Port Ave; one way/round-trip $59/98) offers a daily run to Anchorage. It's more than just public transportation; it's one of the most famous rides in Alaska, complete with glaciers, steep gorges and rugged mountain scenery.

TROLLEY

The **Seward Trolley** (one way adult/child $4/2) runs between the ferry terminal and downtown every half-hour from 10am to 7pm daily.

KENAI FJORDS NATIONAL PARK

Seward is the gateway to Kenai Fjords National Park, created in 1980 to protect 587,000 acres of Alaska's most awesome, impenetrable wilderness. Crowning the park is the massive Harding Ice Field; from it, countless tidewater glaciers pour down, carving the coast into dizzying fjords.

With such a landscape – and an abundance of marine wildlife to boot – the park is a major tourist attraction. Unfortunately, it's also an expensive one. That is why road-accessible Exit Glacier is its highlight attraction, drawing more than 100,000 tourists each summer. Hardier souls can ascend to the Harding Ice Field from the same trailhead, but only experienced mountaineers equipped with skis, ice axes and crampons can investigate the 900 sq miles of ice.

The vast majority of visitors either take a quick trip to Exit Glacier's face or splurge on a tour-boat cruise along the coast. For those who want to spend more time in the park, the coastal fjords are a blue-water kayaker's dream; to reach the area, though, you either have to paddle the sections exposed to the Gulf of Alaska or pay for a drop-off service.

Orientation & Information

Ice-bound inland areas of the park stretch west and northwest of Seward, penetrated only by a few trails and the 8.4-mile-long Exit Glacier Rd, which spurs off the Seward Hwy at Mile 3.7. Some 20 miles south of town the park joins the coastline, taking in such sizable fjords as Aialik Bay, Northwestern Lagoon, McCarty Fjord and North Arm, as well as mountains exceeding 6000ft in height.

Emergency (Ambulance, Fire, Police ☎ 911)

Exit Glacier Nature Center (☼ 9am-8pm) At the Exit Glacier trailhead; has interpretive displays, sells postcards and field guides, and is the starting point for ranger-guided hikes (below).

Kenai Fjords National Park Visitor Center (☎ 224-2125; cnr 4th Ave & S Harbor St; ☼ 8am-6pm) In Seward's small-boat harbor; has information on hiking and camping and issues free backcountry permits.

Sights & Activities

HIKING

Ranger-Led Hikes

At 10am, 2pm and 4pm daily, rangers at the Exit Glacier Nature Center lead free one-hour hikes to the face of the glacier, providing information on the wildlife and natural history of the area. For a more strenuous outing, show up at the nature center on a Saturday at 9am for the guided ascent of the Harding Ice Field Trail. The trek lasts eight hours; pack a lunch and rain gear.

Harding Ice Field Trail

This strenuous and extremly popular 3.5-mile trail follows Exit Glacier up to Harding Ice Field, one of the most extensive in North America. The 936-sq-mile expanse remained undiscovered until the early 1900s, when a map-surveying team discovered that eight coastal glaciers flowed from the exact same system.

DETOUR: EXIT GLACIER

The marquee attraction of Kenai Fjords National Park and one of Alaska's most accessible glaciers, Exit Glacier was named by explorers crossing the Harding Ice Field who found the glacier a suitable way to 'exit' the ice and mountains. Now 3 miles long, it's believed the river of ice once extended all the way to Seward.

From the Exit Glacier Nature Center, the **Outwash Plain Trail** is an easy half-mile walk to the glacier's alluvial plain – a flat expanse of pulverized silt and gravel, cut through by braids of grey meltwater. The **Overlook Loop Trail** departs the first loop and climbs steeply to an overlook at the side of the glacier before returning; don't skip the short spur to Falls Overlook, a scenic cascade off the upper trail. Both trails make for a short hike, not much more than a mile in length; you can return along the half-mile **nature trail** through cottonwood forest, alder thickets and old glacial moraines before emerging at the ranger station. Note how the land becomes more vegetated the farther you get from the ice – the result of having had more time to recover from its glacial scouring.

Despite all the warning signs, some folks still cozy up to the face of the crackling, calving glacier for photos. Please note that this glacier has removed such people from the gene pool before, by dropping large chunks of ice on their heads. It's a great spot to explain global warming *and* natural selection to the kids.

KENAI PENINSULA

Today you can rediscover it via a steep, roughly cut and sometimes slippery ascent to 3500ft; for reasonably fit trekkers, that's a good three- or four-hour trip. Beware of bears; they're common here.

The trek is well worth it for those with the stamina, as it provides spectacular views of not only the ice field but of Exit Glacier and the valley below. The upper section of the route is snow-covered for much of the year; bring a jacket and watch for crevasses, which may be hidden under a thin and unstable bridge of snow. Camping up here is a great idea, but the free, cozy public-use cabin at the top is for emergencies only.

Resurrection River Trail

This 16-mile trail accesses a 72-mile trail system connecting Seward and Hope. This continuous trail is broken only by the Sterling Hwy and provides a wonderful wilderness adventure through a diversity of streams, rivers, lakes, wooded lowlands and alpine areas. It's difficult and expensive to maintain, so expect natural hassles like downed trees, boggy patches and washed-out sections, especially in spring. **Resurrection River Cabin** (p239) is 5½ miles from the trailhead.

The southern trailhead is at Mile 8 of Exit Glacier Rd. The northern trailhead joins the Russian Lakes Trail (p69) 5 miles from Cooper Lake or 16 miles from the Russian River Campground off the Sterling Hwy. The hike from the Seward Hwy to the Sterling Hwy is a 40-mile trip, including Exit Glacier.

PADDLING

Bluewater paddles out of Resurrection Bay along the coastline of the park are for experienced kayakers only; others should invest in a costly drop-off service. You'll be rewarded, however, with wildlife encounters and close-up views of the glaciers from a unique perspective. Most companies can arrange drop-off and pickup; it's about $250 for the round-trip to Aialik Bay and $275 to $300 for the more remote Northwestern Lagoon.

Kayak Adventures Worldwide (☎ 224-3960; www.kayakak.com) is a highly respected, eco-oriented operation that rents kayaks ($40 to $75 per day), guides half- and full-day trips ($59 to $99), and can arrange multiday adventures.

Sunny Cove Sea Kayaking (☎ 224-8810, 800-770-9119; www.sunnycove.com) doesn't rent kayaks, but does arrange a multitude of different trips, including $59 three-hour paddles in Resurrection Bay, $325 full-day journeys in Aialik Bay, and $149 excursions that combine a half-day of paddling with a salmon-bake lunch on Fox Island and a Kenai Fjords cruise.

Miller's Landing (☎ 224-5739, 866-541-5739; www.millerslandingak.com) rents kayaks (single/double $42/52) and equipment, and also provides a water-taxi service as far as Northwestern Fjord.

Weather Permitting Water-taxi (☎ 224-6595; www.watertaxiak.com) and **Alaska Saltwater Lodge** (☎ 224-5271; www.alaskasaltwaterlodge.com) provide pickup and drop-off service throughout the park.

Aialik Bay

This is the more popular arm for kayakers. Many people hire water-taxis to drop them near Aialik Glacier, then take three or four days to paddle south past Pedersen Glacier and into Holgate Arm, where they're picked up. The high point of the trip is Holgate Glacier, an active tidewater glacier that's the main feature of all the boat tours.

Northwestern Lagoon

This fjord is more expensive to reach but much more isolated, with not nearly as many tour boats. The wildlife is excellent, especially the seabirds and sea otters, and more than a half-dozen glaciers can be seen. Plan on three to four days if you're being dropped inside the lagoon.

Tours

The easiest and most popular way to view the park's dramatic fjords, glaciers and abundant wildlife is from a cruise ship. Several companies offer the same basic tours: wildlife cruises (three to five hours) take in Resurrection Bay without really entering the park. Don't bother. Much better tours (eight to 10 hours) explore Holgate Arm or Northwestern Fjord. Some offer a buffet lunch on beautiful Fox Island, which basically means spending an hour picking at trays of overcooked salmon when you could instead be whale watching. Eat on the boat.

With an office base at the small-boat harbor, **Kenai Fjords Tours** (☎ 224-8608, 800-478-3346;

www.kenaifjords.com) goes the furthest into the park (Northwestern Fjord; per adult/child $149/75) and offers the widest variety of options, including an overnight on Fox Island (per person $329). It also does package deals that include rail travel from Anchorage.

Although it has fewer options, **Major Marine Tours** (☎ 224-8030; 800-764-7300; www.majormarine.com) is cheaper and includes a national park ranger on every boat. It has a half-day Resurrection Bay tour (per adult/child $69/34) and a full day viewing Holgate Arm ($122/61). The latter tour is a local favorite.

Owned by Kenai Fjords Tours, **Mariah Tours** (☎ 800-478-8068; www.kenaifjords.com) runs smaller vessels, carries fewer passengers and offers more intimate tours, which are often adapted to the interests of the group. Its full-day outings into the park are per adult/child $145/73.

For flightseeing trips, contact **Scenic Mountain Air** (☎ 224-9152; www.scenicmountainair.com), at Seward airport, which flies over the fjords. Prices start at $139 for 45 minutes and rise to $219 for 1½ hours.

Sleeping

Exit Glacier Campground (Exit Glacier Rd; sites free). Located nine miles from Seward, this is the only formal campground in the park. It has great wilderness sites for tents only and a bearproof food-storage area. If it's full, lots of folks camp free along the rocky river bed paralleling Exit Glacier Rd – bring a mat.

Public-use cabins (☎ 224-3175; www.nps.gov/aplic /cabins/nps_cabins.html; cabins $50) There are three cabins along the fjords, in addition to countless other informal campsites that line the kayak-accessible beaches of Aialik Bay and Northwestern Lagoon. Aialik Cabin is on a beach perfect for hiking, beachcombing and whale watching; Holgate Arm Cabin has a spectacular view of Holgate Glacier; and North Arm is actually much closer to Homer. You'll want to reserve these well in advance through the **Alaska Public Lands Information Center** (☎ 271-2742).

Getting There & Around

To reach the coastal fjords, you'll need to take a tour (opposite) or a water-taxi (opposite).

Getting to Exit Glacier is a bit easier. If you don't have a car, **Exit Glacier Guides** (☎ 224-5569) runs an hourly shuttle to the glacier

between 9:30am and 5pm. The van departs from the Holiday Inn Express at the small-boat harbor and costs $8 round-trip. Otherwise, there are cabs: **Glacier Taxi** (☎ 224-6678) charges $50 for as many people as you can squeeze in.

STERLING HIGHWAY

At **Tern Lake Junction** (Mile 37 Seward Hwy), the paved Sterling Hwy turns off from the Seward Hwy, heading westward through the forests and mountains to Soldotna and then bending south along Cook Inlet toward Homer.

TERN LAKE JUNCTION TO COOPER LANDING

From Tern Lake Junction it's only 58 miles to Soldotna, not much more than an hour's drive. Yet this stretch contains so many hiking, camping and canoeing opportunities that it would take you a month to enjoy them all. Surrounded by the Chugach National Forest and Kenai National Wildlife Refuge, the Sterling Hwy and its side roads pass a dozen trails, 20 campgrounds and an almost endless number of lakes, rivers and streams. Mileposts along the highway show distances from Seward, making Tern Lake Junction, at Mile 37, the starting point of the Sterling Hwy.

This is one of Alaska's top playgrounds, and summer crowds (both Alaskans and tourists) can be crushing at times. Be prepared, during July and August, to stop at a handful of campgrounds before finding an available site.

For good, basic rooms, there's **Sunrise Inn & Café** (☎ 595-1222; Mile 45 Sterling Hwy; r summer $99-125, RV sites $20; gourmet grub $8-15; ☺ 7am-10pm), which also has RV spaces but no campsites. It's a grand place to stop for affordable and outstanding dishes like the vegetarian 4:20 Love Burger or the Hippie Girl breakfast. Beware, however, the Pig Vomit Omelet.

Just past Sunrise Inn, **Quartz Creek Campground** (Mile 0.3 Quartz Creek Rd; sites $13) on the shores of Kenai Lake is crazily popular with RVs and fishers during salmon runs. The campground is so developed that the sites are paved. Tenters may want to continue 3 miles more down Quartz Creek Rd to the USFS **Crescent Creek Campground** (sites $10), which is a little prettier and much more secluded.

The **Crescent Creek Trail**, about half a mile beyond the Crescent Creek Campground, leads 6½ miles to the outlet of Crescent Lake and the USFS's **Crescent Saddle Cabin** (☎ 877-444-6777; www.reserveusa.com; $45). It's an easy walk or bike ride and has spectacular autumn colors in September. Anglers can fish for arctic grayling in the lake during the summer. The **Carter Lake Trail** connects the east end of the lake to the Seward Hwy, with a rough path along the south side of the lake between the two trails.

COOPER LANDING & AROUND
☎ 907/pop 351

After skirting the north end of Kenai Lake, you enter scenic Cooper Landing at Mile 48.4. The picturesque outpost, named for Joseph Cooper, a miner who worked the area in the 1880s, is best known for its rich and brutal combat salmon fishing along the Russian and Kenai Rivers (see the boxed text p248). While rustic log-cabin lodges featuring giant fish freezers are still the lifeblood of this town, the trails and whitewater rafting opportunities attract a very different sort of tourist. Businesses plying fine dining, chakra alignment and other organic amusements are finding fertile ground among the towering mountains.

Orientation & Information
Cooper Landing is largely strung along the Sterling Hwy where the Kenai River flows from Kenai Lake. A few places are on Bean Creek Rd north of the river while others are down Snug Harbor Rd beside the lake.

Cooper Landing Library (☎ 595-1241; Bean Creek Rd; ☉ 1-4pm Mon-Sat; 🖳) Close to Mile 47.7 Sterling Hwy; offers free Internet access after you purchase a $5 library card.

Emergency (Ambulance, Fire, Police ☎ 911)

Wildman's (☎ 595-1456, 866-595-1456; www .wildmans.org; Mile 47.5 Sterling Hwy; ☉ 8am-10pm Mon-Thu, to midnight Fri-Sun) Your basic backcountry superstore, with snacks, booze, espresso beverages, an ATM, laundry and showers ($4).

Sights & Activities
K'BEQ INTERPRETIVE SITE
This riverfront **site** (☎ 283-3633; Mile 52.6 Sterling Hwy; tours self-guided/guided $3/5; ☉ 11am-7pm), run by the local Kenaitzie tribe, is a refreshing

reminder of what this area was like before the flood of sportfishermen. A quarter-mile boardwalk winds past an ancient house pit and other archaeological relics, while interpretive panels address berry-picking, steam bath–building and more traditional methods of catching fish on the Kenai.

HIKING
Cooper Landing is the starting point for two of the Kenai Peninsula's loveliest multiday trails: the 39-mile **Resurrection Pass Trail** (p69) to Hope; and the 21-mile **Russian Lakes Trail** p69), a favorite of fishers and families.

OTHER ACTIVITIES
Alaska River Adventures (☎ 595-2000, 888-836-9027; www.alaskariveradventures.com; Mile 47.9 Sterling Hwy) Runs scenic three-hour floats on the Kenai (per person $49) and four-to-five hour excursions that combine horseback riding and rafting ($169).

Alaska Rivers Company (☎ 595-1226; www.alaska riverscompany.com; Mile 49.9 Sterling Hwy) Runs guided raft trips down the Kenai River (per half/full day $49/108), with the longer trip bumping over some Class III rapids.

Kenai Lake Sea Kayak Adventures (☎ 595-3441; www.kenailake.com; Mile 0.3 Quartz Creek Rd) Its guided three-hour sea-kayak trips on Kenai Lake are a good introduction to paddling, in a stunning setting to boot. It also rents mountain bikes (half/full day $25/35) and leads four-hour bike tours to Crescent Lake ($65).

Alaska Horseman Trail Adventures (☎ 595-1806; www.alaskahorsemen.com; Mile 45 Sterling Hwy) Based behind the Sunrise Inn; it offers horseback rides along Quartz and Crescent Creeks (per half/full day $130/175) and pricier guided overnight trips.

FISHING
Cooper Landing is littered with fishing-guide operations, so you'll have no trouble finding someone to set you up with a rod and reel, take you out in a boat and help you catch your dinner. Most of the fishing on the Upper Kenai is for rainbow trout, Dolly Vardens, and silver and sockeye salmon. Expect to pay at least $150 for a half-day on the water and more than $200 for a full day. Fishing trips are run by numerous companies including the following:
Alaska River Adventures (☎ 595-2000, 888-836-9027; www.alaskariveradventures.com; Mile 47.9 Sterling Hwy),

Alaska Rivers Company (☎ 595-1226; www.alaska riverscompany.com; Mile 49.9 Sterling Hwy)

Gwin's Lodge (☎ 595-1266; www.gwinslodge.com; Mile 52 Sterling Hwy; cabins & chalets $99-159)

Sleeping

Cooper Creek Campground (Mile 50.7 Sterling Hwy; sites $10) This campground has 29 sites, including some right on the Kenai River. Good luck hooking one of those.

Russian River Campground (Mile 52.6 Sterling Hwy; s/d sites $13/20) Located where the Russian and Kenai Rivers merge, this place is beautiful and incredibly popular when red salmon are spawning. It costs $6 just to park there.

Hutch B&B (☎ 595-1270; www.arctic.net/~hutch; Mile 48.5 Sterling Hwy; r incl breakfast $70-99) In a three-story, balcony-ringed lodge, the Hutch's big, simple, clean rooms are the best deal in town.

Alaskan Sourdough B&B (☎ 595-1541; www .alaskansourdoughbb.com; r incl breakfast $120) A lovely B&B that serves pancakes made with a century-old sourdough starter. It also has a wedding chapel where you can make it official with the sweetheart you met on the trail; traditional Yup'ik and standard Christian ceremonies are available.

Gwin's Lodge (☎ 595-1266; www.gwinslodge .com; Mile 52 Sterling Hwy; cabins & chalets $99-159) This classic 1952 log-cabin lodge is a fish-frenzied madhouse when the sockeyes are running. It's got a 24-hour restaurant and a round-the-clock grocery store that books everything from fishing charters to flight-seeing. It's a landmark.

Kenai Princess Lodge (☎ 595-1425, 800-426-0500; www.princess.com; Mile 2 Bean Creek Rd; d $159-299, RV sites $30) This swish Princess Cruises resort is set on a high bluff above the river. The standard rooms are sweet, but spring for a deluxe for the best views.

Eating

Cooper Landing Grocery (☎ 595-1677; Mile 48.2 Sterling Hwy; ☼ 9am-10pm) Has scads of snacks and souvenirs.

Gwin's Lodge (☎ 595-1266; Mile 52 Sterling Hwy; breakfast $5-13, lunches $7-13, dinners $17-25) In addition to other hearty American fare, this jam-packed place serves salmon omelets, salmon chowder, salmon salad, grilled salmon – even salmon-stuffed halibut.

Eagle Crest Restaurant (breakfast & lunch $7-11, dinner $15-30; ☼ 5:30am-10pm) Located at Kenai Princess Lodge, this is rustic-chic and perhaps overpriced.

Getting There & Around

If you're without wheels, your best option for reaching Cooper Landing is **Homer Stage Line** (☎ 868-3914; www.homerstageline.com), which runs daily buses through here from both Anchorage and Homer. From either end, it's $40 per person one way.

KENAI NATIONAL WILDLIFE REFUGE

Once west of the Resurrection Pass trailhead, you enter the Kenai National Wildlife Refuge, managed by the US Fish & Wildlife Service. Impressive populations of Dall sheep, moose, caribou and bear here have attracted hunters from around the world since the early 1900s. In 1941 President Roosevelt set aside 1.73 million acres as the Kenai National Moose Range. The 1980 Alaska Lands Act increased that acreage to almost 2 million and adopted the current name for the refuge.

The **Russian River Ferry** (Mile 55 Sterling Hwy; adult/child $8/4), west of the confluence of the Kenai and Russian Rivers, transports more than 30,000 anglers across the water every summer to some of the finest fishing anywhere. Whether you want to stop for the day or stay overnight in the ferry parking area, it's $9 for cars or tents, $13 for RVs.

The 3-mile **Fuller Lakes Trail** (Mile 57 of the Sterling Hwy) leads to Fuller Lake just above the tree line. The well-marked trail begins with a rapid ascent to Lower Fuller Lake, where you cross a stream over a beaver dam and continue over a low pass to Upper Fuller Lake. At the lake, the trail follows the east shore and then branches; the fork to the left leads up a ridge and becomes a route to the **Skyline Trail**. This route is not maintained and is unmarked above the bush line. It follows a ridge for 6½ miles and descends via the Skyline Trail to Mile 61 of the Sterling Hwy. Those who want to hike both trails should plan to stay overnight at Upper Fuller Lake, where there are several good campsites.

The **Kenai National Wildlife Refuge Visitor Contact Station** (Mile 58 Sterling Hwy; ☼ 10am-4pm), near the junction of Skilak Lake Rd, has up-to-date information on camping, hiking, canoeing and fishing throughout the refuge.

KENAI PENINSULA

COMBAT FISHING

In a place that's all about getting back to nature, there are few sights more unnatural than what happens each summer wherever Alaska's best salmon rivers meet a busy road. When the fish are running, the banks become a human frenzy – a ceaseless string of men, women and children hip-to-hip, hundreds of fishing rods whipping to and fro, the air filled with curses and cries of joy, the waters rippling with dozens of fish dancing on taut and sometimes tangled lines. The banks are a jumble of coolers and tackle boxes and catches-of-the-day. Rub your eyes all you want: the scene is for real. This is combat fishing.

Though combat fishing occurs several places in the state – including on Ship Creek, practically in downtown Anchorage – it reaches its bloody nadir on the Kenai River, and particularly at the spot where the Kenai is joined by the Russian River. There, red (aka sockeye) salmon, averaging six pounds or so, run close to the banks, often congregating in such great numbers that even amid hundreds of anglers, your chances of snagging a fish or two are pretty good.

As with any form of combat, there are subtle rules that guide the chaos. Among them: don't wade out in front of other fishermen, or snap up their spot on the bank if they briefly step away. (On the other hand, don't let the glares of the earlier arrivals dissuade you from taking your proper place in the fray.) Inasmuch as possible, try to give your neighbor space – and whatever you do, don't foul your line with theirs. Most importantly, if you get a bite, shout 'fish on!' so others can reel in their lines and give you room to wrestle your catch. And while you may be tempted to milk the moment for all it's worth, try to get your trophy to shore as quickly as possible. In combat fishing, you don't 'play' a fish, you land it fast, so others can rejoin the fight.

Don't be dissuaded by the term 'combat' fishing. Most of the anglers are tolerant and even supportive of fellow fishermen – indeed, many are there for the camaraderie, taking as much joy in being part of the melee as in landing a fish of their own. If going into battle still doesn't appeal, take heart – the combat zone is usually limited to within a few hundred yards of the closest road. Hike half a mile upriver, and you'll likely have all the fish to yourself.

Skilak Lake Road makes a scenic 19-mile loop off the Sterling Hwy, and provides access to an assortment of popular recreational opportunities. There are five campgrounds along the road. Some, like Hidden Lake and Upper Skilak, cost $10 a night for a vehicle and $5 for a walk-in site, while others are free. All these campgrounds are well marked and, from east to west, are as follows:

Campground	Sites	Location
Hidden Lake	44	Mile 3.6
Upper Skilak Lake	25	Mile 8.4
Lower Ohmer Lake	3	Mile 8.6
Engineer Lake	4	Mile 9.7
Lower Skilak Lake	14	Mile 14.0

The eastern entrance to the **Kenai River Trail** begins at Mile 0.6 of Skilak Lake Rd. A half-mile down this trail are wonderful views of the Kenai River Canyon.

The **Skilak Lookout Trail** starts at Mile 5.5 of Skilak Lake Rd and ascends 2.6 miles to a knob (elevation 1450ft) that has a panoramic view of the mountains and lakes. Plan on four to five hours for the round-trip.

The **Seven Lakes Trail**, a 4.4-mile hike to the Sterling Hwy, begins at Engineer Lake. The trail is easy walking over level terrain and passes Hidden and Hikers Lakes before ending at Kelly Lake Campground on a side road off the Sterling Hwy.

If you choose to stay on the Sterling Hwy past the Skilak Lake Rd junction, a side road at Mile 69 leads south to the **Peterson Lake Campground** (sites free) and **Kelly Lake Campground** (sites free), near one end of the Seven Lakes Trail. **Watson Lake Campground** (Mile 71.3 Sterling Hwy; sites free) has 3 sites. Four miles farther down the highway is the west junction with Skilak Lake Rd.

At Mile 81, the Sterling Hwy divides into a four-lane road, and you soon arrive in the small town of **Sterling** (pop 1800), where the Moose River empties into the Kenai. Sterling meets the usual travelers' needs, with restaurants, lodges, gas stations and small grocery stores.

It also has a hostel of sorts: **Jana House** (☎ 260-4151; Swanson River Rd; campsites/RV sites/dm

$7/12/22), in a vast, renovated schoolhouse. This is by no means an international backpackers hostel, but it does provide clean, affordable bunks for fishermen looking to sleep on the cheap.

Izaak Walton Recreation Site (Mile 82 Sterling Hwy; sites $13), at the confluence of the Kenai and Moose Rivers, is popular among anglers during the salmon runs and with paddlers ending their Swan Lake Route canoe trip at the Moose River Bridge (p82).

Swanson River Road, at Mile 85 of the Sterling Hwy, heads north for 18 miles, with Swan Lake Rd heading east for 12 miles at the end of Swanson River Rd. The roads offer access to the Swanson River and Swan Lake canoe routes and three campgrounds: **Dolly Varden Lake Campground** (Mile 14 Swanson River Rd; sites free), **Rainbow Lake Campground** (Mile 16 Swanson River Rd; sites free); and **Swanson River Campground** (sites free), at the very end of the road. Even without a canoe, you'll enjoy a day or two exploring the trails that connect prized fishing holes.

Across the Sterling Hwy from Swanson River Rd is the entrance to Scout Lake Rd, where you'll find the **Scout Lake Campground** (sites $10) and **Morgans Landing State Recreation Area** (sites $13). This is a particularly scenic area on the bluffs overlooking the Kenai River, a 3½-mile drive from the Sterling Hwy. The **Alaska Division of Parks office** (☎ 262-5581; ☼ 8am-5pm Mon-Fri) for the Kenai Peninsula offers information on both Kachemak Bay State Park to the south and Caines Head State Recreation Area in Seward.

CITY OF KENAI & AROUND
☎ 907/pop 6809

At first blush, Kenai is a sorry sight – an object lesson in poor city planning. It's not convenient or especially picturesque, existing primarily as a support community for the drilling operations at Cook Inlet. It's long been a rare bird: a major Alaskan city with minimal tourism. Lately, though, this faded boomtown has taken some hesitant steps toward wooing visitors – especially those tantalized by the excellent salmon fishing at the mouth of the Kenai River.

This wealth of sustenance has made Kenai one of the oldest continuously inhabited European settlements in Alaska. When Russian fur traders arrived here in 1791, they built their 300-strong colony next to the Dena'ina Indian village of Skitok. With statehood, US troops established a fort at the strategically important site.

The first Russian Orthodox Church on mainland Alaska today presides over a replica of the 1867 fort, which hasn't fully realize its potential as adorable tourist magnet. And then there's the view: Mt Redoubt (the volcano that erupted steam and ash in December 1989) to the southwest, Mt Iliamna at the head of the Aleutian Range and the Alaska Range to the northwest. Nice.

North of town, around Mile 19 of the Kenai Spur Hwy, is Alaska's largest concentration of oil infrastructure outside Prudhoe Bay. Signs prohibit parking along the industrialized strip, but perhaps the site of 15 oil platforms pumping out the highest-quality crude oil in Alaska is best appreciated while your car's burning the very product they work so hard to extract.

Orientation & Information

Located on the busy Kenai Spur Hwy, the city of Kenai is about 10 miles northwest of Soldotna – though with urban sprawl, the two towns almost merge. In Kenai, the highway itself is the main drag, lined with strip malls and franchise stores. The area of interest to visitors is accessed by turning south off the highway onto Main St, which runs past the visitors center to scenic and historic 'Old Town' above the waterfront.

Alaska USA Bank (☎ 800-525-9094; 10576 Kenai Spur Hwy; ☼ 10am-7pm Mon-Fri, noon-4pm Sat) Located inside Carrs Supermarket.

Central Peninsula General Hospital (☎ 262-4404; Marydale Dr) Is just west of the Kenai Spur Hwy.

Kenai Community Library (☎ 283-4378; 163 Main St Loop; ☼ 10am-8pm Mon-Thu, to 5pm Fri & Sat, noon-5pm Sun; ▢) Has free Internet access.

Kenai Visitors & Cultural Center (☎ 283-1991; www .visitkenai.com; ☼ 9am-7pm Mon-Fri, 10am-6pm Sat & Sun) Has all the usual pamphlets and can get last-minute rooms at area B&Bs. The impressive center, built in 1991 to mark the city's 200th anniversary, has a museum (below).

Police (☎ 911, 283-7879)

Post office (Caviar St) Just north of the Kenai Spur Hwy.

Wash-n-Dry (☎ 283-8473; 502 Lake St; ☼ 8am-10pm) Has a laundry and showers ($4.20).

Sights & Activities
KENAI VISITORS & CULTURAL CENTER

In a town without much of a visitor industry, this excellent **visitors center** (☎ 283-1991;

www.visitkenai.com; adult/child $3/free; ☺ 9am-7pm Mon-Fri, 10am-6pm Sat & Sun) is itself among the main attractions. The museum features historical exhibits on the city's Russian heritage, offshore drilling and a room full of stuffed wildlife staring down from the rafters. It also has quality Alaska Native art from around the state. Free movies about the city's strange history are screened, and docents offer free guided tours and classes throughout the summer.

OLD TOWN KENAI
From the visitors center, follow Overland Ave west to what locals refer to as 'Old Town' – an odd amalgam of historic structures and low-rent apartments, all stupendously situated high above the mouth of the Kenai River. You can pick up a free *Walking Tour* pamphlet at the visitors center. Near Cook Inlet, the US military established **Fort Kenay** in 1867 and stationed more than 100 men here. What stands today is a replica constructed as part of the Alaska Centennial in 1967. It's not open to the public.

Across Mission St from the fort is the ornate **Russian Orthodox Church** (☎ 283-4122; ☺ 11am-4pm Mon-Fri), a white-clapboard structure topped with baby blue onion domes. Built in 1895, it's the oldest Orthodox church on mainland Alaska. West of the church overlooking the water is **St Nicholas Chapel**, built in 1906 on the burial site of Father Igumen Nicolai, Kenai's first resident priest.

Head southeast on Mission St, and you'll be traveling along the **Bluff**, a good vantage point to view the mouth of the Kenai River or the mountainous terrain on the west side of Cook Inlet. In the late spring and early summer you can often see beluga as they ride the incoming tides into the Kenai River to feed on salmon.

KENAI BEACH
Down below the bluffs is an oddity in Alaska: a sweeping, sandy beach, ideal for picnicking, Frisbee-chucking and other waterfront fun. There are stellar views of the volcanoes across the inlet, and from July 10 to 31 you can watch hundreds of frantic fishermen dip-net for sockeye salmon at the mouth of the Kenai River. (Sadly, unless you've lived in Alaska for the past year, you can't participate.) The beach can be reached by taking Spruce Dr off Mile 12 of the Kenai Spur Hwy.

STEVENS CENTER FOR TECHNOLOGY
Better known as the **Challenger Center** (☎ 283-2000; www.akchallenger.org; 9711 Kenai Spur Hwy), this flight-simulation facility is refreshingly free of moose heads and mining relics. There are free tours at 11am Monday, Wednesday and Friday, and if you can round up at least 14 people, you can pre-arrange a 'mission,' where in a room packed with old NASA equipment you'll prepare a virtual shuttle for launch, then dock it at the International Space Station ($30). It's a popular synergy-training course for local businesses.

CAPTAIN COOK STATE RECREATION AREA
By following the Kenai Spur Hwy north for 36 miles, you'll first pass the trailer parks and chemical plants of the North Kenai industrial district to this uncrowded state recreation area that encompasses 4000 acres of forests, lakes, rivers and beaches along Cook Inlet. The area offers swimming, camping and the beauty of the inlet in a setting that is unaffected by the stampede for salmon to the south.

The Kenai Spur Hwy ends in the park after first passing Stormy Lake, where you'll find a bathhouse and a swimming area along the water's edge. **Discovery Campground** (sites $10) has 53 sites on the bluff overlooking Cook Inlet, where some of the world's greatest tides ebb and flow. The fishing in Swanson River is great, and this is a fine place to end the Swanson River canoe route (p82).

Sleeping
Finding a last-minute room during summer's king salmon runs can be more challenging than hauling in a 70-pounder, but log onto **Kenai Peninsula B&B Association** (www.kenaipeninsulabba.com) and it'll see what it can do. If you're on a tight budget, head north along the Kenai Spur Hwy, where several motels cater to oil workers and offer lower rates. Kenai adds 10% in bed-and-sales tax to lodging.

Beluga Lookout RV Park (☎ 283-5999; 929 Mission St) This is basically a parking lot with a great view and a gift shop, as well as laundry and showers. During the mid-to-late-July dip-netting season, sites are $35 to $40; the rest of the summer they're just $20.

Harborside Cottages B&B (☎ 283-6162, 888-283-6162; www.harborsidecottages.com; cnr Main St & Riverview Ave; cottage $135-160) This place has five small-but-immaculate bluffside cottages, each equipped with kitchenettes. The views here are spectacular.

Uptown Motel (☎ 283-3660; www.uptownmotel .com; 47 Spur View Dr; r $140-170) Well located, and the big rooms have kitchenettes.

Eating & Drinking

Veronica's Coffee House (☎ 283-2725; 604 Peterson Way; light meals $3-8; ☺ 9am-8pm Mon-Wed, to 9:30pm Thu-Sat, 11am-4pm Sun) In an Old Town log building dating from 1918; serves espressos and healthy sandwiches and hosts open mics, folk jams and live bands.

Little Ski-Mo's Burger-N-Brew (☎ 283-4463; 11504 Kenai Spur Hwy; fast food $6-8; ☺ 11am-11pm Mon-Sat, to 10pm Sun) Across from the visitors center, this is a popular All-American hangout with baseball on the tube and every type of burger known to man.

Ohana's (☎ 283-6292; Mile 16.5 Kenai Spur Hwy; breakfast $5-11, other meals $7-18; ☺ 6am-9pm Mon-Sat, to 3pm Sun) Run by Hawaiian expats, this log-cabin diner north of town has boffo breakfasts and a few island specialties, like a teriyaki burger with ham and pineapple.

Paradisos Restaurant (☎ 283-2222; 11397 Kenai Spur Hwy; dinner $13-35; ☺ 11am-11pm Sun-Fri, to midnight Sat) If you're tired of seafood, head to this longtime favorite for Italian, Greek and Mexican dishes.

Louie's Restaurant (☎ 283-3660; 47 Spur View Dr; dinner $19-29; ☺ 5am-10pm) Under stuffed moose and elk heads in the Uptown Motel, Louie's serves the best surf-and-turf in the city.

Safeway (☎ 283-6360; 10576 Kenai Spur Hwy; ☺ 24hr) Offers the usual groceries, plus it has a deli and salad bar.

Getting There & Around

AIR

Kenai has the main airport on the peninsula and is served by **ERA Aviation** (☎ 283-3168, 800-866-8394; www.flyera.com), which offers 17 daily flights between Anchorage and Kenai. The round-trip fare costs $190.

BICYCLE

Bikes can be rented from **Beluga Lookout RV Park** (☎ 283-5999; www.belugalookout.com; 929 Mission St; per hr/day $5/20), up on the bluffs.

BUS

The **Homer Stage Line** (☎ 868-3914; www.homer stageline.com) makes daily trips from Kenai to Anchorage, Seward and Homer.

TAXI

Alaska Cabs (☎ 283-6000) serves Kenai and Soldotna.

SOLDOTNA

☎ 907/pop 3767

Soldotna, at the junction of the Sterling and Kenai Spur Hwys, would be just another ugly, overcommercialized roadside-service center, interchangeable with a zillion other American towns, save for one fact: a river runs through it, filled to bursting with the biggest salmon on the planet. Indeed, the world's largest sport-caught king salmon was reeled in right here – a 97.2lb behemoth, hooked by local resident Les Anderson in 1985. Biologists believe genetics and the fact that Kenai River salmon often spend an extra year at sea account for their gargantuan size. A trophy salmon elsewhere in Alaska is a 50lb fish, while here, anglers don't get too excited until a king salmon tops 75lbs. Most experts agree it's only a matter of time before the first 100lb king is landed. Until that day, and probably long after it, fast-growing Soldotna will be the most fish-crazy place in Alaska.

Orientation & Information

Situated where the Sterling Hwy crosses the Kenai River, Soldotna sprawls in every direction, including practically to the city of Kenai, some 12 miles northwest along the Kenai Spur Hwy. The intersection of the Spur Hwy and the Sterling Hwy is referred to as the 'Y.'

Central Peninsula General Hospital (☎ 262-4404; Marydale Dr) Is just west of the Kenai Spur Hwy.

Emergency (ambulance, fire, police ☎ 911)

Joyce Carver Memorial Library (☎ 262-4227; 235 S Binkley St; ☺ 9am-8pm Mon-Thu, noon-6pm Fri, from 9am Sat; ☐) Near the post office; has free Internet access.

Post office (175 S Binkley St) Just west of the Kenai Spur Hwy and north of the Soldotna 'Y.'

Soldotna Chamber of Commerce & Visitors Center (☎ 262-2139; www.soldotnachamber.com; ☺ 9am-7pm; per 20 min $5; ☐) Has Internet plus up-to-date fishing reports and can find last-minute rooms in town.

Wash & Dry (☎ 262-8495; 1221 Smith Way; ☺ 24hr summer) Near the intersection of the Kenai Spur and Sterling Hwys at the Soldotna 'Y'; has showers ($4.50) and laundry.

Wells Fargo (☎ 262-4435; 44552 Sterling Hwy) Has cash and an eclectic collection of historical exhibits.

Sights & Activities

SOLDOTNA HOMESTEAD MUSEUM

This **museum** (☎ 262-3832; entry by donation; ⏰ 10am-4pm Tue-Sat, from noon Sun) includes a wonderful collection of homesteaders' cabins spread through six wooded acres in Centennial Park. There's also a one-room schoolhouse (that probably looks a lot more fun than the school you went to), a torture-chamber collection of early dental tools and a replica of the $7.2-million check the US paid Russia for Alaska.

KENAI NATIONAL WILDLIFE REFUGE HEADQUARTERS

Opposite Kalifornsky Beach Rd near the Kenai River is the junction with Funny River Rd. Turn left (east) here and turn right (south) immediately onto Ski Hill Rd, following it for a mile to reach this excellent **information center** (☎ 262-7021; admission free; ⏰ 8am-5pm Mon-Fri, from 9am Sat & Sun). It features displays on the lifecycles of salmon, daily slide shows and wildlife films in its theater, and naturalist-led outdoor programs on the weekends. Three short trails begin at the visitors center and wind into the nearby woods or to a viewing platform on Head-quarters Lake. Ask for a map.

FISHING

From mid-May through September, runs of red, silver and king salmon make the lower Kenai River among the hottest sport-fishing spots in Alaska. If you're green to the scene but want to wet a line, first drop by the visitors center where staff members will assist you in determining where to fish and what to fish for. They can also hook you up with a guide, who'll charge you up to $250 a day but vastly improve your chances of catching dinner – and of not violating the river's fairly Kafkaesque regulations. Rather go it alone? From the shore, you've still got a shot at catching reds (from mid-July to early August) and silvers (late July through August). Try casting from the 'fishwalk' below the visitors center, or from city campgrounds (right). If you don't have your own rod, you can pick up inexpensive gear from **Trustworthy Hardware** (☎ 262-4655; 44370 Sterling Hwy; ⏰ 8am-8pm Mon-Fri, 9am-6pm Sat, from 10am Sun), located right across the highway from Sal's Klond-ike Diner.

Sleeping

Spending the night in Soldotna is a catch-22: outside fishing season there's no reason to stay here; in season, there's nowhere to stay – just about every campsite and room is taken. What's left will cost you dearly. Make reservations. The chamber of commerce can locate last-minute rooms, or call **Accommodations on the Kenai** (☎ 262-2139), a referral service for area B&Bs, lodges and fish camps. The **Kenai Peninsula B&B Association** (www.kenaipeninsulabba.com) has listings for the entire peninsula.

BUDGET

Centennial Park Campground (☎ 262-5299; www.ci.soldotna.ak.us; cnr Sterling Hwy & Kalifornsky Beach Rd; sites $13) Maintained by the city, this camp-ground has boardwalked fishing access to the Kenai River.

Swiftwater Park Campground (☎ 262-5299; www.ci.soldotna.ak.us; cnr E Redoubt Ave & Rinehardt; sites $11.35) Also run by the city; it doesn't have a boardwalk but is still a good place for pulling in prized salmon.

Diamond M Ranch (☎ 283-5227, 866-283-9424; www.diamondmranch.com; Mile 16.5 Kalifornsky Beach Rd; campsites $20-25, RV sites $25-30, s/d $75/80, cabin $55-99) A decade ago, this was just the Martin family farm – but with fishermen constantly asking to camp in their field, they converted it to a tourist megaplex. Nowadays, cows and llamas share space with an extensive campground, cabins and full B&B.

MIDRANGE & TOP END

Riverside House (☎ 262-0500; 877-262-0500; www.riverside-house.com; 44611 Sterling Hwy; r Jul $135-150, r Aug-Jun $80-100, RV sites $15) Never mind the unappealing exterior, this place has big and perfectly tolerable rooms, some of which overlook the river. RVs can park here, but tents aren't allowed.

Kenai River Lodge (☎ 262-4292; www.kenairiverlodge.com; 393 Riverside Dr; r $89-140) Smells like cedar and seems like a winner, and there's a private fishing hole right outside.

Hooligan's Lodge (☎ 262-9951; 44715 Sterling Hwy; r $125) This is a lot to pay for a ho-hum motel room, but if you roll into town without reservations it may be one of the few places available.

Duck Inn (☎ 262-1849; 43187 Kalifornsky Beach Rd; r $70-80) Located 3½ miles out on K-Beach Rd, this inn is a good deal – but don't piss off the bikers drinking in the bar.

Soldotna B&B Lodge (☎ 262-4779; www.soldotna lodge.com; 399 Lovers Lane; r $99-357) This is the luxury place, drawing blue-chip anglers and honeymooners. It has plush rooms, custom fishing charters and rooms with kitchenettes and some shared baths. There's breakfast and a private fishing hole for reds.

Eating & Drinking

Sal's Klondike Diner (☎ 262-2220; 44619 Sterling Hwy; breakfast & lunch $5-9, dinner $9-14; ⏰ 24hr) Being Soldotna's best stab at a tourist trap, this fun diner is jammed with weary travelers, gabbing locals and frantic waitresses. The meals are both good and ample.

Moose is Loose (☎ 760-7861; 44278 Sterling Hwy; snacks $2-7; ⏰ 4:30am-6pm Tue-Sun) This Moose comes with coffee and goodies galore, attracting both tourists and locals.

Mykel's (☎ 262-4305; www.mykels.com; dinner $15-34; ⏰ 11am-9pm Sun-Thu, to 10pm Fri & Sat) The speciality here is high-end steaks and seafood, such as walnut-crusted salmon in raspberry sauce ($22).

Riverside House Restaurant (☎ 262-0500; 44611 Sterling Hwy; lunch $7-10, dinner $15-29; ⏰ 11:30am-10pm) Upscale cuisine is on offer in a gorgeous dining room overlooking the river.

Kaladi Brothers Coffee Co (☎ 262-5115; 315 S Kobuk St; snacks $2-5; ⏰ 6am-7pm Mon-Fri, 7am-9pm Sat, 8am-4pm Sun) Despite the odd location, this is a fun hangout, with good coffee, baked goodies, and art – check out the ceiling tiles.

China Sea Restaurant (☎ 262-5033; 44539 Sterling Hwy; lunch $7-9, dinner $10-14; ⏰ 11am-9pm) Located upstairs in Blazzy's Soldotna Mall, where you'll find a fairly spectacular buffet.

BJ's (cnr Sterling Hwy & Lovers Ln) Insofar as a hobo can have a home, this squat, cinder-block bar is home to the peninsula's favorite minstrel, Hobo Jim. It's a bit of a dive, but that's the way he likes it.

Safeway (10576 Kenai Spur Hwy) This supermarket, just before the Soldotna 'Y' junction, has a deli, salad bar, bakery and Starbuck's.

Getting There & Around

Homer Stage Line (☎ 868-3914; www.homerstageline .com) has buses passing through daily en route to Anchorage ($45) and Homer ($30).

SOUTH TO HOMER

After Soldotna, traffic thins out as the Sterling Hwy rambles south, hugging the coastline and opening up to grand views of Cook Inlet. This stretch is 78 miles long and passes through a handful of small villages near some great clamming areas, ending at the charming town of Homer. Take your time in this area; the coastline and Homer are worth every day you decide to spend there.

Kasilof
☎ 907/pop 473

The fishing village of Kasilof is at Mile 108.8 Sterling Hwy. Turn west on Kalifornsky Beach Rd and travel 3.6 miles to reach the small-boat harbor on the Kasilof River. The Sterling Hwy crosses a bridge over the Kasilof River a mile south of the Kalifornsky Beach Rd turnoff.

Kasilof River State Recreation Site (day-use $5), just across the bridge, has no campsites but is a popular day-use and boat-launch area along a productive river.

Tustumena Lodge (☎ 262-4216; www.tustumena lodge.com; Mile 111 Sterling Hwy; r $45), at the giant 'T,' has cheap lodging in the most rudimentary of rooms. The adjacent bar also boasts the world's largest hat collection – well over 28,000. Amid this jungle of caps it occasionally hosts live music.

At Mile 111.5 of the Sterling Hwy, the Cohoe Loop Rd heads northwest toward the ocean, passing **Cohoe Cove Campground** (☎ 262-1939; sites $10), which is both pretty and pretty packed with anglers. Also along the road is **Crooked Creek State Recreation Area** (sites $10), another top spot for salmon fishing. The 'campground' is a gravel lot where you'll be cheek-by-jowl with your neighbor.

Southeast of the Cohoe Loop Rd intersection on the Sterling Hwy is Johnson Lake Access Rd, which quickly passes the **Johnson Lake Recreation Area** (sites $10), with somewhat boggy open-forest sites for folks who prefer rainbow trout to salmon.

Clam Gulch
☎ 907/pop 164

At Mile 117.4 of the Sterling Hwy, before reaching the hamlet of Clam Gulch, you pass the turnoff to a 2-mile gravel road. Just west on the road is **Clam Gulch State Recreation Area** (day-use $5, sites $10), a gorgeous bluffside spot overlooking a sandy beach renowned for its very productive razor-clam beds. The dirt lot won't tantalize tent campers, but it's a convenient place to park while rooting through the sand for

KENAI PENINSULA

DIGGING FOR CLAMS

Almost all of the beaches on the west side of the Kenai Peninsula (Clam Gulch, Deep Creek, Ninilchik and Whiskey Gulch) have a good supply of razor clams, considered by mollusk connoisseurs to be a true delicacy. Not only do razors have the best flavor, but they're also among the largest of the mollusks. The average razor clam is 3½in long, but most clammers have their heart set on gathering clams that reach 5in, 6in or even 7in in length.

To go clamming, you first have to purchase a sportfishing license (a one-day visitor's license is $10, and a seven-day license is $30). The daily bag limit is 60 clams, but remember – that's an awful lot of clams to clean and eat. Two dozen per person are more than enough for a meal. While the clamming's good from April to August, the best time is July, right before spawning. And though you can dig for clams anytime the tide is out, the best clamming is during extra-low, or 'minus,' tides. The most extreme minus tides occur every two weeks. Consult a tide book – and count on hundreds of other clammers to do the same.

For equipment, you'll need a narrow-bladed clam shovel that can either be purchased or, if you don't feel like hauling it around all summer, rented at many lodges and stores near the clamming areas. You'll also want rubber boots, rubber gloves, a bucket and a pair of pants to which you're not terribly attached.

Once on the beach, you have to play detective. Look for the clam's 'footprint,' a dimple mark left behind when it withdraws its neck. That's your clue to the clam's whereabouts, but don't dig directly below the imprint or you'll break its shell. Shovel a scoop or two next to the mark and then reach into the sand for the clam. You have to be quick, as a razor clam can bury itself and be gone in seconds.

Once you're successful, leave the clams in a bucket of seawater, or better yet, beer, for several hours to allow them to 'clean themselves.' Many locals say a handful of cornmeal helps this process. The best way to cook clams is right on the beach over an open fire while you're taking in the mountain scenery across Cook Inlet. Use a large covered pot and steam the clams in saltwater, or for more flavor, in white wine with a clove of garlic.

Here's where to go:

Clam Gulch This is the most popular and, many say, most productive spot by far. The Clam Gulch State Recreation Area is a half-mile from Mile 118 of the Sterling Hwy, where there's a short access road to the beach from the campground.

Ninilchik The best bet is to camp at Ninilchik View State Campground, located above the old village of Ninilchik. From there, you can walk to beaches for clamming.

Deep Creek Just south of Ninilchik is the Deep Creek State Recreation Site, where there's camping and plenty of parking along the beach.

Whiskey Gulch Look for the turnoff at about Mile 154 of the Sterling Hwy. Unless you have a 4WD vehicle, park at the elbow-turn above the beach.

Mud Bay On the east side of the Homer Spit is Mud Bay, a stretch abundant with Eastern soft-shells, cockles and blue mussels. Some surf clams (rednecks) and razor clams can also be found on the Cook Inlet side of the Spit.

succulent mollusks. If you have a reliable 4WD you can do what the Alaskans do: just motor your way straight onto the beach.

The village of Clam Gulch is less than a mile south of the gravel road on the Sterling Hwy and it has a post office and gas station. The run-down **Clam Shell Lodge** (☎ 262-4211; r $40) provides rooms that are simple in the extreme. Instead, it's best to go for **Clam Gulch Lodge** (☎ 260-3778, 800-700-9555; www.clam gulch.com; Mile 119.6 Sterling Hwy; d $95), which is a delightful family-friendly B&B with stunning views.

Ninilchik

☎ 907/pop 783

For many travelers, Ninilchik, at Mile 135 Sterling Hwy, is merely a stop for gas and a quick look at its Russian church. But this interesting little village is well worth spending a night, either at its stellar hostel, its affordable hotels or one of its numerous campsites boasting volcanic views.

The community is among the oldest on the Kenai Peninsula, having been settled in the 1820s by employees of the Russian-American Company. Many stayed even after imperial Russia sold Alaska to the US, and their descendants form the heart of the present community.

ORIENTATION & INFORMATION

Though Ninilchik's core is found along the Sterling Hwy between the Ninilchik River and Deep Creek, several tourist services – especially RV parks and fishing-charter operations – straggle out to the east along Kingsley and Oilwell Rds. The intriguing Old Ninilchik Village and the waterfront, meanwhile, are west of the highway, accessible via Mission Ave.

Alaskan Angler RV Resort (☎ 800-347-4114; Kingsley Rd) For a shower or laundry facilities.

Emergency (ambulance, fire, police ☎ 911)

Ninilchik General Store (☎ 567-3378; Mile 135.7 Sterling Hwy; ☺ 7am-11pm Mon-Thu, to midnight Fri, 6am-midnight Sat, to 11pm Sun) Has an ATM, lots of fishing and camping gear, and a few tourist-oriented brochures posted out front.

Ninilchik Public Library (☎ 567-3333; Sterling Hwy; ☺ 11am-4pm Mon-Thu, 1-6pm Fri, 11am-2pm Sat; 💻) Just north of Oilwell Rd, has three free Internet terminals.

Post office (Kingsley Rd) Is just past the Alaskan Angler.

SIGHTS & ACTIVITIES

Begin a scenic walk through Alaska's Russian history at the **Village Cache Gift Shop** (☺ 9am-7pm Mon-Sat), a log cabin built in the late 19th century, then completely dismantled and restored, log by log, in 1984. It has Russian and Alaska Native trinkets for sale, and you may be able to pick up a copy of the free *Tour of Ninilchik Village* brochure. **Old Ninilchik Village**, the site of the original community, is a postcard scene of faded log cabins in tall grass and beached fishing boats against the spectacular backdrop of Mt Redoubt.

The most spectacular building is the **Old Russian Church**, reached via a posted footpath behind the Village Cache. Built in 1901, the historic blufftop structure sports five golden onion-domes and commands an unbelievable view of Cook Inlet and the volcanoes on the other side. Adjoining it is a prim Russian Orthodox cemetery of white-picket cribs. Together they make for a photographer's delight on a clear day.

Clamming is Ninilchik's No 1 summer pastime (see Digging for Clams, opposite), however. At low tide, go to either Ninilchik

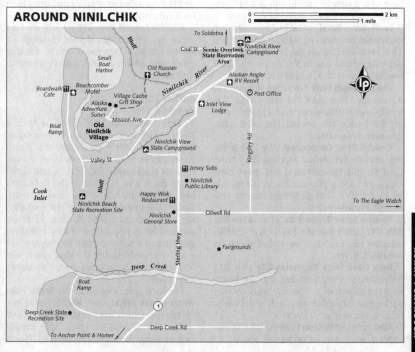

AROUND NINILCHIK

0   2 km
0   1 mile

To Soldotna

Coal St

Scenic Overlook State Recreation Area

Ninilchik River Campground

Small Boat Harbor

Old Russian Church

Bluff

Ninilchik River

Alaskan Angler RV Resort

Beachcomber Motel

Boardwalk Cafe

Village Cache Gift Shop

Alaska Adventure Suites

Mission Ave

Inlet View Lodge

Post Office

Boat Ramp

Old Ninilchik Village

Ninilchik View State Campground

Kingsley Rd

Valley St

Bluff

Jersey Subs

Ninilchik Public Library

Cook Inlet

Happy Wok Restaurant

To The Eagle Watch

Ninilchik Beach State Recreation Site

Ninilchik General Store

Oilwell Rd

Fairgrounds

Deep Creek

Sterling Hwy

Boat Ramp

Deep Creek State Recreation Site

Deep Creek Rd

To Anchor Point & Homer

KENAI PENINSULA

Beach State Recreation Site, across the river from the old village, or Deep Creek State Recreation Site. It costs $5 to park at the state recreation areas. You can either purchase a shovel ($16) and bucket ($5) at the Ninilchik General Store or rent one from the Village Cache.

The main event in Ninilchik is the **Kenai Peninsula State Fair**, the 'biggest little fair in Alaska,' which takes place annually in mid-August.

SLEEPING

Eagle Watch (☎ 567-3905; Mile 3 Oilwell Rd; dm/r $13/35) This hostel, situated on an outrageously scenic and peaceful bluff high above the Ninilchik River, lives up to its name: eagles throng here, feeding on spawned-out salmon in the waters below. The facilities are charmingly rough-hewn but immaculate, and you're free to use the friendly owners' clam shovels and buckets. There's a lockout from 10am to 5pm.

Ninilchik View State Campground (Mile 135.5 Sterling Hwy; sites $10) By far the best of Ninilchik's public campgrounds, it's set atop a wooded bluff with a view of the old village and Cook Inlet. A stairway leads down to the beach.

Beachcomber Motel (☎ 567-3417; www.beachcombermotelrvpark.com; Beach Rd; s/d $65/75, RV sites $25) This place is right on the beach beside the old village, and has half a dozen ultracute rooms, some with kitchenettes.

Ninilchik Beach State Recreation Site (sites $10) Across the river from the old village, this windy spot is little more than a gravel parking lot beside the ocean. The clamming, however, is fantastic.

Ninilchik River Campground (Mile 134.9 Sterling Hwy; sites $10) Across the Sterling Hwy from Coal St; this campground has great river access and some pleasant trails. It's mainly set up for RVs, though tenters may be able to find a grassy patch.

Ninilchik Scenic Overlook State Recreation Area (Mile 134.6 Sterling Hwy; sites $10) It has 25 RV-oriented parking 'sites' on a bluff above the Ninilchik River.

Deep Creek State Recreation Site (Mile 137.2 Sterling Hwy; sites $10) Situated on the beach near the mouth of the creek, this is another parking lot–style campground, with little to offer in the way of privacy.

Alaskan Angler RV Resort (☎ 800-347-4114; www.afishhunt.com; Kingsley Rd; campsites/RV sites $15/30).

A privately owned place where RVers prep 300lb of fresh fish at a time for winter storage. There's a tenting area back in the trees, and guests can rent rods and reels ($7), hip boots ($5) and clam shovels ($5).

Alaska Adventure Suites (☎ 277-1800; www.alaskaadventuresuites.com; suites $165-195) Right beside the Village Cache, has a sizable volcano-view suite and a slightly smaller village-view suite. Both are tricked out with kitchens and all the amenities.

EATING

Boardwalk Café (☎ 567-3388; breakfast $6-9, other mains $5-12; ☯ 9am-9pm) This nautically-inclined stand practically overhangs the crashing surf and serves quality espressos and very fine fish-and-chips. The homemade clam chowder ($3.50) is a must.

Jersey Subs (☎ 567-1018; sub sandwiches $7-11; ☯ 7am-7pm) In a little red shack across from the school; this is a local fave for overstuffed subs.

Happy Wok Restaurant (☎ 567-1060; 15945 Sterling Hwy; mains $8-15; ☯ 10:30am-11pm) This place is near the general store, and provides quality lunch and dinner specials that draw both local fishermen and visiting clam diggers.

Ninilchik General Store (☎ 567-3378; Mile 135.7 Sterling Hwy; ☯ 7am-11pm Mon-Thu, to midnight Fri, 6am-midnight Sat, to 11pm Sun) If you're wanting groceries and fried food, this is where to find them.

Anchor Point
☎ 907/pop 1792

Twenty miles south of Ninilchik is Anchor Point, which is, as a monument here notes, 'the most westerly point on the North American continent accessible by a continuous road system.' Captain Cook christened the site in 1778, after the *Resolution* lost a kedge anchor to the tidal currents. Today, the town is a fishing hot spot during early summer, with Anchor River renowned for its population of king and silver salmon and steelhead trout. Be prepared for massive crowds during the king run in late May and early June; otherwise, it's a sleepy little place.

For local info, stop in at the **Anchor Point Visitor Center** (☎ 235-2600; Mile 156 Sterling Hwy; ☯ 8am-4pm) which has maps, brochures and coffee. For $3 you can pick up a certificate proving you have experienced 'North

DETOUR: NIKOLAEVSK

If the fish aren't running, the best thing to do in Anchor Point is to leave – driving instead to the absolutely intriguing Russian Old Believer settlement of Nikolaevsk. The Old Believers are members of a sect that split from mainstream Russian Orthodoxy in the 1650s, defending their 'old beliefs' in the face of what they considered heretical reforms. Long considered outcasts in Russia, they fled communism in 1917, ending up in Brazil, then Oregon, and then – in 1968 – Alaska, where they finally felt they could enjoy religious freedom while avoiding the corruptive influences of modernity.

Nowadays, Alaska's Old Believers number at most 3000. They're hard-core traditionalists, speaking mainly Russian, marrying in their teens, raising substantial broods of children, and living simply. The men – usually farmers or fishermen – are forbidden from trimming their beards; the women typically cover their hair and are garbed in long dresses. The Old Believers tend to keep to themselves, inhabiting a handful of isolated villages on the Kenai Peninsula, of which Nikolaevsk is the most prominent.

To get there, head 10 miles east on North Fork Rd, which departs the Sterling Hwy in the heart of Anchor Point and winds through hillbilly homesteads and open, rolling forest. Right before the pavement ends, hang a left at Nikolaevsk Rd. Two miles later, you'll enter the village.

At first, you may be disappointed. Apart from the dress and language of the inhabitants (who are often nowhere to be seen), the community appears downright Alaskan: wooden prefab homes, muddy streets, rusting pickup trucks, gardens with gargantuan produce. Look hard, though, and you'll notice subtle Russian touches – the ornate scrollwork on a porch railing, for instance. Impossible to miss is the village's house of worship, the Church of St Nikolas, built in 1983 and sporting an elaborately painted façade and a white-and-blue onion dome. You can look, but don't photograph it unless you get permission.

To really get into the heart of Nikolaevsk, you must follow the signs to the **Samovar Café and B&B** (☎ 235-6867; www.russiangiftsnina.com; mains $5-11; r $39-79; café ☺ 10am-10pm Mon-Fri, to 8pm Sat), which has more than simply the best Russian food on the peninsula, and more than a wonderful collection of cheap and colorful (and pretty basic) accommodations. This small restaurant is a wacky welcome mat into the world of the Old Believers. Nina, the proprietor, is both an electrical engineer and force of nature, painting much of the beautiful artwork on sale and dressing guests up in traditional Orthodox gear for photos, all while stuffing them senseless with borscht, cream puffs and delicious *pelimeny* (Siberian dumplings). She'll then tell you exactly how much to tip. However much it is, it will be well worth one of the most unique dining and cultural experiences that you'll have in Alaska.

America's Most Westerly Highway Point.' For Internet access, staff members will direct you to **Anchor Point Library** (☎ 235-5692; Fritz Rd; ☺ 9am-4:30pm Mon, to 4pm Wed, to 4:30pm Fri, to noon Sat; ☐), adjacent to the VFW (look for the anti-aircraft gun).

Near the turnoff to the library on the Sterling Hwy is the **Blue Bus** (☎ 235-6285; Mile 156.7 Sterling Hwy; fast food $6-9; ☺ 11am-7pm), which features long lines of locals waiting for burritos, sandwiches and charter lunches.

Just down the highway from the visitors center is the turnoff to the Old Sterling Hwy, where you'll find the town's main hotel, the **Anchor River Inn** (☎ 235-8531, 800-435-8531; Sterling Hwy at Old Sterling Hwy; s/d small $54/59, motel $94/99). It has small economy rooms called 'fisherman's specials,' plus larger,

more modern rooms costing twice as much. The adjacent **Anchor River Inn Restaurant** (dinner $15-25, other meals $6-14; ☺ 6am-10pm), the town's only sit-down eatery, serves seafood, steaks and salads.

Progressing down the Old Sterling Hwy you'll come to Anchor Beach Rd and the **Anchor Angler** (☎ 235-8351; 1 Anchor Beach Rd; ☺ 6am-10pm), a tackle shop with the best fishing tips in town, as well as a nifty collection of antique rods and reels. Get hooked up here and go catch some dinner!

On the opposite side of Anchor Beach Rd is the Anchor River State Recreation Area, with five campgrounds. Four of them are on the river while the last one, **Halibut Campground** (Mile 1.5 Anchor Beach Rd; sites $10), has 20 sites and overlooks Cook Inlet Beach. The road ends at a beautiful stretch of sand with good views of Mt Redoubt and Mt Iliamna across the inlet. Almost as intriguing are the huge tractors busily launching fishing vessels into the surf.

If the campgrounds along Anchor Beach Rd seem too busy, backtrack four miles up the Sterling Hwy to **Stariski Creek State Recreation Site** (Mile 152 Sterling Hwy; sites $10), with 16 sites, some right at the edge of a 100ft bluff over the ocean.

HOMER
☎ 907/pop 5332

Among veteran visitors to Alaska, Homer is sacred soil – a mythic realm, like a northern Shangri-La, which bestows itself upon the faithful only after a long, difficult pilgrimage to get there. Hearing the travelers' tales, you half expect to find lotus-eaters and mermaids. Indeed, it's a place where many are lured, and some never leave.

At first blush, though, Homer's appeal might not be evident. The city isn't overhung with mountains like Seward, nor does it have the quaint townscape of Cordova. It sprawls a bit, is choked with tourists, isn't lushly forested, lacks legendary hikes, and has a windswept waterfront that makes kayaking a bitch. And then there's the Homer Spit – a tourist trap you may love to hate.

Stick around for a bit, however, and Homer will make you a believer. For one thing, there's the panorama, and the promise that it holds. Across Kachemak Bay, glaciers and peaks and fjords beckon – a trekkers' and paddlers' playground to which Homer is the portal.

And then there's the vibe: the town is a magnet for radicals, artists and folks disillusioned with mainstream society, who've formed a critical mass here, dreaming up a sort of utopian vision for their city, and striving – with grins on their faces – to enact it. Because of that, this is the arts capital of Southcentral Alaska, with great galleries, museums, theater and music. As well, it's a culinary feast, with more wonderful eateries than most places 10 times its size.

Plus, the weather is hard to beat. The town is protected from the severe northern cold by the Kenai Mountains to the north and east. Winter temperatures rarely drop below 0°F, while summer temperatures rarely rise above 70°F. The annual precipitation is only 28in, much of it snow.

Orientation

Homer lies at the end of the Sterling Hwy, 233 road miles from Anchorage. For tourists, there are two distinct sections of town. The 'downtown' area, built on a sloping hill between high bluffs to the north and Kachemak Bay to the south, lies along – or nearby to – busy Pioneer Ave. Heading eastward, Pioneer Ave becomes rural East End Rd, with a number of other lodging and eating options. The second section of Homer, and certainly the most notorious, is the Homer Spit, a skinny tongue of sand licking halfway across Kachemak Bay. In summer, the Spit is a madhouse of fishing charters and tourist traps; in winter it all but shuts down. Many locals say they assiduously avoid the Spit; many tourists make a beeline there, unaware that there's another side to Homer.

Information

BOOKSTORES

Homer Bookstore (Map p259; ☎ 235-7496; 332 E Pioneer Ave; ☺ 10am-7pm Mon-Sat, noon-5pm Sun) Sells new books to what's clearly a more intellectually demanding market than most. The selection is phenomenal.
Old Inlet Bookshop (Map p259; ☎ 235-7984; 106 W Bunnell Ave; ☺ 11am-6pm daily summer, 11am-5pm Tue-Sat winter) Has stacks and stacks of quality used books.

EMERGENCY
Ambulance, Fire, Police (☎ 911)

LAUNDRY
East End Laundry (Map p260; ☎ 235-2562; Mile 2.9 E End Rd; ☺ 9am-8pm Mon-Sat, 9am-7pm Sun) Also has showers ($4) and is convenient to Seaside Farm.
Sportsman's Supply & Rental (Map p260; ☎ 235-2617; 1114 Freight Dock Rd; ☺ 6am-11pm) Offers showers ($5.50) and laundry right on the Spit.
Washboard Laundromat (Map p259; ☎ 235-6781; 1204 Ocean Dr; ☺ 7am-10pm) Sure, the showers are pricey ($5), but you can stand under them as long as you want.

LIBRARY & INTERNET ACCESS
Computer Needz (Map p259; ☎ 235-5931; 345 W Sterling Hwy; per hr $5; ☺ 9am-6pm Mon-Fri, 10am-5pm Sat; 💻) Has Internet access and digital photo developing.
Homer Public Library (Map p259; ☎ 235-3180; 141 W Pioneer Ave; ☺ 10am-8pm Tue & Thu, 10am-6pm Mon,

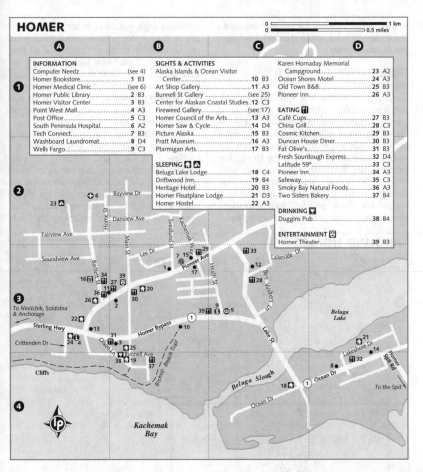

HOMER

0 ———————————— 1 km
0 ———————————— 0.5 miles

Wed, Fri & Sat) Has free Internet access and plenty of books – including Cyrillic texts for the Russian Old Believers in the surrounding settlements. At the time of research, it was slated to relocate to Heath St.

K-Bay Caffé (Map p260; ☎ 235-1551; www.kbay caffe.com; 59415 E End Rd; ⏰ 6:30am-6pm Mon-Fri, 7am-6:30pm Sat, from 7:30am Sun; 🖥) Has free Internet access (donations appreciated) on one computer.

Tech Connect (Map p259; ☎ 235-5248; 432 E Pioneer Ave; ⏰ 9am-5pm Mon-Fri, noon-4pm Sat; per hr $5; 🖥) Offers Internet access.

MEDICAL SERVICES
Homer Medical Clinic (Map p259; ☎ 235-8586; 4136 Bartlett St) Next door to South Peninsula Hospital; for walk-in service.

South Peninsula Hospital (Map p259; ☎ 235-8101; Bartlett St) North of the Pratt Museum.

MONEY
Wells Fargo (☎ 235-8151; 88 Sterling Hwy) For cash this is as good a bank as any.

POST
Post office (cnr Sterling Hwy & Lake St) Sells phonecards.

TOURIST INFORMATION
Halibut Derby Office (☎ 399-2212; Homer Spit Rd; ⏰ 5:30am-8am & 3-8pm) Has a few pamphlets and is the official weigh-in station for the Homer Halibut Derby.
Homer Visitor Center (☎ 235-7740; www.homer alaska.org; 201 Sterling Hwy; ⏰ 9am-7pm Mon-Fri, 10am-6pm Sat & Sun) Has countless brochures but, when

KENAI PENINSULA

we were there, staff members that were less than helpful. Also, it's operated by the chamber of commerce, and only provides info on members.

Sights

HOMER SPIT

Generally known as 'the Spit' (Map p260), this long needle of land – a 4½-mile sand bar stretching into Kachemak Bay – is viewed by some folks as the most fun place in Alaska. Others wish another earthquake would come along and sink the thing. Regardless, the Spit throbs all summer with tourists, who mass here in unimaginable density, gobbling fish-and-chips, quaffing specialty coffees, getting chair massages, purchasing alpaca sweaters, arranging bear-

watching trips, watching theatrical performances, and – oh yeah – going fishing in search of 300lb halibut. The hub of all this activity is the **small-boat harbor**, one of the best facilities in Southcentral Alaska and home to more than 700 boats. Close by is the **Seafarer's Memorial**, which, amid all the Spit's hubbub, is a solemn monument to residents lost at sea.

Beach combing, bald-eagle watching (they seem as common here as pigeons in New York City) and watching recently docked fishermen angling for cute tourist chicks at the Salty Dawg Saloon are all favorite activities. You can also go clamming at Mud Bay, on the east side of the Spit. Blue mussels, an excellent shellfish

AROUND HOMER

INFORMATION	
East End Laundry	1 D1
Halibut Derby Office	2 A3
Sportsman's Supply & Rental	3 A2

SIGHTS & ACTIVITIES	
Bald Mountain Air	4 B3
Harbormaster's Office	5 B3
Pier One Theatre	6 A2
Pratt Museum Harbor Tours	(see 26)
Rainbow Tours	7 B3
Seafarer's Memorial	8 B3
Smokey Bay Air	9 C2
True North Kayak Adventures	10 B3
Yurt on the Spit	11 B3

SLEEPING	
Homer Brewing Company	12 C2
Homer Spit Campground	13 B3
Homer Spit Public Camping	14 A2
Land's End Hotel	15 C3
Room at the Harbor	(see 24)
Seaside Farm	16 D1
Showers	(see 13)
Skyline B&B	17 C1

EATING	
Boardwalk	18 B3
Captain Pattie's	19 B3
General Store	20 B3
Glacier Drive-in	21 A2

Homer Hot Shots	22 A3
K-Bay Caffé	23 D1
Spit Sisters	24 B3

DRINKING	
Bear Creek Winery	25 C1
Salty Dawg Saloon	26 B3

TRANSPORT	
Ferry Office	27 B3
Ferry Terminal	28 B3
Mako's Water Taxi	29 B3

KENAI PENINSULA

overlooked by many people, are the most abundant.

If you'd rather catch your dinner than shovel or buy it, try your luck at the **Fishing Hole**, just before the Pier One Theatre. The small lagoon is the site of a 'terminal fishery,' in which salmon are planted by the state and return three or four years later to a place where they can't spawn. Kings can be caught here from mid-May to the end of June, while silvers run in August. **Sportsman's Supply & Rental** (☎ 235-2617; 1114 Freight Dock Rd; ❤ 6am-11pm), close by, rents rods ($10) as well as rakes and shovels (each $5) for clamming.

PRATT MUSEUM

This recently renovated **museum** (Map p259; ☎ 235-8635; 3779; www.prattmuseum.org; Bartlett St; adult/child $6/3; ❤ 10am-6pm) is fantastic – so much so, it loans exhibits to the Smithsonian. There's lots of local art and Alaska Native artifacts, but a more impressive feature is the interactive displays on the area's wildlife, designed to mesmerize both kids and ex-kids. Particularly cool is the remote gull-cam, which you can rotate to zoom in on Gull Island's roosting birds in real time. More sobering is the Storm Warning Theater, with harrowing tales about fishing on Kachemak Bay, where making a living can end your life. A box of tissues is provided for those brought to tears. And then there's the 'Darkened Waters' exhibit, a stunning and emotional look at the Exxon oil spill. The image of the oil-entombed eagle will wrench your gut.

The Pratt also offers 1½-hour harbor tours ($5) throughout summer at 3pm Thursday to Saturday, leaving from the Salty Dawg Saloon.

ALASKA ISLANDS & OCEAN VISITOR CENTER

More a research facility and **museum** (Map p259; ☎ 235-6961; www.islandsandocean.org; 95 Sterling Hwy; admission free; ❤ 9am-6pm) than a visitors center, this impressive new place has numerous cool interactive exhibits, perhaps the best of which is a room that's a replica seabird colony, complete with cacophonous bird calls and surround-view flocking. There's also a decent film about ship-based marine research, a hands-on discovery lab, and a slate of daily educational programs

and guided walks. It's operated jointly by the Kachemak Bay Research Reserve and the Alaska Maritime National Wildlife Refuge, which, though headquartered in Homer, mainly takes in the distant Aleutian Islands. With the Aleutians as the main focus of the center, many visitors may come away unclear how it all relates to Homer.

CENTER FOR ALASKAN COASTAL STUDIES

This **nonprofit organization** (Map p259; ☎ 235-6667; www.akcoastalstudies.org; 708 Smokey Way; ❤ 9am-5pm Mon-Fri), devoted to promoting appreciation of Kachemak Bay's ecosystem, runs the Carl E Wynn Nature Center (below) and the Peterson Bay Field Station (p272), both of which offer guided hikes and educational programs throughout the summer. Drop by to learn more about their offerings, and to get maps and info about Kachemak Bay State Park. It also operates the **Yurt on the Spit** (Map p260; Homer Spit Rd; ❤ 7:30am-6pm), right behind Mako's Water-Taxi, which does a daily 'Creatures of the Dock' tour at 11am and 2pm ($5).

Activities
HIKING

For all its natural beauty, Homer has few good public trails. For a map of short hiking routes around town, pick up the *Walking Guide to the Homer Area* at the visitors center.

Bishop Creek Trail

This **hike** (Map p260) is a 7-mile waterfront trek from north of Homer back into town (you could do it in reverse, but you're likely to miss the turnoff to the highway). The views of Kachemak Bay and the Kenai Mountains are superb, while the marine life that scurries along the sand at low tide is fascinating.

The trailhead is opposite Diamond Ridge Rd, 5 miles north along the Sterling Hwy. The trail begins by descending along Diamond Creek, then hits the beach. Check a tide book, and leave before low tide and return before high tide. High tides cover most of the sand, forcing you to scramble onto the base of the nearby cliffs. Within 4 miles you'll pass a sea-otter rookery a few hundred yards offshore. The hike ends 3 miles later at Homer's Bishop Park, below the Oceans & Islands Visitor Center.

KENAI PENINSULA

Homestead Trail

This 6.7-mile **trek** (Map p260) from Rogers Loop Rd to the City Reservoir, just off Skyline Dr on Crossman Ridge Rd, is a 2½-mile walk to Rucksack Dr, which crosses Diamond Ridge Rd. Along the way you pass through open meadows with panoramic views of Kachemak Bay and Mt Iliamna and Mt Redoubt on the other side of Cook Inlet. The trek continues another 4.2 miles, following Rucksack Dr and Crossman Ridge Rd to the reservoir. Cars are banned from both dirt roads.

To reach the trail, head out of town on the Sterling Hwy and turn right on Rogers Loop Rd across from the Bay View Inn. The trailhead is a half-mile farther, on your right.

Carl E Wynn Nature Center

Situated on the bluffs that are above Homer, this moose-ridden 140-acre **reserve** (Map p260; ☎ 235-6667; Skyline Dr; admission adults/under-18 $5/3; ⏰ 10am-6pm) is highly recommended for families and anyone interested in the area's ethnobotany. With a few short interpretive nature trails, one of them boardwalked and wheelchair accessible, this is a grand place to learn which plants can be used to heal a cut, condition your hair or munch for lunch. Naturalist-led hikes leave at 10am and 2pm daily in summer. It also has a slate of lectures and other programs; call the center for a schedule.

BIKING

Though Homer lacks formal mountain-biking trails, the dirt roads in the hills above town lend themselves to some great rides, especially along Diamond Ridge Rd and Skyline Dr. For an easy tour, just head out E End Rd, which extends 20 miles east to the head of Kachemak Bay. There's also good biking to be had in Seldovia (p269), an easy day or overnight trip from Homer by water-taxi. To rent a bike and get more recommendations on good routes, head to Homer Saw & Cycle (p267).

HOOKING A HALIBUT IN HOMER

To thousands of tourists who come to Alaska every summer, Homer is the place where you go to catch a halibut. Halibut is a bottom-dweller that, when first born, looks like any normal fish with an eye on each side of its head. But as a halibut feeds exclusively off the bottom, it flattens out and one eye moves to the other side, which has become the 'top' of the fish.

Females are larger than males; in fact, just about every halibut weighing more than 100lb is a female. And almost without fail, a 300lb halibut is hauled out of Kachemak Bay every summer. The state-record halibut tipped the scales at almost 500lb. The average-size fish, however, is closer to 30lb or 40lb.

Anglers use a large hook, usually baited with a chunk of cod or herring and a 40lb weight to take it 200ft to the bottom of the bay, where they proceed to 'jig' (raise and lower the hook slightly) for a fish.

As you can imagine, reeling in a halibut can be quite a workout, and many anglers find it exciting, though these fish are not battlers or jumpers like salmon or trout. Actually getting the fish into the boat can be the most dramatic part, as charter captains often use a club or even a gun to subdue their catch and a gaff to haul it aboard.

There are more than two dozen charter captains working out of the Spit, and they charge anywhere from $160 to $200 for a halibut trip. For a clue who to go with, peruse the board beside the Halibut Derby Office (Map p260), which lists the biggest fish caught that summer, along with who captained the boat. Other than that, the biggest distinction between the charter operations is vessel size: bigger boats bounce around less when the waves kick, meaning greater comfort and less *mal de mer*.

Most captains try to take advantage of two slack tides and often leave at around 6am for a 12-hour trip on the bay. Take warm clothing and rain gear, and pack a lunch or purchase one from a handful of restaurants that sell box lunches. You'll also need a fishing license; non-resident licenses cost $10 for one day, $30 for 7 days. And just in case you reel in the mother of all halibut, be sure to have bought a derby ticket (opposite). Otherwise, you'll wind up with a huge dead fish and no fortune.

KENAI PENINSULA

HOMER ART GALLERIES

The cold, dark season of unemployment has inspired a saying in these parts: 'If you're starving, you might as well be an artist.' Just browsing these great galleries is a treat, and on the **first Friday** of the month, many break out the wine and cheese, and stay open late for a series of openings all over town. This is just the tip of the iceberg – grab a free *Downtown Homer Art Galleries* flyer at the visitors center with many more gallery listings, or stop by the **Homer Council of the Arts** (☎ 235-4288; www.homerart.org; 355 W Pioneer Ave; ⊗ 9am-6pm Mon-Fri), with its own awesome gallery and information on various tours.

Art Shop Gallery (Map p259; ☎ 235-7076; 202 W Pioneer Ave; ⊗ 10am-7pm Mon-Sat, 11am-5pm Sun) Does framing and features a fairly tourist-centric selection of Alaska-wide art and souvenirs.

Bunnell Street Gallery (Map p259; ☎ 235-2662; www.bunnellstreetgallery.org; 106 W Bunnell Ave; ⊗ 10am-6pm Mon-Sat, noon-4pm Sun) An avant-garde place with the priciest and most experimental offerings – definitely the star of the show.

Fireweed Gallery (Map p259; ☎ 235-3411; 475 E Pioneer Ave; ⊗ 10am-7pm Mon-Sat, 11am-5pm Sun) Has a more statewide representation than most of the other galleries. It's got photography, metalwork, oil paintings, jewelry, and is also home to the Kachemak Bay Watercolor Society.

Picture Alaska (Map p259; ☎ 235-2300; 448 E Pioneer Ave; ⊗ 10am-7pm Mon-Sat, 11am-5pm Sun) Specializes in affordable prints and neat little knick-knacks.

Ptarmigan Arts (Map p259; ☎ 235-5345; 471 E Pioneer Ave; ⊗ 10am-7pm Mon-Sat, 10am-6pm Sun) An artist-owned and operated co-op featuring mostly works from the Kenai Peninsula, including jewelry, textiles, Alaska Native pieces, and Homer spruce ash-glaze pottery.

PADDLING

Though, theoretically, you could spend a wavy day paddling in the vicinity of the Spit, you'll find infinitely better scenery and more varied wildlife, and far more sheltered waters, across the bay in the state park (p273). Due to fast currents and massive waves, attempting the wide-open crossing is a poor idea; you're better off taking your kayak across on a water-taxi or renting one from the various companies that maintain fleets of kayaks on the far side.

WHALE WATCHING

Whenever you're out in the bay there's a chance of spotting whales – sometimes you can even spot orca from the tip of the Spit. But only the MV *Rainbow Connection*, operated by **Rainbow Tours** (Map p260; ☎ 235-7272; Homer Spit Rd), runs a dedicated whale-watching tour. The comfortable 65ft vessel leaves Homer at 9am, cruises to Seldovia, and then spends six-plus hours seeking out humpbacks, orcas, minkes, finbacks and gray whales in Kachemak Bay and Kennedy Entrance. The $125 price includes lunch. Be sure to bundle up and bring your binocs.

BEAR WATCHING

Due largely to the density of tourists visiting Homer, the town has become a major departure point for bear-watching trips to the famed bruin haven of Katmai National Park (p289), located on the Alaska Peninsula 100-plus miles southwest by floatplane. Due to the distances involved, these trips cost a pretty penny: expect to pay between $500 and $600 per person for a day trip. However, that may be a small price to pay for the iconic Alaskan photo: a slavering brown bear, perched atop a waterfall, snapping its fangs on an airborne salmon.

Bald Mountain Air (Map p260; ☎ 235-7969; www.baldmountainair.com; Homer Spit Rd; per person $530) runs trips to the park headquarters at Brooks Camp, where countless bears converge to snag salmon ascending Brooks River – and where countless tourists converge to watch them. Once-in-a-lifetime photos are pretty much certain.

Emerald Air Service (Map p260; ☎ 235-6993; www.emeraldairservice.com; Homer Spit Rd; per person $530) is run by respected naturalists and offers a far more wilderness-oriented experience, bypassing Brooks Camp and seeking out bears along isolated Katmai beaches and lakeshores.

Festivals & Events

There's always something happening in Homer, especially in May – check to see what's on at the visitors center.

KENAI PENINSULA

Homer Jackpot Halibut Derby (www.homerhalibut derby.com) May 1 marks the beginning of the five-month, $200,000-plus contest to catch the biggest fish (in 2004, it was a 353-pounder). There are special 'catch and release' prizes for folks unhooking female fish over 100lb. Tickets cost $10, are good for one day of fishing, and can be bought at numerous places in Homer, including the derby office on the spit (p258).

Kachemak Bay Shorebird Festival (☎ 235-7337; www.homeralaska.org/shorebird) Brings hundreds of birders and 100,000 shorebirds to Mud Bay in early May, making it the largest bird migration site along the Alaskan road system. The tidal flats of Homer become the staging area for thousands of birds, including one-third of the world's surfbirds.

Spring Arts Festival A month-long May event that began as an outlet for local artists to display their work and has since evolved into a full-scale festival.

Kachemak Bay Kayak Festival (www.kachemakka yakfest.com) A great time to paddle into town is at the end of May.

Sleeping

Homer has B&Bs galore. There are two reservation services with many, many more listings; **Cabins & Cottages Network** (☎ 235-0191; www.cabinsinhomer.com) and **Homer's Finest Bed & Breakfast Network** (☎ 235-4938, 800-764-3211; www.homeraccommodations.com). Homer adds a 5.5% sales tax to lodging but is considering a bed tax as well.

BUDGET

Homer Hostel (Map p259; ☎ 235-1463; www.homer hostel.com; 304 W Pioneer Ave; dm $22, s/d $47/56) This is a superclean, very well-run hostel perfectly located downtown, and run with unbridled ebullience by Will – a Homer transplant so gung-ho about this place that you too may consider relocating here. He rents bikes and fishing poles and can store your backpacks for $1.

Homer Spit Public Camping (Map p260; Homer Spit Rd; campsites/RV sites $8/15) On the west beach of Homer Spit a catch-as-catch-can tent city springs up every night of the summer. It's a beautiful spot, though often windy, crowded – and sometimes rowdy. The self-registration stand is right across the road from Sportsman's Supply.

Karen Hornaday Memorial Campground (Map p259; campsites/RV sites $8/15) Below the bluffs just north of downtown, this campground is less busy than those on the Spit. It has private, wooded sites with impressive views and is

probably a better choice for families with small children. Unlike the campgrounds on Homer Spit, it has a playground instead of the Salty Dawg Saloon.

Seaside Farm (☎ 235-7850; www.xyz.net/~seaside; E End Rd; campsites $10, dm/r/cabins $15/50/55) Located 5 miles from the city center, this is more like Burning Man than a regulation youth hostel. Campers share a grassy field overlooking Grewingk Glacier and an outdoor cooking pavilion patrolled by roosters; inside are well-worn private rooms and dorms. Some people will be put off by the filth and foul odors; others will find this to be one of those 'experiences' they'd dreamed of having when they hit the trail for Alaska.

Homer Spit Campground (Map p260; ☎ 235-8206; Homer Spit Rd; campsites/RV sites $22/28) Has coin-operated laundry facilities, showers ($3.50) and about 150 bald eagles, which 'the Eagle Lady' has been feeding every winter since 1979. They hang around all summer to keep her company.

MIDRANGE

Driftwood Inn (Map p259; ☎ 235-8019, 800-478-8019; www.thedriftwoodinn.com; cnr Main St & Bunnell Ave; r $69-165, cottages $225, RV sites $32-35) This has a variety of accommodations, including European-style rooms with shared baths, snug, cedar-finished 'ships quarters,' and a cottage with a deck affording some stunning oceanfront views.

Old Town B&B (Map p259; ☎ 235-7558; www.old townbeadandbreakfast.com; 106 W Bunnell Ave; d $95-115) There are beautiful rooms, great views and lots of antiques at this B&B; breakfast is served at Panarelli's Café next door.

Pioneer Inn (Map p259; ☎ 235-5670, 800-782-9655; www.pioneerinn.net; 244 W Pioneer Ave; r $79-109) Has a couple smaller (and thus cheaper) rooms, along with a number of near-luxurious larger suites with kitchenettes.

Room at the Harbor (Map p260; ☎ 299-6767, 299-6868; Homer Spit Rd; s/d $85/100) This establishment has one beautiful room upstairs from Spit Sisters; the private deck overlooks the boat harbor.

Skyline B&B (Map p260; ☎ 235-3832; www.sky linebb.com; 60855 Skyline Dr; r $85-120) Located high on the ridgeline behind the city, this has five rooms with beautiful views of Grewingk Glacier.

Ocean Shores Motel (Map p259; ☎ 235-7775, 800-770-7775; www.akoceanshores.com; 451 Sterling Hwy;

d $99-159) This has clean, spacious but somewhat institutional rooms. Those down by the ocean cost the most; the cheaper ones are up on the hill and lack good views. The owner is a serious kayak buff and worth talking to if you're planning to paddle.

TOP END

Heritage Hotel (Map p259; ☎ 235-7787, 800-380-7787; 147 E Pioneer Ave; r $119-165) Housed in a 1948 log cabin, has an older section with small, ultra-adorable and rustically decorated rooms, plus a newer wing with rooms that are larger but less charming. Guests should sleep easier now that the noisy bar next door has closed.

Beluga Lake Lodge (Map p259; ☎ 235-5995; 204 Ocean Dr Loop; d $89-249) This lodge overlooks its namesake lake and is pleasant and clean; the smallest rooms are cozy while the biggest ones sleep eight and have full kitchens.

Bear Creek Lodging (Map p260; ☎ 235-8484; Bear Creek Dr; www.bearcreekwineryalaska.com; d $225) Situated on a stunning hillside at the Bear Creek Winery, this place has two posh, romantic rooms, a hot tub overlooking the fruit vineyard, and a complimentary bottle of vino beside each bed.

Chocolate Drop B&B (Map p260; ☎ 235-3668, 800-530-6015; www.chocolatedropinn.com; r from $125) More of a lodge than a B&B, this is a stunning log inn overlooking the bay, with an outdoor hot tub and a sauna inside.

Land's End Hotel (Map p260; ☎ 800-478-0400, 235-0420; www.lands-end-resort.com; r $125-210) Located at the end of the Spit; it's considered a luxury hotel for its grand views and storied ambience, but only the pricier rooms really fit that description.

Homer Floatplane Lodge (Map p259; ☎ 877-235-9600, 235-4160; www.floatplanelodge.com; 1244 Lakeshore Dr) There are four slips for floatplanes and a variety of all-inclusive packages on offer, such as a three-nights stay covering lodging, meals and halibut fishing for $1050 (plus 6.5% tax).

Eating

Loosen your belt, because bite for bite, no place in Alaska has the culinary variety of Homer. There are great coffee shops on nearly every corner, an unfair share of eclectic gourmet sandwich joints, and several urbane dining rooms that'll make you forget you're in the boonies. Realize that if you eat on the Spit, you'll pay substantially more than for dining in town.

RESTAURANTS

Homestead (Map p260; ☎ 235-8723; Mile 8.2 E End Rd; dinner $22-36; ☯ 5pm-10pm) Considered the highest-end – and perhaps the most delicious – restaurant in Homer, with appetizers like Kachemak Bay oysters ($14) and mains such as Thai curry ($22) and Sonoran seafood stew ($29). Though the waiters wear black ties, patrons can come as they are (hey, this is Homer, after all). Reservations are recommended.

Fat Olives (Map p259; ☎ 235-8488; 276 Ohlson Ln; dinner $16-26; ☯ 11am-9:30pm) In this chic and hyper-popular pizza joint/wine bar, you could gorge affordably on appetizers like prosciutto-wrapped Alaska scallops or spend a bit more for mains like wood oven–roasted game hen.

Café Cups (Map p259; ☎ 235-8330; 162 W Pioneer Ave; lunch $8-10, dinner $16-21; ☯ 11am-10pm Mon-Sat) This place has a wacky exterior (think Antoni Gaudi) and an equally fun, eclectic yet refined menu, including lunch dishes like the 'cosmic-halibut-by-the-sea-wich' and dinner mains such as chicken coconut curry.

Captain Pattie's (Map p260; ☎ 235-5135; Homer Spit Rd; lunch $7-17, dinner $20-27; ☯ 11am-10pm) This oceanfront eatery has become a Spit institution by selling overpriced seafood to a constant stream of landlubbers. It claims its halibut is Alaska's best, but those in the know order crab.

China Grill (Map p259; ☎ 235-3662; Lake St; buffet $7-10; ☯ 11am-11pm) The $10 dinner buffet may seem overpriced, but the $7 lunch buffet is a deal – especially if you dig (of all things) deviled eggs.

CAFÉS

Cosmic Kitchen (Map p259; ☎ 235-6355; 510 E Pioneer Ave; burritos & sandwiches $6-8; ☯ 9am-8pm Mon-Sat, to 3pm Sun) A hippie twist on the standard diner: on one hand, it has burgers and Budweiser; on the other, you can pay 50¢ extra to have bee pollen added to your $4 mango smoothie.

Duncan House Diner (Map p259; ☎ 235-5344; 125 E Pioneer Ave; breakfast & lunch $6-10; ☯ 5am-3pm) This busy downtown place fries up Homer's best bacon-and-eggs, which it serves until 2pm.

Fresh Sourdough Express (Map p259; ☎ 235-7571; 1316 Ocean Dr; breakfast $6-10, lunch & dinner $6-11; ☺ 7am-9pm) Quite popular with the tourists, it serves 'howling hotcakes' in the morning and buffalo burgers and halibut salad for lunch. Charter-boat lunches are also available.

QUICK EATS

Two Sisters Bakery (Map p259; ☎ 235-2280; 233 E Bunnell Ave; light meals $3-8; ☺ 7am-6pm Mon-Sat, 9am-4pm Sun) A beloved Homer institution with espresso and great fresh-baked bread, plus quiche, soups, salads and pizza by the slice.

Boardwalk (Map p260; ☎ 235-7749; Homer Spit Rd; fast food $2-10; ☺ 11am-11pm) Widely viewed as the best place on the Spit for halibut – tempura-battered, fried and served kabob-style. Notice, however, that fishermen, unlike the tourists, go for the burgers.

K-Bay Caffé (Map p260; ☎ 235-1551; www.kbay caffe.com; 59415 E End Rd; ☺ 6:30am-7pm Mon-Fri, 8am-4pm Sat & Sun; 🖳) Ask any local and they'll tell you: this is the best coffee in town, and well worth the inconvenient drive.

Homer Hot Shots (Map p260; ☎ 235-1272; Homer Spit Rd; snacks $2-5; ☺ 5am-'until I get tired') This has the best coffee on the Spit.

Spit Sisters (Map p260; ☎ 235-4921; Homer Spit Rd; ☺ 5am-4pm) If you're after a feisty girl-power vibe, you've come to the right place. There's a great view overlooking the Small-Boat Harbor, and delicacies to enjoy – apricot scones, blackberry muffins, sticky buns – made by the revered Two Sisters Bakery in town.

Glacier Drive-In (Map p260; ☎ 235-7148; Homer Spit Rd; fast food $2-10; ☺ 11am-8pm Tue-Sun) One of the better cheap eateries on the Spit offering burgers, hot dogs and, of course, fried halibut.

Latitude 59° (Map p259; ☎ 235-5935; 3858 Lake St; light meals $2-5; ☺ 6:30am-5pm Mon-Fri, 9am-4pm Sat) A wonderfully relaxed coffee shop and art gallery serving bagels, pastries, smoothies and espressos.

Fritz Creek General Store (Map p260; ☎ 235-6753; Mile 8.2 East End Rd; quick eats $3-8; ☺ 7am-9pm Mon-Sat, 10am-8pm Sun) A ways from town, but locals say it's worth the drive for the veggie burritos. It also does pizza, tamales, hoagies (sandwiches) and espresso.

GROCERIES

Safeway (Mile 90 Sterling Hwy; ☺ 24hr) On the way to the Spit, this is the best place in town

for groceries, fresh baked breads, deli sandwiches and salads.

Smoky Bay Natural Foods (☎ 235-7252; 248 W Pioneer Ave; ☺ 9:30am-7pm Mon-Fri, 10am-6pm Sat & Sun) A co-op with organic veggies, groceries, herbs and a great bulk foods selection.

Drinking & Entertainment

The bumper sticker says it all: 'Homer, Alaska: A quaint drinking village with a fishing problem.'

Salty Dawg Saloon (Map p260; Homer Spit Rd) Maybe the most storied bar on the Kenai Peninsula, the Salty Dawg is one of those places that's famous for being famous. In the evenings every square foot of its wood shaving–laden floor is packed with tourists singing along to sea shanties, rubbing elbows with the occasional fisherman and paying 50% more for beer than they would elsewhere in town. The lighthouse tower atop the whole party, visible from anywhere in town, stays lit during opening hours.

Homer Brewing Company (Map p260; ☎ 399-8060; 1411 Lakeshore Dr; ☺ noon-7pm Mon-Sat, to 5pm Sun) Isn't a bar, but it does offer 'tours' with free samples of fresh (and some organic) beer – try the broken birch bitter ale.

Bear Creek Winery (Map p260; ☎ 235-8484; Bear Creek Dr; www.bearcreekwineryalaska.com; ☺ 11am-7pm) Wineries are scarcer than vineyards in Alaska, but this impressive family-run operation bottles some fine berry-based wines, plus fireweed mead and rhubarb vino. It conducts tours and tastings daily in the summer and sells its product on-site.

Beluga Lake Lodge Bar & Grill (Map p259; ☎ 235-5995; www.belugalakelodge.com; 204 Ocean Dr Loop; d $89-249) There are big windows overlooking the lake, a wonderful deck, and live music at this bar & grill. When we were there, patrons were tapping their toes to the country-inflected tunes of Atz Kilcher – father of local-girl-turned-pop-star Jewel.

Duggins Pub (Map p259; 120 W Bunnell Ave) This place has an Irish theme, sausage sandwiches made from scratch and Sunday-night performances by the locally renowned band Three-Legged Mule.

Pier One Theater (Map p260; ☎ 235-7333; Homer Spit Rd; admission $16) Live drama and comedy is performed in a 'come-as-you-are' warehouse next to the Fishing Hole on the Spit. Shows start at 8:15pm Friday and Saturday and 7:30pm Sunday during summer.

Homer Theater (Map p259; ☎ 235-6728; cnr Main St & Pioneer Ave) First-run movies are shown here.

Getting There & Around

AIR

The contract carrier for Alaska Airlines, **ERA Aviation** (☎ 235-7565, 800-426-0333; www.flyera .com) provides daily flights between Homer and Anchorage from Homer's airport, 1.7 miles east of town on Kachemak Dr. The advance-purchase fare runs about $117 one way, $211 round-trip.

Smokey Bay Air (Map p260; ☎ 235-1511; www .smokeybayair.com; 2100 Kachemak Dr) offers flights to Seldovia for $27.50 each way.

BICYCLE

Homer Saw & Cycle (☎ 235-8406; 1532 Ocean Dr; ☷ 9am-5:30pm Mon-Fri, 11am-5pm Sat) rents mountain bikes ($25 per day).

BOAT

The Alaska Marine Highway provides twice-weekly service from Homer to Seldovia ($31, 1½ hours) and thrice-weekly service to Kodiak ($72, 9½ hours), with connecting service to Seward as well as the Aleutians. The **ferry terminal** (☎ 235-8449; www.ferryalaska .com) is at the end of Homer Spit.

Rainbow Tours (Map p260; ☎ 235-7272; Homer Spit Rd; one way/round-trip $20/35) offers the inexpensive Rainbow Connection shuttle from Homer to Seldovia. It departs at 9am, gets to Seldovia an hour later, and then returns to take you back to Homer at 5pm. It'll transport your bike for $5 and your kayak for $10.

Many water-taxi operations shuttle campers and kayakers between Homer and points across Kachemak Bay. Though the companies are good and work closely together, the most respected by far is **Mako's Water-taxi** (Map p260; ☎ 235-9055; www.makoswatertaxi.com; Homer Spit Rd). It usually charges per person round-trip $60 with a two-person minimum.

BUS

The **Homer Stage Line** (☎ 868-3914; www.homer stageline.com) runs daily from Homer to Anchorage (one way/round-trip $55/100), Seward ($45/85) and all points in between.

CAR

To obtain an affordable rental car, stop at **Polar Car Rental** (☎ 235-5998; airport). The small dealer has subcompacts for $75 a day.

Kostas Taxi (☎ 399-8008, 399-8115) and **Kachecab** (☎ 235-1950) are fierce rivals, and can get you anywhere around town for a reasonable fare.

SELDOVIA
☎ 907/pop 263

If the tourist-thronged towns of the Kenai Peninsula have left you frazzled, catch a boat to Seldovia, on the south side of Kachemak Bay and in a world of its own. Living up to the nickname 'City of Secluded Charm,' the community has managed to retain much of its old Alaskan character, and can be a restful (and inexpensive) day, or overnight, trip from Homer.

One of the oldest settlements on Cook Inlet, Russians founded the town in the late 18th century and named it after their word *seldevoy*, meaning 'herring bay.' By the 1890s, Seldovia had become an important shipping and supply center for the region, and the town boomed right into the 1920s, with salmon canning, fur farming and, of course, a (short-lived) herring industry.

After the Sterling Hwy to Homer was completed in the 1950s, Seldovia's importance as a supply center began to dwindle. Today it relies primarily on fishing but is making its best stab at becoming a tourist destination. It's a process that's happening in fits and starts: the hiking and biking possibilities here are excellent and the accommodations are plush, but the culinary offerings are limited and the galleries feel a bit like desperate rummage sales. All in all you'll find a village with quaintness to spare, but little tourist infrastructure, which may be the best thing about the place.

Orientation & Information

As the crow flies, Seldovia is about 15 miles southwest of Homer. located on the far side of Kachemak Bay. The community, oriented toward Seldovia Bay and flanked by Seldovia Slough to the west, is laughably compact: a sprinter could tour the downtown in 30 seconds, while the airport is a mere half-mile walk. For a real road trip, head out Jakolof Bay Rd, which runs a whopping 10 or so miles.

The post office is near the corner of Main St and Seldovia St. There's an ATM at Linwood Bar & Grill (p270) but no banks in town.

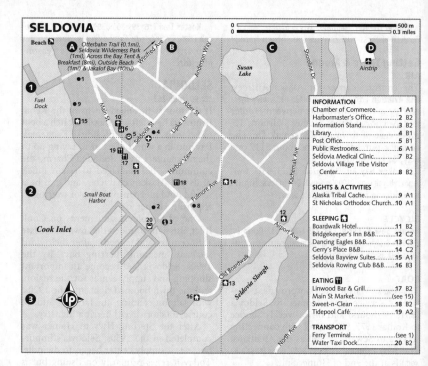

SELDOVIA

| 0 | 500 m |
| 0 | 0.3 miles |

Beach

Otterbahn Trail (0.1mi),
Seldovia Wilderness Park
(1mi), Across the Bay Tent &
Breakfast (8mi), Outside Beach
(1mi) & Jakalof Bay (10mi)

Winfred Ave

Anderson Way

Susan
Lake

Shoreline Dr

Airstrip

Fuel
Dock

Main St

Alder St

Lipke Ln

Kachemak Ave

Seldovia St

Harbor View

Fulmore Ave

Small Boat
Harbor

Airport Ave

Cook Inlet

Old Boardwalk

Seldovia Slough

North Ave

INFORMATION	
Chamber of Commerce..............**1**	A1
Harbormaster's Office.................**2**	B2
Information Stand.......................**3**	B1
Library...................................**4**	B1
Post Office................................**5**	B1
Public Restrooms.......................**6**	A1
Seldovia Medical Clinic...............**7**	B2
Seldovia Village Tribe Visitor	
Center..................................**8**	B2

SIGHTS & ACTIVITIES	
Alaska Tribal Cache....................**9**	A1
St Nicholas Orthodox Church.....**10**	A1

SLEEPING	
Boardwalk Hotel......................**11**	B2
Bridgekeeper's Inn B&B.............**12**	C2
Dancing Eagles B&B..................**13**	C3
Gerry's Place B&B.....................**14**	C2
Seldovia Bayview Suites............**15**	A1
Seldovia Rowing Club B&B.........**16**	B3

EATING	
Linwood Bar & Grill..................**17**	B2
Main St Market....................(see 15)	
Sweet-n-Clean........................**18**	B2
Tidepool Café.........................**19**	A2

TRANSPORT	
Ferry Terminal.......................(see 1)	
Water Taxi Dock.....................**20**	B2

Emergency (ambulance, fire, police ☎ 911)

Harbormaster's Office (☎ 234-7886; ⏱ 8am-9pm) Has baths.

Information stand (Main St) Close to the small-boat harbor, with a few flyers tacked up; several more flyers are available in the Harbormaster's Office.

Library (☎ 234-7662; 250 Seldovia St; ⏱ afternoon Tue, Thu & Sat; 🖳) Has one terminal for Internet access.

Seldovia Chamber of Commerce (www.xyz.net /~seldovia) Its website is great for pretrip planning.

Seldovia Medical Clinic (☎ 234-7825; 250 Seldovia St) Not far off Main St.

Seldovia Village Tribe Visitor Center (☎ 234-7898; www.svt.org; cnr Airport Ave & Main St; Internet per 15min $2; ⏱ 9am-4:30pm; 🖳)

Sweet-n-Clean (☎ 234-7420; 226 Main St; ⏱ 10am-9pm Mon-Sat) Has laundry, showers ($4) and serves as the city's unofficial visitors center, when it's not too busy.

Sights & Activities
SELDOVIA VILLAGE TRIBE VISITOR CENTER

This **visitors center** (☎ 234-7898; www.svt.org; cnr Airport Ave & Main St; ⏱ 9am-4:30pm; 🖳), opened in 2005, attempts to showcase Seldovia's Alaska Native heritage – a unique blend

of Alutiiq (Eskimo) and Tanaina (Indian) cultures. Though enjoyable (especially on a rainy day), the displays are a hodge-podge, featuring artifacts like arrowheads and stone knives dredged up from nearby waters, a series of old photos of Seldovia, and an exhibit about the intricacies of seal hunting. You can buy souvenirs here, and pay to use the public-use Internet terminal ($2 per 15 minutes).

Also run by the Seldovia Native Association is the **Alaska Tribal Cache** (☎ 234-7898; www.alaskatribalcache.com; 234 Main St; ⏱ 10am-6pm Mon-Sat, noon-5pm Sun), across town, which sells jams, jellies and marmalade, all made on-site with fresh wild berries picked by local kids – and shoestring travelers (opposite).

ST NICHOLAS ORTHODOX CHURCH

Seldovia's most popular attraction is this onion-domed **church** (⏱ 1:30-3:30pm Mon-Sat), which overlooks the town from a hill just off Main St. Built in 1891 and restored in the 1970s, the church is open on weekday afternoons, when you can see the exquisite icons inside. Note the chandelier, made from old barrel staves. Though there is no resident clergyman, occasionally the priest from Nanwalek travels here to conduct services.

OUTSIDE BEACH

This beach is an excellent place for wildlife sightings and a little beachcombing. To reach it, follow Anderson Way (Jakolof Bay Rd) out of town for a mile, then head left at the first fork to reach the picnic area at Outside Beach Park. You stand a good chance of spotting eagles, seabirds and possibly even otters here. At low tide, you can explore the sea life among the rocks, and on a clear day the views of Mt Redoubt and Mt Iliamna are stunning.

BERRY PICKING

Seldovia is known best for its blueberries, which grow so thick just outside town that from late August to mid-September you often can rake your fingers through the bushes and fill a two-quart bucket in minutes. You'll also come across plenty of low-bush cranberries and salmonberries, a species not found around Homer. Be aware, however, that many of the best berry areas are on tribal land; before setting out, stop at the **Seldovia Native Association** (☎ 234-7898; 234 Main St) in the same building as the Alaska Tribal Cache, which will sell you a berry-picking permit for a nominal fee. If you're feeling light in the wallet, you may even be able to sell your harvest to the Cache for about $2 per pound – and you can keep as many as you want for personal use.

HIKING

The **Otterbahn Trail** was famously created by local high school students, who dubbed it the 'we-worked-hard-so-you-better-like-it trail.' The trailhead lies behind Susan B English School, off Winfred Ave. Lined with salmonberries and affording great views of Graduation Peak, it skirts the coastline most of the way and reaches Outside Beach in 1½ miles. Make sure you hike it at tides below 17ft, as the last stretch runs across a slough that is only passable (legally – property above 17ft is private) when the water is out.

Two trails start from Jakolof Bay Rd. You can either hike down the beach toward the head of Seldovia Bay at low tide, or you can follow a 4½-mile logging road

to reach several secluded coves. There is also the **Tutka/Jakolof Trail**, a 2½-mile trail to a campsite on the Tutka Lagoon, the site of a state salmon-rearing facility. The posted trail departs from Jakolof Bay Rd about 10½ miles east of town.

The town's newest hike is the rigorous **Rocky Ridge Trail**, where 800ft of climbing will be rewarded with remarkable views of the bay, the town and Mt Iliamna. The trail starts (or ends) on Rocky St and loops back to the road near the airport, covering about 3 miles.

BIKING

Seldovia's nearly carless streets and outlying gravel roads make for ideal biking; mountain bikes can be brought over from Homer or rented from the Boardwalk Hotel (p270). Those looking for a fairly leisurely ride can pedal the 10-mile Jakolof Bay Rd, which winds along the coast nearly to the head of Jakolof Bay. For a more rigorous experience, continue on another six miles beyond the end of the maintained road, climbing 1200ft into the alpine country at the base of Red Mountain.

In the past, fit cyclists could also depart from Jakolof Bay Rd for an epic 30-mile round-trip ride along the rough Rocky River Rd, which cuts across the tip of the Kenai Peninsula to Windy Bay. In recent years washouts have made the road largely impassable; inquire about current conditions.

PADDLING

There are some excellent kayaking opportunities in the Seldovia area. Just north, Eldred Passage and the three islands (Cohen, Yukon and Hesketh) that mark its entrance are prime spots for viewing otters, sea lions and seals, while the northern shore of Yukon Island features caves and tunnels that can be explored at high tide. Even closer are Sadie Cove and Tutka and Jakolof Bays, where you can paddle in protected water, amid interesting geological features and near numerous camping areas along the beaches.

Kayak'Atak (☎ 234-7425; www.alaska.net/~kayaks/; kayaks 1st day single/double $50/80, subsequent days $35/50) rents kayaks and can help arrange transportation throughout the bay. It also offers various guided tours starting from $80, some including a 'gourmet lunch.' Make reservations in advance.

KENAI PENINSULA

Sleeping

You won't have problems finding an excellent room in this town. Note that Seldovian B&Bs are extremely plush – great art, lovely antiques and fabulous views are almost standard.

BUDGET & MIDRANGE

Across the Bay Tent & Breakfast (summer ☎ 235-3633, winter ☎ 345-2571; www.tentandbreakfastalaska.com; tent cabin $63) Located 8 miles from town on Jakolof Bay, this is something a little different. Its cabinlike tents include a full breakfast and transportation from Seldovia. For $95 per day you can get a package that includes all your meals – and dinner could consist of fresh oysters, beach-grilled salmon or halibut stew. The offbeat resort also rents mountain bikes for $25 per day and organizes kayak trips. Bring your sleeping bag.

Dancing Eagles B&B (☎ 234-7627; www.dancingeagles.com; s/d $65/110, cabin $175) On the Old Boardwalk; this rambling collection of rustic yet upscale structures is as close to the ocean as you can be without getting wet. It serves full breakfasts that you can eat on a marvelous outcrop rising from the harbor.

Seldovia Rowing Club B&B (☎ 234-7614; www.seldoviarowingclub.com; 343 Bay St; r $110) Also located on the Old Boardwalk, this place has homey suites decorated with quilts, antiques and owner Susan Mumma's outstanding watercolors. She serves big breakfasts and often hosts inhouse music concerts.

Seldovia Wilderness Park (☎ 234-7643; campsites/RV sites $5/8) About a mile out of town; this is a city-maintained campground on spectacular Outside Beach. You can pay for your site at the ferry terminal or harbormaster's office.

Gerry's Place B&B (☎ 243-7471; s/d $50/70) This is a block from the harbor on Fulmore Ave, and has some of the best rates.

TOP END

Boardwalk Hotel (☎ 234-7816, 800-238-7862; www.alaskaone.com/boardwalkhotel/; 234 Main St; r $109-139) Has big, beautiful rooms with lots of wicker; the pricier ones have huge windows overlooking the bay and small-boat harbor. It also rents bikes (right) and fishing poles ($10 per day).

Bridgekeepers Inn B&B (☎ 234-7535; www.thebridgekeepersinn.com; r $125-135) A cozy place with private baths and full breakfasts; one room has a balcony overlooking the salmon-filled slough.

Seldovia Bayview Suites (☎ 800-478-7898, 234-7631; 381 Main St; r with/without view $139/109) Though the rooms here are sterile and charmless, they're spacious and blessed with beautiful views. The $250 apartment will sleep eight comfortably, plus perhaps 30 on the floor.

Eating

Perhaps the most frustrating thing about Seldovia is that it can sleep far more people than it can feed. When we were there, the dining situation was dire, with one decent restaurant in operation. By the time you visit, this situation will hopefully have changed.

Tidepool Café (☎ 234-7502; 267 Main St; breakfast $6-9, lunch $8-13, dinner $20-25; ◷ 8am-3pm daily, plus 5:30-9pm Wed-Sun) In a sunny space overlooking the harbor, this eclectic eatery serves great wraps, sandwiches and espressos, and has dinner offerings like wasabi halibut ($22) and sweet-chili salmon ($23). Be prepared to queue up out the door.

Sweet-n-Clean (☎ 234-7240; 226 Main St; fast food $3-10; ◷ 11am-9pm Mon-Sat) It serves quality burgers and fried fish on Styrofoam plates while you watch your clothes spin. It's got espressos, too.

Linwood Bar & Grill (☎ 234-7674; 257 Main St; burgers $9-11, pizzas $9-22; ◷ grill 5-10pm) A dark harborfront saloon, which has plenty of cigarette smoke to go with your meal.

Main Street Market (☎ 234-7633; 381 Main St; ◷ 9am-8pm) This is where to go for groceries, liquor, espressos and T-shirts.

Getting There & Around

BICYCLE

If you didn't bring your two-wheeler over from Homer, the Boardwalk Hotel rents mountain bikes (per hour guests/nonguests $15/20). All-day rates are also available.

BOAT

Alaska Marine Highway ferries provide twice-weekly service between Homer and Seldovia ($31, 1½ hours) with connecting service throughout the peninsula and the Aleutians. The **Seldovia ferry terminal** (☎ 234-7886, www.ferryalaska.com) is at the north end of Main St.

Rainbow Tours (☎ 235-7272; drop-off at Homer Spit Rd; one way/round-trip $20/35) offers the inexpensive

DETOUR: ACROSS THE BAY

Opposite Homer but outside Kachemak Bay State Park is a handful of compelling destinations easily accessible by water-taxi.

Gull Island

Halfway between the Spit and Halibut Cove, the 40ft-high Gull Island attracts some 16,000 nesting seabirds: puffins, kittiwakes, murres, cormorants and many more species. If you can cope with the stench, you'll enjoy photographing the birds up close, even if you don't have a 300mm lens.

    Mako's Water-taxi (☎ 235-9055; www.makoswatertaxi.com; Homer Spit Rd) has a one-hour island tour (per person $35, three-person minimum) and a two-hour tour that includes adorable sea otters (per person $50, four-person minimum). Several other companies do Gull Island tours as well.

Halibut Cove

Halibut Cove, an absurdly quaint village of 30 permanent residents, is a place you'll wish you grew up in. In the early 1920s the cove had 42 herring salteries and had over 1000 residents. Today it's home to the noted Saltry restaurant, several art galleries, a warren of boardwalks – but no roads.

    The *Danny J* travels to the cove twice daily. It departs Homer at noon, swings past Gull Island and arrives at 1:30pm. There, you have 2½ hours to explore and have lunch. The ferry returns to the Spit by 5pm and then makes an evening run to the cove for dinner, returning to Homer at 10pm. The noon tour costs $47 per person, while the evening trip costs $25. Make reservations through **Central Charters** (☎ 235-7847, 800-478-7847; www.centralcharter.com), which has an office on the Spit.

    For many couples, dining at the **Saltry** (☎ 296-2223; lunch $11-22, dinner $20-26) makes for the ultimate date, with an outdoor deck over the aquamarine inlet and excellent seafood and vegetarian cuisine. Its lunch seatings are at 1:30pm and 3pm; for dinner it's 6pm or 7:30pm.

    After eating, check out the galleries. **Halibut Cove Experience** (☎ 296-2215) displays the paintings, pottery and sculpture of more than a dozen local artisans – a significant percentage of the adult population. **Cove Gallery** (☎ 269-2207), just up the steps from where the *Danny J* docks, is where Diana Tillion sells her octopus-ink watercolors. The art's not great, but it's worth the visit just to learn how she gets the ink out of the octopi.

    To make Halibut Cove an even more interesting side trip, spend the night. **Quiet Place Lodge** (☎ 296-2212 Jun-Aug, 235-1800 Sep-May; www.quietplace.com) has luxurious facilities and all-inclusive packages that cover transport and meals, while at the more basic **Country Cove Cabins** (☎ 888-353-2683, 296-2257; www.xyz.net/~ctjones/home.htm), you get kitchen facilities where you cook for yourself.

North of Seldovia

In Tutka Bay, Sadie Cove and Eldred Passage are a selection of quality lodges accessed only by water-taxi.

    Otter Cove Resort (☎ 235-7770; www.ottercoveresort.com; cabins $80), located on Eldred Passage, has affordable camping-style cabins near the Sadie Knob Trail, rents kayaks (per single/double $40/70) and guides single- and multiday paddling trips. It is also home to the **Rookery** (lunch $8-13, dinner $12-25; ☽ noon-9pm), serving seafood and steak in a beautiful seaside setting. Round-trip transportation is $20.

    Tutka Bay Wilderness Lodge (☎ 235-3905, 800-606-3909; www.tutkabaylodge.com; r per person from $650) is an all-inclusive resort with chalets, cottages and rooms surrounding the lodge house, where guests enjoy meals with a sweeping view of the inlet and Jakolof Mountain. The accommodations are very comfortable, the food is excellent and the amenities include a sauna, deepwater dock, boathouse and hiking trails. Activities range from clamming to sea kayaking. There's a two-night minimum.

    Sadie Cove Wilderness Lodge (☎ 888-283-7234, 235-2350; www.sadiecove.com; r per person $275) is just to the north of Tutka Bay in Sadie Cove. This wilderness lodge offers similar amenities – cabins, sauna, outdoor hot tub, Alaskan seafood dinners – but it's not quite as elegant or pricey.

KENAI PENINSULA

Rainbow Connection shuttle from Homer to Seldovia. It departs at 9am, gets to Seldovia an hour later, and then returns to take you back to Homer at 5pm. It'll transport your bike for $5 and your kayak for $10.

Mako's Water-taxi (☎ 235-9055; www.makoswater taxi.com; drop-off at Homer Spit Rd; round-trip $85) offers a tour that drops you off at Jakolof Bay, from which you'll be driven to Seldovia. You return to Homer via a short flightseeing trip.

Central Charters (☎ 235-7847, 800-478-7847; www .centralcharter.com; drop-off at Homer Spit Rd, one way/ round-trip $30/45) does a daily six-hour tour from Homer, leaving at 11am, circling Gull Island, and deboarding you in Seldovia to enjoy the village for the afternoon.

PLANE

Smokey Bay Air (☎ 235-1511; www.smokeybayair .com; 2100 Kachemak Dr; each way $27.50) offers a scenic 12-minute flight from Homer, over the Kenai Mountains and Kachemak Bay to Seldovia.

Homer Air (☎ 235-8591; www.homerair.com; one way/round-trip $32/64) flies to Seldovia hourly.

Great Northern Air Guides (☎ 800-243-1968, 243-1968; www.gnair.com; one way about $130) can fly you to Anchorage.

TAXI

For rides out Jakolof Bay Rd or to the airport, try **Jim's Shuttle Service** (☎ 234-7848, 399-8159) or **Seldovia Cab & Limousine** (☎ 234-7830, 299-0831).

KACHEMAK BAY STATE PARK

Stand on Homer Spit and look south, and an alluring wonderland sprawls before you: a luxuriantly green coastline, sliced by fjords and topped by sparkling glaciers and rugged peaks. This is Kachemak Bay State Park, which, along with Kachemak Bay State Wilderness Park to the south, includes 350,000 acres of idyllic wilderness accessible only by bush plane or boat. It was Alaska's first state park. According to locals, it remains the best.

The most popular attraction is Grewingk Glacier, which can be seen across the bay from Homer. Viewing the glacier at closer range means a boat trip to the park and a very popular one-way hike of 3½ miles. Outside the glacier, however, you can easily escape into the wilds by either hiking or kayaking. With more than 40 miles of trails,

plenty of sheltered waterways, numerous campsites and a few enclosed accommodation options, this is a highly recommended outing for a day or three.

Orientation

The park takes in much of Kachemak Bay's south side, extending from Chugachik Island in the northeast to Tutka Bay, east of Seldovia, in the southwest. In places it crosses the peninsula to the Gulf of Alaska; elsewhere, it abuts Kenai National Wildlife Refuge and Kenai Fjords National Park.

Center for Alaskan Coastal Studies (☎ 235-6667; www.akcoastalstudies.org; 708 Smokey Way; ☯ 9am-5pm Mon-Fri) Has maps and information about the park, both at its downtown Homer headquarters off Lake St and at its yurt on the Spit behind Mako's Water-taxi. National Geographic's *Trails Illustrated* map of the park is an excellent resource, depicting hiking routes, public-use cabins, docks and campsites, and it's available here. The Center also operates the Peterson Bay Field Station across the bay (below).

Emergency (ambulance, fire, police ☎ 911)

Mako's Water-taxi (☎ 235-9055; www.makoswater taxi.com; Homer Spit Rd) can give you the lowdown on possible hikes and paddles in the park – and about the logistics of getting over and back.

Sights & Activities

PETERSON BAY FIELD STATION

Though technically it's outside the park, this **field station** (☎ 235-2778), operated by the Center for Alaskan Coastal Studies, provides an excellent introduction to the ecology and natural history of the area. In summer, staff members lead daylong educational tours of the coastal forest and waterfront tide pools; the best intertidal beasties are seen during extremely low, or 'minus,' tides. Inside the station, too, you can get up close and personal with a touch tank full of squishy sea creatures. The cost is $95, which includes the boat ride over from the Spit. For $140 you can combine a morning natural-history tour with an afternoon of guided paddling in Peterson and China Poot Bays. If you want to overnight here, the station has bunks and yurts (p274).

HIKING
Glacier Lake Trail

The most popular hike in Kachemak Bay State Park is this 3½-mile, one-way trail that begins at the Glacier Spit trailhead, near the small Rusty Lagoon Campground. The level, easy-to-follow trek proceeds across the glacial outwash and ends at a lake with superb views of Grewingk Glacier. Camping on the lake is spectacular, and often the shoreline is littered with icebergs. At Mile 1.4 you can connect to the 6½-mile **Grewingk Glacier Trail**, with a hand-tram and access to the face of the glacier. If you don't have time for the entire hike, there are excellent views less than a mile from the tram.

Alpine Ridge Trail

At the high point of the mile-long Saddle Trail, an offshoot of the Glacier Lake Trail, you will reach the posted junction for this 2-mile climb to an alpine ridge above the glacier. The climb can be steep at times but manageable for most hikers with day packs. On a nice day, the views of the ice and Kachemak Bay are stunning.

Lagoon Trail

Also departing from the Saddle Trail is this 5½-mile route that leads to the ranger station at the head of Halibut Cove Lagoon. Along the way it passes the Goat Rope Spur Trail, a steep 1-mile climb to the alpine tundra. You also pass the posted junction of Halibut Creek Trail. If Grewingk Glacier is too crowded for you, follow this trail a half-mile to Halibut Creek to spend the night in a beautiful, but much more remote, valley.

The Lagoon Trail is considered a moderately difficult hike and involves fording Halibut Creek, which should be done at low tide. At the ranger station, more trails extend south to several lakes, as well as Poot Peak and the Wosnesenski River.

Poot Peak

This is a difficult, slick, rocky ascent of 2600ft Poot Peak. The trailhead begins at the Halibut Cove Lagoon, where a moderate 2.6-mile climb along the China Poot Lake Trail takes you to a campsite on the lake. From there, the trail to the peak diverges after the Wosnesenski River Trail junction. For a little over a mile you'll clamber upward through thinning forest until you reach the Summit Spur, where the route climbs even more precipitously to the mountain's lower summit, 2100ft in elevation. From here, reaching the very top involves scaling a shifting wall of scree, a feat that should

be attempted only by those who have some rock-climbing experience. In wet weather, it should be avoided altogether. Getting from the lake to the summit and back will likely take the better part of a day.

Grace Ridge Trail

This is a 7-mile trail that stretches from a campsite at Kayak Beach trailhead to deep inside Tutka Bay in the state park. Much of the hike runs above the tree line along the crest of Grace Ridge, where, needless to say, the views are stunning. There's also access from Sea Star Cove public-use cabin (see p274). You could hike the trail in a day, but it makes a great two-day trek with an overnight camp in the alpine.

Emerald Lake Trail

This steep, difficult 6.4-mile trail begins at Grewingk Glacial Lake and leads to Portlock Plateau. You'll witness firsthand the reclamation of the wasted forest (due to spruce bark beetle damage) by brushy alder and birch, considered delicacies by local wildlife. At Mile 2.1 a spur trail reaches the scenic Emerald Lake, and there are great views of the bay from the plateau. In spring, stream crossings can be challenging.

PADDLING

You can also spend three or four days paddling the many fjords of the park, departing from Homer and making overnight stops at Glacier Spit or Halibut Cove. Think twice before crossing Kachemak Bay from the Spit, however. Although it's only 3½ miles to the eastern shore, the currents and tides are powerful and can cause serious problems for inexperienced paddlers.

A tiny family-run outfit, **Seaside Adventures** (☎ 235-6672; www.seasideadventure.com; trips incl water-taxi half-/full day $90/$130) will show you the bay on kayak complete with running commentary about local flora and fauna, emphasis on fauna.

St Augustine Charters (☎ 299-1894; www.homer kayaking.com; paddles incl water-taxi half-/full-day $85/130) offers rentals from its Peterson Bay Kayak Center, as well as guided paddles. It does multiday excursions, too, involving paddling, trekking along state park trails, and camping at seaside sites.

True North Kayak Adventures (☎ 235-0708; www .truenorthkayak.com), based on Yukon Island, runs half-day paddles amid the eagles overhead and otters for $85, water-taxi included. Once you've spent all that time crossing the bay, however, it makes more sense to spring for the full-day paddle ($135). There are also several multiday options that cross Eldred Passage into Tutka Bay or Sadie Cove. For experienced kayakers, it rents rigid single/double kayaks for $45/65 per day.

Glacier Lake Kayaking & Hiking (☎ 888-777-0930, 235-0755; www.threemoose.com) offers kayaking on Glacier Lake, inside Kachemak Bay State Park, combined with guided hikes.

Sleeping

Camping is permitted throughout Kachemak Bay State Park. Moreover, numerous free, primitive camping areas have been developed, usually at waterfront trailheads or along trails. Consult the Alaska Division of Parks for the locations and facilities.

Center for Alaskan Coastal Studies (☎ 235-6667; www.akcoastalstudies.org; Heath St; ☽ 9am-5pm Mon-Fri) This organization reserves bunks ($20) or yurts ($70) close to its Peterson Bay Field Station, just outside the park. Lodgers can use the kitchen at the field station.

Public-use cabins (☎ 269-8400; 262-5581; www.alaskastateparks.org; $65) There are five cabins, which can be reserved in the park. Three are in Halibut Cove: Lagoon Overlook, with a pair of bunk-beds; Lagoon East Cabin, which has disabled access; and Lagoon West Cabin, a half-mile west of the public dock. Sea Star Cove Cabin, on the south shore of Tutka Bay, is convenient to the Tutka

Lake Trail. China Poot Cabin is accessible by kayak or water-taxi. Make reservations for any of them months in advance.

Yurts (☎ 235-0132; www.nomadshelter.com; $65) There are six of these for rent in the park, maintained by a private operator. All are near the ocean and equipped with bunks and woodstoves. They're located at the mouth of Humpy Creek, at the mouth of Halibut Cove, in China Poot Bay, near the North Eldred Passage Trailhead, and near the northwest and southeast Grace Ridge Trailheads.

Getting There & Around

The state park makes an excellent side trip for anybody who has a tent, a spare day and the desire to escape the overflow of RVers on Homer Spit. A number of water-taxis offer drop-off and pickup service (round-trip $50 to $80). Because boat access to some of the trailheads is tidally dependent, you'll need to work with them to establish a precise rendezvous time and location – and then be sure to stick to it.

Mako's Water-taxi (☎ 235-9055; www.makoswatertaxi.com) is the most respected of Homer's water-taxi services, famed for making timely pick-ups even in foul weather – and for dropping off beer to unsuspecting campers. For most cross-bay destinations it charges $60 per person round-trip with a two-person minimum.

Other good outfits include **Smoke Wagon Water-taxi & Charter** (☎ 235-2947; www.homerwatertaxi.com) and **Tutka Bay Taxi** (☎ 235-7166; www.tutkabaytaxi.com).

Southwest Alaska

Stretching more than 1500 miles, from Kodiak to the western end of the Aleutian Islands, is Southwest Alaska, an island-studded region with stormy weather and a violent past. This is the northern rim of the volcanic chain in the Pacific Ocean known as the Ring of Fire. Forty-six active volcanoes are spread along the Alaska Peninsula and the Aleutians – the greatest concentration anywhere in North America.

Despite the harsh weather and volcanic activity – or maybe because of it – Southwest Alaska is a region of diverse habitats rich in wildlife. It boasts the world's largest bears, on Kodiak Island; Alaska's richest salmon runs, in Bristol Bay; and some of the biggest blue-berries you'll ever pick, on the windswept islands of the Aleutians. From a naturalist's point of view, few places on earth have such abundant wildlife.

From a traveler's point of view, this is as remote as Alaska gets. Southwest Alaska can be divided into four areas: the Kodiak Archipelago with Kodiak Island, the Alaska Peninsula, the Aleutian Islands and Bristol Bay. There are no roads, making the region hard to reach, expensive to visit, and so stormy you better be prepared for weather-bound days at the airport.

But if travel in Alaska is for the adventurous, this is your spot. Even in Alaska there are few adventures like riding a state ferry across the North Pacific, poking around a desolate WWII battlefield or watching 1000lb bears gorge themselves on salmon only 100ft away.

HIGHLIGHTS

- **Best road trip** (p286) – exploring the wild beauty of Kodiak Island along its road system in a rental car

- **Best bear watching** (p290) – seeing giant brown bears snag salmon at Brooks Falls in Katmai National Park & Preserve

- **Best bus tour** (p291) – joining a tour through the barren landscape of Valley of 10,000 Smokes in Katmai National Park & Preserve

- **Most adventurous boat trip** (p285) – boarding the Trusty Tusty for a ferry trip past whales and volcanoes to the Aleutian Islands

- **Best historic site** (p296) – hiking up Dutch Harbor's Mount Ballyhoo to view gun turrets, Quonset huts and other WWII military remains

Katmai National Park & Preserve ★

Kodiak ★

★ Aleutian Islands

Dutch Harbor ★

■ AREA CODE: ☎ 907   ■ POPULATION: 35,500   ■ ELEVATION: MT REDOUBT 10,197FT

SOUTHWEST ALASKA

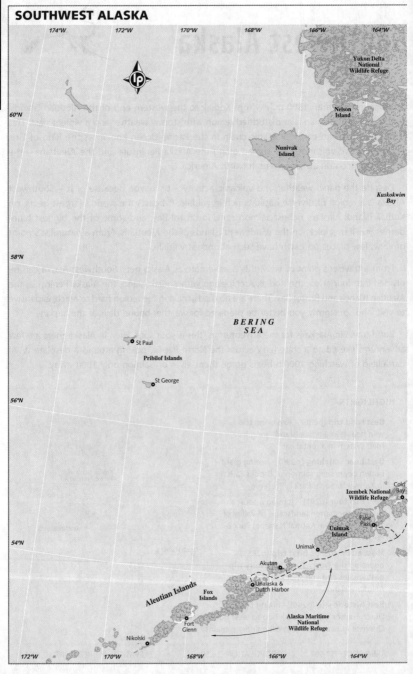

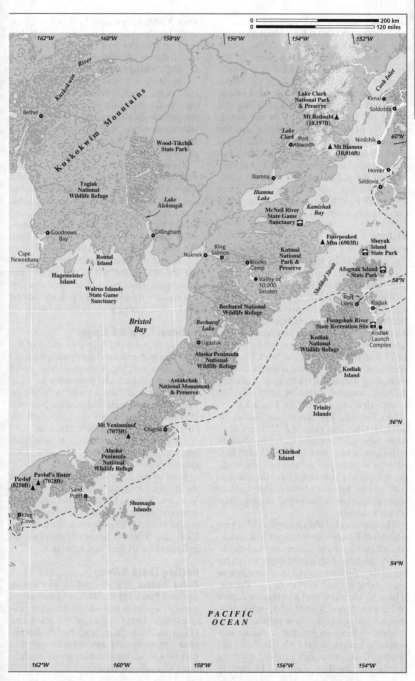

0   200 km
0   120 miles

162°W   160°W   158°W   156°W   154°W   152°W

Kuskokwim River

Bethel

Kuskokwim Mountains

Wood-Tikchik State Park

Cook Inlet

Kenai
Soldotna

Lake Clark National Park & Preserve

Mt Redoubt ▲ (10,197ft)

Lake Clark

Port Alsworth

Ninilchik

▲ Mt Iliamna (10,016ft)

60°N

Togiak National Wildlife Refuge

Lake Aleknagik

Iliamna

Homer

Seldovia

Iliamna Lake

McNeil River State Game Sanctuary

Kamishak Bay

Dillingham

Goodnews Bay

Cape Newenham

Round Island

King Salmon

Naknek

Brooks Camp

Valley of 10,000 Smokes

Katmai National Park & Preserve

Fourpeaked ▲ Mtn (6903ft)

Shuyak Island State Park

Afognak Island State Park

58°N

Hagemeister Island

Walrus Islands State Game Sanctuary

Bristol Bay

Bechatof National Wildlife Refuge

Becharof Lake

Ugashik

Alaska Peninsula National Wildlife Refuge

Shelikof Strait

Port Lions

Kodiak

Pasagshak River State Recreation Site

Kodiak Launch Complex

Kodiak National Wildlife Refuge

Kodiak Island

Aniakchak National Monument & Preserve

Mt Veniaminof (7075ft) ▲

Chignik

Trinity Islands

56°N

Alaska Peninsula National Wildlife Refuge

Chirikof Island

Pavlof (8250ft) ▲ ▲ Pavlof's Sister (7028ft)

Sand Point

King Cove

Shumagin Islands

54°N

PACIFIC OCEAN

162°W   160°W   158°W   156°W   154°W

Climate

With little to protect it from the high winds and storms that sweep across the North Pacific, Southwest Alaska is home to the worst weather in Alaska. Kodiak is greatly affected by the turbulent Gulf of Alaska and receives 80in of rain per year, along with regular blankets of pea-soup fog and occasional blustery winds. On the northern edge of the Pacific, Unalaska and the Alaskan Peninsula receive less rain (annual precipitation ranges from 60in to 70in), but are renowned for unpredictable and stormy weather. Rain, fog and high wind are common. Summer temperatures range from 45°F to 65°F, with the clearest weather often occurring in early summer and fall.

History

More than any other region of the state, Southwest Alaska has the most turbulent history, marked by massacres, violent eruptions and WWII bombings.

When Stepan Glotov and his Russian fur-trading party landed at present-day Dutch Harbor in 1759, there were more than 30,000 Aleuts living on Unalaska and Amaknak Islands. After the Aleuts destroyed four ships and killed 175 fur hunters in 1763, the Russians returned and began a systematic elimination of Aleuts, massacring or enslaving them. It's estimated that by 1830 only 200 to 400 Aleuts were living on Unalaska.

The Russians first landed on Kodiak Island in 1763 and returned 20 years later when Siberian fur trader Gregorii Shelikof established a settlement at Three Saints Bay. Shelikof's attempts to 'subdue' the indigenous people resulted in another bloodbath where more than 1000 Alutiiq Indians were massacred or drowned during their efforts to escape.

The czar recalled Shelikof and in 1791 sent Aleksandr Baranov to manage the Russian-American Company. After an earthquake nearly destroyed the settlement at Three Saints Bay, Baranov moved his operations to more stable ground at present-day Kodiak. It became a bustling port and was the capital of Russian America until 1804 when Baranov moved again, this time to Sitka.

Some violence in Southwest Alaska was caused by nature. In 1912 Mt Katmai on the nearby Alaska Peninsula erupted, blotting out the sun for three days and blanketing Kodiak with 18in of ash. Kodiak's 400 residents briefly escaped to sea on a ship but soon returned to find buildings collapsed, ash drifts several feet high and spawning salmon choking in ash-filled streams.

The town was a struggling fishing port until WWII when it became the major staging area for the North Pacific operations. At one point Kodiak's population topped 25,000, with a submarine base at Women's Bay, an army outpost at Buskin River and gun emplacements protecting Fort Abercrombie.

Kodiak was spared from attack during WWII, but the Japanese bombed Unalaska only six months after bombing Pearl Harbor and then invaded Attu and Kiska Islands (p26). More hardship followed: the Good Friday Earthquake of 1964 leveled downtown Kodiak and wiped out its fishing fleet; the king-crab fishery crashed in the early 1980s; and the *Exxon Valdez* oil spill soiled the coastline at the end of the decade. But this region rebounded after each disaster, and today Unalaska and Kodiak are among the top five fishing ports in the country.

National Parks & Refuges

Southwest Alaska is home to some of the state's largest and most intriguing national parks and refuges. Unfortunately all of them are isolated and expensive to visit. Katmai National Park & Preserve (p289) on the Alaska Peninsula and Kodiak National Wildlife Refuge (p286) are renowned for bear watching. Lake Clark National Park & Preserve (p292), across Cook Inlet from Anchorage, is a wilderness playground for rafters, anglers and backpackers.

Most of the Aleutian Islands and part of the Alaska Peninsula form the huge Alaska Maritime National Wildlife Refuge, headquartered in Homer (p261). The refuge encompasses 3.5 million acres and more than 2500 islands, and is home to 80% of the 50 million seabirds that nest in Alaska.

Getting There & Away

Alaska Airlines (☎ 800-252-7522; www.alaskaair .com) and **PenAir** (☎ 800-448-4226; www.penair.com) service the region and one or the other provides daily flights to Kodiak, King Salmon, Unalaska, Dillingham and Bethel. **Era Aviation** (☎ 800-866-8394; www.eraaviation.com) also flies to Kodiak from a number of destinations throughout Alaska.

The most affordable way to reach the region is via the **Alaska Marine Highway** (☎ 800-642-0066; www.ferryalaska.com), which has stops at Kodiak, Unalaska and a handful of small villages in between.

KODIAK ISLAND

Big and green, wild and remote, Kodiak Island is Alaska's largest island (3670 sq miles) and the US's second largest after the Big Island of Hawaii. It's home to the famed Kodiak brown bear, the world's largest terrestrial carnivore. Fattened by the island's abundant salmon runs, these bears grow to gargantuan proportions – males can weigh up to 1500lb. An estimated 2300 of them live here.

Flying into Kodiak's airport on a sunny day, it's easy to see why it's called the Emerald Isle. Steep green mountains rise up out of an azure blue sea, like a North Pacific version of Bali Hai. Modern-day explorers of the island can find back roads leading to some of the most beautiful deserted beaches in Alaska.

KODIAK
☎ 907 / pop 13,466

Kodiak is a worker's town. Unlike many ports in the Southeast, tourism in Kodiak is nice but not necessary. That's why there's no hostel on the island, no campgrounds near the city and nobody running a shuttle service to the airport.

Everybody is too busy working, primarily at sea. Kodiak sits at the crossroads of some of the most productive fishing grounds in the world and is home to Alaska's largest fishing fleet – 770 boats including the state's largest trawl, longline and crab vessels. The fleet and the 12 shore-based processors account for more than 50% of employment on the island.

Kodiak works hard. It's consistently one of the top five fishing ports in the country and second only to Alaska's Dutch Harbor for value of product and tonnage processed. Since the king-crab moratorium in 1983, Kodiak has diversified to catch everything from salmon, pollack and cod to sea cucumbers. In 1995 Kodiak set a record when 49 million pounds of salmon crossed its docks.

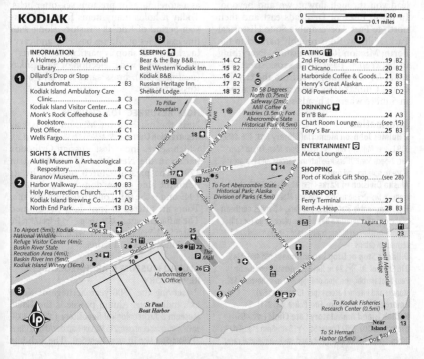

It is also the home to the largest US coast-guard station, while at Cape Narrow at the south end of the island is the Kodiak Launch Complex (KLC), a $38 million low Earth–orbit launch facility.

You'll find residents friendly, lively at night in the bars, often stopping to offer you a lift without a thumb being extended. But in the morning they go to work. This is the real Alaska: unaltered, unassuming and not inundated by the tourism industry, particularly cruise ships. Arrive for the scenery, stay to enjoy outdoor adventures that range from kayaking to photographing a 1000lb bear. But most of all, come to Kodiak to experience Alaska and meet people who struggle at sea to earn a living on the stormy edge of the Pacific Ocean. This is a lesson in life worth the price of an airline ticket from Anchorage.

Orientation

Lucky you if you're arriving in Kodiak on the state ferry. The vessel ties up downtown right next to the Kodiak Island Visitor Center. How convenient is that? There are three main roads in Kodiak that will lead you through downtown and beyond. In town, Rezanof Dr heads east and then north to Fort Abercrombie State Historical Park. Mill Bay Rd is roughly parallel to the north; Mission Rd to the south. Everything in between is basically a cross street. Rezanof Dr also heads west from the city, becomes Chiniak Hwy and reaches the airport in 5 miles where it heads south.

Information

A Holmes Johnson Memorial Library (☎ 486-8686; 319 Lower Mill Bay Rd; ◷ 10am-9pm Mon-Fri, to 5pm Sat, 1-5pm Sun) Offers free Internet access and is a great place to hole up and read.

Alaska Division of Parks (☎ 486-6339; 1400 Abercrombie Dr; ◷ 9am-5pm Mon-Fri) Maintains an office at Fort Abercrombie State Historical Park, 4.5 miles northeast of the city off Monashka Bay Rd, the place to go (or call) for information on hiking trails, state campgrounds and recreation cabins.

Dillard's Stop or Drop Laundromat (☎ 486-2345; 216 Shelikof St; ◷ 24 hr Jun-Sep) Across from the St Paul Boat Harbor, the Stop or Drop also has showers ($8), storage and Internet access (per 15 minutes $2).

Emergency (Ambulance, Fire, Police ☎ 911)

Kodiak Island Ambulatory Care Clinic (☎ 486-6188; Suite 102,1202 Center St; ◷ 9am-8pm Mon-Fri, 10am-6pm Sat) For emergency and walk-in medical care.

Kodiak Island Visitor Center (☎ 486-4782, 800-789-4782; www.kodiak.org; 100 Marine Way; ◷ 8am-5pm Mon-Fri, 10am-4pm Sat) Next to the ferry terminal, with brochures and maps of the city.

Kodiak National Wildlife Refuge Visitor Center (☎ 487-2600; http://kodiak.fws.gov; 1390 Buskin River Rd; ◷ 8am-4:30pm Mon-Fri, noon-4pm Sat) Four miles southwest of the city, near the airport, this office has information on public-use cabins.

Monk's Rock Coffeehouse & Bookstore (☎ 486-0905; 202 W Rezanof Dr; ◷ 10am-6pm Tue-Sat) Weird but cool place with lots of Alaskan titles, Russian Orthodox books and icons and espresso drinks.

Post office (419 Lower Mill Bay Rd) The main post office is just northeast of the library.

Wells Fargo (☎ 486-3216; 202 Marine Way) Has an ATM and a king-crab display in its lobby.

Sights

BARANOV MUSEUM

Housed in the oldest Russian structure in Alaska is **Baranov Museum** (☎ 486-5920; 101 Marine Way; adult/child $3/free; ◷ 10am-4pm Mon-Sat, from noon Sun), across the street from the visitors center. The museum fills the Erskine House, which the Russians built in 1808 as a storehouse for precious sea-otter pelts. Today it holds many items from the Russian period of Kodiak's history along with fine examples of Alutiiq basketry and carvings. The gift shop is particularly interesting, offering a wide selection of *matreshkas* (nesting dolls), brass samovars and other Russian crafts.

HOLY RESURRECTION CHURCH

Near the museum on Mission Rd is **Holy Resurrection Church** (☎ 486-5532; 385 Kashevarof St), which serves the oldest Russian Orthodox parish in the New World, established in 1794. The present church, marked by its beautiful blue onion domes, was built in 1945 and is the third one to occupy this site. Tours are offered at 1pm daily in summer. The adjacent small **gift shop** (◷ 1-4pm Mon-Fri, to 6pm Sat & Sun) is stocked with *matreshkas*, religious books and icons.

ALUTIIQ MUSEUM & ARCHAEOLOGICAL REPOSITORY

Preserving the 7500-year heritage of Kodiak's indigenous Alutiiq people is the **Alutiiq Museum & Archaeological Repository** (☎ 486-7004; www.alutiiqmuseum.com; 215 Mission Rd; adult/child $3/free; ◷ 9am-5pm Mon-Fri, from 10am Sat). The exhibits display one of the largest collections of Alutiiq artifacts in the state, ranging from a kayaker in his waterproof parka of seal gut to a 19th-century spruce-root hat. Take time to explore 'Sharing Words,' an intriguing interactive computer program that uses village elders to teach Alutiiq words and songs in an attempt to save the indigenous language.

ST PAUL BOAT HARBOR
The pulse of this city can be found in its boat harbors. **St Paul Boat Harbor** is downtown and the larger of the two. Begin with the **Harbor Walkway** (Shelikof St), where a series of interesting interpretive displays lines the boardwalk above the docks. Then descend to the rows of vessels, where you can talk to the crews or even look for a job.

FORT ABERCROMBIE STATE HISTORICAL PARK
This military fort, 4.5 miles northeast of Kodiak, off Monashka Bay Rd, and its pair of 8in guns were built by the US Army during WWII for a Japanese invasion that never came. In the end, Kodiak's lousy weather kept the Japanese bombers away from the island. The fort is now a 186-acre state historical park, sitting majestically on the cliffs above scenic Monashka Bay. Between the guns is Ready Ammunition Bunker, which stored 400 rounds of ammunition during the war. Today it contains the small **Kodiak Military History Museum** (☎ 486-7015; adult/child $3/free; ☼ 1-4pm Fri-Mon).

Just as interesting as the gun emplacements are the tidal pools found along the park's rocky shorelines, where an afternoon of searching for sea creatures can be spent. Park rangers lead tidal-pool exploration walks most Saturday and Sunday mornings during the summer. Call the **Alaska Division of Parks** (☎ 486-6339) for exact days and times.

PILLAR MOUNTAIN
From the top of this 1270ft mountain behind the city you'll have excellent views of the surrounding mountains, ocean, beaches and islands. One side seems to plunge directly down to the harbor below, and the other overlooks the green interior of Kodiak Island. Pick up the bumpy dirt road to the top by walking or driving north up Thorsheim Ave and turning left on Maple Ave, which runs into Pillar Mountain Rd.

BUSKIN RIVER STATE RECREATION SITE
Four miles southwest of the city on Chiniak Rd, this 168-acre park includes the Buskin River, where anglers flock for salmon fishing, the best in this part of Kodiak Island. The **Kodiak National Wildlife Refuge Visitor Center** (☎ 487-2600; http://kodiak.fws.gov; 1390 Buskin River Rd; ☼ 8am-4:30pm Mon-Fri, noon-4pm Sat) has numerous displays and films on the island's wildlife, including brown bears. The **Audubon Loop Trail** is a short, self-guided nature trail near the center.

Activities
BEER & WINE TASTING
Within town is the delightful **Kodiak Island Brewing Co** (☎ 486-2537; 338 Shelikof St; ☼ noon-7pm) where brewmaster/owner/tour guide Ben Millstein will give you a short talk about the operation and then let you taste the five beers he brews. His Liquid Sunshine is so good you might walk out with a half-gallon growler ($8) or even a case-sized party pig ($34).

Kodiak is also home to several wineries, fermenting everything (except grapes that is) from rhubarb and salmonberries to wild rose. **Kodiak Island Winery** (☎ 486-4848; www.kodiakwinery.com; Mile 36 Chiniak Hwy; ☼ 1-6pm) is a scenic 36 miles out of town and has tours, a gift shop and, of course, wine tasting.

HIKING
The Kodiak area has dozens of hiking trails, but few are maintained, and trailheads are not always marked. Windfall can make following the track difficult or even totally conceal it. Still, hiking trails are the best avenues to explore the natural beauty of Kodiak Island.

The best source of hiking information is the **Alaska Division of Parks** (☎ 486-6339) or the excellent *Kodiak Audubon's Hiking & Birding Guide* ($12), a large waterproof topographical map with notes on the trails and birds.

For transportation and company on the trail, the local **Audubon Society** (☎ 486-5648) offers group hikes ($2) almost every Saturday and Sunday from May to October, meeting at 9:30am at the ferry terminal. Plant-lovers might consider **Backwoods Botany** (☎ 486-5712, ext 201; tours $25; ☼ 2pm Mon-Fri) and its 2½-hour plant-identification hiking tour of the island.

Barometer Mountain

This popular hiking trail is a steep climb and a 4-mile round-trip to the 2452ft summit. To reach the trailhead, follow Chiniak Rd south of Buskin River Campground and turn right on Burma Rd, the first road immediately after passing the end of the airport's runway. Look for a well-worn trail on the left. The trek, which begins in thick alder before climbing the hogback ridge of the mountain, provides spectacular views of Kodiak and the bays south of the city.

Termination Point

This is another popular hike. The 5-mile loop starts at the end of Monashka Bay Rd and branches into several trails near Termination Point, a spectacular peninsula that juts out into Narrow Strait. Most hiking is done in a lush Sitka spruce forest that shelters you even on the most blustery of days. Be warned, however, that the inland portion of the loop can be confusing at times. If you're nervous about your navigational skills, simply hike the coastal half of the loop and then backtrack.

North Sister Mountain

Starting 150ft up a creek bed a mile before the end of Monashka Bay Rd, this trail (find it on the left side of the creek bed) first leads up steeply through dense brush, but then levels off on alpine tundra. The summit of North Sister (2100ft) is the first peak seen (to your left), about a mile from the trailhead. The other two sisters are also accessible from here.

Pyramid Mountain

Two trails, both starting on Anton Larsen Bay Rd, lead to the top of Pyramid Mountain (2401ft). Avoid the easternmost trail, accessed off the golf course, which is brush-choked and hard going. Instead, continue west to Anton Larsen Pass, where the other trail begins in the parking area on the right. It's a steep but easy-to-follow climb, straight up the mountain 2 miles to the top.

Anton Larsen Pass

This 5-mile loop is a scenic ridge walk and a far easier alpine hike than Barometer Mountain. The trail begins just north of the gravel parking lot at the pass on the left side of Anton Larsen Bay Rd. A well-defined trail leads you through meadows; at a fork the trailheads right to cross a bridge and climbs to a broad alpine ridge. Once on top, use the rolling ridge to skirt a distinctive, glacial valley before descending back to the fork in the trail.

CYCLING

Mountain bikers will find Kodiak's gravel roads interesting to ride on, especially 12-mile Anton Larsen Bay Rd. Leading northwest from near Buskin River Campground, the road crosses a mountain pass and leads to the island's west side, where you will find quiet coves and shorelines to explore. Plan on two hours for the ride to Anton Larsen Bay. Another favorite is Burma Rd, picked up near the airport (see Barometer Mountain left). It can be combined with a stretch of Chiniak Rd for a 12-mile, two- to three-hour loop.

58 Degrees North (☎ 486-6249; 1231 Mill Bay Rd; per 24hr $35; ☉ 10am-6pm Mon-Sat) is an outdoor shop that rents out mountain bikes. If you are planning to do a lot of bike exploration, purchase the *Kodiak Island Mountain Bike Guide* ($8), which outlines 17 rides throughout the island.

PADDLING

With its many bays and protected inlets, scenic coastline and offshore rookeries, much of Kodiak is a kayaker's dream. Paddling around Near and Woody Islands and on to Monashka Bay is a scenic day trip from the downtown area.

Unfortunately, there is nowhere in Kodiak to rent a kayak. However, a growing number of outfitters offer fully equipped tours, either from the harbor or utilizing a mothership to reach more isolated areas of the island. **Mythos Expeditions Kodiak** (☎ 486-5536; www.thewildcoast.com) uses a converted fishing vessel for a variety of guided trips including a day of whale watching from kayaks (per person $200 to $300). **Orcas Unlimited** (☎ 481-1121; www.orcasunlimited.com) has a half-day outing among the harbor islands ($100) and a full-day paddle ($200) to two remote inlets of Kodiak Island.

Kodiak for Children

If the kids are tagging along in Kodiak, cross the Zharoff Memorial Bridge to Near Island, where you'll find several attractions well suited to families. Best of all, they're free.

Kodiak Fisheries Research Center (☎ 481-1800; Trident Way; 🕙 8am-4:30pm Mon-Fri) Opened in 1998 to house the fisheries research being conducted by various agencies, it has an interesting lobby that includes displays, touch tanks and a large aquarium.

North End Park (Trident Way) Reached as soon as you cross the bridge. The small park is laced by forested trails that converge at a stairway to the shoreline. At low tide you can search the tidal pools here for starfish, sea anemones and other marine life.

St Herman Harbor (Dog Bay Rd) A great place to look for sea lions, which often use the Dog Bay Breakwall as a haul-out, while eagles are usually perched in the trees onshore.

Tours

Several companies provide either a city tour of Kodiak or a daylong scenery-viewing tour that includes Baranov Museum, Pillar Mountain and Fort Abercrombie State Historical Park. Call **Alaska Motor Coaches** (☎ 486-3648) or **Kodiak Tours** (☎ 486-3920; www.kodiak tours.com) for full-day or half-day tours that cost $85 or $50 per person.

Kodiak is one place where you should skip the ground tour and hit the water. **Galley Gourmet** (☎ 486-5079, 800-253-6331; www .kodiak-alaska-dinner-cruises.com; dinner $95, brunch $75) Onboard their 42ft yacht, Marty and Marion Owen whip up delicious meals like BBQ king salmon with rhubarb-sage sauce, and serve them on white table linen while you enjoy the coastal scenery. The nightly dinner cruise is 3½ hours; brunch is a two-hour cruise and is offered only on the weekends.

Helios Sea Tours (☎ 486-5310; www.kodiakriver camps.com; half-/full day $150/200) Whale watching and marine-wildlife viewing on a smaller 27ft vessel.

Kodiak Sailing Charters (☎ 486-1732, 866-486-1732; www.kodiaksailingcharters.com; full-day sail 2/3/4 people $1000/1200/1300) Uses a 49ft ketch-rigged sailboat for a full day of sailing that includes whale watching, kayaking and a delicious seafood dinner. Overnight trips are also available.

Festivals & Events

Kodiak Crab Festival The town's best event, it was first held in 1958 to celebrate the end of crabbing season. Today the weeklong event in late May features parades, a blessing of the fleet, foot and kayak races, fishing-skills contests (such as a survival-suit race), and a lot of cooked king crab.

Fourth of July Kodiak celebrates with fireworks that begin at midnight.

Bear Country Music Festival Features country, bluegrass and Alaskan music in mid-July.

State Fair & Rodeo Held on Labor Day weekend at the Bell Flats rodeo grounds.

Sleeping
KODIAK CITY

Lodging is expensive in Kodiak and there's an 11% sales and bed tax on top of all tariffs. The most current list of B&Bs is on the website of the **visitors center** (www.kodiak.org).

Budget

Buskin River State Recreation Site (Mile 4.5, W Rezanof Dr; sites $10) This pleasant, 15-site campground offers secluded tent sites, picnic shelters, pit toilets and trails. It's the closest campground to the city.

Fort Abercrombie State Historical Park (Mile 4, E Rezanof Dr; sites $10) The other camping option, this has 13 wooded sites northeast of Kodiak.

Midrange

Shelikof Lodge (☎ 486-4141; www.shelikoflodge.com; 211 Thorsheim Ave; s/d $70/80; ✗ 🖵) Nicest rooms downtown for what you pay plus a good restaurant and a lounge. A bonus is the airport shuttle service.

Bev's Bed & Make Your Own Darn Breakfast (☎ 486-0834; www.bevsbedandbreakfast.com; 1510 Mission Rd; r $70; ✗) You have to admire the attitude of this B&B proprietor and love the price. The four guestrooms have queen-size beds and private entrances. Outside there is a porch with a barbecue grill; inside is a fully stocked kitchen that you're encouraged to use, especially in the morning.

Russian Heritage Inn (☎ 486-5657; www.geocities .com/russianheritageinn; 119 Yukon St; r $65-95, ste $110; 🖵) In 2005 this 25-room motel received a badly needed face-lift that included new carpets and beds. There are eight economy rooms at $65 a night.

Kodiak B&B (☎ 486-5367; home.gci.net/~mmonroe; 308 Cope St; s/d $85/105; ✗) This longtime B&B is the most convenient to downtown. It's just up the hill from the boat harbor, with two rooms, a friendly owner and nice views.

Bear & the Bay B&B (☎ 486-6154; 206 E Rezanof Dr; r with/without bath $95/75; ✗) A downtown B&B with five guestrooms on two floors. Each floor has a private entrance, kitchen, living room and a deck with a view of both boat harbors.

Top End

Best Western Kodiak Inn (☎ 486-5712, 888-563-4254; www.kodiakinn.com; 236 W Rezanof Dr; s/d from $139/149; 🖵) Kodiak's largest and most upscale motel with 81 rooms downtown along with a fine restaurant, outdoor hot tub and airport-shuttle service.

Buskin River Inn (☎ 487-2700, 800-544-2202; www.kodiakadventure.com; 1395 Airport Way; r $135-145; 💻) In the same league as the Kodiak Inn but located next to the airport. A good choice if you plan to rent a car and explore the island.

AROUND KODIAK
Scattered along the Kodiak road system are numerous B&Bs, lodges and resorts, offering a bed away from town and a serene evening along the coast.

Lagoonside B&B (☎ 486-5445; www.chiniak.net/lagoonside; Mile 36, Chiniak Hwy; s/d incl meals $125/150; ✖ 💻) Near Kodiak Island Winery is this B&B with five guestrooms, four kayaks and a deck that overlooks Jack's Lagoon. Within a 20-minute drive are six salmon streams and in case you catch one there's a BBQ on the deck to grill it.

9th Wave B&B (☎ 486-0838; www.keaconnect.net/jvanatta; Mile 35, Chiniak Hwy; r per night 1st/additional $125/100; ✖ 💻) Also on the rugged coast of Chiniak Bay, an hour's drive from town, is this rustic log home with two guestrooms, private baths and a hot tub.

AAA River Inn (☎ 486-2882, 888-568-2882; www.aaabayview.com; Mile 38, Pasagshak Bay Rd; r $160) A five-guestroom inn next door to the Pasagshak River State Recreation Area with a deck overlooking salmon-rich Pasagshak River. You're so close to the river you can hear the fish jumping.

Eating
Mill Bay Coffee & Pastries (☎ 486-4411; 3833 E Rezanof Dr; breakfast $4-6, lunch $7-10; 🕒 6:30am-7pm Mon-Sat, 8am-5pm Sun; ✖) What's a French chef doing in Kodiak? Joel Chenet's love of hunting is the reason this city is blessed with the best pastries in Alaska, hands down. Get there early: the case is empty of tortes, éclairs and 8in-high apple pies by midafternoon. For a seafood treat try the Kodiak sea burger, a salmon patty topped with crab, shrimp and cream cheese, and served on a toasted brioche bun.

Old Powerhouse (☎ 481-1088; 516 Marine Way; lunch $10-15, dinner $14-21; 🕒 11:30am-2pm & 5-9pm Tue-Thu, 11:30am-2pm & 5-10pm Fri & Sat, 5-9pm Sun; ✖) This Japanese seafood restaurant, located in a historic power plant, offers Kodiak's best

waterfront dining. An outdoor deck and solarium overlook the channel where fishing boats and the state ferry glide right past you. Along with a sushi bar, the restaurant serves excellent *udon* and *soba* noodles as well as *yakisoba* (broiled Japanese noodles).

El Chicano (☎ 486-6116; 103 Center St; lunch $8-10, dinner $15-23; 🕒 11am-9:30pm Sun-Thu, to 10:30pm Fri & Sat) A sprawling restaurant and bar that serves big portions of Mexican food and 'grande' margaritas. There is an outdoor deck for the three days in the summer the sun's out.

2nd Floor Restaurant (☎ 486-8555; 776 W Rezanof Dr; sushi rolls $4-13, dinner $18-26; 🕒 11am-2pm & 5-10pm Sun-Thu, 11am-2pm & 5-11pm Fri & Sat; ✖) Kodiak's other fine Japanese restaurant, with more than 30 types of sushi, much of it made with local seafood.

Henry's Great Alaskan (☎ 486-8844; 512 Marine Way; sandwiches $7-10, dinner $11-25; 🕒 11:25am-10pm Mon-Thu, to 10:30pm Fri & Sat, noon-9:30pm Sun) On the mall in front of the small-boat harbor; burgers, lots of deep-fried seafood, beer on tap and sports on TVs large and small scattered throughout the restaurant.

Harborside Coffee & Goods (☎ 486-5862; 216 Shelikof St; 🕒 6:30am-7pm Mon-Sat, from 7am Sun; ✖) Has a bulletin board listing deckhand jobs and makes the incredibly delicious 'Harborside Mocha.'

Safeway (☎ 481-1500; 2685 Mill Bay Rd; 🕒 6am-midnight) Kodiak's largest and best grocery store has a salad bar, ready-to-eat items and a seating area.

Drinking & Entertainment
Clustered around the city waterfront and small-boat harbor are a handful of bars that cater to Kodiak's fishing industry. If you visit these at night you'll find them interesting places, overflowing with skippers, deckhands and cannery workers drinking hard and talking lively.

Chart Room Lounge (236 W Rezanof Dr) In the Kodiak Inn, its 2nd-floor location allows you to sip a glass of wine with a nice view of the harbor and mountains. An acoustic guitarist on Fridays makes the setting even more mellow.

B'n'B Bar (326 Shelikof St) Across from the harbor, B'n'B claims to be Alaska's oldest bar, having served its first beer in 1899. It's a fishermen's bar; and the giant wall-mounted king crab alone is worth the price of a beer.

THE TRUSTY TUSTY

There are two ways to see a part of the remote region of Alaska called 'the Bush' without flying. One of them is to drive the Dalton Hwy to Prudhoe Bay on the Arctic Ocean. The other is to hop onto the Alaska Marine Highway ferry when it makes its special runs to the eastern end of the Aleutian Islands. The MV *Tustumena*, a 290ft vessel that holds 230 passengers, is one of only two ferries in the Alaska Marine Highway fleet rated as an oceangoing ship; hence its nickname, the 'Trusty Tusty.'

Once a month from May through to September or October, the *Tustumena* leaves Kodiak on a Wednesday, and continues west to Chignik, Sand Point, King Cove, Cold Bay and False Pass, to reach Unalaska and Dutch Harbor by Saturday morning. It leaves again on Saturday afternoon, reaching Kodiak on Monday evening and continuing on to Homer that night.

The boat docks at the smaller villages only long enough to load and unload (one to two hours), which is plenty of time to get off for a quick look around. In Unalaska and Dutch Harbor, the ship stays in port for five or six hours, which is long enough for van tours designed to accommodate ferry passengers.

This is truly one of the best bargains in public transportation. The scenery and wildlife are spectacular. You'll pass the perfect cones of several volcanoes, the treeless but lush green mountains of the Aleutians and distinctive rock formations and cliffs. Whales, sea lions, otters and porpoises are commonly sighted, and birdlife abounds. More than 30 species of seabirds nest in the Aleutians, and 250 species of bird migrate through here. Diehard birders are often on board sighting albatross, auklets, cormorants and puffins. If you don't know a puffin from a kittiwake, you can attend daily presentations by naturalists from the US Fish & Wildlife Service (USFWS).

Viewing wildlife and scenery depends, however, on the weather. It can be an extremely rough trip at times, deserving its title 'the cruise through the cradle of the storms.' On the runs in fall, 40ft waves and 80-knot winds are the norm, and no matter when you step aboard, you'll find barf bags everywhere on the ship – just in case. The smoothest runs are from June to August.

Cabins are available and are a worthwhile expense if you can afford it (double $247 each way). The trip is long, and the Tusty's solarium isn't as comfortable as most of the Southeast ferries for cabinless sleeping. If you plan to sleep there, make sure you bring a good sleeping pad. Also bring a good book. On days when the fog surrounds the boat, there is little to look at but the waves lapping along the side.

The round-trip fare for walk-on passengers to Dutch Harbor from Kodiak is $516; if you begin and end in Homer, it's $618. Travelers who want to spend more time in Unalaska and Dutch Harbor can fly back with **Alaska Airlines** (☎ 800-426-0333; www.alaskaair.com) through one of its contract carriers **PenAir** (☎ 800-448-4226; www.penair.com), though a one-way flight back to Anchorage will set you back $400 to $500.

Tony's Bar (518 Marine Way) This drinking hole in the mall calls itself 'the biggest navigational hazard on Kodiak.'

Mecca Lounge (302 Marine Way) Open mic on Wednesday, karaoke on Thursday, and rock and roll booming across its dancefloor on Friday and Saturday.

Getting There & Away

Both **Alaska Airlines** (☎ 487-4000, 800-252-7522) and its contract carrier **ERA Aviation** (☎ 487-4363, 800-866-8394; www.eraaviation.com) fly to Kodiak daily. Fares range between $260 and $350 depending on when you go and if the ticket is an advance purchase. The airport is 5 miles south of Kodiak on Chiniak Rd.

Other than the offerings from a few motels, there is no shuttle service into town. **Alaska Cab** (☎ 481-3400) charges $17 for the ride downtown.

Alaska Marine Highway's MV *Tustumena* stops at Kodiak several times a week, coming from either Seward ($73) or Homer ($65), and stopping twice a week at Port Lions, a nearby village on Kodiak Island. Once a month the 'Trusty Tusty' continues west to Unalaska and Dutch Harbor ($258 one way from Kodiak).

The **ferry terminal** (☎ 486-3800, 800-526-6731; 100 Marine Way) is right in the middle of downtown, so it's easy to explore Kodiak even if you're just in port for an hour or two.

Getting Around

The cheapest car rental in Kodiak is **Rent-A-Heap** Airport Terminal (☎ 487-4001); Port of Kodiak Gift Shop (☎ 486-8550; 508 Marine Way), with used, two-door compacts for $37 a day plus 37¢ per mile. If you're planning to drive around the island, that mileage rate will quickly drain your funds. **Budget Rent-A-Car** (☎ 487-2261; Airport Terminal) offers compacts for $60 a day with unlimited mileage.

AROUND KODIAK

More than 100 miles of paved and gravel roads head from the city into the wilderness that surrounds Kodiak. Some of the roads are rough jeep tracks, manageable only by 4WD vehicles, but others can be driven or hitched along to reach isolated stretches of beach, great fishing spots and superb coastal scenery.

South of Kodiak, Chiniak Rd winds 48 miles to Cape Greville, following the edge of three splendid bays. The road provides access to some of Alaska's best coastal scenery and opportunities to view sea lions and puffins offshore, especially at Cape Chiniak near the road's southern end.

Just past Mile 30 of Chiniak Rd is the junction with Pasagshak Bay Rd, which continues another 16.5 miles due south. Along its way it passes **Pasagshak River State Recreation Site** (Mile 8.7, Pasagshak River Rd) with 12 free

campsites near a beautiful stretch of rugged coastline 45 miles from town. This small, riverside campground is famous for its silver and king-salmon fishing and for a river that reverses its flow four times a day with the tides. These scenic areas, not the city, are the true attractions of Kodiak Island.

To find a bed for the night, see p284.

Kodiak National Wildlife Refuge

This 2812-sq-mile preserve, which covers the southern two-thirds of Kodiak Island, all of Ban and Uganik Islands and a small section of Afognak Island, is the chief stronghold of the Alaska brown bear. An estimated 2300 bears reside in the refuge and the surrounding area, which is known worldwide for brown-bear hunting and to a lesser degree for salmon and steelhead fishing. Birdlife is plentiful: more than 200 species have been recorded, and there are 600 breeding pairs of eagles that nest within the refuge. Flowing out of the steep fjords and deep glacial valleys and into the sea are 117 salmon-bearing streams that account for 65% of the total commercial salmon harvest in Kodiak.

The refuge's diverse habitat ranges from rugged mountains and alpine meadows to wetlands, spruce forest and grassland. No roads enter the refuge, and no maintained trails lie within it. Cross-country hiking is extremely hard, due to thick brush. Access

---

THE BEARS OF KODIAK

The Kodiak Archipelago is home to a wide range of land mammals, including river otters, Sitka black-tailed deer, Roosevelt elk and mountain goats. But almost everybody arrives hoping to catch a glimpse of just one animal – the Kodiak bear. This subspecies of the brown bear, *Ursus arctos middendorffi*, is the largest land carnivore in the world. Males normally weigh in at more than 800lb but have been known to exceed 1500lb. Females usually weigh in at 400lb to 600lb. From late April to June, the bears range from sea level to midelevations and feed on grasses and shrubs. In July many graze in alpine meadows. But from mid-July to mid-September the bears congregate at streams to gorge themselves on spawning salmon. The runs are so heavy that the bears often become selective, and many feast only on females and then eat only the belly portion containing the eggs. The carcass they toss aside is immediately devoured by scavengers-in-waiting such as red foxes, bald eagles and seagulls.

Biologists estimate there are 3000 brown bears living in the archipelago, or one bear per 1.5 sq miles, with more than 2300 on Kodiak Island itself. That's more than three times the number of brown bears in the rest of the USA. But you won't see any near the city of Kodiak or even from the road system. Like most wild animals, Kodiak bears are often secretive around humans. They are most active in early morning and late evening and spend much of their time in dense alder thickets. The best time to see the bears is during the salmon-feeding period from July to September and the most common way to do this is with a bear-sighting flight or with an outfitter as part of a unique wilderness experience (see opposite).

into the park is by charter plane or boat out of Kodiak, and most of the refuge lies at least 25 air miles away.

Like most wilderness areas in Alaska, an extensive trip into the refuge is something that requires advance planning and some money. Begin before you arrive in Alaska by contacting the **Kodiak National Wildlife Refuge Visitor Center** (☎ 487-2600; http://kodiak.fws .gov; 1390 Buskin River Rd, Kodiak, AK 99615).

If you're looking for somewhere to sleep, the Kodiak office of the US Fish & Wildlife Service (USFWS) administers eight cabins in the refuge, none accessible by road. The closest to Kodiak are Uganik Lake Cabin and Veikoda Bay Cabin. The rate is $30 a night and the cabins are reserved through four lotteries throughout the year. If all dates are not booked in the lottery, the open dates are booked by phone on a first-come, first-served basis. Contact the refuge visitors center for more information.

BEAR WATCHING

What most people really want to see in the refuge are the massive brown bears. But if you're limited to just a day or two in Kodiak, the only feasible way to do this is through an air charter. Just about every air-charter company in town offers a bear-watching flight in which you fly over remote shorelines in the refuge looking for bruins. The length of flights and the number of times you land differ from one 'tour' to the next but generally a four-hour trip that includes landing and photographing bears feeding on salmon will cost $400 to $450 per person with a two-person minimum.

Among the many air services offering bear tours are **Andrew Airways** (☎ 487-2566; www.andrew airways.com), **Bear Quest Aviation** (☎ 486-2327, 800-304-2327; www.bearquestaviation.com), **Kodiak Air Service** (☎ 486-4446) and **Sea Hawk Air** (☎ 486-8282, 800-770-4295; www.seahawkair.com).

If you have more time, a much more adventurous way of seeing the bears is through **Kodiak Treks** (☎ 487-2122; www.kodiaktreks.com), which offers low-impact, small-group bear-watching trips from its remote lodge on an island in Uyak Bay. Harry Dodge, a noted bear biologist, leads guests from the lodge, by boat and boot, to various viewing spots in the bay. You'll spend the day hiking and watching anywhere from a handful to more than two dozen bears. The cost is $275 per

person per day and covers lodging, meals and equipment but not your charter flight to Uyak Bay. This is an excellent way to experience the refuge, but plan at least three days at the lodge to include other activities such as kayaking and fishing.

Afognak Island State Park

Afognak Island lies just north of Kodiak Island in the archipelago. Some 75,000 acres of Afognak are protected in the pristine Afognak Island State Park, which has two public-use cabins: Laura Lake Cabin and Pillar Lake Cabin. The cabin at Pillar Lake is a short walk from a beautiful mile-long beach. Both cabins are accessed by floatplane, cost $35 a night, and are reserved through **Alaska Division of Parks & Outdoor Recreation** (☎ 486-6339; www.alaskastateparks.org). You can also check the cabin availability and make reservations six months in advance online.

Shuyak Island State Park

The northernmost island in the Kodiak Archipelago, remote and undeveloped Shuyak is 54 air miles north of Kodiak. It's only 12 miles long and 11 miles wide, but almost all of the island's 47,000 acres are taken up by Shuyak Island State Park, featuring forests of virgin Sitka spruce and a rugged shoreline dotted with secluded beaches. Otters, sea lions and Dall porpoises inhabit offshore waters, while black-tailed deer and a modest population of the famous Kodiak brown bear roam the interior.

Kayakers enjoy superb paddling in the numerous sheltered inlets, coves and channels – the area boasts more protected waterways than anywhere else in the archipelago. Most of the kayaking takes place in and around Big Bay, the heart of the state park. From the bay you can paddle and portage (carrying your boat and gear over a trail between two bodies of water) to four public cabins and other protected bays, where you can explore numerous islands and maybe even sight an occasional humpback whale.

The park's four cabins are on Big Bay (which has a ranger station and visitors center), Neketa Bay and Carry Inlet. The cabins ($65 per night) are cedar structures with bunks for eight, woodstoves, propane lights and cooking stoves but no running water. Shuyak Island cabins are reserved the same way as Afognak Island cabins (above).

ALASKA PENINSULA

Due west of Kodiak Island is the Alaska Peninsula, stretching 550 miles from Cook Inlet to its tip at False Pass. The rugged volcanic arm includes Alaska's largest lakes – Lake Clark, Iliamna Lake and Becharof Lake – and some of the state's most active volcanoes. Birds, marine mammals, brown bears and other wildlife are plentiful on the peninsula, and anglers from around the world come here to fish for trophy rainbow trout and five species of salmon.

The Alaska Marine Highway stops at four small communities along the Alaska Peninsula on its way to the Aleutians, but the peninsula's most popular attraction, Katmai National Park & Preserve, has turned King Salmon into the main access point. Two other natural preserves attract the interest of travelers: McNeil River State Game Sanctuary and Lake Clark National Park & Preserve.

KING SALMON

☎ 907 / pop 404

The residents of King Salmon are mostly government employees, living in a vast, wide, open landscape on the beautiful Naknek River. The town is a little rough around the edges and, along with the relative lack of people, this gives King Salmon a quiet, edge-of-the-world appeal.

Just under 300 air miles from Anchorage, King Salmon is the air-transport hub for Katmai National Park & Preserve (opposite) and most visitors see little more than the airport terminal and the float dock where they catch a flight into the park.

Information

King Salmon's post office is about a mile west of the airport, but you can purchase stamps and mail letters at the visitors center.

AC Value Center (☎ 246-6109; 100 Eskimo St; ⏱ 7am-9pm) By King Salmon Mall; sells some camping gear and supplies.

Camai Medical Center (☎ 246-6155; 211 School Rd; ⏱ 9am-5pm Mon-Fri) For anything routine, get yourself to Naknek's medical center, which is on call for emergencies.

Emergency (ambulance, fire, police ☎ 911)

Katmai National Park Headquarters (☎ 246-3305; ⏱ 8am-4:30pm Mon-Fri) A block from the terminal in King Salmon Mall; turn right as you exit the terminal.

Rangers can answer any questions that might have stumped the knowledgeable visitors-center staff.

King Ko Inn (☎ 246-3377; 100 Airport Rd; ⏱ 8am-6pm) Has laundry facilities with showers. At $10 for a shower, think twice about how clean you want to be.

King Salmon Visitor Center (☎ 246-4250; ⏱ 8am-5pm) The National Park Service (NPS), USFWS and the two area boroughs operate this center, next door to the airport terminal. The center has natural-history displays and videos, and sells an excellent selection of books and maps (including topographic maps).

Wells Fargo (☎ 246-3306; King Salmon Mall) Has an ATM.

Sleeping

Lodging here is hideously expensive, so most visitors try to avoid spending the night, but if you haven't made campground or lodge reservations at Katmai National Park & Preserve, you'll have to overnight in King Salmon and visit the park as a day trip. The bed tax is 10%.

If you're hauling backpacking equipment, one option is to just wander down the road away from town and set up camp on the riverbank. Just remember that winds can be murderous here, so you'd best have a tent that can withstand strong gusts.

Dave's World/R&G Boat Rental (☎ 246-3353, 246-8651; Municipal Dock 1; rgbrakna@bristolbay.com; campsites $8, 4-person cabins $75) Has a 160-acre spread you can camp on. Most of the area is across the Naknek River from King Salmon, a $5 (round-trip) skiff ride away. Dave has another small camping area by the office on the town side, but it tends to be swampy if it has just rained. If you need lodging in King Salmon, Dave's three rustic cabins are the best deal in town.

Antlers Inn (☎ 246-8525, 888-735-8525; antlersinn@bristolbay.com; s/d without bath $110/130, campsites $20) A reasonably priced option with a friendly family-run atmosphere. It's right 'downtown' on Eskimo Creek and rooms share bathrooms, microwave and coffeemaker. Outside is a place to pitch tents and a shower building.

King Ko Inn (☎ 246-3377, 866-234-3474; www.kingko.com; 100 Airport Rd; cabin s/d $175/190; 💻) Friendly, comfortable and adjacent to the airport terminal. It offers 16 cabins with private baths; eight of them have kitchenettes. The King Ko is also home to the liveliest bar in town.

Quinnat Landing Hotel (☎ 246-3000, 800-770-3474; www.quinnat.com; Mile 1, Eskimo Creek Rd; s/d $250/270)

With 48 rooms, Quinnat is the largest hotel in the area and ritzy for this part of the world. But that's not saying much, and King Salmon's not a good place for a splurge.

Eating

Soup, great *panini* sandwiches, salads, quiches and other healthy stuff are all available at **Fireweed Café** (☎ 246-3122; King Salmon Mall; sandwiches $8, salads $7; ☆ 11am-3pm Mon-Fri; ☒).

Both King Ko Inn and Quinnat Landing Hotel have full-service restaurants. Or you might try **Eddie's Fireplace Inn** (☎ 246-3435; Airport Rd; breakfast $10-12, dinner $12-25; ☆ 7am-10pm), an atmospheric bar across the street from King Ko with a kitchen open all day.

Getting There & Away

Alaska Airlines (☎ 800-252-7522; www.alaskaair.com) flies up to six times daily between Anchorage and King Salmon during the summer. The advance-purchase round-trip fare is $350 to $400. **PenAir** (☎ 800-448-4226; www.pen air.com) also offers service from Anchorage to King Salmon.

KATMAI NATIONAL PARK & PRESERVE

In June 1912 Novarupta Volcano erupted violently and, with the preceding earthquakes, rocked the area now known as Katmai National Park & Preserve. The wilderness was turned into a dynamic landscape of smoking valleys, ash-covered mountains and small holes and cracks fuming with steam and gas. Only one other eruption in historic times, on the Greek island of Santorini in 1500 BC, displaced more ash and pumice.

If the eruption had happened in New York City, people living in Chicago would have heard the explosion; the force of the eruption was 10 times greater than the 1980 eruption of Mt St Helens in the state of Washington. For two days people in Kodiak could not see a lantern held at arm's length, and the pumice, which reached half the world, lowered the temperature in the northern hemisphere that year by 2°F. In history books, 1912 is remembered as the year without a summer, but the most amazing aspect of this eruption, the most dramatic natural event in the 20th century, was that no-one was killed. Katmai is that remote.

In 1916 the National Geographic Society sent Robert Grigg to explore the locality. Standing at Katmai Pass, the explorer saw

for the first time the valley floor with its thousands of steam vents. He named it the Valley of 10,000 Smokes and the name stuck. Grigg's adventures revealed the eruption's spectacular results to the world, and two years later, the area was turned into a national monument. In 1980 the monument was enlarged to 4.2 million acres and designated a national park and preserve.

Although the fumaroles no longer smoke and hiss, the park is still a diverse and scenic wilderness, unlike any other in Alaska. It ranges from glaciated volcanoes and ash-covered valleys to island-studded lakes and a coastline of bays, fjords and beaches. Wildlife is abundant, with more than 30 species of mammals, including large populations of brown bears, some weighing over 1000lb. Katmai is also a prime habitat for moose, sea lions, arctic foxes and wolves. The park's many streams and lakes are known around the state for providing some of Alaska's best trout and salmon fishing.

Information

Katmai National Park & Preserve (☎ 246-2100, 246-3305; www.nps.gov/katm; PO Box 7, King Salmon, AK 99613) is not a place to visit on a whim. Because of the cost of reaching the park, it's best to spend at least four days or more here to justify the expense.

The park's summer headquarters is Brooks Camp, on the shores of Naknek Lake, 35 miles from King Salmon. The camp is best known for Brooks Falls, which thousands of bright-red sockeye salmon attempt to jump every July, much to the interest of bears and tourists. In the middle of the wilderness, this place crawls with visitors (and bears) during July, when as many as 300 people will be in Brooks Camp and the surrounding area in a single day.

When you reach the camp on a floatplane, take a good look; bears are usually seen lumbering along the beach between the lodge and the planes pulled up on the sand. If the coast is clear, you're directed to go to the NPS Visitor Center, where you are enrolled in the 'Brooks Camp School of Bear Etiquette,' a mandatory 20-minute bear orientation. Among the things you learn is that bears have the right-of-way here; if a brownie lies down right on the trail and takes a nap, no visitors use the trail until it wakes up and moves on. These 'bear jams' have been known to last hours.

Rangers at the center also answer questions, help you fill out backcountry permits, stage a variety of interpretive programs and sell books and maps.

Most visitors come between mid-June and mid-July, when the salmon and brown bears are at their peak. Unfortunately, mosquitoes, always heavy in this area, are also at their peak. The best time for hiking and backpacking trips is from mid-August to early September, when the fall colors are brilliant, the berries ripe and juicy and the insects scarce. Be prepared for frequent storms. In fact, be ready for rain and foul weather at any time in Katmai, and always pack warm clothing.

Activities

BEAR WATCHING

Katmai has the world's largest population of protected brown bears (more than 2000). At Brooks Camp they congregate around Brooks River to benefit from the easy fishing for sockeye salmon. Most of this occurs in mid-June to mid-July, when 40 to 60 bears gather along a half-mile stretch of the Brooks River. In that month it is near impossible to get a campsite, a cabin or even a spot on the observation decks without planning months in advance. The bear activity then tapers off in late July and August, when the animals follow the salmon up into the streams feeding into Brooks Lake. It increases again in September as the bears return to the lower rivers to feed on spawned-out fish. That said, a few brown bears can be seen in the Brooks Camp area during summer; a couple of younger ones always seem to be hanging around.

Brooks Camp has three established viewing areas. From the lodge, a dirt road leads to a floating bridge over the river and the first observation deck – a large platform dubbed 'Fort Stevens' by rangers, for the Alaskan senator who secured the funding for it. From here you can see the bears feeding in the mouth of the river or swimming in the bay. Continue on the road to the Valley of 10,000 Smokes, and in half a mile a marked trail winds to Brooks Falls. Two more viewing platforms lie along this half-mile trail. The first sits above some riffles that occasionally draw sows trying to keep their cubs away from aggressive males at the falls.

The last deck, at the falls, is the prime viewing area, where you can photograph the salmon making spectacular leaps or a big brownie at the top of the cascade waiting with open jaws to catch a fish. At the peak of the salmon run, there might be eight to 12 bears here, two or three of them atop the falls themselves. The observation deck holds 40 people, and in early to mid-July it will be crammed with photographers, forcing rangers to rotate people on and off.

HIKING

Hiking and backpacking are the best ways to see the park's unusual backcountry. Like Denali National Park in Alaska's interior, Katmai has few formal trails; backpackers follow river shores, lake shores, gravel ridges and other natural routes. Many hiking trips begin with a ride on the park bus along the dirt road to the Valley of 10,000 Smokes. The bus will also drop off and pick up hikers along the road. The one-way fare is $51.

The only developed trail from Brooks Camp is a half-day trek to the top of **Dumpling Mountain** (2520ft). The trail leaves the ranger station and heads north past the campground, climbing 1.5 miles to a scenic overlook. It then continues another 2 miles to the mountain's summit, where there are superb views of the surrounding lakes.

PADDLING

The area has some excellent paddling including the Savonoski River Loop, a five- to seven-day adventure for experienced paddlers. Other popular treks include a 30-mile paddle from Brooks Camp to the **Bay of Islands** and a 10-mile paddle to Margot Creek, which has good fishing and lots of bears.

Lifetime Adventures (☎ 746-4644, 800-952-8624; www.lifetimeadventures.net) rents out folding kayaks (double/single daily $65/55, weekly $280/245) that you pick up either in Anchorage or King Salmon. The company also offers a self-guided Savonoski Loop trip for $750 per person that includes air transport from Anchorage to King Salmon, an air charter with a kayak to Bay of Islands and a return from Brooks Camp.

Once in the park, you can rent canoes (per hour/day $12/40) and kayaks (per hour/day $16/60) from Brooks Lodge. Remember that winds can be strong here and the lakes are big. Accomplished paddlers should have no problem, but the conditions can sometimes get dangerous for novices.

Tours

INDEPENDENT TOURS

The only road in Katmai is 23 miles long. It's a scenic traverse of the park that leads from the lodge past wildlife-inhabited meadows and river valleys and ends at Overlook Cabin, which has a sweeping view of the Valley of 10,000 Smokes. **Katmailand** (☎ 243-5448, 800-544-0551; www.katmailand.com; 4125 Aircraft Dr, Anchorage, AK 99502) runs the lodge at Brooks Camp. It has a daily bus to Overlook Cabin and back, which leaves at 9am, with three hours at the cabin, and returns to the lodge at 4:30pm. Most visitors take the bus round-trip as a tour, but backpackers sometimes use the bus one-way to or from the valley (per person $51).

Each bus carries a ranger who talks during the bus trip and leads a short hike from the cabin into the valley below. Views from the cabin include almost 12 miles of barren, moonlike valley where the lava oozed down, with snowcapped peaks beyond. It's an amazing sight.

The fare for the tour is a steep $88 per person (with a packed lunch $96), but if the weather isn't too bad most people feel it's money well spent. Sign up for the tour at the Katmailand office across from the lodge as soon as you arrive at Brooks Camp. The bus is filled most of the summer, and you often can't get a seat without making a reservation a day or two in advance.

Brooks Lodge also offers an hour-long flightseeing tour around the park for $130 per person (two people minimum).

PACKAGE TOURS

Because of the logistics of getting there and the need to plan and reserve so much in advance, many visitors arrive in Katmai as part of a one-call-does-it-all package tour. A shockingly large number are part of a one-day visit, spending large sums of money for what is basically an hour or two of bear watching. At the height of the season in July there can easily be 20 floatplanes or more lined up on the beach at Brooks Camp. **Katmailand** (☎ 243-5448, 800-544-0551; www.katmailand.com) Offers packages that include round-trip transportation from Anchorage to Brooks Camp, lodging and park fees but not meals. The double-occupancy price for two/three nights per person is $1072/1357. There is a sizable discount if you come in August when there are fewer bears at Brooks Falls: a one-day trip from Anchorage per person is $519.

Quinnat Landing Hotel (☎ 246-3000, 800-770-3474; www.quinnat.com) On offer are packages where you stay at the King Salmon hotel but fly into Brooks Camp for bear watching or a Valley of 10,000 Smokes tour. Its one-night tour, which includes a full day in the park and air transport from Anchorage, is $678 for a single ($842 for a double). Two nights at the hotel with two days in the park is $1455 for a single ($1176 for a double).

Lifetime Adventures (☎ 746-4644, 800-952-8624; www.lifetimeadventures.net) If you have the time, this offers a seven-day camping adventure that includes hiking in the Valley of 10,000 Smokes, biking the road back to Brooks Camp and kayaking near Margot River. The cost is $1700 per person and includes the flight from Anchorage, charters into the park, all equipment and guides.

Sleeping & Eating

If you plan to stay at Brooks Camp, either at the lodge or in the campground, you must make reservations. No walk-ins are accepted, so if you don't have reservations, you're limited to staying in King Salmon and visiting the park on day trips.

Campground reservations are accepted only by telephone from the first working day of January; call the **National Park Reservation Service** (☎ 800-365-2267, 301-722-1257; http://reservations.nps.gov). It might be easier to win the New York lottery than to obtain a campground reservation for the prime July bear-watching season. Often the campsites for July are completely booked within the first week of January. Camping is $8 per person per night and limited to a maximum of seven nights. If you don't have a reservation, you don't get a site.

Important: the 15-site campground holds a maximum of 60 people, and reservations are made by person, not by site. If you don't provide the names of everyone in your party when you make your reservation, space will be held for just one person. Woe to the reservation-maker who gave only his or her name, then found on arrival that the campground had no room for the other members of the party. It's happened.

Brooks Lodge (per person d/tr/q $317/220/172) has 16 basic but modernized, cabin-style rooms, each with two bunk beds and a private bath with shower. Cabins are usually rented as part of package tours that include transportation from Anchorage and park fees. Book a cabin at least several months in advance. During July there is a three-night maximum stay. For reservations contact **Katmailand** (☎ 243-5448, 800-544-0551; www.katmailand.com).

DETOUR: MCNEIL RIVER STATE GAME AREA

The McNeil River State Game Sanctuary, just north of Katmai National Park & Preserve on the Alaska Peninsula and 250 miles southwest of Anchorage, is famous for its high numbers of brown bears from July to August. This spot is world renowned among wildlife photographers, and every great bear-catches-salmon shot you've ever seen was most likely taken either here or the Brooks River. Often, 20 or so brown bears will feed together where McNeil River Falls slows the salmon, providing an easy meal; up to 80 have congregated here at one time.

The Alaska Department of Fish & Game has set up a viewing area and allows 10 visitors per day for a four-day period to watch the bears feed. From a camp, park guides lead a 2-mile hike across sedge flats and through the thigh-deep Mikfik Creek to the viewing area on a bluff. There you can watch the bears feed less than 60ft away, in a series of rapids and pools where the salmon gather between leaps. Though an expensive sidetrip for most visitors, watching and photographing giant brown bears at such close range is a once-in-a-lifetime experience.

July is the prime month for bear watching. Most visitors depart for McNeil River from Homer with a round-trip air charter that costs around $300 per person. Among the Homer-based air services offering flights to McNeil River is **Bald Mountain Air Service** (☎ 235-7969, 800-478-7969; www.baldmountainair.com).

Visits to the game sanctuary are on a permit basis only – by lottery – and your odds of drawing a permit from the lottery are less than one in five; applications are received from around the world. You can apply online at the **Alaska Department of Fish & Game – Division of Wildlife Conservation** (☎ 267-2182; www.wildlife.alaska.gov/mcneil; 333 Raspberry Rd, Anchorage, AK 99518-1599) or request an application by mail. Return your application (by mail only) with a $25 per person nonrefundable fee by March 1 for the lottery draw. Permits are drawn for 10 people a day for four-day periods; you must be self-sufficient, with camping equipment and food. The user fee for the sanctuary is $350 for non-Alaskans. Despite the fee, if your name is drawn, by all means take advantage of this rare opportunity in wildlife photography.

A store at Brooks Camp sells limited supplies of freeze-dried food, white gas (for camp stoves), fishing equipment, flies and other odds and ends...such as beer. You can also sign up for the all-you-can-eat meals at Brooks Lodge without renting a cabin (renters pay too); it's adult/child $12/8 for breakfast, $18/12 for lunch and $28/20 for dinner. Also in the lodge is a lounge with a huge stone fireplace, soft chairs and bar service in the evening.

Getting There & Away

Most visitors to Katmai fly into King Salmon on **Alaska Airlines** (☎ 800-252-7522; www.alaskaair .com). Once you're in King Salmon, a number of air-taxi companies offer the 20-minute floatplane flight out to Brooks Camp. **Katmai Air** (☎ 243-5448, 800-544-0551 within Alaska; www.katmai land.com/air-services), the Katmailand-affiliated company, charges $156 for a round-trip.

Also check with **Quinnat Landing Hotel** (☎ 246-3000, 800-770-3474; www.quinnat.com) about getting jet-boat transport to Brooks Camp. The hotel suspended the daily service in 2005 but is planning to resume it in 2006.

LAKE CLARK NATIONAL PARK & PRESERVE

Apart from backpacking enthusiasts and river runners, few tourists arrive in Alaska knowing about Lake Clark National Park & Preserve despite it being only 100 miles southwest of Anchorage. Yet Lake Clark offers some of the most spectacular scenery of any park in the state. The Alaska Range and Aleutian Range meet within this 5625-sq-mile preserve; among the many towering peaks are Mt Iliamna and Mt Redoubt, two active volcanoes that can be clearly seen from Anchorage.

The park made news in 1990 when Mt Redoubt erupted after 25 dormant years. The volcano roared back to life, sending ash into the air and creating a cloud that closed the Anchorage International Airport and forced officials to distribute 10,000 face masks to the residents of central Kenai Peninsula to protect against inhaling the fine powder.

Along with its now-famous volcanoes, the park has numerous glaciers, spectacular turquoise lakes (including Lake Clark, the park's centerpiece), and three designated wild rivers that have long been havens for river runners. Wildlife includes brown and black bears, moose, red foxes, wolves and Dall sheep on the alpine slopes, and caribou roam the western foothills. The park's watershed is one of the world's most important producers of red salmon, contributing 33% to the US catch.

For any pretrip planning contact the **park headquarters** (☎ 271-3751; www.nps.gov/lacl; 4230 University Dr, Suite 311, Anchorage); after you arrive a **ranger station** (☎ 781-2218; ⏰ 8am-4:30pm Mon-Fri) in Port Alsworth has displays and videos on the park and sells a limited selection of maps and books.

Activities

HIKING

Lake Clark is another remote park best suited to the experienced backpacker. Most extended treks take place in the western foothills north of Lake Clark, where the open and relatively dry tundra provides ideal conditions for hiking.

The 50-mile historic **Telaquana Trail**, first used by indigenous Dena'ina Athabascans and later by fur trappers and miners, is the park's best cross-country route. It begins on Lake Clark's north shore, near the Athabascan village of Kijik, and ends near Telaquana Lake. In between, you pass through boreal forests, ford glacial rivers and cross the fragile alpine tundra along the western flank of the Alaska Range.

Less experienced backpackers can be dropped off at the shores of the many lakes in the area to camp and undertake day hikes. Among the more popular are **Twin Lakes**, where dry tundra slopes provide for easy travel to ridges and great views. Along the lower lake there is a backcountry patrol cabin that is usually staffed during the summer and good fishing throughout the area. You will most likely encounter fly-in, day-use fishing parties from Anchorage as well as a few rafters and other backpackers.

RIVER RUNNING

Float trips down any of the three designated wild rivers are spectacular and exciting, with waterways rated from Class III to Class IV. The best way to handle a boat rental is through **Alaska Raft & Kayak** (☎ 561-7238, 800-606-5950; www.alaskaraftandkayak.com; 401 W Tudor Rd, Anchorage; ⏰ 9am-6pm Mon-Sat), which rents inflatable kayaks and canoes (per day $60) and

14ft to 16ft rafts (per day $90) in Anchorage. The shop will also deliver the boat to **Lake Clark Air** (☎ 781-2208, 888-440-2281; www.lakeclarkair .com) in Anchorage for your flight into the national park and pick it up when you return.

Chilikadrotna River

Beginning at Twin Lakes, this river offers a good adventure for intermediate rafters. Its steady current and narrow course winds through upland spruce and hardwood forest, draining the west flank of the Alaska Range. From the lakes to a pickup (locally known as takeout) on the Mulchatna River is a 60-mile, four-day float with some Class III stretches.

Tlikakila River

This fast but small glacial river flows from Summit Lake to upper Lake Clark through a narrow, deep valley within the Alaska Range. The 46-mile trip takes three days and hits a few stretches of Class III water. The hiking in tundra around Summit Lake is excellent, and from there you make a portage to the river.

Mulchatna River

Above Bonanza Hills, this river is a shallow, rocky channel from its headwaters at Turquoise Lake with stretches of Class III rapids. Below the hills, the Mulchatna River is an easy and leisurely float. Plan on two days to float from the lake to the end of Bonanza Hills. The entire river is a 220-mile run to the Nushagak River.

Sleeping

Port Alsworth is on Lake Clark's southeastern shore and serves as the main entry point into the park. **Farm Lodge** (☎ 781-2208, 888-440-2281; www.thefarmlodge.com; r per person/with 3 meals $100/150) provides lodging and three meals, or just a bed and breakfast. The inn also operates a flying service for backpacking drop-offs and river trips.

Iliamna, a small village located 30 miles south of the park, serves as another jump-off spot for trips into Lake Clark National Park & Preserve. Near town is **Roadhouse Inn B&B** (☎ 571-1272; r per person/with meals $100/145) with food service and courtesy transportation.

Getting There & Away

You can reach Iliamna through **PenAir** (☎ 800-448-4226; www.penair.com), which has two flights a day from Anchorage for $350 to $400 for a round-trip. From Iliamna, you have to charter a plane to your destination within the park through air-taxi operators such as **Iliamna Air Taxi** (☎ 571-1245). The alternative is to fly into Port Alsworth. **Lake Clark Air** (☎ 781-2208, 888-440-2281; www.lakeclarkair.com) offers daily flights to Port Alsworth from Anchorage for a round-trip fare of $350.

THE LOWER PENINSULA

Most visitors to the little fishing villages on the western peninsula arrive on the Alaska Marine Highway's MV *Tustumena*, which goes from Kodiak to Unalaska and Dutch Harbor (p285). The ferry usually stops long enough for visitors to get out and walk from one end of a village to the other, and for most people, that's ample. If you decide to stay over at any village, you'll be able to find food and shelter, and then return to Anchorage through **PenAir** (☎ 800-448-4226; www.penair.com). A one-way flight from the peninsula communities to Anchorage is a $375 to $425 ticket.

On the northwest coast of Popof Island, **Sand Point** (☎ 383-2696; sptcity@arctic.net) is the largest commercial fishing base in the Aleutians with a population of 900. It was founded in 1898 by a San Francisco fishing company as a trading post and cod-fishing station but also bears traces of Aleut, Scandinavian and Russian heritage. The town's **St Nicholas Chapel**, a Russian Orthodox church, was built in 1933 and is now on the National Register of Historical Places.

At the Alaska Peninsula's western end, near the entrance to Cold Bay is **King Cove** (☎ 497-2340; amscity@arctic.net), founded in 1911 when a salmon cannery was built. Today, with a population of 723, it is a commercial fishing base and home to Peter Pan Seafoods, whose salmon cannery is the largest operation under one roof in Alaska.

On the west shore of the same bay is **Cold Bay** (☎ 532-2401; coldbayak@arctic.net), with a population of 90. A huge airstrip was built here during WWII; today it's the third-longest in the state, making Cold Bay the transport center for the entire Aleutian chain. You can still see Quonset huts and other remains from the WWII military buildup.

A 10-mile road also links the town to **Izembek National Wildlife Refuge** (☎ 532-2445, 877-836-6332; www.r7.fws.gov/nwr/izembek), which was created in 1960 to protect some 142 bird spe-

cies, mainly the Pacific black brant (a type of goose). Almost the entire North American brant population of 150,000 birds arrives in spring and fall during the annual migration, to feed on the large eelgrass beds in Izembek Lagoon. When the salmon are running, brown-bear densities in the refuge can be among Alaska's highest: as many as six bears per mile along some streams.

ALEUTIAN ISLANDS

Remote, rarely visited and extremely expensive to do so, the Aleutian Islands is a jagged arc where the Pacific plate of the earth's crust is violently forcing its way under the North American plate.

For most visitors the Aleutians is limited to two stops aboard the Alaska Marine Highway's MV *Tustumena* (p285); your first stop in the Aleutians is **False Pass** (☎ 548-2319; cityoffalsepass@ak.net), a small fishing village with a population of 62 on the tip of Unimak Island, looking across a narrow passage at the Alaska Peninsula.

UNALASKA & DUTCH HARBOR

☎ 907 / pop 4366

Unalaska, on Unalaska Island, and its sister town Dutch Harbor, on Amaknak Island, are at the confluence of the North Pacific and the Bering Sea, one of the world's richest fisheries. Dutch Harbor is the only natural deepwater port in the Aleutians, and more than 400 vessels call here each year from as many as 14 countries. The two towns are connected by the 500ft Bridge to the Other Side.

In summer the area's population can double with the influx of cannery workers who process seafood, mostly crab and pollack. Dutch Harbor is a transport center for the Bristol Bay salmon fishery. Since 1988 the towns have led the nation in both volume and value of seafood processed. There are five major seafood plants, whose 2000 workers churn out more than 800 million pounds of seafood annually for export. Offshore fishing vessels, ranging from 70ft crab boats to 700ft floating processors, employ more workers.

Dutch Harbor is the site of the canneries and fish-processing plants, and is something of an industrial park. Unalaska is where most residents live and, despite the large influx of transient workers, it can be

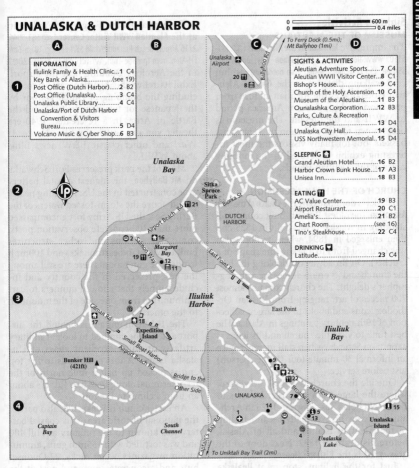

UNALASKA & DUTCH HARBOR

0 — 600 m
0 — 0.4 miles

INFORMATION
Iliulink Family & Health Clinic...**1** C4
Key Bank of Alaska..............(see **19**)
Post Office (Dutch Harbor).....**2** B2
Post Office (Unalaska)............**3** C4
Unalaska Public Library............**4** C4
Unalaska/Port of Dutch Harbor
 Convention & Visitors
 Bureau.................................**5** D4
Volcano Music & Cyber Shop...**6** B3

SIGHTS & ACTIVITIES
Aleutian Adventure Sports.......**7** C4
Aleutian WWII Visitor Center....**8** C1
Bishop's House.......................**9** C4
Church of the Holy Ascension..**10** C4
Museum of the Aleutians.........**11** B3
Ounalashka Corporation..........**12** B3
Parks, Culture & Recreation
 Department...........................**13** D4
Unalaska City Hall...................**14** C4
USS Northwestern Memorial..**15** D4

SLEEPING
Grand Aleutian Hotel..............**16** B2
Harbor Crown Bunk House....**17** A3
Unisea Inn.............................**18** B3

EATING
AC Value Center....................**19** B3
Airport Restaurant.................**20** C1
Amelia's................................**21** B2
Chart Room......................(see **16**)
Tino's Steakhouse.................**22** C4

DRINKING
Latitude.................................**23** C4

---

a charming and friendly town if you have the time to enjoy it. Unfortunately, people returning on the ferry really don't. To stay longer, you can either splurge on an expensive airline ticket before you get there or be reckless and arrive hoping to pick up a cheaper one in town. Either way, a few days in Unalaska can be a refreshing cure for anybody who is suffering from an overdose of RVers, cruise ships and tour buses.

Information

Emergency (ambulance, fire, police ☎ 911)
Iliuliuk Family & Health Clinic (☎ 581-1202; 34 LaVelle Ct; ☼ walk-in 8:30am-6pm Mon-Fri, 7am-5pm Sat) Just off Airport Beach Rd near Unalaska City Hall; has walk-in and 24-hour emergency service.

Key Bank of Alaska (☎ 581-1300; Salmon Way) Next to AC Value Center in Dutch Harbor; has a 24-hr ATM.
Post office Dutch Harbor (Airport Beach Rd); Unalaska (82 Airport Beach Rd) The Dutch Harbor post office is next to AC Value Center near Salmon Way.
Unalaska Public Library (☎ 581-5060; 64 Eleanor Dr; ☼ 10am-9pm Mon-Fri, noon-6pm Sat & Sun) Near the 5th St Bridge, offers free Internet access.
Unalaska/Port of Dutch Harbor Convention & Visitors Bureau (☎ 581-2612, 877-581-2612; www .unalaska.info; cnr 5th & Broadway, Unalaska; ☼ 8am-5pm Mon-Fri) This place maintains a small visitors center stocked with brochures, and a gallery of local and regional artists.
Volcano Music & Cyber Shop (☎ 581-4238; Unisea Mall, Suite 202; per hr $10; ☼ noon-5pm Fri & Sat) For Internet access in Dutch Harbor.

Sights & Activities

MUSEUM OF THE ALEUTIANS

The impressive **Museum of the Aleutians** (☎ 581-5150; www.aleutians.org; 314 Salmon Way; adult/child $5/free; ☺ 9am-5pm Tue-Sat, from noon Sun), within easy walking distance of the Grand Aleutian Hotel, traces the Aleutian culture from prehistory and the Russian America period to WWII and the present. The museum is best known for its collection of Aleut grass baskets, but for many visitors the most interesting exhibit is devoted to the mummy caves of the Aleutian Islands.

CHURCH OF THE HOLY ASCENSION

Unalaska is dominated by the **Church of the Holy Ascension**, the oldest Russian-built church still standing in Alaska. It was built in 1825 and then enlarged in 1894, when its floor plan was changed from to a *pekov* (the shape of a crucifix). On Broadway overlooking the bay, the church and its onion domes are a photographer's delight. The church contains almost 700 pieces of art, ranging from Russian Orthodox icons and books to the largest collection of 19th-century paintings in Alaska. The best time to view the church and its icons is at 6pm on Saturday when staff members give an informal 30-minute tour ($5 per person) just before service.

Outside the church is a small graveyard, where the largest grave marker belongs to Baron Nicholas Zass. Born in 1825 in Archangel, Russia, he eventually became bishop of the Aleutian Islands and all of Alaska, before his death in 1882. Next door to the graveyard is the **Bishop's House**.

Just for the halibut, stop in at **Unalaska City Hall** (☎ 581-1251; 43 Raven Way; ☺ 8am-5pm Mon-Fri), up on the hill on the way to Dutch Harbor; the lobby holds a replica of the world-record halibut, a 459-pounder caught locally.

ALEUTIAN WWII NATIONAL HISTORIC AREA

In 1996 the US Congress created this 134-acre **national historic area** to preserve the bloody history of the WWII battles on the Aleutian Islands. The park is unique because the Alaska Native **Ounalashka Corporation** (☎ 581-1276; www.ounalashka.com; 400 Salmon Way; ☺ 8am-5pm Mon-Fri), not the Federal Government, owns and manages it, with NPS providing only technical assistance.

To learn about the 'Forgotten War,' begin at the **Aleutian WWII Visitor Center** (☎ 581-9944; 2716 Airport Beach Rd; adult/child $5/free; ☺ 10am-6pm Fri-Mon, from 1pm Tue-Thu), which opened in 2002 in the Aerology Building near the airport. Exhibits relive the Aleutian campaign, including the bombing of Dutch Harbor by the Japanese for two days in 1942 and the Battle of Attu. In a re-created 1940-era theater you can watch the film *Alaska At War!* and other classic B&W news films about WWII.

Most of the park preserves Fort Schwatka on **Mt Ballyhoo**, the highest coastal battery ever constructed in the US. Looming nearly 1000ft above the storm-tossed waters of the Bering Sea, the US Army fort encompassed more than 100 concrete observation posts, command stations and other structures built to withstand earthquakes and 100mph winds. The gun mounts here are still among the best preserved in the country and include tunnels that allowed gunners to cart ammunition from one side of the mountain to the other.

The 1634ft mountain is behind the airport and can be climbed to look at military artifacts or enjoy excellent views of Unalaska Island. A dirt road leads to the top and is picked up half a mile north of the ferry terminal along Ballyhoo Rd. It's about an hour's climb to the top.

An easier climb is **Bunker Hill**, also part of the national historic area. This coastal battery was known to the military as Hill 400 and was fortified with 155mm guns, ammunition magazines, water tanks, 22 Quonset huts and a concrete command post at the top. You can hike to the peak of Bunker Hill along a gravel road picked up just after crossing the bridge to Amaknak Island.

More war history can be found in Unalaska by following Bayview Rd to the southeast end of town. In a picturesque hillside graveyard along the bay is the **USS Northwestern Memorial**. Launched in 1889, the passenger and freight ship was retired in 1937, then repaired by the military in 1940 to serve as a floating bunkhouse. It was bombed during the attack on Dutch Harbor and burned for five days. In 1992, for the 50th anniversary of the event, the propeller was salvaged by divers and is now part of the memorial to those who died during the Aleutian campaign.

HIKING & PADDLING

Sitka Spruce Park, within Dutch Harbor, is a national historical landmark where three of six trees planted by Russians in 1805 have somehow survived where all other foliage can't. Because of the treeless environment, however, hiking is easy here. And don't worry about bears – there aren't any.

The area has few developed trails, but an enjoyable day can be spent hiking to **Uniktali Bay**, a round-trip of 8 to 10 miles. From Captains Bay Rd, turn east on a gravel road just before you pass Westward Cannery. Follow the road for a mile to its end; a foot trail continues along a stream. In 2 miles, the trail runs out, and you'll reach a lake in a pass between a pair of 2000ft peaks. Continue southeast to pick up a second stream that empties into Uniktali Bay. The bay is an undeveloped stretch of shoreline and a great place to beachcomb. From time to time, glass floats from Japanese fishing nets wash ashore.

Before hiking Mt Ballyhoo, Bunker Hill or just about anywhere outside town, you must obtain a permit (per day per person/family $6/10) from the **Ounalashka Corporation** (☎ 581-1276; www.ounalashka.com; 400 Salmon Way; ☉ 8am-5pm Mon-Fri) in Dutch Harbor near Margaret Bay. Also check with Unalaska's **Parks, Culture & Recreation Department** (PCR; ☎ 581-1297; 37 S 5th St; ☉ 9am-5pm Mon-Fri), in the community center (next to the visitors center). PCR offers organized hikes in summer that are highly worthwhile if you're in the area longer than just the ferry stop.

The many protected harbors, bays and islands of Unalaska Island make for ideal sea-kayaking conditions. The scenery is stunning and the wildlife plentiful. It is possible to encounter Steller's sea lions, sea otters and harbor porpoises. **Aleutian Adventure Sports** (☎ 581-4489; www.aleutianadventure.com; W Broadway) has single/double kayak rentals for $69/89 per day.

Sleeping

Rooms are expensive in Unalaska and Dutch Harbor and there are not a lot of them. Check with the visitors center, which was trying to organize some B&Bs at the time of research. On top of the prices listed below you have to add an 8% sales and bed tax.

Grand Aleutian Hotel (☎ 581-3844, 866-581-3844; www.grandaleutian.com; 498 Salmon Way; s/d $159/179)

With more than 100 rooms and suites, this is the only full-service, tourist-class place in either town. Rooms are large and feature queen- or king-size beds.

Unisea Inn (☎ 581-3844; Gilman Rd; s/d $99/110) Across the street from Intersea Mall, this is sandwiched between a shipyard and a fish-processing plant. It's operated by the Grand Aleutian Hotel; guests check in at the Grand Aleutian and are shuttled over.

Harbor Crown Bunk House (☎ 581-6337; 68 Gilman Rd; per person daily/weekly $70/335) Harbor Crown Seafoods in Dutch Harbor runs this bunkhouse and during the summer opens it up to visitors. Rooms are split between men and women and hold two to four people. You share the baths with construction workers and crewmembers on R&R, but it's hard to beat the price.

It is possible to camp outside of town, but most of the land is owned by **Ounalashka Corporation** (☎ 581-1276; www.ounalashka.com; 400 Salmon Way), from whom you'll need to obtain a permit before setting up your tent. Permits cost $6 per person ($10 per family) per day.

Eating & Drinking

Chart Room (☎ 866-581-3844; cnr Airport Beach Rd & Salmon Way; dinner $20-40; ☉ 6am-11pm; ✗) The best restaurant in the Aleutian Islands is on the 2nd floor of the Grand Aleutian Hotel, where every table commands a view of Margaret Bay. The Chart Room is best known for the seafood buffet it sets up every Wednesday ($30), featuring locally caught halibut, salmon and king crab. It's such a popular feast you need to make reservations.

Tino's Steakhouse (☎ 581-4288; Broadway; lunch $10-11, dinner $16-28; ☉ 10am-10pm Mon-Sat) A good bet for Mexican or American food. Try the house specialty, halibut ceviche ($13), or the homemade soup ($4).

Amelia's (☎ 581-2800; Airport Beach Rd; breakfast & lunch $9-10, dinner $12-25; ☉ 6am-11pm) Head to this place in Dutch Harbor for a good breakfast or an extensive dinner menu that includes burgers, pasta, steaks and Mexican.

Airport Restaurant (☎ 581-6007; breakfast & lunch $8-12, dinner $10-23; ☉ 9am-11pm Mon-Sat, to 10pm Sun; ✗) This restaurant would be popular even if it wasn't at an airport notorious for bad weather. The breakfasts are large and for dinner you can go either American or Asian. It also has a bar if your plane is really late.

AC Value Center (☎ 581-1245; 100 Salmon Way; ☿ 8am-10pm) In its grocery department there is a deli, an Eastern counter and even a seating area for when your money runs out before your plane arrives.

Latitude (☎ 581-1271; cnr 2nd St & Bayview Rd) Had a wild past that's still legendary, when it used to be the Elbow Room. Today Latitude is a tame and friendly place for a beer.

Getting There & Around

The airport is on Amaknak Island, 3 miles from Unalaska. The ferry terminal is even farther north, on Amaknak Island off Ballyhoo Rd. Cab fare to downtown Unalaska costs $11 to $13 from the airport, or $14 to $16 from the ferry. Cabs are readily available all over Dutch Harbor and Unalaska.

Another way to get around is to hire a mountain bike. The extensive, lightly used dirt roads left over from the WWII buildup make great mountain bike trails. You can hire a mountain bike from **Aleutian Adventure Sports** (☎ 581-4489; W Broadway) for $25 a day.

Other than the once-a-month ferry, the only other way of getting out of Unalaska and Dutch Harbor is flying. The town is serviced by **PenAir** (☎ 800-448-4226; www.penair .com) but you book the ticket through **Alaska Airlines** (☎ 800-252-7522; www.alaskaair.com). There are three to four flights daily and a round-trip ticket is $900 to $1000.

BRISTOL BAY

The pristine lakes and rivers that empty into Bristol Bay support the world's largest run of red salmon, as well as the other four Pacific species – king, silver, chum and pink. The largest town is the region is Bethel (population 5888) but during the summer the spawning runs turn Dillingham into the world's salmon capital and the departure point into a paradise for sportfishing. From June through September anglers from around the world shell out several thousand dollars each to stay at exclusive fly-in fishing lodges scattered throughout the region.

The top attraction is Wood-Tikchik State Park, the largest state park in the country and a destination for wilderness adventure. Equally interesting is Round Island, a remote island in Bristol Bay that is a major walrus haul-out site from April to November.

DILLINGHAM

☎ 907 / pop 2422

Commercial fishing has made Dillingham the largest community in the Bristol Bay region. The first cannery was built in 1884 and today Icicle, Peter Pan, Trident and Unisea all operate fish-processing plants in the city, handling mostly salmon.

Dillingham serves as the jumping-off point for trips to Wood-Tikchik State Park, Round Island and the region's numerous fishing lodges. The airport is located 2.5 miles west of town and the only place you can drive to is Lake Aleknagik, the southernmost lake in the Wood River chain and connected to Dillingham by a 23-mile gravel road that was built in 1960. At the end of the road you'll find **Lake Aleknagik State Recreation Site**, which has a free seven-site campground.

Information

Bristol Bay Area Health Corporation (☎ 842-5201; 6000 Kanakanak Rd; ☿ walk in 8am-5pm Mon-Fri) Has walk-in and 24-hour emergency care.

Dillingham Library(☎ 842-5610; 348 D St; ☿ 10am-6pm Mon-Fri, to 2pm Sat) Offering free Internet access in the same building as the Dillingham Museum and visitors center.

Dillingham Visitor Center (☎ 842-5115; 348 D St; ☿ 10am-6pm Mon-Fri, to 2pm Sat)

Emergency (ambulance, fire, police ☎ 911)

Wells Fargo (☎ 842-5284; 512 Seward St) Has an ATM.

Sleeping

Dillingham has a number of hotels and lodges, but the price of accommodations here is on the high side, partly because of the 10% bed tax. There's the **Bristol Inn** (☎ 842-2240, 800-764-9704 within Alaska; 104 Main St; s/d $151/165) but it's pricey for what you get. Better to book a room at a B&B, which will throw in breakfast and free transport from the airport. The **Beaver Creek B&B** (☎ 842-7332, 866-252-7335; www.dillinghamalaska.com; 1800 Birch Cr; per person per night $80; ✕) is 4 miles from town and has three rooms in a house and several cottages and cabins nearby.

Getting There & Away

Dillingham is serviced by **PenAir** (☎ 800-448-4226; www.penair.com) and **Alaska Airlines** (☎ 800-252-7522; www.alasakaair.com) with five flights daily in the summer from Anchorage. An advance-purchase round-trip ticket costs from $375 to $425.

WOOD-TIKCHIK STATE PARK

At 2500 sq miles, Wood-Tikchik is the country's largest state park. Thirty miles north of Dillingham, the park preserves two large systems of interconnecting lakes that are the important spawning grounds for Bristol Bay's salmon. Wildlife in the park includes brown and black bears, beavers, moose, foxes and wolves. The fishing for arctic char, rainbow trout, dolly varden, grayling, salmon and northern pike is excellent. All five species of Pacific salmon spawn in the park.

With the exception of the 11 expensive fishing lodges in or just outside the park,

Wood-Tikchik is almost totally undeveloped. You'll find some well-used campsites here and there, but no formal campgrounds and no trails. Even the park's ranger station is outside the park, at Lake Aleknagik.

For park information, contact **Wood-Tikchik State Park** (in Dillingham late May–late Sep ☎ 842-2375, in Anchorage year-round ☎ 269-8698; www.dnr.state.ak.us /parks/units/woodtik.htm).

Activities

PADDLING

The park is an ideal place for a wilderness canoe or kayak trip. Several companies in

---

DETOUR: PRIBILOF ISLANDS

The Pribilofs are a five-island archipelago marooned in the Bering Sea, 300 miles from Alaska's mainland and 750 from Anchorage. They're desolate, foggy and windswept but overrun with wildlife, making them a far-flung tourist attraction. The two tiny communities – St Paul (population 494) and St George (population 137) – are the world's largest indigenous Aleut villages, but the human numbers here pale in comparison to the staggering quantity of seals and birds.

The Pribilofs' charcoal-colored beaches host a mad scene each summer, as a million fur seals, having spent the year at sea between California and Japan, swim ashore to breed and raise their young. The barking throng is the largest gathering of sea mammals in the world. Meanwhile, the islands' dizzying ocean-cliffs become home to extensive bird rookeries. More than 2.5 million seabirds, ranging from common murres and crested auklets to tufted puffins and cormorants, nest here, making the Pribilofs the largest seabird colony in the Northern Hemisphere. It's easy to reach the cliffs to photograph the birds, and blinds have been erected on beaches in some places to observe wildlife. During the breeding months of June, July and August, more than 230 species of birds have been sighted, the reason many hard-core birders say the Pribilofs are a sort of avian Serengeti.

Every summer there are roughly 1000 visitors to St Paul, the largest island at 14 miles long by 8 miles wide. Rough roads ring the island and the community has a hotel and a store, but not much else. Camping is not permitted on the island.

Because of the strict regulations and limited facilities, most travelers take package tours here. **Alaska Birding & Wildlife Tours** (☎ 877-424-5637; www.alaskabirding.com) offers a variety of packages from Anchorage, including a three-day tour for $1361, which covers airfare, accommodations and transportation to the beaches and rookeries (but not meals).

The alternative, though not a whole lot cheaper, is to travel to the island on your own. **PenAir** (☎ 243-2323, 800-448-4426; www.penair.com) flies from Anchorage to St Paul for $864 round-trip. The three-story **King Eider Hotel** (☎ 546-2477; 523 Tolstoi St; r per person $125) has Spartan accommodations and shared baths but will arrange for a tour guide if you request one. Dining is at the airport cafeteria or via the grocery store. Consider taking extra rations and trail snacks; food is expensive even by Alaskan standards. Make sure you also pack good rain gear, warm socks and binoculars for watching the wildlife. You can leave behind the mosquito spray, bear bells and sunglasses.

Perhaps a more unique experience, which still allows you to see an immense amount of wildlife, is to travel independently to St George, a smaller and much less visited island. Since St George isn't that big (only 5 miles wide) you can hike to within view of the wildlife. Accommodations are available at the 10-room, shared-bath **St George Hotel** (s/d $129/199), a designated national historical landmark, where you can cook your own meals in the downstairs kitchen. **St George Tanaq Corporation** (☎ 272-9886; www.stgeorgetanaq.com) in Anchorage can reserve a room; PenAir will fly you there.

Dillingham rent inflatable kayaks, rafts or canoes. **Fresh Water Adventures** (☎ 842-5060; www.fresh-h2o.com) rents out a few 20ft inflatable kayaks for $25 a day, or catarafts for $80 to $100 a day.

Wood River Lakes

These lakes, in the park's southern half, are connected by shallow, swiftly moving rivers. For that reason, most parties are flown in and paddle out, returning to Dillingham via the Wood River. A popular spot to put in is at Lake Kulik. From there the paddle toward Dillingham is a trip of close to 140 miles requiring from 10 to 14 days. A drop-off at Lake Kulik costs around $650.

This route eliminates the need for a pick-up flight and is an easy paddle for most intermediate canoeists. However, the eight fishing lodges on these lakes all use power-boats in certain locations.

Tikchik Lakes

In the park's northern half, and much more remote than the Wood River lakes, are these six lakes. Flat-water kayaking is popular on these lakes, and those interested in river floating can get dropped off on Nishlik or Upnuk Lake and travel along the Tikchik

River into Tikchik Lake. You can be picked up there or continue your journey by floating the Nuyakuk and Nushagak Rivers to one of several Alaska Native villages where air-charter flights are available back to Dillingham. A drop-off costs around $1300 to Nishlik Lake and $1105 to Upnuk Lake.

The upper lakes are more challenging and more costly to experience. But the scenery – mountains, pinnacle peaks and hanging valleys surrounding the lakes – is impressive, and there will be far less motorboat activity, if any at all.

The paddling season is from mid-June, when the lakes are finally free of ice and snow, until early October, when they begin to freeze up again. Be prepared for cool and rainy weather and pack plenty of mosquito repellent. Be cautious; sudden winds on the open lakes can create whitecap conditions, and white water may exist on many of the connecting streams.

Getting There & Away

To reach Wood-Tikchik State Park, contact any of the floatplane charter companies in Dillingham, including **Fresh Water Adventures** (☎ 842-5060; www.fresh-h2o.com) based at the Dillingham Airport.

Denali & the Interior

A grand expanse of forest and alp sweeping from Anchorage to Fairbanks to Canada, the Interior has been immortalized by poets, picked over by miners and popularized in the quirky 1990s TV series *Northern Exposure*. Here is Alaska's heartland: dogsleds and gold pans, roadhouses and fish wheels, moose on the side of the road and a seemingly endless stretch of pavement disappearing into the mountains.

At the heart of this heartland is Mt McKinley, North America's highest peak at 20,320ft, and Denali National Park & Preserve, Alaska's best-known spot for hiking, camping and mountain-climbing. It's also the stomping ground of grizzlies, moose, caribou, wolves and Dall sheep, whose visibility here is unmatched anywhere else in the country.

Aside from Talkeetna, McCarthy and Eagle, the towns here aren't as charming as the coastal ones. But on the upside, the Interior's summer weather is hotter, its skies drier, its days longer, its expanses more expansive, and its characters…well, they're over the top.

Best of all, the Interior can be enjoyed by even the most budget-minded traveler because it's accessible by road. The greater part of Alaska's highway system forms a triangle including Alaska'a two largest cities, Anchorage and Fairbanks, and allows cheap travel by bus, train, car or hitchhiking to the places in between.

HIGHLIGHTS

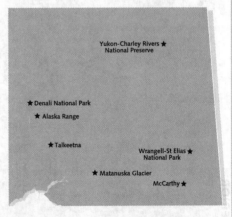

- **Best gazing and gourmandizing** – flightseeing over the eye-popping Alaska Range (p324), then dining at one of Talkeetna's fine restaurants (p326)

- **Best way to play it cool** – glacier hiking in Denali National Park (p314), Wrangell-St Elias National Park (p348), or Matanuska Glacier (p343)

- **Best way to find yourself** – losing yourself in the trackless backcountry of Denali National Park (p313)

- **Best place to visit before it totally changes** – offbeat McCarthy (p347); what every town should be, but may not be for long

- **Best way to go with the flow** – paddling a canoe through Yukon-Charley Rivers National Preserve (p339) between Eagle and Circle

Yukon-Charley Rivers ★
National Preserve

★ Denali National Park
★ Alaska Range

★ Talkeetna

Wrangell-St Elias ★
National Park

★ Matanuska Glacier

McCarthy ★

■ AREA CODE: ☎ 907　　■ POPULATION: 99,290　　■ ELEVATION: MT MCKINLEY 20,320FT

DENALI & THE INTERIOR

THE INTERIOR

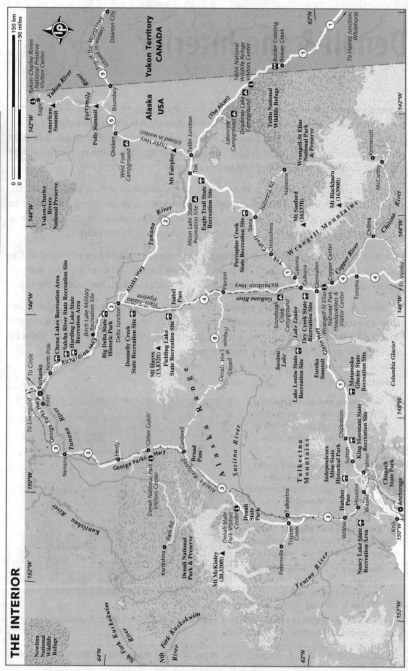

Climate

In this region of mountains and spacious valleys, the climate varies greatly and the weather can change on a dime.

In January, temperatures can sink to −60°F for days at a time; in July, they often soar above 90°F. The norm for the summer is long days with temperatures of 60°F to 70°F. However, it's common for Denali National Park to experience at least one snowfall in the lowlands between June and August.

Here, more than anywhere else in the state, it's important to have warm clothes while still being able to strip down to a T-shirt and hiking shorts. Most of the area's 10in to 15in of annual precipitation comes in the form of summer showers, with cloudy conditions common, especially north of Mt McKinley. In Denali National Park, Mt McKinley tends to be hidden by clouds more often than not.

History

If archaeologists are correct, Interior Alaska was the corridor through which the rest of the continent was peopled, as waves of hunter-gatherers migrated across the Bering Land Bridge to points south. Ancestors of the region's present native group, the Athabaskans, are thought to have been here at least 6000 years.

It wasn't until the 1800s that the first white people began to trickle in. At first, the newcomers were mainly traders: Russians, who established posts along the lower Yukon and Kuskokwim Rivers, and Britons, who began trading at Fort Yukon, on the upper Yukon River, in the 1840s. Next came prospectors, whose discoveries transformed this region. The first major gold rush in the Interior was in the Fortymile district in the 1880s; similar rushes subsequently gave rise to many Interior communities. At the turn of the last century Talkeetna began as a supply center for gold miners working the Susitna River region. Miners took up permanent residence in Eagle, on the Canadian border, in 1898, and in nearby Chicken around the same time. Kantishna, in Denali National Park, got its start from a gold rush in 1905. Copper originally drew settlers to what is now the Interior's other major national park, Wrangell-St Elias: in 1900, some of the world's richest veins led to the birth of Kennecott and McCarthy.

Transportation projects brought the next wave of growth. In 1914, Congress agreed to fund the building of the US' northernmost railroad, from Seward to Fairbanks. At the peak of construction, 4500 workers labored along the route, and their base camps became boomtowns. In 1915 Talkeetna was made the headquarters of the Alaska Engineering Commission, which was responsible for pushing the line north to the Tanana River. From there, Nenana – previously just a trading post – became the base for the anchor leg to Fairbanks.

Two decades later, during WWII, the building of the Alcan had the same effect on the eastern Interior: both Tok and Delta Junction got their start as highway construction camps. Another three decades after *that* came the biggest undertaking the Interior has ever seen: the laying of the $8 billion Trans-Alaska Pipeline, which transects Alaska, paralleling Richardson Hwy before running northward to the Arctic Ocean.

National & State Parks

Alaska's Interior holds two marquee national parks and one impressive national preserve.

The big name here, of course, is Denali National Park (p304), which is blessed with the continent's mightiest mountain, abundant megafauna such as moose and bears, and enough untrammeled backcountry to flee the gazillions of tourists who flock here aboard RVs, trains and tour buses. Crowding is less a problem in gargantuan Wrangell-St Elias National Park (p345), located in the region's southeast corner, with even more peaks, glaciers and wild creatures than Denali, but with just a fraction of the visitors and infrastructure.

Finally, up in the Interior's northeast is Yukon-Charley Rivers National Preserve (p338), located at the nexus of two of the state's legendary waterways, and experienced mainly by folks paddling the Yukon River.

Getting There & Around

Compared to most places in the developed world, the Interior is a trackless hinterland; for Alaska, however, it's got roads galore.

DENALI & THE INTERIOR

Highways such as George Parks, Alcan, Richardson, Tok Cutoff & Glenn, Denali and Taylor crisscross the place, making it a good area to own or rent an auto.

Lacking that, a few long-haul bus companies keep busy here, most notably **Alaska Direct Bus Line** (☎ 800-770-6652), traveling the Alcan and Tok Cutoff & Glenn Hwy, and **Alaska/Yukon Trails** (☎ 479-2277, 800-770-7275), covering George Parks and Taylor Highways, and the Alcan.

The corridor from Anchorage to Fairbanks is, in Alaskan parlance, the Railbelt, traversed daily in summer by the **Alaska Railroad** (☎ 265-2494, 800-544-0552; www.alaskarailroad.com). The train is a mellow, scenic alternative to driving, with depots at two of the Interior's must-see destinations: Talkeetna and Denali National Park.

Of course, much of Alaska's heartland *isn't* accessible by road or rail – and for that, there's the old Great Land standby: the bush plane. Even small Interior towns usually have airstrips and scheduled flights, and the region's national parks are normally abuzz with flightseeing excursions.

DENALI NATIONAL PARK

Encompassing both the north and south flanks of the Alaska Range, 237 miles from Anchorage and about half that distance from Fairbanks, Denali National Park is an immense subarctic wilderness centered on Mt McKinley – North America's highest peak and an overwhelming sight when caught on a clear day. At 20,320ft, the peak of this massif is almost 4 miles high, but what makes it stunning is that it rises from an elevation of just 2000ft. From Park Rd, you'll see 18,000ft of rock, snow and glacier reaching for the sky. In contrast, Mt Everest, the world's highest mountain at 29,028ft, rises only 11,000ft from the lofty Tibetan Plateau.

But it's not just this signature mountain that makes Denali National Park special. The park is also home to three dozen species of mammals, ranging from lynx, marmots and Dall sheep to foxes and snowshoe hares, and 167 different bird species, including the impressive golden eagle. Most visitors, however, want to see four beasts in

DENALI NATIONAL PARK – PARK ROAD

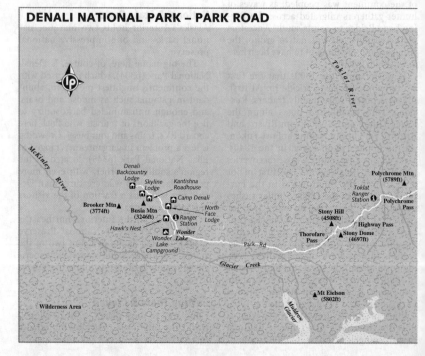

particular: moose, caribou, wolf and everybody's favorite, the brown, or grizzly, bear. Here at Denali, unlike most wilderness areas in the country, you don't have to be a backpacker to view this wildlife – people who never sleep in a tent have excellent, once-in-a-lifetime opportunities to get a close look at these magnificent creatures roaming free in their natural habitat.

It might not have turned out this way but for the efforts of naturalist and noted hunter Charles Sheldon. In 1905, gold finds had prompted a stampede to Kantishna, near Mt McKinley, and big-game hunters followed in their wake. Sheldon, stunned by the destruction they had caused, mounted a campaign to protect the area. The result was Mt McKinley National Park. In 1923, when the railroad arrived, 36 visitors enjoyed the splendor of Denali. As a result of the 1980 Alaska National Interest Lands Conservation Act, the park was enlarged by 4 million acres, redesignated and renamed Denali National Park and Preserve.

Nowadays visitors come here in droves; the park receives around 400,000 of them annually. The National Park Service (NPS) has a never-ending job trying to keep all those people from overrunning the park and destroying its wilderness character, while still ensuring that each is able to get some kind of quality experience.

Unique visitor-management strategies have been created at the park and generally they've been successful. As a result, Denali National Park is still the great wilderness it was 10 or 20 years ago. The entrance area has changed, but the park itself hasn't, and a brown bear meandering on a tundra ridge still gives the same quiet thrill as it did when the park first opened nine decades ago.

Orientation

Denali National Park and Preserve occupies a whopping 6 million acres of Interior Alaska, largely flanking George Parks Hwy from just north of Talkeetna clear to Healy, bestriding the Alaska Range and sprawling westward into the headwaters of the Kuskokwim River.

In all this wilderness there's only one road: the 92-mile Park Rd, which turns west off

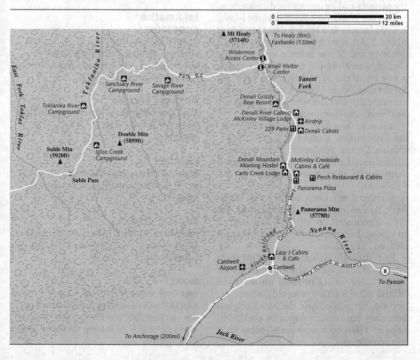

Mile 237 of George Parks Hwy, a mile south of Denali Park's main lodging and business district. The park entrance area, where most visitors congregate, extends a scant 4 miles up Park Rd. The shuttle and tour buses taking visitors into the park depart from this area, and the park headquarters, visitor center and main campground are all here.

Almost immediately on Park Rd you'll come to Riley Creek Campground, the park's largest, most developed campground. Also here is Riley Creek Mercantile, a small store and shower-house serving the campground. Across Park Rd from the store is one end of Jonesville Trail, a handy shortcut for pedestrians heading toward the business district on George Parks Hwy.

Heading west a few hundred yards on Park Rd will make you reach the Wilderness Access Center (WAC, opposite), at Mile 0.5. Here you'll pay your park entrance fee, arrange campground and bus bookings and alight the buses that lead into the park center. In a trailer across the parking lot is the Backcountry Information Center (BIC, opposite), where backpackers get backcountry permits and bearproof food containers.

Past the WAC, Park Rd crosses the Alaska Railroad tracks and reaches a traffic circle at Mile 1.5. Arc right from the circle and you'll come to the Murie Science and Learning Center, where you can learn about research going on in the park; follow the circle left for the new Denali Visitor Center, which has extensive displays and where the rangers will field every question imaginable.

Just next door is the extensive, cafeteria-style restaurant, Morino Grill, and the adjoining Denali Bookstore. Also nearby is the train station, where the Alaska Railroad stops on its run between Anchorage and Fairbanks.

Another 2 miles beyond the traffic circle, Park Rd comes to Park Headquarters, the NPS administration office. It's of interest to visitors because it is the site of the park's sled-dog kennels.

Past Park Headquarters, Park Rd leads another 80-odd miles west into the heart of the park. It ends at a privately owned island of land called Kantishna, an old gold-mining enclave that was outside the park's original boundary but was enveloped by park additions in 1980. Four wilderness lodges lie in this remote area.

Back out on George Parks Hwy and heading north, you'll almost immediately cross the Nenana River into the park's main business district, a strip locally known as Glitter Gulch. You'll love it – it makes the coolest whooshing noise as you zoom past. If you must stop, however, you'll find a schlock-to-substance ratio that's off the charts. At Glitter Gulch's north end is McKinley Chalet Resort, a large hotel complex that's the park's northernmost shuttle-bus stop. About 11 miles north of here on the highway is the town of Healy, which has a few places to stay.

Five miles south of Park Rd on George Parks Hwy is McKinley Village, another lodging area and the southernmost stop for the park shuttle bus.

About 12 miles south of the park entrance is Carlo Creek, where a small pocket of civilization holds some outstanding lodging and dining options, including the excellent Denali Mountain Morning Hostel. This is a great area to spend your nights; you can escape the park crowds here, but you need a vehicle unless you stay at the hostel, which runs four shuttles per day to the WAC.

Information
BOOKSTORES
Denali Bookstore (Mile 1.5 Park Rd; ☉ 9am-9pm) Across from the Denali Visitor Center. It has field guides, topographic maps, coffee-table books, Alaskan literature and park ranger action figures (dig it!).

INTERNET ACCESS
Black Bear Coffee House (☎ 683-1656; Mile 238.5 George Parks Hwy; per 15 min $3; ☉ 6:30am-10pm) In Glitter Gulch.

LAUNDRY
Riley Creek Mercantile (☎ 683-9246; Mile 0.2 Park Rd; ☉ 7am-9pm) Showers ($4), and coin-op laundry facilities.

MEDICAL SERVICES
Healy Clinic (☎ 683-2211; Healy Spur Rd) In the Tri-Valley Community Center, 13 miles north of the park and a half mile east of George Parks Hwy.

MONEY
Lynx Creek Store (☎ 683-2548; ☉ 7am-11:30pm) In the heart of Glitter Gulch, this gas station-cum-grocery store-cum-liquor store has an ATM. The closest full-service banks are in Fairbanks and on George Parks Hwy at Talkeetna Spur Rd junction.

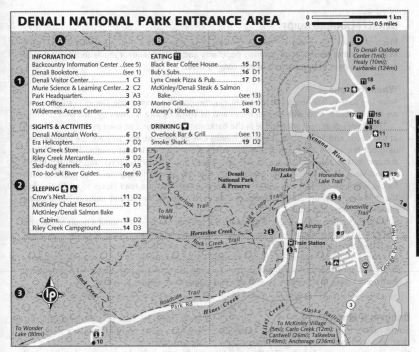

DENALI NATIONAL PARK ENTRANCE AREA

0 — 1 km
0 — 0.5 miles

INFORMATION
Backcountry Information Center ..(see 5)
Denali Bookstore.........................(see 1)
Denali Visitor Center....................1 C3
Murie Science & Learning Center...2 C2
Park Headquarters.......................3 A3
Post Office...................................4 D3
Wilderness Access Center.............5 D2

SIGHTS & ACTIVITIES
Denali Mountain Works................6 D1
Era Helicopters...........................7 D2
Lynx Creek Store.........................8 D1
Riley Creek Mercantile.................9 D2
Sled-dog Kennels.......................10 A3
Too-loó-uk River Guides...........(see 6)

SLEEPING
Crow's Nest...............................11 D2
McKinley Chalet Resort..............12 D1
McKinley/Denali Salmon Bake
  Cabins....................................13 D2
Riley Creek Campground...........14 D3

EATING
Black Bear Coffee House.............15 D1
Bub's Subs.................................16 D1
Lynx Creek Pizza & Pub..............17 D1
McKinley/Denali Steak & Salmon
  Bake...................................(see 13)
Morino Grill...........................(see 1)
Mosey's Kitchen........................18 D1

DRINKING
Overlook Bar & Grill.................(see 11)
Smoke Shack.............................19 D2

To Denali Outdoor
Center (1mi);
Healy (10mi);
Fairbanks (124mi)

Nenana River

Denali
National Park
& Preserve

Horseshoe
Lake

Horseshoe
Lake Trail

Jonesville
Trail

To Mt
Healy

Mt Healy Overlook Trail

Taiga Loop Trail

Horseshoe Creek

Rock Creek Trail

Train Station

Airstrip

Roadside Trail

Park Rd

Hines Creek

Rock Creek

Riley Creek

Alaska Railroad

George Parks Hwy

To Wonder
Lake (80mi)

To McKinley Village
(5mi); Carlo Creek (12mi);
Cantwell (26mi); Talkeetna
(149mi); Anchorage (236mi)

DENALI & THE INTERIOR

OUTDOOR GEAR & SUPPLIES

Denali Mountain Works (☎ 683-1542; Mile 239 George Parks Hwy; ⏱ 9am-9pm) Affiliated with Too-loó-uk River Guides (p315), this jam-packed Glitter Gulch store can sell you just about anything you'd need for the backcountry. They also rent tents, stoves and other outdoor gear.

POST & COMMUNICATIONS

As of 2005, the post office was still housed in a trailer next to Riley Creek Campground. It may end up elsewhere when all the new construction dust settles.

TOURIST INFORMATION

Backcountry Information Center (BIC; ☎ 683-9510; Mile 0.5 Park Rd; ⏱ 9am-6pm) If you want to overnight in Denali's backcountry you'll need to come to the BIC, just across the parking lot from the WAC. Here, rangers can explain the backcountry quota system, help you find an available backcountry 'unit' that matches your interests and skills, and issue you with the free backcountry permit.

Denali Visitor Center (☎ 683-2294; www.nps.gov /dena; Mile 1.5 Park Rd; ⏱ 9am-9pm) Officially opened in 2005, this 14,000-sq-ft, $5-million facility is the place to come for an executive summary of Denali National Park. Upstairs there's a giant table-top relief map giving you the

lay of the land; downstairs there are museum-quality displays on the area's natural and human history; and every half hour in the theater the beautifully photographed, unnarrated film *Heartbeats of Denali* provides a peek at the park's wildlife and scenery. Near the building's entrance is a streamlined selection of park literature, including the NPS' indispensable *Alpenglow* booklet, which functions as a user's manual to Denali. At peak times, the two staffers at the info desk are swamped with queries, but if you're willing to wait they can probably answer any question you dream up.

Murie Science & Learning Center (☎ 683-1269; Mile 1.5 Park Rd; ⏱ 8:30am-4:30pm) With some fascinating hands-on exhibits in its front lobby, this is the place to come for information on research taking place in the park. It also serves as Denali's winter visitor center.

Wilderness Access Center (WAC; ☎ 683-9274; Mile 0.5 Park Rd; ⏱ 5am-8pm) This place, which used to be Denali's main visitor center, still maintains a general-purpose info desk. The WAC's main function, however, is as the park's transport hub and campground-reservation center. You'll also pay the park-entrance fee here: $10/20 per person/family, which is good for seven days. Finally, there are espressos, muffins and other last-minute snacks, and a tiny gear store with freeze-dried meals, mosquito repellent, camping gas and so on.

DENALI & THE INTERIOR

DENALI PLANNING GUIDE

Much of Alaska can be experienced by the seat of your pants, but due to Denali National Park's fleeting summer season, overwhelming popularity and the consequent regulations instituted to protect it, it pays to be prepared before coming here.

When to Come

From late June to late August, despite cool, cloudy conditions and drizzle, Denali's campgrounds are full, its road is busy with shuttle buses and its entrance area is cheek by jowl with tourists.

The hordes disappear once you're in the backcountry, and aren't an issue in the 'frontcountry' in early June and September. The latter month can be pleasant; not only are the visitors thinning out but so are the bugs. This is also when there are the clearest skies and most brilliant autumn foliage. However shuttle buses (your ticket into the backcountry) stop running in the second week of September. The winners of a four-day vehicle lottery (held the previous July) follow, when 400 private cars a day are allowed entry. Then the road closes to all traffic until the following May. By late September the snow has usually arrived and another backpacking season has come and gone.

Winter visitation is the lowest of the year, so if you can handle −40*F and 4½ hours of daylight you'll have the place almost to yourself. Riley Creek Campground stays open in winter and camping is free, though the water and sewage facilities don't operate. Most area lodges are closed, but you might try Healy. You can use the unplowed Park Rd and the rest of the park for cross-country skiing and snowshoeing (bring your own equipment, as rentals are unavailable) or dogsledding. Earthsong Lodge (p318) offers several different dogsled adventures in winter.

Dangers & Annoyances

Some hikers fear Denali's grizzlies so much that to avoid one they would plunge into the nearest river. Bad move. In the park's history, no visitor has ever been killed by a bear. Rather, most tourist fatalities here are at the hands of frigid, snowmelt-swollen waterways. If your hiking route intersects a river that's thigh-high or deeper, scout for a broad, braided, shallow place to ford, or time your crossing for early morning when meltwaters typically subside. Undo the waistbelt on your pack so it won't pin you underwater, face upstream, and, if possible, use a walking stick to help you stagger across.

Sights & Activities

PARK ROAD

Park Rd begins at George Parks Hwy and winds 92 miles through the heart of the park, ending at Kantishna, an old mining settlement and the site of several wilderness lodges. Early on, park officials envisaged the onset of bumper-to-bumper traffic jams along this road and wisely closed almost all of it to private vehicles. With few exceptions, motorists can drive only to a parking area along the Savage River at Mile 14, a mile beyond the Savage River Campground. To venture further along the road you must walk, bike, be part of a concessionaire-run tour, or, most popularly, take a park shuttle or camper bus.

If you're planning to spend the day riding the buses, pack plenty of food and drink. It can be a long, dusty ride, and in the park there are no services save for toilets and, at the Toklat Ranger Station, bottled water. Carry a park map so you know where you are and what ridges or riverbeds appeal to you for hiking.

Shuttle Buses

Shuttle buses are aimed at wildlife watchers and day hikers. They aren't fancy, comfortable, high-tech wonders but big, clunky school-bus-style affairs. On board, passengers armed with binoculars and cameras scour the terrain for animals, most of which are so accustomed to the rambling buses that they rarely run and hide. When someone spots something and yells 'stop!' the driver pulls over for viewing and picture taking. The drivers are concessionaire employees, not NPS naturalists, but they provide unofficial natural-history information en route. Some are better at this than others.

Day hikers don't need a backcountry permit and can get off shuttle buses anywhere along Park Rd. After hiking, produce your

What to Bring

Don't arrive in Denali expecting to outfit an expedition once you get there. Save for one small shop in Glitter Gulch (Denali Mountain Works) and a tiny nook in the WAC, no-one sells camping gear.

Groceries are even less available. Double-check your equipment before leaving Anchorage or Fairbanks; Denali is not the place to discover your stove won't light or your tent stakes are back in Kansas. For a list of suggested backpacking items, see p66, or peruse the backcountry-gear checklist on the Denali National Park website.

Reservations

Before showing up in Denali it's worthwhile to have secured advance reservations for campsites and, to a lesser degree, shuttle buses. Do so through the **Denali National Park Reservation Service** (☎ 272-7275, in the USA 800-622-7275; www.reservedenali.com). Payment is by credit card. You can reserve online for the following year beginning December 1; phone reservations start February 15 for the same year.

Sites in four of Denali's five campgrounds – Riley Creek, Savage River, Teklanika and Wonder Lake – can be reserved in advance. The campgrounds are hugely popular, so visitors without advance reservations will likely have difficulty getting a site on a walk-in basis. Reservations for the Sanctuary River Campground are available only by walk-in at the WAC.

Up to 65% of bus seats are available through advance reservation; the other 35% are set aside for in-person reservations at the WAC. The latter can be made no more than two days in advance.

bus-ticket stub and flag down the next bus that comes along. (Due to space considerations, you might have to wait a bus or two during peak season.) Many park visitors hop on and off buses several times in one day.

Certain buses head into the park as early as 5:15am; the last ones are back by around 10:15pm. It's wise to reserve a seat as far in advance as possible (see opposite). The cost varies based on how far you're riding: free to Savage River (Mile 15), $18.50 as far as Toklat River (Mile 53), $32.50 to Wonder Lake (Mile 85) and $35.50 to Kantishna. There's also a three-for-two pass, allowing three days of travel for the price of two.

Camper Buses

The alternative to the shuttle buses are the less crowded, informal camper buses, aimed at ferrying overnight campers, backpackers and cyclists, and offering ample space to stow gear. To take these buses you must have a campsite or backcountry unit reserved along Park Rd, or be toting a bicycle. If you don't have a campground booking, you can't ride *out* on the camper bus, but you can probably hitch a ride *back* on one (a recommended course of action). The buses cost $23.75 to anywhere along the road. As with shuttles, it's good to reserve as far ahead as possible.

Points of Interest

Mt McKinley is not visible from the park entrance or the nearby campgrounds and hotel. Your first glimpse of it comes between Mile 9 and Mile 11 of Park Rd, if you're blessed with a clear day. (The rule of thumb stressed by the NPS rangers is that Mt McKinley is hidden two out of every three days, but that's a random example – it could be clear for a week and then hidden for the next month.) While 'the Great One' might not be visible for most of the first 15 miles, this is the best stretch to spot moose because of the proliferation of spruce and especially willow, the animal's favorite food.

From Savage River, the road dips into the Sanctuary and Teklanika River valleys, and Mt McKinley disappears behind the foothills. Both these rivers are in excellent hiking areas, and three of the five backcountry campgrounds lie along them. Sanctuary River Campground (Mile 22) is the most scenic, and it's a good base camp for hiking up Primrose Ridge.

The closed Igloo Creek Campground (Mile 34; see p316) lies among some spruce woods along the creek.

From here you can make an easy day hike into the Igloo and Cathedral Mountains to spot Dall sheep.

After passing through the canyon formed by the Igloo and Cathedral Mountains, the road ascends to 3880ft Sable Pass (Mile 38.5). The canyon and surrounding mountains are excellent places to view Dall sheep, while the pass is known as a prime habitat for Toklat brown bears. From here, the road drops to the bridge over the East Fork Toklat River (Mile 44). Hikers can trek from the bridge along the riverbanks both north and south.

Polychrome Pass Overlook (Mile 47) is a rest stop for the shuttle buses and it's popular with visitors. This scenic area, at 3500ft, has views of the Toklat River to the south. The alpine tundra above the road is good for hiking, as you can scramble up ridges that lead north and south of the rest-stop shelter.

During 2006 and possibly 2007, **Toklat Ranger Station** (Mile 53) will feature interpretive displays and offer ranger-led programs, including an hour-long tundra hike at 1pm daily. To make it here in time for the hike, reserve a shuttle bus leaving the WAC by 9am. The station is functioning as a temporary visitor center until the overhaul and reopening of Eielson Visitor Center (Mile 66), on the far side of Thorofare Pass (3900ft). Several day and overnight hikes are still possible from the Eielson area, including one around Mt Eielson and another to Muldrow Glacier.

Past Eielson, Park Rd drops to the valley below, passing a sign for **Muldrow Glacier** (Mile 74.4). At this point, the glacier lies about a mile to the south, and the terminus of the 32-mile ice floe is clearly visible, though you might not recognize it because the ice is covered with a mat of plant life. If the weather is cloudy and Mt McKinley and the surrounding peaks are hidden, the final 20 miles of the bus trip will be a ride through rolling tundra and past numerous small lakes known as kettle ponds. Study the pools of water carefully to spot beavers or waterfowl.

Wonder Lake Campground (Mile 84) is a place where the beauty of Mt McKinley is doubled on a clear day, with the mountain's reflection on the lake's surface.

Ironically, the heavy demand for the 28 sites at Wonder Lake and the numerous overcast days caused by Mt McKinley itself prevent the majority of visitors from ever seeing this remarkable panorama. If you do experience the reddish sunset on the summit reflecting off the still waters of the lake, cherish the moment.

The campground is on a low rise above the lake's south end and is only 26 miles from the mountain. Those who come on the early buses can gain another hour at the lake by getting off and picking up a later bus for the trip back. Keep in mind that those famous McKinley-reflected-in-the-lake photos are taken along the northeast shore, 2 miles beyond the campground, so you might want to save some time for hiking.

Kantishna (Mile 90) is mainly a destination for people staying in the area's private lodges. Here, the buses turn around, and begin the long trip back to the WAC.

WILDLIFE WATCHING

Because hunting has never been allowed in the park, professional photographers refer to animals in Denali as 'approachable wildlife.' That means bears, moose, Dall sheep and caribou aren't as skittish here as in other regions of the state. For this reason, and because Park Rd was built to maximize the chances of seeing wildlife by traversing high open ground, the national park is an excellent place to view a variety of animals.

Roughly 1800 moose roam the north side of the Alaska Range, and the most spectacular scene in Denali comes in early September, when the bulls clash their immense racks over breeding rights to a cow. Moose are almost always found in stands of spruce and willow shrubs (their favorite food), making backpackers especially wary when plowing blindly through those areas of thick groundcover.

All the park's caribou belong to the Denali herd – one of 13 herds in Alaska – which presently numbers around 2000 animals. The herd's entire range, from its calving grounds to its wintering site, lies within Denali National Park and Preserve. The best time to spot caribou is often in late summer, when the animals begin to band into groups of six to a dozen, in anticipation of the fall migration. Caribou are easy to spot, as the rack of a bull often stands 4ft high and appears to be out of proportion with the rest of his body.

Consider yourself lucky if you spot a wolf in the park. Denali is home to a fluctuating population of the animals, with current numbers below 100. In summer, when small game is plentiful, the packs often break down and wolves become solitary hunters. Then, visitors stand a chance of seeing a lone wolf crossing Park Rd.

The park holds an estimated 200 grizzly bears, usually inhabiting tundra areas, and another 200 black bears, which avoid the grizzlies and tend to stick to the forests. Since Denali's streams are mostly fed by glaciers, the fishing is poor, and bears must rely on vegetation for 85% of their diet. This accounts for their small size. Most male grizzlies here range from only 300lb to 600lb while their cousins on the salmon-rich coasts can easily top 1000lb.

In addition to moose, caribou, wolves and bears, Denali is home to 35 other species of mammal – from wolverines to mice – as well as 167 varieties of bird, 10 types of fish, and a lone amphibian, the wood frog.

RANGER-LED ACTIVITIES

If you're hesitant about venturing into the wilds on your own, or merely looking to kill some time until your desired back-country unit opens, Denali offers a daily slate of worthwhile ranger-led hikes and presentations.

Sled-Dog Demonstrations

Denali is the only US national park where rangers conduct winter patrols via dog team. In summer, the huskies serve a different purpose: amusing and educating the legions of tourists who sign up for the park's free daily tours of the sled-dog kennels, and dog demonstrations. The 40-minute show takes place at Park Headquarters at 10am, 2pm and 4pm. Free buses head there from the visitor center, departing 40 minutes before each start time.

Campground Programs

Each evening throughout the summer, rangers converge on the Riley Creek, Savage River and Teklanika Campgrounds to present 45-minute talks on Denali's wildlife and natural history. You're welcome to show up even if you're not camping there. Riley Creek programs commence at 8pm; Savage River and Teklanika talks take place at 7:30pm.

Entrance-Area Hikes

To join a ranger on an easy, guided stroll (ranging from a half hour to 2½ hours) along the park's entrance area trails, check out the schedule at the visitor center and show up ready to hike at the appointed departure time.

Discovery Hikes

These are moderate-to-strenuous, three- to five-hour hikes departing from Park Rd. The location varies from day to day; you can find out the schedule at the visitor center. Sign up there one or two days in advance to ensure a space (last-minute walk-ups are accepted if there's room), then head to the WAC to reserve a shuttle ticket to wherever the hike is happening. Be sure to pack rain gear, food and water.

DAY HIKING

Even for those who have neither the desire nor the equipment for an overnight trek, hiking is still the best way to enjoy the park and to see the land and its wildlife. You can hike virtually anywhere here that hasn't been closed due to the impact on wildlife. For a day hike (which doesn't require a permit), just ride the shuttle bus and get off at any valley, riverbed or ridge that grabs your fancy. Popular areas for cross-country day hiking off Park Rd include the Teklanika River, Cathedral Mountain, the Toklat River, the tundra areas near Eielson Visitor Center and Polychrome Pass.

The park has few trails; most hiking is cross-country over open terrain. Nature trails exist at some of the rest stops along Park Rd, and while you won't get lost following these trails, neither will you experience the primal thrill of making your own route across the landscape. A good compromise for those unsure of entering the backcountry on their own is to take a ranger-led Discovery Hike.

Park Entrance Area

A few short, maintained trails web the park entrance area. The **Horseshoe Lake Trail**, accessed at Mile 1.2 of Park Rd by the railroad crossing, is a leisurely 1½-mile walk through the woods to an overlook of an oxbow lake, followed by a steep trail to the water. Follow the tracks north a short way to the wide gravel path. The **Taiga Trail**, also commencing from the railroad tracks, turns west from the Horseshoe Lake Trail and leads to both Mt Healy Overlook Trail and Rock Creek Trail.

The moderate 2.3-mile **Rock Creek Trail** leads west to the park headquarters and dog kennels. It's far easier hiking this trail downhill from the headquarters end, where the trail begins just before Park Rd. From here it crosses Rock Creek but doesn't stay with the stream. Instead, it climbs a gentle slope of mixed aspen and spruce forest, breaks out along a ridge with scenic views of Mt Healy and George Parks Hwy, and then begins a rapid descent to its end at the Taiga Trail.

Mt Healy Overlook Trail

This is the longest maintained trail in the entrance area, and the only one in the vicinity that truly lets you escape the crowds. It's a popular trail among day hikers as it provides a good workout and the reward of fine views over the Nenana River valley, Healy Ridge and other ridgelines. The trail veers off the Taiga Trail and makes a steep climb up Mt Healy, ascending 1700ft in 2½ miles. Plan on three to five hours for the hike.

Once on the trail, you soon cross a bridge over **Horseshoe Creek**, after which there's a moderately steep climb through a forest of spruce mixed with aspen and alder. After a mile you reach a scenic viewpoint where you can gaze upon Mt Fellows to the east and the Alaska Range to the south. At this point, the trail moves from stunted spruce into thickets of alder, and at the base of a ridge begins a series of switchbacks. You reach **Halfway Rock**, a 12ft boulder, at 1.2 miles. The steep climb continues, with the switchbacks becoming shorter, and at 1.6 miles you move from a taiga zone of alder to the alpine tundra: a world of moss, lichen, wildflowers and incredible views. Keep an eye out for the large hoary marmots, a northern cousin of the groundhog, and the pika, a small relative of the rabbit.

In the final 0.4 miles the trail emerges below **Mt Healy Overlook**. You then curve steeply around the ridge to emerge at the rocky bench that is the overlook. Views from here are excellent. Sugar Loaf Mountain, at 4450ft, dominates the eastern horizon, and above the overlook to the northwest is the actual summit of Mt Healy. If you have binoculars, search the slopes to the north for Dall sheep. If the weather is clear, look to the southwest for the Mt McKinley massif, some 80 miles away. From the overlook (3425ft), hardy hikers can climb another mile to the high point of Healy Ridge (4217ft), or another 2 miles to the summit of Mt Healy (5700ft).

Polychrome Pass Circuit

One cross-country route you might consider off Park Rd is Polychrome Pass Circuit, an 8-mile trek that will challenge fit, experienced day hikers. (Less studly souls might want to do it as an overnight, which requires a permit.) This hike traverses one of the park's most scenic areas. The brilliantly colored rocks of Polychrome Pass are the result of volcanic action some 60 million years ago. Today the multicolored hills and mountains, including Polychrome Mountain (5790ft) and Cain Peak (4961ft), are a stunning sight in the low-angle light of a clear Alaskan summer day.

The route begins on the west side of Park Rd's bridge across East Fork Toklat River (Mile 42.7). Downstream, or north from the bridge, the East Fork flows as a braided river across a wide gravel bar for almost 8 miles until it enters a 7-mile-long canyon. During periods of low to medium water levels the river is braided enough for a safe crossing. If the water is high, you might run into problems; while you follow the river along its west bank, deep channels may force you to climb up and around bordering cliffs.

It's 1½ miles along the gravel bars from Park Rd to the first major tributary flowing out of the hills south of Polychrome Mountain. Head upstream (south) along the unnamed tributary for another 1½ miles, fording to its west side at the best possible crossing. Just before the stream enters a mile-long canyon, a low pass will appear to the west. It's a 200ft ascent to the pass.

From the top of the pass, it's an easy stroll down into the next valley where two streams converge. Keep in mind that the valley forms a natural travel corridor for wildlife, including brown bears. As you hike down the valley, the scenery is dominated by the northern slopes of **Polychrome Mountain**, whose colors justify its name. In early summer search the slopes for Dall sheep.

Within half a mile upstream from the confluence the stream enters a narrow canyon filled with willow, birch and alder. You'll probably have to ford the stream a few times. Be wary as you travel through the canyon. Your visibility will be limited by the brush, and bears often pass through here. Clap your hands, sing songs, argue loudly about politics. Do anything to make noise.

After a mile of bushwhacking through the canyon the stream breaks out into a wide area of the valley, where travel is far easier (though at times boggy and wet). Within another mile you arrive at the source of the stream, a small lake frequented by waterfowl. The lake is less than a quarter mile north of Park Rd.

The easiest way to return to Polychrome Pass rest area is to hike along the road, enjoying the views to the south of Toklat River, other valleys and, if you're lucky, Mt McKinley. Those who want one last climb can skip the easy road route and climb the 4000ft ridge due east of the lake. Toward the end it becomes steep and the earth underfoot is loose. Eventually you reach the 4200ft high point and from there follow the ridgeline to a low saddle at its north end. Head east from this pass, cross the bushy ravine and then climb a final hill which lies across from Polychrome Pass rest area. You'll probably see people on top of the hill, viewing Polychrome Mountain during their short bus stop.

BACKPACKING

For many, the reason to come to Denali is to escape into the backcountry for a truly Alaskan experience. Unlike many parks in the Lower 48, Denali's rigid restrictions ensure you can trek and camp in a piece of wilderness all your own, even if it's just for a few days.

The park is divided into 87 backcountry units, and in 43 only a regulated number of backpackers (usually from four to six) are allowed at a time. You have to obtain a free permit for the unit you want to overnight in. You may spend a maximum of seven nights in any one unit, and a maximum of 30 consecutive nights in the backcountry.

Obtain permits at the Backcountry Information Center, where you'll find wall maps with the unit outlines and a quota board indicating the number of vacancies in each unit. Permits are issued only a day in advance, and the most popular units fill up fast. It pays to be flexible: decide what area you're aiming for, and be prepared to take any zone in that area. If you're picky, you might have to wait several days until your choice opens up.

After you decide where you want to go among the open units, the next step is to watch the required backcountry orientation video, followed by a brief safety talk that covers, among other things, proper use of the bear-resistant food containers (BRFCs) you'll receive free of charge with your permit. The containers are bulky, but they work – they've reduced bear encounters dramatically since 1986. You'll then be given your permit and can head over to the WAC to buy topographic maps and a ticket for the camper bus ($23.75) to get you out to the starting point of your trip.

Units 1, 2, 3 and 24 surround the park entrance and are often available. You could spend a night or two here, checking in at the BIC each morning awaiting a more favorable place deeper in the park.

For the best overview of the different units in the park, purchase *Backcountry Companion for Denali National Park* by Jon Nierenberg (Alaska National History Association). It's available at the WAC for $8.95.

It's important to realize that Denali is a trailless park, and the key to successful backcountry travel is being able to read a topographic map. Riverbeds are easy to follow and make excellent avenues for the backpacker, but they always involve fording water. Pack a pair of tennis shoes or rafters' sandals for this.

Ridges are also good routes to hike along if the weather isn't foul. The tree line in Denali is at 2700ft, and above that you'll usually find tussock or moist tundra – humps of watery grass that make for sloppy hiking. In extensive stretches of tussock, the hiking has been best described as 'walking on basketballs.' Above 3400ft you'll encounter alpine or dry tundra, which generally makes for excellent trekking.

Regardless of where you're headed, remember that 5 miles is a full-day trip for the average backpacker in Denali's backcountry.

BIKING

No special permit is needed to cycle on Park Rd, but biking off-road is prohibited. Camper buses will carry bikes, but only two at a time and only if you have a reservation. Many cyclists ride the bus in and bike back out, carrying their gear and staying at campsites they've reserved along the way. It's also possible to take an early-morning bus in, ride for several hours and catch a bus back the same day.

DENALI IN...

One Day

If you have only a day in Denali National Park, there's only one option: the park bus. Take it all the way to Wonder Lake and back and it'll eat up your whole day and leave you saddle sore. Instead, take the bus only as far as the Toklat Ranger Station (or Eielson Visitor Center, when it reopens). That's still a long journey, but if you get on an early-morning bus you'll have time for a nice day hike before you have to return. Plenty of wildlife can be seen between the park entrance and Toklat or Eielson, and you'll have the opportunity to see Mt McKinley, weather permitting, so you won't be missing much by not riding all the way to Wonder Lake.

Two Days

Try to get a permit for an overnight backpacking trip somewhere in the park. One of the popular backcountry units might be available, but even if it's not, a night spent anywhere in the backcountry is worth the price of admission. If you don't want to backpack, you could certainly day hike for two days (or two months!). Start by going to the Wilderness Access Center (WAC) on the first day and joining a ranger-led Discovery Hike (advance reservations usually required) or just talk to the rangers and get a feel for where you might want to day hike along Park Rd. Spend the rest of the day tramping up Mt Healy Overlook Trail, which starts near the entrance area, or check out the sled-dog presentation at Park Headquarters. On the second day take the bus to wherever you decided to day hike.

Three or More Days

With this amount of time you'll be able to go backpacking or get in a lot of day hiking. Day hikers might consider buying the 'three days for the price of two' bus ticket – you can then use the bus to access different areas of Park Rd for day hikes on consecutive days. The three-for-two ticket is also a nice hedge against bad weather – if you don't use a day, you haven't lost anything, but if the skies clear and the mountain appears on day three, you'll be glad you had the ticket. If you tire of the tundra and you can afford it, you could also take a raft trip down the Nenana River or a flightseeing excursion over the park.

You can rent bikes at **Denali Outdoor Center** (☎ 683-1925, 888-303-1925; www.denaliout doorcenter.com; Mile 240.5 George Parks Hwy), which charges $25 for a half day, $40 for a full day, or $35 per day for two days or more. Rates include a helmet, water bottle, tools and lock.

Tours

PARK ROAD

The park shuttle buses are the most common 'tours' along Park Rd, but there are others, none especially noteworthy.

Park co-concessionaire **Aramark** (☎ 800-622-7275, 272-7275; www.reservedenali.com) offers a five-hour Natural History Tour ($57.50) to Primrose Ridge, a four- to five-hour Tek-lanika Tundra Wilderness Tour ($59.50) to the Teklanika River Overlook, and a six- to eight-hour Tundra Wildlife Tour ($80) to Toklat River. All include narration, hot drinks and a snack or box lunch.

The other co-concessionaire, Doyon, runs **Kantishna Roadhouse** (☎ 800-942-7420; www.seed enali.com), which offers a one-day bus tour ($125) along Park Rd to Kantishna (p316). There you get an interpretive tour of the area, lunch in the dining hall and either gold panning or a sled-dog demo before returning on the bus. Or you can return on a sightseeing flight for an extra charge.

FLIGHTSEEING

Most flightseeing around Denali leaves from Talkeetna, but some companies also operate out of the park area.

Denali Air (☎ 683-2261; www.denaliair.com) charges around adult/child $260/130 for a narrated flight of about an hour around the mountain. Flights leave from the company's airstrip at Mile 229.5 of George Parks Hwy.

Era Helicopters (☎ 683-2574, 800-843-1947; www .eraaviation.com) will take you up on a 50-minute Mt McKinley tour ($269) or a 75-minute flight that includes a glacier landing ($369). Heli-hiking trips are also available. The helipad is on the north side of the Nenana River bridge, at the south end of Glitter Gulch.

Fly Denali (☎ 683-2899, 866-733-7768; www.flyde nali.com) is based in Healy and has tours of various durations and routes. Their three-hour flight includes the only glacier landing available from the park entrance ($325).

Kantishna Air Taxi (☎ 683-1223; www.katair .com) flies out of Kantishna and Healy. The company offers hour-long flightseeing excursions around Mt McKinley ($145 per person from Kantishna, $190 from Healy); direct flights between Kantishna and the park entrance ($195); and flights from Kantishna to the park entrance with a 20-minute detour by Mt McKinley ($245). Two versions of a bus-out/fly-back day tour are also available.

You may be able to get cheaper flightseeing deals with a couple of smaller-scale local operators:

Alaska Timberline Aviation (☎ 683-2121, 877-683-2121; www.alaskaflighttours.com; Healy)

Atkins Guiding & Flying Service (☎ 768-2143; Cantwell)

RIVER RAFTING

Thanks to Denali Park tourists, the Nenana River is the most popular white water rafting area in Alaska. The river's main white-water stretch begins near the park entrance and ends 10 miles north, near Healy. It's rated Class III (see p78) and involves standing waves, rapids and holes with names such as 'Coffee Grinder' in sheer-sided canyons. South of the park entrance the river is much milder, but to many it's just as interesting as it veers away from both the highway and the railroad, increasing your chances of sighting wildlife. Raft companies offer guided trips on both stretches.

Denali Outdoor Center (☎ 683-1925, 888-303-1925; www.denalioutdoorcenter.com; Mile 240.5 George Parks Hwy) is located on the canyon rim north of Glitter Gulch and is universally considered the finest rafting outfit, with good equipment, a safety-first philosophy and friendly guides. Its canyon and scenic runs each last two hours and cost $70; you can combine the two for a half-day, $95 excursion. The center also offers inflatable-kayak tours ($75).

Too-loó-uk River Guides (☎ 683-1542; www.alaska one.com/tooloouk; Mile 239 George Parks Hwy) is af-filiated with Denali Mountain Works (p307) and runs guided wilderness raft trips across the state, including a two-day paddle on the Nenana River from just north of Cantwell to Healy ($350 per person).

Sleeping

Denali Park occasionally stuns visitors who arrive in late afternoon or early evening seeking lodging: the cruise-ship companies book vast numbers of rooms here for their package tourists. You definitely want something reserved – even if it's just a campsite – before you show up. And expect to pay more than you'd expect. The Denali Borough charges a 7% accommodations tax on top of the prices listed below.

INSIDE THE PARK

Kantishna (an inholding) excepted, lodgings are not available inside park boundaries, so if you want overnight shelter within the park you'll need a tent or RV.

For information on reserving campsites, see p308. If you don't have a reservation, you'll probably have to find lodging outside the park for the first night or two before you can secure a campsite.

Riley Creek Campground (Mile 0.2 Park Rd; walk-in/drive-in sites $12/19) At the park's main entrance and within earshot of George Parks Hwy, this is Denali's largest and most developed campground and is the only one open year-round. It has 146 sites, piped-in water, flush toilets and evening interpretive programs. As the park's main campground, it's favored by RVers. But it's also spacious, so campers shouldn't feel overwhelmed, and the location is convenient to Riley Creek Mercantile, the WAC and Glitter Gulch.

Savage River Campground (Mile 13 Park Rd; sites $18) Despite its name, this is a mile short of the actual river. It's one of only two campgrounds with a view of Mt McKinley. The 33 sites can accommodate both RVs and tents, with such amenities as flush toilets, piped-in water and evening presentations.

Sanctuary River Campground (Mile 23 Park Rd; sites $9) This is the next campground down the road from Savage River. On the banks of a large glacial river, the seven sites are for tents only and can't be reserved in advance. While there's no piped-in water, Sanctuary River is a great area for day hiking. You can either head south to trek along the river or climb

DENALI & THE INTERIOR

DEVELOPMENT AT DENALI

If you've visited Denali before and are plotting a return, brace yourself: though the backcountry endures as it has for eons, George Parks Hwy and park entrance areas have been transformed.

First there's Glitter Gulch: the east side, once merely chaotic, is now a full-blown dog's breakfast, with countless shops hawking Subway sandwiches, Jeep safaris, Harley Davidson paraphernalia and trinkets featuring moose.

Hell-bent traffic through the Gulch has been calmed by traffic lights (which flash yellow in the seven-month off-season), and the old Hail-Mary pedestrian crossing over the Nenana River bridge has been superseded by a parallel footbridge.

On the west side of the Gulch, small-scale operators such as Denali Outdoor Center and Bub's Subs have been displaced by the area's twin titans, Aramark and Princess, which now own everything between the highway and the river. By the time you read this they'll have installed hundreds more cookie-cutter hotel rooms here.

In the park entrance area, the changes – most dating to 2005 – are more positive. Beside the train station, the vast new Denali Visitor Center – designed to be largely solar-powered, constructed of local wood and stone, and costing $2 million for its exhibits alone – is a streamlined, stately portal to the park. Nearby, the Morino Grill, though not a culinary delight, has finally given tourists a place to grab a bite in the park. The adjoining Denali Bookstore has the best gifts and literature in the area.

The former Visitor Access Center, or VAC, is now the Wilderness Access Center, or WAC. It's the scene of considerably less bedlam now that it's not trying to be all things to all park visitors. And the Murie Science & Learning Center, which opened in late 2004, provides park researchers with lab and office space while offering tourists a peek at science in Denali.

There are a few more changes to come, most notably a new visitor center at Eielson along Park Rd, which will hopefully be ready by 2007. There may be upgrades to existing rest-stops along the road, as well as short, formal trails in the immediate vicinity of Eielson and Wonder Lake. The entrance area may also see new trails – possibly a bike path from the visitor center to the Gulch, and a hiking trail to the McKinley Village area.

Other developments are more theoretical. For years there has been talk of opening a second gateway to the park with a visitor center and perhaps a road on the south side of the Alaska Range, where's there's great hiking, better fishing, and the clearest views of Denali National Park's main attraction, Mt McKinley.

Mt Wright or Primrose Ridge to the north for an opportunity to photograph Dall sheep.

Teklanika River Campground (Mile 29 Park Rd; sites $16) In 2005 tent camping (not RV camping) was stopped here due to wolf activity, but that may soon change. There are 53 sites, flush toilets, piped-in water and evening programs. You can drive to this campground, but once here you must park your vehicle until you're ready to return to Riley Creek.

Igloo Creek Campground (Mile 34 Park Rd) This small waterless tent-camping area has been closed for some time due to wolf-denning in the vicinity, but it may reopen. The day hiking around here is excellent, especially the numerous ridges around Igloo Mountain, Cathedral Mountain and Sable Pass that provide good routes into alpine areas.

Wonder Lake Campground (Mile 85 Park Rd; sites $16) This is the jewel of Denali campgrounds,

thanks to its eye-popping views of Mt McKinley. The facility has 28 sites for tents only but does offer flush toilets and piped-in water. If you're lucky enough to reserve a site, book it for three nights and then pray that the mountain appears during one of the days you're there. Also, pack plenty of insect repellent and maybe even a headnet: the bugs are vicious in midsummer.

KANTISHNA
Kantishna, on private property at the end of Park Rd, provides the ultimate lodging location. Here, surrounded by parkland, you'll feel as close to nature as you can get without taking rubber off your Vibram soles. Several places lie out here, though only the Camp Denali properties have views of the mountain. Most Kantishna options may be in the splurge category, but remember that rates

include round-trip transportation from the park entrance, meals and guided activities. All require reservations far in advance – six months isn't overdoing it.

Midrange

Skyline Lodge (☎ 683-1223; www.katair.com; r $155) This small, solar-powered, two-room place serves as Kantishna Air Taxi's base of operations. Guests have use of a common kitchen, dining area, bathroom, shower and decks overlooking the Kantishna Valley. Breakfast is included, but you're on your own for other meals, and you'll have to take the park shuttle to get here.

Top End

Camp Denali (☎ 683-2290; www.campdenali.com; cabins per person per night $400) Verging on legendary, Camp Denali has been the gold standard among Kantishna lodges for the last half-century. Widely spread across the ridgeline, the camp's simple, comfortable cabins elegantly complement the backcountry experience while minimizing impact on the natural world. Think of it as luxury camping, with gourmet meals, guided hikes, killer views of the mountain, and staff so devoted to Denali that you'll come away feeling like the beneficiary of a precious gift. The camp requires stays of at least three nights, meaning you'll be shelling out at least $1200. So start saving pennies – this is the real deal.

North Face Lodge (☎ 683-2290; www.campdenali.com; per person per night $400) Affiliated with Camp Denali and just down the hill, this is a more traditionally appointed lodge complete with en suite bath and all the comforts of home. You gain amenities here, but you lose that extra intimacy with the land that Camp Denali provides.

Hawk's Nest (cabin $425) This is another Camp Denali option, 1½ miles distant. Rent this one and you get it all to yourself, but without Camp Denali's food, transportation, guided activities or evening programs.

Denali Backcountry Lodge (☎ 644-9980, 800-841-0692; www.denalilodge.com; per person per night $375) The last lodge on this end of the road, this is a great-looking place on the banks of Moose Creek with comfortable modern cabins and common areas. Transport, meals and guided activities are included.

Kantishna Roadhouse (☎ 459-2120, 800-942-7420; www.kantishnaroadhouse.com; per person per night $360)

Owned by park co-concessionaire Doyon, Kantishna Roadhouse has clean modern cabins, a beautiful new dining room, a bar and guided activities. It has a nice location on Moose Creek, but of all the Kantishna lodgings it feels the most corporate.

MCKINLEY VILLAGE

Six miles south of the park entrance is McKinley Village, which is served by the park shuttle bus.

Budget

Denali Grizzly Bear Resort (☎ 683-2696; www.alaskaone.com/dengrzly; Mile 231.1 George Parks Hwy; sites $19, tent cabin $26-30, cabin $52-188) This place offers wooded campsites, platform tent cabins, and 23 well-spaced wood-frame cabins in various configurations – some have a private bath, some have a kitchen, some have both, and some are old historical cabins with tons of Alaskan character. The big cabins sleep six. Communal amenities include hot showers and laundry facilities.

Midrange & Top End

Denali River Cabins (☎ 683-8000, 800-230-7275; www.seedenali.com; Mile 231 George Parks Hwy; cabin $139-169) This Doyon-operated place offers cozy, cedar-scented, double-occupancy, modern cabins with private bath. Some cabins have decks with the Nenana River rushing past.

McKinley Village Lodge (☎ 800-276-7234; Mile 231.1 George Parks Hwy; r $219) The shuttle bus stops at this place, an upscale lodge (with restaurant and bar) run by Aramark.

Denali Cabins (☎ 644-9980, 888-560-2489; www.denali-cabins.com; Mile 229 George Parks Hwy; cabin d $139-219) Two miles further south, this place has private-bath cabins, a sauna and two outdoor hot tubs.

CARLO CREEK

Further south at Carlo Creek, you'll find a variety of reasonably priced camping and lodging options. This is one of the best areas to stay, as it's both scenic and away from the tourist hubbub.

Budget

Denali Mountain Morning Hostel (☎ 683-7503; www.hostelalaska.com; dm $25, d $65-100; ▣) Among the best hostels in Alaska, this rustic, forested place offers accommodations in its main building and in several outlying cabins by the banks of babbling Carlo Creek. Amenities include kitchen facilities, clean showers, Internet and a free shuttle that runs to the WAC four times daily. The hostel rents out backpacking gear and sells organic and bulk foods. Highly recommended.

Midrange & Top End

Carlo Creek Lodge (☎ 683-2576; www.carlocreek.com; cabins with/without bath $102/77, sites $12, RV sites with/without hookups $19/14, all sites per person plus $4) In a nice setting on the opposite bank of Carlo Creek, this lodge has a couple of affordable shared-bath cabins and a nice wooded campground. Each site has a picnic table, a firepit with barbecue grill, and a shelter under which you could pitch a tent in bad weather. Communal amenities include a laundry room and showers.

Perch Restaurant & Cabins (☎ 683-2523, 888-322-2523; www.denaliperchresort.com; cabin with/without bath $115/85) Also in Carlo Creek, this place has a small cluster of tightly spaced double-occupancy cabins. Rates include breakfast at the Perch, which is one of the park area's best restaurants.

McKinley Creekside Cabins (☎ 683-2277, 888-533-6254; www.mckinleycabins.com; cabins $139-189) Across from the hostel, this place has well-maintained private-bath cabins, some with kitchenettes.

GLITTER GULCH

Glitter Gulch contains the mangy lion's share of park lodgings. This area's only redeeming feature is convenience, and that can't begin to make up for its total lack of compatibility with the spectacular natural world surrounding it.

McKinley/Denali Salmon Bake Cabins (☎ 683-2733; www.denaliparksalmonbake.com; Mile 238.5 George Parks Hwy; cabins with/without bath $105/59) 'The Bake' has 12 cabins, including a couple of barebones shared-bath tent cabins that are by far the cheapest digs in Glitter Gulch.

Crow's Nest (☎ 683-2723, 888-917-8130; www.denali crowsnest.com; Mile 238.5 George Parks Hwy; cabins $159) Up on the hill behind the gas station, these modern log cabins, though a little tightly spaced, have common front porches with great views.

HEALY

Healy, 12 miles north of the park entrance, has a range of lodging options.

EarthSong Lodge (☎ 683-2863; www.earthsong lodge.com; Mile 4 Stampede Rd; r $125-175) North of Healy, off Mile 251 George Parks Hwy, this place rents out 12 private-bath cabins above the tree line at 1900ft – just a short climb away from stunning views of Mt McKinley. In the evening you can help feed the 30 sled dogs. Proprietor Jon Nierenberg, a former Denali ranger, quite literally wrote the book (see p313) on hiking in the park's backcountry.

Denali Dome Home B&B (☎ 683-1239; www.denali domehome.com; Mile 0.5 Healy Spur Rd; r with breakfast $145) In a huge, intriguing geodesic house, this is the best B&B in Healy. The owners are absolute oracles of wisdom when it comes to Denali Park, and do a bang-up job with breakfast.

Motel Nord Haven (☎ 683-4500, 800-683-4501; www.motelnordhaven.com; Mile 249.5 George Parks Hwy; r $122-150) Pricey but pleasantly comfortable, this motel offers 28 rooms, all with private bath, satellite TV and phone; kitchen suites are available. In summer, rates include continental breakfast in the dining room.

Park's Edge (☎ 683-4343; Mile 0.5 Hilltop Rd; www .parks-edge.com; small cabin/deluxe cabin $100/125) This place offers neat log cabins. The smaller cabins sleep two to three people, while the larger ones sleep up to six – good value for families or small groups. To get there, turn onto Otto Lake Rd at Mile 247 George Parks Hwy, then turn right onto Hilltop Rd.

Eating

Groceries are extremely limited and expensive in the Denali Park area, so stock up in Fairbanks, Anchorage or Wasilla before coming here. Inside the park itself there are no restaurants except the Morino Grill.

RESTAURANTS

229 Parks (☎ 683-2567; www.229parks.com; Mile 229 George Parks Hwy; dinner $18-33; 🕑 6:30pm-11am, 5-10pm) South of McKinley Village on George Parks Hwy, this lovely new establishment is at once epicurean and ardently environmental, emphasizing organic and locally grown foods. The menu changes daily, but when we were there offerings included tangerine duck salad ($17) and crimini-crusted rack of elk ($33).

Perch Restaurant (☎ 683-2523; Mile 224 George Parks Hwy; breakfast buffet $7.50, dinner $19-30; 🕑 6am-9am, 5-9pm) At Carlo Creek, this is among Denali's best fine-dining restaurants, specializing in seafood, pasta and wild game. Try the king salmon with cranberry-horseradish sauce ($20) or the caribou medallions wrapped in bacon ($26).

McKinley/Denali Steak & Salmon Bake (☎ 683-2733; Mile 238.5 George Parks Hwy; breakfast & lunch $8-13, dinner $10-18; ⏱ 5am-1:30am) 'The Bake' is as garish and off-kilter as Glitter Gulch itself. It has sourdough-pancake breakfasts and, for dinner, king salmon plates.

Overlook Bar & Grill (☎ 683-2723, 888-917-8130; Mile 238.5 George Parks Hwy; sandwiches & burgers $9-18; ⏱ 11am-11pm) Way up on the hill over Glitter Gulch, the Overlook gets raves for its view and beer list, but razzes for slow and haphazard service. It does steak, seafood, pasta and poultry.

CAFÉS

Panorama Pizza Pub (☎ 683-2624; Mile 224 George Parks Hwy; pizzas $5-17; ⏱ noon-midnight) Comparatively new but already beloved, this Carlo Creek eatery offers good beer, burgers, and pizza pies with names like the Vegghead and the Runnin' Chicken. You get a discount if you're staying across the road at the Denali Mountain Morning Hostel.

McKinley Creekside Café (☎ 683-2277; Mile 224 George Parks Hwy; breakfast $8-11, lunches $8-12, dinner $17-24; ⏱ 6am-10pm) Down at Carlo Creek, this café with a sunny deck has a hearty mountain woman breakfast on offer and, for dinner, Alaskan amber-glazed salmon ($17). If you're taking a bus into the park they'll pack you a lunch.

Lynx Creek Pizza & Pub (☎ 683-2547; Mile 238.6 George Parks Hwy; pizza slices $4; ⏱ 11am-midnight) Owned by Princess, this Glitter Gulch fixture has a small pub with log-cabin atmosphere and a nice outdoor patio. The pizza wedges are sizable and the taste is tolerable.

Morino Grill (Mile 1.5 Park Rd; mains $8-9; ⏱ 11am-7pm) This cafeteria-style establishment in a barnlike structure beside the visitor center is the only eatery within the park. It has burgers, paninis and small pizzas, as well as seafood chowder and reindeer stew. When we were there it was a madhouse, and staff were in a less-than-pleasant mood.

Black Bear Coffee House (☎ 683-1656; Mile 238.5 George Parks Hwy; sandwiches $8; ⏱ 6:30am-10pm) Situated on the Glitter Gulch boardwalk, this place has good coffee, plus bagels, pastries and deli sandwiches.

QUICK EATS

Bub's Subs (☎ 683-7827; Mile 238.5 George Parks Hwy; sandwiches $7-13; ⏱ 10am-10pm) Among Denali denizens, no eatery is better loved than Bub's. When we were there they were closed for renovations and locals were palpably depressed. Thankfully, they've since reopened.

Mosey's Kitchen (☎ 683-5019; Mile 238.5 George Parks Hwy; Mexican munchies $4-12; ⏱ 11am-10pm) In a trailer at the north end of the Glitter Gulch boardwalk, Mosey's does $5 halibut tacos, which are a favorite of park-area employees.

GROCERIES

Lynx Creek Store (☎ 683-2548; Mile 238.4 George Parks Hwy; ⏱ 7am-11:30pm) Situated in Glitter Gulch, this gas-station-cum-convenience-store-cum-liquor-store has the widest range of groceries in the park area. Seriously. Good luck finding fresh produce.

Riley Creek Mercantile (☎ 683-9246; Mile 0.2 Park Rd; ⏱ 7am-11pm) Next to the Riley Creek Campground, it has a few groceries, as well as espressos, deli sandwiches and wraps.

Wilderness Access Center (☎ 683-9274; Mile 0.5 Park Rd; ⏱ 5am-8pm) The center has an extremely limited array of backpacker-oriented foods.

Drinking & Entertainment

McKinley/Denali Steak & Salmon Bake (☎ 683-2733; Mile 38.5 George Parks Hwy) 'The Bake' in Glitter Gulch has recently become *the* venue for live music, with DJs or performers every night in the nonsmoking bar.

Smoke Shack (Mile 238.2 George Parks Hwy) Up the hill near the south end of Glitter Gulch, this bar has pub grub on the menu, a decent array of libations, and a thumpin' dance floor that's often packed with youthful park employees.

Overlook Bar & Grill (☎ 683-2723, 888-917-8130; Mile 238.5 George Parks Hwy) For chillin' and chattin', it's hard to beat the scenically situated Overlook.

Getting There & Around

Located on George Parks Hwy about four hours north of Anchorage and two hours south of Fairbanks, Denali is easily accessible. Once here, you'll find the area between Glitter Gulch and McKinley Village well served by public transport. North or south of there you may need your own car, though Denali Mountain Morning Hostel in Carlo Creek now provides limited transport to the WAC.

BUS

Both northbound and southbound bus services are available from Denali National Park.

Alaska/Yukon Trails (☎ 479-2277; 800-770-7275) has southbound buses that pick up at the Lynx Creek Store, visitor center and railroad station around noon, reaching Anchorage ($76 one way) by 5:45pm, and northbound buses leaving Denali around 1pm and getting to Fairbanks ($46 one way) at 3:40pm.

Park Connection (☎ 245-0200, 800-208-0200; www .alaskacoach.com) runs between Denali and points south of there, including Anchorage ($69) and Seward ($118). It leaves Anchorage at 1:30am and arrives at Denali at 8:30pm; or leaves Denali at 7:45am and arrives in Anchorage at 1:30pm.

There's one northbound bus and one southbound bus each day.

TRAIN

The most enjoyable way to arrive or depart from the park is aboard the **Alaska Railroad** (☎ 265-2494, 800-544-0552; www.alaskarailroad.com), with its viewing-dome cars that provide sweeping views of Mt McKinley and the Susitna and Nenana River valleys along the way. All trains arrive at the depot beside the new visitor center, only staying long enough for passengers to board. The northbound train arrives in Denali at 3:45pm and reaches Fairbanks at 8:15pm. The southbound train arrives in Denali at noon and gets in to Anchorage at 8:15pm. Tickets aren't cheap: the one-way fare from Denali National Park to Anchorage is $129; from Denali to Fairbanks it's $54.

PLANE

Talkeetna Aero Services (☎ 733-2899, 888-733-2899; www.talkeetnaaero.com), based in Talkeetna, offers air transportation to/from Talkeetna.

COURTESY BUSES & SHUTTLES

The free Riley Creek Loop Bus makes a circuit through the park entrance area, picking up at the visitor center every half hour and stopping at the Horseshoe Lake trailhead, WAC and Riley Creek Campground.

The park also has a free Dog Sled Demo Bus, which departs the visitor center en route to the Park Headquarters 40 minutes before each show (p311).

If you want to head north along George Parks Hwy to Glitter Gulch or south as far as McKinley Village, you can catch Aramark's courtesy shuttles.

From 6:30am until 11:30pm they make a circuit between the McKinley Village Lodge, WAC, visitor center and McKinley Chalet Resort.

Many other lodgings run buses to and from the WAC and visitor center. Most notable among them is the four-runs-per-day **Denali Mountain Morning Hostel shuttle** (☎ 683-7503), which heads from Carlo Creek to the WAC at 6:45am and 8:30am, and picks up at the WAC at 5:30pm and 9:30pm. Nonguests pay $5.

TAXI

If the bus won't work for you, try one of the Healy-based taxi companies. **Caribou Cab** (☎ 683-5000) charges around $30 for a ride between Healy and the park entrance, so you'll want some fellow travelers to help split the cost.

GEORGE PARKS HIGHWAY

Between Alaska's metropolis, Anchorage, and its second-biggest city, Fairbanks, is more wilderness than exists in most nations: a vastness of forests, rivers and tundra plains, punctuated by the skyscraping Alaska Range. Through it all cuts George Parks Hwy, beginning at the junction with Glenn Hwy 35 miles north of Anchorage and ending 327 miles away in Fairbanks. Known simply as Parks Hwy, it's the straightest path to Denali National Park . Mileposts indicate distances from Anchorage. Wasilla, at Mile 42.2, is covered in the Anchorage chapter (p206).

NANCY LAKE STATE RECREATION AREA

Located along the Nancy Lake Pkwy at Mile 67.3 of George Parks Hwy, this **state recreation area** (☎ 495-6273; day-use $5, sites $10) is one of Alaska's few flat, lake-studded parks, offering camping, fishing, canoeing and hiking. Although it lacks the dramatic scenery of the country to the north, the 22,685-acre area can be peaceful on weekdays – and thronging with Anchorage and Mat-Su residents on weekends. Pick up a map at the fee station at Mile 1.3 of Nancy Lake Parkway, as the area can be confusing.

Activities

PADDLING

Lynx Lake Loop is the most popular canoe trail. It is a two-day, 16-mile trip passing through 14 lakes and over an equal number of portages. The route begins and ends at the posted trailhead for the Tanaina Lake Canoe Trail at Mile 4.5 of the parkway. The portages are well marked, and many of them are planked where they cross wet sections. The route includes 12 backcountry campsites, accessible only by canoe, but bring a camp stove because campfires are prohibited in the backcountry.

The largest lake on the route is Lynx Lake, and you can extend your trip by paddling south on the lake to the point where a portage leads off to six other lakes and two more primitive campsites on Skeetna Lake.

You can rent canoes at the long-established **Tippecanoe Rentals** (☎ 495-6688; www.paddle alaska .com), which has a rental shed at South Rolly Lake Campground. Rates begin at $20 for an eight-hour day, $50 for two days, $65 for three days and $75 for four to seven days.

HIKING

The park's major hiking route is the Red Shirt Lake Trail (Mile 6.5 of Nancy Lake Parkway), which begins at the entrance of the South Rolly Lake Campground at the end of the parkway. It leads 3 miles south, primarily on high ground, and ends at Red Shirt Lake's north end. Along the way you'll pass Red Shirt Overlook, offering scenic views of the surrounding lake country, and the Chugach Mountains on the horizon.

The trail ends at a group of backcountry campsites along the lake. Tippecanoe Rentals (see above) keeps canoes at the lake; if you want to use one you must pay and pick up your paddles and life vests before hiking in.

Sleeping

Nancy Lake State Recreation Area offers two road-accessible campgrounds, numerous backcountry campsites and 13 public-use cabins. The backcountry campsites are first-come-first-served, while the cabins can be rented for up to five nights. They cost between $35 and $50 per night and come in various sizes, sleeping from four to eight people.

Four of the cabins are on Nancy Lake; three of these can be reached via a short hike from the Nancy Lake Pkwy. Four more cabins are on Red Shirt Lake, but these require a 3-mile hike in and then a short canoe paddle. The cabin on Bald Lake is accessed by a quarter-mile hike. The other four cabins are on the Lynx Lake canoe route, with three on Lynx Lake and one on James Lake. The cabins are popular. Reserve them through the **Alaska Division of Parks** (☎ 745-3975; Mile 0.7 Bogard Rd; www.alaskastateparks.org), either online or in person at their Wasilla office.

South Rolly Lake Campground (sites $10), a drive-in campground, has 98 secluded sites; it's so large that you stand a good chance of finding an open site even on the weekend. It also has a canoe-rental shed.

Nancy Lake State Recreation Site (sites $10), just off George Parks Hwy south of the entrance to the parkway, is the only other vehicle-accessible campground. It's not nearly as nice as South Rolly Lake, though. The campground has 30 sites.

WILLOW

☎ 907 / pop 1856

In the 1970s Willow, at Mile 69 of George Parks Hwy, was a sleepy little village that became famous for its controversial selection as the new Alaskan capital that was to be moved from Juneau. The move was put on the back burner in 1982, however, when funding for the immense project was defeated in a general state election. The issue is ongoing. The move still hasn't been approved, but in the meantime Willow has grown – with land speculators arriving in anticipation of it becoming the capital and with general population growth creeping ever further out from Anchorage and Wasilla.

To many travelers heading north, Willow offers the first overwhelming view of Mt McKinley. If the day is clear, 'the Great One' dominates the skyline. Actually, just about anything would dominate the skyline of this sparse little town.

In a pinch, sardine-style camping is available at **Willow Creek State Recreation Area** (sites $10), where the 140-site 'campground' – really just a parking lot near the Susitna River – caters to king salmon fishers unconcerned about the lack of privacy. To get there, follow the signs a few miles west from Mile 70.8 of George Parks Hwy.

TALKEETNA

☎ 907 / pop 844

At Mile 98.7 of George Parks Hwy, a spur road heads 14½ miles north to Talkeetna, the place that perhaps best matches the rest of the world's fantasies of what an Alaskan town must be like.

A turn-of-the-20th-century gold-mining center, Talkeetna has retained much of its early Alaskan flavor: log cabins and geriatric clapboard storefronts line the streets, dogs and unconventional people run hither and yon, and – despite a tourism boom that's

transforming the face of Main St – there's still not a McDonald's or Wal-Mart in sight.

Nothing so defines Talkeetna as its relationship with the peaks on its northwestern horizon. Among alpinists, the community is famed as the staging area for ascents of Mt McKinley, Mt Foraker, the Moose's Tooth and other dizzying summits, the very names of which jump-start the saliva glands of mountaineers the world over. In late spring and early summer an international coterie of climbers fills every bed in town. On their way to or from grand successes or humbling failures (which occasionally include death), they cut loose at the bars and eat mass quantities of non-freeze-dried food in every restaurant in town.

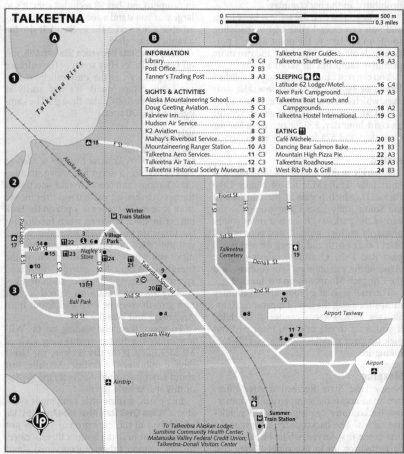

TALKEETNA

0 ——— 500 m
0 ——— 0.3 miles

INFORMATION
Library..............................1 C4
Post Office........................2 B3
Tanner's Trading Post...........3 A3

SIGHTS & ACTIVITIES
Alaska Mountaineering School.....4 B3
Doug Geeting Aviation............5 C3
Fairview Inn......................6 A3
Hudson Air Service................7 C3
K2 Aviation.......................8 C3
Mahay's Riverboat Service.........9 B3
Mountaineering Ranger Station....10 A3
Talkeetna Aero Services..........11 C3
Talkeetna Air Taxi...............12 C3
Talkeetna Historical Society Museum..13 A3

Talkeetna River Guides.............14 A3
Talkeetna Shuttle Service..........15 A3

SLEEPING
Latitude 62 Lodge/Motel...........16 C4
River Park Campground............17 A3
Talkeetna Boat Launch and
    Campgrounds..................18 A2
Talkeetna Hostel International....19 C3

EATING
Café Michele.....................20 B3
Dancing Bear Salmon Bake.........21 B3
Mountain High Pizza Pie..........22 A3
Talkeetna Roadhouse..............23 A3
West Rib Pub & Grill.............24 B3

It's not just the climbers who make Talkeetna interesting. Equally fascinating are the community's other subcultures: the intrepid aviators forever buzzing overhead as they ferry climbers and sightseers to the mountains, the end-of-the-road bushrats who've come here to carve an unbridled life out of the Alaskan wilds, the seasonal flocks of fresh-faced hippie chicks and nature boys, and the plethora of leftists who've made the Green Party the top vote-getter here in past elections.

Amazingly, all these folks mix fairly fluidly, forming a town with an intense community spirit and a powerful appeal to visitors. After spending a day or two here – fishing, flightseeing, glacier trekking or just drinking in the local scene – you'll likely see the truth in the town's unofficial motto: 'Talkeetna: Where the road ends and life begins.'

Orientation & Information

Though famed for its proximity to the mountains, Talkeetna sits in flat, lushly wooded country near the confluence of the Susitna, Talkeetna and Chulitna Rivers (the town gets its name from a Tanaina word meaning 'river of plenty').

A few visitor services are strung along the Talkeetna Spur Rd into town, but almost everything you'll need is within a stone's throw of Main St, which begins with a 'Welcome to Beautiful Downtown Talkeetna' sign at the town park and ends a few blocks later at the riverbank.

Library (☎ 733-2359; Mile 13.5, Talkeetna Spur Rd; ⏰ 11am-6pm Mon-Wed & Fri, 11am-7pm Thu, noon-5pm Sat; 💻) Just south of town. Offers free Internet access.

Matanuska Valley Federal Credit Union (☎ 733-4891; 0.3 Mile Talkeetna Spur Rd) Just up from George Parks Hwy. Has the area's only full-service bank.

Post Office (Spur Rd near Main St; ⏰ 9am-5pm Mon-Fri)

Sunshine Community Health Center (☎ 733-2273; Mile 4.4 Talkeetna Spur Rd) Will get that grizzly-bear tooth out of your tush.

Talkeetna–Denali Visitors Center (☎ 733-2688, 800-660-2688; www.alaskan.com/talkeetnadenali) At the junction of George Parks Hwy and Talkeetna Spur Rd, provides remarkably frank recommendations and is far more helpful than the privately owned places in town that call themselves visitor centers.

Tanner's Trading Post (☎ 733-2621; Main St; ⏰ 7am-9pm) Has an ATM, a laundromat and showers.

Sights

TALKEETNA HISTORICAL SOCIETY MUSEUM

A block south of Main St is this **museum** (☎ 733-2487; admission $3; ⏰ 10:30am-6pm), a small complex of restored buildings. The town's 1936 schoolhouse features an exhibit devoted to Don Sheldon (the bush pilot who pioneered landing climbers high on Mt McKinley's glaciers for a better shot at the peak), as well as artifacts on trapping and mining. The complex also includes a fully furnished trapper's cabin and a train depot. But the most fascinating building by far is the Section House. Inside you'll find a 12ft by 12ft relief model of Mt McKinley surrounded by Bradford Washburn's famous mural-like photos of the mountain. An exhibit devoted to the town's best-known climber, Ray 'the Pirate' Genet, is also on display.

MOUNTAINEERING RANGER STATION

Whether you're intrigued by high-altitude alpinism or boggled by it, this **ranger station** (☎ 733-9110; cnr 1st & B Sts; ⏰ 8am-6pm) provides an excellent window into that rarefied world. In addition to coordinating the numerous expeditions to Mt McKinley during the spring and summer, the station functions as a visitor center, with maps, books, photos and video presentations about the Alaska Range, as well as climbing-club flags from around the world and signed ice axes from successful ascents. Rangers offer presentations daily; a full calendar is posted.

TALKEETNA CEMETERY

The most solemn way to appreciate the effect of the mountain on Talkeetna is to visit the **cemetery**, a restful spot set among tall trees on 2nd St, just off Talkeetna Spur Rd near the airport.

Don Sheldon's grave is the most prominent, with the epitaph 'He wagered with the wind and won'. The Mt McKinley Climber's Memorial includes a stone for Ray Genet, despite the fact that his body was never removed from the slopes of Mt Everest. The most touching sight, however, is a memorial with the names and ages of all the climbers who've died on Mt McKinley and neighboring peaks.

Particularly grim was the *annus horribilis* of 1991, when 11 lives were lost.

SCALING THE MOUNTAIN

So, has gazing up at lordly Mt McKinley infected you with summit fever?

If so, you're suffering from a century-old sickness. James Wickersham, the US district judge in Alaska, made the first documented attempt to scale Denali, reaching the 7500ft mark of the 20,320ft peak in 1903. His effort inspired a rash of ensuing bids, including Dr Frederick Cook's 1906 effort (which he falsely claimed was a success) and the 1910 Sourdough Expedition, where four Fairbanks miners, carrying only hot chocolate, donuts and a 14ft spruce pole, topped out on the North Peak only to realize it was 850ft lower than the true, more southerly summit.

Success finally came in 1913 when Hudson Stuck, Henry Karstens, Robert Tatum and Walter Harper reached the top on June 7. From there they saw the spruce pole on the North Peak to verify the claims of the Sourdough Expedition.

The most important date for many climbers, however, is 1951. That year, Bradford Washburn arrived and pioneered the West Buttress route, by far the preferred avenue to the top. Not long after, Talkeetna's two most famous characters – Ray 'the Pirate' Genet and Don Sheldon – began to have an impact on the climbing world. Genet was an Alaskan mountaineer who made a record 25 climbs up Mt McKinley, while Sheldon was a legendary glacier pilot. The two worked closely in guiding climbers to the top and, more importantly, rescuing those who failed. Sadly, the town lost both in quick succession, with Sheldon dying of cancer in 1975 and Genet freezing to death on Mt Everest four years later.

Nowadays, Denali's storied mountaineering history adds considerably to the mythic business of scaling the peak. Between 1000 and 1300 climbers attempt it each year, spending an average of three weeks on the slopes. About 85% use the West Buttress route, which involves flying in a ski plane from Talkeetna to the 7200ft Kahiltna Glacier and from there climbing for the South Peak, passing a medical/rescue camp maintained by mountaineering clubs and the National Park Service (NPS) at 14,220ft.

In a good season, when storms are not constantly sweeping across the range, more than 50% will be successful. In a bad year that rate falls below 40%, and several climbers may die.

If you're a seasoned alpinist you can mount an expedition yourself, or be among the 25% of Mt McKinley climbers who are part of guided ascents. Of the licensed guiding companies, only one is local: **Alaska Mountaineering School** (☎ 733-1016; www.climbalaska.org; Third St), which charges $4500 to lead you up the mountain.

Folks without high-altitude credentials would be better off opting for one of the company's one-, two- or three-day glacier treks on the shoulders of the mountain – a fine way to get a taste of what the mountaineers endure, but at an altitude that isn't life-threatening. These excursions cost from $690 to $1200, which covers the glacier flight and all the gear you'll need for the experience of a lifetime.

FAIRVIEW INN

Closed in 2005, it would be an absolute travesty if this **inn** (Main St) failed to reopen. Though not an official museum, it might as well be. Founded in 1923 to serve as the overnight stop between Seward and Fairbanks on the newly constructed Alaska Railroad, the inn is listed on the National Register of Historic Places. Its old plank-floored saloon is classic Alaska: its walls are covered with racks of antlers, various furry critters (including a grizzly on the ceiling) and lots of local memorabilia. One corner holds Talkeetna's only slot machine; another is devoted to President Warren G Harding. When the railroad was finished in 1923, Harding arrived in Alaska and rode the rails to the Nenana River, where he hammered in the golden spike. Talkeetna locals swear (with grins on their faces) that he stopped at the Fairview Inn on the way home, was poisoned, and wound up dying in San Francisco less than a week later. Ever since, the Fairview has remained a fine place to be poisoned.

Tours
FLIGHTSEEING

When in Talkeetna, it's pretty much mandatory to go flightseeing around Mt McKinley. It's not cheap, but on a clear day it's so worthwhile that it's one of the best bargains in this expensive state.

There are five local flightseeing operations, all well established, all similar with regards to safety, professionalism and price, and all recipients of fawning reviews from their customers. Most offer three different tours: a circuit of Mt McKinley, a ski-equipped landing on one of its glaciated flanks, and a wildlife tour when the peak is clouded over.

The main difference between the companies is the planes they use: some have small aircraft that stay below 12,000ft but can weave in and out of canyons like gnats on steroids, while others fly higher, taking you into the thin air around the 20,320ft summit, where from April to mid-July you might even be able to spy climbing parties slogging toward the top. Also, some planes have above-window wings, meaning you get a less obstructed view of the scenery.

Decide what sort of trip works best for you and ask the right questions before you sign up. Plan on spending anywhere from around $140 to $290 per person for a flight, depending on flight length (usually between one and two hours) and whether you want to land on a glacier or circle the summit.

The companies all have their offices near the airstrip, a short jaunt across the railroad tracks from downtown.

Doug Geeting Aviation (☎ 733-2366, 800-770-2366; www.alaskaairtours.com)

Hudson Air Service (☎ 733-2321, 800-478-2321; www.hudsonair.com)

K2 Aviation (☎ 733-2291, 800-764-2291; www.flyk2.com)

Talkeetna Aero Services (☎ 733-2899, 888-733-2899; www.talkeetnaaero.com)

Talkeetna Air Taxi (☎ 733-2218, 800-533-2219; www.talkeetnaair.com)

TOWN & RIVER TOURS

The town walking tour led by **Mountain Light Adventures** (☎ 733-1237; www.mountainlightadventures.com) offers a glimpse into the gold-rush, railroad and alpine history of this legendary little community. It runs twice daily, at 8:30am and 6:30pm, and costs $24. Meet at the 'Welcome to Beautiful Downtown Talkeetna' sign at the beginning of Main St.

To get out onto Talkeetna's many nearby waterways, sign up with **Talkeetna River Guides** (☎ 733-2677; www.talkeetnariverguides.com; Main St), who'll put you in a raft for a placid two-hour float on the Talkeetna River ($54) or a four-hour float on the Chulitna River, through Denali State Park ($99).

Fishing around Talkeetna is absurdly good, with runs of every species of Pacific salmon plus grayling, rainbow trout and Dolly Varden. **Mahay's Riverboat Service** (☎ 733-2229; www.mahaysriverboat.com; Spur Rd) will equip you with fishing gear and take you where the fish are biting. A five-hour charter is $150; for eight hours it's $200.

Sleeping

The Matanuska-Susitna Borough charges a 5% accommodations tax on top of the prices listed below.

BUDGET

River Park Campground (sites $10) This informal place at the end of Main St is a bit scruffy, but close to the river and the action. No RVs.

Talkeetna Hostel International (☎ 733-4678; www.talkeetnahostel.com; I St; sites $15, dm $27, s/d $60/75; office 🕑 9am-2pm, 4-9pm; 🖳) In a quiet neighborhood a 10-minute walk from Main St, this well-loved but not-too-worn hostel has coed dorm rooms, two private rooms, a shared kitchen, showers, free Internet access and great advice about what to do in Talkeetna. In climbing season, when they rent out even couch and floor space, reservations are key. To get here, take 2nd St (the airport road) off Talkeetna Spur Rd; you'll pass I St on the way to the runway at the end of the road.

Talkeetna Boat Launch & Campgrounds (☎ 733-2604; sites $13) East of the tracks at the north end of F St, this tree-shrouded campground offers sites near the Talkeetna River and has restrooms, showers ($4) and a small store. If it seems off the beaten path, ask about the shortcut through the woods to downtown.

Talkeetna Roadhouse (☎ 733-1351; www.talkeetna roadhouse.com; Main St; dm $21, s/d $48/63) This place is the real Alaskan deal. It dates from 1917 and hosts scores of climbers in season. It has seven small private rooms with shared bath, and a bunkroom.

MIDRANGE & TOP END

Latitude 62 Lodge/Motel (☎ 733-2262; Mile 13.5 Talkeetna Spur Rd; s/d $63/74) If downtown Talkeetna is just too hippie-dippy for you, there's always this place, with hunting-lodge decor that includes plenty of pelts and skulls.

Talkeetna Alaskan Lodge (☎ 733-9500, 888-959-9590; www.talkeetnalodge.com; Mile 12.5 Talkeetna Spur Rd; r $249-539) This is a newish and luxurious Alaska Native corporation–owned place with

TALKEETNA BLUEGRASS FESTIVAL

Of all the summer shindigs that get things shakin' in this great state, none is as famed as the **Talkeetna Bluegrass Festival** (www.talkeetnabluegrass.com; tickets $35, Sunday-only $10), a four-day party coinciding with the first weekend in August. Called 'Alaska's greatest campout' and likened to Woodstock itself, the event has been an annual ritual for over 20 years. Now too big for downtown Talkeetna (attendance in past years has reportedly approached 5000 people), it takes place on a 142-acre site at Mile 102 of George Parks Hwy.

If the festival has outgrown Talkeetna, it's also outgrown bluegrass. Alaskan folk, blues and rock bands dominate the bill, and though there's music on stage 20 hours a day (and round-the-clock jamming in the campground), you're less likely to hear banjo-pickin' than to find yourself slam-dancing in a mud-soaked mosh-pit or gyrating to strobe-lit techno. The Fairview Inn used to rectify this situation, booking a bluegrass band or two during the event, but unless that establishment reopens there may be little recourse for true bluegrass fans.

For a long time, the festival was notorious for being a big bacchanal, with revelers split into two factions: the drinkers, who tended to get rowdy and sloppy, and the nondrinkers, who indulged abundantly in other synapse-seducing substances. In recent years organizers have worked to clean up the event's image, creating a less rambunctious family-camping area, deploying an internal 'security' squad called the Karma Kontrol, and accepting an increased police presence to crack down on drunk driving, vandalism and the like. Still, in true Alaskan live-and-let-live fashion, the festival remains the sort of whoop-up where folks enjoy beer for breakfast and often let a lot more than just their hair down.

153 rooms/suites, a restaurant and lounge. The hillside setting offers great views of Mt McKinley. Prices drop dramatically before June and after August.

Eating & Drinking
RESTAURANTS
Café Michele (☎ 733-5300; www.cafemichele.com; cnr Talkeetna Spur Rd & 2nd St; lunch $13-17, dinner $18-29; ⏲ 11am-4pm, 5:30-10pm) The town's best food and most upscale atmosphere can be found here, either inside the bright and spotless dining room or out on the flower-bedecked patio. Prices are steep, but worth it. Owner-chef Michele Camera-Faurot subscribes to the food-as-art school; try the superb soy-ginger salmon. Fine wines and good imported/craft beers are also available.

Talkeetna Roadhouse (☎ 733-1351; Main St; breakfast $8-12, sandwiches $4-8; ⏲ 6:30am-3pm) This venerable, colorful establishment has the best breakfasts in town. Half-orders are adequate; fulls are mountain-sized. The restaurant also doubles as a bakery, cooking up giant cinnamon rolls in the morning.

CAFÉS & QUICK EATS
Mountain High Pizza Pie (☎ 733-1234; Main St; pizza slices $3.50, sandwiches $5-11; ⏲ 11:30am-11pm) This arty, airy downtown establishment makes fabulous pizzas with names such as 'the

Yentna' and 'the Grizzly.' They've also got lots of microbrews available.

West Rib Pub & Grill (☎ 733-3354; Main St; burgers & sandwiches $7-10; ⏲ 11:30am-2am) At the back of Nagley's Store, this is good to soak in Talkeetna's live-and-let-live vibe, rubbing shoulders with visitors and locals alike. It's got burgers, salmon and halibut, plenty of craft brews, and, if sunny, outdoor seating.

Dancing Bear Salmon Bake (cnr Main St & Talkeetna Spur Rd; mains $4-10; ⏲ 11am-9pm) This roadside stand serves up reindeer hotdogs, buffalo bratwursts, steamy buttered fiddlehead ferns, and, of course, halibut and salmon.

Getting There & Around
AIR
You can stay in Talkeetna and get a ride up to Denali National Park with **Talkeetna Aero Services** (☎ 733-2899, 888-733-2899; www.talkeetna aero.com). The company offers a day-trip package from Talkeetna to Denali National Park ($295) that includes round-trip flights, lunch and a bus tour in the park; for an extra $50 you can get a flightseeing diversion thrown in. If you just want a ride to the park and back, it's $135 each way.

BUS
There are a couple of options for busing between Talkeetna and points up and down

George Parks Hwy. In the climbing (which starts in spring) and summer season, **Talkeetna Shuttle Service** (☎ 733-1725, 888-288-6008; www.denalicentral.com) runs twice a day between Anchorage and Talkeetna, departing the big city at 8am and 5pm and Talkeetna at 11am and 4pm. The fare is $55/100 one-way/round-trip.

Alaska/Yukon Trails (☎ 479-2277; 800-770-7275) plies the whole George Parks Hwy, leaving Anchorage daily at around 7am, getting to downtown Talkeetna around 9am and continuing northbound through Denali Park to Fairbanks. The reverse trip departs Fairbanks around 8:45am daily, leaves downtown Talkeetna at 3:45pm and reaches Anchorage around 5:45pm. The one-way fare between Talkeetna and Anchorage is $79; to or from Fairbanks it's $94.

TRAIN

The **Alaska Railroad** (☎ 265-2494, 800-544-0552; www.alaskarailroad.com) runs a couple of trains that stop in Talkeetna. From mid-May to mid-September, the *Denali Star* stops daily on its run between Anchorage and Fairbanks. The one-way adult fares are: Anchorage to Talkeetna $80; Talkeetna to Denali $75; Talkeetna to Fairbanks $103.

The *Hurricane*, sometimes called the 'Local' or the 'Bud Car,' provides a local rural service from Thursday through Sunday in the summertime. It's a flag-stop train, departing Talkeetna at 12:15pm for the trip north to Hurricane Gulch, where it turns around and heads back the same day. This 'milk run' takes you within view of Mt McKinley and into some remote areas. It also allows you to mingle with local residents, something not as easy to do on the express train (*Denali Star*). Round-trip adult fare is $72.

DENALI STATE PARK

At 324,240-acres, Denali State Park is the fourth-largest state park in Alaska and is roughly half the size of Rhode Island. The entrance is at Mile 132.2 of George Parks Hwy. The park covers the transition zone between the coastal region and the spine of the Alaska Range, and provides numerous views of towering peaks, including Mt McKinley and the glaciers on its southern slopes.

Some say on a clear day the panorama of Mt McKinley here is the most spectacular view in North America. The park is largely undeveloped but does offer a handful of turnoffs, trails, two rental cabins and three campgrounds that can be reached from George Parks Hwy, which runs through the park.

It may share the same name and a border with the renowned national park to the north, but Denali State Park is an entirely different experience. Because of its lack of facilities you need to be better prepared for your hiking and backpacking adventures. But this may be the park's blessing, for it also lacks the crowds, long waits and tight regulations of Denali National Park.

At the height of the summer season, experienced backpackers may want to consider the state park as a hassle-free and cheaper alternative.

Information

The **Denali State Park Visitor Center** (Mile 147 George Parks Hwy; ◷ 9am-6pm) is at the Alaska Veterans Memorial, just north of Byers Lake Campground. It has a few maps and brochures, for a price, but due to budget cuts it mostly sells candy bars and pop to the tour-bus crowd.

Activities

There are several excellent hiking trails and alpine routes in the park. Keep in mind that in the backcountry, open fires are allowed only on the gravel bars of major rivers. Pack a stove if you plan to camp overnight.

Troublesome Creek Trail begins at a posted trailhead in the parking area at Mile 137.6 of George Parks Hwy and ascends along the creek until it reaches the tree line, where you enter an open area with alpine lakes and mountain views. From here the route is marked only by rock cairns as it heads north to Byers Lake. The 15-mile backpacking trip to Byers Lake Campground is of moderate difficulty, but if you're more adventurous, you can continue to Little Coal Creek Trail, a 36-mile trek above the tree line. Views from the ridges are spectacular. Numerous black bears feeding on salmon gave the creek its name. Because of them, the trail is usually closed to hikers from July to September.

Byers Lake Loop Trail is an easy 4.8-mile trek around the lake. It begins at Byers Lake Campground and passes six hike-in campsites on the other side, 1.8 miles from the posted trailhead.

328 GEORGE PARKS HIGHWAY •• Cantwell & Broad Pass

Kesugi Ridge Traverse is a difficult route that departs from Byers Lake Trail and ascends its namesake ridge. Once on the ridge, you follow a route north to Little Coal Creek Trail at the park's north end. Little Coal Creek Trail leads back to George Parks Hwy. The 27.4-mile route is well marked with cairns and flags.

If you're contemplating this trek, remember that it's far easier for hikers to access the ridge along Little Coal Creek Trail than it is to hike from Byers Lake Trail, which is a much steeper climb.

Little Coal Creek Trail departs from Mile 163.8 of George Parks Hwy, ascending to the alpine areas of Kesugi Ridge. From there you continue to the summit of Indian Mountain, an ascent of about 3300ft, or continue along the ridge to either Byers Lake or Troublesome Creek. Within 3 miles Little Coal Creek Trail climbs above the tree line at a spot known as the North Fork Birdhouse, a great place to set up an alpine camp for the night. It's a 9-mile round-trip to Indian Peak and 27.4 miles to Byers Lake.

Sleeping

Lower Troublesome Creek Campground (Mile 137.2 George Parks Hwy; sites $10) This place has toilets, drinking water and 20 walk-in sites just yards from the parking lot.

Byers Lake Campground (Mile 147 George Parks Hwy; sites $10) As well as 73 sites, this campground offers access to walk-in sites along the loop trail around the lake, and to the state park's Byers Lake Cabins 1 and 2. You can drive to one; the other is a half-mile hike away. Each is $50 a night and must be reserved in advance, online at the **Alaska Division of Parks** (☎ 745-3975; www.alaskastateparks.org; Mile 0.7 Bogard Rd) in Wasilla.

Denali Viewpoint North Campground (Mile 162.7 George Parks Hwy; sites $10) This place has 20 sites and with the exception of some charming walk-in sites, it is basically a parking lot; but the views are stunning. You overlook the Chulitna River while Mt McKinley overwhelms you from above. Interpretive displays and a spotting scope help you enjoy the panorama.

Mt McKinley Princess Wilderness Lodge (☎ 733-2900, 800-426-0500; www.princessalaskalodges.com; Mile 133 George Parks Hwy; r $139-179) On the park's south edge, this is Princess Cruises' deluxe entry in the area.

CANTWELL & BROAD PASS

The northern boundary of Denali State Park is at Mile 168.5 George Parks Hwy. Situated at Mile 203.6, **Broad Pass** (2300ft) is a dividing line: rivers to the south drain into Cook Inlet, while waters to the north flow to the Yukon River. The area is at the tree line and worth a stop for some hiking. The mountain valley, surrounded by tall white peaks, is unquestionably one of the most beautiful spots along George Parks Hwy or the Alaska Railroad – both use the low gap to cross the Alaska Range.

North from the pass, George Parks Hwy descends 6 miles to Cantwell (pop 220), at the junction with Denali Hwy. Here you'll find gas pumps, convenience stores and accommodations, including **Lazy J Cabins & Café** (☎ 768-2414; www.homestead.com/lazy_j/home.html; Mile 210 George Parks Hwy; sites $20; cabins $100; r with bath $120; café ☾ 7am-11pm), with somewhat overpriced, pine-panelled rooms and small but functional cabins.

NENANA

☎ 907 / pop 549

The only significant town between Denali National Park and Fairbanks is Nenana (nee-na-nuh, like 'banana') at Mile 305 of George Parks Hwy, which lies at the confluence of the Nenana and Tanana (tan-uh-naw, not like 'banana') Rivers. Though the big industry here is barging freight downstream, for visitors and northerners alike the community is most famous for the Nenana Ice Classic, an eminently Alaskan game of chance in which prognosticators attempt to profit by guessing when the ice will break up on the Nenana River (p330).

There's lots of info on the Ice Classic at the very helpful **Nenana Visitor Center** (☎ 832-9953; Mile 304.5 George Parks Hwy; ☾ 8am-6pm), located at the entrance to town in a one-room log cabin (note the sod roof abloom with wildflowers). Outside you'll find the Taku Chief river tug, which once pushed barges along the Tanana River.

Historically, Nenana was little more than a roadhouse until it was chosen as the base for building the northern portion of the Alaska Railroad in 1916. The construction camp quickly became a boomtown that made history on July 15, 1923, when President Warren G Harding arrived to hammer in the golden spike on the north side of the Tanana.

DENALI & THE INTERIOR

BACK INTO THE WILD

Just north of Healy, the Stampede Trail turns off George Parks Hwy and heads west into the bush. On April 28, 1992, 24-year-old Chris McCandless hiked 20 miles along this road, intending to live off the land for an indefinite length of time. Less than four months later, he was dead.

Not raised an outdoorsman, McCandless was from an upper-class East Coast family. He graduated from Emory University and was headed for law school – or so his parents thought. Instead he loaded a few belongings into his old Datsun and hit the road, leaving his family and his entire way of life behind. When the Datsun gave out, he abandoned it in the Arizona desert, burned his money and set out on foot. Roaming the country from one end to the other, he worked when necessary as an itinerant laborer, but stuck to a quest to find nirvana in a simple nomadic life eschewing all materialism.

In 1992 that quest took him to Alaska, where he hoped to brave his biggest challenge – to live alone, off the land, in the bush…a primal pioneer existence many generations removed from the comfortable hand he'd been dealt in life. When he hiked out along the Stampede Trail, he had intentionally forsaken a map, and he carried with him little more than a .22 rifle, a 10lb bag of rice and a load of paperback books ranging from Thoreau to Tolstoy. He came upon an abandoned bus, and here he made his 'home.' For three months he hunted small game, killed one moose and gathered edible plants for sustenance, but then something quickly went wrong.

Author Jon Krakauer, who chronicled McCandless' story in his book *Into the Wild* (New York: Doubleday, 1996) believes McCandless died of starvation after relying too heavily on the seed pods of the otherwise edible wild potato for a food source. Unlike the rest of the plant, the seeds contain a toxin that prevents the body from deriving energy from its food supply. When McCandless realized he was getting weak and tried to hike out, the Teklanika River – which had been a fordable stream in April when he came into the Bush – had become a swollen torrent he was unable to cross. Without a map, he had no way of knowing that he was near a gauging station with a cable tram across the river, or that he was in close reach of a USFS cabin with emergency food supplies. McCandless retreated to the bus, finally passing away in mid-August 1992.

Since the publication of Krakauer's book, the bus where McCandless lived and died has become a shrine. Like visitors to Jim Morrison's grave, pilgrims by the hundred have come to pay homage to someone who, they maintain, lived life strictly on his own terms. They scratch their initials into the bus, leave flowers and survival equipment, and write reflective comments in a register at the site. This is seen as totally ridiculous by many Alaskans, who consider McCandless nothing more than a city boy who didn't respect the rigors of life in the Alaskan Bush and paid the price.

If you want to make your own pilgrimage to Alaska's most famous bus, you'd be wisest to do it in winter, when the Teklanika is stilled by cold and when **EarthSong Lodge** (☎ 683-2863; www.earthsonglodge.com; Mile 4 Stampede Rd; r $125-175) runs dogsled trips along the Stampede Trail. Otherwise, aim for spring or fall, when the water crossings are less hazardous. And no matter when you go, ask advice from locals, pack a map and respect Ma Nature – you don't want Chris McCandless' journey to be your own.

The sickly Harding, the first president ever to visit Alaska, missed the golden spike the first two times, or so the story goes, but finally drove it in to complete the railroad.

In preparation for the president's arrival, the Nenana train station was built in 1922 at the north end of A St. Extensively restored in 1988 it's now on the National Register of Historic Places. The building includes the jumbled **Alaska Railroad Museum** (☎ 832-5500; admission free; ☉ 9:30am-6pm), which displays not just railroad memorabilia but local artifacts ranging from ice tongs to animal traps. East of the station, a monument commemorates Harding's visit. On Front and Market Sts, **St Mark's Episcopal Church** dates from 1905. The interior has many beautiful handcrafted features including an altar with traditional Athabascan beadwork.

Down on the river you might see some **fish wheels** at work during the late-summer salmon runs. These traditional traps scoop fish out of the water as they swim upstream to spawn. The riverfront is also home to the

DENALI & THE INTERIOR

BREAKING THE ICE IN NENANA

For stir-crazy Alaskans, nothing heralds the end of winter like the break-up of ice on the nearest river. It's a subject of much anticipation everywhere in the state – but nowhere more than in Nenana, where this seasonal guessing game has become the state's preeminent gamble.

The Nenana Ice Classic began in 1917 when cabin-feverish Alaska Railroad surveyors pooled $800 and bet on when the ice would disintegrate on the frozen Tanana River. Eight decades later the wager is the same, but the stakes are much higher, with a 2005 jackpot of $285,000.

Anyone can play: just shell out $2.50 for a ticket and register your guess, down to the month, day, hour and minute. Though tickets are on sale throughout Alaska from February 1 to April 5, in the summer they can be purchased only in Nenana. Most tourist-oriented places in town sell them, including the Rough Woods Inn and the Tripod Gift Shop across from the visitor center.

Come next spring, the first movement of the ice will be determined by a 'tripod' which stands guard on the Tanana, 300ft from shore. Any surge will dislodge the tripod, which tugs on a cord, which in turn stops a clock on shore. The exact time on the clock will determine the winner.

And when will it happen? Your prediction is as good as anybody's. The earliest break-up came at 3:27pm on April 20, 1940. The latest was 11:41am, May 20, 1964. The vast majority were between April 29 and May 12. And it almost never happens between midnight and 9am.

But don't get too excited: no matter what time you guess, many others will likely guess the same – meaning that if you win, your payout will likely be just a fraction of the jackpot.

You can view a replica of the Ice Classic tripod and past books of guesses – vast tomes some 4in thick – at the Nenana Visitor Center. You can usually see the next Nenana Ice Classic tripod even if you're not getting off the train. During the summer, it's on the banks of the Tanana River near the depot, ready to be positioned on the ice in February during the town's Tripod Raising Festival.

Alfred Starr Nenana Cultural Center (☎ 832-5520), which has been closed in recent years but may reopen to inform visitors about local culture and history.

Sleeping & Eating

Nenana Valley RV Park (☎ 832-5230; cnr 4th & B Sts; campsites $5, RV sites $10-15) Has spots for tenters in a grassy expanse near the visitor center.

Rough Woods Inn & Café (☎ 832-5299; www .roughwoodsinn.biz; 623 N A St; r $65-130; breakfast & lunch $6-9, dinner $16-29) Right on A St, has large but somewhat worn rooms, most with kitchenettes. One room sleeps up to seven people. The café is the essence of home cookin'.

DENALI HIGHWAY

A highway in only the titular sense, the Denali Hwy is basically a gravel road from Cantwell, just south of Denali National Park on George Parks Hwy, to Paxson on Richardson Hwy. Considered one of Alaska's most stunning drives, this 135-mile route was opened in 1957 as the only road to the national park. It became a secondary route after George Parks Hwy was completed in 1972. Now it's open only from mid-May to October, it sees just a trickle of tourists, hunters and anglers.

Most of the highway is at or near tree line, running along the foothills of the Alaska Range and through glacial valleys where you can see stretches of alpine tundra, enormous glaciers and braided rivers. All that scenery is a blessing, because the road itself, though perfectly passable in a standard auto, is slow going. Due to washboarding and hairpin curves you'll likely average just 35mph, taking six hours from end to end. Better yet, make fat-tire fun out of it; the highway in its rough-and-tumble state has become a favorite for mountain-bikers.

Hikers can reach the surrounding backcountry via numerous trails off the highway, though few are marked and most are trafficked by ATVs.

There are also several popular paddling routes in the area. Ask locals at the roadhouses for information and take along topographic maps that cover the areas you intend to trek or paddle.

There are no established communities along the way, but the roadhouses provide food, beds and sometimes gas. Most of the development is at the Paxson end of the highway. If you're driving, fill up with gas at Paxson or Cantwell.

Cantwell to Tangle Lakes

The junction at Cantwell is at Mile 133.8 of the Denali Hwy. Within 3 miles pavement ends, rough gravel takes over, and the road ascends into the sort of big-sky territory that will dominate it for the duration.

Fifteen miles along, at Mile 118, you'll reach a put-in for the silt-choked Nenana River, which can be paddled in Class I to II conditions from here to George Parks Hwy, 18 river miles distant. Novices will want to pull out there; after George Parks Hwy it gets way hairier.

At Mile 104, just before a bridge over the Brushkana Creek, is the Bureau of Land Management's (BLM) Brushkana Creek Campground. If you've brought your rod you can try your hand at catching grayling and Dolly Varden in the fast-flowing waters.

Another fishing possibility is Butte Lake, at the end of the **Butte Lake Trail** (Mile 94 Denali Hwy), a willow-lined, 5-mile ATV track. Nearly opposite the trailhead is a pull-off with excellent mesa-top views of the Alaska Range.

Several potential hiking trails, none signposted, branch off the highway in the dozen or so miles after Gracious House Lodge, a roadhouse at Mile 82. One of them is the **Snodgrass Lake Trail**, which begins from a parking area between Mile 80 and Mile 81 and leads 2 miles south to Snodgrass Lake, known for its good grayling fishing.

Just over the Susitna River is the **Denali Trail** (Mile 79 Denali Hwy), more of a gravel road, which begins on the highway's north side at a 'Clearwater Creek Controlled Use Area' sign. The 6-mile route winds to the old mining camp of Denali, first established in 1907. A few old buildings still remain. Several mining trails branch off the trail, including an 18-mile route to Roosevelt Lake from Denali Camp. The area can provide experienced hikers with a good two- to three-day trip.

At Mile 56 a bridge crosses Clearwater Creek; outhouses and informal campsites are nearby. Another 14 miles on is the MacLaren River Lodge, just before you cross the MacLaren River.

On the river's far side is **Crazy Dog Kennels** (☎ 978-6812, 822-5424; www.dogsleddenali.com), the summer operation of Yukon Quest champ John Schandelmeier and his wife, Zoya DeNure. Impassioned about their pups,

they run the only dog-yard in Alaska that rescues unwanted sled dogs and turns them into racers. A tour of the kennel is $10 per person; it's nice if you call ahead.

From here, the highway ascends **MacLaren Summit** (Mile 37 Denali Hwy), at 4086ft one of the highest highway passes in the state. The summit offers great views of Mt Hayes, Hess Mountain and Mt Deborah to the west and MacLaren Glacier to the north.

At Mile 32, at a parking lot on the highway's north side, signage marks the trailhead of the 2-mile **Glacier Lake Trail**. Another 7 miles down the highway you'll cross Rock Creek Bridge, where the signposted **Landmark Gap Trail** leads north 3 miles to Landmark Gap Lake, at an elevation of 3217ft. You can't see the lake from the highway, but you can spot the noticeable gap between the Amphitheater Mountains.

SLEEPING & EATING

The Denali Hwy between Cantwell and Tangle Lakes features scores of pull-offs ideal for informal camping.

Brushkana Creek Campground (Mile 104.3 Denali Hwy; sites $6) This place offers 22 not-very-private sites, a picnic shelter, drinking water and a meat rack for the hunters who invade the area in late summer and fall.

Gracious House Lodge (☎ 333-3148, summer 259-1111; www.alaskaone.com/gracious; Mile 82 Denali Hwy; tents $10, s/d with bath $110/110, without bath $75/95; café ☻ 8am-8pm) This half-century-old establishment is a collection of cabins, trailers and Quonset huts with killer views of the mountains. The proprietors offer flightseeing, lodging and meals, and are particularly proud of their biscuits and pies.

MacLaren River Lodge (☎ 822-7105; Mile 42 Denali Hwy; www.maclarenlodge.com; dm $20, r without bath $60, cabin $125; café ☻ 7am-10pm) This lodge has unplumbed rooms in an ATCO trailer plus a new, bath-equipped cabin that sleeps up to six people.

Tangle Lakes To Paxson

After several miles of lonely road, the Denali Hwy suddenly gets busier and better-maintained as it descends into the Tangle Lakes area, a magnet for birders, anglers and paddlers. Pavement begins around Mile 21. Most of the lakes – as many as 40 in spring – can be seen from the Wrangell Mountain Viewpoint at Mile 13.

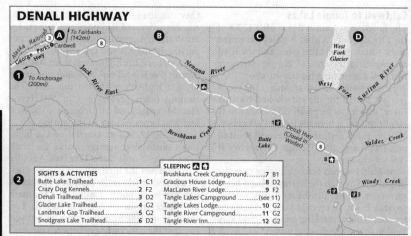

DENALI HIGHWAY

SIGHTS & ACTIVITIES
Butte Lake Trailhead..........................1 C1
Crazy Dog Kennels..............................2 F2
Denali Trailhead..................................3 D2
Glacier Lake Trailhead.........................4 G2
Landmark Gap Trailhead.....................5 G2
Snodgrass Lake Trailhead...................6 D2

SLEEPING
Brushkana Creek Campground..........7 B1
Gracious House Lodge........................8 D2
MacLaren River Lodge........................9 F2
Tangle Lakes Campground ....(see 11)
Tangle Lakes Lodge...........................10 G2
Tangle River Campground...............11 G2
Tangle River Inn...............................12 G2

ACTIVITIES

Paddling

The **Delta River Canoe Route** is a 35-mile paddle that starts at Tangle Lakes Campground (right) and ends a few hundred yards from Mile 212.5 of Richardson Hwy. Cross Round Tangle Lake and continue to Lower Tangle Lake, where you must make a portage around a waterfall. Below it is a set of Class III rapids that you must either line for 2 miles or paddle if you have an experienced hand. Every year many canoeists damage their boats beyond repair on these rapids and then have to hike 15 miles back out to the Denali Hwy. The remainder of the route is a much milder trip.

The **Upper Tangle Lakes Canoe Route** is easier and shorter than the Delta River route but needs four portages, which aren't marked but are easy to work out in the low-bush tundra. All paddlers trying this route must have topo maps. The route starts where the Denali Hwy crosses the Tangle River, passing through Upper Tangle Lake before ending at Dickey Lake, 9 miles to the south. There is a 1.2-mile portage into Dickey Lake.

From here, experienced paddlers can continue by following Dickey Lake's outlet to the southeast into the Middle Fork of the Gulkana River. For the first 3 miles the river is shallow and mild, but then it plunges into a steep canyon where canoeists have to contend with Class III and IV rapids. Most canoeists choose to line their boats carefully or make a portage. Allow seven days for the entire 76-mile trip from Tangle Lakes to Sourdough Creek Campground on the Gulkana River off Richardson Hwy.

Hiking

The unsignposted **Swede Lake Trail** (Mile 15 Denali Hwy) leads south 3 miles to Swede Lake, passing Little Swede Lake at the 2-mile mark. Beyond here it continues to the Middle Fork of the Gulkana River, but the trail is extremely wet at times and suitable only for off-road vehicles. Anglers fish the lakes for trout and grayling. Inquire at the Tangle River Inn (below for directions to the trail and an update on its condition.

SLEEPING

Tangle River Campground (Mile 21.7 Denali Hwy; sites free) Located right at the put-in for the Delta River canoe route, this seven-site campground is extremely popular; good luck finding a spot.

Tangle Lakes Campground (Mile 21.5 Denali Hwy; sites free) On the shores of Round Tangle Lake, this 22-site campground was free at time of research, but likely won't remain so.

Tangle River Inn (☎ 822-3970; www.tangleriverinn.com; Mile 20 Denali Hwy; dm $30, r $70-109) This is a popular stop for anglers, with a quality café in a log building overlooking the lakes. You may experience the proprietor holding forth in the dining room, possibly lambasting environmentalists.

Tangle Lakes Lodge (☎ 822-4202; Mile 22 Denali Hwy; cabins $75) Offers log cabins (without bath), a bar and a restaurant. For $88 you get a cabin-and-canoe combo.

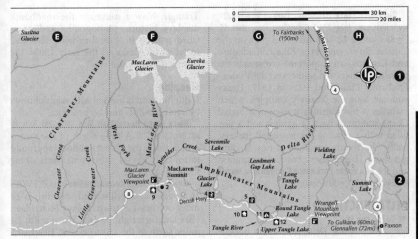

THE ALCAN/ALASKA HWY

One of the world's legendary roadways, the Alaska Hwy reaches 1390 miles from Dawson Creek, British Columbia to Delta Junction, Alaska. Another 98 miles from Delta Junction to Fairbanks, though nominally Richardson Hwy, are almost universally considered the final leg of the Alcan, and are herein treated as such.

The Alaska Hwy was famously punched through the wilderness in a mere eight months in 1942, which was part of a WWII effort to protect Alaska from expansionist Japan (p28). Commonly known as the Alcan, short for 'Alaska-Canada Military Highway,' it remains the only year-round overland route that links the 49th state to the Lower 48.

Approximately 300 of its miles, paved and well maintained, are within Alaska, between Fairbanks and the Yukon Territory border.

FAIRBANKS TO DELTA JUNCTION

From Fairbanks, Richardson Hwy runs 98 relatively unscenic miles to Delta Junction. From there, the Richardson continues to the south via Glennallen to Valdez, while the Alcan branches off and passes through Tok en route to Canada.

Chena Lakes Recreation Area (Mile 346.7 Richardson Hwy; day-use $4, sites $10) was the last phase of an Army Corps of Engineers flood-control project prompted by the Chena River's flooding of Fairbanks in 1967.

Two separate parks make up the area, offering nature paths, paved trails and swimming as well as canoe, sailboat and paddleboat rentals. Three campground loops provide access to around 80 sites.

Unless you're really keen on in-line skating, the whole thing feels a bit overdeveloped for Alaska.

Salcha River State Recreation Site (Mile 323.3 Richardson Hwy; sites $10) offers access to the Salcha and Tanana Rivers for fishing and boating. It has a basic camping area on a gravel bar, plus the reservable **Salcha River Public-Use Cabin** (www.dnr.state.ak.us/parks/cabins; per night $25) right by the boat dock. To reach the state recreation site, turn in at the Salcha Marine boat dealership.

Harding Lake State Recreation Area (Mile 321.5 Richardson Hwy; sites $10), 43 miles from Fairbanks, has a highly developed campground with over 90 sites, a ranger office, picnic shelters, horseshoes, volleyball, swimming, canoeing, and fishing (Arctic char and pike) in the natural lake. Five group walk-in sites are on the water.

Birch Lake Military Recreation Site (Mile 305.5 Richardson Hwy; sites $10) is jam-packed on weekends, when the lake is abuzz with personal watercraft and the parking lot is filled with noisy kids on tricycles.

At Mile 277.7 you'll come to Quartz Lake State Recreation Area, a large camping area (p334).

Big Delta State Historical Park (☎ 895-4201; www.rikas.com; Mile 274.5 Richardson Hwy; sites $5; ☷ 8am-8pm), a 10-acre historical park on the Tanana River, preserves Rika's Roadhouse and Landing, an important crossroads for travelers, miners and soldiers on the Valdez–Fairbanks Trail from 1909 to 1947. Today you can tour the leisurely complex, which includes a blacksmith's museum, a Signal Corps station, a barn, a garden and a pen filled with menacing domesticated turkeys. Sadly, the roadhouse itself is now a giant gift shop. There's also a rustic campground and the à la carte **Packhouse Pavilion Restaurant** (sandwiches $4-7; ☷ 9am-5pm).

DELTA JUNCTION
☎ 907 / pop 984
For most visitors, Delta Junction is notable for a technicality: it proclaims itself the end of the Alcan, as the famous highway joins Richardson Hwy here to complete the route to Fairbanks. The community began as a construction camp and picked up its name from the junction between the two highways. Nowadays it's an overtly religious place (among the multitude of churches, some have special RV parking), functioning as a service center for travelers, for the area's burgeoning agricultural community, and for nearby Fort Greely, a key cog in America's nascent missile-defense shield. The big Deltana Fair, with giant vegetables, livestock shows and parades, is on the last weekend of July.

Information
Delta Community Library (☎ 895-4102; 2291 Deborah St; ☷ 10am-6pm Mon-Thu, 10am-7pm Fri, 10am-5pm Sat, 1-5pm Sun; ☐) The best place in town to check your email. It shares a building with City Hall.
Delta Junction Visitor Center (☎ 895-5068, 877-895-5068; Mile 1422 the Alcan; ☷ 8am-8pm summer) More of a gift shop than a visitor center, this place is usually jammed with RVers clamoring to purchase 'End-of-the-Alaska-Highway' certificates ($1).

Sights
Across the parking lot from the visitor center is **Sullivan Roadhouse** (admission free; ☷ 9am-6pm). The classic log structure was built in 1906 and served travelers along the Fairbanks–Valdez Trail until 1927. It was placed on the National Register of Historic Places in 1979 and in 1997 was moved, log by log, from Fort Greely to its present location in the

Triangle. Now a museum, the roadhouse displays historic photographs and excavated artifacts in several exhibits dedicated to travel in Alaska in the early 1900s, the so-called 'roadhouse era.'

Sleeping
Delta Junction is blessed with scads of nearby campgrounds and no bed tax.
Delta State Recreation Site (Mile 267 Richardson Hwy; sites $10) A mile north of the visitor center, this is the closest public campground to town. It has 24 sites, some overlooking the local airstrip.
Clearwater State Recreation Site (sites $10) With 16 wooded and well-spaced sites, this is 13 miles northeast of town. Follow Richardson Hwy and turn right on Jack Warren Rd, 2.4 miles north of the visitor center. Head 10½ miles east and look for signs to the campground. (If you're heading into Delta Junction from Tok, you can go directly to the campground by turning north on Clearwater Rd, at Mile 1415 of the Alcan, then right at the T intersection with Jack Warren Rd.) Most of the sites overlook Clearwater Creek, which has a good grayling fishery.
Quartz Lake State Recreation Area (Mile 277.8 Richardson Hwy; sites $10) Covering 600 acres north of town, this area has 16 campsites in the loop and many more RV sites in an overflow parking area. A trail from the campground leads over to nearby Lost Lake, where there are 12 more campsites. The Alaska Department of Natural Resources' reservable **Glatfelder** and **Quartz Lake** public-use cabins (www.dnr.state.ak.us /parks/cabins/north; per night $25) are other options.
Kelly's Alaska Country Inn (☎ 895-4667; www .kellysalaskacountryinn.com; 1616 Richardson Hwy; s/d $89/99) Two blocks north of the visitor center, this recently remodeled place has spacious, clean rooms, some with kitchenettes.
Alaska 7 Motel (☎ 895-4848; Mile 270.3 Richardson Hwy; r $80) Located 4 miles north of the visitor center, the 16 rooms include small fridges and microwaves.

Eating
Buffalo Center Diner (☎ 895-5089; 1680 Richardson Hwy; breakfast $6-9, lunch $9-12, dinner $14-20; ☷ 6am-10pm) Across from the IGA, this is certainly the town's busiest restaurant and would be your standard roadside diner save for the emphasis on local buffalo products. Try a bowl of buffalo black-bean chili ($4.75).

Pizza Bella (☎ 895-4841; 265 Richardson Hwy; ⏲ 4pm-10pm Mon-Sat) This place is locally recommended for its pizza and is conveniently located opposite the visitor center.

IGA Food Cache (Mile 266 Richardson Hwy; ⏲ 6:30am-9pm Mon-Sat, 9am-8pm Sun) A half-mile north of the visitor center, this is a market with a bakery, deli and an espresso cart, plus homemade soup and other ready-to-eat items to go. It's the place to go in the morning for coffee, a pastry and a bit of local news.

Getting There & Away

Alaska Direct Bus Line (☎ 800-770-6652) stops in Delta Junction Sundays, Wednesdays and Fridays on its run between Fairbanks ($43) and Tok ($27). From Tok you can continue to Whitehorse, Glennallen or Anchorage.

TOK

☎ 907 / pop 1439

Tok, 92 miles up the Alcan from the Canadian border, is the first Alaskan town motorists on multiweek pilgrimages from the Lower 48 will encounter. Thus, this hodgepodge of gas stations, motels and RV parks is viewed with a strange, out-of-proportion reverence, like a sort of pearly gates opening onto heavenly Alaska. The town was born in 1942 as a construction camp for the highway, and was originally called Tokyo Camp until anti-Japanese sentiment caused locals to shorten it to Tok. From here, the rest of the state beckons: the Alcan heads 206 miles northwest to Fairbanks, Tok Cutoff and Glenn Hwy reaches 328 miles southwest to Anchorage, and the Taylor Hwy curls back 161 miles to Eagle.

Information

Alaska Public Lands Information Center (☎ 883-5667; www.nps.gov/aplic; Mile 1314 the Alcan; ⏲ 8am-7pm) This center provides decent information on the state's parks and outdoor activities. On a clear day the center's large picture window frames the Alaska Range.

Chickadee Business Network (☎ 883-2665; www.chickadee.net; ⏲ noon-9pm; 🖳 per 15 mins $2.50) Located just down the Tok Cutoff from the Alcan.

Tok Mainstreet Visitors Center (☎ 883-5775; ⏲ 8am-7pm Mon-Sat, 10am-7pm Sun) Near the corner of the Tok Cutoff and the Alcan, this massive 7000-sq-ft lodge is said to be Alaska's largest log structure. Along with racks of brochures, pay phones and rest rooms, the center contains displays on wildlife, gold panning and the construction of the Alcan.

Sleeping

BUDGET

Tok River State Recreation Site (Mile 1309 the Alcan; sites $15) On the Tok River's east bank, this is 4½ miles east of Tok and has 27 campsites, a boat launch, picnic shelter, water, toilets and a telephone.

Moon Lake State Recreation Site (Mile 1331 the Alcan; sites $15) Fourteen sites sit next to placid Moon Lake, 17 miles west of Tok on the Alcan.

Tok International Hostel (☎ 883-3745; Mile 1322.5 the Alcan; dm $10) Located an inconvenient 8 miles west of town on the Alcan and then a mile south on Pringle Dr, this wooded place feels a bit like a squatters' camp, what with all the rotting outbuildings and sundry junk. Guests stay in a 10-bed tent cabin.

MIDRANGE & TOP END

Off the Road House B&B (☎ 883-5600; www.offthe roadhouse.net; Mile 1318.5 of the Alcan; s/d $75/85, cabin s/d $65/75) By far the most appealing lodging in Tok is this backwoods oasis, where Helga, a German-born artist, offers rooms and cedar-shingled cabins, full breakfasts and 'good philosophical conversation'. To get here, head west to Mile 1318.5 of the Alcan, then follow the progressively worsening gravel lane 1½ miles south and east.

Burnt Paw Cabins (☎ 883-4121; www.burntpaw cabins.com; r $109) Just west of the cut-off junction, this place offers four modern sod-roof cabins, each with private bath and decorated with a different Alaskan theme.

Snowshoe Motel (☎ 883-4511; snowshoe@aptalaska .net; s/d $72/77) On the Alcan near the visitor center, this motel has clean, super-sized rooms with views from the second story.

Young's Motel (☎ 883-4411; Mile 1313 the Alcan; s/d $78/86) Right behind Fast Eddy's restaurant, this place has functional but unremarkable rooms.

Eating

Fast Eddy's (☎ 883-4411; Mile 1313.3 the Alcan; burgers $7-11, pizza $14-22; ⏲ 6am-11pm) Perhaps the most famous eatery on the Alcan, big and bustling Fast Eddy's is a step above your average diner. It seems everyone who drives the highway stops in here.

Gateway Salmon Bake (☎ 883-5555; Mile 1313.1 the Alcan; ⏲ 4pm-9pm) Next to Fast Eddy's, serves up fare ranging from $8 halibut burgers to a $20 combination plate with salmon, halibut and reindeer sausage.

DENALI & THE INTERIOR

Three Bears Grocery (☎ 883-5195; 1314 the Alcan; ☾ 7am-10pm) Across the Alcan from the Alaska Public Lands Information Center. It has a decent selection of groceries and a few baked goods.

Getting There & Away
BUS
The buses of **Alaska Direct Bus Line** (☎ 800-770-6652) all pass through Tok on Sundays, Wednesdays and Fridays, stopping at the village Texaco a short distance southeast of the highway junction down the Alcan. From there they head northwest to Fairbanks ($70), southwest to Anchorage ($92), and southeast to Whitehorse ($125), where you can transfer to a bus to Skagway.

Alaska/Yukon Trails (☎ 479-2277, 800-770-7275) runs buses daily between Fairbanks and Tok ($55 one way with a two person minimum), continuing on over Taylor and Top of the World Hwys to Dawson City, Yukon.

HITCHHIKING
For many backpackers, the most important item at the Tok Mainstreet Visitors Center is the message board. Check out the board or display your own message if you're trying to hitch a ride through Canada along the Alcan. It's best to arrange a ride in Tok and not wait until you reach the international border. In recent years, the Canadian customs post at the border has developed a reputation as one of the toughest anywhere in the world. It's not unusual to see hitchhikers, especially Americans, turned back at the border for having insufficient funds.

TAYLOR HIGHWAY
Taylor Hwy runs 161 miles north from Tetlin Junction, 13 miles east of Tok on the Alcan, through the lovable tourist trap of Chicken and on to the sleepy, historic community of Eagle on the Yukon River. Save for recent wildfire scarring it's a scenic drive, ascending Mt Fairplay, Polly Summit and American Summit, all over 3500ft. Until recent years the route was infamously rough, though these days the only white-knuckle stretch is the last 65 miles from Jack Wade Junction to Eagle.

The highway takes paddlers to both the Fortymile River and the Yukon-Charley Rivers National Preserve, and also offers much off-road hiking. As on the Denali

Hwy, many of the trailheads are unmarked, making it necessary to have the appropriate topographic maps. Many trails are off-road-vehicle tracks that hunters use heavily in late summer and fall.

By Alaskan standards summer traffic is light to moderate until you reach Jack Wade Junction, where the majority of vehicles continue east to Dawson City, Yukon, via the Top of the World Hwy (opposite). Hitchhikers aiming for Eagle from the junction will have to be patient. If you're driving, leave Tok or Dawson with a full tank of gasoline, because roadside services are limited.

The first section of the Taylor, from Tetlin Junction (Mile 0) to just shy of Chicken, is now paved. Within 9 miles of Tetlin Junction you'll begin to climb Mt Fairplay (5541ft). At Mile 35 a lookout near the summit is marked by trash cans and an interpretive sign describing the history of Taylor Hwy. From here you should see superb views of Mt Fairplay and the valleys and forks of Fortymile River to the north. The surrounding alpine area offers good hiking for those wanting to stretch their legs.

The first state campground is the 25-site **West Fork Campground** (Mile 49 Taylor Hwy; sites $8), which recent forest fires nearly incinerated. Travelers packing gold pans can try their luck in West Fork River, which is the first access point for a canoe trip down Fortymile River.

Chicken
☎ 907 / pop 21
After crossing a bridge over Fortymile River's Mosquito Fork at Mile 64.4, Taylor Hwy enters dusty Chicken, once a thriving mining center and now more of a punchline than an actual community. The town's name allegedly originated at a meeting of resident miners in the late 1800s. As the story goes, they voted to dub their new tent-city 'Ptarmigan,' since that chickenlike bird was rampant in the area. Trouble is, no-one could spell it. The town's name has been Chicken ever since.

In retrospect, it was a savvy move: Nowadays, folks flock here for 'Go peckers!' coffee mugs and 'I got laid in Chicken' ballcaps. Profiting the most seems to be the **Chicken Creek Café, Liquor Store & Saloon** (www.chickenalaska .com; breakfast $5-11, lunch & dinner $9-12; café ☾ 7am-9pm), on a spur road 300 yards north of the bridge. Their gift shop is extensive, the saloon has hats from every corner of the world, and the café, unsurprisingly, features lots of chicken on the menu.

Just across the road is **Chicken Gold Camp** (☎ 235-6396; www.yukonalaska.com/chickengold; campsites/RV sites $10/14; cabins with breakfast $75; café ⓨ 7:30am-7:30pm), where you can pitch a tent and consume paninis, ice cream and espressos. For $5 there's also gold panning or tours of the Pedro Gold Dredge, which worked creeks in the area from 1959 to 1967. For $25 they also have recreational kayaks available for half-day floats on the Fortymile River.

Slightly further along on Taylor Hwy is Chicken's final tourist lure, **The Goldpanner** (www.chickenak.com; Mile 66.8 Taylor Hwy; campsites/RV sites $10/14; ⓨ 8am-6pm), with more camping and gold panning, plus a three-hole golf course, and, for $5, tours of some of Chicken's historic cabins across the road.

Just north of Chicken is Chicken Creek Bridge, built on tailing piles from the mining era. The creek, and most other tributaries of the Fortymile River, are covered from one end to the other by active mining claims, and often you can see from the highway suction from dredges looking for gold. The bridge over South Fork (Mile 75.3) marks the most popular access point for the Fortymile River canoe route.

Fortymile River

Historic Fortymile River, designated as Fortymile National Wild River, offers an excellent escape into scenic wilderness for paddlers experienced in lining their canoes around rapids. It's also a step back into Alaska's goldrush era; the river passes abandoned mining communities, including Franklin, Steele Creek and Fortymile, as well as some present-day mining operations. The best place to start paddling is at the bridge over South Fork, because the access points south of here on Taylor Hwy are often too shallow for an enjoyable trip.

Many canoeists paddle the 40 miles from South Fork bridge to the bridge over O'Brien Creek, at Mile 113 of Taylor Hwy. This two- to three-day trip involves three sets of Class III rapids. For a greater adventure, continue past O'Brien Creek and paddle the Fortymile into the Yukon River; from here, head north to Eagle at the end of the Taylor Hwy. This trip is 140 miles long and takes seven to 10 days. You'll need to line several sets of rapids in Fortymile River. Such an expedition requires careful planning.

Eagle Canoe Rentals (☎ 547-2203; www.aptalaska .net/~paddleak), in Eagle, is the closest place to get an expedition-worthy canoe or raft for your trip.

South Fork Bridge to Eagle

Shortly after the South Fork put-in for Fortymile River, Taylor Hwy reaches **Walker Fork Campground** (Mile 82 Taylor Hwy; sites $8), which lies on both sides of the highway and has 18 sites, tables, firewood and a short trail to a limestone bluff overlook.

DETOUR: TOP OF THE WORLD HIGHWAY

From Jack Wade Junction, Dawson City, one of the North's most intriguing, fun-drunk towns is just 79 miles distant – and almost all downhill. You reach this grail of the Klondike Gold Rush and now an irreverent tourist mecca, via the Top of the World Hwy. The route begins with a 13-mile dirt stretch sometimes called the Boundary Spur Rd, which heads to the one-horse community of Boundary (where there's gas, gifts and food, if anyone's home) and then 4 miles beyond to the international border – the continent's northernmost roadcrossing. Be forewarned: Canadian customs is open only from 8am to 8pm Alaska time; arrive too late and you'll be camping in the parking lot until morning. Beyond the border the highway – mainly paved now, but with lots of gravel patches under repair – lives up to its name, twisting along high-country ridgetops with flabbergasting views and all sorts of offroad hiking options. After 66 miles of this you'll wind your way down to the Yukon River, where for now a wonderful car ferry (but soon, lamentably, an efficient, modern bridge) will convey you across the water to Dawson.

If you're without wheels, you can ride along the Top of the World Hwy with **Alaska/Yukon Trails** (☎ 479-2277, 800-770-7275), whose buses come this way each day in summer from Fairbanks ($162 one way) and Tok ($99 one way). For more on Dawson City, consult Lonely Planet's *British Columbia*, which covers the Yukon Territory.

DENALI & THE INTERIOR

On the roadside at Mile 86 is the decaying **Jack Wade Dredge**, which operated from 1900 to 1942. When we were there you could climb inside the guts of it, but safety fears may soon put an end to this.

The Top of the World Hwy meets Taylor Hwy at **Jack Wade Junction** (Mile 95.7 Taylor Hwy). From here, the route north to Eagle isn't for the faint of heart. Almost immediately it becomes washboarded, cliff-clinging and crazily twisty; in places it's so narrow the phrase 'one lane' seems generous. It's the worst stretch of highway in Alaska, requires at least two hours to safely negotiate, and should be avoided by RVs.

Soon after the junction you'll climb to **Polly Summit** (3550ft) and then begin a very steep descent to the bridge over O'Brien Creek (Mile 113 Taylor Hwy), a common take-out for Fortymile River trips.

Primitive camping is possible at Mile 135, on the south side of a bridge over North Fork Solomon Creek. This is a former BLM campground that has not been maintained in years. Eight miles on is **American Summit** (3650ft), with excellent alpine views and hiking possibilities. Eagle is reached 18 miles later, after a long descent to the Yukon River.

Eagle
☎ 907 / pop 115

One of the better-preserved boomtowns of the Alaskan mining era, Eagle is a quaint hamlet of log cabins and clapboard houses, inhabited by folks who seem disarmingly cosmopolitan. The original settlement, today called Eagle Village, was established by the Athabascans long before Francois Mercier arrived in the early 1880s and built a trading post in the area. A permanent community of miners took up residence in 1898. A year later, the US Army decided to move in and build a fort as part of its effort to maintain law and order in the Alaskan Interior. Judge Wickersham established a federal court at Eagle in 1900, and the next year President Theodore Roosevelt issued a charter that made Eagle the first incorporated city of the Interior.

Eagle reached its peak at the turn of the 20th century, when it boasted a population of more than 1500 residents, some of whom went so far as to call their town the 'Paris of the North,' though that was hardly the case. The overland telegraph wire from Valdez

arrived here in 1903. This new technology proved particularly useful to the famous Norwegian explorer Roald Amundsen, who hiked overland to Eagle in 1905 after his ship froze in the Arctic Sea off Canada. From the town's telegraph office, he sent word to the world that he had just navigated the Northwest Passage. Amundsen stayed two weeks in Eagle and then mushed back to his sloop. Nine months later, the ship reached Nome, completing the first successful voyage from the Atlantic to the Pacific Ocean across the Arctic Ocean.

The gold strikes of the early 1900s, most notably at Fairbanks, began drawing residents away from Eagle and caused the removal of Judge Wickersham's court to the new city in the west. The army fort was abandoned in 1911, and at one point, it is said, the population of Eagle dipped to nine residents, seven of whom served on the city council. When the Taylor Hwy was completed in the 1950s, however, the town's population increased to its present level. In the late 1970s, noted author John McPhee arrived, rented a cabin for part of a year and worked on his bestseller *Coming into the Country*, which immortalized life in Eagle, Alaska.

INFORMATION
Yukon-Charley Rivers National Preserve Visitor Center (☎ 547-2233; www.nps.gov/yuch; ⊗ 8am-5pm) The headquarters for the Yukon-Charley Rivers National Preserve is the best place for info, not just on the 3906-sq-mile preserve but on Eagle proper. It's on the banks of the Yukon River, off 1st Ave beside the downtown airstrip. Inside you can buy books, use the reference library or watch a video about the Yukon-Charley Rivers National Preserve.

SIGHTS & ACTIVITIES
Tours
Residents say Eagle has the state's largest 'museum system,' boasting five restored turn-of-the-20th-century buildings. If you're spending a day here, the best way to see the buildings and learn the town's history is to head to **Judge Wickersham's Courthouse** (cnr Berry St & 1st Ave) at 9am, when the **Eagle Historical Society** (☎ 547-2325; www.eagleak.org) commences its three-hour town walking tour. For $5 you'll see the Courthouse, **Eagle City Hall**, the Log Church, Fort Egbert, **Redmen Hall**, the **Customs Building Museum** and **Amundsen Park**, where

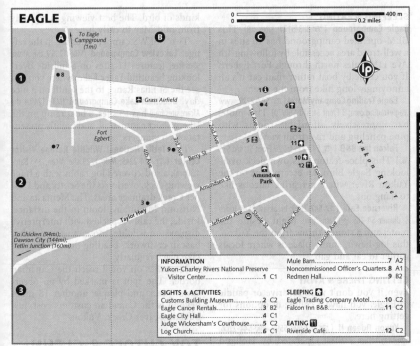

EAGLE

INFORMATION	
Yukon-Charley Rivers National Preserve Visitor Center	1 C1

SIGHTS & ACTIVITIES	
Customs Building Museum	2 C2
Eagle Canoe Rentals	3 B2
Eagle City Hall	4 C1
Judge Wickersham's Courthouse	5 C2
Log Church	6 C1

Mule Barn	7 A2
Noncommissioned Officer's Quarters	8 A1
Redmen Hall	9 B2

SLEEPING	
Eagle Trading Company Motel	10 C2
Falcon Inn B&B	11 C2

EATING	
Riverside Café	12 C2

a plaque commemorates explorer Roald Amundsen's visit. Tours may be available at other times through special arrangement.

To the north of town is **Fort Egbert**, which can be reached from the Taylor Hwy via 4th Ave. The BLM has restored the old army fort, which once contained 37 buildings; among the structures are the restored mule barn, carriage house, doghouse and officers' quarters, which are clustered together in one section of the fort.

You can wander past it on your own but the Eagle Historical Society tour is the only way to go inside.

Paddling

During its heyday, Eagle was an important riverboat landing for traffic moving up and down the Yukon.

Today it's a departure point for the many paddlers who float along the river through the Yukon-Charley Rivers National Preserve. The 150-mile trip extends from Eagle to Circle, at the end of the Steese Hwy northeast of Fairbanks; most paddlers take six to 10 days, though some require as few as three.

It's not a difficult paddle, but it must be planned carefully. Kayakers and canoeists should come prepared for insects, but can usually camp either in public-use cabins or on open beaches and river bars, where winds keep the bugs at bay. They also need to be prepared for extremes in weather; freezing nights can be followed by daytime temperatures of 90°F.

Eagle Canoe Rentals (☎ 547-2203; www.aptalaska.net/~paddleak; Taylor Hwy), as you enter town, provides canoes for travel between Dawson City, Eagle and Circle. Pick up the boat at either the **Dawson City River Hostel** (☎ 867-993-6823) or at the shop in Eagle and then leave it in Circle. A four-day rental between Dawson City and Eagle is $110; a five-day rental between Eagle and Circle is $185. **Everts Air Alaska** (☎ 450-2350; tatondukflying.com) may be able to make a flag stop in Circle to get you back to Eagle; otherwise you're looking at a two-stage flight through Fairbanks or a very long drive.

For information in advance, contact the Yukon-Charley Rivers National Preserve Visitor Center (opposite).

SLEEPING & EATING

Eagle Campground (☎ 883-5121; sites $8) This BLM-operated campground has 16 sites in a well-treed area accessible by following 4th Ave 11½ miles north through Fort Egbert. If you come by boat rather than car it's an annoyingly long hike from the river.

Eagle Trading Company Motel (☎ 547-2220; www .eagletrading.com; 3 Front St; s/d $60/70) This motel has impressively affordable rooms with pine paneling and riverfront views.

Falcon Inn B&B (☎ 547-2254; 220 Front St; s/d $75 /85) This place features its own deck overlooking Eagle Bluff, an escarpment on the Yukon River where peregrine falcons like to hang out.

Riverside Café (☎ 547-2220; breakfast $5-8, lunch & dinner $4-16; ☻7am-7pm) Right beside the motel and a stone's throw from the Yukon, this log-hewn, sunny place is where locals gather to eat and gab.

GETTING THERE & AWAY

Even if you don't want to drive or paddle to Eagle, you have a couple of options for getting here.

Yukon Queen II (☎ 867-993-5599, 800-544-2206; one-way/return $90/180) Operated by Holland America, this 110-passenger tour boat plies the river between Eagle and Dawson City, covering the 102-mile distance at 35 knots – and irritating many local boaters, who complain of swamped vessels and disturbed fishing nets.

Everts Air Alaska (☎ 450-2350; tatondukflying .com) Flies to Eagle most days of the week from Fairbanks.

TOK TO CANADA

The journey from Tok (Mile 1314) to the Canadian border comprises 92 winding miles of the Alcan: paved but often frostheaved, and weaving through low-slung mountains and vast wetlands. Thirteen miles east of Tok is Tetlin Junction, where Taylor Hwy branches off toward Eagle, with connections via the Top of the World Hwy to Dawson City .

Shortly after the junction you'll reach the 730,000-acre **Tetlin National Wildlife Refuge** (☎ 883-5312; http://tetlin.fws.gov), which skirts the highway's south side all the way to the border. Waterlogged by countless lakes, marshes, streams and rivers, the refuge is a home or migratory pit-stop for nearly 200

kinds of bird. The best viewing is typically from mid-May to early June.

Two USFWS campgrounds are in the refuge. **Lakeview Campground** (Mile 1256.7 the Alcan; sites free) features 11 sites on a hillside overlooking beautiful Yager Lake, where you can see the St Elias Range to the south on a nice day. **Deadman Lake Campground** (Mile 1249.4 the Alcan; sites free) has 15 sites, a boat ramp on the lake, a short nature trail, and nightly presentations by rangers.

The **Tetlin National Wildlife Refuge Visitor Center** (☎ 774-2245; Mile 1229 the Alcan; ☻ 8am-4:30pm), a sod-covered log cabin with a huge viewing deck, overlooks the Scotty and Desper Creek drainage areas. The Mentasta and Nutsotin Mountains loom in the distance. Inside, the cabin is packed with interpretive displays on wildlife, mountains and Athabascan craftwork; beading demonstrations take place regularly.

Ten miles on you'll reach the Canadian border. The spot is marked by an observation deck and plaque; another 18 miles beyond is the Canadian customs post, just outside Beaver Creek, Yukon.

TOK CUTOFF & GLENN HIGHWAY

Despite being the quickest path from the Alcan to Anchorage, the paved Tok Cutoff and Glenn Hwy seem at times almost eerily untraveled. That's a bonus for those who *do* come this way, as this 328-mile route, graced by both the Wrangell and Chugach Mountains, offers some of the best hiking, paddling and scenery-gawking in the state. Glennallen and Palmer are significant-sized communities along the way.

TOK CUTOFF

Narrow and forest-flanked, the Tok Cutoff runs 125 miles from Tok to Gakona Junction. There, it meets Richardson Hwy, which heads 14 miles south to Glennallen, the eastern terminus of Glenn Hwy.

The first of only two public campgrounds on Tok Cutoff pops up at Mile 109.5 as you drive south from Tok. **Eagle Trail State Recreation Site** (sites $15), near Clearwater Creek, has 35 sites, drinking water and toilets. The historic **Valdez-Eagle Trail**, which at one time

DETOUR: NABESNA ROAD

For connoisseurs of roads less traveled, Alaska offers few lonelier motorways than the Nabesna Rd, jutting 42 miles south from the Tok Cutoff into the northern reaches of Wrangell-St Elias National Park.

Turning onto the Nabesna Rd from the Cutoff you'll find yourself in a place the signs call Slana (pop 110). Somewhere back through the trees there's an Alaska Native settlement on the north banks of the Slana River, where fish wheels still scoop salmon during the summer run. Also in the area are more recent settlers: in the early 1980s this was one of the last places in the USA to be opened to homesteading.

Before continuing, stop in at the NPS **Slana Ranger Station** (☎ 822-5238; Mile 0.2 Nabesna Rd; 🕑 8am-5pm), where you can get info about road conditions and possible hikes, purchase USGS maps, peruse displays and collect the free *Nabesna Road Guide*.

In the 4 miles between the ranger station and the park entrance you'll pass a handful of accommodations. The log-frame **Nabesna House B&B** (☎ 822-4284; www.nabesnahouse.com; Mile 0.8 Nabesna Rd; s/d $65/75) offers appealing attic rooms, serves up breakfasts of blueberry pancakes and reindeer sausage, and will let you cook other meals in the kitchen. More offbeat is **Huck Hobbit's Homestead** (☎ 822-3196; sites per person $5, cabins per person $20), a wind-and-solar-powered wilderness retreat off Mile 4 of Nabesna Rd; the last half mile is accessible only by hiking or driving an ATV. The three cabins include beds, sheets and a cooking area; be sure to bring your own food. Stay an extra day here – the scenery is beautiful – and splurge on a canoe trip down the Slana River for $50 per canoe.

Upon entering the park proper the Nabesna Rd turns to gravel. It's manageable in a 2WD vehicle for the first 29 miles, but after that several streams flow over it, making it impassable in high water. Although there are no formal campgrounds along the road, primitive sites, often with picnic tables and outhouses, exist at several waysides. Maintenance ends at Mile 42, though a rough track continues 4 miles to the private Nabesna Gold Mine, a National Historic Site.

For a comparatively easy hike, try the 4-mile **Caribou Creek Trail** (Mile 19.2 Nabesna Rd), which ascends 800ft from the road to a dilapidated cabin with unbeatable views of the surrounding peaks. A tougher day trek is the 5-mile **Skookum Volcano Trail** (Mile 36.2 Nabesna Rd), which climbs 2800ft through a deeply eroded volcanic system, ending at a high alpine pass frequented by Dall sheep. From there you can either retrace your steps or follow the rocky streambed another 3 miles back down to the road.

extended clear to Eagle on the Yukon River, now provides just a leisurely 20-minute stroll in the vicinity of the campground. Look for the posted trailhead near the covered picnic shelters.

Another 45 miles southwest along the highway, just north of the Nabesna Rd junction, is the 240-acre **Porcupine Creek State Recreation Site** (Mile 64.2 Tok Cutoff; sites $15), offering 12 wooded sites in a scenic spot along the creek. A mile north along the highway you'll find a historical marker and splendid views of Mt Sanford (16,237ft), a dormant volcano.

Officially, the Tok Cutoff ends at Gakona Junction, 125 miles southwest of Tok, where it merges with Richardson Hwy. Nearby is **Gakona Lodge** (☎ 822-3482; www.gakonalodge.com; Mile 2 Tok Cutoff; r $50-95, cabins $125), a lovely log roadhouse dating from 1905 that's listed on the National Register of Historic Places. It has a dining room, a bar, nine lodge rooms and three cabins.

From Gakona Junction, follow Richardson Hwy 14 miles south to Glenn Hwy junction.

GLENN HIGHWAY

Among Alaska's most jaw-dropping drives, the Glenn runs 189 miles from Richardson Hwy at Glennallen through the Chugach Range to Anchorage, merging with George Parks Hwy just after Palmer. Appropriately, most of this corridor was recently declared a National Scenic Byway. Along the route, outdoor opportunities abound: there's great alpine hiking around Eureka Summit, easy access to the humbling Matanuska Glacier, and some of the state's best white water in the nearby Matanuska River.

Glennallen

☎ 907 / pop 115

Glennallen is referred to by its civic fathers as 'the hub' of Alaska's road system, which is appropriate, because despite the impressive vistas (which include several peaks over 12,000 feet) most travelers will find little to do here but leave. Located at the axis of the Glenn and Richardson Hwys, the town is a supply center for those going to Wrangell-St Elias National Park. Lots of fishing and hunting guides live here.

The **Greater Copper River Valley Visitor Center** (☎ 822-5555; ☽ 9am-7pm) is at the junction of the Glenn and Richardson Hwys. West along the Glenn is the only full-service bank in the Copper Valley region, a **Wells Fargo** (☎ 822-3214; Mile 187.5 Glenn Hwy), which has an ATM.

For camping, your best bet is the very peaceful, spruce-shrouded **Dry Creek State Recreation Site** (Mile 117.5 Richardson Hwy; sites $12), 5 miles northeast of town on Richardson Hwy. In town, you can camp at **Northern Nights Campground** (☎ 822-3199; www.alaska-rv-campground-glennallen-northernnights.net; Mile 188.7 Glenn Hwy; campsites/RV sites $12/20; ☽ 8am-8pm), where showers are $3.

Otherwise, there's Glennallen's only hotel, the **Caribou Hotel** (☎ 822-3302, 800-478-3302; www .caribouhotel.com; Mile 186.9 Glenn Hwy; main hotel r $139-195, annex s/d $59/69). The lack of competition shows. Rooms in the main building are nice but overpriced; the work-camp-style annex, however, would be okay for budget travelers. At the adjoining **Caribou Hotel Restaurant** (breakfast $5-11, lunch $5-9, dinner $11-20; ☽ 7am-10pm) you can dine on meals geared to Middle American retirees: among the offerings is 'tender beef liver.'

For hitchhikers, Glennallen is notorious as a place for getting stuck (especially at Glenn Hwy junction) when trying to thumb a ride north to the Alcan. Luckily, buses are available. **Alaska Direct Bus Lines** (☎ 800-770-6652) passes through town every Sunday, Wednesday and Friday en route to Anchorage ($65) and Tok ($27). Call them for departure times and pick-up locations.

The vans of **Backcountry Connection** (☎ 822-5292, in Alaska 866-582-5292; www.alaska-backcountry -tours.com) go to and from McCarthy in Wrangell-St Elias National Park daily in summer for $89 round-trip (see p350). You need to make a reservation.

Tolsona Creek to Matanuska Glacier

West of Glennallen, Glenn Hwy slowly ascends through woodland into wide-open high country, affording drop-dead views of the Chugach and Talkeetna Mountains, and limitless hiking opportunities.

The first campground west of Glennallen is **Tolsona Wilderness Campground** (☎ 822-3865; tolsona.com; Mile 173 Glenn Hwy; campsites/RV sites $14/21), a private facility with more than 90 sites bordering Tolsona Creek. Water is available, along with coin-operated showers and laundry facilities.

A lookout marks the trailhead for the **Mae West Lake Trail**, a short hike away from Mile 169.3 of Glenn Hwy. This mile-long trail leads to a long, narrow lake fed by Little Woods Creek. The trailhead for the **Lost Cabin Lake Trail** is at another pull-out on the south side of the highway at Mile 165.8. The trail winds 2 miles to the lake and is a berry-picker's delight from late summer to early fall.

At Mile 160 a 19-mile spur road runs north to scenic **Lake Louise State Recreation Area** (campsites $15), which has 52 campsites in two campgrounds and is popular among Alaskans keen on swimming, boating and angling for grayling and trout. A few lodges and numerous private cabins are on the lake as well.

Little Nelchina State Recreation Site (Mile 137.4 Glenn Hwy; sites free), just off Glenn Hwy, has 11 campsites but, due to state budget cuts, no services.

From Little Nelchina River, Glenn Hwy begins to ascend, and Gunsight Mountain comes into view (you have to look hard to see the origin of its name). From Eureka Summit you can see both Gunsight Mountain and the Chugach Mountains to the south, the Nelchina Glacier spilling down in the middle and the Talkeetna Mountains to the northwest. This impressive, unobstructed view extends to the west, where the highway drops into the river valley that separates the two mountain chains. **Eureka Summit** (Mile 129.3 Glenn Hwy) is the highway's highest point (3322ft).

Just after the summit, at Mile 126.4, lies one of numerous trailheads for the old **Chickaloon-Knik-Nelchina Trail**, a gold miner's route used before Glenn Hwy was built. Today it's an extensive trail system extending to Palmer and beyond. The system is not maintained regularly, and hikers attempting any part of it should have good outdoor experience and the right topographic maps. You'll have to share the trail with off-road vehicles.

The trailhead for the **Belanger Pass Trail**, on Martin Rd (Mile 123.3 of Glenn Hwy), is signposted. Usually miners and hunters in off-road vehicles use it to travel into the Talkeetna Mountains. The views from Belanger Pass, a 3-mile hike, are excellent and well worth the climb. From the 4350ft pass, off-road-vehicle trails continue another 3½ miles north to Alfred Creek, then eventually lead around the north side of Syncline Mountain past active mining operations.

Two miles west of the Belanger Pass trailhead at Mile 121 is **Tahneta Pass**. Half a mile further on you can view the 3000ft pass at a scenic turnoff. East of the turnoff lies Lake Liela, with Lake Tahneta beyond it.

Squaw Creek Trail is another miners' and hunters' trail that begins at Mile 117.6 of Glenn Hwy and merges into the Chickaloon-Knik-Nelchina Trail. It begins as an off-road-vehicle trail, then extends 3½ miles to Squaw Creek and 9½ miles to Caribou Creek after ascending a low pass between the two. Although the trail can be confusing at times, the hike is a scenic one, with the Gunsight, Sheep and Syncline Mountains as a backdrop.

From here Glenn Hwy begins to descend, and the surrounding scenery becomes stunning as the road heads toward the Talkeetna Mountains, passing a Sphinx-like rock formation known as the Lion's Head at Mile 114. A half mile beyond it the highway reaches the first view of Matanuska Glacier. To the north is Sheep Mountain – aptly named, as you can often spot Dall sheep on its slopes.

Sheep Mountain Lodge (☎ 745-5121, 877-645-5121; www.sheepmountain.net; Mile 113.5 Glenn Hwy; cabin $135) is among the finest and most scenically situated lodges along Glenn Hwy, featuring a café, a bar, a sauna, cabins and bunkrooms without bath. You can squeeze four people into these rooms for $60, but you'll need to bring your own sleeping bags. There's great hiking nearby, and the restaurant has the area's best eating.

Four miles down the road are the idyllic **Tundra Rose Guest Cottages** (☎ 745-5865; in Alaska 800-315-5865; www.tundrarosebnb.com; Mile 109.5 Glenn Hwy; cottages $90-125), in a glacier-view setting that's as pretty as the name implies. The owners serve quality meals at their nearby Grandview RV Park.

Matanuska Glacier to Palmer

One of Alaska's most accessible ice tongues, **Matanuska Glacier** nearly licks Glenn Hwy, stretching 27 miles from its source in the Chugach Mountains. Some 18,000 years ago it was way bigger, covering the area where the city of Palmer is today.

You can get to the glacier via **Glacier Park Resort** (☎ 745-2534; Mile 102 Glenn Hwy; sites $10), which charges $12.50 to follow its private road to a parking lot at the terminal moraine. From there, a self-guided trail will take you a couple of hundred yards onto the gravel-laced ice itself; to go further, duck into the nearby office of **MICA Guides** (☎ 800-956-6422; www.micaguides.com), where you'll be outfitted with a helmet, crampons and trekking poles, and led on a 1½-hour glacier tour ($35), a three-hour trek ($70) or a six-hour ice-climbing excursion ($130).

If you want to pitch your tent hereabouts you can either camp at Glacier Park's rough campsites, or head back up the hill to **Matanuska Glacier State Recreation Site** (Mile 101 Glenn Hwy; sites $15), where there are 12 tree-shrouded campsites just steps away from outrageous glacier vistas.

The **Purinton Creek Trail** starts at Mile 91 of Glenn Hwy, leading 12 miles to the foot of Boulder Creek (most of the final 7 miles is a trek along the river's gravel bars). The Chugach Mountains scenery is excellent, and you'll find good camping spots along Boulder Creek.

There's good camping, too, at the 22-site **King Mountain State Recreation Site** (Mile 76 Glenn Hwy; sites $15), a scenic campground on the banks of the Matanuska River with views of King Mountain to the southeast.

Across the highway from the campground is the headquarters of **Nova** (☎ 745-5753, 800-746-5753; www.novalaska.com; Mile 76 Glenn Hwy, Chickaloon), one of Alaska's pioneering rafting companies, which runs the Matanuska River daily. They offer a mild 2½-hour float at 10:30am (adult/child $75/40) and a wilder one, which features Class IV rapids around Lion's Head Wall, at 9:30am and 2pm ($80-85 per person). From early June to mid-July there's also the extremely popular evening Lion's Head trip, departing at 7pm and including a riverside cookout.

For lower-key fun – perhaps a picnic and a stroll through the clovers – try the **Alpine Historical Park** (☎ 745-7000; Mile 61 Glenn

Hwy; admission free; ◐ 9am-7pm), encountered just before passing through Sutton. The park contains several buildings, including the Chickaloon Bunkhouse and the original Sutton post office, which now houses a museum. Inside, displays are devoted to the Athabascan people, the 1920 coal-boom era of Sutton and the building of Glenn Hwy.

Almost 12 miles beyond Sutton is the junction with the Fishhook-Willow Rd, which provides access to Independence Mine State Historical Park (p206). The highway then descends into the agricultural center of Palmer.

From Palmer, Glenn Hwy merges with George Parks Hwy and continues south to Anchorage, 43 miles away.

RICHARDSON HIGHWAY

The Richardson Hwy, Alaska's first highway, runs 266 miles from Fairbanks to Valdez. However, the 98-mile stretch between Fairbanks and Delta Junction is popularly considered part of the Alcan, and our coverage of the Richardson thus begins at Delta Junction, where the Alcan branches away to the east. Because the mile markers on the Richardson start in Valdez, drivers traveling from north to south will find the numbers descending.

The Richardson was originally scouted in 1919 by US Army Captain WR Abercrombie, who was looking for a way to link the gold town of Eagle with the warm-water port of Valdez. At first it was a telegraph line and footpath, but it quickly turned into a wagon trail following the turn-of-the-20th-century gold strikes at Fairbanks.

Today the road is a scenic wonder; it cuts through the Chugach Mountains and the Alaska Range while providing access to Wrangell-St Elias National Park. Along the way it passes waterfalls, glaciers, five major rivers and the Trans-Alaska Pipeline, which parallels the road most of the way.

DELTA JUNCTION TO GLENNALLEN

Richardson Hwy runs 151 relatively untrafficked miles from Delta Junction to Glennallen, first ascending the Delta River drainage, crossing Isabel Pass over the Alaska Range, then paralleling the Gulkana

and Gakona Rivers to Gakona Junction. Here, the road joins the Tok Cutoff for the final 14 miles to Glenn Hwy junction at Glennallen. This route has plenty of curves, hills and frost-heaves, but is otherwise in fine condition.

Donnelly Creek & Around

After departing Delta Junction's 'Triangle,' where the Alcan merges with Richardson Hwy at Mile 266, the highway soon passes Fort Greely (Mile 261) and, a few minutes later, the Alaska Pipeline's Pump Station No 9.

A turnoff at Mile 243.5 offers one of the best views you'll get of the pipeline, as it plunges beneath the highway. Interpretive signage provides an overview of the pipeline's history and engineering, including a fascinating explanation of how 'thermal siphons' protect the permafrost by sucking heat from areas where the pipeline is buried. There are also spectacular panoramas to the southwest of three of the highest peaks in the Alaska Range. From south to west, you can see Mt Deborah (12,339ft), Hess Mountain (11,940ft) and Mt Hayes (13,832ft).

Another interesting turnoff, at Mile 241.3, overlooks the calving grounds of the Delta buffalo herd to the west. In 1928, 23 bison were relocated here from Montana for the pleasure of sportsmen and today they number more than 400. The animals have established a migratory pattern that includes summering and calving along the Delta River. If you have binoculars you may be able to spot dozens of the beasts.

The first public campground between Delta Junction and Glennallen is just after Mile 238, where a short loop road leads west of the highway to **Donnelly Creek State Recreation Site** (sites $10), which has 12 sites. This is a great place to camp, as it's seldom crowded and is extremely scenic, with good views of the towering Alaska Range. Occasionally the Delta bison herd can be seen from the campground.

At Mile 225.4 you'll find a viewpoint with picnic tables and a historical marker pointing out what little ice remains of **Black Rapids Glacier** to the west. The glacier became known as the 'Galloping Glacier' after its famous 3-mile advance in the winter of 1936, when it almost engulfed the highway.

Across from the marker, the easy **Rapids Lake Trail**, 0.3-miles long, winds through wildflowers to Black Rapids Lake.

From here, the highway ascends into alpine country and the scenery turns gonzo, with the road snaking under sweeping, scree-sided peaks. At Mile 200.5, a gravel spur leads 2 miles to the west to **Fielding Lake State Recreation Site** (sites free), where a willow-riddled 17-site campground sits in a lovely area above the tree line at 2973ft. The state's **Fielding Lake Cabin** (www.dnr.state.ak.us/parks/cabins; per night $25) is also available here by online reservation.

In another 3 miles the highway crests its highest point, **Isabel Pass** (3000ft). The pass is marked by a historical sign dedicated to Captain Wilds Richardson, after whom the highway is named. From this point you can view Gulkana Glacier to the northeast and the Isabel Pass pipeline camp below it.

For much of the next 12 miles the highway parallels the frothing headwaters of the Gulkana River as it pours toward Paxson.

Paxson & Around

At Mile 185.5 of Richardson Hwy, the junction with the Denali Hwy, you'll find the small service center of Paxson (pop 40).

You can gas up and even grab a snack at the hulking Paxson Inn, but a better place to spend the night is **Denali Highway Cabins** (☎ 822-5972; www.denalihwy.com; r $130), a couple of hundred feet up the Denali Hwy, where there are modern log cabins along the Gulkana River and various hiking, birding and float trips available.

Ten miles south on Richardson Hwy, a gravel spur leads 1½ miles west to **Paxson Lake BLM Campground** (campsites/vehicle sites $3/6) with 50 sites around the lakeshore. For experienced boaters, this is a potential put-in for white-water trips on the Gulkana River.

Over the next 20 miles, Richardson Hwy descends from the Alaska Range, presenting sweeping views of the Wrangell Mountains to the southeast and the Chugach Mountains to the southwest.

Sourdough Creek & Gulkana River

At Mile 147.5 of Richardson Hwy, the BLM's 42-site **Sourdough Creek Campground** (sites $6) provides canoeists and rafters access to the popular Gulkana River. Located in scrubby forestland that bugs seem to

love, the campground has a boat launch, a fishing deck and trails leading to a river observation shelter.

From here, the river can be floated 35 fairly placid miles down to the highway bridge at Gulkana (Mile 126.8), making for a pleasant one- or two-day paddle. Harder-core canoeists can put in up the highway at Paxson Lake, turning the trip into an 80-mile excursion. Those first 45 miles, however, involve several challenging rapids, including the Class IV Canyon Rapids. Although there's a short portage around these rapids, rough Class III waters follow.

All the land from Sourdough Creek Campground south belongs to the Ahtna Native Corporation, which charges boaters to camp. The exceptions – three single-acre sites – are signposted along the riverbanks and have short trails leading back to the highway. Raft rentals and shuttle services for many of the area's rivers, including the Gulkana, can be arranged through **River Wrangellers** (☎ 822-3967, 888-822-3967; www.alaskariverwrangellers.com) in Gakona.

From the take-out at the Gulkana River Bridge you are 3 miles south of Gakona Junction, where Tok Cutoff heads northeast to Tok, and 11 miles north of Glennallen, where Richardson Hwy intersects with Glenn Hwy.

WRANGELL-ST ELIAS NATIONAL PARK

Created in 1980, Wrangell-St Elias is the country's largest national park. Stretching north 170 miles from the Gulf of Alaska, it encompasses 13.2 million acres of mountains, foothills and river valleys bounded by the Copper River to the west and Canada's Kluane National Park to the east. Together, Kluane and Wrangell-St Elias National Parks make up almost 20 million acres and encompass the greatest expanse of valleys, canyons and towering mountains in North America, including the continent's second- and third-highest peaks (and nine of the 16 highest peaks in the US).

This area is a crossroads of mountain ranges. To the north are the Wrangell Mountains; to the south, the Chugach Mountains. Thrusting from the Gulf of Alaska and clashing with the Wrangell Mountains are the St Elias Mountains. Indeed, as the park brochure observes, 'the peaks' sheer numbers quickly quell your urge to learn their names'.

Spilling out from the peaks are extensive ice fields and more than 100 major glaciers, including some of the world's largest and most active.

The Bagley Ice Field found near the coast is 127 miles long, making it the largest sub-polar mass of ice in North America. The Malaspina Glacier, which pours out of the St Elias Mountains between Icy Bay and Yakutat Bay, is larger than Rhode Island.

Wildlife in Wrangell-St Elias National Park is more diverse and plentiful than in any other Alaskan park. Species include moose, black and brown bears, Dall sheep, mountain goats, wolves, wolverines, beavers and three of Alaska's 11 caribou herds.

Despite these wonders, Wrangell-St Elias remains a true wilderness park, with few visitor facilities or services of any kind.

Orientation & Information

The Richardson Hwy borders the park's northwest corner, and two rough dirt roads penetrate its interior. The Nabesna Rd (p341), cutting into the park's northern reaches, is seldom traveled; the most popular access by far is McCarthy Rd, at the end of which are the historic mining towns of McCarthy and Kennecott. Today, offbeat McCarthy provides lodging, food and other services to park visitors; Kennecott, meanwhile, is largely a living museum, owned and maintained by the National Park Service.

Wrangell-St Elias National Park Headquarters & Visitor Center (☎ 822-7440; www.nps.gov/wrst; Mile 106.8 Richardson Hwy; ☯ 8am-6pm), outside Copper Center, 10 miles south of Glenn Hwy-Richardson Hwy junction, is the best place for info and trip suggestions. You can also pick up topographic maps, view displays and videos on the park, and leave your backpacking itinerary.

Other park offices include the **Chitina Ranger Station** (☎ 823-2205; ☯ 10am-4:30pm Wed-Mon) at the end of the Edgerton Hwy, the **McCarthy Visitor Contact Station** (☎ 823-2305; ☯ 9:30am-4:30pm), in a kiosk just before the end of Mc-Carthy Rd, the **Kennecott Visitor Contact Station** (☎ 554-4417; ☯ 9am-5:30pm) on the main road in Kennecott, the **Slana Ranger Station** (☎ 822-5238; ☯ 8am-5pm), for visitors heading down the Nabesna Rd, and the **Yakutat Ranger Station** (☎ 784-3295; ☯ 8am-5pm Mon-Sat), if you're exploring the park's southeastern coastal regions.

Sights & Activities
MCCARTHY ROAD

Edgerton Hwy and McCarthy Rd combine to provide a 92-mile route into the heart of Wrangell-St Elias National Park, ending at the footbridge across the Kennicott River to McCarthy.

The 32-mile Edgerton Hwy, fully paved, begins at Mile 82.6 of Richardson Hwy. If you want to camp before reaching the park, the best bet is lovely **Liberty Falls State Recreation Site** (Mile 24 Edgerton Hwy; sites $10), where the eponymous cascade sends its waters rushing past several tent platforms.

The end of Edgerton Hwy is 10 miles beyond, at little Chitina (pop 118), the last place you can purchase gas. There's a grocery store here too, and a café, an art gallery and a ranger station. Backpackers can camp along the 3-mile road south to O'Brien Creek or beside Town Lake.

At Chitina, the McCarthy Rd begins, auspiciously enough, by passing through a single-lane notch blasted through a granite outcrop. From here 60 miles eastward you'll be tracing the abandoned Copper River & Northwest Railroad bed that was used to transport copper from the mines to Cordova. Though your $40-a-day rental car can usually travel this stretch during the summer, the route is rugged and ill-maintained, is a lane-and-a-half wide at best, and often seems intent on shaking your teeth loose. If you average 30mph, you're flying.

The first few miles offer spectacular views of the Chugach Mountains, the east-west range that separates the Chitina Valley lowlands from the Gulf of Alaska. Peaks average 7000ft to 8000ft. You'll also cross the mighty Copper River, where it's possible to see a dozen fish wheels or, if your timing is right, hordes of dipnetters who descend in July and August to scoop up red and king salmon.

To accommodate these hordes, a small, free **campground** with eight sites sits next to the east side of the Copper River Bridge. There are countless informal campsites on the riverbanks.

Silver Lake Campground (Mile 11 McCarthy Rd) is a commercial facility with sites, canoe rentals for Silver Lake, and other limited services – gas not being one of them. At Mile 14.5 you'll reach the access road to the trailheads for the Dixie Pass, Nugget and Kotsina Trails, across from the Strelna airstrip.

At Mile 17 of McCarthy Rd sits the one-lane, 525ft-long **Kuskulana River Bridge**, long known as 'the biggest thrill on the road to McCarthy.' Built in 1910, this historic railroad span is a vertigo-inducing 238ft above the bottom of the gorge. Though the state has added guard rails and new planks and thus taken some of the thrill out of the crossing, the view of the steep-sided canyon and rushing river from the bridge is awesome, and well worth the time to park at one end and walk back across it.

After rattling through another 43 miles of scrubby brush and thick forest – with few good mountain vistas and not many diversions en route – the road ends at the Kennicott River. If you're driving in, that's as far as you can go; to get into McCarthy, you cross the river on a footbridge and walk a short distance into the tiny town. If you're staying at a lodge or campground on the road side of the river, you can leave your car there; otherwise, you can park at a private parking lot right by the bridge for $10 a day.

Built in 1996, the footbridge replaced the hand-pulled trams the state erected when the original bridge was washed out in 1981. The trams, open platforms with two benches facing each other, were a classic way to enter McCarthy, but as tourism began to boom they were viewed as neither efficient nor safe. On a busy Friday afternoon, for instance, when you had to wait an hour or two for a ride across the river, four or five people and a mountain bike would be loaded on the tram. It was a crazy scene, encapsulating that bit of Alaska most of us came looking for, and gave rise to the most popular saying in McCarthy: 'Every day is Saturday once you cross over on the tram.'

MCCARTHY
☎ 907 / pop 66

Most local services are in the hamlet of McCarthy, an erstwhile ghost town so funky and cool you'll want to haunt the place yourself. Facing the Kennicott Glacier's terminal moraine and just a stone's throw from the river, the tiny community is a car-free idyll, where the handful of gravel roads wind past rotting cabins and lovingly restored boomtown-era buildings. Alas, in the past few years the place has been 'discovered,' but the summer population still hits only about 200, and just a quarter stick it out for the winter.

Once you've crossed the Kennicott River on the footbridge, follow the road across another footbridge and about half a mile further to the unstaffed **McCarthy-Kennecott Historical Museum**, an old railroad depot featuring historical photographs, a few mining artifacts and a model of McCarthy in its heyday (donations are appreciated). At the museum, the road bends back 500ft into downtown (such as it is) McCarthy, or continues toward Kennecott, 4½ miles up the road.

Historically, the two towns have always been different. Kennecott was a company town, self-contained and serious. McCarthy, on the other hand, was created in the early 1900s for miners as a place of 'wine, women and song'. In other words, it had several saloons, restaurants and a red-light district. The spirit remains lively today.

KENNICOTT

In 1900 miners 'Tarantula Jack' Smith and Clarence Warner reconnoitered Kennicott Glacier's east side until they arrived at a creek and found traces of copper. They named the creek Bonanza, and was it ever – the entire mountainside turned out to hold some of the richest copper deposits ever uncovered. In the Lower 48, mines were digging up ore that contained 2% copper. Here, the veins would average almost 13%, while some contained as much as 70%.

Eventually, a group of investors bought the existing stakes and formed the Kennecott Copper Corporation, named when a clerical worker misspelled Kennicott (which is why, nowadays, the town is spelled with an 'e' while the river, glacier, and other natural features get an 'i'). First the syndicate built its railroad: 196 miles of track through the wilderness, including the leg that's now McCarthy Rd and Cordova's famous Million Dollar Bridge. The line cost $23 million before it even reached the mines in 1911.

The syndicate then built the company town of Kennecott, a sprawling red complex that included offices, the crushing mills, bunkhouses for the workers, company stores, a rec hall, wooden tennis courts and a school, all perched on a mountainside above the Kennicott Glacier. From 1911 until 1938 the mines operated around the clock, produced 591,000 tons of copper and reported a net profit of more than $100 million.

By 1938 most of the rich ore had been exhausted, and in November that year the mine closed permanently. With the exception of a steam turbine and two large diesel engines, everything was left behind, and Kennecott became a perfectly preserved slice of US mining history.

Unfortunately, when the railroad bed was converted to a road in 1974, Kennecott also became the country's biggest help-yourself hardware store. Locals were taking windows, doors and wiring, while tourists were picking the town clean of tools, railroad spikes and anything else they could haul away as souvenirs.

Despite the pillage, Kennecott remains a beautiful ruin. The mill, where the ore was crushed and the copper concentrated, towers above the surrounding buildings and still has tram cables leading up to the mountain mines. The rest of the buildings, including bunkhouses, worker's cottages and the train depot and power plant, still perch high above Kennicott Glacier. Strewn among these structures are countless antique mining relics such as ore cars, hand carts and boilers.

In 1998 the NPS purchased the mill, power plant and many of the buildings from private owners as the first step to restoring them. The project of saving this unique piece of Alaskan history will undoubtedly take years. Until then, you will have to be content with strolling through the center of town and admiring the mining history by peeping through the windows. Keep in mind that many of the buildings are still privately owned, and it is illegal to enter them. For more information, stop in at the small **National Park Service Visitor Center** on Kennecott's main drag, where rangers give regular talks on the area, show films and lead nature walks.

You can reach Kennecott from McCarthy on foot by walking or cycling up the main road (the old railroad grade), a 4½-mile trek. There's also a van service in McCarthy, or you can hitch a ride in summer when a trickle of traffic runs between the two towns.

HIKING
You can buy US Geological Society (USGS) topographic maps at **Fireweed Arts & Crafts** (☎ 554-4500; ☒ 9:30am-6:30pm), on the main drag in Kennecott. If you just want to wander through Kennecott on your own, stop at

the visitor center and pick up a copy of the *Walking Tour of Kennecott* ($3).

Beginning from Kennicott Glacier Lodge, the **Root Glacier Trail** is a 3-mile round-trip route past the mine ruins to the sparkling white-and-blue ice. Hike northwest of town and continue past an unmarked junction to Bonanza Mine, less than a quarter mile away. Along the way you cross Jumbo Creek; a plank upstream makes fording this creek easy in normal water conditions. Another half mile further on campsites overlook the end of Root Glacier; nearby you'll find an outhouse and a storage bin (to keep bears out of your food).

You can climb the glacier, but use extreme caution if you're inexperienced or lack proper equipment (crampons, ice ax, etc). A safer alternative is to follow the rough trail up the lateral moraine. The path continues another 2½ miles, providing excellent views of the ice. For this trek, you'll need the USGS topographic maps *McCarthy B-6* and *McCarthy C-6*.

Another excellent hike from Kennecott is the alpine **Bonanza Mine Trail**. It's a round-trip of almost 8 miles and a steep uphill walk all the way. Plan on three to five hours to hike up if the weather is good and half that time to return. The trail is actually a rough dirt road to the tree line and starts just north of town at a junction that makes a sharp 180-degree turn up the mountain. Once above the tree line the view is stunning, and you can clearly see the mountain where the mine still sits. To reach the mine you have to trek up a rocky slope to the remaining bunkhouse, shafts and tram platform. Water is available at the top, but carry at least a quart (1 liter) if the day is hot.

Tours
HIKING
St Elias Alpine Guides (☎ 554-4445, 888-933-5427; www.steliasguides.com), with offices in McCarthy and on Kennecott's main road, runs the only tours that go inside Kennecott's mine buildings ($25). They can also equip you with crampons for half-day hikes on Root Glacier ($50) or take you on a full-day alpine hike to the mining ruins at the base of Castle Mountain ($95). If you've got a spare month, consider joining an ascent of 18,000ft Mount St Elias – but if you have to ask the price, you can't afford it.

The other local guiding firm, also extremely experienced, is **Kennicott Wilderness Guides** (☎ 554-4444, 800-664-4537; www.kennicottguides.com), whose offerings include full-day ice-climbing excursions for $110, overnight stays on the Root Glacier for $185, and fly-in day-trips to the remarkable Donoho Lake area for $235.

RIVER RUNNING

Where there are mountains and melting glaciers, there's sure to be white water. **Copper Oar** (☎ 554-4453, 800-523-4453; www.copperoar.com), with an office on the west side of the Kennicott River, offers a half-day 'paddle and pedal' package, involving one hour of rafting down the Class III Kennicott River followed by a five-mile mountain bike ride ($80 to $95, depending on the group size). For a full-day float, they combine the Kennicott with the Nizina and a portion of the Chitina River and return you to McCarthy by bush plane. The high point is going through the vertical-walled Nizina Canyon. This trip costs $245 to $265 per person (two person minimum).

St Elias Alpine Guides (☎ 554-4445, 888-933-5427; www.steliasguides.com) offers a similar Nizina trip for a similar price. Both they and Copper Oar also do multiday floats.

FLIGHTSEEING

If the day is clear, splurge on a flightseeing tour of the surrounding mountains and glaciers. Both **McCarthy Air** (☎ 554-4440, 888-989-9891; www.mccarthyair.com) and **Wrangell Mountain Air** (☎ 554-4411, 800-478-1160; www.wrangellmountainair.com), with offices on McCarthy's main drag have a fantastic reputation, offering a wide range of scenic flights and charging around $80/150/190 per person (two person minimum) for around 35/70/90 minutes.

Sleeping

BUDGET

One day the NPS may open a campground near the end of McCarthy Rd on the river's west side. Until then, private campgrounds are the only option. There are several near the road's end, including one run by the Pilgrim family, a brood of biblical back-to-the-landers who famously pissed off the NPS a few years back by driving a bulldozer through the park to their inholding.

Glacier View Campground (☎ 554-4490; sites $15, cabin $85) A half mile back from the river,

this place has stony sites, hot showers ($5), mountain bikes (half/full day $10/20), and the best reputation of the bunch.

Kennicott River Lodge & Hostel (☎ 554-4441, winter 941-447-4252; dm $28, cabin $100) A short walk from road's end is this beautiful two-story log lodge with outlying private and dormitory cabins offering glacier views. There's a great communal kitchen and common room, a bright outhouse and a Finnish sauna.

MIDRANGE & TOP END

Lancaster's Backpackers Hotel (☎ 554-4402; www.mccarthylodge.com; s/d $48/68; 🖥️) In the heart of McCarthy, this hotel has very popular shared-bath private rooms, a communal cooking area and Internet access ($3 for 20 minutes).

Ma Johnson's Hotel (☎ 554-4402; www.mccarthylodge.com; s/d $109/159) This place was built in 1923 and has been restored into a posh living museum with lots of hardwood, red velvet, and mining antiques from the area. The price includes a full breakfast and round-trip transportation from the footbridge.

Kennicott Glacier Lodge (☎ 258-2350, 800-582-5128; www.kennicottlodge.com; s/d $169/189) This may be the fanciest place around, but its rooms have shared bath. The lodge sits on a hill overlooking the till-covered glacier, offering superb views from a long front porch and lawn. Rates include transport and a tour. For $285 per couple you can get the same package with meals.

McCarthy B&B (☎ 554-4433; www.mccarthy-kennicott.com/mccarthybb; r $110) By Glacier View Campground, this B&B has cabins and in-house rooms, all with private bath.

Eating & Drinking

For middle-of-nowhere mining towns, McCarthy and Kennecott offer surprisingly good grub.

Roadside Potatohead (hotdogs, burgers, burritos $5-10; 🕙11am-8pm) As offbeat as McCarthy itself, this screened-in cabin off the town's main drag will satisfy your burger, spud and espresso needs.

McCarthy Lodge (☎ 554-4402; www.mccarthylodge.com; lunch $8-13, dinner $9-17; 🕙7am-10pm) In the heart of McCarthy, this eatery serves up quality wraps and sandwiches for lunch, and mains such as halibut cioppino for dinner.

Kennicott Glacier Lodge (☎ 258-2350, 800-582-5128; www.kennicottlodge.com; breakfast $8-14, lunch $7-10, dinner $24-30; 🕙7am-10am, noon-3pm, 7pm-10pm)

This may have the area's most upscale dining room, with family-style dinners, for which you'll need a reservation. Even if you don't stay at the lodge, have at least one meal on the front porch, drinking in the spectacular view of peaks and glaciers.

The Golden Saloon (☎ 554-4402) Beside the McCarthy Lodge, this is the area's only true bar, with pool, frequent live music and an always intriguing cast of drinkers. There's bar food until 10pm.

Glacier View Campground (☎ 554-4490; hotdogs & burgers $7-11) The snack-stand at this campground has buffalo burgers that have been known to corrupt vegetarians.

Getting There & Around

AIR

Ellis Air (☎ 822-3368, 800-478-3368; www.ellisair.com) flies from Anchorage via Gulkana at 8:30am Wednesdays and Fridays, arriving in McCarthy at 11am and then returning. Fares are $299/550 one-way/round-trip from Anchorage or $109/200 from Gulkana.

Wrangell Mountain Air (☎ 554-4411, 800-478-1160; www.wrangellmountainair.com) offers daily scheduled flights between McCarthy and Chitina for around $175 round-trip. The service doubles as a flightseeing trip that includes five glaciers and the mountaintop mines on Bonanza Peak. If you have more money than time, you might consider the company's one-day fly-in tours of the park. The eight-hour trip ($329 per person) includes flightseeing from Glennallen to McCarthy, lunch at the Kennicott Glacier Lodge, guided tours of Kennecott and McCarthy, and a flight back.

BUS

Backcountry Connection (☎ 822-5292, 866-582-5292; www.alaska-backcountry-tours.com) departs Glennallen at 7am daily in summer, reaching Chitina at 8:30am and the McCarthy footbridge at 11:30am. After a four-hour layover – enough time to see McCarthy and the ruins at Kennecott – the van returns to Glennallen, arriving at 8pm. The round-trip fare for the same day is $89; one-way costs $70. You'll need to make a reservation.

McCarthy–Kennicott Community Shuttle (☎ 554-4411; one way $5) runs vans between McCarthy and Kennecott from 9am to 7pm daily. Pickup at the footbridge is on the hour; in downtown Kennecott it's on the half-hour.

BICYCLE

Mountain bikes outnumber cars here, as most locals and travelers use them to get around the area. Those old mining roads and trails, which are tough on vehicles, are ideal for fat-tire bikes, making McCarthy something of a cyclist's paradise. If you have your own bike, you can walk it across the footbridge. If not, you can rent a mountain bike at Glacier View Campground.

GLENNALLEN TO VALDEZ

One of Alaska's most spectacular drives, the 115 miles of Richardson Hwy between Glennallen and Valdez lead through a paradise of snowy summits, panoramic passes and gorgeous gorges.

Glaciers ooze down from the snow-capped mountains like frosting melting off a cake, while waterfalls cascade in sugary streams down verdant slopes and off sheer cliffs, occasionally bathing the road itself in clouds of cool, sweet-scented mist.

Nine miles south of Glennallen is a turnoff to the Wrangell-St Elias National Park Visitor Center, where you can get the low-down on the vast, mountainous park that covers nearly everything between there and Canada. To enter the park proper you'll need to head 25 miles down Richardson Hwy to Edgerton Hwy, which leads to McCarthy Rd – a dead-end gravel route bumping and potholing its way 96 miles into the heart of Wrangell-St Elias National Park.

Just south of the visitor center, at Mile 106, Old Richardson Hwy loops off the main highway, offering access to Copper Center. Old Richardson Hwy rejoins the Richardson Hwy at Mile 100.2.

At Mile 102 of Richardson Hwy is **Copper River Princess Wilderness Lodge** (☎ 800-426-0500; www.princesslodges.com; Brenwick Craig Rd, off Mile 102 Richardson Hwy; r $139-179). This hilltop luxury establishment is for shopaholics and usually full of Princess tour groups, but sometimes offers big discounts on its website.

You'll reach a lookout over **Willow Lake** at Mile 87.6. The lake can be stunning on a clear day, with the water reflecting the Wrangell Mountains, a 100-mile chain that includes 11 peaks over 10,000ft. The two most prominent peaks visible from the lookout are Mt Drum, 28 miles to the northeast, and Mt Wrangell, Alaska's largest active volcano, to the east. Mt Wrangell is 14,163ft, and on some days

---

DETOUR: COPPER CENTER

The Richardson Hwy bypasses **Copper Center**, but don't you do the same. This quaint village of 445 residents, reached by detouring a few miles down Old Richardson Hwy, is prettily situated on the sockeye-salmon-rich Klutina River and offers a handful of worthwhile sights.

Long used by Ahtna Indians, Copper Center at the turn of the last century was an important pitstop for thousands of prospectors stampeding to the Klondike and Fairbanks goldfields. While a decidedly slower pace prevails these days, the region's diverse history can be relived at the **George Ashby Museum** (☎ 822-5285; Mile 101 Old Richardson Hwy; admission by donation; ☷ 11am-5pm). Inside the log cabin and the nearby Trail of '98 Museum Annex are area relics including Russian religious artifacts, Alaska Native baskets, and mining memorabilia from the Kennecott mines.

Next door is **Copper Center Lodge** (☎ 822-3245; www.coppercenterlodge.com; Mile 101 Old Richardson Hwy; r $109-139; breakfast $5-13, lunch $8-13, dinner $12-29; ☷ dining room 5am-9:30pm), founded in 1897 and still functioning as a classic Alaskan roadhouse. The place offers either shared- or private-bath, and in the morning you can get a plate of sourdough pancakes made from a century-old starter recipe.

Also on Old Richardson Hwy is **Chapel on the Hill** (admission free), a half-mile north of the Klutina Bridge. This picturesque log chapel was built in 1942. Inside you can often see a slide show about the chapel and the Copper Center area.

---

you can see a plume of steam rising from its crater.

Squirrel Creek State Campground (Mile 79.6 Richardson Hwy; sites $10) offers a scenic 25-site camping area on the banks of the creek. Some pull-through spaces are available, and you can fish for grayling and rainbow trout in Squirrel Creek.

Fourteen miles further along you'll reach what used to be the Little Tonsina River State Recreation Site. Though it's closed, a path leads down to the water, where anglers can fish for Dolly Varden most of the summer.

At Mile 28.6, the turnoff to **Worthington Glacier State Recreation Area** leads you to the glacier's face via a short access road. The recreation area includes outhouses, picnic tables and a large, covered viewing area. The mile-long **Worthington Glacier Ridge Trail** begins at the parking lot and follows the crest of the moraine. It's a scenic hike that follows the edge of the glacier, but exercise caution. Never hike on the glacier itself due to its unstable crevasses. Thompson Pass and the surrounding area above the tree line are ideal for tramping; hikers will have few problems climbing through the heather.

Above the tree line the weather can be windy and foul as the highway ascends toward **Thompson Pass** at Mile 26. Several scenic turnoffs near the pass (2678ft) allow lucky early summer visitors to ooh and aah at a riot of wildflowers. This spot also holds most of Alaska's snowfall records, including 62in

of snow in a 24-hour period in December 1955. Despite this, the pass is seldom closed; a squadron of mega-sized plows labors almost continuously here in winter.

Blueberry Lake State Recreation Site (Mile 24.1 Richardson Hwy; sites $15) offers 15 sites and several covered picnic shelters in a beautiful alpine setting surrounded by lofty peaks. Often during summer all the sites will be taken by RVs, but it's easy for backpackers to find a spot near the trails to pitch their tents. There's good fishing for rainbow trout in the nearby lakes.

At Mile 14.8, you'll reach the northern end of **Keystone Canyon**, which holds an abandoned hand-drilled tunnel that residents of Valdez began but never finished when they were competing with Cordova for the railroad to the Kennecott copper mines. A historical marker briefly describes how nine companies fought to develop the short route from the coast to the mines, leading to the 'shootout in Keystone Canyon'.

For the next 2 miles you'll pass through the canyon, where the smooth dark rock walls contrast extravagantly with the pure foamy white waterfalls pouring over them. Two magnificent waterfalls are here: spectacular Bridal Veil Falls and, half a mile further, Horsetail Falls. Large turnouts at both allow you to get out and fill your lungs with the pure ionized air.

Leaving the canyon at Mile 12.8 the road begins a long, gradual descent into Valdez.

Fairbanks & Around

Perhaps the best description of Fairbanks is its visitor bureau slogan: 'extremely Alaska.' The community here is one of a kind (even for Alaska). Fairbanks has central log cabins, summer baseball and golf games that go all night, a college campus from which students can view the continent's highest mountain, and more sled dogs than there are horses in Kentucky.

Visitors can be forgiven for not immediately adoring the place. Although it's Alaska's second-largest city, Fairbanks seems uninterested in attracting visitors. Its tourist development is minimal and its downtown feels down-and-out. But travelers willing to linger may be thankful they did. To start with, there's the weather: perpetual summer daylight combined with some of the warmest, driest conditions in the state. (You might not want to stick around for winter, when temperatures drop below freezing for months.)

Then there are the people. Locals are hardy and independent because they have to be. Their 'partners in adversity' bond helps them endure, and that endurance, more than the log cabins or the midnight sun, is the city's trademark. It's made locals more colorful, louder and a degree more boastful than most Alaskans, exemplifying the Alaskan ethic of 'work hard, play hard, drink hard.' And it's made almost every Fairbanks resident a bona fide character.

Here, perhaps more than anywhere else in Alaska, to enjoy yourself you really *have* to befriend a local or two. They'll get you out of the city – out to the surrounding mountains, rivers, lakes and hot springs – and show you why enduring this place is so worthwhile.

HIGHLIGHTS

- **Best place to get steamed** (p373 & p370) – soaking in Fairbanks-area hot springs, including Manley Hot Springs and Chena Hot Springs

- **Best way to develop an appetite** (p369) – paddling down the Chena River to one of Fairbanks' fine waterfront dining rooms

- **Best culture clash** (p360 & p365) – visiting the remarkable Museum of the North, then kicking up your heels at a rowdy local saloon

- **Most enjoyable way to feel insignificant** (p359) – gazing skyward at the northern lights, which are nowhere as vivid as in Fairbanks

- **Guiltiest pleasure** (p358) – forsaking art galleries and alpine trails for a day at Alaska's own Disneyland, Pioneer Park

■ AREA CODE: ☎ 907	■ POPULATION: 85,500	■ ELEVATION: MT PRINDLE 5286FT

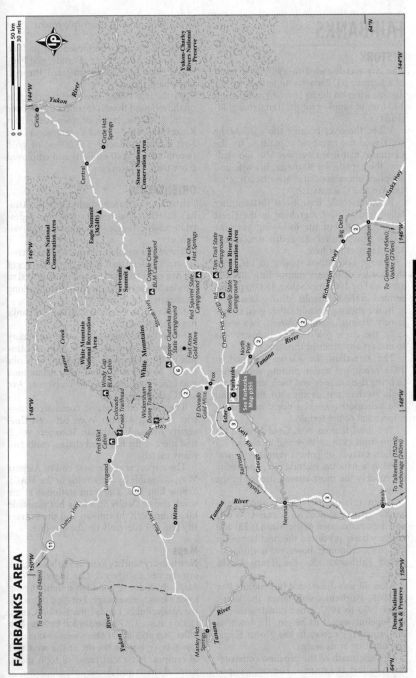

FAIRBANKS AREA

FAIRBANKS & AROUND

FAIRBANKS

HISTORY

The city was founded in 1901, as a result of a journey ET Barnette undertook up the Tanana River on the SS *Lavelle Young* – with 130 tons of supplies for the Tanacross gold-fields.

When the river became too shallow, he convinced the riverboat captain to try the Chena. When that river was also too shallow, the captain set Barnette, his wife and supplies ashore at what is now the corner of 1st Ave and Cushman St.

Barnette could have been just another failed trading-post merchant in the Great White North, but the following year the Italian prospector Felix Pedro struck gold 12 miles north of here.

A large boomtown sprang to life amid the hordes of miners stampeding into the area, and by 1908 more than 18,000 people resided in the Fairbanks Mining District.

In the ensuing decade, other gold rushes largely drained the population, but ironically, the city's gold-mining industry was to outlast any other in the state.

The arrival of the Alaska Railroad in 1923 prompted major mining companies to bring their money and their three-story-high mechanized dredges to the region. The behemoths worked nonstop, making mincemeat of the terrain.

The most famous one, Gold Dredge No 8, ran from 1928 to 1959 and recovered 7.5 million ounces of gold. Eventually it was listed as a national historic site, and today is probably the most viewed dredge in the state.

When mining activity declined, Fairbanks' growth slowed to a crawl. WWII and the construction of the Alcan (p28) and military bases produced the next booms in the city's economy; however, nothing affected Fairbanks like the Trans-Alaska Pipeline.

After oil was discovered in Prudhoe Bay in 1968, Fairbanks was never the same. From 1973 to 1977, when construction of the pipeline was at its height, the town, as the principal gateway to the North Slope, was bursting at its seams.

The aftermath of the pipeline construction was just as extreme. The city's popu-lation shrank and unemployment crept toward 25%.

The oil industry bottomed out in 1986 with the declining price of crude, and Fairbanks, like Anchorage, suffered through more hard times.

By the late 1990s, however, the city was on the rebound thanks to tourism and, once again, gold. Just north of town is the Fort Knox Gold Mine – Alaska's largest. In 2004 Fort Knox produced 338,000oz of gold (worth nearly $140 million) and employed more than 420 workers.

ORIENTATION

Fairbanks, the transportation hub for Alaska's Interior, is a messy, sprawling, pedestrian-phobic tangle of highways and rail yards.

The rather desolate downtown is centered around Golden Heart Plaza, on the corner of 1st Ave and Cushman St, and spreads west to Cowles St, east to Noble St and south along Cushman St to Airport Way.

Cushman is the closest thing Fairbanks has to a main street.

Several miles northwest is the university area, which consists of the hilltop campus of the University of Alaska Fairbanks (UAF), as well as student bars, restaurants and other businesses along University Ave and College Rd.

The city's other major commercial district is along Airport Way, between University Ave and Cushman St, where you'll find most of the fast-food chains, malls and many motels.

The airport is at the west end of Airport Way, accessible by car, shuttle or the MACS Yellow Line bus. The train station is at the south end of Danby St, a long but plausible hike from both downtown and the university and not currently on the bus line.

Maps

Nearly every touristy joint in Fairbanks gives out the free *Campers & Car Travelers' City Map*, which does a good job simplifying the town's knotty streetscape. For topo maps, try the Alaska Public Lands Information Center (p356). Also, UAF's **Geophysical Institute Map Office** (Map p355; ☎ 474-6960; www.gi.alaska.edu; 930 Koyukuk Dr; ☒ 8am-5pm Mon-Fri), at the west end of campus, has a vast range of topo maps, nautical charts and Arctic maps.

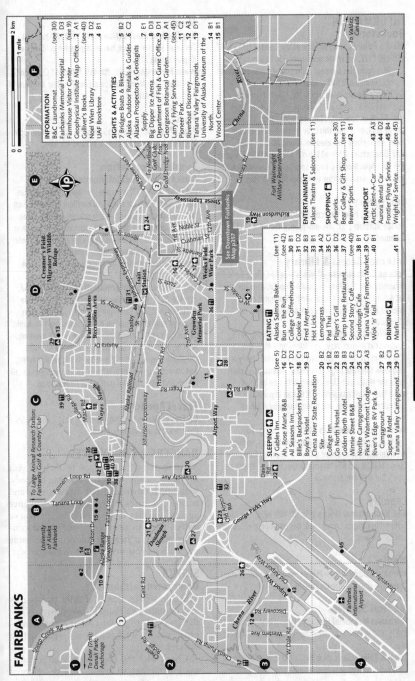

FAIRBANKS

0   1 mile
0   2 km

INFORMATION
B&C Laundromat..........................(see 30)
Fairbanks Memorial Hospital............1 D3
Farmhouse Visitor Center...............(see 9)
Geophysical Institute Map Office.......2 A1
Gulliver's Books.........................(see 40)
Noel Wien Library.......................3 D2
UAF Bookstore...........................4 B1

SIGHTS & ACTIVITIES
7 Bridges Boats & Bikes................5 B2
Alaska Outdoor Rentals & Guides.......6 C2
Alaskan Prospectors & Geologists
  Supply...............................7 E1
Big Dipper Ice Arena...................8 D3
Department of Fish & Game Office.......9 D1
Georgeson Botanical Garden............10 A1
Larry's Flying Service.................(see 45)
Pioneer Park..........................11 C2
Riverboat Discovery...................12 A3
Tanana Valley Fairgrounds.............13 D1
University of Alaska Museum of the
  North...............................14 B1
Wood Center...........................15 B1

SLEEPING
7 Gables Inn...........................(see 5)
Ah, Rose Marie B&B....................16 D2
All Seasons Inn.......................17 D2
Billie's Backpackers Hostel...........18 C1
Boyle's Hostel........................19 E3
Chena River State Recreation
  Site................................20 B2
College Inn...........................21 B2
Go North Hostel.......................22 B3
Golden North Motel....................23 B3
Minnie Street B&B.....................24 E2
Norlite Campground....................25 C3
Pike's Waterfront Lodge...............26 A3
River's Edge RV Park &
  Campground..........................27 B2
Super 8 Motel.........................28 C3
Tanana Valley Campground..............29 D1

EATING
Alaska Salmon Bake....................(see 11)
Bun on the Run........................(see 42)
College Coffeehouse...................30 B1
Cookie Jar............................31 D2
Fred Meyer............................32 B3
Hot Licks.............................33 B1
Lemongrass............................34 A2
Pad Thai..............................35 C1
Player's Grill........................36 D2
Pump House Restaurant.................37 A3
Second Story Cafe.....................(see 40)
Sourdough Cafe........................38 C1
Tanana Valley Farmers Market.........39 C1
Wok 'n' Roll..........................40 B1

DRINKING
Marlin................................41 B1

ENTERTAINMENT
Palace Theatre & Saloon...............(see 11)

SHOPPING
Artworks..............................(see 30)
Bear Galley & Gift Shop...............(see 11)
Beaver Sports.........................42 B1

TRANSPORT
Arctic Rent-A-Car.....................43 A3
Aurora Rental Car.....................44 D2
Frontier Flying Service...............45 B4
Wright Air Service....................(see 45)

See Downtown Fairbanks Map p357

INFORMATION

Bookstores

Alaska Public Lands Information Center (Map p357; ☎ 456-0527; www.nps.gov/aplic/; 250 Cushman St; ☺ 9am-6pm) Has a decent collection of works on natural history, wildlife and indigenous culture.

Gulliver's Books (Map p355; ☎ 474-9574; www.gullivers-books.com; 3525 College Rd; ☺ 9am-10pm Mon-Fri, 9am-8pm Sat, 11am-6pm Sun) Next to Campus Corner Mall, near UAF, this is by far the best bookstore in town, selling new and used books and Alaskan titles.

UAF Bookstore (Map p355; ☎ 474-6858; 504 Tok Lane; ☺ 8am-5pm Mon-Fri, noon-5pm Sat) In Constitution Hall on campus, has highbrow texts plus Alaskan titles.

Emergency

Ambulance, Fire, Police (☎ 911)

Police station (☎ non-emergency 450-6500; 911 Cushman St)

Internet Access & Library

College Coffeehouse (Map p355; 3677 College Rd at University Ave; ☺ 7am-midnight Mon-Fri, 8am-midnight Sat & Sun) In Campus Corner Mall; 15 minutes of Internet time free with any drink purchase, or $2 per 15 minutes.

Noel Wien Library (Map p355; ☎ 459-1020; 1215 Cowles St at Airport Way; ☺ 10am-9pm Mon-Thu, 10am-6pm Fri, 10am-5pm Sat) This excellent library is a long walk from the Log Cabin Visitor Information Center (take the MACS Blue Line). Along with free Internet and a large Alaskana section, it has an impressive collection of paintings and prints, many by Alaskan artists.

Second Story Café (Map p355; 3525 College Rd; ☺ 9am-9pm Mon-Fri, 9am-7pm Sat, 11am-5pm Sun) Near University Ave; above Gulliver's Books by Campus Corner Mall. It has free Internet access (with a 30-minute limit), but only one terminal.

Laundry

B&C Laundromat (Map p355; ☎ 479-2696; ☺ 7am-9:30pm) In Campus Corner Mall; has coin-operated laundry and $3 showers.

Media

Fairbanks Daily News-Miner (www.news-miner.com) Covers the city, the Interior and the Bush.

Medical Services

Fairbanks Memorial Hospital (Map p355; ☎ 452-8181; 1650 W Cowles St) Emergency care; south of Airport Way.

Tanana Valley Clinic (Map p357; ☎ 459-3500 24hr; 1001 Noble St; ☺ 8am-8pm Mon-Sat) For minor problems.

Money

Key Bank of Alaska (Map p357; ☎ 459-3362; 100 Cushman St) Downtown; has an impressive gold nugget display and an ATM.

Wells Fargo (Map p357; ☎ 459-4300; 613 Cushman St; ☺ 10am-5pm Mon-Thu, 10am-6pm Fri) Near Key Bank of Alaska; has an ATM.

Post

Post office (Map p357; 315 Barnette St; ☺ 10am-6pm Mon-Fri) Downtown, between 3rd and 4th Aves.

Tourist Information

Alaska Public Lands Information Center (Map p357; ☎ 456-0527; www.nps.gov/aplic/; 250 Cushman St; ☺ 9am-6pm) For maps and excellent information on state and national parks, wildlife refuges and recreation areas, head to APLIC, two blocks south of the Chena River in the Courthouse Square building's basement. The center has exhibits and video programs, a small theater that screens nature films four times daily, and staff that can assist with trip-planning.

Log Cabin Visitor Information Center (Map p357; ☎ 456-5774; www.explorefairbanks.com; 550 1st Ave at Cushman St; ☺ 8am-7pm summer; ☐) The main source of tourist information is this always-busy Fairbanks Convention and Visitors Bureau's center, which overlooks the Chena River. The many services include a recorded telephone message (☎ 456-4636) listing weekly events and attractions, racks of brochures, courtesy phones to call motels and B&Bs, helpful staff – but no restrooms.

Travel Agencies

US Travel (Map p357; ☎ 452-8992; 1211 Cushman St) For a ticket to anywhere but here.

DANGERS & ANNOYANCES

More than most places you're likely to visit in Alaska, downtown Fairbanks can be seedy, with much down-and-out drunkenness and occasional cases of harassment. Violence against tourists is very rare, but if you've gotten used to dropping your guard consider raising it here by following the same precautions you would in any major city.

SIGHTS

Downtown Fairbanks

Much has been done recently to beautify and revitalize Fairbanks' downtown. While the area can still seem a bit of a wasteland – especially on weekends – it's well worth a wander.

Check with the Log Cabin Visitor Information Center to see if they've reissued their downtown walking tour guide. Then head out the door into **Golden Heart Plaza** (Map p357), a pleasant riverside park in the city center. In the middle of the plaza is an impressive bronze statue, *The Unknown First Family,* which depicts an Athabascan family braving the elements.

Heading west along 1st Ave's pretty waterfront promenade you'll see a half-dozen old log cabins and several historic buildings, including **St Matthew's Episcopal Church,** a beautiful log structure built in 1905 and rebuilt in 1948 after it burned down. **Immaculate Conception Church** (Map p357), just across the Chena River Bridge from Golden Heart Plaza, was built in 1904 and moved to its present location in 1911. It's

a national historic monument and features beautiful painted-glass windows.

Fairbanks Community Museum (Map p357; ☎ 457-3669; 410 Cushman St; admission free; ☼ 10am-6pm Tue-Sat), though not thrilling, merits a visit on a rainy day. This homespun place traces the city's history mainly through old photos and newspaper clippings.

More interestingly, the museum is home to the **Yukon Quest Cache,** with a gift shop and displays devoted to the city's seminal dog-sled race. Like a handful of other Alaskan towns, Fairbanks bills itself as the dog mushing capital of the world. The Yukon Quest, taking place each February, covers 1023 miles between here and Whitehorse along many of the early trails used by trappers,

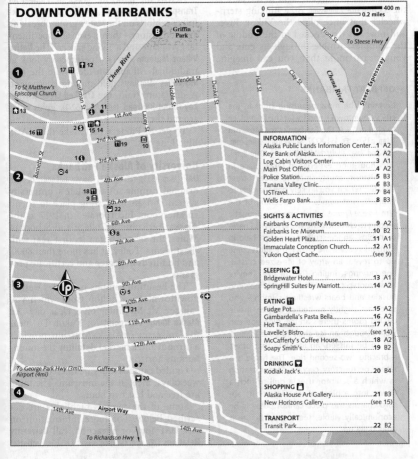

DOWNTOWN FAIRBANKS

INFORMATION	
Alaska Public Lands Information Center...1	A2
Key Bank of Alaska............................2	A2
Log Cabin Visitors Center...................3	A1
Main Post Office..............................4	A2
Police Station.................................5	B3
Tanana Valley Clinic.........................6	B3
USTravel.......................................7	B4
Wells Fargo Bank.............................8	B3

SIGHTS & ACTIVITIES	
Fairbanks Community Museum...............9	A2
Fairbanks Ice Museum.......................10	B2
Golden Heart Plaza..........................11	A1
Immaculate Conception Church...........12	A1
Yukon Quest Cache.....................(see 9)	

SLEEPING ⌂	
Bridgewater Hotel............................13	A1
SpringHill Suites by Marriott...............14	A2

EATING ⌷	
Fudge Pot......................................15	A2
Gambardella's Pasta Bella..................16	A2
Hot Tamale....................................17	A1
Lavelle's Bistro.........................(see 14)	
McCafferty's Coffee House.................18	A2
Soapy Smith's.................................19	B2

DRINKING ⌷	
Kodiak Jack's..................................20	B4

SHOPPING ⌷	
Alaska House Art Gallery....................21	B3
New Horizons Gallery..................(see 15)	

TRANSPORT	
Transit Park....................................22	B2

FAIRBANKS & AROUND

miners and the postal service. Though less famous than the Iditarod (p34), mushers will attest that the Quest is tougher, forcing teams to climb four mountains over 3000ft high and run along hundreds of miles of the frozen Yukon River. While the Iditarod has 25 rest stops, the Quest has only six.

Pioneer Park

Fairbanks' guiltiest pleasure is this 44-acre **theme park** (Map p355; ☎ 459-1087; Airport Way at Peger Rd; ☑ 11am-9pm), formerly known as Alaskaland. It may sound corny, but suspend your cynicism and you'll dig this vacation from your vacation. Entry is free, though some of the rides and attractions involve nominal fees.

The most prominent sight in the park is the **SS Nenana** (admission $3), a hulking sternwheeler that once plied the Yukon River and now sits dry-docked in the middle of the complex. Amble through its guts and you'll learn more than you can imagine about Alaska's river-travel heyday. Other of the park's historical relics include the railroad car that carried President Warren Harding to the golden-spike ceremony in 1923, and a century-old carousel that still offers rides to the young and young-at-heart.

Near Peger Rd is the Alaska Salmon Bake (p364), while the park's Gold Rush Town – a street of relocated cabin-cum-gift shops – has the Palace Theatre and Saloon (p365). Nearby is the **Pioneer Museum** (admission free), mainly a jumble of antiques ostensibly chronicling the history of Fairbanks. This is also where, six times daily, you can catch the 40-minute **Big Stampede Show** (admission $4), reenacting gold-rush days.

Across the park, the geodesic **Pioneer Air Transportation Museum** (admission $2) is chock-full of exhibits on the state's groundbreaking aviation history – there's even an experimental gyroplane and a 'flying saucer.' The **Native Village Museum** offers a perfunctory look at traditional Athabascan life, while the **Mining Valley** displays gold-mining equipment. A miniature train, the **Crooked Creek & Whiskey Island Railroad** (adult/child $2/1), gives rides around the park.

To get to Pioneer Park, take the MACS Blue Line bus.

University of Alaska Fairbanks

UAF (Map p355; ☎ 474-7211; www.uaf.edu) is the original campus of the state's university system and an interesting place to spend an afternoon. Incorporated in 1917 as the Alaska Agricultural College and School of Mines, the school began its first year with six students. Today, it has more than 8000, and hundreds of degree and certificate programs.

The beautiful campus is 4 miles west of downtown, on a hilltop from which you can see Mt McKinley on a clear day. An **Alaska Range viewpoint** on Yukon Dr, near the University of Alaska Museum, provides a turnout and a marker detailing the mountainous horizon.

Guided campus tours are offered at 10am weekdays; meet at the museum. The tours are free and last two hours.

Some of the campus highlights are described below. For more information on any UAF tour or attraction, call **University Relations** (☎ 474-7581) or visit UAF's website.

OFFBEAT FAIRBANKS

Certainly the most bemusing sight in the city's downtown – and by far the best place to chill out – is the **Fairbanks Ice Museum** (Map p357; ☎ 451-8222; www.icemuseum.com; 500 2nd Ave; adult/child $11/6; ☑ 10am-8pm). This hour-long experience takes place in the historic, musty-smelling Lacey Street Theater, which you'll likely have largely to yourself. First comes the screening of the film *Freeze Frame,* which employs dramatic editing to chronicle the World Ice Art Championships, an ice-sculpting contest held in Fairbanks each March. Then the lights come up to reveal an array of life-sized crystalline carvings ringing the theatre. They're all stereotypical Alaskan scenes – howling huskies and bears wrestling salmon – and some are slightly melted or broken. Inside chilled rooms there's an ice-igloo you can walk through, an ice-chair to pose in, and, not to be missed, an ice-slide that offers a bracing two-second ride. The finale is a rather perfunctory carving demonstration in which a sculptor uses a drill to etch a flower into a block of ice. Despite its absurd charms this place cannot possibly be economically viable; see it soon before it goes belly up.

THE NORTHERN LIGHTS

Fairbanks' best attraction is also its furthest-flung: the aurora borealis, better known as the northern lights. The aurora is a phenomenon of physics taking place 50 to 200 miles above the Earth. As solar winds flow across the upper atmosphere, they hit gas molecules, which light up much like the high-vacuum electrical discharge of a neon sign. The result is a solar-powered lightshow of ghostly, undulating colors streaming across the sky. In the dead of winter, the aurora often illuminates the night for hours. Other evenings 'the event,' as many call it, lasts less than 10 minutes, with the aurora spinning into a giant green ball and then fading. Milky green and white are the most common colors; red auroras are the rarest. In 1958 the northern sky was so 'bloody' with brilliant red auroras that fire trucks rushed out to the hills surrounding Fairbanks, expecting to find massive forest fires.

This polar phenomenon has been seen as far south as Mexico, but Fairbanks is the undisputed aurora capital. Somebody in northern Minnesota might witness fewer than 20 'events' a year and in Anchorage around 150, but in Fairbanks you can see the lights an average of 240 nights a year. North of Fairbanks, the number begins to decrease, and at the North Pole the lights are visible for fewer than 100 nights a year.

Regrettably, from May to mid-August there's too much daylight in Alaska to see an 'event,' but generally in late summer the aurora begins to appear in the Interior and can be enjoyed if you're willing to be awake at 2am. By mid-September the lights are dazzling, and people are already asking, 'did you see the lights last night?'

The best viewing in Fairbanks is in the outlying hills, away from city lights. The University of Alaska Fairbanks is also a good spot to view the aurora.

FAIRBANKS & AROUND

To reach the campus, take MACS Red or Blue Line buses to UAF's Wood Center.

WOOD CENTER & CONSTITUTION HALL

A good place to start exploring the campus is **Wood Center** (Map p355; ☎ 474-7037; 505 Yukon Dr; ⏰ 7:30am-5:30pm Mon-Fri), where the information desk provides the *UAF Campus Map & Visitors' Guide* and the latest scoop on university events. This student center and general meeting place also holds a cafeteria, espresso stand, pizza parlor, pub and an outdoor patio. Next door is Constitution Hall, where territorial delegates drafted the constitution for statehood. Now it houses the **UAF Bookstore** (☎ 474-7348; ⏰ 8am-5pm Mon-Fri, noon-5pm Sat).

GEORGESON BOTANICAL GARDEN

On the edge of campus is the Agricultural and Forestry Experiment Station, where the university dabbles in growing vegetables of mythical proportions, and small grains like barley, wheat and oats that seem best suited for the short Alaskan growing seasons. Ironically, the station's grain fields are ideal places to spot Sandhill cranes, an endangered species in the rest of the country.

On the station grounds is the 5-acre **Georgeson Botanical Garden** (Map p355; ☎ 474-1944; www.uaf .edu/salrm/gbg; W Tanana Dr; admission $2; ⏰ 8am-8pm),

a perfect picnicking spot that's a riot of wildflowers, herbs, fruits and gigantic vegetables. You can look around independently anytime during opening hours, and guided tours are offered on Fridays at 2pm.

To reach the station take Tanana Loop west from the lower campus, bear left at the fork onto W Tanana Dr and continue for a mile.

LARGE ANIMAL RESEARCH STATION

UAF's **Large Animal Research Station** (Map p355; ☎ 474-5724; www.uaf.edu/lars) keeps herds of musk oxen, reindeer and caribou to study their unique adaptations to a sub-Arctic climate. Viewing areas outside the fenced pastures allow a free look at the herds anytime, but bring binoculars, as the animals don't always cooperatively graze nearby. The facility itself can only be seen on guided walks.

The hour-long tours (adult $10, child free) take place daily at 1:30pm and 3:30pm, while half-hour walks ($6) occur throughout the day. A gift shop sells, among other things, raw *qiviut* (musk-ox wool). To reach the station, head north from campus on Farmers Loop Rd, bear left onto Ballaine Rd, and then turn left again on Yankovich Rd and continue 1.2 miles to the site.

UNIVERSITY OF ALASKA MUSEUM

In an architecturally abstract igloo-and-aurora-inspired edifice, near the west end of the campus, is one of Alaska's finest museums, the **University of Alaska Museum of the North** (Map p355; ☎ 474-7505; www.uaf.edu/museum; 907 Yukon Dr; adult/child $5/3; ⊗ 9am-7pm), where a recent $42-million overhaul has doubled the facility's size and further amplified its impact. Inside, you'll find the Gallery of Alaska, which examines the geology, history and unusual aspects of each region of the state, and where you can view the museum's most famous exhibit, Blue Babe: a 36,000-year-old bison found preserved in the permafrost by Fairbanks-area miners. In the new wing is a temporary-exhibit space as well as the permanent Rose Berry Alaska Art Gallery, where northern works ranging from ancient ivory carvings to contemporary photographs are intermixed in an egalitarian fashion. In the museum's auditorium, two programs run several times daily (additional fee): *Northern Inua* showcases Alaska Natives' songs, dances and athletic events, while *Dynamic Aurora* is a multimedia look at historical perspectives on, and modern research into, the northern lights. Rounding out the museum are a gift shop specializing in authentic Alaska Native crafts, a coffee shop selling espressos, sandwiches and salads, a sitting room with comfy couches to help stave off 'museum fatigue,' and a viewing deck with here-to-infinity views of the Alaska Range.

ACTIVITIES

As befits an Alaskan university town, Fairbanks has plenty to keep outdoor enthusiasts enthusiastic. Much of the best trekking and paddling, however, is well out of town, meaning those without wheels will need transportation.

Hiking

Unlike Anchorage or Juneau, Fairbanks doesn't have outstanding hiking on its doorstep. The best trail for an extended backpacking trip is the impressive **Pinnell Mountain Trail** (p73) at Mile 85.5 and Mile 107.3 of the Steese Hwy. For a variety of long and short hikes, head to the Chena River State Recreation Area.

For more information, stop at the Alaska Public Lands Information Center, or at UAF's Geophysical Institute Map Office.

CREAMER'S FIELD

A handful of trails, each less than 2 miles round trip, wind through the farmlands and forests of **Creamer's Field Migratory Waterfowl Refuge** (Map p355), an old dairy farm that's become a birders' paradise. The Alaska Department of Fish and Game seeds the area with bird-luring plants, attracting more than 100 species annually, including sandhill cranes. The **Farmhouse Visitor Center** (Map p355; ☎ 459-7307; 1300 College Rd at Danby St; ⊗ 10am-5pm), adjacent to the Fish and Game office and reached by the MACS Red Line, has trail guides, bug spray and a list of recent sightings.

Volunteers lead one-hour nature walks at 7pm Monday through Friday and 9am Wednesday.

UNIVERSITY OF ALASKA FAIRBANKS

UAF's backyard is laced with peaceful walking and biking trails, some several miles in length, that will introduce you to the woods and wildlife on Fairbanks' northwestern outskirts.

Along the way you may find evidence of ongoing research projects; be sure not to touch them.

For a rough overview of the trails, consult the *UAF Campus Map* – free at the Wood Center.

Biking

Fairbanks has a fine network of bike routes in and around the city. Bike paths begin at 1st Ave and Cushman St and extend all the way past Pioneer Park, across the Chena River, to UAF and the George Parks Hwy. Shoulder bikeways lead you out of town. One of the more popular rides is to head north on Illinois St from downtown, and then loop around on College Rd and Farmers Loop Rd–University Ave for a 17-mile ride. Pick up a free *Bikeways Map* at the Log Cabin Visitor Information Center.

Alaska Outdoor Rentals & Guides (Map p355; ☎ 457-2453; www.akbike.com; Pioneer Park; ⊗ 10am-7pm) is located on the river behind Pioneer Park and rents mountain bikes for $27 per day. **Go North Hostel** (Map p355; ☎ 479-7272,

866-236-7272; www.gonorthalaska.com; 3500 Davis Rd) also has mountain bikes for $27 a day. **7 Bridges Boats & Bikes** (Map p355; ☎ 479-0751; www.7gablesinn .com; 4312 Birch Lane), at the 7 Gables Inn & Suites, rents road bikes for $15 a day and mountain bikes for $20 a day.

Paddling

The Fairbanks area offers a wide variety of canoeing and kayaking opportunities from leisurely day to overnight trips into the surrounding area; for extended backcountry expeditions, see p78, or visit the Alaska Public Lands Information Center.

Several local places rent boats and run shuttles to put-ins and take-outs: Alaska Outdoor Rentals & Guides will set you up with a canoe for $41 a day and, for another $15, pick you up at downstream locations like Pike's Landing or the Pump House Restaurant; Go North Hostel has canoes for $35 per day or $190 per week, can help with trip-planning and will transport you to and from rivers throughout the Interior; and 7 Bridges Boats & Bikes provides canoes and a shuttle service: canoes are $35 a day and transport costs $2 a mile, with a $10 minimum.

AROUND TOWN

An afternoon can be spent paddling the Chena River; its mild currents let you paddle upstream as well as down. You can launch a canoe from almost any bridge crossing the river, including Graehl Landing near the north side of Steese Hwy, where locals like to paddle upstream and then float back down.

From 7 Bridges Boats & Bikes you can drop a canoe in the Chena River, head downstream and into the quiet Noyes Slough and complete the loop by paddling east back into the river, a 13-mile round-trip journey.

CHENA & TANANA RIVERS

Those looking for an overnight – or even longer – paddle should try a float down the Chena River from Chena Hot Springs Rd, east of Fairbanks, or a pleasant two-day trip down the Tanana River. The popular Tanana trip usually begins from the end of Chena Pump Rd and finishes in the town of Nenana, where you can return with your canoe to Fairbanks on the Alaska Railroad. This 60-mile trip can be done in a single day but would require 10 to 12 hours of serious paddling.

CHATANIKA RIVER

For a one-day trip, the Chatanika River can be paddled for 28 miles west from Cripple Creek BLM (Bureau of Land Management) Campground at Mile 60 of the Steese Hwy (see Map p353). The route parallels the road until the Upper Chatanika River State Recreation Area at Mile 39. Many local paddlers avoid the complexities of shuttling this stretch by leaving a bicycle chained at the take-out and pedaling back to their car. Extended trips on the Chatanika River are possible; you can paddle another 17 miles to a bridge at Mile 11 of the Elliott Hwy.

Gold Panning

If you've been bitten by the gold bug, Fairbanks is an ideal area to try your hand at gold panning. Start at **Alaskan Prospectors & Geologists Supply** (Map p355; ☎ 452-7398; 504 College Rd), which sells all the necessary equipment for recreational prospecting. It stocks books, pamphlets and videos that can help you strike it rich, and even offers panning instructions.

The next stop should be the Alaska Public Lands Information Center, which distributes a helpful sheet entitled 'Where Can I Pan for Gold Without Getting Shot?' Popular places in the area include the Discovery Claim on Pedro Creek (off the Steese Hwy, across from the Felix Pedro Monument), and several other locations further up the Steese Hwy.

TOURS
Organized Tours

Riverboat Discovery (Map p355; ☎ 479-6673, 866-479-6673; www.riverboatdiscovery.com; Mile 4.5 Airport Way; adult/child $47/32) Departing at 8:45am and 2pm daily, this 3½-hour tour navigates the Chena River via historic sternwheeler, stopping at a replica of an Athabascan village as well as the riverfront home and kennels of Susan Butcher, four-time winner of the Iditarod.

Fairbanks Historical City Tour (☎ 474-0286, 800-770-3343; www.riversedge.net; 4140 Boat St; adult/child $25/10) Departing from River's Edge RV Park & Campground, this four-hour motorcoach tour leaves daily at 8:30am and visits downtown, the Trans-Alaska Pipeline, and the UAF Museum and Botanical Gardens.

Gray Line (Map p357; ☎ 451-6835; 1980 S Cushman St; adult/child $60/32) Offers a four-hour 'Discover the Gold Tour' that departs at 9am and noon, and includes Gold Dredge No 8, the Trans-Alaska Pipeline and lunch.

Gold Panning & Mine Tours

Gold Dredge No 8 (Map p369; ☎ 457-6058; www
.golddredgeno8.com; 1755 Old Steese Hwy N; adult/child
$19/13) Off the old Steese Hwy at Mile 10 Goldstream Rd,
this five-deck, 250ft dredge was built in 1928, operated
until 1959, and was named a national historic site in 1984.
Today perhaps Alaska's most visited dredge, No 8 is still
making money. There are on-the-hour one-hour tours
from 9:30am to 3:30pm daily; for an additional fee you
can also indulge in gold panning and the all-you-can-eat
Miner's Lunch.

El Dorado Gold Mine (Map p353; ☎ 479-6673, 866-
479-6673; www.eldoradogoldmine.com; Mile 1.3 Elliott
Hwy; adult/child $30/20) This daily two-hour train tour on
a mile-long narrow-gauge track winds through a reconstructed mining camp and culminates with visitors panning
gold-laden dirt.

Flightseeing Tours

The Arctic Circle may be an imaginary line,
but it's become one of Fairbanks' biggest
draws, with small air-charter companies
doing booming business flying travelers on
sightseeing excursions across it. Companies
offering Arctic Circle 'flightseeing' trips:

Larry's Flying Service (Map p355; ☎ 474-9169; www
.larrysflying.com) Offers a 1¾-hour air-only tour, or a
three-hour trip with an hour-long ground tour of Fort
Yukon, just north of the circle.
Alaska Flying Tours (☎ 457-4424, 888-326-4424;
www.alaskaflyingtours.com)
Northern Alaska Tour Co (☎ 474-8600, 800-474-
1986; www.northernalaska.com)
Trans Arctic Circle Treks Ltd (☎ 479-5451, 800-336-
8735; www.arctictreks.com)

FESTIVALS & EVENTS

Summer solstice celebrations Taking place on June
21 when the sun shines for almost 23 hours, events
include footraces, arts and crafts booths and the traditional midnight sun baseball game, which pits the Alaska
Goldpanners against an Alaskan rival team in a bright-as-
day night game.
Golden Days Fairbanks' largest summer happening,
staged the third week of July, commemorates Felix Pedro's
discovery of gold, with games and events ranging from
rubber-ducky races to horse-and-rider shootouts. If you
show up without a Golden Days button or garter, you risk
being locked up in the mobile jail.
World Eskimo-Indian Olympics (☎ 452-6646; www
.weio.org) Held annually on the second-to-last weekend in
July at the Big Dipper Ice Arena (Map p355), this four-day
event attracts indigenous people from across the North,
who display their athletic prowess in contests like the
Alaska High Kick and test their pain thresholds in games

such as the Knuckle Hop. There's also dancing, cultural
performances and plenty of traditional regalia.
Fairbanks Summer Arts Festival (☎ 474-8869;
www.fsaf.org) In the last two weeks of July on the UAF
campus, this festival features numerous concerts and
workshops in the performing and visual arts.
Tanana Valley State Fair (www.tananavalleyfair.org)
In early to mid-August at the fairgrounds on College Rd
(Map p355), Alaska's oldest fair has sideshows, entertainment, livestock contests (including one for 'poultry
and rabbit showmanship') and produce of immense
proportions.

SLEEPING

Fairbanks offers all manner of lodging options, from tents to tony resorts. Most of
the campgrounds are along Airport Way,
University Ave and College Rd, while hostels are scattered throughout the city. There
are more than 100 B&Bs, many of which are
in the downtown area; visit the Log Cabin
Visitor Information Center for brochures.
Fairbanks has an 8% bed tax that is not
included in the prices below.

Budget

HOSTELS

Go North Hostel (Map p355; ☎ 479-7272, 866-236-7272;
www.gonorthalaska.com; 3500 Davis Rd; wall-tent dm $20,
sites $8 plus $8 per person) Fairbanks' best hostel
houses backpackers in four comfortable wall
tents, offers communal cooking in a bright
kitchen-cabin, and boasts a dazzling array
of services, including gravel-ready vehicle
hire, camping-gear-package rentals, canoe-
trip shuttles and guided backcountry expeditions. Though a fair walk from anywhere
of interest, it's on the MACS Yellow Line
bus route.

Billie's Backpackers Hostel (Map p355; ☎ 479-
2034; www.alaskahostel.com; 2895 Mack Rd; sites $15, dm
$25, r $75) Right off the MACS Red Line and
not far from the university, Billie's is somewhat sloppy and slightly worn but remains
Fairbanks' most popular hostel. It offers
the typical amenities, plus free use of bikes.
Make reservations, as this place is regularly
full in summer.

CAMPING

Chena River State Recreation Site (Map p355; walk-in
sites/campsites/RV sites $10/15/22) This 29-acre park
is on the Chena River, off University Ave just
north of Airport Way (not to be confused
with the Chena River State Recreation Area,

east of Fairbanks). The lushly wooded campground has 61 sites, tables, toilets, fireplaces, water and a boat launch. It's served by the MACS Blue Line.

Pioneer Park (Map p355; ☎ 459-1095; Airport Way at Peger Rd; sites $10; four nights maximum) If you just want to park the van or RV and don't need facilities or a hook-up, you can spend the night in the parking lot here.

Tanana Valley Campground (Map p355; ☎ 456-7956; www.tananavalleyfair.org/campground.shtml; 1800 College Rd; campsites $10; RV sites $14-16) This campground has lots of trees, plus showers and laundry facilities. It's open 24 hours.

Norlite Campground (Map p355; ☎ 474-0206; 1660 Peger Rd; campsites $15; RV sites $21-25) Just south of Airport Way and the entrance to Pioneer Park, this slightly scruffy place has showers and laundry facilities.

River's Edge RV Park & Campground (Map p355; ☎ 474-0286, 800-770-3343; www.riversedge.net; 4140 Boat St; campsites $19, RV sites $27-30) Near the corner of Airport Way and George Parks Hwy, this large campground is better suited to RVs than campers. It's on the Chena River and has showers, laundry facilities, a shuttle service and access to the city's bike-trail system.

Midrange

Ah, Rose Marie B&B (Map p355; ☎ 456-2040; www.akpub.com/akbbrv/ahrose.html; 302 Cowles St; s/d $60/75) Just west of downtown, this highly recommended place has four homey rooms. Avuncular owner John Davis prides himself on his breakfasts.

7 Gables Inn & Suites (Map p355; ☎ 479-0751; www.7gablesinn.com; 4312 Birch Lane; r $90-130, apt $150) This B&B, just off the Chena River, is entered via a hothouse garden and offers plush rooms, some with Jacuzzis, as well as private apartments. Full breakfasts have an international theme, like eggs in curry sauce and Norwegian farmers' omelets.

Super 8 Motel (Map p355; ☎ 451-8888, 800-800-8000; 1909 Airport Way at Wilbur St; r $125-144) Corporate and totally characterless but clean and efficient. It's near Pioneer Park and has a free shuttle service to the airport and train station.

Golden North Motel (Map p355; ☎ 479-6201, 800-447-1910; www.goldennorthmotel.com; 4888 Old Airport Rd; s/d $69/74) This friendly, helpful place may be the cheapest respectable motel in town. Rooms tend to be on the small side.

College Inn (Map p355; ☎ 474-3666; 700 Fairbanks St; s/d without bath $59/69) Reeks of marijuana and has a flophouse feel, but the price is hard to beat.

Top End

Pike's Waterfront Lodge (Map p355; ☎ 456-4500, 877-774-2400; www.pikeslodge.com; 1850 Hoselton Rd; r from $210) An upscale place on the banks of the Chena River. Its amenities include a steam room and sauna, exercise facilities and a deck on the river.

Minnie Street B&B Inn (Map p355; ☎ 456-1802, 888-456-1849; www.minniestreetbandb.com; 345 Minnie St; r with/without bath $145/115) North of the river from downtown, this spacious B&B provides full breakfasts and bountiful advice on what to do around Fairbanks.

All Seasons B&B Inn (Map p357; ☎ 451-6649, 888-451-6649; www.allseasonsinn.com; 763 7th Ave; r $135-175) On a quiet residential street downtown, the All Seasons has a great sun porch and nine lovingly furnished rooms that can accommodate a variety of sleeping arrangements.

Bridgewater Hotel (Map p357; ☎ 452-6661, 800-528-4916; www.fountainheadhotels.com; 723 1st Ave; r $149) Overlooks the Chena River and caters largely to the tour-group crowd.

SpringHill Suites by Marriott (Map p357; ☎ 451-6552, 877-729-0197; www.springhillsuites.com; 575 1st Ave; r $159-189) Offers sparkling, spacious corporate suites right across from the Log Cabin Visitor Information Center downtown.

EATING

If your taste buds have atrophied from all the quick-and-dirty diner fare in Alaska's Interior, take heart: in Fairbanks, you'll nurse them back to life. Though fast-food franchises dominate the scene, there are quality quick eats near the university, excellent fine dining downtown and on the city's outskirts, and some quality midrange places amid the sprawl of Airport Way. Best, and most surprising of all, yummy Thai joints are just about everywhere.

University Area
RESTAURANTS

Pad Thai (Map p355; ☎ 479-1251; 3400 College Rd; mains $10-13; ☯ 11am-9:30pm) In a sunny shack next to the Marlin bar, this is among the most popular of Fairbanks' many Thai restaurants. For dessert, try the fried banana with honey and ice cream ($4.50).

Sourdough Café (Map p355; ☎ 479-0523; University Ave at Cameron St; breakfast $6-11, burgers & sandwiches $6-9; ⏰ 6am-10pm) Considered by many to be the town's best diner, this place, just down University Ave from campus, serves up sourdough pancakes all day long.

CAFÉS

College Coffeehouse (Map p355; ☎ 374-0468; 3677 College Rd; ⏰ 7am-midnight Mon-Fri, 8am-midnight Sat & Sun; ▯) In Campus Corner Mall, this is one of the best spots in Fairbanks to pick up on the city's off-beat vibe. There's fancy coffee and great smoothies, but food is limited to bagels, brownies and the like. They often have live music.

Second Story Café (Map p355; ☎ 474-9574; 3525 College Rd; wraps & sandwiches $7; ⏰ 9am-9pm Mon-Fri, 9am-7pm Sat, 11am-5pm Sun; ▯) Above Gulliver's Books, this place whips up espressos, *chai* and smoothies, as well as killer wraps and sandwiches.

QUICK EATS

Wok 'n' Roll (Map p355; ☎ 455-4848; 3535 College Rd; dishes $6-9; ⏰ 11am-9pm Mon-Sat) Adjacent to Campus Corner Mall, this is good for quick, cheap Chinese food.

Bun on the Run (Map p355; ⏰ 7am-5pm Mon-Fri, 9am-4pm Sat) In a pink trailer in the Beaver Sports parking lot, the Bun cranks out delicious pastries and has quite a following.

Hot Licks (Map p355; ☎ 479-7813; www.hotlicks.net; 3453 College Rd; ⏰ noon-11pm Mon-Sat, noon-10pm Sun) On warm days, the line for the homemade ice cream here is insane. Find out why with a double-scoop cone of their fresh Alaska blueberry ($4).

Tanana Valley Farmers Market (Map p355; ☎ 456-3276; www.tvfmarket.com; College Rd at Caribou Dr; ⏰ 11am-4pm Wed, 9am-4pm Sat) The market sells fresh produce, baked goods, local handicrafts and more. Come in late August and you can buy a 20lb cabbage, enough for a month's supply of coleslaw.

Downtown

RESTAURANTS

Gambardella's Pasta Bella (Map p357; ☎ 457-4992; 706 2nd Ave; lunch $7-12, dinner $11-21; ⏰ 11am-10pm Mon-Sat, 4-10pm Sun) *The* place for Italian food in Fairbanks, with luscious pasta dishes, gourmet subs, pizzas and homemade bread. There's an outdoor café that's a delight during Fairbanks' long summer days.

Lavelle's Bistro (Map p357; ☎ 450-0555; 575 1st Ave; mains $16-33; ⏰ 4:30-9pm Sun & Mon, 4:30-10pm Tue-Sat) Chic, urbane and blessedly devoid of 'Last Frontier' kitsch, Lavelle's has a wine list as long as your arm and mains that include potato-crusted salmon and 'the best meatloaf you've ever had.'

Hot Tamale (Map p357; ☎ 457-8350; 112 N Turner St; dinner $10-13; ⏰ 10am-9pm) Across the Chena River from the Log Cabin Visitor Information Center, this is the place to try affordable Mexican food.

Soapy Smith's (Map p357; ☎ 451-8380; 543 2nd Ave; lunch $10-13, dinner $14-25; ⏰ 11am-9pm) Though Smith was a Skagway character who died before Fairbanks even existed, this place has good burgers in saloon-style environs.

CAFÉS & QUICK EATS

McCafferty's Coffee House (Map p357; ☎ 456-6853; 408 Cushman St; soups $4; ⏰ 7am-6pm Mon-Thu, 7am-11pm Fri, 10am-11pm Sat, 10am-4pm Sun) Arty without being pretentious, this espresso emporium also serves soups and baked goods. Live music adds atmosphere on Friday and Saturday nights.

Fudge Pot (Map p357; ☎ 456-3834; 515 1st Ave; soup & sandwich $10; ⏰ 9am-7pm Mon-Fri, 10am-6pm Sat, 10am-4pm Sun) A convenient but touristy place opposite the Log Cabin Visitor Information Center, with basic sandwiches and, unsurprisingly, pots of fudge ($12 per pound).

Airport Way & Other Areas

Alaska Salmon Bake (Map p355; ☎ 452-7274, 800-354-7274; www.akvisit.com; ⏰ 5-9pm) Hungry souls should take in the touristy, tasty, tongue-in-cheek salmon bake at Pioneer Park. For $28 you choose between all-you-can-eat grilled salmon, halibut, cod, prime rib and countless sides. After dinner, head over to the Palace Theatre for the Golden Heart Revue. A $2 shuttle bus is available from major hotels.

Pump House Restaurant (Map p353; ☎ 479-8452; Mile 1.3 Chena Pump Rd; www.pumphouse.com; dinner mains $18-36; ⏰ 11:30am-2pm & 5-11pm) Located 2 miles from downtown, this is the best place to turn dinner into an evening, or to enjoy a great Sunday brunch. A pump house during the gold-mining era, the building is now a national historic site. The atmosphere is classic gold rush; inside and out there are artifacts and relics from the city's mining era. Steak, seafood and wild game dominate the menu, and you can also enjoy a drink on the outdoor deck while watching the boat traffic on the Chena. The MACS Blue Line goes by here.

Two Rivers Lodge (Map p369; ☎ 488-6815; dinner $25-47; ✆ 5-10pm Mon-Fri, 3-10pm Sat & Sun) A high-end lodge 16 miles out on Chena Hot Springs Rd. Its rustic décor, complete with bearskin rugs, is in keeping with the natural setting. Steak, seafood and poultry are the focus, with mains like almond-coated halibut and pheasant with apricots.

Lemongrass (Map p355; ☎ 456-2200; 388 Old Chena Pump Rd; mains $7-13; ✆ 11am-4pm & 5pm-10pm) Ignore the out-of-the-way, strip-mall setting – Fairbanks' best Thai food and most gracious service is found here.

Cookie Jar (Map p355; ☎ 479-8319; 1006 Cadillac Ct; breakfast $4-10; ✆ 6:30am-8:30pm Mon, 6:30am-9pm Tue-Sat, 8am-7pm Sun) Bizarrely situated behind a pair of car dealerships off Danby St, locals flock here for the all-day breakfast.

Player's Grill (Map p355; ☎ 456-7427; 1694 Airport Way; lunch $7-12, dinner $11-19; ✆ 7:30am-9pm) Down the road from Pioneer Park, this place is popular among Fairbanksans for its ribs and burgers, generous portions and reasonable prices.

Fred Meyer (Map p355; ☎ 474-1400; cnr Old Airport Rd & Airport Way; ✆ 7am-11pm) This airplane hangar–sized store has every grocery imaginable, plus bulk foods, an extensive salad bar and all sorts of ready-to-eat fare. A sister store is at the intersection of the Old Steese Hwy and Johansen Expressway.

DRINKING & ENTERTAINMENT

As Alaska's second-biggest city, Fairbanks always has something on the go. For a low-down on live music, movies and such, check the listings in *FBX Square*, printed each Thursday in the *Fairbanks Daily News-Miner* (p356). Other publications with the skinny on events include *AK This Month* and the *Anchorage Press*, both available for free around town.

Bars & Live Music

Fairbanks' watering holes are the best places to meet locals, groove to soothing tunes or ignite the dance floor. If you're here in September after classes begin, head to University Pub, in the Wood Center at UAF, for live music and a college atmosphere.

Marlin (Map p355; 3412 College Rd) This subterranean dive hosts Fairbanks' edgiest musical acts most nights of the week. It's located opposite Gulliver's Books, a stone's throw from campus.

Kodiak Jack's (Map p357; 537 Gaffney Rd) At the south end of downtown, this is a kick-up-yer-heels country-dance spot attracting a sizable military crowd.

Pump House Saloon (Map p355; Mile 1.3 Chena Pump Rd) Enjoys the riverfront ambience of the Pump House Restaurant (opposite), but with a bar menu that won't break the bank. Check out the solid mahogany bar and the antique Brunswick pool table.

Blue Loon (p369) Seven miles southwest of town in Ester, this is where the DJs rock the dancehall and, every so often, major-label groups like the Cowboy Junkies and Violent Femmes come to play.

Saloon Shows

Rowdy saloons – throwbacks to the mining days – are the area's specialty, though now they're for tourists, not sourdoughs.

Palace Theatre & Saloon (Map p355; ☎ 456-5960; www.akvisit.com; adult/child $16/8) At Pioneer Park, this saloon comes alive at night with honkytonk piano, cancan dancers and other acts in the *Golden Heart Revue*. The large stage show purportedly answers the question: 'Why would anyone want to build a town in this godforsaken swamp, and why would that town survive for more than 90 years?' Showtime is 8:15pm nightly. Dinner at the park's nearby Alaska Salmon Bake (opposite) takes place before the show.

Malamute Saloon (p368) Seven miles west of Fairbanks in Ester, the Malamute puts on perhaps one of the best locally produced acts in Alaska. Shows are nightly during summer, and $2 bus transportation from Fairbanks is available.

Theater

Fairbanks Shakespeare Theatre (☎ 457-7638, 877-750-9455; www.fairbanks-shakespeare.org) Performs Shakespeare classics at various times and in different venues around Fairbanks. Check the website for a complete schedule of upcoming shows.

Spectator Sports

The **Goldpanners** (☎ 451-0095; www.goldpanners.com) is Fairbanks' entry in the collegiate-level Alaska Baseball League, which also includes teams from Anchorage, Mat-Su Valley and

---

FAIRBANKS MIDNIGHT SPORTS

Tourists aren't the only folks made manic by Alaska's endless summer days. Fairbanksans, all too aware that darkness and cold are just around the corner, go into overdrive from May to September playing outdoors at all hours of the night.

The most revered of the city's wee-hour athletic activities is the Midnight Sun Baseball Game, held every solstice since 1906 without artificial light and, thus far, never canceled due to darkness. For the past four decades the game has pitted the local Goldpanners against an Alaska Baseball League rival. The contest is invariably the most popular of the season, and when the first pitch is hurled at 10:30pm the sun is still well above the horizon. By midnight – when play pauses for the traditional singing of the Alaska Flag Song – the sun is low, and at the end of nine innings it's gone. Its glow, however, lights the sky until sunrise, two hours later.

If you're more a fan of links than diamonds, Fairbanks also has a couple of golf courses where you can tee up well past your bedtime. **North Star Golf Club** (☎ 457-4653; www.northstargolf.com; 330 Golf Club Dr; 18 holes weekdays/weekends $25/28) is an 18-hole course where visitors can start a round as late as 10pm. The USGA-approved course bills itself as 'America's Northernmost Golf Course.' Also in the area is the venerable **Fairbanks Golf & Country Club** (☎ 479-6555; 1735 Farmers Loop Rd; 9 holes $20), a nine-hole course open until 2am in June and July. Listed hazards at the courses include moose, marmot and sandhill crane.

Kenai Peninsula. Games are played mid-June through July at **Growden Memorial Park** (Map p355; cnr Wilbur St & 2nd Ave; ticket $10), starting at 7pm. Don't miss the Midnight Sun Baseball Game on June 21 – it's a century-old tradition.

SHOPPING
Arts & Crafts
Artworks (Map p355; ☎ 479-2563; Campus Corner Mall; ☼ 10am-6pm Mon-Fri, 10am-5pm Sat) Next to the College Coffeehouse, this place has lots of glass, ceramics and oil paintings, plus a limited quantity of aboriginal carvings and musk ox–wool weavings.

Alaska House Art Gallery (Map p357; ☎ 456-6449; cnr 10th Ave & Cushman St; ☼ 11am-7pm Mon-Sat) In a log building at the south end of downtown, the gallery specializes in indigenous and native-themed creations. Artists can often be found on the premises demonstrating their talents or telling stories.

Bear Gallery & Gift Shop (Map p355; ☎ 456-6485; Pioneer Park; ☼ 11am-9pm) Run by the Fairbanks Arts Association and located upstairs in the Alaska Centennial Center for the Arts in Pioneer Park, this gallery showcases an ever-changing array of local artists.

New Horizons Gallery (Map p357; ☎ 456-2063; 509 1st Ave; ☼ 9:30am-7pm Mon-Sat, noon-5pm Sun) Just across from the Log Cabin Visitor Information Center, this gallery has a huge but somewhat stereotypical selection of Alaska-themed works.

Outdoor Gear
Beaver Sports (Map p355; ☎ 479-2494; www.beaver sports.com; 3480 College Rd; ☼ 10am-7pm Mon-Sat, 11am-5pm Sun) This is *the* place for outdoor gear in Fairbanks, with mountain bikes, mountaineering boots and mountains of every other species of wilderness equipment. Also, there's a handy message board for exchanging info with fellow adventurers or securing used gear.

GETTING THERE & AWAY
Air
Alaska Airlines (☎ 800-252-7522; www.alaskaair.com) flies direct to Anchorage (where there are connections to the rest of Alaska, the Lower 48 and overseas), Barrow and Seattle. The round-trip advance-purchase fare to Anchorage is around $240; to Seattle it's about $420. **Frontier Flying Service** (☎ 474-0014, 800-478-6779; www.frontierflying.com) also visits Anchorage daily, charging $128 (one way) or $249 (round trip). **Air North** (☎ in USA 800-764-0407, in Canada 800-661-0407; www.flyairnorth.com) flies thrice-weekly to Whitehorse, but it'll cost you around $495.

In summer, **Condor (Thomas Cook)** (☎ in USA & Canada 800-524-6975, in Germany 01-803-333 130; www .condor.com) operates a weekly service direct to and from Frankfurt, Germany, for about $1300 return.

For travel into the Bush, try Frontier Flying Service, **Larry's Flying Service** (☎ 474-9169; www .larrysflying.com) or **Wright Air Service** (☎ 474-0502,

800-478-0502; www.wrightair.net). All have offices off University Ave on the airport's east side, and together they provide scheduled flights to more than 50 communities, including Bettles (Gates of the Arctic National Park), Fort Yukon, Kotzebue, Galena and Nome.

Bus

Long-distance bus services are available from **Alaska Direct Bus Line** (☎ 800-770-6652), which makes a Fairbanks–Whitehorse run ($180 one way) on Sunday, Wednesday and Friday. Along the way it stops at Delta Junction ($43), Tok ($70), Beaver Creek ($92) and Haines Junction ($153). At Tok, you can transfer to a bus for Glennallen and Anchorage. At Whitehorse you can catch the company's bus to Skagway.

Travel down the George Parks Hwy to Denali Park, Talkeetna and Anchorage with **Alaska/Yukon Trails** (☎ 479-2277, 800-770-7275). It departs from the Log Cabin Visitor Information Center in Fairbanks at 8:45am, arriving at Denali National Park's Visitor Access Center at 11:55am, downtown Talkeetna around 3:45pm and Anchorage around 5:30pm. The company also has a daily service to Dawson City, Yukon Territory, via the Taylor Hwy, leaving at 8:30am and arriving at 6:45pm.

Car & Motorcycle

If you're driving to Fairbanks from Canada, you'll likely be coming up the Alaska Hwy (p333). It's a good 12 hours from Whitehorse to Fairbanks, with little save for Tok and a few other highway-service communities en route. From Anchorage, it's six hours to Fairbanks up George Parks Hwy.

Train

The **Alaska Railroad** (☎ 458-6025, 800-544-0552; www.alaskarailroad.com) leaves Fairbanks daily at 8:15am from mid-May to mid-September. The train gets to Denali National Park at noon and Anchorage at 8:15pm. The new **train station** (⏱ 6:30am-3pm) is at the south end of Danby St. The one-way fare to Denali National Park is $54, and $179 to Anchorage.

GETTING AROUND
To/From the Airport

Fairbanks International Airport (☎ 474-2500; www.dot.state.ak.us/faiiap/) is at the west end of Airport Way, 4 miles from town and beyond walking distance of anywhere you'll want to get to.

MACS Yellow Line (☎ 459-1011) bus swings by here eight times a day between 6:30am and 8pm, charging $1.50 and taking you past some Airport Way motels and the Go North Hostel en route to the downtown transfer station.

Alpenglow Shuttles (☎ 479-2277, 800-770-7275; www.akalpenglow.com) will convey you from the airport to destinations throughout Fairbanks for $7.

Or grab a cab, for which you'll have to pay around $18 to go downtown.

Car

Considering Fairbanks' noncentralized streetscape, as well as the worthwhile drives beyond town, you'll likely want a vehicle while you're here. If you don't have your own there are lots of rental options to choose from, including the national franchises at the airport. Of the companies listed here, the last two are probably the only ones in town that will allow their cars on gravel highways, such as the Steese, Elliott and Dalton.

Aurora Rental Car (Map p355; ☎ 459-7033, 800-849-7033; 1000 Cadillac Court), located at the intersection of Danby and Johansen Expressway, charges $35 a day for a compact with unlimited mileage.

Arctic Rent-A-Car (Map p355; ☎ 479-8044; www.arcticrentacar.com; 4500 Dale Rd), near the airport, rents out compacts for around $50 a day with 200 free miles, 30¢ a mile after that, and charges a $189 drop-off fee for a one-way rental between Anchorage and Fairbanks.

Dalton Highway Auto Rentals (Map p355; ☎ 474-3530; www.daltonhighway.com; Fairbanks International Airport) rents vehicles tricked out for trips on Alaska's roughest roads. Cars are $139 a day and Jeeps $189 a day, with 250 free miles a day and 35¢ per mile after that.

Go North (Map p355; ☎ 479-7272, 866-236-7272; www.gonorthalaska.com; 3500 Davis Rd) has gravel-road-ready SUVs for $114 per day with unlimited miles, or camper-equipped pickups from $150 per day.

Public Transportation

The **Metropolitan Area Commuter Service** (MACS; ☎ 459-1011; www.co.fairbanks.ak.us/transportation) provides a local bus service in the Fairbanks area from around 6:30am to 7:30pm Monday to Friday, with limited service on Saturday and none on Sunday. **Transit Park** (Map p357; cnr Cushman St & 5th Ave) is the system's central

---

DETOUR: NORTH POLE

Well, it *seemed* like a good idea: back in the 1940s, a development corporation bought up a sleepy homestead southeast of Fairbanks and, in a bid to attract toy manufacturers, named it North Pole. Though the Fortune 500 companies never came knocking, a steady stream of smirking tourists and their starry-eyed kids have been wandering through ever since.

Today this community of 1500 souls is 15 minutes (12 miles) south of Fairbanks on the Richardson Hwy. It would be a forgettable clutch of churches and fast-food franchises save for its name and its year-round devotion to the Yuletide. Here you'll find holiday decorations and trimmings glimmering beneath the midnight sun. You can wander down Mistletoe Lane, do your wash at Santa's Suds Laundromat, or sleep in the shadow of a 45ft-tall Kris Kringle at **Santaland RV Park** (☎ 488-9123, 888-488-9123; www.santalandrv.com; campsites/RV sites $17/26). The schtick really kicks in during December, when radio stations from around the world call City Hall with disc jockeys asking what the temperature is, or if 'Santa Claus really lives there.' And at the **North Pole Post Office** (325 S Santa Claus Lane) hundreds of thousands of letters arrive annually simply addressed to 'Santa Claus, North Pole, Alaska.'

The town's biggest attraction is **Santa Claus House** (☎ 488-2200, 800-588-4078; www.santaclaushouse.com; 101 St Nicholas Dr off Richardson Hwy; ☉ 8am-8pm), between the North Pole exits. The sprawling barnlike store holds endless aisles of Christmas ornaments and toys, a live Santa to listen to your Christmas wishes, a giant statue of Santa, and the 'North Pole' – a candy-striped post.

---

hub – all six bus routes stop here. The three lines of most interest to travelers are the Yellow Line, which goes to the airport; the Blue Line, which runs to the library, Pioneer Park and the university; and the Red Line, which goes from the hospital on the south side of Airport Way to downtown, then out to the university via College Rd. The fare on all routes is $1.50, or you can purchase an unlimited day pass for $3.

Taxi

Cabs charge $2.70 per mile, adding up in 10¢ increments. Try **Alaska Cab** (☎ 455-7777), **Eagle Cab** (☎ 455-5555) or **Fairbanks Taxi** (☎ 452-3535).

AROUND FAIRBANKS

ESTER

pop 1811

Seven miles southwest of Fairbanks on the George Parks Hwy is the so-called 'Peoples Republic of Ester' – a scattering of back-road cabins that are home to professors, artists and other off-beat folks all united, it seems, in their desire to prevent their town from being swallowed up by Fairbanks. Ester was established in 1906, when miners made a sizable gold strike at Ester Creek. Soon this was a thriving community of 15,000, with three hotels and five saloons. The town came back to life in the 1920s when the Fairbanks

Exploration Company began a large-scale mining operation. Most of Ester's historical buildings date from that era and were either built by the company or moved from Fox, just a few miles north of Fairbanks.

Gold mining still takes place in the hills surrounding Ester, but the town is best known as the home of Ester Gold Camp and its Malemute Saloon. The restored mess hall and bunkhouse from the mining camp have become a regular stop for every tour bus out of Fairbanks. An evening here can be enjoyable; before then, there's very little to do.

Sleeping & Eating

Ester Gold Camp (☎ 479-2500, 800-676-6925; www.akvisit.com/ester.html; s/d $65/76, campsites/RV sites $10/15) An old miners' bunkhouse, it has minimalist and well-worn rooms that share a bathroom with their neighbor; camping is also available. Dinner is an all-you-can-eat feast, served dining-hall-fashion in a room with hardwood floors and mining antiques. The regular buffet is excellent and includes halibut, chicken, reindeer stew, corn on the cob and great biscuits, among other things. The price is $19, or $30 with crab.

Entertainment

Malemute Saloon Show (☎ 479-2500, 800-676-6925; www.akvisit.com/malemute.html; adult/child $15/7.50) This show takes place in one of those classic Alaskan bars: sawdust on the floors, junk –

er, excuse me – mining artifacts in the rafters, and patrons tossing peanut shells everywhere. The stage show, which combines skits, songs, Robert Service poetry and tunes from the Sawdust String Band, is one of the funniest in Alaska. Show time is 9pm nightly. For $2, bus transportation to and from major Fairbanks hotels is available.

Blue Loon (☎ 457-5666; www.theblueloon.com; Mile 352.5 George Parks Hwy) One of the Fairbanks area's most popular nightspots, with live bands and DJs, dancing, food and lots of good beer.

CHENA HOT SPRINGS ROAD

This fireweed-lined, forest-flanked corridor parallels the languid Chena River 56 miles east off the Steese Hwy to the Chena Hot Springs Resort, the closest to Fairbanks and also the most developed. The road is paved and in good condition. From Mile 26 to Mile 51 it passes through Chena River State Recreation Area, a 397-sq-mile preserve encompassing the river valley and nearby alpine areas and has some of the Fairbanks area's best hiking, canoeing and fishing.

Activities
PADDLING

With no whitewater and comparatively few other hazards, the peaceful Chena River offers a variety of day and multiday canoeing possibilities in the area, with access points all along Chena Hot Springs Rd. For more details on paddling here, see p84.

HIKING

The 15-mile **Granite Tors Trail** loop provides access into an alpine area with unusual tors: isolated pinnacles of granite rising out of the tundra.

The first set is 6 miles from the trailhead but the best group lies 2 miles further along the trail. The entire trail is a five- to eight-hour trek gaining 2700ft in elevation, with a free-use shelter midway. The trailhead is in the Tors Trail State Campground, at Mile 39 of the Chena Hot Springs Rd.

Angel Rocks Trail is a 3.5-mile loop trail that leads to Angel Rocks: large granite outcroppings near the north boundary of Chena River State Recreation Area. It's a moderate day's hike; the elevation gain is 900ft and the rocks are less than 2 miles from the road. The trail is also the first leg of the Angel Rocks–Chena Hot Springs Traverse, a more difficult 8.3-mile trek that ends at the Chena Hot Springs Resort, at the end of Chena Hot Springs Rd. Roughly halfway along the traverse is a free-use shelter.

The posted trailhead for Angel Rocks is just south of a rest area at Mile 49 of the Chena Hot Springs Rd. The lower trailhead for the Chena Dome Trail is practically across the street.

The upper trailhead for the **Chena Dome Trail** (p72) is at Mile 50.5 of Chena Hot Springs Rd. The trail follows the ridge for almost 30 miles in a loop around the Angel Creek drainage area; the first 3 miles to the tree line make an excellent day hike.

FAIRBANKS & AROUND

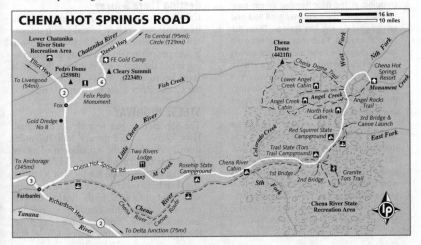

CHENA HOT SPRINGS ROAD

Sleeping & Eating

Chena Hot Springs Rd offers a number of sleeping options, including three popular state-run campgrounds and seven public-use cabins. Two of the cabins are on the road while the rest are accessible via (often very wet) hikes. The cabins vary in size, sleeping between four and nine people, and can be reserved via the **Alaska Division of Parks** (☎ 451-2705; www.alaskastateparks.org).

Rosehip State Campground (Mile 27 Chena Hot Springs Rd; sites $10) Has a nature trail and 36 well-treed, well-spaced sites, some right on the riverbank.

Tors Trail State Campground (Mile 39.5 Chena Hot Springs Rd; sites $10) Twenty-four sites in a stand of spruce, with a canoe launch on the Chena River. Across the highway is the trailhead for the Granite Tors Trail.

Red Squirrel State Campground (Mile 42.8 Chena Hot Springs Rd; sites $10) With ad-hoc sites in a grassy area overlooking a placid pond, this is the least appealing of the area's campgrounds.

Lower Angel Creek Cabin (per night $25) This place is 3.6 miles along an ATV trail from Mile 50.5 of Chena Hot Springs Rd.

Chena River Cabin (Mile 32.2 Chena Hot Springs Rd; per night $40) A newer, road-accessible cabin in a stand of spruce and birch overlooking the river.

HOT SPRINGS NEAR FAIRBANKS

Back when Alaskan gold prospectors were stooping in the near-freezing creeks panning for gold, the Fairbanks area had one saving grace – the hot springs. There are several around Fairbanks, and all were quickly discovered and used by the miners as a brief escape from Alaska's ice and cold. Today, the same mineral water, ranging in temperature from 120°F to 150°F, soothes the aches and pains of freezing travelers and sore hikers passing through.

The hot springs include Chena Hot Springs, 56 miles east of Fairbanks; Circle Hot Springs (closed at the time of writing), 135 miles northeast of Fairbanks on the Steese Hwy; Tolovana Hot Springs, 100 miles west of Fairbanks on the Elliot Hwy; Hutlinana Warm Springs, 129 miles west of Fairbanks on the Elliott Hwy; and Manley Hot Springs, at the end of the Elliott Hwy.

North Fork Cabin (Mile 47.7 Chena Hot Springs Rd; per night $40) Further down the road, it also has access to the river.

Chena Hot Springs Resort (☎ 451-8104, 800-478-4681; www.chenahotsprings.com; Mile 56.6 Chena Hot Springs Rd; campsites & RV sites $20, r $120-220, cabins & yurts with outhouse $65-200) Don't be put off by the word 'resort' – there's nothing snobby about this come-as-you-are complex at the end of Chena Hot Springs Rd. Its burbling waters were discovered by gold miners in 1905, quickly making it the premier place to soak for residents from booming Fairbanks. Over a century later the place offers something for everyone, from quick dips to multiple days of lodging, meals and amusement. The resort has a pretty good **restaurant** (breakfast $7-10, lunch $9-11, dinner $15-26; ☻ 7am-10pm) and a bar decorated with Yukon Quest memorabilia.

At the heart of a 40-sq-mile geothermal area, the **Chena springs** produce a steady stream of water that, at 156°F, must be cooled before you can even think about bathing in it. The facility has several indoor and outdoor tubs, Jacuzzis and pools, including what amounts to a boulder-ringed artificial lake with a fountain at its center. If you've just come to soak it costs $10 (adult) or $7 (child), open 7am to midnight. Other activities include mountain biking, hiking, horseback riding, and fishing the local streams for grayling. Guided activities are available. In winter, this is one of the best places in the world to view the aurora.

Getting There & Away

Call the Chena Hot Springs Resort to book its shuttle-van service; round-trip transportation from Fairbanks is $90 for one person, or $45 per person for two or more. Hitchhiking is not the grand effort it is on the Elliott Hwy, because of the heavy summer usage of the Chena River State Recreation Area.

STEESE HIGHWAY

The superscenic but severely lonely Steese Hwy follows an old miners' trail 162 miles from Fairbanks to the Athabascan village of Circle, on the Yukon River. This hilly and winding road is paved for the first 53 miles, and then has a good gravel base to the mining settlement of Central. In the final 30 miles it narrows and becomes considerably rougher and more twisty. While an interesting drive, the route's main attraction – Circle Hot

Springs – was closed at the time of research. If it doesn't reopen, this trip may not be worth the trouble; inquire at the Log Cabin Visitor Information Center (p356) in Fairbanks.

The Steese Hwy starts at the junction of Airport Way and the Richardson Hwy. From there it passes the beginning of Chena Hot Springs Rd at Mile 4.6, and then the Elliott Hwy at Mile 11, near Fox. The center of Fairbanks Mining District, Fox has a few worthwhile watering holes, eateries and attractions.

Howling Dog Saloon (Mile 11 Old Steese Hwy) This saloon serves ales and lagers from the Silver Gulch Brewery (across the road), and hosts local and out-of-town bands.

Turtle Club (☎ 457-3883; Mile 10 Old Steese Hwy; dinner $18-30; ☷ 6-10pm Mon-Sat, 5-9pm Sun) This place has a roadhouse atmosphere and is reputed for its prime rib.

For information on the Gold Dredge No 8, see p362.

Fox to Central

On the Steese Hwy, the **Felix Pedro Monument** (Mile 16.6 Steese Hwy) commemorates the miner whose gold strike gave birth to Fairbanks. The stream across the highway – now known as Pedro Creek – is where it all happened. You'll likely see amateur goldpanners there 'looking for color.'

At Mile 27.9 take a sharp turn up a hill to reach the **FE Gold Camp** (☎ 389-2414; Mile 27.9 Steese Hwy; sandwiches $7-11, dinner $12-24; r $55, dm $25; ☷ 6am-9pm), a national historic site with a charmingly rustic bar and restaurant.

There are also hostel-style accommodations, with quaint shared bathrooms. The camp was built in 1925 for the dredging that went on from 1927 to 1957 and removed an estimated $70 million in gold (at yesterday's prices).

A few miles beyond, the landscape opens up, revealing expansive vistas as well as evidence of recent forest-fire activity. **Upper Chatanika River State Recreation Area** (Mile 39 Steese Hwy; sites $10) is the first public campground along the Steese and has 24 sites, some right on the riverbank. Have your bug dope handy – this is mosquito country. People with canoes can launch their boats here, and the fishing for grayling is good.

Cripple Creek BLM Campground (Mile 60 Steese Hwy; walk-in sites/drive-up sites $3/6), the next campground along, has 18 sites (including six

walk-in sites with no vehicle access), tables, water and a nearby nature trail. It's the uppermost access point to the Chatanika River canoe route.

Access points for the **Pinnell Mountain Trail** are at Mile 85.6 and Mile 107 of the Steese Hwy. The first trailhead is Twelvemile Summit, which offers remarkable alpine views and is often snowy well into June. Even if you have no desire to undertake the three-day trek, the first 2 miles is an easy climb past unusual rock formations.

The **Birch Creek canoe route** begins at Mile 94 of the Steese Hwy, where a short road leads down to a canoe launch on the creek. The wilderness trip is a 140-mile paddle to the exit point, at Mile 147 of the highway. The overall rating of the river is Class II, but there are some Class III and Class IV parts that require lining your canoe.

Eagle Summit (Mile 107 Steese Hwy), 3624ft in elevation, has a parking area for the second trailhead of the Pinnell Mountain Trail. A climb of less than a mile leads to the mountaintop, the highest point along the Steese Hwy and a place where the midnight sun can be observed skimming the horizon around the summer solstice. On a clear day, summiting here can feel like ascending to heaven. The peak is also near a caribou migration route.

Central

pop 102

At Mile 127.5 the Steese Hwy reaches Central, where pavement briefly takes over. Though the settlement once offered a range of visitor services, the closure of the hot springs down the road has resulted in fewer tourist options here. Locals are keeping their fingers crossed the springs will reopen.

HISTORY

Originally referred to on maps as Central House, the town began as a supply stop on the trail from Circle City to the surrounding creeks of the Circle Mining District. Central became a town in the 1930s, thanks largely to the Steese Hwy, which was built in 1927. Then in the late 1970s and early 1980s the town experienced something of a second gold rush.

With the price of the metal bouncing between $300 and $400 an ounce, miners were suddenly making a fortune sluicing the streams. One miner alone, Jim Regan, recovered 26,000 ounces of gold from the Crooked Creek area between 1979 and 1986. Even more interesting was a diamond unearthed by miners in 1982. Nicknamed Arctic Ice, it was the first ever discovered in Alaska.

Although mining activity has dwindled in recent years and most efforts are now small family operations, the miners' distrust of anybody or any agency threatening their right to make a living is still evident throughout town, especially at the bars.

Also, if you're keen to try some panning yourself, avoid claim-jumping at all costs. The safest places are wherever the Steese Hwy crosses a creek or stream, since the road is public land.

SIGHTS & ACTIVITIES

One of the best museums of any small Alaskan town is the **Circle District Historical Society Museum** (☎ 520-1893; Mile 127.5 Steese Hwy; admission $1; ☒ noon-5pm) in Central. Established in 1984, the main portion of the museum is a large log lodge that houses a miner's cabin, exhibits on early mining equipment and dog-team freight and mail hauling, and the Yukon Press – the first printing press north of Juneau, which produced Interior Alaska's first newspaper.

The most interesting display is the museum's collection of gold nuggets and gold flakes recovered and donated by local miners. This display, more than anything else, will help you understand why they continue to tear away at the hills and streams in an effort to find the precious metal.

Outside in a large barn is a collection of dog sleds and other large artifacts, including an unusual covered wagon – covered with metal, not cloth.

The museum also has a small video area with tapes on mining and a variety of other topics, a gift shop and a visitor information area.

EATING & DRINKING

At the time of writing, just about the only culinary option in Central was the unappealing **Steese Roadhouse** (☎ 520-5800; breakfast $6-9, lunch $6-9, dinner $13-15; ☒ 8am-10pm Mon-Thu, 8am-midnight Fri & Sat, 8am-8pm Sun), where, despite half-hearted service, locals crowd the bar to bad-mouth the government.

Circle

pop 99

Beyond Central, in what may be Alaska's *least* scenic stretch of road, the Steese Hwy passes the exit point of the Birch Creek canoe route at Mile 147 and heads to Circle (Mile 162). Much of this area is low-lying, burned-over, muddy and mosquito-ridden. Also, the road is almost humorously circuitous: at times, you'll be driving through your own dust.

Circle itself is an Alaska-Native village on the banks of the broad Yukon River. Before the Dalton Hwy opened it was the northernmost point you could drive to – as a large sign in the center of town still proclaims.

Though 50 miles south of the Arctic Circle, miners who established the town in 1896 thought they were near the imaginary line and gave Circle its present name. After gold was discovered in Birch Creek, Circle became a bustling town of 1200 with two theaters, a music hall, eight dance halls and 28 saloons. It was known as the 'largest log-cabin city in the world' until the Klondike gold rush (1897–98) reduced its population and the river gobbled up much of the original townscape.

Today Circle has zero attractions, but that's OK: you can spend an hour or two wandering past the shacks and shanties, appreciating the fish wheels in folks' backyards and the distinctive flat-bottomed river skiffs used to negotiate the Yukon. You may even find someone to take you on the river; look for signs or ask at the **Yukon Trading Post** (☎ 773-1217; ☒ 10am-noon & 3-6pm), the only place in town to get meals or alcohol.

At the boat-ramp where the Steese Hwy meets the river there's ostensibly a public **campground** (sites $5), but it's overgrown and, worse, a party spot for people from downriver villages. For several years an ambitious but unfinished log motel has stood nearby. Basic groceries, snacks and gas for your return trip can be gotten just up the road at the **HC Company Store** (☎ 773-1222).

Getting There & Away

Hitchhiking is more difficult on the Steese Hwy than on Chena Hot Springs Rd, though people this far north are good about stopping. Still, you have to consider your time schedule and patience level before attempting this road.

You can try renting a vehicle in Fairbanks, but you'll have to go with a company that permits driving on gravel roads (see p367). If you want to fly, **Warbelow's Air Ventures** (☎ 474-0518, 800-478-0812; www.warbelows.com), in Fairbanks, has regular flights to Circle for $196 round trip.

ELLIOT HIGHWAY

From the crossroad with the Steese Hwy at Fox, just north of Fairbanks, the Elliott Hwy extends 152 miles north and then west to Manley Hot Springs, a small settlement near the Tanana River.

The first half is paved, the rest is gravel, and there's no gas and few services until you reach the end. Diversions along the way are comparatively few, but the leisurely, scenic drive, coupled with the disarming charms of Manley Hot Springs, make it a worthwhile one- or two-day road trip.

Lower Chatanika River State Recreation Area (Mile 11 Elliott Hwy) is a 570-acre park offering fishing, boating and camping opportunities along the Chatanika River. The area has two free, informal campgrounds: **Whitefish** and **Olnes Pond**.

At Mile 28 of the Elliott Hwy is the Wickersham Dome Trailhead parking lot and an information box. From here, trails lead to Borealis-Le Fevre's and Lee's cabins. **Lee's Cabin** (Sun-Thu/Fri & Sat $20/25) is a 7-mile hike in and has a large picture window overlooking the White Mountains and a loft that comfortably sleeps eight. **Borealis-Le Fevre Cabin** (Sun-Thu/Fri & Sat $20/25) is a 19-mile hike over the Summit Trail. Reserve through the **Bureau of Land Management office** (BLM; ☎ 474-2251) in Fairbanks.

At Mile 57, where a bridge crosses the Tolovana River, there's an old BLM campground that's no longer maintained, but there's still a turnoff here. The fishing here is good for grayling and northern pike, though the mosquitoes are of legendary proportions. Nearby is the start of the **Colorado Creek Trail** to Windy Gap BLM Cabin. Check with the BLM office in Fairbanks about use of the cabin during the summer.

Off Mile 62, 10 miles before the junction with the Dalton Hwy, a 500ft spur leads from the road to **Fred Blixt Cabin** (Sun-Thu/Fri & Sat $20/25). This public-use cabin should be reserved in advance through the BLM office in Fairbanks.

Livengood (*lye*-ven-good), 2 miles east of the highway at Mile 71, has no services and is little more than a scattering of log shanties. Here, the Elliott Hwy swings west and in 2 miles, at the junction of the Dalton Hwy, pavement ends and the road becomes a rutted, rocky lane. Traffic evaporates and until Manley Hot Springs you may not see another vehicle.

In short order the Elliot Hwy ascends to a high subalpine ridge, which it follows for miles, and on clear days affords views of Mt McKinley to the south.

The open country invites off-road hiking, and the breeze is often strong enough to keep mosquitoes at bay.

The rustic, privately-managed **Tolovana Hot Springs** (☎ 455-6706; www.mosquitonet.com/~tolovana; cabins $30-120) can be accessed via a taxing 11-mile overland hike south from Mile 93. Facilities consist of two cedar tubs bubbling with 125°F to 145°F water, plus, a quarter mile up the valley, two cedar cabins that must be reserved in advance. The trailhead isn't signposted; contact the managers for directions.

At Mile 110 is the paved 11-mile road to the small Athabascan village of **Minto** (population 207), which isn't known for welcoming strangers.

Beyond Minto, the Elliot Hwy briefly becomes winding and hilly, and then suddenly, at Mile 120, there's chip-sealing for the next 17 miles. Hutlinana Creek is reached at Mile 129, and a quarter mile east of the bridge is an 8-mile creekside trail to **Hutlinana Warm Springs**, an undeveloped thermal area with a 3ft-deep pool.

The springs are visited mainly in winter; in summer, the buggy bushwhack seems uninviting.

From the bridge it's another 23 miles southwest to Manley Hot Springs.

Manley Hot Springs
pop 73

The town of Manley Hot Springs may be one of the loveliest discoveries you'll make in Alaska. At the end of a long, lonely road, here's a gem of a town, full of friendly folks, well-kept log homes and luxuriant gardens. Located between Hot Springs Slough and the Tanana River, the community was first homesteaded in 1902 by JF Karshner, just as the US Army Signal Corps arrived to put in a telegraph station. A few years later, as the place boomed with miners from the nearby Eureka and Tofty districts, Frank Manley arrived and built a four-story hotel. Most of the miners are gone now, but Manley's name – and the spirit of an earlier era – remains. In modern times the town has been a hotbed of high-level dog-mushing: champs like Charlie Boulding, Joe Redington Jr and four-time Iditarod winner Susan Butcher have all lived here.

Just before crossing the slough you pass the town's namesake **hot springs** (☎ 672-3231, 672-3171; admission $5; ⊙ 24hr). Privately owned by famously hospitable Chuck and Gladys Dart, bathing happens within a huge, thermal-heated greenhouse that's a veritable Babylonian garden of grapes, Asian pears and hibiscus flowers.

Deep in this jungle are three spring-fed concrete tubs, each burbling at different temperatures. Pay your money, hose yourself down, pluck some fruit and soak away in this deliriously un-Alaskan setting.

Across the slough and 3 miles beyond the village is the broad Tanana River, just upstream from its confluence with the Yukon. Frank Gurtler of **Manley Boat Charters** (☎ 672-3271; fishing charters per hr $60, tours per person per hr $15) can take you to catch salmon, char and grayling, or just show you the sights along the waterway.

SLEEPING & EATING

Manley Roadhouse (☎ 672-3161; r with/without bath $90-125/65; breakfast $7-10, lunch mains $7-11, dinner mains $11-22; ⊙ 8am-10pm) Facing the slough, this antique-strewn, century-old establishment has clean, uncomplicated rooms and is the social center of town. The bar boasts an impressive array of beers while the restaurant offers locally caught king salmon.

Cabin (☎ 672-3231, 672-3171; cabin $50) If the roadhouse doesn't suit, the Darts offer a charmingly tumbledown cabin with the warm creek gurgling past the back door.

Public campground (sites $5) The town also has a slough-front campground just past the bridge. Pay at the roadhouse.

Manley Trading Post (☎ 762-3221; ⊙ 10am-5pm) You will find groceries, gas, liquor and the post office here.

Getting There & Away

With so little traffic on Elliot Hwy, hitching is ill-advised – though if someone *does* come along, they'll likely take pity on you. Alternatively, you can rent a vehicle in Fairbanks (p367), but you'll have to go with a company that permits driving on gravel roads. Finally, **Warbelow's Air Ventures** (☎ 474-0518, 800-478-0812; www.warbelows.com), in Fairbanks, has regular flights to Manley Hot Springs for $140 round-trip.

The Bush

For most Alaskans, the Bush is mythic and it's hard to pin down. Some say it's wherever roads don't reach; others say that it's 'Indian Country,' where Alaska Natives outnumber Whites. Many think of it as 'out there' – an amorphous wild vastness.

It's enough to know the Bush is a world apart. The state's most pristine wilderness lies here, in parks and preserves without tourist infrastructure. Traditional villages, where subsistence is a means of survival, and homesteads, with ingenious residents, lie hidden across the region.

But despite this purity and exoticism, only a trickle of tourists makes it to the Bush. Cost, more than mountains or rivers, isolates the place. With few exceptions, flying is the only way to travel into the area. Once here, there are few facilities and most are expensive.

We've split the Bush into two sections: Western Alaska and Arctic Alaska. The former is largely a treeless, mountainous and wetland expanse, bordered by the Bering Sea. The most visited place is Nome, with a gold-rush legacy, plus a network of scenic gravel highways that offer unparalleled access to the backcountry. Arctic Alaska has the Brooks Range and the tundra of the North Slope, lands of nightless summers and dayless winters. Alaska's northernmost village, Barrow, draws a few tourists, while intrepid motorists hit the Dalton Hwy and backpackers go to Gates of the Arctic National Park and Preserve, an intriguing place for a wilderness adventure that's slowly becoming more accessible and more affordable.

HIGHLIGHTS

- **Best road trip, even if it kills your car** (p386) – driving along the jarring Dalton Highway, Alaska's most scenic, surreal auto route

- **Best way to get rich and tan** (p379) – sifting through the sands of Nome's Golden Sands Beach, which still produce the occasional glittering nugget

- **Best place to really rough it** (p391) – tackling the Gates of the Arctic National Park, where there are no beaten paths to peel away from

- **Most otherworldly destination** (p394) – visiting frigid, fascinating Barrow will make other Alaskan towns seem boringly all-American

- **Most northerly nightmare** (p389) – exploring Deadhorse, a postapocalyptic petroleum camp so ugly that it's intriguing

Barrow ★
Deadhorse ★
Gates of the Arctic National Park ★   ★ Dalton Hwy
Golden Sands Beach ★

THE BUSH

| ■ AREA CODE: ☎ 907 | ■ POPULATION: 36,000 | ■ ELEVATION: MT MICHELSON 8855FT |

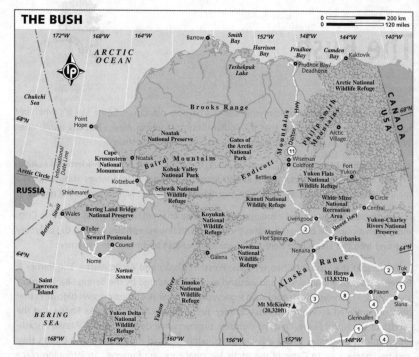

THE BUSH

Climate

Due to its geographical diversity, the Bush is a land of many climates. In inland areas, winter holds sway from mid-September to early May, with ceaseless weeks of clear skies, negligible humidity and temperatures colder than anywhere else in America. Alaska's all-time low, minus 80°F, happened at Prospect Creek Camp, just off the Dalton Hwy. Closer to the ocean, winter lingers even longer but is incrementally less chilly.

During the brief summer, visitors to the Bush should be prepared for anything. Barrow and Prudhoe Bay may demand a parka; July highs there often don't hit 40°F. Along the Dalton Hwy and around Nome, the weather is famously variable. Intense heat – stoked by the unsetting sun – can be as much a concern as cold.

History

The history of the Bush is largely the history of Alaska Natives. By their own accounts, they've been here since the beginning. Archeologists say it's been slightly less long; perhaps 6000 years for the ancestors of today's Athabascans, and about 3000 years for the Inupiat, Yup'ik and Aleut. Either way, they displayed remarkable ingenuity and endurance, thriving as fishermen, hunters and gatherers until Europeans arrived.

That happened in the 1800s, with traders and missionaries setting up shop in numerous communities along the Western Alaska coast, and with whalers entering the Bering Sea in midcentury, expanding into the Arctic Ocean, and virtually decimating the bowhead whale population by 1912. The most climactic event in the Bush, however, was the gold rush at Nome, trigged in 1898 by the 'Three Lucky Swedes' (p378). The stampede drew 20,000 people to the Seward Peninsula, giving the region, ever so briefly, the most populous town in Alaska. Nome remains the only significant non-Native community in the Bush.

Over the past century, progress in transportation, communications and social services further transformed the region. 'Bush planes' made the area relatively accessible, and towns like Barrow, Kotzebue, Nome and Bethel became commercial hubs, giving services to the smaller villages in their orbit. Political and legal battles brought more schools and better healthcare, and the 1971 *Alaska Native Claims Settlement Act* provided the region with some jobs. Today, anywhere you go in the Bush you'll find residents engaged in a fine balancing act – coping with the challenges of the 21st century, while at the same time struggling to keep their millennia-old values, practises and links to the land.

National & State Parks

The Bush has several national parks and preserves, but generally they can't be reached by car, are devoid of visitor services and are for hearty adventurers only. Most famous is Gates of the Arctic National Park (p391), spanning the spires of the Brooks Range and offering spectacular hiking and paddling. Near Kotzebue is Kobuk Valley National Park, known for the Great Kobuk Sand Dunes and the oft-paddled Kobuk River (p385). The mountain-ringed Noatak National Preserve is just to the north of there, with the quite popular Noatak River (p385). And to the southwest, between Nome and Kotzebue, is Bering Land Bridge National Preserve, which commemorates the peopling of the Americas and is experienced largely by visitors to Serpentine Hot Springs (p384).

Getting There & Around

The Bush is, almost by definition, roadless. You can drive (or be driven) up the Dalton Hwy (p390), but everywhere else is fly-in only. Alaska Airlines (p381) is the main carrier connecting urban Alaska to Bush hubs like Nome, Kotzebue and Barrow; from there, regional airlines fly to smaller villages or provide air-taxi service into the wilderness. In Nome, an insular road network also reaches out to a few surrounding destinations.

WESTERN ALASKA

NOME

☎ 907 / pop 3473

Nome, in so many ways, is the Alaskan archetype: a rough-hewn, fun-loving, undying Wild West ghost town, thriving at the uttermost edge of the planet. With America's biggest concentration of Whites north of the

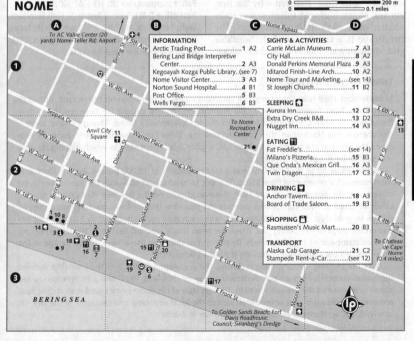

NOME

0 _____ 200 m
0 _____ 0.1 miles

Nome Bypass

INFORMATION
Arctic Trading Post.................1 A2
Bering Land Bridge Interpretive
  Center.................................2 A3
Kegoayah Kozga Public Library..(see 7)
Nome Visitor Center................3 A3
Norton Sound Hospital............4 B1
Post Office..............................5 B3
Wells Fargo............................6 B3

SIGHTS & ACTIVITIES
Carrie McLain Museum.............7 A3
City Hall.................................8 A2
Donald Perkins Memorial Plaza .9 A3
Iditarod Finish-Line Arch........10 A2
Nome Tour and Marketing.....(see 14)
St Joseph Church...................11 B2

SLEEPING
Aurora Inn............................12 C3
Extra Dry Creek B&B..............13 D2
Nugget Inn...........................14 A3

EATING
Fat Freddie's.......................(see 14)
Milano's Pizzeria..................15 B3
Que Onda's Mexican Grill.......16 A3
Twin Dragon........................17 C3

DRINKING
Anchor Tavern.....................18 A3
Board of Trade Saloon...........19 B3

SHOPPING
Rasmussen's Music Mart........20 B3

TRANSPORT
Alaska Cab Garage.................21 C2
Stampede Rent-a-Car...........(see 12)

To AC Value Center (20 yards) Nome-Teller Rd; Airport

W 5th Ave
Bering St
W 4th Ave
Seppala Dr
Alley Way
C St
W 2nd Ave
W 1st Ave
Front St

Anvil City Square
Warren Place
W 3rd Ave
Division St
King's Place
W 2nd Ave
Lanes Way
Federal Way
Spokane Ave

To Nome Recreation Center

E 6th Ave
E 5th Ave
E 3rd Ave
E 4th Ave
E St
F St

Steadman St
E 1st Ave
Moore Way

To Chateau de Cape Nome (0.4 miles)

E Front St

BERING SEA

To Golden Sands Beach; Fort Davis Roadhouse; Council; Swanberg's Dredge

THE BUSH

tree line, the town is at once familiar and exotic: on one hand, with paved streets, grassy public squares, many saloons (more than in the rest of Bush Alaska combined) and palpable gold-rush history, it has the infrastructure like the rural West.

On the flipside, there's the setting: hard against the ice-choked Bering Sea, cut off from the continental road system, closer to Siberia than to Anchorage, and patrolled by polar creatures like musk oxen and reindeer.

Of the three major towns in the Bush, Nome, Kotzebue and Barrow, Nome is the most affordable and best setup for travelers. It has a range of accommodations, from top-notch hotels to free camping on the beach, a fine visitors center, and friendly watering holes in which to meet the locals. It lacks the vibrant aboriginal culture of Kotzebue and Barrow, but Nome has something else the other two don't: roads. No trip to Nome would be complete without renting a pickup truck to see the remarkable outlying region.

Orientation & Information

Watched over by 1062ft Anvil Mountain and washed – sometimes battered – by the Bering Sea, Nome is among the most scenically situated of Alaska's Bush communities. The streetscape is a compact, orderly, walkable grid, stretching six blocks from the boulder-reinforced waterfront back into the tundra, and reaching about 18 blocks from the harbor at the western edge of town to the famed Golden Sands beach in the east. Most visitor-oriented businesses are concentrated along a half-dozen blocks of the remarkably broad Front St, overlooking the cold, grey ocean.

Arctic Trading Post (☎ 443-2686; 67 Front St; ☽ 7:30am-10pm) Has a good selection of books on the region and the Iditarod.

Bering Land Bridge Interpretive Center (☎ 443-2522; 179 Front St; ☽ 8am-5pm Mon-Fri) Diagonally across from the visitors center, in the Sitnasuak Native Corporation Building. This NPS center is the best place to go for information on hiking, fishing and wildlife in the area.

Emergency (☎ 911)

Kegoayah Kozga Public Library (☎ 443-6627; 223 Front St; ☽ noon-8pm Mon-Thu, to 6pm Fri & Sat) Has been in operation since 1902, offers free Internet access and includes a section of rare and 1st-edition books.

Nome Visitor Center (☎ 443-6624; www.nomealaska .org; 301 Front St; ☽ 9am-9pm) Make this your first stop in Nome; the extremely helpful staff will load you with brochures.

Norton Sound Hospital (☎ 443-3311; cnr 5th Ave & Bering St) There is a 19-bed facility with a 24-hour emergency medical service as well as a pharmacy.

Police (nonemergency ☎ 443-5262; 500 Bering St)

Post office (240 E Front St) Next to the Wells Fargo Bank.

Wells Fargo (☎ 443-7688; 109A Front St) In the historic Miner's and Merchant's Bank Building (dating from 1904); has an ATM accessible round-the-clock.

THREE LUCKY SWEDES

In September 1898 Jafet Lindeberg, Erik Lindblom and John Brynteson hit the jackpot. Although newcomers from Scandinavia with only eight weeks' mining experience between them, they found gold in Anvil Creek, just a few miles outside present-day Nome. Though one of them – Lindeberg – was Norwegian, they were dubbed the 'Three Lucky Swedes.' Their discovery triggered the greatest stampede on Alaskan soil, a 'poor man's gold rush' in which digging for gold was said to be easier than stealing it.

By the following year, 'Anvil City' was a tent metropolis of 10,000 people. Among them was John Hummel, a prospector from Idaho. Too sick to head inland to search the tundra creeks, he stayed near the ocean and, in July 1899, discovered gold on the beaches. News of the 'golden sands' resulted in 2000 stampeders working the shoreline that summer, panning more than $1 million in gold dust. It was a banner year, with each man recovering $20 to $100 of gold per day on the edge of the Bering Sea. When the news finally reached Seattle in 1900, it set off yet another stampede of hopeful miners. By the end of that year there were 20,000 people in the town that is now called Nome, making it Alaska's largest city.

Over the ensuing century, mining slowed, the population fizzled and the township suffered numerous disasters. Fires all but destroyed Nome in 1905 and 1934, and a violent Bering Sea storm overpowered the sea walls in 1974. Though little of the community's gold-rush architecture remains and mining is now almost irrelevant to the local economy, the character of the city has survived. Today, Nome is as colorful as any town in Alaska.

Sights & Activities

CENTRAL NOME

Begin at the Nome Visitor Center (opposite) and pick up a copy of its walking-tour brochure. The center has a dozen albums with historic photos and a few exhibits, including a mounted musk ox. Outside, overlooking the seawall, is the **Donald Perkins Memorial Plaza**, featuring a collection of old mining detritus, including dredge buckets. During Nome's golden heyday there were more than 100 gold dredges in the area, and each one had hundreds of these buckets to scoop up gravel and dirt. Today you'll see the buckets all over town, often used as giant flowerpots. On the seawall near the plaza is a wooden platform that provides views of the Bering Sea and Sledge Island.

Across the street is the Bering Land Bridge Interpretive Center (opposite) in the Sitnasuak Native Corporation Building. The center is dedicated to Beringia, the 1000-mile-wide landmass that linked Alaska and Siberia until about 10,000 years ago. Archaeologists believe that the first people to arrive in Alaska, along with a variety of animals, used this land bridge. The center has displays on mammoths, early Alaska Native culture and reindeer herding, and a series of short videos that are shown on request.

In a lot next to the city hall is the **Iditarod finish-line arch**. The huge wooden structure, a distinctly bent pine tree with burls, is raised over Front St every March in anticipation of the mushers and their dogsled teams ending the 1049-mile race here. The original arch fell apart after the 1999 race and, Nome, in a basically treeless region, sent out a call for help throughout the state to find a new one. The present pine was located near Hope, on the Kenai Peninsula.

To the east of the visitors center on Front St is **Carrie McLain Museum** (☎ 443-2566; 223 Front St; admission free; ✆ 9am-5:30pm) in the basement of the Kegoayah Kozga Public Library. There are displays on Native culture and local reindeer-cultivation efforts, but the focus is the gold rush and Nome's history in the early 20th century. See the preserved body of Fritz the sled dog, one of the leaders of the famed 1925 race to deliver diphtheria serum to Nome, which inspired the Iditarod.

Among the historic buildings listed in the walking tour is **St Joseph Church**. It overlooks Anvil City Sq at Bering St and 3rd Ave. Built in 1901, when there were 30,000 people living in Nome, this huge church was originally located on Front St, and the electrically lit cross at the top of the building was used as a beacon for seamen. By the 1920s the population of the city had plummeted to less than 900 and the Jesuits abandoned the structure. The church was used for storage by a mining company before the city purchased it in 1996, moving it to its present location and restoring it as a multipurpose building. You'll have to admire it from the outside, as it will likely be locked. Also in the square are statues of the Three Lucky Swedes (looking more somber than lucky) plus dozens of dredge buckets, the 'world's largest gold pan' and a grassy expanse just right for picnicking or Frisbee.

GOLDEN SANDS BEACH

A very interesting afternoon can be spent at Nome's Golden Sands Beach, stretching a mile east of town along Front St. At the height of summer a few local children may be seen playing in the 45°F water, and on Memorial Day (in May), more than 100 masochistic residents plunge into the ice-choked waters for the annual Polar Bear Swim.

Usually more numerous than swimmers here are gold prospectors, as the beach is open to recreational mining. Miners will set up camp along the shore and work the sands throughout the summer. The serious miners rig their sluice and dredging equipment on a small pontoon boat and anchor it 100yd offshore to suck up the more productive sand along the bottom. Others set up sluice boxes at the edge of the water. Miners are generally friendly, and occasionally you can even coax one to show you his gold dust and nuggets. If you catch the fever, practically every gift shop and hardware store in town sells black plastic gold pans. As you're panning, think about the visitor who in 1984 and found a 3½in nugget that weighed 1.29oz at the east end of the seawall.

After walking along the beach to Fort Davis Roadhouse (which, sadly, was shuttered and for sale at time of research) return along Front St to see **Swanberg's Gold Dredge** near the Nome Bypass junction. The dredge was in operation until the 1950s before being passed on to the city for its historic value. Near the dredge is a rusty collection of other mining equipment.

HIKING

If you're well prepared and the weather holds, the backcountry surrounding Nome can be a hiker's heaven. Though there are no marked trails in the region, the area's three high-ways offer perfect access into the tundra and mountains. What's more, the lack of trees and big, rolling topography make route-finding fairly simple: just pick a point and go for it. For those who'd like a little more direction, a seven-page list of suggested day hikes is available from the Nome Visitor Center (p378). If you're setting off on anything more than a stroll up the nearest ridgeline, a map is a good idea; topo maps can be purchased at **Rasmussen's Music Mart** (☎ 443-2798; 103 Federal Way; ✆ noon-6pm Mon-Sat), operated by avid local hiker (and former mayor) Leo Rasmussen.

Also providing great info on local trekking is the Bering Land Bridge Interpretive Center (p378). At time of research, they were leading very popular free **guided day hikes** on most Saturdays throughout the summer.

The climb up 1062ft **Anvil Mountain** is the closest hike to Nome and the only one that can be easily pulled off without a car. Follow the Teller Hwy 3.5 miles from town to Glacier Creek Rd, which takes you directly onto the mountain. After the road veers left, look for a smooth route up the slope and commence your climb. It's about one mile round-trip to the summit, ascending through wonderful wildflower patches. At the top you'll find the giant parabolic antennae of the Cold War–era White Alice Communications System, plus great views of town and the ocean as well as the Kigluaik Mountains farther inland.

Tours

Nome Discovery Tours (☎ 443-2814; discover@cgi .net) The most intimate, highly recommended tours run by local raconteur Richard Beneville offer everything from two-hour evening tundra-exploration drives ($40) to full-day excursions to Teller, where you'll drop in on an Inupiat family, or to Council, with fishing along the way ($150).
Nome Tour & Marketing (☎ 443-2651, 877-443-2323; www.nomenuggetinn.com) Based out of the Nugget Inn, this caters mainly to larger package-deal groups, though independents are welcome. It operates three tours daily in the summer, each costing $75. The six-hour history-oriented tour includes gold panning at the Little Creek Mine and a hands-on dog-mushing demonstration, while the four-hour wildlife tour heads out along the highways in search of birds and beasts. The two-hour Alaska Native–culture demonstration focuses on Inupiat hunting, dancing and athletic contests.

Sleeping

Nome tacks on 9% bed and sales taxes to its accommodations.

BUDGET

If the weather's good, sleeping out may be the way to go in Nome. There's free water-front camping on Golden Sands Beach in a mile-long stretch running east from town to the Fort Davis Roadhouse; pitch your tent beside those of miners sifting the sands for glittering nuggets.

Across the road is an outhouse and pavilion in the small public park at Nome By-pass. Showers are available ($5) at the **Nome Recreation Center** (☎ 443-5431; cnr D St & 6th Ave; ✆ 5:30am-10pm Mon-Fri).

Further from town it's unofficially permissible to camp just about anywhere: simply hike away from the road corridor, avoid private property and active mining claims, and clean up after yourself. Also, on the Kougarok Rd is the BLM's (Bureau of Land Management) lovely, free Salmon Lake Campground (p383).

MIDRANGE & TOP END

If you want a roof over your head, the options are all comparatively expensive.

There are a few B&Bs in town, plus hotels ranging from seedy (the Polaris; avoid it!) to semiluxurious.

Chateau de Cape Nome (☎ 443-2083; east end of E 4th Ave; r with/without breakfast $130/100) Spectacularly situated overlooking the tundra on the edge of town, this is Nome's most colorful B&B. The owner, Cussy Kauer, is a descendent of gold rush–era pioneers, and her place is a trove of local history. There's also a live reindeer out back – and plenty of stuffed and mounted beasts inside.

Extra Dry Creek B&B (☎ 443-7615; sbabcock@gci .net; 607 E F St; s/d $100/125) More like a rental apartment than a B&B, this pristine suite (named for an apparently desiccated waterway outside of town), has a full kitchen stocked with breakfast fixings that you prepare yourself.

Aurora Inn (☎ 443-3838, 800-354-4606; www.auro rainnome.com; Front St at Moore Way; d $130-220) There's no question this is Nome's nicest hotel, but is it just a little too nice? With a sauna, laundry facilities and kitchenettes in some rooms, the Aurora has plenty of amenities – but none of the devil-may-care charm of its hometown.

THE BUSH

Nugget Inn (☎ 443-4189, 877-443-2323; 315 Front St; r $129) In the thick of things downtown, the Nugget has 45 smallish rooms, about half with ocean views. Have no fear: the downstairs bar closes at midnight.

Eating

In a town where the Glue Pot is a popular restaurant, you can't have much hope for the culinary scene. And sadly, in 2005 Nome's only fine-dining establishment, the Fort Davis Roadhouse, was out of business – though there's a chance it may reopen.

Fat Freddie's (☎ 443-5899; 306 Front St; breakfast $7-13, lunch $7-14, dinner $19-24; ☼ 6am-10pm) Nome's local café is built right on the breakwater, with great views and lots of chin-wagging locals.

Qué Onda's Mexican Grill (☎ 443-3986; 235 Front St; mains $13-17; ☼ 11am-10pm Mon-Sat, from 4pm Sun) Currently the highest-end place in town. It serves up huge portions of decent south-of-the-border fare, as well as burgers, in a lowlit, saloonesque environment.

Milano's Pizzeria (☎ 443-2924; Front St; pizza $11-33; ☼ 11am-11pm Mon-Sat, from 3pm Sun) Located in the Old Federal Building, it also serves Japanese dinners, Italian mains and burgers.

Twin Dragon (☎ 443-5552; cnr Front & Steadman Sts; lunch $8; ☼ 11am-11pm Mon-Sat, from 3pm Sun) This has good Chinese food. There's a two-person

dinner special for $20 that may be the best-priced meal in town.

AC Value Center (☎ 443-2243; cnr Bering St & Nome Bypass; ☼ 7:30am-9pm Mon-Sat, 10am-7pm Sun) This is the cheap-eats option. The supermarket has a bakery, espresso counter and a deli with ready-to-eat items.

Drinking & Entertainment

Even by Alaskan standards, drinking in Nome is legendary. Among the early bar owners was Wyatt Earp, the gunslinger at the OK Corral (see below). All but two of the bars are clustered around one another on Front St. The **Board of Trade Saloon** (212 Front St), dating back to 1900, claims to be the oldest bar on the Bering Sea and is certainly the most notorious. It's the place to go for late-night live music. For a quieter hangout where you can sit and chat with locals, try **Anchor Tavern** (114 Front St), which has a good selection of beer on tap.

Getting There & Around

Nome is serviced by **Alaska Airlines** (☎ 443-2288, 800-468-2248; www.alaskaair.com), which offers at least three daily flights from Anchorage for about $430. Two of those flights also route through Kotzebue; visiting both Bush communities will cost you around $530. If you want to fly to Nome from Fairbanks,

---

WYATT EARP IN ALASKA

A bit of the Old West found its way to Nome when Wyatt Earp and his wife arrived at the end of the 1890s. Earp was a former marshal and noted gunslinger who teamed up with Doc Holiday to win the famous shootout at the OK Corral in Tombstone, Arizona.

But when Earp heard about the Klondike Gold Rush in 1899, he packed his bags and left Arizona to seek his fortune, though not as a prospector – Earp was above working a rocker box or getting his suits dirty. Rather he headed to Alaska to do what one friend had suggested to him: 'mine the miners.'

While on the road, Earp read about Alaska's new boomtown and quickly switched his destination; after the spring thaw of 1899 he arrived at Nome on a steamer with his wife, Josie. Teaming up with a partner, Earp immediately built the Dexter – the first two-story, wooden structure in what was basically still a tent city full of prospectors. It was Nome's largest and most luxurious saloon, with 12ft ceilings and 12 plush clubrooms upstairs, and was located only a block from 'the Stockade,' the city's red-light district.

Earp's timing was amazing. By July of that year John Hummel had discovered gold on the beaches, and the 2000 men who stampeded to the city that summer had by early fall recovered $1 million in gold dust and nuggets.

Wyatt Earp managed to fleece his share of that gold. By October 1901, having already endured two winters on the Bering Sea, the Earps left Nome with, as legend has it, $80,000 – a fortune at that time. You can see pictures of Earp on the streets of Nome, and some of the turn-of-the-century gambling devices used in town, at the Carrie McLain Museum on Front St.

THE BUSH

you can go direct aboard **Frontier Flying Service** (☎ 450-7200; 800-478-6779; www.frontierflying .com) six days a week for about $380.

Many people see Nome on package tours. Alaska Airlines runs day trips out of Anchorage for $395 (including airfare and a Nome Tour and Marketing excursion) and overnight stays for $515 (including airfare, tour, and lodging at the Nugget Inn).

Once on the ground, Nome's airport is a little more than a mile from town. If the day is nice, it's a pleasant walk. If not, a cab ride is $5 per person.

Only two places in Nome rent cars. Both offer unlimited mileage in an area of the state where there is very limited mileage. **Stampede Rent-A-Car** (☎ 443-3838, 800-354-4606; cnr Front St & Moore Way) is in the Aurora Inn and offers SUVs and pickups for $90 a day. **Alaska Cab Garage** (☎ 443-2939; at 4th Ave & Steadman St) has pickups, 4WD pickups and Suburbans for $75 to $85 a day. When budgeting for a rental, keep in mind that gas in Nome is extremely spendy.

Hitchhiking is possible, and locals are really good about picking people up. But you must be patient – and willing to sit in the back of an open pickup on very dusty roads.

AROUND NOME

Radiating east, north and northwest from Nome are its finest features: three gravel roads, each offering passage into very different worlds, and each providing a full-day adventure at minimum. While Nome can seem dirty and rundown, the surrounding country is stunning – think sweeping tundra, crystal-clear rivers, rugged mountains and some of the best chances in Alaska to see waterfowl, caribou, bears and musk ox. But be prepared: there's no gas and few other services along Nome's highways; instead, you'll encounter road-shrouding dust, as well as rocks determined to ravage your tires. Going slow is key. Take twice as long as you would on pavement.

Nome–Council Road

This 73-mile route, which heads northeast to the old mining village of Council, is perhaps the best excursion if you have time for just one of Nome's roads. For the first 30 miles

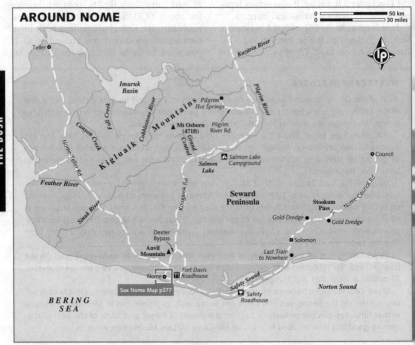

AROUND NOME

0 — 50 km
0 — 30 miles

Teller
Kuzitrin River
Imuruk Basin
Pilgrim River
Canyon Creek
Fall Creek
Pilgrim Hot Springs
Kigluaik Mountains
Cobblestone River
Mt Osborn (471ft)
Pilgrim River Rd
Grand Central
Nome-Teller Rd
Salmon Lake Campground
Council
Salmon Lake
Feather River
Sinuk River
Kougarok Rd
Seward Peninsula
Nome-Council Rd
Stookum Pass
Gold Dredge
Gold Dredge
Dexter Bypass
Anvil Mountain
Solomon
Last Train to Nowhere
Nome
Fort Davis Roadhouse
See Nome Map p377
Safety Sound
Safety Roadhouse
Norton Sound

BERING SEA

THE BUSH

THE LAST TRAIN TO NOWHERE

In all of Bush Alaska, it's almost certainly the most-photographed landmark: a set of steam locomotives, utterly out of place and out of time, moldering on the Arctic tundra at the continent's edge, hundreds of miles from the nearest functioning railway. Dubbed the Last Train to Nowhere, the three engines first plied the elevated lines of New York City in the 1880s, until Manhattan switched from steam to electric-driven trains. In 1903 the upstart Council City & Solomon River Railroad purchased the locomotives and transported them north, hoping to profit by servicing inland mines from the coast. Though the company surveyed some 50 miles of potential track, only half of that was built. By 1907 the operation went belly up. Six years later, a powerful storm sealed the Last Train's fate, destroying the Solomon River railroad bridge and stranding the engines on the tundra forever. Truly, it was the end of the line.

---

it hugs the glimmering Bering Sea coastline, passing an outstanding, and motley, array of shacks, cabins, tepees and Quonset huts, used by Nome residents as summer cottages and fish camps. On sunny days, miles of beaches beckon – but note how far inland autumn storms have tossed driftwood. At Mile 22 the road passes **Safety Roadhouse** (a dollar bill–bedecked dive of a watering hole) and then crosses the birders' wonderland of Safety Sound. Ten miles further along is Bonanza Crossing, on the far side of which is the **Last Train to Nowhere** (see above), a series of locomotives abandoned in the tundra in 1907 by the Council City & Solomon River Railroad. Just to the north is the ghost town of Solomon, which originally established in 1900 and once boasted a population of 1000 and seven saloons. The town was destroyed by a storm in 1913, and although it was relocated to higher ground, it was further decimated by the 1918 flu epidemic. In 2005 there were plans to open a B&B in a renovated schoolhouse here; check with the Nome Visitor Center about its status.

Near Mile 40 you pass the first of two **gold dredges** within a couple of miles of each other. By 1912 almost 40 dredges worked the Seward Peninsula, and today many are still visible from the Nome road system. The two on this road are in the best shape and are the most picturesque. Nome–Council Rd begins climbing after passing the second dredge and reaches **Stookum Pass** at Mile 53. There's a parking area at the pass, so you can pull off and admire the views or take a hike on the nearby ridges.

The road ends at Mile 73 at **Council**. Actually, the road ends at the banks of the Niukluk River, and Council is on the other side. Most of the houses here are weekend getaways for

people living in Nome. There are very few, if any, year-round residents. Locals drive across the river – with the water often reaching their running boards. Tourists with rental vehicles should stay put. There are no services or shops in Council, but the Niukluk is an excellent place to fish for grayling.

Kougarok Road

Also known as Nome–Taylor Rd, Kougarok Rd leads 86 miles north from Nome, through the heart of the Kigluaik Mountains. There are a few artifacts from the gold-rush days along the way, and the best mountain scenery and hiking in the Nome area. You can access the highway two ways: from its juncture off the Nome–Council Rd just east of town, or via the Dexter Bypass, which spurs off the Nome–Teller Rd a few miles northeast of Nome.

The Kigluaiks spring up almost immediately, flanking the road until around Mile 40, where the free, BLM-operated **Salmon Lake Campground** are beautifully situated at the north end of the large Salmon Lake. The facility features nine willow-girdled sites with tables, fire rings and an outhouse. The outlet for the Pilgrim River, where you can watch sockeye salmon spawn in August, is nearby.

Just before Mile 54 is Pilgrim River Rd, a rocky lane that heads northwest. The road climbs a pass where there's great ridge walking, then descends into a valley dotted with small tundra lakes. Less than 8 miles from Kougarok Rd, Pilgrim River Rd ends at the gate of **Pilgrim Hot Springs**. A roadhouse and saloon was located here during the gold rush, but burnt down in 1908. Later there was an orphanage for children who lost their parents in the 1918 influenza epidemic. The

Catholic Church managed the orphanage until 1942. Today the hot springs are privately owned and somewhat dilapidated, but if you contact caretaker Louie Green (☎ 443-5583) ahead of time, you'll likely get permission to walk inside for a soak.

Kougarok Rd crosses Pilgrim River at Mile 60, the Kuzitrin River at Mile 68 and the Kougarok Bridge at Mile 86. This is one of the best areas to look for herds of musk oxen. At all three bridges, you can fish for grayling, Dolly Varden and salmon, among other species.

After the Kougarok Bridge, the road becomes a rough track, impassable to cars. The extremely determined, however, can shoulder a pack and continue overland a very challenging, boggy, unmarked 30-plus miles to Serpentine Hot Springs, inside the Bering Land Bridge National Preserve. A free, first-come-first-served bunkhouse-style cabin there sleeps 15 to 20, and there's a bathhouse for slipping into the 140° to 170° F waters. Almost no-one hikes both ways; consider chartering in or out. Check around to see who's currently making the flight; in recent years it's been variable.

Nome–Teller Road

This road leads 73 miles (a one-way drive of at least two hours) to Teller, a year-round, subsistence Inupiat village of 241 people. The landscape en route is vast and undulating, with steep climbs across spectacular rolling tundra. Hiking opportunities are numerous, as are chances to view musk oxen and a portion of the reindeer herd communally owned by families in Teller. The huge **Alaska Gold Company dredge**, which operated until the mid-1990s, lies just north of Nome on the Nome–Teller Rd.

The road also crosses a number of rivers that drain the south side of the Kigluaik Mountains, all of them offering fishing opportunities. The Snake (spanned near Mile 8), Sinuk (Mile 26.7) and Feather rivers (Mile 37.4) are three of the more productive waterways for Arctic grayling, Dolly Varden and salmon. Ten miles from Teller you'll crest a ridge that affords sublime views of Port Clarence, with the village of Brevig Mission on the far side.

Teller lies at the westernmost end of the westernmost road in North America. This wind-wracked community overlooks the slate waters of the Bering Sea and stretches along a tapering gravel spit near the mouth of Grantley Harbor. Roald Amundsen, one of the greatest figures in polar exploration, returned to earth here after his legendary 70-hour airship flight over the North Pole on May 14, 1926. In 1985 Teller again made the headlines when Libby Riddles, then a Teller resident, became the first woman to win the Iditarod.

Though Teller is a scenic place – witness the fishnets set just offshore, and the salmon hanging from racks on the beach – there's little for a visitor to do.

Still, out of respect for the residents (who are likely tired of drive-by gawkers from Nome), park your car and ask one of the village kids for directions to the tiny community store. There you can buy a snack and perhaps a handmade craft, supporting the Teller economy and facilitating interaction with the locals.

KOTZEBUE
☎ 907/pop 3130

Situated 26 miles above the Arctic Circle on the shores of the Chukchi Sea, Kotzebue – named after Polish explorer Otto von Kotzebue, who arrived here in 1816 – is one of Alaska's northernmost hubs. It could also be considered the state's biggest Alaska Native village. Unlike other aboriginal centers such as Bethel and Barrow, Kotzebue lacks a substantial white population. About 90% of residents are Inupiat, and – despite the financial injection provided by the massive Red Dog zinc mine, 90 miles north of town – eons-old hunting-and-gathering practises are the lifeblood of the community.

While this sounds exotic, take heed: it's a hard place for visitors to penetrate. There's no Alaska Native food at local restaurants (curiously, all six are run by Korean Americans), local hotels are sterile and costly, and there are few easy ways to meet people and get out on the land or water. Moreover, in-town attractions are practically nonexistent, especially since the closure of the once-impressive museum (though a new one, run by the park service, was in the planning stages at press time).

Thus, most visitors to Kotzebue will either want to be en route to wilderness expeditions in the surrounding parklands (charter flights from town can get you into nearby Noatak and Bering Land Bridge national preserves and Kobuk Valley National Park) or be satisfied with a sort of antiholiday, involving wandering the mere 17 miles of streets and being thankful global tourism hasn't made it this far.

Orientation & Information

Utterly flat and treeless, encircled by ocean, and devoid of any notable landmarks, Kotzebue presents a less-than-compelling visage to the new arrival. The township is tiny and compact, making it extremely walkable, and the streets, most of which are gravel, form a fairly sensible (if insufficiently signposted) grid. The airport is on the south edge of town. The most interesting road, Shore Ave, where the two hotels and several restaurants are located, is on the west edge, literally feet from Kotzebue Sound. A few blocks back from the water is broad, straight, paved Third Ave, which cuts through the center of the community.

Arctic Blues Coffeeshop (☎ 442-2554; per 10 min $2; ☯ 7:30am-5:30pm Mon-Fri, 9am-4pm Sat) Right at the airport, has Internet, espresso, some Alaska Native crafts, plus the highly recommended books of locals Nick Jans and Seth Kanter.

Chukchi Consortium Library (☎ 442-2410; 604 3rd Ave; ☯ noon-8pm Mon-Fri, to 6pm Sat) Is within the landing craft–shaped Chukchi College building and has free Internet (when the connection's working).

Emergency (☎ 911)

Innaigvik Public Lands Information & Education Center (☎ 442-3890; cnr 2nd Ave & Lakes St; ☯ noon-8pm Tue-Fri, to 4pm Sat) Maintained by the National Park Service (NPS), this is the best visitor resource in town, with ample info on the region's 9 million acres of parklands and on Kotzebue in general. It has displays on the area's natural history, plus topo maps and a small gift shop.

Maniilaq Health Center (☎ 442-3321; 436 5th Ave) Can handle medical emergencies.

Police (nonemergency ☎ 442-3351; 258B Third Ave)

Post office (Shore Ave) Next to the First Baptist church.

Wells Fargo (☎ 442-3258; cnr 2nd Ave & Lagoon St) Has an ATM accessible all hours.

Sights & Activities

AROUND TOWN

Perhaps the most interesting thing to do in Kotzebue is just stroll down Shore Avenue, where the old and new Arctics collide. On the beach, elders gut seals and dry salmon in preparation for the long winter ahead; meanwhile, youth skim their supercharged snowmachines across the water, wowing their buddies on shore. Across the road, a long line of caribou antler–adorned, weather-battered shacks stands as testament to the endurance of this place. Shore Ave also offers the best views of the midnight sun as it rolls along the horizon, painting the sea reddish gold with reflected light. From early June the sun doesn't set for almost six weeks.

Also of interest is a large **cemetery** in the center of town, where spirit houses have been erected over many of the graves.

The Innaigvik Public Lands Information & Education Center (left) has information on the large tracts of public land in this corner of the state and videos and displays on wildlife and Alaska Native culture.

For local art, check out the **Northwest Arctic Borough Giftshop** (☎ 442-2500; Lagoon St btwn 2nd & 3rd Ave; ☯ 8am-4:30pm Mon-Fri), with an extensive array of masks, birch-bark baskets, sealskin moccasins and mammoth-bone carvings. They're hoping to soon open a new art center, which will be half gallery and half workshop, at the corner of Second Ave and Lake St.

PADDLING

Kotzebue provides access to some of the finest river running in Arctic Alaska. Popular trips include the Noatak, the Kobuk, the Salmon (which flows into the Kobuk) and the Selawik (which originates in the Kobuk lowlands and flows west into Selawik Lake). Trips along the Kobuk National Wild River often consist of floats from Walker Lake traveling 140 miles downstream to the villages of Kobuk or Ambler. From these villages there are scheduled flights to both Kotzebue and Bettles, another departure point for this river. **Bering Air Service** (☎ 442-3943; www.beringair.com) can transport you and your gear from either Kobuk or Ambler to Kotzebue. Most of the river is rated Class I, but some lining of boats may be required just below Walker Lake and for a mile through Lower Kobuk Canyon. Paddlers usually plan on six to eight days for the float.

The **Noatak National Wild River** is a 16-day, 350-mile float from Lake Matcharak to the village of Noatak, where Bering Air has scheduled flights to Kotzebue. However, the numerous access lakes on the river allow it to be broken down into shorter paddles. The entire river is rated from Class I to II. The upper portion, in the Brooks Range, offers much more dramatic scenery and is usually

THE BUSH

accessed from Bettles (p393). The lower half, accessed through Kotzebue, flows through a broad, gently sloping valley where hills replace the sharp peaks of the Brooks Range. The most common trip here is to put in at Nimiuktuk River where, within an hour of paddling, you enter the 65-mile-long Grand Canyon of the Noatak, followed by the 7-mile-long Noatak Canyon. Most paddlers pull out at Kelly River, where there's a ranger station with a radio. Below the confluence with the Kelly, the Noatak becomes heavily braided.

For more information contact the Innaigvik Public Lands Information & Education Center (p385) before you depart for Alaska.

Canoes, rafts and outdoor gear are available through **Northwest Alaska Backcountry Rentals** (☎ 442-3944; northwestalaska@yahoo.com) in Kotzebue.

Tours

Arctic Circle Education Adventures (Jun-Aug ☎ 442-6013, Sep-May ☎ 276-0976; www.fishcamp.org) has a couple offerings that may well be the best way to crack the nut of Kotzebue. If you're just in town for the day, its four-hour custom tour ($200) will take you to look for birds – from swans to short-eared owls – explore the tundra and meet Inupiat residents. Better yet, stick around for a few days and get the real Bush experience at owner LaVonne Hendricks' fish camp, five miles south of town, where you can hike, beachcomb and participate in the local subsistence lifestyle. The cost is $150 per person per night with a minimum two-night stay, and includes transport, family-style meals and lodging in well-maintained plywood cabins.

Sleeping & Eating

Kotzebue doesn't have a public campground or hostel. In theory, backpackers are welcome to hike south of town along the gravel beach in search of ad hoc campsites. However, you may have to trek for over an hour to get beyond the private fish camps and associated stench of rotting seal entrails. Unfortunately, the most desirable alternative to camping, a B&B at 227 Lagoon St, was changing ownership in 2005 and may no longer provide lodging. Kotzebue adds 12% sales and bed taxes to lodging.

Nullagvik Hotel (☎ 442-3331; www.nullagvik.com; 308 Shore Ave; r $161) This three-story edifice is the

purplish color of Pepto Bismol and ringed with thermal siphons to keep it from melting the permafrost. Rooms are decent and modern, and some overlook the ocean.

Bayside Hotel (☎ 442-3600; 303 Shore Ave; r $125; restaurant ✷ 7am-11pm Mon-Sat, from 8am Sun) A cheaper, less appealing hotel two doors down from Nullagvik. Its restaurant has breakfasts from $7 to $16, lunches $7 to $11, dinners $11 to $25; it has waterfront booths and high-backed chairs – this is what passes for ambience in Kotzebue. Alas, the Korean and American fare is nothing special.

Empress Chinese Restaurant (☎ 442-4304; Shore Ave; mains $6-17; ✷ 11am-11pm Mon-Sat) Next door to the Bayside, this place has more Spartan decor and a similar menu, but better food.

Arctic Tern (☎ 442-3331; 308 Shore Ave; breakfasts $6-14; lunches & dinners $8-13; ✷ 6am-10pm Mon-Sat, to 9pm Sun) In the Nullagvik Hotel, this waterfront restaurant was focusing on fajitas, *huevos rancheros* (corn tortilla with fried eggs and a sauce of tomato, chili and onion) and other Mexican dishes when we were there.

AC Store (☎ 442-3285; cnr 5th Ave & Bison St; ✷ 8am-10pm Mon-Sat, 9am-9pm Sun) This supplies your basic groceries.

Getting There & Around

Alaska Airlines (☎ 800-426-0333, 442-3474; www.alaskaair.com) flies from Anchorage to Kotzebue three times daily for about $400 round-trip. You can also purchase a round-trip ticket from Anchorage with stopovers in both Nome and Kotzebue for around $530. From Fairbanks to Kotzebue, you can travel with **Frontier Flying Service** (☎ 450-7200, 800-478-6779; www.frontierflying.com) five days a week for about $380 return.

If you need a cab, **B&D Taxi** (☎ 442-2244) can get you there for $3.

ARCTIC ALASKA

DALTON HIGHWAY

There are precious few adventures to be had while sitting down – but then, most road trips aren't on the legendary Dalton Hwy. Also known as the Haul Rd, this punishing truck route rambles 414 miles from Alaska's Interior to the North Slope, paralleling the Trans-Alaska Pipeline to its source at the supergiant Prudhoe Bay Oil Field. The highway reaches further north than any other on the continent, and is the only way to motor to the stunning Brooks Range and the Arctic. If you're steeled for multiple days aboard a gravel rollercoaster – dodging hell-on-wheels big-rigs, risking bankruptcy if you need a tow, and (almost) reaching the edge of the Earth – it's a helluva trip.

Fueled by crude-oil fever, the Dalton was built in a whirlwind five months in 1974. For the ensuing two decades, however, it was effectively a private driveway for the gas companies, until a bitter battle in the state legislature opened it to the public. Even now, though, you can't drive clear to the Arctic Ocean: due to security concerns the road ends just shy of the oilfields, at the sprawling industrial camp of Deadhorse. From there the 'beach' is 8 miles distant, accessible only via a corporate tour (p390).

Though the Dalton is slowly being tamed – since 2000 around 130 miles have been paved – it's still not a road that suffers fools. In summer the 28ft-wide corridor is a dusty minefield of potholes, its embankments littered with blown tires. Paint scratches and window chips are inevitable, which is why most car-rental companies don't allow their vehicles here. There are few services, such as telephones, tire repair, fuel and restaurants, and none for the final 225 miles from Wiseman to Deadhorse.

The road is open year-round, but you should only tackle it between late May and early September, when there's virtually endless light and little snow and ice. Drive with headlights on, carry two spares, and always slow down and swing wide for oncoming trucks. Only the reckless exceed 55mph; expect a 40mph average and two hard days to reach Deadhorse. Other alternatives are to join one of the various van tours up the highway (p390), or drive halfway – to the Coldfoot truck stop – and from there catch a Prudhoe-bound shuttle-bus (p390), letting the pros negotiate the roughest stretch while you can gawk at the best scenery.

Mile 0 of the Dalton is at the junction with the Elliott Hwy, 84 miles from Fairbanks. Immediately, the Haul Rd announces itself: the pavement ends and the blind curves and technical pitches begin. At Mile 25, there's a lookout with good views of the pipeline crossing Hess Creek. Near the Hess Creek Bridge are serviceable campsites among the trees.

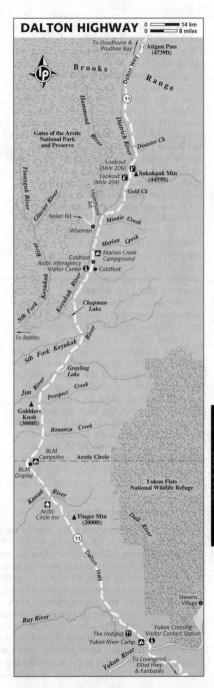

THE BUSH

The highway begins descending toward the Yukon River at Mile 47, and the silvery ribbon of pipeline can be seen reaching into the distance. At Mile 56, the 2290ft-long, wooden-decked **Yukon River Bridge** carries you and the pipeline across the silty, broad river – the only place where the legendary waterway is spanned in Alaska. On the far bank, turn right and pass under the pipeline to reach the BLM's **Yukon Crossing Visitor Contact Station** (9am-6pm Jun-Aug), staffed by an affable retired couple and featuring displays on the road and the terrain you're about to enter. It also has copies of the handy 24-page *Dalton Highway Visitor Guide*.

On the opposite side of the highway is a vast muddy lot and **Yukon River Camp** (☎ 474-3557; r $89; breakfast $9-12, lunch $8-10, dinner $19-22; 9am-9pm), a utilitarian truck stop with work camp–style rooms, showers ($6), costly gas, a gift shop, and not-half-bad food. An alternative is the agglomeration of temporary structures called the **Hotspot** (☎ 451-7543; r $95; 10am-midnight), five miles north, with similar accommodations but cheaper fuel. Its burgers are famous up and down the highway.

Around Mile 70, as the road clambers back out of the river valley, burned-over patches of forest appear, a legacy of the wildfires that scorched the majority of the Interior in 2004. Pavement starts at Mile 90 – a mixed blessing, given its potholed, frost-heaved state. Soon the highway ascends to an alpine area, with the 40ft-high granite tor of Finger Mountain beckoning to the east. At Mile 98, a windy BLM wayside offers great cross-tundra hiking to other tors, plus berry picking and views of the sprawling flats of the Kanuti National Wildlife Refuge to the west. A steep descent takes you past the homesteader-operated **Arctic Circle Inn** (☎ 457-9080, 800-932-4468; www.arctic circleinn.com; Mile 103 Dalton Hwy; cabin $75), with a gift shop, snacks and rustic lodging. Twenty minutes beyond is the inn's namesake, Alaska's most famous imaginary feature.

From **Gobbler's Knob** (Mile 132) northward, the pyramids of the Brooks Range begin to dominate the scene. In the next 50 miles you'll cross several grayling-rich streams, including Prospect Creek, which, in January 1971, experienced America's lowest-ever temperature, 80°F. Then, at Mile 175, in a mountain-rimmed hollow, you'll arrive in **Coldfoot**. Originally named Slate Creek, the area was first settled by miners in 1898. When a group of greenhorns got 'cold feet' at the thought of wintering in the district they headed south, and the community was renamed accordingly. It was a ghost town by 1912, but its moniker, at least, was revived in 1981, when Iditarod musher Dick Mackey set up an old school bus here and began selling hamburgers to Prudhoe Bay–bound truck drivers.

Nowadays, with an airstrip, post office and trooper detachment, you might expect Coldfoot to be a quaint Arctic hamlet. No such luck. The place consists mainly of **Coldfoot Camp** (☎ 474-3500, 866-474-3400; www.coldfoot camp.com), a plug-ugly truck stop with the last **gas** (24hrs) until Deadhorse, plus Spartan rooms in the **Slate Creek Inn** (r $165) and a **restaurant** (breakfast $6-13, lunch & dinner $8-14; 6am-midnight) with passable diner-style fare and a photo collection of jackknifed 18-wheelers. At **Frozen Foot Saloon** (6pm-10pm) – Alaska's northernmost bar – you can sip microbrews

---

DETOUR: THE ARCTIC CIRCLE

Motoring up a spruce- and aspen-studded ridge at Mile 115 of the Dalton Hwy, it looms into view: the Arctic Circle. OK, not really. Truth is, if it weren't for the green highway sign, you'd miss it: an unassuming BLM wayside marking the only place in America where you can drive to 66° 33′ N latitude. If you're willing to brave the horseflies and mosquitoes (they're sadistic here), pull over for a photo-op before the large circumpolar map, and check out the viewing platform with interpretive signage discussing northern Alaska's seasonal cycles. You can even take advantage of the nice picnic sites among the trees, or the rudimentary campground 450yd up the hill.

But don't come rolling up here on the solstice, expecting the midnight sun. See those mountains to the north? The golden orb ducks behind them at the magical moment – and then the bugs *really* start biting. To view El Sol all night (and having driven this far, you might as well), continue to **Gobbler's Knob**, a hilltop lookout at Mile 132 where there's a pullover, an outhouse and, if you scale the hill to the east on the first night of summer, perpetual sun.

on a deck overlooking (and oversmelling) idling trucks. The exhaust, it seems, keeps the bugs down.

A world apart is the **Arctic Interagency Visitors Center** (☎ 768-5209; ⏰ 10am-10pm Jun-Aug), on the opposite side of the highway. This impressive $5 million structure opened in 2004 and features museum-quality displays about the Arctic and its denizens. It has ultrahelpful staff, a schlock-free gift shop and nightly nature presentations – the best show in town.

As the visitors-center employees will tell you, the area's best lodging is down the highway. Campers should proceed 5 miles north to **Marion Creek Campground** (Mile 180; sites $8). This 27-site campground almost always has space and is situated in an open spruce forest with stunning views of the Brooks Range.

Those seeking a bed – or wanting an antidote to Coldfoot's culture of the quick-and-dirty – should push on to **Wiseman** (population 24), a century-old log-cabin village accessible via a short dirt spur road at Mile 189. The only authentic town on the Dalton, Wiseman occupies an enviable spot, overhung by peaks and fronting the Middle Fork of the Koyukuk River. Its heyday was 1910, when it replaced the original Coldfoot as a hub for area gold miners. Many buildings from that era still stand, including those of **Arctic Getaway Cabin & Breakfast** (☎ 678-4456; www.arcticgetaway.com), which offers a sunny, two-person cabin for $90 and an antique-laden four-person house for $150. Next door, cheaper but more institutional, are the rooms at **Boreal Lodge** (☎ 768-4566; www.boreallodge.com; s/d without bath $55/75). Once upon a time the **Wiseman Historical Museum**, near the entrance to town, was open to the public, but Northern Alaska Tour Company (p390) has purchased it and admits only its own clients.

Those wanting erudition should instead follow the signs to the cabin of Wiseman's wiseman, Jack Reakoff, an engaging and surprisingly urbane trapper who sells crafts and will discourse at length about local history and wildlife.

North from Wiseman the Dalton skirts the east edge of **Gates of the Arctic National Park** (p391). Dall sheep are often visible on the mountain slopes, and the scenery goes into overdrive. By Mile 194 the first views appear of the massive wall of **Sukakpak Mountain** (4459ft) looming dead ahead. Just before

Mile 204 is a lookout with a half-mile trail to Sukakpak's face, while soon after, even taller promontories arise – imposing black talus cones, 7000ft high, riven by glacier-carved valleys. At Mile 235 you kiss the woods goodbye: the famed **Last Spruce**, though recently girdled by a vandal's ax, stands stately even in death near a turnout on the highway's east side.

The ascent of **Atigun Pass** (Mile 242) is where the real fun begins. At an elevation of 4739ft this is the highest highway pass in Alaska, and marks the continental divide. While clawing your way 2 miles up the washboarded 12% grade, watch for downward-bound trucks and try to ignore the guardrails mangled by rockslides and avalanches. The view from the top – with the Philip Smith Mountains to the east and the Endicotts to the west – will steal your breath away.

The Brooks Range is largely behind you once you reach the turnoff for the undeveloped **Galbraith Lake Campground** at Mile 275. From here on it's all rolling tundra, where hiking and camping options are limitless, wildflowers and berries grow in profusion, and wildlife is far easier to spot. Especially at the beginning and end of summer, migrating waterbirds throng roadside ponds, and caribou – members of the 31,000-head Central Arctic herd – often graze nearby. Also, keep an eye out for weird polar phenomena such as pingos – protuberant hills with a frozen center – and ice-wedge polygons, which shape the tundra into bizarre geometric patterns.

You'll know the coast draws near when the weather turns dire. Even in summer, wind, fog and bitter cold are de rigueur at the Arctic Ocean. The gloom sets the mood for your arrival at the dystopia of **Deadhorse**, the world's northernmost anticlimax. Centered around Lake Colleen, this is no town – nobody lives here permanently – but a sad expanse of aluminum-clad warehouses, machinery-laden lots and workmen counting the moments until they return south. Don't even think about camping: the tundra is a quagmire and the gravel pads are plied by speeding pickups. Having come all this way, you can either turn around (after gassing up with what is, ironically, some of America's costliest petrol), or do what locals do: hole up in a hotel and watch cable TV.

THE BUSH

Arctic Caribou Inn (☎ 659-2368, 877-659-2368; www
.arcticcaribouinn.com; r $125) and the **Prudhoe Bay
Hotel** (☎ 659-2449; www.prudhoebayhotel.com; dm/r with
bath $90/110), both near the airport and under
the same ownership, aren't froufrou but are
a shockingly good deal because the price
includes quality café-style meals – the only
food service in Deadhorse. (Note that Prudhoe Bay Hotel's ensuite bath can be accessed
by two separate bedroom doors.) What dif-
ferentiates the two places is that, because the
Caribou is more tourist-oriented, its gift shop
has espressos rather than porno mags. Souvenirs and sundries can also be bought at the
Prudhoe Bay General Store (☎ 659-2412; ☽ 9am-
9pm), located on the town's east edge and containing the **post office** (☎ 659-2669). Send Mom
a postcard from the top of the world!

Tours
Various companies run similar tours:
Arctic Caribou Inn Oilfield Tour (☎ 659-2368,
877-659-2368; www.arcticcaribouinn.com; tours $38) This
two-hour ordeal is the only way to gain access to the oil
fields and the ocean. Taking place several times daily, it
begins with a cloying corporate video and continues with a
perfunctory bus ride to the waterfront, where you have the
option of taking a quick, frigid dip. You must sign up for
this tour a day in advance in order to clear security.
Northern Alaska Tour Company (☎ 800-474-1986,
474-8600; www.northernalaska.com) This is the granddaddy
of the Dalton Hwy tour companies, offering all sorts of
packages, including a three-day van trip to Prudhoe Bay for
$749 that includes lodging at Wiseman and Deadhorse and
flights back to Fairbanks. Food is not covered.
Trans Arctic Circle Treks (☎ 800-336-8735, 479-5451;
www.arctictreks.com) Charges $799 for a similar tour, also
covering lodging but not food.

Getting There & Around
BUS
There's a scheduled van service between Fairbanks and Prudhoe Bay that, among other
things, drops off backpackers along the way.
Dalton Highway Express (☎ 474-3555; www.dalton
highwayexpress.com) makes the run daily during
the summer, spending overnight at Deadhorse and giving you time to take an early-
morning oil-field tour before returning the
next day. The round-trip fare to the Arctic

THE ALASKA PIPELINE
Love it or loath it, if you're driving Alaska's Richardson or Dalton Hwys, the Trans-Alaska Pipeline
will be your traveling companion. The steely tube, 4ft wide and 800 miles long, parallels the highways from Prudhoe Bay on the Arctic Ocean down to Valdez, Alaska's northernmost ice-free port.
En route, it spans 800-odd waterways and three mountain ranges, transporting about one million
barrels of crude oil per day – 15% of the US's domestic production – to tankers waiting in Prince
William Sound. If drilling had taken place in the Arctic National Wildlife Refuge, it would have
contributed to this flow. However in late 2005 the energy bill was rejected by the US Senate.

Before construction began in 1975, the debate over the pipeline was among America's hardest-
fought conservation battles. Both sides viewed themselves as defenders of the Last Frontier, with
boosters viewing the project as a grand act of Alaskan pioneering and opponents calling it an
affront to all that's wild and wonderful about the 49th state. Since the pipeline's completion –
two years and $8 billion later – the late University of Alaska president William R Wood likened it
to 'a silken thread, half-hidden across the palace carpet.' Many have had less kind words for it.

For about 380 of its miles, the Trans-Alaska Pipeline – like most pipelines elsewhere – runs
underground. Elsewhere it can't, because the 150° to 180°F oil it carries would melt the permafrost. It's in those places – particularly where it crosses the highway – that you'll get your best
look at the line. Especially good views can be had at Mile 243.5 of the Richardson Hwy south
of Delta Junction, and on the Dalton at the Yukon River crossing as well as at the spur road to
Wiseman.

Be forewarned, however: it's a bad move to get too close to the pipeline, much less to fold,
bend, spindle or mutilate it. After September 11, 2001, officials identified the pipe as Alaska's No
1 terrorist target, ramping up security and for a while even operating a checkpoint on the Dalton
Hwy. Their fears aren't entirely unfounded: in 1978, a mystery bomber near Fairbanks damaged
the pipeline with explosives, spilling some 670,000 gallons of oil. Then, in 2001, a drunken hunter
shot it with a .338-caliber rifle, and 285,000 gallons spewed out. Officials say the pipeline has
been shot – with no result – at least 50 other times.

Circle is $120, Wiseman and Coldfoot $150, Galbraith Lake $210 and Deadhorse $290. If you drive to Coldfoot and catch the shuttle northward, it's $150 round-trip.

CAR

Finding somebody to rent you a car in Fairbanks for travel on the Dalton is a major challenge. Don't even bother with the used-car firms or most national franchises. **Arctic Outfitters** (☎ 474-3530; www.daltonhighway.com) has sedans equipped with two spare tires for $139 a day, or $99 per day for four days or more. **GoNorth** (☎ 479-7272, 866-236-7272; www.gonorth alaska.com) rents SUVs and pickups, as well as bed-equipped campers that start at around $150 per day with unlimited mileage.

GATES OF THE ARCTIC NATIONAL PARK & PRESERVE

The Gates of the Arctic National Park & Preserve is one of the world's finest wilderness areas. Covering 13,125 sq miles, it straddles the ragged spine of the Brooks Range, America's northernmost chain of mountains, and sprawls 800 miles from east to west. The sparse vegetation is mainly shrubbery and tundra; animals include grizzlies, wolves, Dall sheep, moose, caribou and wolverines. There's great fishing for grayling and Arctic char in the clear streams, and for lake trout in the larger, deeper lakes.

Within the park are dozens of rivers to run, miles of valleys and tundra slopes to hike and, of course, the 'gates' themselves: Mt Boreal and Frigid Crags, which flank the north fork of the Koyukuk River. In 1929 Robert Marshall found an unobstructed path northward to the Arctic through these landmark peaks and his name for the passage has stuck ever since.

The park contains no visitor facilities, campgrounds or trails, and the National Park Service is intent upon maintaining its virgin quality. Therefore, rangers urge a six-person limit on trekking parties. As well, they've begun strongly encouraging visitors to get off the (literally) beaten path, possibly avoiding such increasingly busy corridors as the Noatak River.

Unguided trekkers, paddlers and climbers entering the park should be well versed in wilderness travel; they should also check in at one of the ranger stations for a backcountry orientation and updates on river hazards and bear activity. To avoid confrontations with bears, campers are required to carry bearproof food canisters, checked out free-of-charge from the ranger stations.

Orientation & Information

Bettles is the main gateway to Gates of the Arctic, offering meals, lodging and transport into the backcountry. Other visitors fly in from Coldfoot on the Dalton Hwy, or hike in from nearby Wiseman.

Arctic Interagency Visitors Center (p389) In Coldfoot; has info for those accessing the park from the Dalton Hwy.

Bettles Ranger Station (☎ 692-5494; www.nps.gov /gaar; ⏱ 8am-5pm) In a log building less than a quarter-mile from the airstrip, it also serves as a visitors center and has displays depicting the flora and fauna of the Brooks Range, a small library, and books and maps for sale.

Sights & Activities

HIKING

Most backpackers enter the park by way of charter air-taxi, which can land on lakes, rivers or river bars, and which are usually caught from Bettles. Once on the ground you can follow the long, open valleys for extended treks or work your way to higher elevations where open tundra and sparse shrubs provide good hiking terrain. One of the more popular long-distance treks is the four- to five-day hike from Summit Lake through the Gates to Redstar Lake. Less-experienced backpackers often choose to be dropped off and picked up at one lake and explore the surrounding region on day hikes from there. Lakes ideal for this include Summit Lake, the Karupa lakes region, Redstar Lake, Hunt Fork Lake or Chimney Lake.

The only treks that don't require chartering a plane are those beginning from the Dalton Hwy that lead into several different areas along the eastern border of the park. Stop at the Arctic Interagency Visitor Center in Coldfoot (p389) for advice and assistance in trip planning. Then drive north to your access point into the park. Many backpackers stop at Wiseman, which provides access to several routes, including the following trails.

Nolan/Wiseman Creek Area

Head west at the Wiseman exit just before Mile 189 of the Dalton Hwy and hike along the Nolan Rd, which passes through Nolan, a hamlet of a few families, and ends at Nolan Creek. You can then reach Wiseman Creek

THE BUSH

and Nolan Creek Lake, which lies in the valley through which Wiseman and Nolan Creeks run, at the foot of three passes: Glacier, Pasco and Snowshoes. You can hike from any of these passes to Glacier River, which can be followed to the north fork of the Koyukuk for a longer hike.

Lower Hammond River Area

From Wiseman, go north by hiking along the Hammond Rd, which can be followed for quite a way along the Hammond River. From the river you can explore the park by following one of several drainage areas, including Vermont, Canyon and Jenny Creeks. The latter heads east to Jenny Creek Lake.

PADDLING

Floatable rivers in the park include the John, the north fork of the Koyukuk, the Tinayguk,

the Alatna and the middle fork of the Koyukuk River from Wiseman to Bettles. The headwaters for the Noatak and Kobuk are in the park.

The waterways range from Class I to III in difficulty. Of the rivers, the Koyukuk's north fork is especially popular, because of the location and challenge – the float starts in the Gates's shadow and goes downstream 100 miles to Bettles through Class I and II waters. Canoes and rafts can be rented in Bettles and then floated downstream to the village.

Upper Noatak

The best-known river and the most popular for paddlers is the upper portion of the Noatak, due to the spectacular scenery as you float by the sharp peaks of the Brooks Range and because it's a mild river that many canoeists can handle on an unguided journey.

DETOUR: ALASKA NATIONAL WILDLIFE REFUGE

Seldom has so much furore involved a place so few have ever been. The Alaska National Wildlife Refuge (ANWR, *an*-wahr) is a 19.6 million–acre wilderness in Alaska's upper-right-hand corner, straddling the eastern Brooks Range from the treeless Arctic Coast to the taiga of the Porcupine River Valley. For years the refuge has been at the core of a white-hot debate over whether to drill for oil beneath its coastal plain, thought to contain 10.4 billion barrels of crude oil.

Advocates, including a sizable majority of Alaskans, say drilling will create jobs, reduce gas prices and heighten America's energy security – and with modern technology, they say, it can be done with nearly zero environmental impact. Opponents – environmentalists and, most famously, the Gwich'in Athabascans who've long frequented the refuge's southern reaches – argue ANWR should remain pristine, particularly for the sake of the 150,000-head porcupine caribou herd, which calves on the coastal plain. Moreover, they say, the amount of oil in ANWR is a drop in the bucket: it would likely last America just six months, considering the US consumes 20 million barrels annually.

If all the Sturm und Drang has you curious about coming here, you'll need to be prepared. There are no visitor facilities of any sort, and even reaching the refuge can be a trick (requiring quite a bit of gas, unless you travel like a caribou). There's only one place ANWR can be accessed by car: just north of Atigun Pass on the Dalton Hwy, where the road and the refuge briefly touch. You could hike in from there, but you'll still be nowhere near the coastal plain, and unlikely to see the embattled caribou.

To get deeper into ANWR, you will need to fly there. Numerous charter companies can be hired; for a list, consult the refuge's website (arctic.fws.gov). A few, like Coldfoot-based **Coyote Air Service** (☎ 678-5995, 800-252-0608; www.flycoyote.com), operate organized flightseeing trips, such as its three-hour caribou-spotting excursion. There are also plenty of outfitters who operate trips in the refuge. Most, including excellent **Alaska Discovery** (☎ 800-586-1911, 780-6226; www.akdiscovery.com), float the Kongakut, Sheenjek, Hulahula or other rivers; some, such as **ABEC's Alaska Adventures** (☎ 888-424-8907, 457-8907; www.abecalaska.com), lead multiday backpacking excursions along the porcupine caribou migration route. Several companies have even more unorthodox offerings: for instance, **Arctic Wild** (☎ 888-577-8203; www.arcticwild.com) conducts a nine-day yoga course in the refuge.

No matter what you choose to do in ANWR, though, you'd be wise to come soon. By the time you read this, drilling may already have begun; see p30.

The most common trip is a 60-mile float that begins near Portage Creek and ends at a riverside lake near Kacachurak Creek, just outside the park boundary. This float is usually completed in five to seven days. It involves some Class II and possible Class III stretches of rapids toward the end. During the busy summer season, from about mid-July to the end of August, other parties may be encountered on the river and aircraft may be heard delivering visitors to the area.

Guided Tours

A few guide companies run trips through the Gates of the Arctic National Park & Preserve. They include **Sourdough Outfitters** (☎ 692-5252; www.sourdoughoutfitters.com), **ABEC's Alaska Adventures** (☎ 888-424-8907, 457-8907; www .abecalaska.com) and **Arctic Wild** (☎ 888-577-8203, 479-8203; www.arcticwild.com).

Sourdough Outfitters also arranges unguided expeditions with drop-off and pickup air services for independent backpackers. Among its options are an eight-day backpacking adventure from Summit Lake to Chimney Lake and a seven-day combination of backpacking and canoeing the North Fork of the Koyukuk. The company rents inflatable canoes and rafts for $35 to $50 per day, depending on the boat's size.

Bettles Lodge (☎ 692-5111; bttlodge@alaska.net) also runs float trips and rents rafts and inflatable canoes for $45/35 a day.

Getting There & Away

Access to the park's backcountry is usually accomplished in two steps, with the first being a scheduled flight from Fairbanks to Bettles. Check out **Bettles Air Service** (☎ 800-770-5111, 692-5111), which makes regular flights to Bettles for $270 round-trip. The second step is to charter an air-taxi from Bettles to your destination within the park. A Cessna 185 on floats holds three passengers and costs around $225 per hour. Most areas in the park can be reached in under two hours. If you're in Bettles, check with **Brooks Range Aviation** (☎ 800-692-5443, 692-5444; www.brooksrange -alaska-wilderness-trips.com) or Bettles Air Service for air charters.

Alternatively, you can drive up the Dalton Hwy (p390) to the Coldfoot/Wiseman area, and access the park from there, either hiking in or chartering with **Coyote Air Service** (☎ 678-5995, 800-252-0608; www.flycoyote.com).

BETTLES

☎ 907/pop 31

This small village serves as the major departure point to the Gates of the Arctic National Park & Preserve. Founded by Gordon C Bettles in 1900 as a trading post, Bettles was originally 6 miles down the middle fork of the Koyukuk River. Riverboats would work their way up the Koyukuk and unload their supplies in Bettles. The supplies were then transported to smaller scows and horsedrawn barges. The smaller boats would then take the cargo to the mining country further upriver.

WWII brought a need for a major airstrip in Arctic Alaska, and the Civil Aviation Agency (now the Federal Aviation Administration) chose to construct one upriver from Bettles. Eventually the entire village moved to the airstrip. Today Bettles has the distinction of being the smallest incorporated city in Alaska.

Sights & Activities

If you find yourself with an unexpected day in Bettles, which can easily happen in August, take a hike up to **Birch Hill Lake**. The trailhead is unmarked but can be located by first heading to the Evansville Health Clinic. Next to it is a small brown house, and the trail can be found just to the right of the house. It's a 3-mile trek to the lake and can get swampy. Wear rubber boots.

Sleeping & Eating

Camping is allowed behind the Bettles Flight Service building, off the runway at the north edge of the aircraft parking area, where you'll find BBQ grills. It would be just as easy to pitch a tent on the gravel bars along the middle fork of the Koyukuk River.

Bettles Lodge (☎ 800-770-5111, 692-5111; www .bettleslodge.com; dm/s/d $15/115/135; ✗) Just off the runway, has a variety of accommodations available. The original inn is a classic Alaskan log lodge with a restaurant, a small tavern and bush pilots constantly wandering through in their hip boots.

Aurora Lodge (s/d $135/160; ✗) Part of the Bettles Lodge complex; it has eight rooms, and there's a bunkhouse hostel.

Sourdough Outfitters (☎ 692-5252; www.sour doughoutfitters.com; dm $30, cabin s/d $75/80) For indoors, it has showers ($4) and a laundry service. The cabins sleep up to four people.

THE BUSH

Bettles Lodge Restaurant (breakfast $10-12, dinner $12-15; 8am-8pm) It has hamburgers with fries for $10. Sign up for dinner if you plan to eat there. The other option for food is a café run by Sourdough Outfitters, which has the usual Bush Alaska selection and prices to match.

Getting There & Around

See p393 for information on how to access the area.

BARROW

907/pop 4351

Barrow is the northernmost settlement in the USA, the largest Inupiat community in Alaska, and one of the most distinctive places you'll likely ever visit. Situated 330 miles above the Arctic Circle, it's a flat, bleak, fogbound place, patrolled by polar bears and locked in almost perpetual winter. It's also a town of surprising contradictions.

On one hand, Barrow's wealth is famous: due to the spoils of North Slope petroleum, it boasts facilities, such as its Inupiat Heritage Center, which are totally unexpected in a town this size. On the flipside, it's an Arctic slum, packed with ramshackle structures wallowing in frozen mud.

It's also at once ancient and modern. Inupiat have dwelled here for a least two millennia, and nowadays they still run the place. Barrow, as the seat of the North Slope Borough (a countylike government covering an area larger than Nebraska) is the administrative and commercial hub of Alaska's Far North. Yet locals have retained much of their traditional culture, best symbolized by the spring whale harvests and seen during the Nalukataq Festival, staged in June to celebrate successful hunts.

For tourists, however, Barrow's appeal isn't so much its Inupiat culture as its novel latitude. They come to see the midnight sun (which doesn't set for 82 days from May to early August), and say they've been at the top of the world.

The vast majority of the 7000-plus visitors who arrive every summer are traveling as part of a package tour. Barrow is an expensive side trip for independent travelers.

Orientation & Information

Barrow lies along the northeasterly trending shore of the icebound Chukchi Sea, and is divided into two distinct sections. Directly north of the airport is Barrow proper, home to most of the hotels and restaurants and interlaced with a warren of gravel streets, including Stevenson St, which runs along the water. North of Isatquaq, or Middle Lagoon, is Browerville, a more residential area that also has the heritage center, post office and grocery store.

Emergency (ambulance, fire, police 911)

North Slope Borough Public Information Office (852-0215; PO Box 60, Barrow, AK 99723) You can contact this place for information in advance of your trip.

Police (nonemergency 852-6111)

Post office (cnr Eben Hobson & Tahak Sts) Can send your postcards from the top of the world.

Samuel Simmonds Memorial Hospital (852-4611; 1296 Agvik St) Will either fix you up or arrange a medevac flight to Fairbanks.

Tuzzy Consortium Library (852-1720; 5421 North Star St; noon-9pm Mon-Thu, to 5pm Fri & Sat) In the same building as the Inupiat Heritage Center, has free Internet and lots to read when the weather's bad.

Wells Fargo (852-6200; cnr Agvik & Kiogak Sts) Has a 24-hour ATM.

Sights & Activities

The main thing to do at the top of the world is bundle up and stand on the shore of the Arctic Ocean, gazing toward the North Pole. You can stroll the gravel roads that parallel the sea to view umiaks (Inupiat skin boats), giant jawbones of bowhead whales, fish-drying racks and the jumbled Arctic pack ice that even in July spans the horizon. On the waterfront opposite Apayauk St at the south end of town is **Ukpiagvik**, the site of an ancient Inupiat village marked by the remains of semi-subterranean sod huts.

Follow the shore 12 miles northeast of the city and you'll come to **Point Barrow**, a narrow spit of land that's the northernmost extremity of the US (though not, as locals sometimes claim, North America). In the winter and spring this is where polar bears den; in the summer it's the featured stop of organized tours. The buses never actually reach the tip, as the road ends several miles short of it. To continue on, you must walk or rent an ATV – and watch out for bears.

Among Barrow's manmade attractions, by far the most impressive is the **Inupiat Heritage Center** (Ahkovak St; admission $5, 8:30am-noon, 1-5pm Mon-Fri, 2-6pm Sat). This 24,000-sq-ft facility houses a museum, gift shop and a large multipurpose room where traditional dancing-and-drumming performances take place each afternoon. The show is worth the additional $10, and afterwards, local craftspeople assemble in the lobby to sell masks, whalebone carvings and fur garments. In the center's galleries, well-curated displays include everything from poster-sized B&W portraits of local elders to a 35ft-long replica of a bowhead skeleton.

Opposite Barrow's airport is the **Will Rogers & Wiley Post Monument**, a six-sided cenotaph memorializing the famous comedian and his legendary pilot, who died together in 1935 when their plane stalled and crashed into a river 15 miles south of here. At the time, Rogers was on a comedy tour en route from Fairbanks to Siberia.

Festivals & Events

The **Nalukataq Festival** is held in late June, when the spring whaling hunt has been completed. Depending on how successful the whaling captains have been, the festival lasts from a few days to more than a week. It's a rare cultural experience if you're lucky enough to be in Barrow when it happens. One Inupiat tradition calls for whaling crews to share their bounty with the village, and during the festival you'll see families carry off platters and plastic bags full of raw whale meat. Dishes served include *muktuk*, the pink blubbery part of the whale, which is boiled, pickled or even eaten raw with hot mustard or soy sauce. It's an acquired taste and usually too tough and chewy for outsiders.

The main event of the festival is the blanket toss, in which locals gather around a sealskin tarp and pull it tight to toss people into the air – the effect is much like bouncing on a trampoline. The object is to jump as high as possible (supposedly replicating ancient efforts to spot game in the distance) and inevitably there are a number of sprains and fractures.

Tours

Arctic Adventure Tours (☎ 852-3800) Offers the most intimate two-hour wildlife tour to Point Barrow to look for polar bears, marine life such as walrus and a variety of migrating birds. The cost is $60 per person.

Tundra Tours (☎ 852-3900, 800-882-8478; www .tundratours.com) The major package-tour operator, using buses to show sightseers the town and tundra. A blanket

toss and Alaska Native–dance performance is included in the six-hour excursion, which costs $75 per person. You can be certain your long-suffering Inupiat guide is bored silly by the whole toe-dipping ritual during the stop at the Arctic Ocean.

Sleeping

Camping is ill advised around Barrow, due to curious, carnivorous polar bears. That means you'll be paying a pretty penny to put a roof over your head.

King Eider Inn (☎ 852-4700, 888-303-4337; www .kingeider.net; 1752 Ahkovak St; r $170-275; ✕ 🖳) This is by far the most inviting, upscale hotel in Barrow, with log furniture, numerous kitchenette units, free Internet and a sauna. If you've come this far, the expense may be worth it.

Barrow Airport Inn (☎ 852-2525; 1815 Momegana St; r $115; ✕) It has 14 somewhat worn but quite tolerable rooms. Some have kitchenettes and, inexplicably, portable fans.

Top of the World Hotel (☎ 800-882-8478, 852-3900; www.topoftheworldhotel.com; 1200 Agvik St; r $165) Large, soulless but centrally located, the Top of the World is where most package-tour visitors stay.

UIC-NARL Hostel (☎ 852-7800; r per person $75) These shared-facility rooms, used mainly by the local community college, are the cheapest around, but inconveniently, they're several miles north of town.

Eating

Osaka (☎ 852-4100; 980 Stevenson St; breakfast $10-14, lunch & dinner $9-25; ⊙ 7am-midnight Mon-Sat, to 11pm Sun) Located diagonally across from the Top of the World Hotel, this place has pretty good all-American breakfasts, plus sushi that even Japanese tourists approve of.

Brower's Café (☎ 852-3456; 3220 Brower Hill; burgers $8-12; ⊙ 11am-11pm Mon-Thu, to midnight Fri & Sat) This beachfront structure was built in the late 19th century by Charles Brower, an American whaler, and has whaling antiques inside and a whale-jawbone arch out front. Nowadays it's Barrow's best burger joint (with about 10 varieties), and hosts what's almost certainly America's northernmost karaoke night.

Pepe's North of the Border (☎ 852-8200; 1204 Agvik St; mains $8-22; ⊙ 7am-10pm) Co-located with the Top of the World Hotel, this 'northernmost Mexican restaurant in the world' has achieved renown thanks to the tireless

THE BUSH

Barrow-boosting efforts of owner Fran Tate. The food is decent, but it's the tour group–oriented antics that make this a surreal experience.

AC Store (☎ 852-6711; cnr Stuaqpak & Agvik Sts; ☺ 8am-10pm Mom-Sat, 9am-9pm Sun) It has quick eats and groceries at diet-inducing prices.

Getting There & Around

The only way to reach Barrow is to fly. **Alaska Airlines** (☎ 800-468-2248, 852-4653; www.alaskaair.com) charges about $470 for a round-trip, advance-purchase ticket from Fairbanks and about $560 from Anchorage.

Such fares make package tours attractive. A same-day excursion, which includes airfare from Fairbanks and a town tour, but not meals, is $415 through Alaska Airlines, or $565 ($465 for double occupancy) if you want to stay overnight.

Once on the ground, the airport is an easy stroll from all three hotels, and most other points of interest can be reached by walking as well. If bad weather blows in, however, cabs are available for $5. Try **Arctic Cab** (☎ 852-2227), **Barrow Taxi** (☎ 852-2222) or **City Cab** (☎ 852-5050). Cars can be rented through **UIC Auto Rental** (☎ 852-2700).

Directory

CONTENTS

PRACTICALITIES

- Alaska has more than 30 daily, weekly and trade newspapers. The largest daily, the closest thing to a statewide newspaper, is the top-rated *Anchorage Daily News*, recipient of several Pulitzer prizes.

- Radio stations are all over Alaska. In small, isolated towns public radio is a crucial outlet for news and entertainment.

- Voltage in Alaska is 110V – the same as everywhere else in the USA.

- There is no national sales tax in the USA and no state sales tax in Alaska. But towns have a city sales tax plus a bed tax that supports the local tourism bureau.

- Almost every town in Alaska has a laundromat, the place to go to clean your clothes or take a shower. A small load of clothes costs $3 to $5, plus $1 to $2 for the dryer. A shower is $3 to $5.

- US distances are in feet, yards and miles. Dry weights are in ounces (oz), pounds (lb) and tons, and liquids are in pints, quarts and gallons (4 quarts). The US gallon is about 20% less than the imperial gallon. See the conversion chart on the inside front cover of this book.

ACCOMMODATIONS

Alaska offers typical US accommodations (motels, hotels and B&Bs) and many that are not; a cabin in the mountains, lodges in the middle of a wilderness. Advance bookings are wise because the Alaskan tourist season is short, and in places such as Juneau, Skagway and Denali National Park, rooms fill quickly. If you arrive with a tent, are renting a car and have a flexible itinerary, then finding a place to bed down at night is not a problem.

The rates listed in this book are all for high season: June through August. The listed rates do not include local taxes, which are covered for each town at the start of the Sleeping sections. In most towns you will be hit with a local sales tax *and* a bed tax, with the combination ranging from 5% to the 12% for cities such as Anchorage and Juneau.

B&Bs

For travelers who want nothing to do with a tent, B&Bs can be an acceptable compromise between sleeping on the ground and sleeping in high-priced motels and lodges. Some B&Bs are bargains, and most are cheaper than major hotels, but plan on spending $70 to $120 per night for a double room.

Many visitor centers have sections devoted to the B&Bs in their area, and courtesy booking phones. Details about specific B&Bs are in the regional chapters. You can also call the following B&B reservation services to book rooms in advance of your trip.

Alaska Private Lodgings (☎ 907-235-2148; www
.alaskabandb.com) Anchorage & Southcentral.
Anchorage Alaska Bed & Breakfast Association
(☎ 907-272-5909, 888-584-5147; www.anchorage-bnb.com)
Bed and Breakfast Association of Alaska (www
.alaskabba.com) Statewide.
Fairbanks Association of Bed & Breakfasts (www
.ptialaska.net/~fabb)
Ketchikan Reservation Service (☎ 800-987-5337;
www.ketchikan-lodging.com)
Mat-Su Bed & Breakfast Association (www.alaska
bnbhosts.com)

Camping & Cabins

Camping is king in Alaska and with a tent
you'll always have cheap accommodations
in the Far North. There are state, federal
and private campgrounds from Ketchikan
to Fairbanks. Nightly fees are from $6 to $10
for rustic public campgrounds and from
$25 to $30 to park your recreation vehicle
in a deluxe private campground with a full
hook-up. Many towns that cater to tourists will have a municipal campground or
several commercial campgrounds nearby.
See p58.

Most public agencies, including the Alaska
Division of Parks and the US Forest Service,
have rustic cabins in remote backcountry
areas, renting them out for $25 to $50 per
night, see p58).

Hostels

Thanks to an influx of backpackers and
foreign travelers each summer, hostels offering budget accommodations in Alaska
increases almost annually. There are now
almost 50, with six in Anchorage, nine in the
Southeast and two in tiny McCarthy. What
isn't increasing is the **Hostel International-
American Youth Hostels** (www.hiayh.org) in Alaska;
there are now only two left, in Ketchikan
and Sitka.

The rest of Alaska's hostels are for backpackers, offering budget bunkroom facilities
without all the rules, regulations or chores
of a Hostel International member. Nightly
fees are from $10 at Juneau International
Hostel (p143) to $28 for the Anchorage
Guest House (p185). Most are around $22
a night. When you consider the access to a
kitchen for cheap eats, hostels are the first
step in making Alaska affordable. It's the
main reason older travelers and families are
using them.

For more information on Alaska's hostels
see the website of the **Alaska Hostel Association**
(www.alaskahostelassociation.org) before your trip.

Hotels & Motels

Hotels and motels are often the most expensive lodgings you can book. Although
there are bargains, the average double room
in a budget hotel costs $70 to $90, a midrange motel is $100 to $170 and a top-end
hotel $170 to well above $200 a night.

The drawback with hotels and motels is
that they tend to be full during summer.
Without being part of a tour or having advance reservations, you may have trouble
finding a bed available in some towns.

Rental Accommodations

The best place in Alaska for a weeklong rental
is Girdwood (p197), the delightful ski town 37
miles southeast of Anchorage. **Alyeska Accommodations**(☎ 907-783-2000, 888-783-2001; www.alyeska
accommodations.com) can arrange for subletting
one of many privately owned condomini-
ums in Girdwood for $110 to $172 per night.
Also check **Vacation Rentals by Owner** (www.vrbo
.com), which has almost 50 Alaskan homes.

Resorts

Resorts – upscale hotels that have rooms,
restaurants, pools and onsite activities – are
not as common in Alaska as elsewhere in the
USA but are increasing due to large companies, such as Princess Tours. The finest is
Girdwood's Alyeska Resort (p199), with a
four-star hotel at the base of its ski runs. If
you're near Fairbanks, go to the Chena Hot
Springs Rd to spend some days at Chena Hot
Springs Resort (p370) for good food, log cabins and a soak in an outdoor hot tub.

University Accommodations

There are not many universities in Alaska
and what few there are don't open their
dorms to summer tourists. The exception is
Sitka's Sheldon Jackson College (p129).

ACTIVITIES

Backpacking, kayaking and canoeing are
covered in the Wilderness Hikes & Paddles
chapter (p64), which has 18 trips that most
travelers can arrange themselves. Mountain
biking, fishing, rock climbing and surfing are
in the Alaska Outdoors chapter. For companies that offer activity tours see p416.

BUSINESS HOURS

Banks and post offices in Alaska are generally open from 9am to 5pm Monday to Friday and sometimes on Saturday mornings. Other business hours vary, but many stores are open 9am to 10pm Monday to Friday, 10am to 6pm Saturdays and noon to 5pm Sundays. For restaurant opening hours see p42.

CHILDREN

Alaska is a great place for families. Infant needs, such as disposable diapers and formula, are available in most cities, towns and villages. Children aged two through 11 receive a 50% discount on **Alaska Marine Highway** (☎ 907-465-3941, 800-642-0066; www .ferryalaska.com), and infants travel free. The Alaska Railroad, bus companies and other transportation companies   extend hefty discounts to kids as do museums, national parks and other attractions that charge entry fees.

For general information on traveling with kids, read Lonely Planet's *Travel with Children*. For more particulars on kid-orientated sights try *Going Places: Alaska & Yukon for Families* by Nancy Thalia Reynolds.

Practicalities

If your family is outdoorsy, Alaska can be a relatively affordable place once you've arrived. A campsite is cheap compared to a motel room, and hiking, backpacking and wildlife watching are free. Even fishing is free for children, as Alaska does not need anglers under the age of 16 to have a fishing license.

The key to any Alaskan adventure is to match the hike or activity to your child's ability and level of endurance. Children lacking outdoor experience might have a tough time with a weeklong kayak trip in Glacier Bay or the Chena Dome Trail near Fairbanks. On the other hand, the easy Resurrection Pass Trail can be handled by most children (even aged six or seven) if their packs are light.

If your children are younger than five years to partake in a wilderness trip, consider a rental cabin in Tongass or Chugach National Forest (see p58). Most cabins are reached by floatplane, an exciting start to any adventure for a child, Floatplanes allow you to bypass long hikes with heavy backpacks into the area, yet offer a remote place and often good chance to see wildlife or catch fish.

CLIMATE

From the north to the south Alaska's climate changes drastically. The following climate charts extend from Barrow to Juneau and will provide a glimpse of temperatures and precipitation for whenever you plan to visit. For more on climate see p12 or p47.

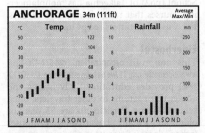

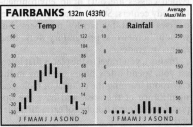

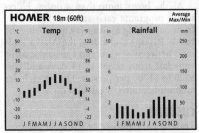

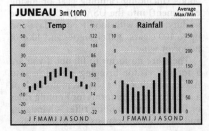

DIRECTORY

COURSES

Alaska is an outdoor classroom and outfitters are the key to learning a new activity. Almost every kayak guiding company has a half-day, learn-to-paddle outing in which they teach basic kayaking skills in a calm setting and then lead you on a short trip. The cost is $40 to $60 per person and includes all equipment. The Ascending Path (p198) of Girdwood has an excellent three-hour introduction to rock climbing while the Alaska Mountaineering School (p62) of Talkeetna has mountaineering courses that range from six to 12 days. For a list of outfitters see p416.

Elderhostel

This nonprofit **organization** (☎ 877-426-8056; www.elderhostel.org; 11 Ave de Lafayette, Boston, MA 02110-1746) provides educational adventures and academic programs to older travelers, often senior citizens. Participants are 55 years or older, and usually stay at college campuses (when classes are out) or in environmental study centers. Students take college-level courses taught by faculty members, but without homework, preparatory work, final exams or grades.

In short, you travel to the places that interest you, spend a few hours each day in the classroom learning the cultural or biological significance of the area, and have the opportunity to join a number of extracurricular activities.

Alaska hosts more than a dozen Elderhostel programs each summer that range from day hiking in Skagway to cruising the Inside Passage and riding the Alaska Railroad between Seward and Fairbanks. Most trips last from seven to 14 days and cost $900 to $1700 per person. The fee includes accommodations, meals and classes.

CUSTOMS

Travelers are allowed to bring all personal goods (including camping gear or hiking equipment) into the USA and Canada free of duty, along with food for two days and up to 100 cigars, 200 cigarettes and 40oz of liquor or wine.

There are no forms to fill out if you are a foreign visitor bringing a vehicle into Alaska, whether it is a bicycle, motorcycle or a car, nor are there forms for hunting rifles or fishing gear. Hunting rifles – handguns and automatic weapons are prohibited –

must be registered in your own country, and you should bring proof of registration. There is no limit to the amount of money you can bring into Alaska, but anything over $5000 must be registered with customs officials.

Keep in mind that endangered-species laws prohibit transporting products made of bone, skin, fur, ivory etc, through Canada without a permit. Importing and exporting such items into the USA is also prohibited. If you have any doubt about a gift or item you want to purchase, call the **US Fish & Wildlife Service** (☎ 907-271-6198) in Anchorage.

Hunters and anglers who want to ship home their salmon, halibut or the rack of a caribou can do so easily. Most outfitters and guides will make the arrangements for you, including properly packaging the game. In the case of fish, most towns have a storage company that will hold your salmon or halibut in a freezer until you are ready to leave Alaska. When frozen, seafood can usually make the trip to any city in the Lower 48 without thawing.

DANGERS & ANNOYANCES

Alaska is a relatively safe place with most of its dangers and annoyances occurring not in the cities but out in the woods. For how to deal with insects and Paralytic Shellfish Poisoning (PSP) that affects some shellfish see the Health chapter (p419).

Bears

Too often travelers decide to skip a wilderness trip because they hear too many bear stories. Your own equipment and outdoor experience should determine whether you take a trek into the woods, not the possibility of meeting a bear on the trail.

The Alaska Department of Fish & Game emphasizes that the probability of being injured by a bear is one-fiftieth the chance of being injured in a car accident on any Alaskan highway.

The best way to avoid bears is to follow a few commonsense rules. Bears charge only when they feel trapped, when a hiker comes between a sow and her cubs or when enticed by food. Sing or clap when traveling through thick bush, so you don't surprise a bear. Don't camp near bear food sources or in the middle of an obvious bear path. Stay away from thick berry patches, streams choked with salmon or beaches littered with bear droppings.

Leave your pet at home; a frightened dog only runs back to its owner, and most dogs are no match for a bear. Set up the spot where you will cook and eat 30 to 50 yards away from your tent. In coastal areas, many backpackers eat in the tidal zone, knowing that when the high tide comes in all evidence of food will be washed away.

At night, try to place your food sacks 10ft or more off the ground by hanging them in a tree, placing them on top of a tall boulder or putting them on the edge of a rock cliff. In a treeless, flat area, cover up the food sacks with rocks. A bear is not going to see the food bags; it's going to smell them. By packaging all food items in resealable plastic bags, you greatly reduce the animal's chances of getting a whiff of your next meal. Avoid odoriferous foods, such as bacon or sardines, in areas with high concentrations of bears. Women should avoid wearing scented cosmetics, including deodorant, as the smell attracts bears. Women who are menstruating should be sure to place used tampons/sanitary napkins in plastic bags and store them in bear-resistant containers up with the suspended food bag.

And please, don't take food into the tent at night. Don't even take toothpaste, hand lotion, suntan oils or anything with a smell. If a bear smells a human, it will leave; anything else might encourage it to investigate.

ENCOUNTERING A BEAR

If you do meet a bear on the trail, *do not* turn and run, it will outrun you. Stop, make no sudden moves and begin talking calmly to it. Bears have extremely poor eyesight, and speaking helps them understand that you are there. If it doesn't take off right away, back up slowly before turning around and leaving the area. A bear standing on its hind legs is not on the verge of charging; it's only trying to see you better. When a bear turns sideways or begins making a series of woofing sounds, it is only challenging you for space. Just back away slowly and leave. If the animal follows you, *stop* and hold your ground.

Most bear charges are bluffs, with the animal veering off at the last minute. Experienced backpackers handle a charge in different ways. Some people throw their packs 3ft in front of them, which will often distract the bear long enough for the person to back away. Other backpackers fire a handheld signal flare over the bear's head (but never at it) in an attempt to use the noise and sudden light to scare it away. If an encounter is imminent, drop into a fetal position, place your hands behind your neck and play dead. If a bear continues biting you after you have assumed a defensive posture, then you must fight back vigorously.

Some people carry guns to fend off bear charges. Shooting a charging bear is a skilled operation if you are a good shot, a foolish one if you are not. You must drop the bear with one or two shots, as a wounded bear is extremely dangerous.

Other people are turning to defensive aerosol sprays that contain red pepper extract. These sprays cost $40 to $50 each and have been used with some success for protection against bears. They are effective at a range of 6 to 8 yards but must be discharged downwind. If not, you will just disable yourself.

Security

Due to a lack of large cities, Alaska is basically a safe place to carry your money, credit cards and traveler's checks. Still, you want to be careful when moving through normally busy places like airport terminals. Don't flaunt your money when making a purchase, and avoid placing a wallet in your back pocket. Always keep some money stashed away in another location, in case you do lose your wallet or purse.

DISABLED TRAVELERS

Thanks to the American Disabilities Act, many state and federal parks are installing wheelchair-accessible sites and rest rooms in their campgrounds. You can call the **Alaska Public Lands Information Center** (☎ 907-271-2599) to receive a map and campground guide to such facilities. The Alaska Marine Highway ferries, the Alaska Railroad, and many bus services and cruise ships are also equipped with wheelchair lifts and ramps to make their facilities easier to access. Chain motels and large hotels in cities and town have rooms set up for disables guests, some wilderness guiding companies such as **Alaska Discovery** (p416) are experienced in handling wheelchair-bound clients in rafting and kayaking expeditions.

When planning your trip, contact **Access Alaska** (☎ 907-248-4777; www.accessalaska.org) for tourist information on accessible services and sites within the state. National organization that can help include **Access-Able Travel Source** (☎ 303-232-2979; www.access-able.com) and **Society for Accessible Travel & Hospitality** (☎ 212-447-7284; www.sath.org).

DISCOUNT CARDS
Senior Cards
The best seniors card for US travelers to carry is the one issued by the **American Association of Retired Persons** (AARP; ☎ 888-687-2277; www.aarp.org), which can be obtained for $12.50 if you're over the age of 50 (you don't even need to be retired).

Student & Youth Cards
Occasionally student discounts are available in which case your university identification is a handy thing to have. The demise of Hostelling International in Alaska – there are now only two sanctioned hostels – makes its HI card of little use in the far north.

EMBASSIES & CONSULATES
US Embassies & Consulates
The following is a list of US Embassies in other countries.

Australia (☎ 02-6214-5600; http://canberra.usembassy.gov; Moonah Place, Yarralumla, ACT 2600)
Canada (☎ 613-238-5335; http://canada.usembassy.gov; 490 Sussex Dr, Ottawa, Ontario K1N 1GB)
France (☎ 1-4312-2222; http://france.usembassy.gov; 2 Ave Gabriel, 75382 Paris)
Germany (☎ 30-238-5174; http://berlin.usembassy.gov; Neustädtische Kirchstrasse, 10117 Berlin)
Japan (☎ 3-224-5000; http://tokyo.usembassy.gov; 1-10-5 Akasaka, Minato-ku, Tokyo 107-8420)
Netherlands (☎ 70-310-2209; http://thehague.us embassy.gov; Lange Voorhout, 102, 2514 EJ, The Hague)
New Zealand (☎ 4-462-6000; http://wellington.us embassy.gov; 29 Fitzherbert Terrace, Thorndon, Wellington)
UK (☎ 20-7499-9000; http://london.usembassy.gov; 24/31 Grosvenor Sq, London W1A 1AE)

Embassies & Consulates in Alaska
There are no embassies in Alaska, but there are a handful of foreign consulates in Anchorage to assist overseas travelers with unusual problems such as the following.

Denmark (☎ 907-279-7611; 3111 C St, Ste 100, Anchorage, AK 99503)
France (☎ 907-222-6232; 2606 C St, Ste 3, Anchorage, AK 99503-2640)
Germany (☎ 907-274-6537; 425 G St, Ste 650, Anchorage, AK 99501)
Italy (☎ 907-563-4378; PO Box 242241, Anchorage, AK 99524-2241)
Japan (☎ 907-562-8424; 3601 C St, Ste 1300, Anchorage, AK 99503-5928)
UK (☎ 907-786-4848; 3211 Providence Drive, Anchorage, AK 99508-8000)

FESTIVALS & EVENTS
Alaskan regional festivals in Alaska include these ones. See the list of Alaskan festivals in the Getting Started chapter (p14).

April
Garnet Festival – Wrangell's weeklong celebration of gem stones and bald eagles.
Alaska Folk Festival (www.juneau.com/aff) – Juneau comes alive music in rainy April.

May
Kodiak Crab Festival – Grab a plate and dig into all the king crab you can eat.
Copper River Delta Shorebird Festival (www.cord ovachamber.com) – Birds and birders invade Cordova.
Kachemak Bay Shorebird Festival – If the birders aren't gathering in Cordova than they're nesting in Homer.
Little Norway Festival – Be a Viking for a day in Petersburg and feast on seafood at night.
Juneau Jazz & Classics (www.jazzandclassics.org) – The Capital City's jazziest festival.
Great Alaska Craft Beer & Homebrew Festival (third week of May; www.haines.ak.us) – Microbrews go head-to-head in Haines for best Alaskan beer.

June
Polar Bear Swim – The water's fine in Nome. Just watch out for the icebergs.
Nalukataq (Whaling Festival) – Head to Barrow for a taste of muktuk (whale blubber).
Summer Solstice – The baseball game starts at midnight in Fairbanks.
Summer Solstice Festival – Small town fun and a short parade in Moose Pass.
Gold Rush Days (www.juneaugoldrush.com) – Loggers and miners take over Juneau.
Midnight Sun Festival – A parade, BBQ and Folk Fest under 22 hours of sun in Nome.
Summer Music Festival (www.sitkamusicfestival.org) – Chamber music, concerts and a lot of culture in beautiful Sitka.

Colony Days – Celebrating the arrival of the first farmers to Palmer.

Mayor's Midnight Sun Marathon (www.mayors marathon.com) – Celebrate the longest day of the year with a 26-mile run in Anchorage.

July

Bear Paw Festival – Home of the Slippery Salmon Olympics or racing with a dead fish through Eagle River.

Golden Days – When Fairbanks cheers on the hairiest legs and the biggest moustaches.

Forest Faire – Artists and musicians gather in the magical woods of Girdwood.

Soapy Smith's Wake – Locals and tourists toast Skagway's most loveable scoundrel at his grave site.

Moose Dropping Festival – When Talkeetna is invaded by Mountain Mothers to the delight of men everywhere.

Bear Country Music Festival – Yee haa! Foot-stomping music in Kodiak.

Bluegrass Festival (www.talkeetnabluegrass.com) – More than 30 bluegrass bands jam for 20 of the 24 hours a day. Wild fun under the midnight sun in Talkeetna!

Mt Marathon Race – Alaska's most popular mountain race is in Seward. Sign-up early!

August

Tanana Valley Fair – Big veggies, livestock and a rodeo in Fairbanks.

Gold Rush Days – Five days of bed races, dances and fish feeds in Valdez.

Southeast Alaska State Fair – Along with produce and pig races, Haines is filled with musicians for the coinciding Bald Eagle Music Festival.

Blueberry Arts Festival – Arts, crafts and blueberry muffins in Ketchikan.

Kenai Peninsula State Fair – A town fair in Ninilchik.

Alaska State Fair (www.alaskastatefair.org) – Palmer's Showcase for 100-pound cabbages and the best Spam recipes in the state.

Silver Salmon Derby – Big fish and big money in Seward.

September

State Fair & Rodeo – Breakin' broncos on Labor Day in Kodiak.

October

Alaska Day Celebration – Sitka dresses the part on the day when Alaska was transferred to USA.

November

Whalefest (www.sitkawhalefest.org) – Whales galore in Sitka, so many you don't even need a boat to view them.

Alaska Bald Eagle Festival (www.baldeaglefestival .org) – There's more eagles in Haines than tourists at this festival.

FOOD

Many travelers are surprised that food prices in a Fairbanks or Anchorage supermarket are not that much higher than what they're paying at home. Then they visit their first restaurant and a glance of the menu sends them into a two-day fast.

Alaskan restaurants are more expensive than most other places in the country because of the short tourist season and the high labor costs of the waiters and chefs. Restaurants can be divided into budget, midrange and upscale.

Dinner is usually an $8 to $10 affair in a budget café, $10 to $20 in midrange restaurant and usually $25 and higher at an upscale place. Refer to the Food & Drink chapter (p40) for more details on eating in Alaska.

GAY & LESBIAN TRAVELERS

The gay community in Alaska is far smaller and much less open than in major US cities, and Alaskans in general are not as tolerant to diversity. In 1998 Alaska, along with Hawaii, passed a constitutional amendment banning same-sex marriages.

In Anchorage, the only city in Alaska of any real size, you have **Identity Inc** (☎ 907-258-4777; www.identityinc.org), which has a gay and lesbian helpline, and even openly gay clubs and bars. But most of the other cities do not have such an active gay community, and in rural Alaska, same-sex couples should exercise discretion.

HOLIDAYS

Public holidays for Alaskan residents include the following and on any of these days state and federal offices might be closed, bus services curtailed, shop and store hours reduced:

New Year's Day January 1.
Martin Luther King Day Third Monday in January.
Presidents' Day Third Monday in February.
Seward's Day Last Monday in March.
Easter Sunday in late March or early April.
Memorial Day Last Monday in May.
Independence Day (aka Fourth of July) July 4.
Labor Day First Monday in September.
Columbus Day Second Monday in October.
Alaska Day October 18.
Veterans' Day November 11.
Thanksgiving Day Fourth Thursday in November.
Christmas Day December 25.

DIRECTORY

INSURANCE

A travel insurance policy to cover theft, loss, and medical problems is a good idea. Coverage depends on your insurance and type of ticket but should cover delays by striking employees or company actions or a cancellation of a trip. Such coverage may seem expensive but it's nowhere near the price of a trip to Alaska or the cost of a medical emergency in the USA.

Some policies offer lower and higher medical-expense options; the higher ones are chiefly for countries such as the USA, which have extremely high medical costs. There is a wide variety of medical and emergency repatriation policies and its important to talk to your health care provider for recommendations. See also the Health chapter (p418) for more information.

For insurance on car rentals see the Transportation chapter (p410).

The following companies offer travel insurance.

Access America (☎ 866-807-3982; www.access america.com; PO Box 71533, Richmond, VA 23286-4684)
Europ Assistance (☎ 0870 737 5720; www.europ -assistance.co.uk; Sussex House, Perrymount Rd, Haywards Health, West Sussex, RH16 1DN, UK)
Insuremytrip.com (800-487-4722; insuremytrip.com; PO Box 511, East Greenwich, RI 02818-0511)

INTERNET ACCESS

It's easy to surf the Net, make online reservations or retrieve email in Alaska. Most towns, even the smallest ones, have Internet access at libraries, hotels and Internet cafés. Access ranges from free at the library and from $3 to $10 an hour at Internet cafés. If you are hauling around a laptop, wi-fi is common in Alaska at bookstores, motels, coffee shops, airport terminals, even bars. For the best websites for travelers headed for Alaska see the Getting Started chapter (p15)

LEGAL MATTERS

Despite the history of marijuana in Alaska – it was legal for personal use from 1975 to 1990 – possession of small amounts are now a misdemeanor punishable by up to 90 days in jail and a $1000 fine. The use of other drugs is also against the law, resulting in severe penalties, especially for cocaine, which is heavily abused in Alaska.

The minimum drinking age in Alaska is 21 and a government-issued photo ID (passport or drivers license) will be needed if a bartender questions your age. Alcohol abuse is also a problem in Alaska, and it's a serious problem if you are caught driving under the influence of alcohol (DUI). The blood alcohol limit in Alaska is 0.08% and the penalty for a DUI is three-month driver's license revocation, at least three days in jail and a $1500 fine.

If you are stopped by the police for any reason while driving, remember there is no system of paying on-spot-fines and bribery is not something that works in Alaska. For traffic violations the officer will explain your options to you and violations, such as speeding, can often be handled in the mail with a credit card.

MAPS

Unlike many places in the world, Alaska has no shortage of accurate maps. There are detailed USGS topographical maps to almost every corner of the state, even though most of it is still wilderness, while every visitor center has free city and road maps that are more than adequate to get from one town to the next.

For trekking in the backcountry and wilderness areas, the US Geological Survey (USGS) topographic maps are worth the $6-per-quad cost. USGS topo maps come in a variety of scales, but hikers prefer the smallest scale of 1:63,360, with each inch equal to a mile. Canoeists and other river runners can get away with the 1:250,000 map.

In Anchorage the **USGS Earth Science Information Center** (☎ 907-786-7011; Grace Bldg, Alaska Pacific University; ☺ 8:30am-4:30pm Mon-Fri) has topo maps for the entire state. You can also order maps in advance directly from **USGS** (☎ 888-275-8747; www.usgs.gov). Or you can view and order custom topo maps and digital maps from cartography websites such as **Topozone** (☎ www.topozone.com) or **Mytopo** (☎ 406-446-1007, 877-587-9004; www.mytopo.com). A customized, waterproof topo is $10,

MONEY

All prices quoted in this book are in US dollars unless otherwise stated. The US dollar is divided into 100 cents (¢). Coins come in denominations of 1¢ (penny), 5¢ (nickel), 10¢ (dime), 25¢ (quarter) and the seldom seen 50¢ (half dollar). Quarters are the most commonly used coins in vending machines and parking meters, so it's handy to have a stash of them. Notes, commonly called bills, come in $1, $2, $5, $10, $20, $50 and $100 denominations. Keep in mind that the Canadian system is also dollars and cents but is a separate currency and worth less than American dollars. For exchange rates, see inside front cover.

ATMs

Alaska is expensive so ATMs are everywhere; banks, gas stations, supermarkets, airports and even some visitor centers. At most ATMs you can use a credit card (Visa, MasterCard etc), or a debit card as well as ATM card that is linked to the Plus or Cirrus ATM networks.

Cash

Hard cash still works. It may not be the safest way to carry funds, but nobody will hassle you when you purchase something with US dollars. Most businesses along the Alcan in Canada will also take US dollars though they often burn you on the exchange rate.

Credit Cards

There are probably some isolated stores somewhere in Alaska that don't accept credit cards, but not many. Like in the rest of the USA, Alaskan merchants are ready and willing to accept just about all major credit cards. Visa and MasterCard are the most widely accepted cards, but American Express and Discovery are not far behind. In short, having some plastic money is good security for the unexpected on any major trip.

Places that accept Visa and MasterCard are also likely to accept debit cards. If you are an overseas visitor, check with your bank at home to confirm that your debit card will be accepted in the USA.

Moneychangers

Wells Fargo, (☎ 800-956-4442; www.wellsfargo.com) the nation's sixth largest bank, is the dominant player in Alaska with more than 400 branches, 16 in Anchorage alone. Wells Fargo can meet the needs of most visitors; including changing currency and 24-hr ATMs. Though opening hours vary from branch to branch, you can usually count on them being open 10am to 3pm Monday to Friday, and Wednesday and Friday evenings.

Tipping

Tipping in Alaska, like in the rest of the USA, is expected. The going rate for restaurants, hotels and taxis is about 15%.

Traveler's Checks

Other ways to carry your funds include the time-honored method of traveler's checks. The popular brands of US traveler's checks, such as AmEx and Visa, are widely used around the state and will be readily cashed at any store, motel or bank in the major tourist areas of Alaska.

PHOTOGRAPHY & VIDEO
Airport Security

For those still using film, security personnel at US airports will visually inspect it as part of carry-on luggage. But this should only be done with high-speed film. Airport X-ray machines are safe for film with an ASA of 100 or 200 and in this post-9/11 era hassling airport security over film gets you in trouble quickly.

Film & Equipment

The most cherished items you can take home from your trip are photos of Alaska's powerful scenery. Much of the state is a photographer's dream, and your shutter finger will be set clicking by mountain and glacier panoramas, bustling waterfronts and the diverse wildlife encountered during paddling and hiking trips.

A compact, fixed-lens, point-and-shoot 35mm or digital camera is OK for a summer of backpacking in the North Country. But if you want to get serious about photography, you need either a 35mm camera with interchangeable lenses or a digital camera with at least 5 megapixels and zoom capabilities. To photograph wildlife in its natural state, a 135mm or larger telephoto lens is needed to make the animal the main object in the picture. Any lens larger than 135mm on a film camera will probably also require a tripod to eliminate camera shake, especially during low-light conditions. A wide-angle lens of 35mm, or better still 28mm, adds considerable dimension to scenic views, and a fast (f1.2 or f1.4) 50mm 'normal' lens will provide you with more opportunities for pictures during weak light.

If you want simplicity, check out the latest zoom lenses. They are much more compact than they have been in the past and provide a sharpness that's more than acceptable to most amateur photographers. A zoom from 35mm to 105mm is ideal.

Film is readily available in Alaska and in cities and large towns will be priced $9 to $12 for a roll of 36 exposures depending on the speed and type. For more on cameras and photography read Lonely Planet's *Travel Photography* book.

POST
Postal Rates
US Postal Service (800-275-8777; www.usps.com) rates for 1st-class mail within the USA are 39¢ for letters up to 1oz (24¢ for each additional ounce) and 24¢ for postcards. International airmail rates are 84¢ for a 1oz letter and 96¢ for each additional ounce. International postcard rates are 55¢ for Canada and Mexico (75¢ for other countries) and aerograms are 75¢.

For heavier items, postal rates within the USA is $4.20 for 2lbs or less. It's faster to use private carriers in Alaska such as **United Parcel Service** (800-742-5877; www.ups.com) or **Federal Express** (800-463-3339; www.fedex.com) for shipping packages home.

Sending & Receiving Mail
For travelers, especially those from overseas, tripping through Canada into Alaska, it's best to wait until you're in the USA to mail home packages. Generally, you'll find the US postal service is half as expensive and twice as fast as its Canadian counterpart.

To receive mail while traveling in Alaska, have it sent c/o General Delivery to a post office along your route. You can receive mail at any post office that has its own five-digit zip (postal) code. Mail is usually held for 10 days before it's returned to sender; you might request your correspondents to write 'hold for arrival' on their letters. Mail should be addressed like this:

Your Name
c/o General Delivery
Town, AK zip code
USA

Although everybody passes through Anchorage (zip code 99501), it's probably better to have mail sent to smaller towns like Ketchikan, Seward or Delta Junction. Zip codes for any Alaskan town are on the US Postal Service website (www.usps.com).

SHOPPING
Alaska abounds with gift shops, with items often much too tacky for our taste. Moose nuggets will be seen from one end of the state to the other, but even if they are varnished, you have to wonder who is going to wear earrings or a necklace made of animal scat. More interesting, and much more affordable than gold-nugget jewelry, is what is commonly called Arctic opal. The blue and greenish stone was uncovered in the Wrangell Mountains in the late 1980s, and is now set in silver in a variety of earrings, pins and other pieces.

Want a keepsake T-shirt or jacket? Avoid the gift shops in Anchorage and Fairbanks and head for the bookstores at the University of Alaska campuses, which have an interesting selection of clothing that you won't find anywhere else.

Authentic Alaska Native–carved pieces, whether in ivory, jade or soapstone, are exquisite, highly prized and expensive. A 6-inch carving of soapstone, a soft stone that indigenous people in western Alaska carve and polish, costs $150 to $300, depending on the carving and the detail. Jade and ivory will cost even more, up to $100 per inch in a carving. When shopping for such artwork, be especially conscious of who you are purchasing from. Non-Native art, sometimes carved in places as far away as Bali, is often passed off and priced as Alaska Native–produced.

If you're considering investing in Native art look for the Silver Hand label, guaranteeing the item was made by a Alaska Native artist. For other art and items that made by non-Alaska Natives, the state has created a Made In Alaska logo with a polar bear on it. For more on Native art see The Culture chapter (p35) or contact the **Alaska State Council on the Arts** (907-269-6610; www.aksca.org).

SOLO TRAVELERS
Maybe it's that Klondike spirit of adventure or the lack of large cities but solo travelers are common in Alaska. Such travelers will find it easy to strike up conversations with locals in small towns, with waitresses if they grab a stool at the counter and bartenders if they're sitting alone at the bar. Hostels receive a large influx of solo travelers during the summer and the openness of campgrounds lends itself well to meeting other travelers. Women in particular will book nights at established

B&Bs, knowing they will find friendly conservation, a sense of security and a lot of local knowledge and contacts.

The main concern of most solo travelers in Alaska is how safe is hiking, backpacking or paddling alone in the wilderness. That depends on your skill level and where you're headed. There are lots of solo hikers every summer on the popular Chilkoot Trail (p66), not nearly as many trekking through some remote national park in the Arctic. If you do decide to go solo in the wilderness, leave a detailed itinerary with the park service or the bush pilot dropping you off and seriously consider carrying some type of communication like an emergency two-way radio. An even better plan is to hook-up with an outfitter on a guided trip (p416) where most likely you'll meet other solo travelers.

TELEPHONE
Cell Phones
Cell phones work in Alaska and Alaskans (especially teenagers) love them as much as anywhere else in the USA. When calling home or locally in cities and towns reception is excellent but overall, in a state this large, cell phone coverage can be unpredictable and sporadic at times. Many injured climbers have been plucked off mountains in the middle-of-nowhere after calling for help on their cell phone. But drive north of Auke Bay in Juneau and it's hard to use your cell phone to make a dinner reservation downtown. The culprit in many cases are mountains and the rugged terrain.

Still most travelers find their cell phones to be more useful than not. Before you head north, however, check your cell phone provider's roaming agreements and black out areas.

Phone Codes
Telephone area codes are simple in Alaska: the entire state shares 907, except Hyder, which uses 250. In this guidebook, the area code is always 907, unless a different one is listed before the phone number. If you're calling from abroad the country code for the USA is ☎ 1.

Phonecards
Every little town and village in Alaska has public pay phones that you can use to call home if you have a phone card or a stack of quarters. There's a wide range of phone cards that are sold in amounts of $5, $10 and $20, and are available at airports, in many convenience stores and Internet cafés. The best way to make international calls is to first purchase a phonecard.

TIME
With the exception of several Aleutian Island communities and Hyder, a small community on the Alaskan/British Columbian border, the entire state shares the same time zone, Alaska Time, which is one hour earlier than Pacific Standard Time – the zone in which Seattle, Washington, falls. When it is noon in Anchorage, it is 4pm in New York, 9pm in London and 7am the following day in Melbourne, Australia.

TOURIST INFORMATION
The first place to contact when planning your adventure is the **Alaska Travel Industry Association** (ATIA; ☎ 907-929-2200; www.travelalaska.com; 2600 Cordova St, Ste 201, Anchorage, AK 99503), the state's tourism marketing arm. From the ATIA you can request a copy of the *Alaska State Vacation Planner,* an annually updated magazine; a state highway map; and schedules for the Alaska Marine Highway ferry service and the Alaska Railroad.

Travel information is easy to obtain once you are on the road, as almost every city, town and village has a tourist contact center, whether it is a visitor center, a chamber of commerce or a hut near the ferry dock. These places are good sources of free maps, information on local accommodations, and directions to the nearest campground or hiking trail.

Most trips to Alaska pass through one of the state' three largest cities. All have large visitors bureaus that will send out city guides in advance include the following.

Anchorage Convention & Visitors Bureau (☎ 907-276-4118; www.anchorage.net)

Fairbanks Convention & Visitors Bureau (☎ 907-456-5774, 800-327-5774; www.explorefairbanks.com)

Juneau Convention & Visitors Bureau (☎ 907-586-1737, 800-587-2201; www.traveljuneau.com)

TOURS
Because of the size of the state and its distance from the rest of the country, Alaska is the land of cruise ships and packaged

WORKING IN ALASKA

Opportunities for astronomical wages for jobs on the Trans-Alaska Pipeline and other high-paying employment are, unfortunately, either exaggerated or nonexistent today. Alaska usually has the highest unemployment rate in the country. In 2005 unemployment was above 7% most of the year and as high as 20% in small towns during the winter.

If you lack a work visa or other proper documentation, search out tourist-related businesses such as hotels, restaurants, bars and resorts that need additional short-term help to handle the sudden influx of customers. The smaller the business, the more likely the employer will be to pay you under the table. Other cash-paying jobs, whether housecleaning or stocking shelves, can sometimes be found by checking bulletin boards at hostels or the student unions at the various University of Alaska campuses. Be forewarned, however, that if you are a foreigner in the USA with a standard nonimmigrant visa, you are expressly forbidden to take paid work in the USA and will probably be deported if you are caught working illegally.

If you are a US citizen or have a green card, finding some kind of work during the summer is usually not a problem, but be realistic about what you will be paid and look in the right places.

If you have access to the Internet, you can get a list with descriptions of job openings at the **Alaska Department of Labor Job Bank** (www.labor.state.ak.us). These positions are located across the state and descriptions include education requirements, salary and contract address. You'll find jobs in the online classified ads of Alaska's largest newspapers: *Anchorage Daily News* (www.adn.com), *Fairbanks News Miner* (www.news-miner.com) and the *Juneau Empire* (www.juneauempire.com).

Once in the state, you can stop at one of the **Alaska Job Centers** (www.jobs.state.ak.us/offices/index.html) run by the Department of Labor. There are 24 centers in Alaska, including four in Anchorage. Check the department's website for addresses and phone numbers.

tours. For information on tours, including companies that handle specialized activities such as biking and wilderness trips, see the Transportation chapter (p416).

VISAS

Since 9/11, obtaining a visa for entering the USA has become much more difficult. Apply early to avoid delays. Overseas travelers will need at least one visa, possibly two. Obviously, a US visa is needed, but if you're taking the Alcan or the Alaska Marine Highway ferry from Prince Rupert in British Columbia, you'll also need a Canadian visa. The Alcan begins in Canada, requiring travelers to pass from the USA into Canada and back into the USA again.

Canadians entering the USA must have proof of Canadian citizenship, such as a passport; visitors from other countries in the Visa Waiver Program (see right) may not need a visa. Visitors from all other countries need to have a US visa and a valid passport. On the website of the **US State Department** (www.travel.state.gov) there is 'Temporary Visas To The US' page with tips on how and where to apply for a visa and what to do if you're denied.

Note that overseas travelers should be aware of the process to re-enter the USA.

Sometimes visitors get stuck in Canada due to their a single-entry visa into the USA, used when passing through the Lower 48. Canadian immigration officers often caution people whom they feel might have difficulty returning to the USA. More information about visa and other requirements entering Canada is available on the website of the **Canada Border Services Agency** (www.cbsa-asfc.gc.ca).

VISA WAIVER PROGRAM

The Visa Waiver Program (VWP) lets citizens of some countries go to the USA for tourism for up to 90 days without having a US visa. Currently there are 27 participating countries in the VWP, including Austria, Australia, Belgium, Denmark, Finland, France, Germany, Iceland, Ireland, Italy, Japan, The Netherlands, New Zealand, Norway, Spain, Sweden, Switzerland and the UK.

Under the program you *must* have a round-trip or onward ticket that is nonrefundable in the USA, a machine-readable passport (with two lines of letters, numbers and<<< at the bottom) and be able to show evidence of financial solvency.

If you're getting a new passport, note that requirements are even tighter. Under current regulations, passports issued between

Seafood Industry

July is the month to hang around the harbors looking for a fishing boat desperate for help, and the best cities to be in are Kodiak, Cordova, Dillingham and Dutch Harbor, where boats are based that work fish runs in Prince William Sound and Bristol Bay, or Ketchikan, Petersburg and Sitka for boats that work the Southeast.

Deckhands and crewmembers usually earn a percentage of the catch. Occasionally they are paid hourly rates from $11 to $13 an hour.

Finding cannery work is possible, as most positions don't require experience and burnout is common in this trade. Seafood processors and fillers at canneries earn between $6 and $8 an hour and work eight to 12 hours a day, seven days a week, when the fish are in. On the slime line you have to endure working in cold, wet conditions and be physically able to stand on your feet for long hours.

Tourism

At resorts you can seek out work as a dishwasher, maid, chef or janitor. The pay is often between $7 and $10 an hour. Waiters earn less, usually lower than $6 per hour, but benefit from tips.

Tour companies you can contact in advance include the following:

Alaska Sightseeing (☎ 800-580-0072; www.cruisewest.com)
Alaska Travel Adventures (☎ 907-789-0052; www.alaskaadventures.com)
Alaska Wildland Adventures (☎ 907-783-2928; www.alaskawildland.com)
Denali & Glacier Bay Park Resorts (☎ 800-727-5272; www.coolworks.com/aramarkak)
Gray Line of Alaska (☎ 208-281-3535; www.graylineofalaska.com)
Princess Tours (☎ 907-550-7711; www.princesslodges.com)

October 26, 2005 and October 25, 2006 must be machine-readable and have a digital photograph on the data page. Passports issued after October 25, 2006 must be machine-readable and include an integrated chip with biometric information from the data pages.

If you have a passport issued *before* October 26, 2005 it will still be accepted for travel as long as it's machine-readable. In other words, there is *no* need to get a new passport until your current one expires.

VOLUNTEER VACATIONS

For many travelers the only way to enjoy Alaska is to volunteer. You won't get paid, but you're often given room and board, and work in a spectacular setting. Most volunteer roles are with federal or state agencies. The Bureau of Land Management (BLM) uses 300 volunteers annually who do tasks from office work and upkeep on campgrounds to working on the National Historic Iditarod Trail. The US Forest Service has an even larger program.

For a volunteer vacation contact the following agencies can be contacted during the winter.
BLM-Alaska (☎ 907-267-1203; www.ak.blm.gov; 6681 Abbott Rd W 7th Ave, Anchorage, AK 90507)

Tongass National Forest (☎ 907-225-3101; www .fs.fed.us/r10/tongass; 648 Mission St, Ketchikan, AK 99901)
Chugach National Forest (☎ 907-743-9500; www .fs.fed.us/r10/chugach; 3301 C Street, Ste 300, Anchorage, AK 99503-3998)
Alaska State Parks (☎ 907-269-8708; www.alaska stateparks.org; 550 W 7th Ave, Ste 1380, Anchorage, AK 99501-3561)
Student Conservation Association (☎ 603-543-1700; www.thesca.org; PO Box 550, Charlestown, NH 03603)

WOMEN TRAVELERS

While most violent crime rates are lower here than elsewhere in the USA, women should be careful at night in unfamiliar neighborhoods in cities like Anchorage and Fairbanks or when hitching alone. Use common sense; don't be afraid to say no to lifts. If camping alone, have pepper spray and know how to use it. Alaska is much less hassle for women traveling solo than most other states.

The excellent **Alaska Women's Network** (www .alaskawomensnetwork.org) has listings of women-owned B&Bs and travel agencies across the state. **Arctic Ladies** (☎ 907-783-1954, 877-783-1954; www.arcticladies.com) arranges women-only trips. The Anchorage **Planned Parenthood** (☎ 907-563-2229; 4001 Lake Otis Parkway) offers contraceptives and medical advice and services.

Transportation

THINGS CHANGE

The information in this chapter is particularly vulnerable to change; prices for international travel are volatile, routes are introduced or cancelled or both, schedules change, special deals come and go, and rules and visa requirements are amended. Get opinions, quotes and advice from as many airlines and travel agents as possible and make sure you understand how a fare (and any ticket you may buy) works before you part with your hard-earned money. The details given in this chapter should be regarded as pointers and are not a substitute for your own careful, up-to-date research.

GETTING THERE & AWAY

Many travelers from the Lower 48 think that a trip to Alaska is like visiting another state of the USA. It isn't. Getting to the North Country is as costly and complicated as traveling to a foreign country.

If you're coming from the US mainland, there are three ways of getting to Alaska: driving the Alcan (also known as the Alaska Hwy), taking a ferry or cruise ship up the Inside Passage or flying in from a number of cities.

If you're coming from Asia or Europe, it's become harder to fly directly to Alaska as few international airlines maintain a direct service to Anchorage. Today most international travelers come through the gateway cities of Seattle, Los Angeles, Minneapolis and Vancouver to Alaska.

ENTERING THE COUNTRY

Since the 9/11 terrorist attacks, air travel in the USA has changed and you can now expect extensive baggage screening procedures and personal searches. In short, you're going to have to take your shoes off. Non-US citizens, especially residents from Middle Eastern, Asian and African countries, should be prepared for an exhaustive questioning process at immigration.

Although the process is time-consuming, once finished most visitors will be allowed into the country. Crossing the border into Alaska from Canada used to be a relaxed process – US citizens often passed across with just a driver's license. Following the terrorist attacks this process has become more complicated, and both US residents and international travelers can expect more substantial questioning and possible vehicle searches.

Passport

If you are traveling to Alaska from overseas, you need a passport. Even Canadian citizens should carry one, as a driver's license alone may not be enough to satisfy some customs officials. Make sure your passport does not expire during the trip, and if you are entering the USA through the Visa Waiver Program (VWP) you *must* have a machine-readable passport. For more on VWP or visas see p408. If you are traveling with children, it's best to bring a photocopy of their birth certificates.

AIR
Airports

The vast majority of visitors to Alaska, and almost all international flights, fly into **Ted Stevens Anchorage International Airport** (ANC ☎ 907-266-2525; www.dot.state.ak.us/anc). International flights arrive at the north terminal; domestic flights arrive at the south terminal and a complimentary shuttle service runs between the two every 15 minutes. You'll find bus services, taxis and car-rental companies at both terminals. The airport has the usual services, including pay phones, ATMs, currency exchange and **baggage storage** (☎ 907-248-0373; per bag per day $5-7), on the ground level of the south terminal.

Airlines

Airlines providing services Alaska include the following.

Air Canada (AC; ☎ 888-247-2262; www.aircanada.com)
Alaska Airlines (AS; ☎ 800-426-0333; www.alaska air.com)
America West Airlines (HP; ☎ 800-235-9292; www .americawest.com)
American Airlines (AA; ☎ 800-443-7300; www.aa.com)
Asiana Airlines (OZ; ☎ 800-227-4262; http://fly asiana.com)
China Airlines (CI; ☎ 800-227-5118; http://usa .china-airlines.com)
Condor Airlines (DE; ☎ 800-524-6975; www.condor.de)
Continental Airlines (CO; ☎ 800-525-0280; www .flycontinental.com)
Delta Air Lines (DL; ☎ 800-221-1212; www.delta.com)
ERA Aviation (7H; ☎ 800-866-8394; www.era aviation.com)
Frontier Flying (2F; ☎ 800-432-1359; www.frontier flying.com)
Korean Air (KE; ☎ 800-438-5000; www.koreanair.com)
Mavial/Magadan Airlines (H5; ☎ 907-248-2994)
Northwest Airlines (NW; ☎ 800-225-2525; www .nwa.com)
PenAir (KS; ☎ 800-448-4226; www.penair.com)
United Airlines (UA; ☎ 800-241-6522; www.united.com)

Tickets

Due to its lack of direct and international flights, Anchorage, and thus Alaska, is not the most competitive place for airfares. Begin any ticket search by first checking travel websites like **Expedia** (www.expedia.com), **Orbitz** (www.orbitz.com) and **Travelocity** (www .travelocity.com). Also check the websites of airlines that service Alaska, particularly **Alaska Airlines** (www.alaskaair.com), as they often have Internet specials offered nowhere else. While the Internet is a great way to comparison shop, you should still call the airline's toll-free number or a travel agent before booking the ticket. Sales representatives know how to modify the ticket (and lower its price) by changing departure days or rerouting stopovers.

FROM THE USA
Seattle serves as the major hub for flights into Alaska. Alaska Airlines owns the lion's share of the market with two dozen flights per day to Anchorage as well as direct flights to Ketchikan, Juneau and Fairbanks. United, Delta, American, Northwest and Continental all offer Seattle–Anchorage flights.

You can also book a nonstop flight to Anchorage from a number of other US cities. Northwest Airlines flies nonstop from Minneapolis, Detroit and Houston. Delta flies in from Atlanta, New York and Salt Lake City. Continental flies non-stop from Houston, Newark, Minneapolis and Portland and United Airlines from Chicago, Denver and San Francisco. American Airlines arrives in Anchorage from St Louis and Dallas; American West from Las Vegas and Phoenix. Alaska Airlines, naturally, flies nonstop to numerous cities; Los Angeles, Denver, Chicago, Phoenix, Portland and Las Vegas among others.

FROM CANADA
During the summer Air Canada flies nonstop from Vancouver to Anchorage, as does Alaska Airlines. For most Canadians it is far cheaper to fly on a US airline, such as Northwest, changing planes at its hubs in Minneapolis or Detroit, then continuing on to Anchorage. Another option is to fly to Whitehorse and then fly **Air North** (in Canada ☎ 800-661-0407; www .flyairnorth.com) to Fairbanks.

FROM UK & IRELAND
Continental Airlines has London–Anchorage flights that require you to change planes in Houston. United Airlines offers a similar flight, changing planes in Seattle.

Popular discount travel agencies in the UK include **STA Travel** (☎ 0870-160-0599; www .statravel.co.uk), **Travel Bag** (☎ 0800-082-5000; www .travelbag.co.uk) and **Flightbookers** (☎ 0870-814-0000; www.ebookers.com).

FROM CONTINENTAL EUROPE
From Paris, Delta Airlines has a daily flight to Anchorage during summer, with a change of planes in Atlanta. Continental Airlines has a daily Paris–Anchorage flight with a connection in Newark. Similar flights can be arranged from Frankfurt through Northwest Airlines and United Airlines. Check out Condor Airlines, the charter air operation

of Thomas Cook, which offers a nonstop, weekly service between Anchorage and Frankfurt from May to October.

In France, recommended ticket agencies are **Nouvelles Frontieres** (☎ 0825-000-747; www .nouvelles-frontiers.fr) and **Anyway** (☎ 0892-893-892; www.anyway.com). In Germany there's **STA Travel** (☎ 01805-456-422; www.statravel.de) and **Expedia** (www.expedia.de).

FROM ASIA
Northwest Airlines partners with Alaska Airlines to offer daily flights from Tokyo to Anchorage, changing planes in Seattle. There is a nonstop service from Seoul to Anchorage with Korean Airlines, Asiana Airlines and United Airlines. There is also a daily nonstop service between Taipei and Anchorage with China Air.

STA Travel is proliferating in Asia, with branches in Singapore (☎ 6737-7188; www.sta travel.com.sg), Hong Kong (2736-1618; www.statravel .com.hk) and Japan (☎ 03-5391-2922; www.statravel .co.jp).

FROM AUSTRALIA & NEW ZEALAND
Qantas has flights from Sydney to Los Angeles with direct connections on Alaska Airlines to Anchorage. In Australia, **STA Travel** (☎ 1300-733-035; www.statravel.com.au) and **Flight Centre** (☎ 133-133; www.flightcentre.com.au) are the main dealers in cheap airfares.

Air New Zealand has a similar agreement with Alaska Airlines. **STA Travel** (☎ 0508-782-872; www.statravel.co.nz) and **Flight Centre** (☎ 0800-243-544; www.flightcentre.co.nz) also have offices in Auckland.

LAND
What began as the Alaska–Canada Military Hwy is today the Alcan (the Alaska Hwy). This amazing 1390-mile road starts at Dawson Creek in British Columbia, ends at Delta Junction and in between winds through the vast wilderness of northwest Canada and Alaska. For those with the time, the Alcan is a unique journey north. The trip is an adventure in itself: the road is a legend among highways, and completing (or surviving) the drive is a feather in anyone's cap.

There are several ways of traveling the Alcan: bus, car or a combination of Alaska Marine Highway ferry and bus. For the road's history see p28. For more on border crossings see p410 and p408.

Bus
A combination of buses will take you from Seattle via the Alcan to Anchorage, Fairbanks or Skagway, but service is limited and a round-trip ride on a bus from Seattle to Anchorage is not cheaper than flying. From Seattle, **Greyhound** (☎ 800-661-8747; www .greyhound.com) goes to Whitehorse, a two-day ride. From Whitehorse, **Alaska Direct** (☎ 907-277-6652, 800-770-6652) leaves three days a week for Anchorage.

Car & Motorcycle
Without a doubt, driving your own car to Alaska allows you the most freedom. You can leave when you want, stop where you feel like it and plan your itinerary as you go along. It's not cheap driving to Alaska, and that's not even considering the wear and tear and the thousands of miles you'll put on your vehicle.

The Alcan is now entirely paved and, although sections of jarring potholes, frost heaves (the rippling effect of the pavement caused by freezing and thawing) and loose gravel still exist, the infamous rough conditions of 30 years ago no longer prevail. Food, gas and lodging can be found almost every 20 to 50 miles along the highway, with 100 miles being the longest stretch between fuel stops.

On the Canadian side, you'll find kilometer posts (as opposed to the mileposts found in Alaska), which are placed every 5km after the zero point in Dawson Creek. Most Alcan veterans say 300 miles a day is a good pace – one that will allow for plenty of stops to see the scenery or wildlife.

Along the way, **Tourism Yukon** (☎ 800-789-8566; www.touryukon.com) operates a number of visitor centers stocked with brochures and maps:
Beaver Creek (☎ 867-862-7321; Mile 1202 Alcan)
Haines Junction (☎ 867-634-2345; Kluane National Park Headquarters)
Watson Lake (☎ 867-536-7469; Alcan & Campbell St)
Whitehorse (☎ 867-667-3084; 2nd St & Hanson Ave)

Hitchhiking
Hitchhiking is probably more common in Alaska than it is in the rest of the USA, and more so on rural dirt roads such as the McCarthy Rd and the Denali Hwy than on the major paved routes. But this doesn't mean it's a totally safe way of getting around. Hitchhiking is never entirely safe in any country and we don't recommend it. That

said, if you're properly prepared and have sufficient time, thumbing the Alcan can be an easy way to see the country, meet people and save money.

The Alcan seems to inspire the pioneer spirit in travelers who drive along it. Drivers are good about picking up hitchhikers, much better than those across the Lower 48; the only problem is that there aren't enough of them.

Any part of the Alcan can be slow, but some sections are notorious. The worst is probably Haines Junction, the crossroads in the Yukon where southbound hitchhikers get stranded trying to thumb a ride to Haines in Southeast Alaska.

If you'd rather not hitchhike the entire Alcan, take the Alaska Marine Highway ferry from Bellingham, WA, to Haines and start hitchhiking from there; you'll cut the journey in half but still travel along the highway's most spectacular parts.

SEA

As an alternative to the Alcan, you can travel the Southeast's Inside Passage. From that maze of a waterway, state ferries and cruise ships then cut across the Gulf of Alaska to towns in Prince William Sound.

Ferry

Travel on the state ferries is a leisurely and delightful experience. The midnight sun is warm, the scenery stunning and the possibility of sighting whales, bald eagles or sea lions keeps most travelers at the side of the ship.

Alaska Marine Highway (☎ 907-465-3941, 800-642-0066; www.ferryalaska.com) runs ferries equipped with observation decks, food services, lounges and solariums with deck chairs. You can rent a stateroom for overnight trips, but many travelers head straight for the solarium and unroll their sleeping bags on deck chairs.

The ferries to Alaska depart from either Bellingham, WA, or Prince Rupert, BC, and then continue on to Ketchikan in Alaska. Most ferries then depart for Wrangell, Petersburg, Sitka, Juneau, Haines and Skagway before heading back. From Haines you can drive north and within a couple of hours pick up the Alcan. A trip from Bellingham to Juneau takes 2½ to four days, depending on the route.

Seven ships ply the waters of Southeast Alaska and once a month the MV *Kennicott*

makes a special run from Southeast Alaska across the Gulf of Alaska to Valdez and Whittier. This links the Southeastern routes of the Alaska Marine Highway ferries to the South-central portion that includes such ports as Homer, Seward, Kodiak and Cordova. This sailing is extremely popular because it allows travelers to skip the long haul over the Alcan. Book it long before you arrive in Alaska.

If the Alaska Marine Highway ferries are full in Bellingham, head to Port Hardy at the north end of Vancouver Island where **BC Ferries** (☎ 250-386-3431, 888-223-3779; www.bcferries.com) leave for Prince Rupert, BC. From this Canadian city, you can transfer to the Alaska Marine Highway and continue to Southeast Alaska on ferries not as heavily in demand as those in Bellingham.

RESERVATIONS

The ferries are extremely popular during the peak season (June to August). If boarding in Bellingham, you should have reservations for a cabin or vehicle space and you need a reservation even if you're just a walk-on passenger.

The summer sailing schedule comes out in December; to get it, view it online or book reservations contact the **Alaska Marine Highway** (☎ 800-642-0066; www.ferryalaska.com). When reserving space, you must know the ports you want to visit along the route, with exact dates. Stopovers are not free; rather, tickets are priced on a port-to-port basis.

All fares listed in this book are for adults (ages 12 and older) but do not include a fuel surcharge – generally around 10% but that could change – that is now added to cover the skyrocketing cost of diesel.

Cruises

Alaska has boomed as a cruise-ship destination since 9/11. At the height of the May to September season five to seven ships could visit a port like Ketchikan in a single day and effectively double its population. Keep that in mind when considering seeing Alaska on a cruise. At times the stampede of cruise-ship passengers can be overwhelming in towns such as Juneau and Skagway.

For a good overview of Alaska cruises go to **CruiseMates** (www.cruisemates.com). Some of the popular cruises include the following.
Holland America (☎ 877-724-5425; www.hollandamerica.com)

Norwegian Cruise Line (☎ 866-625-1166; www.ncl.com)

Princess Cruises (☎ 800-421-5522; www.princess.com)

Radisson Cruises (☎ 877-505-5370; www.rssc.com)

Royal Caribbean (☎ 866-562-7625; www.royal caribbean.com)

ORGANIZED TOURS

Package tours can often be the most afford-able way to see a large chunk of Alaska, if your needs include the better hotels in each town and a full breakfast every morning. But they move quickly, leaving little time for an all-day hike or other activities.

Companies that offer Alaska packages include the following.

Cruise West (☎ 800-888-9379; www.cruisewest.com)

Gray Line (☎ 800-478-6388; www.graylineofalaska.com)

Green Tortoise Alternative Travel (☎ 800-867-8647; www.greentortoise.com)

Knightly Tours (☎ 800-426-2123; www.knightly tours.com)

GETTING AROUND

Traveling around Alaska is unlike traveling in any other state in the country. The over-whelming distances between regions and the fledgling public transportation system make getting around Alaska almost as hard as it is to get there in the first place.

AIR

As a general rule, if there are regularly scheduled flights to your destination, they will be far cheaper than charter flights on the small airplanes known in Alaska as 'bush planes.' This is especially true for **Alaska Air-lines** (☎ 800-426-0333; www.alaskaair.com).

Alternatively, here is a list of regional carriers.

Era Aviation (☎ 800-866-8394; www.eraaviation.com)

Frontier Flying (☎ 800-432-1359; www.frontier flying.com)

LAB (☎ 907-766-2222; www.labflying.com)

PenAir (☎ 800-448-4226; www.penair.com)

Bush Planes

When you want to see more than the road-side attractions, go to a dirt runway or small airfield outside a town and climb into a bush plane. With 75% of the state inac-cessible by road, these small, single-engine planes are the backbone of intrastate trans-port. They carry residents and supplies to desolate areas of the Bush, take anglers to some of the best fishing spots in the country and drop off backpackers in the middle of prime, untouched wilderness.

In the larger cities of Anchorage, Fair-banks, Juneau and Ketchikan, it pays to compare prices before chartering a plane. In most small towns and villages, however, you'll be lucky if there's a choice. In the re-gional chapters, bush flights are listed under the town or area where they operate.

Bush aircraft also include floatplanes, which land and take off on water, and beach-landers with oversized tires that can use rough gravel shorelines as air strips. Fares vary with the type of plane, its size, the number of pas-sengers and the amount of flying time. On average, chartering a Cessna 185 that can carry three passengers and a limited amount of gear will cost up to $290 for an hour of fly-ing time. A Cessna 206, a slightly larger plane that will hold four passengers, costs up to $350, while a Beaver, capable of hauling five passengers with gear, costs on average $420 an hour. When chartering a plane to drop you off at an isolated Forest Service (USFS) cabin or a wilderness trail, you must pay for both the air time to your drop-off point and for the return to the departure point.

Double-check all pickup times and places when flying to a wilderness area. Bush pilots fly over the pickup point and if you're not there, they usually return to base, call the authorities and still charge you for the flight. Always schedule extra days around a charter flight. It's not uncommon to be 'socked in' by weather for a day or two until a plane can fly in. Don't panic: they know you're there.

BICYCLE

For those who want to bike it, Alaska offers a variety of cycling adventures on paved roads during long days with comfortably cool temperatures. A bike can be carried on Alaska Marine Highway ferries for an additional fee and is a great way to explore the Southeast and Prince William Sound.

Most road cyclists avoid gravel, but biking the Alcan (an increasingly popular trip) does involve riding over some short gravel breaks in the paved asphalt. Mountain bikers (p60), on the other hand, are in heaven on gravel roads such as Denali Hwy in the Interior .

Anchorage's **Arctic Bicycle Club** (☎ 907-566-0177; www.arcticbike.org) is Alaska's largest bicycle club and sponsors a wide variety of road-bike and mountain-bike tours during the summer. Its website includes a section on touring Alaska for visiting cyclists.

If you arrive in Alaska without a bike see the regional chapters for the towns with rentals.

BOAT

Along with the Southeast, the **Alaska Marine Highway** (☎ 907-465-3941, 800-642-0066; www.ferry alaska.com) also services Southcentral and Southwest Alaska. Three ferries, including the new high-speed catamaran, MV *Chenega,* connect 17 communities, including Cordova, Valdez, Whittier, Seward, Homer and Kodiak.

Once a month from May through September the MV *Tustumena* makes a special run along the Alaska Peninsula to Aleutian Islands (p285).

Other ferry services in the Southeast include **Inter-Island Ferry Authority** (☎ 866-308-4848; www.interislandferry.com), which services Ketchikan and Prince of Wales Island and **Chilkat Cruises & Tours** (☎ 888-766-2103; www .chilkatcruises.com) which connects Skagway and Haines.

BUS

Regular bus service within Alaska is very limited, and companies come and go with alarming frequency. The following companies have been around for a number of years:

Alaska Direct Bus Line (☎ 800-770-6652, 907-277-6652) Whitehorse, Palmer, Glennallen, Tok, Skagway, Fairbanks and Anchorage.

Alaska Park Connection (☎ 888-277-2757; www .alaskacoach.com) Anchorage, Denali National Park and Seward.

Alaska Yukon Trails (☎ 888-600-6001) Talkeetna, Wasilla, Denali National Park, Nenana, Fairbanks and Anchorage.

Dalton Highway Express (☎ 907-474-3555; www .daltonhighwayexpress.com) Fairbanks and Prudhoe Bay.

Homer Stage Line (☎ 907-868-3914; www.homer stageline.com) Anchorage, Cooper Landing, Soldotna and Homer.

Seward Bus Line (☎ 907-563-0800; www.seward buslines.net) Anchorage and Seward.

Talkeetna Shuttle Service (☎ 888-288-6008; www .denalicentral.com) Anchorage and Talkeetna.

Yukon Alaska Tourist Tours (☎ 866-626-7383 outside Whitehorse ☎ 867-668-5944 in Whitehorse; www .yukonalaskatouristtours.com) Whitehorse and Skagway.

CAR & MOTORCYCLE

Not a lot of roads reach a lot of Alaska but what pavement there is leads to spectacular scenery. That's the best reason to tour the state in a car or motorcycle, whether you arrive with yours or rent one. With personal wheels you can stop and go at will and sneak away from the RVers and tour buses.

Rental & Purchase

For two or more people, car rental is an affordable way to travel, far less expensive than taking a bus or a train. At most rental agencies, you'll need a valid driver's license, a major credit card and you'll also need to be at least 21 years old. It is almost always cheaper to rent in town rather than at the airport because of extra taxes levied on airport rentals. Also be conscious of the per-mile rate of a rental. Add up the mileage you aim to cover and then choose between the 100 free miles per day or the more expensive unlimited mileage plan.

Advantage Car & Van Rental (☎ 888-877-3585) Anchorage.

Denali Car Rental (☎ 800-757-1230) Anchorage.

Rent-A-Wreck (☎ 800-478-1606) Fairbanks.

Valley Car Rental (☎ 907-775-2880) Wasilla.

MOTORHOME

RVers flock to the land of the midnight sun in astounding numbers. This is the reason why more than a dozen companies, almost all of them based in Anchorage, will rent you a motorhome. Renting a recreational vehicle is so popular you have to reserve them four to five months in advance.

Alaska Economy RVs (☎ 800-764-4625; www.go alaska.com)

Alaska Motorhome Rentals (☎ 800-254-9929; www.alaskarv.com)

Clippership Motorhome Rentals (☎ 800-421-3456; www.clippershiprv.com)

Great Alaskan Holidays (☎ 888-225-2752; www .greatalaskanholidays.com)

Automobile Associations

AAA (☎ 800-332-6119; www.aaa.com), the most widespread automobile association in the USA, has two offices in Alaska: **Anchorage South Service Center** (☎ 907-344-4310) and **Fairbanks Service Center** (☎ 907-479-4442). Both offer the usual service including maps, discounts and emergency road service.

TRANSPORTATION

Fuel & Spare Parts

Gas is widely available on all the main highways and tourist routes in Alaska. In Anchorage and Fairbanks the cost of gas will only be 10¢ to 15¢ per gallon higher than in the rest of the country. Along the Alcan, in Bush communities such as Nome and at that single gas station on a remote road, they will be shockingly high.

Along heavily traveled roads, most towns will have a car mechanic, though you might have to wait a day for a part to come up from Anchorage. In some small towns, you might be out of luck. For anybody driving to and around Alaska, a full-size spare tire and replacement belts are a must.

Insurance

Liability insurance, which covers damage you may cause to another vehicle, is required when driving in Alaska but not always offered by rental agencies because most Americans are already covered by their regular car insurance. Agencies offer Collision Damage Waiver (CDW) to cover damage to the rental car in case of an accident. This can up the rental fee by $10 to $15 a day and many have deductibles as high as $1000. It's better, and far cheaper, to arrive with rental car insurance obtained through your insurance company, as a member of AAA or as a perk of many credit cards including American Express. Even if the credit card has an annual fee of $60 to $100, you'd still be better off subscribing to one for the car insurance alone.

Road Conditions & Hazards

For road conditions, closures and other travel advisories for the Alaska highway system, even while you're driving, contact the state's **Alaska511** (in Alaska ☎ 511, outside Alaska ☎ 866-282-7577; http://511.alaska.gov).

ORGANIZED TOURS
Small Cruises

Unlike the 'Sheratons-at-Sea' that carry up to 3000 passengers and have eight bars on board, small cruise ships handle less than 100 passengers. They are more expensive than the larger ships and you usually have to fly to Alaska – not Seattle or Vancouver – to board them. But you'll enjoy a far more personal cruise, with an opportunity for close views of the scenery and wildlife that drew you to Alaska in the first place.

American West Steamboat Co (☎ 800-434-1232; www.americanweststeamboat.com) Offers cruises of the Southeast in a sternwheeler.

Glacier Bay Cruiseline (☎ 800-451-5952; www.glacierbaycruiseline.com) Eight- to 10-day cruises in Prince William Sound, the Southeast and Glacier Bay, and trips designed for families.

Lindblad Expeditions (☎ 800-397-3348; www.expeditions.com) Offers kayaking, wilderness walks and Zodiac excursions during eight-day cruises in the Southeast.

Activity Tours

Whether you want to climb Mt McKinley, kayak Glacier Bay or peddle from Anchorage to Fairbanks, there's a guide company willing to put an itinerary together, supply the equipment and lead the way. Guide companies are also listed in regional chapters.

ABEC's Alaska Adventures (☎ 877-424-8907; www.abecalaska.com) Rafting and backpacking the Arctic National Wildlife Refuge and Gates of the Arctic National Park.

Alaska Discovery (☎ 800-586-1911; www.akdiscovery.com) Kayaking Glacier Bay, bear viewing at Pack Creek and raft trips on the spectacular Tatshenshini River.

Alaskabike.com (☎ 907-245-2175; www.alaskabike.com) Fully supported cycle tours along the George Parks, Richardson and Glenn Hwys.

Arctic Treks (☎ 907-455-6502; www.arctictreksadventures.com) Treks and rafting in the Gates of the Arctic National Park and the Arctic National Wildlife Refuge.

Arctic Wild (☎ 888-577-8203; www.arcticwild.com) Floats and treks in the Brooks Range and Arctic National Wildlife Refuge.

CampAlaska (☎ 800-376-9438; www.campalaska.com) Camping tours with hiking, rafting and other activities.

Sourdough Outfitters (☎ 907-692-5252; www.sourdoughoutfitters.com) Paddling and backpacking trips to the Gates of the Arctic National Park, Noatak and Kobuk Rivers.

St Elias Alpine Guides (☎ 888-933-5427; www.steliasguides.com) Mountaineering, rafting, trekking and glacier-skiing at Wrangell-St Elias National Park.

Tongass Kayak Adventures (☎ 907-772-4600; www.tongasskayak.com) Kayaking LeConte Glacier & Tebenkof Bay Wilderness in Southeast.

TRAIN
Alaska Railroad

It took eight years to build it (p195), but today the Alaska Railroad stretches 470 miles from Seward to Fairbanks, through spectacular scenery. You'll save more money traveling by bus down the George Parks Hwy, but few travelers regret booking a seat on the Alaska Railroad and viewing pristine wilderness from the train's comfortable cars.

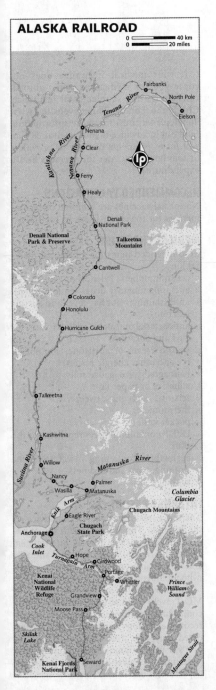

ALASKA RAILROAD

SERVICES

The Alaska Railroad operates a year-round service between Fairbanks and Anchorage, as well as summer services (from late May to mid-September) from Anchorage to Whittier and from Anchorage to Seward.

The most popular run is the 336-mile trip from Anchorage to Fairbanks, stopping at Denali National Park. Northbound, at Mile 279 the train passes 46 miles of Mt McKinley, a stunning sight from the viewing domes on a clear day. It then slows down to cross the 918ft bridge over Hurricane Gulch.

The ride between Anchorage and Seward may be one of the most spectacular train trips in the world. From Anchorage, the 114-mile trip begins by skirting the 60-mile-long Turnagain Arm on Cook Inlet and then swings south, climbs over mountain passes, spans deep river gorges and comes within half a mile of three glaciers.

The Anchorage–Whittier service, which includes a stop in Girdwood and passes through two long tunnels, turns Whittier into a fun day trip. So does riding Alaska Railroad's *Hurricane Turn*, one of America's last flag-stop trains, which departs from Talkeetna (p195).

RESERVATIONS

You can reserve a seat and purchase tickets, even online, through **Alaska Railroad** (☎ 800-544-0552; www.akrr.com); highly recommended for the Anchorage–Denali service in July and early August. See regional chapters for prices and departures.

White Pass & Yukon Route

Built during the height of the Klondike Gold Rush, the White Pass & Yukon Railroad (p168) is still the incredible ride it must have been for the miners. The narrow gauge line has one of the steepest gradients in North America: it climbs from sea level in Skagway to 2885ft at White Pass in only 20 miles. The mountain scenery is fantastic, the old narrow-gauge cars intriguing and the trip is a must for anyone passing through Southeast Alaska. It can also be used for transport to Whitehorse and by backpackers on the Chilkoot Trail (p66).

Given all that, reservations are highly recommended anytime during the summer. Contact **White Pass & Yukon Route** (☎ 800-343-7373; www.whitepassrailroad.com) for information.

Health

CONTENTS

There is a high level of hygiene found in Alaska, so most common infectious diseases will not be a significant concern for travelers. Also superb medical care and rapid evacuation to a major hospital is available.

BEFORE YOU GO

INSURANCE

The cost of health care in the USA is extremely high, and Alaska is no exception. Health insurance is essential in the USA, where some hospitals will refuse care without evidence of insurance. It's essential to purchase travel health insurance if your regular policy doesn't cover you when you're abroad.

A wide variety of policies are available, so check the small print. Be sure that the policy does not exclude wilderness trekking, mountaineering, kayaking, whitewater rafting or any other activities you might be participating in while traveling in Alaska, or you may have a difficult time settling a claim. It is also prudent to be sure that the policy specifically covers helicopter evacuation, the most common way of reaching troubled backpackers in Alaska's wilderness areas.

Bring any medications you may need in their original containers, clearly labeled. A signed, dated letter from your physician that describes all medical conditions and medications, including generic names, is also a good idea.

If your medical insurance does not cover you for medical expenses abroad, consider getting supplemental insurance. Check the Lonely Planet website (www .lonelyplanet.com) for more information. Find out in advance if your insurance plan will make payments directly to providers or reimburse you later for overseas health expenditures.

RECOMMENDED VACCINATIONS

No special vaccines are required or recommended for travel to Alaska, or the USA.

MEDICAL CHECKLIST

Recommended items for a personal medical kit:

- acetaminophen (Tylenol) or aspirin
- anti-inflammatory drugs (eg ibuprofen)
- antihistamines (for hay fever and allergic reactions)
- antibacterial ointment (eg Bactroban) for cuts and abrasions
- steroid cream or cortisone (for poison ivy and other allergic rashes)
- bandages, gauze, gauze rolls
- adhesive or paper tape
- scissors, safety pins, tweezers
- thermometer
- pocket knife
- DEET-containing insect repellent for the skin
- permethrin-containing insect spray for clothing, tents and bed nets
- sunblock

INTERNET RESOURCES

There is a wealth of travel health advice on the Internet. The World Health Organization publishes a superb book, *International Travel and Health*, which is revised annually and is available online at no cost at www .who.int.ith/.

Another website of general interest is MD Travel Health at www.mdtravelhealth. com, which provides complete travel health recommendations for every country, updated daily, also at no cost.

It's usually a good idea to consult your government's travel-health website before departure, if one is available:

Australia (www.dfat.gov.au/travel/)
Canada (www.phac-aspc.gc.ca/tmp-pmv/index.html)
UK (www.dh.gov.uk/PolicyAndGuidance/HealthAdvice
ForTravellers)
USA (www.cdc.gov/travel/)

IN TRANSIT

JET LAG & MOTION SICKNESS

Since a great deal of travel in Alaska is done by boat and much of the overland travel is over rough, unsurfaced roads, motion sickness can be a real problem for those prone to it. Eating lightly before and during a trip will reduce the chances of motion sickness. If you are susceptible to motion sickness, try to find a place that minimizes disturbance – near the wing on aircrafts, close to midships on boats and near the center of buses. Fresh air or watching the horizon while on a boat usually helps; reading or cigarette smoke doesn't. Commercial motion-sickness preparations, which can cause drowsiness, have to be taken before the trip commences; when you're feeling sick it's too late. Ginger (available in a capsule) and peppermint (including mint-flavored sweets) are natural preventatives.

IN ALASKA

AVAILABILITY & COST OF HEALTH CARE

In general, if you have a medical emergency, the best bet is to find the nearest hospital and go to its emergency room. In many small Alaskan villages health clinics serve as hospitals but might not have 24-hour emergency services, in which case call 911 for immediate assistance. If the problem isn't urgent, you can call a nearby hospital for a referral to a local physician or a walk-in clinic. Either one would be cheaper than a trip to the emergency room.

Pharmacies are common throughout Alaska, and in small villages they are usually part of the health clinic. You might find some medications, which are over the counter in your home country, require a prescription in the USA and, as always, if you don't have insurance to cover the cost of the medication, they can be shockingly expensive.

INFECTIOUS DISEASES

In addition to more common ailments, there are several infectious diseases that are unknown or uncommon outside North America. Most are acquired by mosquito or tick bites.

Giardiasis

Giardiasis, commonly known as giardia and sometimes called 'beaver fever,' is caused by an intestinal parasite (*Giardia lamblia*) present in contaminated water. The symptoms are stomach cramps, nausea, a bloated stomach, watery and foul-smelling diarrhea, and frequent gas. Giardia can appear several weeks after you have been exposed to the parasite. The symptoms may disappear for a few days and then return; this çan go on for several weeks. Metronidazole, known as Flagyl, or tinidazole, known as Fasigyn, are the recommended drugs for treatment.

HIV & AIDS

As with most parts of the world, HIV infection occurs throughout the USA, including Alaska. You should never assume, on the basis of somebody's background or appearance, that they're free of this or any other sexually transmitted disease.

West Nile Virus

These infections were unknown in the USA until a few years ago, but have now been reported throughout the country. The exception is Alaska, which at the time of writing still had no reported cases of West Nile Virus.

The virus is transmitted by culex mosquitoes, which are active in late summer and early fall and generally bite after dusk. Most infections are mild or asymptomatic, but the virus may infect the central nervous system, leading to fever, headache, confusion, lethargy, coma and sometimes death. There is no treatment for the virus. For the latest update on West Nile Virus in Alaska go to the **US Geological Survey website** (http://west nilemaps.usgs.gov/).

ENVIRONMENTAL HAZARDS
Altitude Sickness

At high altitudes, acute mountain sickness (AMS) can occur and may be fatal. In the thinner atmosphere of the high mountains, lack of oxygen causes many individuals to

HEALTH

suffer headaches, nausea, nosebleeds, shortness of breath, physical weakness and other symptoms that can have very serious consequences, especially if combined with heat exhaustion, sunburn or hypothermia. There is no hard and fast rule as to how high is too high: AMS has been fatal at altitudes of 10,000ft, although it is much more common above 11,500ft. For mild cases, everyday painkillers such as aspirin will relieve symptoms until the body adapts. Avoid smoking, drinking alcohol, eating heavily or exercising strenuously. Most people recover within a few hours or days. If the symptoms persist, it is imperative to descend to lower elevations. A number of other measures can prevent or minimize AMS:

- Ascend slowly. Have frequent rest days, spending two to three nights at each rise of 3000ft. If you reach a high altitude by trekking, acclimatization takes place gradually, and you are less likely to be affected than if you fly directly to high altitude.
- It is always wise to sleep at a lower altitude than the greatest height reached during the day if possible. Also, once above 10,000ft, care should be taken not to increase the sleeping altitude by more than 1000ft per day.
- Drink extra fluids. The mountain air is dry and cold, and moisture is lost as you breathe. Evaporation of sweat may occur unnoticed and result in dehydration.
- Eat light, high-carbohydrate meals for more energy.
- Avoid alcohol as it may increase the risk of dehydration.
- Avoid sedatives.

Hypothermia

Perhaps the most dangerous health threat in Alaska's Arctic regions is hypothermia. Hypothermia occurs when the body loses heat faster than it can produce it and the core temperature of the body falls. It is surprisingly easy to progress from very cold to dangerously cold due to a combination of wind, wet clothing, fatigue and hunger, even if the air temperature is above freezing point.

Dress in layers for insulation – silk, wool and some of the new artificial fibers are all good insulating materials. A hat is important, as a lot of heat is lost through the head. A strong, waterproof outer layer is essential, as keeping dry is vital. Carry basic supplies, including food containing simple sugars to generate heat quickly, and lots of fluid to drink.

Symptoms of hypothermia are exhaustion, numb skin (particularly toes and fingers), shivering, slurred speech, irrational or violent behavior, lethargy, stumbling, dizzy spells, muscle cramps and violent bursts of energy. Irrationality may take the form of sufferers claiming they are warm and trying to take off their clothes.

To treat hypothermia, first get the victim out of the wind and rain, remove the victim's clothing if it's wet and replace it with dry, warm clothing. Give the victim hot liquids – not alcohol – and some high-calorie, easily digestible food like chocolate, trail mix or energy bars. This should be enough for the early stages of hypothermia, but it may be necessary to place victims in warm sleeping bags and get in with them. Do not rub victims; instead allow them to slowly warm themselves.

Insect Bites & Stings

Alaska is notorious for its biting insects. In the cities and towns you have few problems, but out in the woods you'll have to contend with a variety of insects, including mosquitoes, black flies, white-socks, no-see-ums and deer flies. Coastal areas, with their cool summers, have smaller numbers of insects than the Interior. Generally, camping on a beach where there is some breeze is better than pitching a tent in the woods. In the end, just accept the fact that you will be bitten.

Mosquitoes can often be the most bothersome pest. They emerge from hibernation before the snow has entirely melted away, peak in late June and are around until the first frost. You can combat mosquitoes by wearing light colors and a snug-fitting parka, and by tucking the legs of your pants into your socks or boots.

The most effective protection by far is a high-potency insect repellent; the best contain a high percentage of DEET (diethyltoluamide), the active ingredient. A little bottle of Musk Oil or Cutters can cost $6 or $7 (they contain 100% DEET), but it's one of the best investments you will make.

Unfortunately, repellents are less effective against black flies and no-see-ums. Their season runs from June to August, and their bite is far more annoying. The tiny no-see-um bite is a prolonged prick, after which the surrounding skin becomes inflamed and itches intermittently for up to a week or more. Unlike the mosquito, these insects will crawl into your hair and under loose clothing in search of bare skin.

Thus, the best protection, and a fact of life in Alaska's backcountry, is to wear long-sleeved shirts, socks that will allow you to tuck your pants into them and a snug cap or woolen hat. You also see many backcountry travelers packing head nets. They're not something you wear a lot, as it can drive you crazy looking through mesh all day, but when you really need one a head net is a lifesaver.

Other items you might consider are bug jackets and an after-bite medication. The mesh jackets are soaked in insect repellent and kept in a re-sealable plastic bag until needed. Some people say bug jackets are the only effective way to keep no-see-ums at bay. After-bite medications contain ammonia and are rubbed on; while this might drive away your tent partner, it does soothe the craving to scratch the assortment of bites on your arms and neck.

Paralytic Shellfish Poisoning

In recent years, Paralytic Shellfish Poisoning (PSP) has become a problem in Alaska. State officials urge people not to eat mussels, clams or snails gathered from unmonitored Alaskan beaches. PSP is possible anywhere in Alaska, and within 12 hours of consuming the infected shellfish, victims experience symptoms of tingling or numbness in the lips and tongue (which can spread to the fingers or toes), loss of muscle coordination, dizziness, weakness and drowsiness. To get an update on the PSP situation, or to find out which beaches in the state are safe to clam, check the **Division of Environmental Health website** (www.dec .state.ak.us/eh/fss/seafood/psp/psp.htm).

Rabies

This disease is found in Alaska, especially among small rodents such as squirrels and chipmunks in wilderness areas; it is caused by a bite or scratch from an infected animal. Any bite, scratch or even lick from a mammal should be cleaned immediately and thoroughly. Scrub with soap and running water, and then clean with an alcohol or iodine solution. If there is any possibility that the animal is infected, medical help should be sought immediately.

Sunburn & Windburn

Alaska has long hours of sunlight during the summer, and the sun's rays are even more intense when they are reflected off snow or water. Sunburn and windburn should be primary concerns for anyone planning to spend time trekking or paddling. The sun will burn you even if you feel cold, and the wind will cause dehydration and skin chafing. Use a good sunscreen and a moisture cream on exposed skin, even on cloudy days. A hat provides additional protection, and zinc oxide or some other barrier cream for your nose and lips is recommended for people spending any time on the ice or snow.

Reflection and glare off ice and snow can cause snow blindness, so high-protection sunglasses, known by many locals as 'glacier goggles,' should be considered essential for any sort of visit on or near glaciers.

Water

Tap water in Alaska is safe to drink, but you should purify surface water taken from lakes and streams that is to be used for cooking and drinking. The simplest way to purify water is to boil it thoroughly. Remember that at high altitude, water boils at a lower temperature, so germs are less likely to be killed.

If you are trekking in the wilderness, this can be handled easily by investing in a high-quality filter. Filters such as First Need or MSR's Waterworks are designed to take out whatever you shouldn't be drinking, including *Giardia lamblia*. They cost between $50 and $100 and are well worth it.

HEALTH

Glossary

Alcan or **Alaska Hwy** – the main overland route into Alaska; although the highway is almost entirely paved now, completing a journey across this legendary road is still a special accomplishment; the Alcan begins at the Mile 0 milepost in Dawson Creek (northeastern British Columbia, Canada). It heads northwest through Whitehorse, the capital of the Yukon Territory, and officially ends at Delta Junction (Mile 1422), 101 miles southeast of Fairbanks

AMS – Acute Mountain Sickness; occurs at high altitudes and may be fatal

ANWR – Arctic National Wildlife Refuge; the 1½-million-acre wilderness area that oil-company officials and Alaskans have been pushing hard to open up for oil and gas drilling

ATV – All-Terrain Vehicle

aurora borealis or **northern lights** – the mystical snakes of light that weave across the sky from the northern horizon; it's a spectacular show on clear nights and can occur at almost any time of the year; the lights are the result of gas particles colliding with solar electrons; best viewed from the Interior, away from city lights, between late summer and winter

bidarka – a skin-covered sea kayak used by the Aleuts

blanket toss – a traditional activity of the Inupiat, in which a large animal skin is used to toss a person into the air

BLM – Bureau of Land Management; the federal agency that maintains much of the wilderness around and north of Fairbanks, including cabins and campgrounds

blue cloud – what Southeasterners call a break in the clouds

breakup – when the ice on rivers suddenly begins to melt, breaks up and flows downstream; many residents also use this term to describe spring in Alaska, when the rain begins, the snow melts and everything turns to mud and slush

bunny boots – large, oversized and usually white plastic boots used extensively in subzero weather to prevent the feet from freezing; much to the horror of many Alaskans, the company that manufactured the boot announced in 1995 it would discontinue the style

Bush, the – any area in the State that is not connected by road to Anchorage or is not part of the Alaska Marine Hwy

cabin fever – a winter condition in which cross-eyed Alaskans go stir-crazy in their one-room cabins because of too little sunlight and too much time spent indoors

cache – a small hut or storage room built high off the ground to keep supplies and spare food away from roaming bears and wolves; the term, however, has found its

way onto the neon signs of everything from liquor stores to pizza parlors in the cities

calve – (of an ice mass) to separate or break so that a part of the ice becomes detached

capital move – the political issue that raged in the early 1980s, concerning moving the state capital from Juneau closer to Anchorage; although residents rejected funding the move north in a 1982 state election, the issue continues to divide Alaska

cheechako – tenderfoot, greenhorn or somebody trying to survive their first year in Alaska

chum – not your mate or good buddy, but a nickname for the dog salmon

clear-cut – a hated sight for environmentalists: an area where loggers have cut every tree, large and small, leaving nothing standing; the first view of a clear-cut in Alaska, often from a ferry, is a shocking sight for a traveler

d-2 – the lands issue of the late 1970s, which pitted environmentalists against developers over the federal government's preservation of 156,250 sq miles of Alaskan wilderness as wildlife reserves, forests and national parks

Eskimo ice cream – an Inupiat food made of whipped animal fat, berries, seal oil and sometimes shredded caribou meat

fish wheel – a wooden trap powered by a river's current that scoops salmon or other large fish out of a river into a holding tank

freeze-up – that point in November or December when most rivers and lakes ice over, signaling to Alaskans that their long winter has started in earnest

glacier fishing – picking up flopping salmon along the Copper River in Cordova after a large calving from the Childs Glacier strands the fish during the August spawning run; practiced by both bears and people

humpie – a nickname for the humpback or pink salmon, the mainstay of the fishing industry in the Southeast

ice worm – a small, thin black worm that thrives in glacial ice and was made famous by a Robert Service poem

Iditarod – the 1049-mile sled-dog race run every March from Anchorage to Nome. The winner usually completes the course in less than 14 days and takes home $50,000.

Lower 48 – an Alaskan term for the continental USA

moose nuggets – hard, smooth little objects dropped by moose after a good meal; some enterprising resident in Homer has capitalized on them by baking, varnishing and trimming them with evergreen leaves to sell during Christmas as Moostletoe

mukluks – lightweight boots of seal skin trimmed with fur, made by the Inupiaq

muktuk – whale skin and blubber; also known as *maktak*, it is a delicacy among Inupiat and is eaten in a variety of ways, including raw, pickled and boiled

muskeg – the bogs in Alaska, where layers of matted plant life float on top of stagnant water; these are bad areas in which to hike

NANA – Northwest Alaska Native Association; a Native corporation

no-see-um – nickname for the tiny gnats found throughout much of the Alaskan wilderness, especially in the Interior and parts of the Brooks Range

NPS – National Park Service; administers 82,656 sq miles in Alaska and its 15 national parks include such popular units as Denali, Glacier Bay, Kenai Fjords and Klondike Gold Rush National Historical

NRRS – National Recreation Reservation Service

Outside – to residents, any place that isn't Alaska

Outsider – to residents, anyone who isn't an Alaskan

permafrost – permanently frozen subsoil that covers two-thirds of the state but is disappearing due to global warming

petroglyphs – ancient rock carvings

portage – an area of land between waterways over which paddlers carry their boats

potlatch – a traditional gathering of indigenous people held to commemorate any memorable occasion

qiviut – the wool of the musk ox, often woven into garments

RV – Recreational Vehicles (motor homes) that are driven by RVers.

scat – animal droppings; however, the term is usually used to describe bear droppings. If the scat is dark brown or bluish and somewhat square in shape, a bear has passed by; if it is steaming, the bear is eating blueberries around the next bend

scrimshaw – hand-carved ivory from walrus tusks

solstice – the first day of summer on June 21 and the first day of winter on December 21; in Alaska, however, solstice is celebrated on the longest day of the year

sourdough – any old-timer in the state who, it is said, is 'sour on the country but without enough dough to get out' newer residents believe the term applies to anybody who has survived an Alaskan winter; the term also applies to a 'yeasty' mixture used to make bread or pancakes

Southeast sneakers – the tall, reddish-brown rubber boots that Southeast residents wear when it rains, and often when it doesn't; also known as 'Ketchikan tennis shoes,' 'Sitka slippers' and 'Petersburg pumps' among other names

Squaw Candy – salmon that has been dried or smoked into jerky

stinkhead – an Inupiat 'treat' made by burying a salmon head in the sand; leave the head to ferment for up to 10 days then dig it up, wash off the sand and enjoy

taku wind – Juneau's sudden gusts of wind, which may exceed 100mph in the spring and fall; often the winds cause horizontal rain, which, as the name indicates, comes straight at you instead of falling on you; in Anchorage and throughout the Interior, these sudden rushes of air over or through mountain gaps are called 'williwaws'

tundra – often used to refer to the vast, treeless Arctic plains

UA – University of Alaska

ulu – a fan-shaped knife that indigenous Alaskans traditionally used to chop and scrape meat; now used by gift shops to lure tourists

umiaks – leather boats made by the Inupiat people

USFS – US Forest Service; oversees the Tongass and Chugach National Forests, and the 190 cabins, hiking trails, kayak routes and campgrounds within them

USFWS – US Fish & Wildlife Service; administers 16 federal wildlife refuges in Alaska, more than 120,312 sq miles

USGS – US Geological Society makes topographic maps, including those covering almost every corner of Alaska

Behind the Scenes

THIS BOOK

This 8th edition of *Alaska* was written by Jim DuFresne and Aaron Spitzer. Jim, the coordinating author, wrote the front and back chapters as well as Southeast Alaska, Anchorage & Around and Southwest Alaska; Aaron wrote the Prince William Sound, Kenai Peninsula, Denali & the Interior, Fairbanks & Around, and the Bush chapters. Dr David Goldberg wrote the Health chapter. The 7th edition was written by Jim DuFresne, Paige R Penland and Don Root, and Jim DuFresne wrote all earlier editions. This guidebook was commissioned in Lonely Planet's US office and produced by the following:

Commissioning Editors Jay Cooke, Emily K Wolman
Coordinating Editor Melissa Faulkner
Coordinating Cartographer Andrew Smith
Coordinating Layout Designers Pablo Gastar, David Kemp
Managing Cartographer Alison Lyall
Assisting Editors Lutie Clark, Jackey Coyle, Barbara Delissen, Carly Hall, Liz Heynes, Cahal McGroarty, Dianne Schallmeiner, Laura Stansfield, Louisa Syme
Assisting Cartographers Clare Capell, Jody Whiteoak
Assisting Layout Designers Wibowo Rusli
Cover Designer Candice Jacobus
Color Designer Michael Ruff
Project Managers Chris Love, Rachel Imeson

Thanks to Sally Darmody, Martin Heng, Adriana Mammarella, Jacqui Saunders, Gabrielle Wilson, Celia Wood

THANKS
JIM DUFRESNE

It's good to return to Alaska. The state may be changing but the friendships I made long ago are as strong and as close as ever. Thanks to Sue and Jeff Sloss of Juneau, Jeff Brady of Skagway, and Todd Hardesty and Ed Fogels of Anchorage for that enduring friendship and hospitality that only Alaskans can give. Others who steered me in the right direction include Lori Stepansky of Haines, Pam Foreman of Kodiak, Abby Peterson of Unalaska, Tammy Bruce and Anna Neidig of Wasilla, Janilyn Heger of Skagway, Stu Vincent of Prince of Wales Island, Erika Siegel and Jeanette Anderson Moores of Anchorage, and John Beiler and Becky Janes of Juneau.

AARON SPITZER

As they say in the Bush, *quyana cakneq* to the countless Alaskans who helped me get the low-down on the Great Land, and whose extroversion, candor and colorfulness is perhaps the very best thing about the North. Thanks especially to Peggy Wilcox and Theo Graber, whose dog-filled Anchorage home has repeatedly been the perfect decompression chamber. Big kudos, too, to my commissioning editor, Jay Cooke (who guided me through this, my first major Lonely Planet undertaking, and tolerated being carpet-bombed with questions), and to lead author Jim DuFresne (whose earlier versions of this guide helped inspire my polar peregrinations in the first place). And Ally, I mean this – *mahsi cho*.

THE LONELY PLANET STORY

The story begins with a classic travel adventure: Tony and Maureen Wheeler's 1972 journey across Europe and Asia to Australia. There was no useful information about the overland trail then, so Tony and Maureen published the first Lonely Planet guidebook to meet a growing need.

From a kitchen table, Lonely Planet has grown to become the largest independent travel publisher in the world, with offices in Melbourne (Australia), Oakland (USA) and London (UK). Today Lonely Planet guidebooks cover the globe. There is an ever-growing list of books and information in a variety of media. Some things haven't changed. The main aim is still to make it possible for adventurous travelers to get out there – to explore and better understand the world.

At Lonely Planet we believe travelers can make a positive contribution to the countries they visit – if they respect their host communities and spend their money wisely. Every year 5% of company profit is donated to charities around the world.

OUR READERS

Many thanks to the hundreds of travelers who used the last edition and wrote to us with helpful hints, useful advice and interesting anecdotes:

Darlinda Alexander, Kelly Atlee, Janet Ball, Susan Barnett, Terra Beaton, Norm & Bobbie Bennett, Brian & Caryl Bergeron, Jim Brenock, Mike Busby, Leslie Campbell, Gregory E Carpenter, Stella Carson, Rosemary Clark, Paul Cloutman, Silvio Conti, Vicki Daniels, Lien de Brouckere, Geoffrey DeGraff, Brenda Drinkwater, Zbynek Dvorak, Charlotte Dyhr, Richard Edwards, Roni & Manny Elder, Greg Enderby, Elizabeth & Alan Fieldus, Tapan Ganguli, John Grant, Lotte Grant, Diane Hansen, Mary Anne Harrar, Sarasvati Hewitt, Jim Hiebert, Graham Holey, Nick & Sue Howes, Graham Hunt, Adi Ilarde, Jeroen Immerzeel, Sven Kindt, Meron Langsner, Kenn Leonhardt, Susan Lofranco, Rich Lowenberg, Nina McKenna, Michaele Mansfeld, Karen & Gav Milton, Mat Mitcheson, Julia Mitzel, Dennis Mogerman, John & Oliver Monti-Masel, Tim Murphy, Elizabeth Murray, Peter Mynors, Jed Nancarrow, Do & Paula Noble, Peter Norris, Grant James O'Neill, Rob & Marlene Palich, Yves Pelster, Nicholas Photinos, Olivier Potreau, Lynette Reed, Martin Reichgott, Duane W Roller, Heather Rowland, Safia Rubaii, Lois Rubain, Richard Ryan, Jennifer A Sacco, Ray Sims, Jo Ann Slate, Kristine K Stevens, Judy & David Stockton, Eddie Summerfold, Scott Sutton, Gary Theilman, Bruce Thomson, Annerieke van Hoek, Chris Vassbotn, Arlyn Walford, Mary Ellen Walford, Clive Walker, Katherine Warren, Laura Weaver, Brian Williams, Mike Wold, Robin M Young, Val Young, Steven Youra

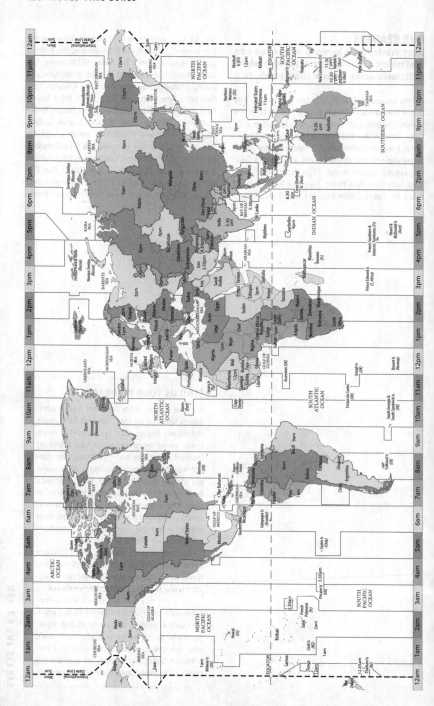

Index

INDEX

Index

000 Map pages
000 Photograph pages

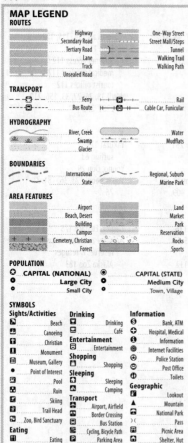

MAP LEGEND

ROUTES

Highway	One-Way Street
Secondary Road	Street Mall/Steps
Tertiary Road	Tunnel
Lane	Walking Trail
Track	Walking Path
Unsealed Road	

TRANSPORT

Ferry	Rail
Bus Route	Cable Car, Funicular

HYDROGRAPHY

River, Creek	Water
Swamp	Mudflats
Glacier	

BOUNDARIES

International	Regional, Suburb
State	Marine Park

AREA FEATURES

Airport	Land
Beach, Desert	Market
Building	Park
Campus	Reservation
Cemetery, Christian	Rocks
Forest	Sports

POPULATION

CAPITAL (NATIONAL)	CAPITAL (STATE)
Large City	Medium City
Small City	Town, Village

SYMBOLS

Sights/Activities
- Beach
- Canoeing
- Christian
- Monument
- Museum, Gallery
- Point of Interest
- Pool
- Ruin
- Skiing
- Trail Head
- Zoo, Bird Sanctuary

Eating
- Eating

Drinking
- Drinking
- Café

Entertainment
- Entertainment

Shopping
- Shopping

Sleeping
- Sleeping
- Camping

Transport
- Airport, Airfield
- Border Crossing
- Bus Station
- Cycling, Bicycle Path
- Parking Area

Information
- Bank, ATM
- Hospital, Medical
- Information
- Internet Facilities
- Police Station
- Post Office
- Toilets

Geographic
- Lookout
- Mountain
- National Park
- Pass
- Picnic Area
- Shelter, Hut

LONELY PLANET OFFICES

Australia
Head Office
Locked Bag 1, Footscray, Victoria 3011
☎ 03 8379 8000, fax 03 8379 8111
talk2us@lonelyplanet.com.au

USA
150 Linden St, Oakland, CA 94607
☎ 510 893 8555, toll free 800 275 8555
fax 510 893 8572
info@lonelyplanet.com

UK
72–82 Rosebery Ave,
Clerkenwell, London EC1R 4RW
☎ 020 7841 9000, fax 020 7841 9001
go@lonelyplanet.co.uk

Published by Lonely Planet Publications Pty Ltd
ABN 36 005 607 983

© Lonely Planet Publications Pty Ltd 2006

© photographers as indicated 2006

Cover photographs: Frost settles on man's hair while enjoying Circle's hot springs in extremely cold temperatures, Workbook Inc/Photolibrary (front); Kodiak brown bear mother and cubs beside the McNeil River, Mark Newman/Lonely Planet Images (back). Many of the images in this guide are available for licensing from Lonely Planet Images: www.lonelyplanetimages.com.

Printed by SNP Security Printing Pte Ltd, Singapore

Lonely Planet and the Lonely Planet logo are trademarks of Lonely Planet and are registered in the US Patent and Trademark Office and in other countries.

Lonely Planet does not allow its name or logo to be appropriated by commercial establishments, such as retailers, restaurants or hotels. Please let us know of any misuses: www.lonelyplanet.com/ip.

Although the authors and Lonely Planet have taken all reasonable care in preparing this book, we make no warranty about the accuracy or completeness of its content and, to the maximum extent permitted, disclaim all liability arising from its use.